LIVES

OF THE

LORD CHANCELLORS OF ENGLAND.

Eng. by W. Wellstood New York

LORD CAMPBELL

James Cockcroft & Co. New York

LIVES

OF

THE LORD CHANCELLORS

AND

KEEPERS OF THE GREAT SEAL

OF

ENGLAND,

FROM THE EARLIEST TIMES TILL THE REIGN OF QUEEN VICTORIA.

BY
LORD CAMPBELL.

SEVENTH EDITION.

ILLUSTRATED.

VOL. I.

WILDSIDE PRESS

PREFACE
TO
THE FOURTH EDITION.

A NEW Edition of "THE LIVES OF THE CHANCELLORS" being called for, I have employed this Long Vacation in carefully revising the whole work, and I now offer it to the public in as perfect a state as I can hope that it may ever attain. The minute criticisms which it has undergone in print, the private communications which I have received from friendly readers, and my own subsequent researches, have enabled me to correct various mistakes in the text, and to enrich the notes with valuable illustrations and references.

As I despair of further improvements, the work is now stereotyped. I should have been glad if there had been no change in the appearance of the page or the number of the volumes; but, with a view to make it accessible to all who may have a taste for such reading, I have followed the example of my distinguished friend Mr. Hallam, and adopted a form of publication which admits of a considerable reduction in price, and, avoiding double columns, may be agreeable to the eye of the reader.

In taking a final leave of the public as author of this work. I beg leave respectfully to proffer my warm and sincere thanks for the kind manner in which it has been received by the English nation, and by our brethren in the United States of America, where it has been often reprinted, and has been praised beyond its merits.

Hartrigge, Roxburghshire,
  October 25, 1856.

PREFACE

TO

THE FIRST EDITION.

WHEN suddenly freed, in the autumn of 1841, from professional and official occupations, I revelled for a while in the resumption of my classical studies, and in the miscellaneous perusal of modern authors. By degrees I began to perceive the want of a definite object: I recollected what Lord Coke and Lord Bacon say of the debt due from every successful lawyer to his profession; and I felt within me a revival of the aspiration after literary fame, which, in my most busy days, I was never able entirely to extinguish. Having amused myself with revising for the press "a Selection of my Speeches at the Bar and in the House of Commons," I resolved to write " THE LIVES OF THE CHANCELLORS."

It is for others to judge how this work is executed, but I am more and more convinced that the subject is happily chosen. " HISTORIES," says Lord Bacon, " do rather set forth the pomp of business than the true and inward resorts thereof. But LIVES, if they be well written, propounding to themselves a person to represent, in whom actions both greater and smaller, public and private, have a commixture, must of necessity contain a more true, native, and lively representation."[1] In writing the lives of those who have successively filled a great office there

---

[1] Advancement of Learning.

is unity of design as well as variety of character and incident, and there is no office in the history of any nation that has been filled with such a long succession of distinguished and interesting men as the office of Lord Chancallor or Lord Keeper of the Great Seal of England. It has existed from the foundation of the monarchy; and although mediocrity has sometimes been the recommendation for it,—generally speaking, the most eminent men of the age, if not the most virtuous, have been selected to adorn it. To an English statesman as well as an English lawyer the narrative ought to be particularly instructive, for the history of the holders of the Great Seal is the history of our constitution as well as of our jurisprudence. There is even a sort of romance belonging to the true tale of many of those who are to be delineated, and the strange vicissitudes of their career are not exceeded by the fictions of novelists or dramatists.

I foresaw the difficulties that would beset me—sometimes from the want and sometimes from the superfluity, of materials. Struggling with these, I have attempted to present to the reader a clear and authentic account of all who have held the Great Seal of England from the earliest times—adapting the scale of my narrative to the varying importance of what is to be told, and trying as I proceed to give a glimpse of the most important historical events, and of the manners of the age.

If I have failed, it will not have been for the want of generous assistance. I wish to speak with the most heartfelt gratitude of the kindness which I have experienced. I have been treated like a shipwrecked mariner cast on a friendly shore—every one eagerly desirous to comfort and to cherish him. In not one single instance since I entered on the undertaking, when I have applied for assistance, have I met with a rebuff; on the contrary, the most eager and disinterested disposition has been evinced to oblige me. Such good offices I have to boast of, not less from political opponents than from political associates, and my thanks are peculiarly due to many clergymen of the Church of England to whom I was personally unknown, and who have devoted much time and trouble in furnishing me with extracts from parish registers, copies of epitaphs, and other local information.

In rapidly traveling through a period of above a thousand years, I am well aware that I must have committed many mistakes, and have passed by, without discovering, much interesting matter. I shall receive very thankfully any information with which I may be favored, either privately or in print, to enable me to correct errors and to supply omissions.

I hope that I have shown myself free from any party or sectarian bias. The great principles of civil and religious liberty I ever wish boldly to avow, and resolutely to maintain; but I believe that I have fairly appreciated the acts and characters of those whose Lives I have had in hand, without being swayed by the consideration whether they were Roman Catholics or Protestants—Whigs or Tories. I must request the candid reader not to judge by any particular expression, or any particular Life, but by the whole scope and tendency of the work.

Horace Walpole seeks to deter all who have ever touched a Great Seal from engaging in such a task, by observing, after his criticisms on the historical labors of Sir Thomas More, Lord Bacon, and Lord Clarendon, "It is hoped no more Chancellors will write our story till they can divest themselves of that habit of their profession—apologising for a bad cause."[1] My object has been uniformly to reprobate violence and fraud, and to hold up integrity and consistency for applause and imitation.

I regret the length into which I have been drawn; but, after a careful revision, I have found little that I could omit without injury to my design; and when due regard

[1] Historic Doubts.

PREFACE.

is had to the number of persons whose history was to be narrated, and to the multitudinous facts to be introduced, I am not without hopes that I may receive some credit for condensation.

It will be seen that this "First Series" comes down to the Revolution of 1688. I was advised to begin with the Chancellors during the eighteenth century, and to travel back, after the precedent of Hume. Such a plan would have had advantages, the recent Lives being generally considered the most interesting; but as I profess to give the history of our jurisprudence, I thought that I should best succeed by starting from its sources, and following the course which it has run.

I calculate that the work will be completed in two additional volumes, for which I have already made considerable preparations, and which, if my life and strength be preserved to me I shall ere long lay before the public. Little interruption to study is offered by the political business of the House of the Lords, and although I resolve still regularly to atend the hearing of Appeals and Writs of Error there, and the meetings of the Judicial Committee of the Privy Council, a considerable portion of the year is left entirely under my own control. That the "Second Series" may be less defective, I earnestly request the communication of any scarce tracts or unpublished MSS. which are likely to be of service to me.

If the work should be worthily finished, my ambition is, that it may amuse the general reader; that it may afford some instruction to those who wish to become well acquainted with our constitutional history; and above all, that it may excite the young student of the law to emulation and industry, and cofirm in his mind the liberal and honorable maxims which ought ever to govern the conduct of an English Barriser.

Stratheden House,
Nov. 1, 1845.

PREFACE

TO

THE SECOND EDITION.

IN presenting to the public a Second Edition of my First Series of the "LIVES OF THE LORD CHANCELLORS OF ENGLAND," I would rather expose myself to the imputation of vanity than of ingratitude; and I must therefore express my warm thanks for the favor with which the book has been received. I may truly say, that within a few weeks after its publication "it was on every table, and almost on every toilette." Though founded on historical records, and having solid instruction for its object, it has been as generally read as popular works of fiction, aiming at nothing beyond amusement.

I must especially return my thanks for the kind manner in which, without regard to politics, the book has been treated in periodical publications — quarterly, monthly, weekly, and daily. Gentlemen who have written these criticisms have done ample justice to any merits which they discovered, and have forborne to dwell upon mistakes which could not have escaped them.

I am only aware of one objection that has been seriously urged against me as a writer,—and this I confess I have not at all attempted to correct,—that, forgetting the "dignity of history," my style is sometimes too familiar and colloquial. If I err here, it is on principle and by design. The felicity of my subject consists in the great variety of topics which it embraces. My endeavor has been to treat them all appropriately. If, in analyzing the philosophy of Bacon, or expounding the judgments of Nottingham, or drawing the character of Clarendon, I have forgotten the gravity and severity of diction suitable to the ideas to be expressed, I acknowledge myself liable to the gravest censure; but in my opinion the skillful biographer, when he has to narrate a ludicrous incident, will rather try to imitate the phases of Mercutio than of Ancient Pistol—

"Projicit ampullas et sesquipedalia verba."

I cannot yet understand why, in recording a jest in print, an author should be debarred from using the very language which he might with propriety adopt if he were telling it in good society by word of mouth.

Stratheden House,
    April 22, 1846,

CONTENTS

OF

THE FIRST VOLUME.

INTRODUCTION.

	PAGE
Of the Origin, Functions, and Jurisdiction of the Office of Lord Chancellor in England, ...	1

CHAP.

I.—Of the Chancellors under the Anglo-Saxon Kings. . .   32

II.—Of the Chancellors from the Conquest to the Reign of Henry II., ...   40

III.—Life of Lord Chancellor Thomas à Becket, . . .   61

IV.—Chancellors from the Resignation of Thomas à Becket to the Death of Henry II., ...   100

V.—Chancellors during the Reign of Richard I., . . .   104

VI.—Chancellors during the Reign of King John, . , .   116

VII.—Chancellors during the Reign of Henry III. till the Appointment of Queen Eleanor as Lady Keeper of the Great Seal, ... - .   123

VIII.—Life of Queen Eleanor, Lady Keeper of the Great Seal,   134

IX.—Lord Chancellors from the Resignation of Lady Keeper Queen Eleanor till the Death of Henry III., . .   141

X.—Chancellors and Keepers of the Great Seal during the Reign of Edward I. till the Death of Lord Chancellor Burnel, ...   156

CONTENTS.

CHAP.		PAGE
XI.	Chancellors and Keepers of the Great Seal from the Death of Lord Chancellor Burnel during the Remainder of the Reign of Edward I., ...	169
XII.	Chancellors during the Reign of Edward II., . .	192
XIII.	Chancellors and Keepers of the Great Seal from the Commencement of the Reign of Edward III. till the Appointment of Sir Robert Bourchier, the First Lay Lord Chancellor, ...	201
XIV.	Chancellors and Keepers of the Great Seal from the Appointment of Sir Robert Bourchier till the Appointment of William of Wickham, ...	223
XV.	Chancellors and Keepers of the Great Seal from the Appointment of William of Wickham till the Death of Edward III., ...	245
XVI.	Chancellors and Keepers of the Great Seal from the Commencement of the Reign of Richard II. till the Second Chancellorship of William of Wickham, .	261
XVII.	Chancellors and Keepers of the Great Seal from the Second Chancellorship of William of Wickham till the End of the Reign of Richard II., . . .	279
XVIII.	Chancellors and Keepers of the Great Seal during the Reign of Henry IV., ...	292
XIX.	Chancellors during the Reign of Henry V., . . .	303
XX.	Chancellors from the Commencement of the Reign of Henry VI. till the Death of Cardinal Beaufort, .	313
XXI.	Chancellors during the Reign of Henry VI. from th Appointment of Cardinal Kempe till the Death of Lord Chancellor Waynflete, ...	322
XXII.	Chancellors during the Reign of Henry VI. from the Appointment of George Neville, Bishop of Exeter, till the Death of Lord Chancellor Fortescue, . .	243
XXIII.	Chancellors in the Reign of Edward IV., . . .	357
XXIV.	Chancellors during the Reigns of Edward V. and Richard III., ...	374

CONTENTS.

Chap.	Page
XXV.—Chancellors and Lord Keepers from the Accession of Henry VII. till the Appointment of Archbishop Warham as Lord Keeper, ...	386
XXVI.—Life of Archbishop Warham, Lord Chancellor of England, ...	398
XXVII.—Life of Cardinal Wolsey from his Birth till his Appointment as Lord Chancellor, ...	411
XXVIII.—Life of Cardinal Wolsey from his Appointment as Lord Chancellor till his Fall, ...	426
XXIX.—Life of Cardinal Wolsey from his Fall till his Death, .	458

LIVES

OF THE

LORD CHANCELLORS OF ENGLAND.

INTRODUCTION.

OF THE ORIGIN, FUNCTIONS, AND JURISDICTION OF THE OFFICE OF LORD CHANCELLOR IN ENGLAND.

BEFORE entering upon the Lives of the individuals who have successively filled the office of Lord Chancellor in England, I propose to take a general view of its origin, functions, and jurisdiction,—reserving for future consideration a more detailed account of the progressive changes which it has from time to time undergone.

The etymology of the word "Chancellor" sheds such a feeble and doubtful light on the subject of our inquiry, that I must decline engaging in the great controversy, whether "Cancellarius" be derived from "cancellare" or "cancelli"?—from the act of *cancelling* of the king's letters patent when granted contrary to law, or from the *little bars* used for fencing off from the multitude the recess or chancel in which sat the doorkeeper or usher of a court of justice. Of the former opinion a distinguished champion is John of Salisbury, who flourished in the reign of Henry II., and in the verses prefixed to his Polycraticon thus glorifies the Chancellor:

> Hic est qui leges regni cancellat iniquas,
> Et mandata pii principis æqua facit." [1]

So when Lord Chancellor Gardyner, in the reign of Queen Mary, presiding on the woolsack, in the sight of all the

---

[1] See 4 Inst. 88. 3 Bl. Com. 47.

2   ORIGIN OF OFFICE OF CHANCELLOR.

Lords, cut off from a bill certain clauses to which the Commons had dissented, he said, "I now do rightly the office of a Chancellor."[1]

But more weight will probably be attached to the authority of Gibbon, who, after exposing the profligate conduct of the Emperor Carinus in having selected his favorites, and even his ministers, from the dregs of the populace, and intrusted a "*Chancellor*" with the government of the city, observes, "This word, *so humble in its origin*, has by a singular fortune risen into the title of the first great office of state in the monarchies of Europe."[2]

It would likewise be foreign to our purpose (though very curious) to trace the steps by which, under the later Roman Emperors, the "Cancellarius," like "the Justice-clerk" in Scotland, from being a humble scribe or secretary, came to be invested with high judicial powers. Nor should I be justified in inquiring how the office passed from the Roman Emperors to that body ever emulous of imperial state—the Roman Church, in which every bishop had his "Chancellor,"—or into the manner in which the office was established, with a great variety of powers and duties, in the different states on the continent of Europe founded by the Northern invaders, who, clinging to their own institutions, were fond of borrowing titles from the

---

[1] "Die Veneris videlicet, 4º. Januarii," (1 & 2 Ph. & Mar. 1554-5).

"Hodie allatæ sunt a Domo Communi tres Billæ; quarum.

"*Prima.*—For the repealing of all outlawries and other attainders had or made against Richard Pate, Bishop, William Peytoo, and others.

"*Secunda.*—That persons dwelling in the country shall not sell divers wares in cities and towns corporate, by retail.

"*Tertia.*—Repealing all statutes, articles, and provisions made against the See Apostolick of Rome since the 20th year of King Henry the Eighth; and for the establishment of all spiritual and ecclesiastical possessions and hereditaments conveyed to the laity, with two new provisoes added thereto by the Commons; and also a request that the two clauses, containing nineteen lines, and concerning the Bishops of London, &c., and the Lords Wentworthe, &c., should be clearly put out. Whereof one of the provisoes, for the manner of the penning thereof, being misliked to the House, another 'o the same effect was commanded to be drawn, which being three times read, and agreed unto by the whole House, except the Viscount Montacute, and the Bishops of London, and Coven. and Lichef., was sent down to the Commons, where being also thrice read and agreed unto, it was brought up again as an act fully assented unto by both Houses; *nor the said nineteen lines were not razed nor taken out of the Act : but the Chancellor, in the sight of all the Lords, with a knife, cut them, saying these words,* "I NOW DO RIGHTLY THE OFFICE OF A CHANCELLOR.'"—Lords Journals, vol. i. p. 484.

[2] Dec. and Fall, ii. 99; and see Casaubon and Salmasius ad Hist. Aug. 253.

conquered. Our business here is exclusively with "the Chancellor of the Kings of England."

This office has existed from the most remote antiquity. The almost fabulous British King Arthur is said to have appointed a Chancellor.[1] The Anglo-Saxon monarchs, from Ethelbert downwards, certainly had such an officer, although we must not therefore assent to the statement of Lord Coke, that the Chancery dispensed justice as an ordinary tribunal, in the reign of King Alfred. The office then existed, but, as we shall see hereafter, centuries elapsed before it assumed the functions of a COURT.— How the office originally sprung up in England, and what it has since become, it will now be my endeavor to describe.

With us the King has ever been considered the fountain of justice. In very early times, as he could not himself in person decide all controversies and remedy all wrongs, tribunals were constituted, over which deputed judges presided, to carry the law into execution. Still, applications were made to him personally by injured parties for redress; these were to be referred to the proper forum, and process was to be made out for summoning the adversary, and directing that after both sides had been heard, the appropriate relief should be administered. To assist him in this department the King employed a secretary, on whom by degrees it was entirely devolved; and this officer, on a statement of facts by the complainant, framed writs or letters, in the king's name, to the judges, by which suits were instituted. Forms were adopted, to be always followed under similar circumstances, and a place was named to which all suitors might resort to be furnished with the means of obtaining justice. This was the *officina justitiæ* called CHANCERY, and the officer who presided over it was called CHANCELLOR.[2]

Again, grants of dignities, of offices, and of lands were made by the king. It was necessary that these grants should be framed and authenticated by an officer well

---

[1] Mirror of Justices.
[2] "Every one was to have a remedial writ from the King's Chancery, according to his plaint," of which the following is the most ancient form:—
"Rex, &c." [to the Judge]. "Questus est nobis *A*. quod *B*., &c. Et ideo tibi (vices nostras in hac parte committentes) præcipimus quod causam illam audias et legitimo fine decidas."—*Mirror of Justices*, 8. See Fitzh. Nat. Brevium.

versed in the laws and customs of the kingdom; and it was found convenient to employ for this purpose the same person who superintended the commencement of suits between subject and subject. Here we have the other great branch of the pristine duties of Chancellor.

These writs and grants in the earliest times were verified merely by signature. From the art of writing being little known, seals became common; and the king, according to the fashion of the age, adopted a seal with which writs and grants were sealed. This was called the GREAT SEAL, and the custody of it was given to the Chancellor.[1]

But how are we to account for the important function which has immemorially belonged to this officer, of "Keeper of the King's Conscience"? From the conversion of the Anglo-Saxons to Christianity by the preaching of St. Augustine, the king always had near his person a priest, to whom was intrusted the care of his chapel, and who was his confessor. This person, selected from the most learned and able of his order, and greatly superior in accomplishments to the unlettered laymen attending the Court, soon acted as private secretary to the king, and gained his confidence in affairs of state. The present demarcation between civil and ecclesiastical employments was then little regarded, and to this same person was assigned the business of superintending writs and grants,— with the custody of the Great Seal.

For ages to come the Chancellor had no separate judicial power, and was not considered of very high dignity in the state, and the office was chiefly courted as a stepping-stone to a bishopric, to which it almost invariably led. Particular individuals holding the Great Seal acquired a great ascendancy from their talents, but among the Anglo-Saxons the Chancellor was not generally a conspicuous member of the government, and in the early Anglo-Norman reigns he ranked only sixth of the great officers under the Crown, coming after the Chief Justiciar, the Constable, the Mareschal, the Steward, and the Chamberlain. At this time the Chief Justiciar was by far the greatest subject, both in rank and power.[2] He was gen-

---

[1] It has generally been supposed that Edward the Confessor was the first English sovereign who used a seal; but Dudgale shows that there were some grants under seal as far back as King Edgar. Dug. Off. ch. 2.
[2] Madd. Exch. b. 1.

erally taken from among the high hereditary barons; his functions were more political than judicial; he sometimes led armies to battle; and when the sovereign was beyond the sea, by virtue of his office, as regent he governed the realm.[1]

The office of Chancellor rose into importance from the energy of A'Becket, Longchamp, and other ambitious men who held it;[2] but it was only in the end of the reign of Henry III., or the beginning of the reign of Edward I., that its supremacy was established. Till then the *Aula Regia* existed,—of which the Chief Justiciar was president, and in which all causes of importance, of whatever description, were decided.

The origin of the different courts in Westminster Hall, as they now exist, may be distinctly traced to the disruption of this great tribunal—like the formation of the planetary system from the nebulous matter of which some philosophers tell us it is composed. The Chancellor always sat as a member of the *Aula Regia*, and from his usual duties and occupations he must have been its chief legal adviser.[3] In all probability, early in its history, the

---

[1] Hence comes the title of the "Lords Justices," appointed to represent the King in England in the reigns of George I. and George II.; and of the "Lords Justices" now appointed to act in Ireland in the absence of the Lord Lieutenant.

There was likewise from very remote times a Grand Justiciar in Scotland with very arbitrary power. In that country when the Judges going the circuit approach a royal burgh, the Lord Provost universally comes out to meet them—with the exception of Aberdeen,—of which there is by tradition this explanation. Some centuries ago, the Lord Provost, at the head of the magistrates, going out to meet the Grand Justiciar at the Bridge of Dee, the Grand Justiciar, for some imaginary offense, hanged his Lordship at the end of the Bridge,—since which the Lord Provost of Aberdeen has never trusted himself in the presence of a Judge beyond the walls of the city.—*Ex relatione* of a very venerable person who has filled the office—now called LORD JUSTICE GENERAL.

[2] The office of Chancellor in France appears to have arisen into great importance by the same means. "Magnitudinem virorum qui eo munere [Cancellarii] fungebantur, vires decusque illi attulis e crediderim, ut ab exiguis initiis ad tantam majestatem pervenerit."—*Paul. Encycl. de rebus gestis Francon.* p. 104, a.

[3] He was wont to act, together with the Chief Justiciar and other great men, in matters of revenue at the Exchequer, and sometimes with the other justiciars itinerant in their circuits. About the beginning of King Henry the Second's reign, there were pleas in the county of Kent holden "before the King's Chancellor, and before Henry de Essex, the King's Constable," and "before the Chancellor and the Earl of Leicester." Amerciaments were set upon several persons in Worcestershire by "the Chancellor and Stephen de

different branches of judicial business which came before it were allotted to the consideration of particular members most conversant with them; and while matters of chivalry might be decided by the opinion of the constable and mareschal, the validity of the king's grants would be referred to him whose duty it was to authenticate them, and proceedings by virtue of mandatory writs or commissions, under the Great Seal, could best be judged of by the same person who had issued them. So, questions arising out of "petitions of right," "*monstrans de droit*," and "traverses of office,"—where a complaint was made that the King had been advised to do any act, or was put in possession of any lands or goods, to the prejudice of a subject, would be naturally referred to "the Keeper of his Conscience."[1]

The officer to whom such references were made by degrees became a separate judge; and hence the origin of what is considered the common-law jurisdiction of the Chancellor.

It is certain, that almost immediately after the establishment of the Court of King's Bench for criminal law, the Common Pleas for civil suits, and the Exchequer for the revenue, all extraordinary cases of a juridical nature being reserved for the King in council,—the Chancellor held a separate independent court, in which the validity of royal grants was questioned by *scire facias*, and the other matters were discussed which I have supposed to have been previously referred for his opinion, to guide the decision of the Aula Regia. To assist in this new separate jurisdiction, officers were appointed, and they had the privilege of suing and being sued in all personal actions in the court to which they were attached. These proceedings were carried on in accordance with the rules and maxims of the common law.

Here then we have the Chancellor with two great occupations:—the first, his earliest one, of supplying writs to suitors who wished to litigate in other courts; the second, the decision of a peculiar class of suits as a judge. According to ancient simplicity, the place where he carried on the business of his office was divided between the

Segrave;" and in the counties of Nottingham and Derby by the same persons.—*Madd. Exch.* cap. 2, p. 42.

[1] Gilbert's History of the Exchequer, p. 8.

"Hanniper" or hamper, in which writs were stored up; and the "Petty-bag," in which were kept the records and proceedings in the suits to be decided by himself.[1] Thus did the Chancellor decide all matters of law that might arise by his own authority, subject to a writ of error to the King's Bench; but he had no power to summon a jury; and issue being joined on a question of fact, he at once handed over the record to the King's Bench, where the suit proceeded, and was finally disposed of.[2]

This "common-law jurisdiction" of the Chancellor has been generally carried back to the reign of Edward I.—by some much higher,—and the validity of it has never been questioned;—but his "Equitable Jurisdiction," which has become of infinitely greater importance, has been supposed to be a usurpation, and not to have been exercised till the reign of Richard II., upon the introduction of uses and trusts of real property, and the invention of the writ of subpœna by John of Waltham, Bishop of Salisbury. After much investigation, I must express my clear conviction, that the Chancellor's *equitable* is an indubitable and as ancient as his *common-law* jurisdiction, and that it may be traced in a manner equally satisfactory.

The silence of Bracton, Glanvil, Fleta, and other early juridical writers, has been strongly relied upon to disprove the equitable jurisdiction of the Chancellor; but they as little notice his common law jurisdiction, most of them writing during the subsistence of the Aula Regia; and they all speak of the Chancery, not as a *court*, but merely as an *office* for the making and sealing of writs.[3] There are no very early decisions of the Chancellors on points of law, any more than of equity, to be found in the Year Books, or old Abridgments. It was formerly objected, that there were no Bills or Petitions in Chancery extant

---

[1] Even now a distinction is made between the "hanniper" side and the "petty-bag" side of the court.

[2] I have followed the authority of Blackstone (Com. vol. iii. 49); but Mr. Macqueen, in his very learned and valuable treatise "On the Appellate Jurisdiction of the House of Lords," has collected weighty decisions and arguments to show that the writ of error from the petty-bag or common-law side in Chancery was directly to Parliament. This jurisdiction is now regulated by stat. 12 and 13 Vic. c. 109, s. 39.

[3] The first law book which treats of the judicial powers of the Lord Chancellor is the 'Diversiteé des Courtes," written in the end of the fifteenth or beginning of the sixteenth century, tit. *Chancery*, fol. 296.

of an earlier date than the time of Henry VI., but by the labors of the Record Commissioners many have been discovered of preceding reigns. Till the 17th Richard II., when the statute was made giving the Chancellor power to award damages or costs to the defendant on the plaintiff's suggestions being proved to be false, there was little use in filing or preserving them, and from that era we have them in abundance.

By "equitable jurisdiction" must be understood the extraordinary interference of the Chancellor, without common-law process, or regard to the common-law rules of proceeding, upon the petition of a party grieved, who was without adequate remedy in a court of common law; whereupon the opposite party was compelled to appear and to be examined, either personally or upon written interrogatories; and evidence being heard on both sides, without the interposition of a jury, an order was made *secundum æquum et bonum*, which was enforced by imprisonment. Such a jurisdiction had belonged to the Aula Regia, and was long exercised by Parliament;[1] and when Parliament was not sitting, by the king's ordinary council. Upon the dissolution of the Aula Regia many petitions, which Parliament or the Council could not conveniently dispose of, were referred to the Chancellor, sometimes with and sometimes without assessors. To avoid the circuity of applying to Parliament or the Council, the peti-

---

[1] Audley *v.* Audley, 40 Edward III. This, the earliest instance I have found of a suit for a specific performance, is fully reported in the close roll of that year. By a deed executed in contemplation of the marriage of Nicholas son of James Lord Audley, he had covenanted to settle lands in possession or reversion to the amount of 400 marks. After the marriage, Elizabeth, the wife, petitioned the King in parliament that Lord Audley should be ordained to perform the covenant. The King caused the defendant to come before the Chancellor, the Treasurer and the justices and other "sages" assembled in the Star Chamber. The Lady Audley "showed forth her grievances;" that is to say, she declared them by word of mouth, and produced the indenture of covenant. A demurrer put in on the part of the defendant was overruled; and after various proceedings before the Chancellor and Treasurer in the Council, performance of the covenant was at last obtained.

One of the most remarkable examples of Parliament acting as a court of equity is William Lord Clynton's case, in the 9th of Hen. V., where William de la Pole, a feoffee to uses, was compelled to reconvey his lordship's estates. This might possibly have proceeded on the ground of parliamentary privilege. I believe the records of the Court of Chancery, although they prove the exercise of the equitable jurisdiction of the Chancellor much further back, do not show any example so early of compelling the execution of a trust. R. P. 9 H. 5.

tion was very soon, in many instances, addressed originally to the Chancellor himself. For some ages these extraordinary applications for redress were received by the Parliament, by the Council, and by the Chancellor concurrently. The Parliament by degrees abandoned all original equitable jurisdiction, acting only as a court of appeal in civil cases, and taking original cognizance of criminal cases on impeachment by the Commons; but it will be found that the Council and the Chancellor long continued equitably to adjudicate on the same matters, and that there were the same complaints and statutes directed against both.

From various causes, however, the equitable jurisdiction of the Council gradually declined. The proper and immemorial business of the Chancellor being the preparation of writs,—where a case occurred to which no known writ was properly applicable, and in which the common-law courts could not grant redress, he took it into his own hands,—and having heard both parties, gave relief. Again, where the proceedings in the courts of law under writs which he had issued were grossly defective and inequitable, he was naturally called upon to review them, and to prevent judgments which had been fraudulently obtained from being carried into effect.

Another source of equitable jurisdiction to the Chancellor, of considerable importance, though little noticed, arose from the practice of enrolling in Chancery covenants and agreements, releases of right, and declarations of uses, and of securing the performance of these deeds by a recognizance acknowledged before the Chancellor, and entered upon the close rolls. On applications for writs of execution by reason of the alleged forfeiture of the recognizance, the Chancellor was of course bound to hear both parties, and to make such decree between them as justice required.

For the sake of fees to the Chancellor and his officers, great encouragement was given to suitors resorting to Chancery, and from the distinguished ability of the men presiding there, who were assisted by the Master of the Rolls and the other Masters,—ecclesiastics well skilled in the civil law,—the business was more systematically and effectively transacted than before the Council, which has ever been a tribunal without fixity in its members or regularity in its proceedings. These various causes combining, the equitable jurisdiction of the Council fell into desuetude, like that of the Parliament; and in the Court of Chancery that admirable system of equity which we boast of in England, and which with our common law has been adopted by our brethren in America, was gradually developed and matured.

It is thus a great mistake to suppose that the clerical expedient of a conveyance to uses, for the purpose of evading the statutes of mortmain, gave rise to the equitable jurisdiction of the Chancellor, or that he at first interfered only in cases of trust binding on the conscience. From the researches of the Record Commissioners it appears that his equitable jurisdiction was well established long anterior to the time when such cases came before him, and that the earliest applications to him for relief were from those who suffered by direct violence and the *combinations* of great men, against which they were unable to gain redress by the ordinary process of law.[1] Then followed cases in which it was necessary to correct the absurdities of the common-law judges, who in their own courts laid down rules utterly subversive of justice,[2]—or in which, from multiplicity of parties, disability to sue, intricacy of accounts, suppression of documents, facts being exclusively in the knowledge of the adverse party, the importance of specific relief, and the urgent necessity for preventing irremediable damage to property,—trial by jury and common-law process afforded no adequate remedy. The maxim of the common-law judges, that if a man accepted the conveyance of land as a trustee, they could only look to the *legal estate*, and they would allow him to enjoy it discharged of the trust, was not the earliest, nor for a long time the most usual, ground for seeking relief in equity.[3]

---

[1] A bill in Chancery still alleges "combination and confederacy,"—which, if specially charged, ought to be denied by the answer.

[2] As, for example, that where a claim was founded on a deed detained in the hands of another, no action could be maintained; that if a deed of grant were lost, the thing granted was lost with it; and that a man was liable to pay money due by deed twice over, if on payment he had omitted to take an acquittance under seal.

[3] Even so late as the reign of Charles II. it was *vexata questio* whether an action on the case could be maintained by cestui que trust against the trustee. See Barnardiston *v* Soame, 7 St. Tr. 443; 1 Vernon, 344 n.

I must likewise observe, that there was not by any means the constant struggle between the two jurisdictions of common law and equity which is generally supposed At times, from personal enmity, from vanity, from love of power, and from love of profit, Chancellors and Chief Justices came into unseemly collision, and in this warfare they resorted unsparingly to the artillery of injunctions, attachments, writs of habeas corpus, indictments, and præmunires. But, generally speaking, the common-law judges co-operated harmoniously with the Chancellor, and recognized the distinction between what might fitly be done in a court of law and in a court of equity. He sometimes consulted them before issuing a subpœna to commence the suit. In hearing causes, if not satisfied with the advice of the Master of the Rolls and the Masters in Chancery (his ordinary council), he was from the earliest times in the habit of calling in the assistance of some Justices or Barons; and questions of extraordinary importance he adjourned into the Exchequer Chamber, that he might have the opinion of all the twelve.[1]

For the benefit of the general reader I may here be permitted to make a few observations upon the Chancellor's supposed *prætorian* power, or *nobile officium*. It is a common opinion that English equity consists in the judge acting upon his own notions of what is right, always softening the rigor of the common law when he disapproves of it, and dispensing with the application to particular cases of common-law rules allowed to be generally wise,—so that he may reach justice according to the circumstances of each particular case, in pursuance of the suggestion of Lord Bacon,—" Habeant Curiæ Prætoriæ potestatem tam subveniendi contra rigorem legis quam supplendi defectum legis."[2] But with us there is no scope for judicial caprice in a court of equity more than elsewhere. Our equitable system has chiefly arisen from supplying the defects of the common law, by giving a remedy in classes of cases for which the common law had

---

[1] From this practice the decrees ran, *Per curiam Cancellariæ et omnes Justitiarios ;* sometimes, *Per decretum Cancellarii ex assensu omnium Justitiarium ac aliorum ac aliorum de Concilii Domini Regis præsentium.* Again, *Ideo consideratum est per curiam de assensu Johannis Fortescue, Capitalisis Justitiarii Domini Regis ad placita tenenda, ed diversorum aliorum Justitiariorum et servientium ad legem in curiæ præsenilum.*—Seld. Off. Lord Ch. § 3.

[2] De Augmentis Scient. lviii. ; Aphor. 35.

provided none, and from a universal disregard by the equity judge of certain absurd rules of the common law, which he considers inapplicable to the whole category to which the individual case under judgment belongs.[1] In former times *unconscientious* Chancellors, talking perpetually of their *conscience*, have decided in a very arbitrary manner, and have exposed their jurisdiction to much odium and many sarcasms.[2] But the preference of individual opinion to rules and precedents has long ceased: "the doctrine of the court" is to be diligently found out and strictly followed ; and the Chancellor sitting in equity is only to be considered a magistrate, to whose tribunal are assigned certain portions of forensic business, to which he is to apply a well-defined system of jurisprudence,—being under the control of fixed maxims and prior authorities, as much as the judges of the courts of common law. He decides "secundum arbitrium boni veri ;" but when it is asked, "Vir bonus est quis ?" the answer is, "Qui consulta patrum, qui leges juraque servat."[3]

There was long great doubt and difficulty with respect to the mode of reviewing the decrees of the Lord Chancellor on the equity side of the court ; but, after a violent parliamentary struggle, it was at last settled, in the reign

---

[1] Notwithstanding the rudeness and defects of the common law, we should ever remember its favor to personal liberty, and its admirable machinery for separating law and fact, and assigning each to a distinct tribunal; wherein it excels all other systems of jurisprudence which have appeared. We should likewise bear in mind that it offered many specific remedies, which, after the improvement of equitable jurisdiction, fell into desuetude.

[2] The most celebrated is the saying of Selden: "Equity is a roguish thing; for law we have a measure. Equity is according to the conscience of him who is Chancellor, and as that is larger or narrower, so is equity. It is all one as if they should make the standard for the measure we call a *foot* 'a chancellor's foot.' What an uncertain measure would this be ? One chancellor has a long foot ; another a short foot ; a third, an indifferent foot: it is the same thing in the chancellor's *conscience.*"—*Table Talk.*

[3] "The discretion of a judge is the law of tyrants; it is always unknown ; it is different in different men ; it is casual, and depends upon constitution, temper, and passion. In the best, it is oftentimes caprice ; in the worst it is every vice, folly, and passion to which human nature is liable."—*Lord Camden.*

See 2 P. Wms. 752; 1 Bl. Com. 47; Story's Equity, i. 30; Maddocks' Chancery, i. 29 ; Correspondence between Lord Hardwicke and Lord Kames ; Tyler's life of Lord Kames, 230 ; Cooper's Letters ; Sur la Cour de la Chaucellerie ; Abuses and remedies of Chancery, by George Norbury ; Harg. Law Tracts ; and two pieces concerning Suits in Chancery by Subpœna, temp. H. VIII., likewise in Harg. Law Tracts,—both exceedingly curious.

MISCELLANEOUS JURISDICTION.

of Charles II., that an appeal lies from them to the House of Lords.

There are other judicial functions to be exercised by the Chancellor in his own court, which I ought to notice. In conjunction with the common-law judges, he is a guardian of personal liberty; and any one unlawfully imprisoned is entitled to apply to him for a writ of HABEAS CORPUS, either in term or in vacation.[1] So the Chancellor may at any time grant PROHIBITIONS to restrain inferior courts from exceeding their jurisdiction, though he listens with reluctance to such motions when they may be made to the King's Bench, whose habits are better adapted to this sort of business.[2]

The Chancellor has an exclusive authority to restrain a party from leaving the kingdom, where it appears that he is purposely withdrawing himself from the jurisdiction of the court, to the disappointment of honest creditors. This is effected by the writ " *ne exeat regno,*" issuing under the Great Seal;—a high prerogative remedy, which, as it affects personal liberty, is granted with great circumspection, particularly where foreigners are concerned.[3]

It is the province of the Chancellor to issue a writ under the Great Seal " *de coronatore eligendo,*" directed to the sheriff, and requiring the freeholders of the county to choose a coroner.[4] He also decides in the Court of Chancery questions arising as to the validity of the election.[5] And upon complaint against a coroner for neglect of duty, or upon an allegation of incapacity,—as from being confined in prison,—or of incompetency,—as from mental derangement or habits of extreme intemperance, — the Chancellor may remove him from his office.[6]

Anciently the Chancellor took cognizance of riots and conspiracies, upon applications for surety of the peace; but this criminal jurisdiction has been long obsolete, although articles of the peace still may be, and sometimes are, exhibited before him.[7]

---

[1] Crawley's Case, 2 Swanst. 6.
[2] Per Lord Redesdale, 2 Sch. & Lef. 136. See 4 Inst. 81; 2 P. Wms. 202.
[3] De Carriere *v.* Calonne, 4 Vess. 577. See Beames' Writ *Ne exeat regno* and Beames' Chancery Orders, p. 39.
[4] F. N. B. 163; 1 Black. 347.
Re Coron. Co. Stafford, 2 Russ. 475.
[5] Ex parte Parnell, 1 Jac. & W. 451; Ex parte Palsey, 3 Drur. & War. 34.
[6] Tunnicliffe *v.* Tunniclife, A.D. 1823; Williams *v.* Williams, A.D. 1841.

The Chancellor had a most important jurisdiction in *Bankruptcy*, which arose partly from the commissions for distributing the effects of insolvent traders being under the Great Seal, and partly from the powers directly given to him by act of parliament. The proceeding is here generally by Petition, in which case there is no appeal; but on questions of difficulty the Court makes its equitable machinery ancillary to this summary jurisdiction; and, a bill being filed, the matter may be carried to the House of Lords. The weight of this branch of business, which was at one time nearly overwhelming, has been greatly lightened by the appointment of permanent Commissioners and Vice-Chancellors; but the Chancellor still retains a general superintendence over bankruptcy.

It has been a common opinion that the Chancellor has no jurisdiction whatever in lunacy by virtue of his office, and that this jurisdiction is entirely derived from a special authority under the royal sign manual, which might be conferred on any one else. But I clearly apprehend that a commission "*de idiota*," or "*de lunatico inquirendo*," would issue at common law from the Court of Chancery under the Great Seal, and that the Lord Chancellor, without any special delegation for this purpose, would have authority to control the execution of it, and to make orders for that purpose. The sign manual takes its origin from stat. 17 Edw. 2, c. 9, by which the rents and profits of the estates of idiots are given to the Crown, and form part of the royal revenue. During the existence of the Court of Wards and Liveries, the management of the estates of idiots and lunatics was entrusted to it, and since has been delegated to the Chancellor. Being a fiscal matter, the warrant is countersigned by the Lord High Treasurer, or Lords Commissioners of the Treasury.[1]

So much may for the present suffice respecting the forensic character of the Lord Chancellor; and I now proceed to give a rapid sketch of his other functions.

---

[1] I was obliged to investigate this matter during the short time I had the honor to hold the Great Seal of Ireland. By an oversight, the usual warrant under the sign manual respecting lunatics had not in the first instance been delivered to me, but I found that I might safely make some orders in lunacy before I received it. On such matters, perhaps, the appeal ought to be to the House of Lords, although the appeal respecting others comprehended in the special delegation be to the Sovereign in Council. See 3 Bl. Com. 48, 427 Story's Equity, ii. 542; In Re Fitzgerald, 2 Sch. & Lef. 432, 151.

It is said by Selden that the Chancellor is a privy councillor by virtue of his office; but this can only mean that he is entitled to offer the king advice, as any peer may do; —not that by the delivery of the Great Seal to him he is incidentally constituted a member of the Privy Council, with the powers lawfully belonging to the office of a privy councillor; for no one can sit in the Privy Council who is not by the special command of the Sovereign appointed a member of it; and, as far back as can be traced, the Lord Chancellors who were not privy councillors previous to their elevation have been sworn of the Privy Council, like other great officers of state.[1]

He certainly is *ex officio* Prolocutor or Speaker of the House of Lords, whether he be a peer or not. Without any commission or express authority for the purpose, he always presides there when present. This privilege is said to belong to him by *prescription*, and he has enjoyed it many centuries, although in the reigns of Richard I., John, and Henry III. (within time of legal memory) it was exercised by the Chief Justiciar. The Crown may by commission name others to preside in the House of Lords in the absence of the Chancellor; and, no speaker appointed by the Crown being present, the Lords of their own authority may choose one of themselves to act as speaker,—which they now often do in hearing appeals;— but all these speakers are immediately superseded when the Chancellor enters the House.[2]

By 25 Edw. 3, c. 2, to slay him in the execution of his office is high treason. By 31 Hen. 8, c. 10, he has precedence above all temporal peers, except the king's sons, nephews, and grandsons, whether he be a peer or a commoner. If he be a peer, he ought regularly to be placed at the top of the dukes' bench, on the left of the throne; and if a commoner, upon " the uppermost sack in the par-

---

[1] See Selden's Office of Lord Chancellor, § 3. It has often been said that the Lord Mayor of London is a privy councillor by virtue of his office, but for this there is not the slightest pretense, although he is styled "right honorable," and on a demise of the Crown joins with the aldermen and other notables in recognizing the title of the new sovereign.

[2] Lord Chief Baron Gilbert suggests that the Chancellor sits on the woolsack as steward of the King's Court Baron, and draws an ingenious but fanciful parallel between the Court Baron of a manor and the House of Lords. Gilb. Ev. 42.—By an old standing order of the House of Lords, his constant attendance there is required.

liament chamber, called the Lord Chancellor's woolsack."[1] For convenience, here he generally sits, though a peer, and here he puts the question, and acts as prolocutor; but this place is not considered within the House, and when he is to join in debate as a peer, he leaves the woolsack, and stands in front of his proper seat, at the top of the dukes' bench.

If he be a commoner, notwithstanding a resolution of the House that he is to be proceeded against for any misconduct as if he were a peer, he has neither vote nor deliberative voice,[2] and he can only put the question, and communicate the resolutions of the House according to the directions he receives.[3]

From very early times the Chancellor was usually employed on the meeting of a new parliament to address the two Houses in the presence of the King, and to explain the causes of their being summoned,—although this was in rare instances done by the Chief Justice of the King's Bench, and by other functionaries.[4]

Whether peer or commoner, the Chancellor is not, like the Speaker of the Commons, moderator of the proceeding of the House, in which he seems to preside; he is not addressed in debate; he does not name the peer who is to be heard; he is not appealed to as an authority on points of order; and he may cheer the sentiments expressed by his colleagues in the ministry.[5]

---

[1] There are woolsacks for the Judges and other assessors, as well as for the Lord Chancellor. They are said to have been introduced into the House of Lords as a compliment to the staple manufacture of the realm; but I believe that in the rude simplicity of early times a sack of wool was frequently used as a sofa—when the Judges sat on a hard wooden BENCH, and the advocates stood behind a rough wooden rail, called the BAR.

[2] From the manner in which the journals are kept, it might have been inferred that the Chancellor, or Keeper of the Great Seal, though a commoner, was considered a member of the House. Thus, in the times of Sir Nicholas Bacon, his presence is recorded as if he were a peer, under the designation of "*Custos Mag. Sig.;*" and the same entries continue to be made with respect to Sir N. Wright and Sir R. Henley. So, on the 22nd Nov. 1830, there is an entry in the list of peers present, "*Henricus Brougham Cancellarius,*" but he had no right to debate and vote till the following day, when the entry of his name and office appears in the same place, "Dominus Brougham et Vaux Cancellarius."

[3] Lord Keeper Henley, till raised to the peerage, used to complain bitterly of being obliged to put the question for the reversal of his own decrees, without being permitted to say a word in support of them.

[4] See Elsynge on Parliaments, p. 137.

[5] This arises from a proper distrust of a Speaker holding his office during

On the trial of a peer for treason or felony, either before the House of Lords or before selected peers when parliament is not sitting, the presidentship of the Lord Chancellor is suspended, and a Lord High Steward is especially appointed *pro hac vice* by the Crown. This arose from the Lord Chancellor, in early times, being almost always an ecclesiastic, who could not meddle in matters of blood. Since the Chancellor has been a layman, he has generally been nominated Lord High Steward; but then he becomes "His Grace," and presides in a different capacity.[1] On the impeachment of commoners (which can only be for high crimes and misdemeanors)[2] he presides as in the ordinary business of the House.

The Chancellor was once a most important criminal judge, by ruling the Court of Star Chamber. Here he alone had a right to speak with his hat on; and if the councillors present were equally divided, he claimed a double vote, whether for acquitting or convicting.[3] While this arbitrary tribunal flourished in the plentitude of its power under the Tudors and Stuarts,—with a view to proceedings here rather than in the Court of Chancery was the Great Seal often disposed of;—but since the abolition of the Star Chamber, the Chancellor has been released from taking any part in criminal proceedings, unless on the rare occasions of impeachments, and the trials of peers.[4]

the pleasure of the Crown, and necessarily an active political partisan; but most inconvenient consequences follow from there being no moderator in an assembly which is supposed to be the most august, but is probably the most disorderly in the world.

[1] On the late trial of the Earl of Cardigan, Lord Denham was appointed and acted as Lord High Steward, on account of the temporary illness of Lord Chancellor Cottenham.

[2] So settled in Fitzharris's case, temp. Car. II. See Lives of Shaftesbury and North.

[3] Hudson's Star Chamber, 2 Coll. Jur. 31; 4 Inst. 63.

[4] Various statutes, now repealed, delegated to the Chancellor functions in aid of the criminal law. Thus by 2 H. 5, st. 1, c. 29, he was enabled to issue writs of proclamation in cases of bloodshed; and 35 H. 5, c. 1, the like power was granted to him for the apprehension of fugitive servants embezzling the goods of their masters, to be exercised with the advice of the Chief Justice of either Bench, or of the Chief Baron of the Exchequer. Till the late new modelling of the courts of error, he likewise, by 31 E. 1, c. 12, sat in the Exchequer Chamber to decide writs of error from the Court of Exchequer. He is now, *ex officio*, a member of the Central Criminal Court, and of the Judicial Committee of the Privy Council; but he is not expected to attend in the

Still he presides at "the trial of the Pyx," when a jury of goldsmiths determine whether new coinages of gold and silver be of the standard weight and fineness, and the Master of the Mint be entitled to his *quietus*.

Since the institution of justices of the peace in the reign of Edward III., instead of the conservators of the peace formerly elected by the people,—to the Lord Chancellor has belonged the power of appointing and removing them throughout the kingdom.[1] Upon this important and delicate subject, he generally takes the advice of the Lord Lieutenant, or Custos Rotulorum, in each county; but when any extraordinary cases arises, it is his duty, and his practice, to act upon his own judgment.

He nominates, by his own authority, to many important offices connected with the administration of Justice, and he is by usage the adviser of the Crown in the appointment to others still more important,—including the Puisne Judges in the three superior courts in Westminster Hall.[2]

He is patron of all the king's livings of the value of 20*l*. and under, in the king's books.[3] These he was anciently obliged to bestow upon the clerks in Chancery, King's Bench, Common Pleas, and Exchequer, who were all in orders; but he can now dispose of them according to his notions of what is due to religion, friendship, or party.

He is visitor of all colleges and hospitals of royal foundation; and representing the Sovereign as *parens patriæ*, he has the general superintendence of all charitable uses, and is the guardian of all infants who stand in need of his protection.

former, and in the latter only in cases of great difficulty. Till the accession of the present Queen, the Chancellor had a most painful duty to perform, in advising on the report of the Recorder of London in what cases the law should be allowed to take its course; but convictions in the metropolis are now left as those at the Assizes with the Judges and the Secretary of State. 7 W. 4 & 1 Vic. c. 77.

[1] See 1 Ed. 3, st. 2 c. 16; 28 Hen. 6, c. 11.

[2] Lord Eldon likewise claimed the patronage of the office of Chief Baron, as belonging to the Great Seal; but this, since the Court of Exchequer was reformed, has been supposed to belong to the Prime Minister,—of course with the concurrence of the Cabinet and the Sovereign.

He formerly appointed the Masters in Chancery; but, by a most useful reform, these officers are now abolished. 14 & 15 Vic. c. 83.

[3] The limit to be used to be twenty marks; but since the new *valor beneficiorum* in the time of Henry VIII., *pounds* are supposed to have been substituted for *marks*.

KEEPER OF THE GREAT SEAL.

The custody of the royal conscience may possibly be considered one of the obsolete functions of the Chancellor, for he is no longer a casuist for the Sovereign as when priest, chaplain, and confessor; and it is now merely his duty, like other sworn counselors, to give honest advice, for which he is responsible in parliament. I may observe, however, that the Chancellor has in all ages been an important adviser of the Crown in matters of state as well as a great magistrate. The Chancellor in former times was frequently prime minister; and although Earl Clarendon in the reign of Charles II. is the last who ostensibly filled this situation, his successors have always been members of the Cabinet, and have often taken a leading part, for good or for evil, in directing the national councils.

There is a distinction which it may be convenient that I should explain between the title of "Chancellor" and " Keeper of the Great Seal." As we have seen, there was in very early times always an officer called "the Chancellor," *kat exochen,* or " King's Chancellor," to distinguish him from the Chancellors of bishops or of Counties Palatine. He generally was intrusted with the personal custody of the Great Seal; but occasionally while there was a Chancellor, the seal was delivered to another person who was called " Custos sigilli," or " Vicecancellarius," and did all the duties of the office connected with the sealing of writs and grants, and the administration of justice,—accounting for all fees and prequisites to the Chancellor. In the 28th of Henry III. a statute passed to check this practice : " Si rex abstulerit sigillum a Cancellario, quicquid fuerit interim sigillatum irritum habeatur." However, the attempt to prevent such a deputation soon failed. Chancellors going upon embassies, or visiting their dioceses, or laid up by long sickness, could not themselves use the seal, and were unwilling to surrender the office to a rival, from whom there might have been great difficulty in recovering it when he had tasted its sweets. Wherefore, in defiance of the law,—on all such occasions while they retained the favor of the Sovereign, they handed over the seal to a *" lieu-tenant"* from whom they could at any time demand it back. By-and-by, between the death, resignation, or removal of one Chancellor and the appointment of another, the Great

Seal, instead of remaining in the personal custody of the Sovereign, was sometimes intrusted to a temporary keeper, either with limited authority (as only to seal writs), or with all the powers, though not with the rank, of Chancellor. At last, the practice grew up of occasionally appointing a person to hold the Great Seal with the title of "Keeper," where it was meant that he should permanently hold it in his own right, and discharge all the duties belonging to it. Queen Elizabeth, ever sparing in the conferring of dignities, having given the Great Seal with the title of "Keeper" to Sir Nicholas Bacon, objections were made to the legality of some of his acts, —and to obviate these, a statute was passed [1] declaring that "the Lord Keeper of the Great Seal for the time being shall have the same place, pre-eminence, and jurisdiction as the Lord Chancellor of England." Of course there have never since been a Chancellor and the Keeper of the Great Seal concurrently, and the only difference between the two titles is, that the one is more sounding than the other, and is regarded as a higher mark of royal favor. During the seventeenth and eighteenth centuries various instances occurred of the Great Seal being delivered to a "Lord Keeper," who not rarely, for acceptable service, has been raised to the dignity of "Lord Chancellor;" but since the commencement of the reign of George III., the title of "Lord Chancellor" has always been conferred in the first instance with the Great Seal, and "Lord Keepers" probably will be seen no more.

We have still to treat of "Lords Commissioners of the Great Seal,"—whom it may continue convenient to appoint. From very early times there had been a custom of occasionally giving the Great Seal into the joint custody of several persons, who held it under the Chancellor, or while the office was vacant. Immediately after the Revolution, in 1689, Sergeant Maynard and two other lawyers were appointed by a commission under the Great Seal to execute the office of Lord Chancellor. Doubts were started as to their powers and precedence, which gave rise to the 1 W. & M. c. 21, enacting "that commissioners so appointed should have all the authority of Lord Chancellor or Lord Keeper, one of them being empowered to hear interlocutory motions, and the presence of

[1] 5 Eliz. c. 18.

two being required at the pronouncing of a decree or affixing the Great Seal to any instrument;—the commissioners to rank next after peers and the Speaker of the House of Commons."

On the union with Scotland, the Chancellor was designated "Lord High Chancellor of Great Britain," and now his proper title is " Lord High Chancellor of Great Britain and Ireland,"—the Great Seal which he holds testifying the will of the Sovereign as to acts which concern the whole empire, although there are certain patents confined in their operations to Scotland and Ireland respectively, which still pass under the separate Great Seals appropriated to those divisions of the United Kingdom.[1]

The appointment to the office of Lord Chancellor in very remote times was by patent or writ of Privy Seal, or by suspending the Great Seal by a chain around the neck:[2] but for many ages the Sovereign has conferred the office by simply delivering the Great Seal to the person who is to hold it, verbally addressing him by the title which he is to bear. He then instantly takes the oaths,[3] and he is clothed with all the authority of the office, although usually, before entering upon the public exercise of it, he has been installed in it with great pomp and solemnity.

The proper tenure of the office is *during pleasure*, and it is determined by the voluntary surrender of the Great

---

[1] By Art. XXIV. of the union with Scotland, it is provided that there shall be one Great Seal for the United Kingdom. There is no such provision in the Act for the union with Ireland; and s. 3 of 39 & 40 G. 3, c. 67, provides that the Great Seal of Ireland may continue to be used as theretofore. But patents of peerage of the United Kingdom, treaties with foreign states, and other imperial acts, are under the seal held by our Lord Chancellor, who is, therefore, in some sense, the Chancellor of the empire, although he has no judicial jurisdiction beyond the realm of England.

[2] "Forma cancellarium constituendi, regnante Henrico Secundo, fuit appendendo magnum Angliæ sigillum ad collum cancellarii electi." See 4 Inst. 87; Camden, p. 131.

[3] The oath of office consists of six parts: "1. That well and truly he shall serve our Sovereign Lord the King and his people in the office of Chancellor. 2. That he shall do right to all manner of people, poor and rich, after the usages of the realm. 3. That he shall truly counsel the King, and his counsel he shall layne* and keep. 4. That he shall not know nor suffer the hurt or disheriting of the King, or that the rights of the Crown be decreased by any means as far as he may let it. 5. If he may not let it, he shall make it clearly and expressly to be known to the King, with his true advice and counsel. 6. And that he shall do and purchase the King's profit in all that he reasonably may. as God him help."—4 Inst. 88.

* An old Norman word signifying *to conceal.*

Seal into the hands of the Sovereign, or by his demanding it in person, or sending a messenger for it with a warrent under the Privy Seal or Sign Manual. There have been grants of the office of Chancellor for life and for a time certain, but these Lord Coke pronounces to be illegal and void; and, while its political functions remain, the person holding it must necessarily be removable with the other members of the administration to which he belongs.

I must now make a few observations respecting the Great Seal and the mode of applying it. It is considered the emblem of sovereignty,—the *clavis regni*,—the only instrument by which on solemn occasions the will of the Sovereign can be expressed.[1] Absolute faith is universally given to every document purporting to be under the Great Seal, as having been duly sealed with it by the authority of the Sovereign.[2]

The law, therefore, takes anxious precautions to guard against any abuse of it. To counterfeit the Great Seal is high treason,[3] and there are only certain modes in which the genuine Great Seal can be lawfully used.

Letters patent ought always to state the authority under which they have passed the Great Seal. In early times we find such notices as these: "By the king himself," "By the king himself and all the council," "By the petition of the council," "By the king himself and the great council," "By the king and council in full parliament," "By letters of the king himself of the signet," "By petition in parliament," "By the king's own word of mouth."

To guard against grants improperly passing under the Great Seal, an ordinance was made in 1443,[4] requiring that the Chancellor should not fix the Great Seal to a grant without authority under the Privy Seal; but this was not by any means rigorously observed. Thus, in 1447, Henry

[1] 1 Hale's Pleas of the Crown, ch. xvi.
[2] The most striking illustration of this maxim is given by the course pursued by Parliament in 1788 and 1811, when, from the mental alienation of George III., the royal authority was completely in abeyance. Commissions, without any royal warrant, were produced under the Great Seal for opening Parliament and giving the royal assent to the Regency Bill, and in point of law they were supposed to express the deliberate will of him who in point of fact was unconscious of these proceedings.—*Parl. Hist.* vol. xxvii. 1162; *Parl. Deb.* vol. xviii. 830, 1102.
[3] 25 Ed. 3.
[4] 25 Hen. 6.

VI. having pardoned a person who had been convicted of high treason, a letter sealed with "the signet of the eagle" was sent to the Chancellor, commanding him to make out a pardon to him under the Great Seal, with this P.S.: "When the Privy Seale shall come into the countrey, wee shall sende you your suffycient warrant in this behalf."

Another instance of this king's disregard of the official forms intended to prevent the Crown from acting without the sanction of its advisers we have in the negotiation of his marriage. In 1442 instructions were issued under the Great Seal empowering ambassadors therein named to treat for an alliance with the *eldest* daughter of the Count of Armagnac; but the King afterwards wished to "set it general," that he might have the choice of any one of the Count's daughters. Instead of causing so important a variation from the original instructions to be executed in a proper manner under the Great Seal, it was merely expressed in a private letter from the King to the ambassadors under "the signet of the eagle;"—the King thus trying to excuse the irregularity—" And forasmuch as ye have none instructions of this form but this only which proceedeth of our own motion, desiring therefore that ye, notwithstanding all other, do the execution thereof, we have signed this letter of our own hand, the which as yet, wot well, we be not much accustomed for to do in other case." The ambassadors declined to act upon that letter, and informed the King that, "according to their simple wits," it had altogether superseded their commission. They therefore prayed for new powers; and another commission was "issued under the Great Seal, which expressly authorized them to select any one of the Count's daughters for consort to His Majesty."[1]

On many occasions, King Edward IV. enforced directions in the letters to the Chancellor for using the Great Seal, by adding his commands in his own handwriting. Thus Kirkham, the Master of the Rolls, while he had the custody of the Great Seal, having hesitated to make out letters of safe-conduct for a Spanish ship without a warrant under the Privy Seal, the King ordered a letter to be sent to him under the signet, expressing surprise at his non-compliance with the former request, and com-

[1] Journal of Bishop Beckington, p. 6.

manding him that, immediately on sight of that letter he should make out and deliver the instrument, and that he should afterwards have further warrant if necessary. "Alt eit," the King adds, " our speech to you, us thinketh, was sufficient warrant." And at the bottom he wrote, with his own hand, "Sir, we will the premises be sped without delay."[1]

Some riots having occurred at Bristol, the Chancellor was ordered by a letter signed by the King, and sealed with the signet, to make a commission for the trial of the offenders; and Edward wrote on it with his own hand, "Cosyn, yff ye thynke ye schall have a Warrant, ye may have on made in dew forme; We pray you hyt fayle not."[2]

In 1479 the Chancellor was ordered to grant letters patent of a corody to one of the King's servants on his petition signed by the King, who wrote under it, "My Lord Chanseler, Wee praye you spede thys Bille, and take hyt for your warrant."

Towards the end of his reign Edward directed a writ for an inquisition to be made out for the benefit of his "Lady Mother" by a letter to the Chancellor, concluding thus:—" This we wol you speed in any wise, as our trust is in you;" adding, in his own hand, "My Lord Chanseler, thys most be don."[3]

Much greater irregularities, in this respect, prevailed under the Tudors and the Stuarts; and the practice became not very uncommon for the Sovereign, where an instrument of doubtful legality was to pass, to affix the Great Seal to it with his own hand.

Since the Revolution in 1688, when the principles of responsible government were fully established, the Great Seal could only be lawfully used by a Lord Chancellor, Lord Keeper, or Lords Commissioners; and unless with respect to the sealing of writs and commissions of course, for which the delivery of the Seal to them is sufficient authority, there must be a warrant under the royal sign manual for the preparation of "a bill" or draught of the proposed patent. This, when prepared, is superscribed

---

[1] Ex. orig. in Turr. Lond.
[2] Warrant here evidently means letters of Privy Seal, without which the King doubted whether his order would be obeyed.
[3] Ex orig. in Turr. Lond.

ADOPTION OF NEW GREAT SEAL.

by the Sovereign, and sealed with the Privy Signet in the custody of a secretary of state; then it sometimes immediately passes under the Great Seal, in which case it is expressed to be "per ipsum regem," "by the king himself;" but in matters of greater moment, the bill, so superscribed and sealed, is carried to the keeper of the Privy Seal, who makes out a writ of warrant thereupon to the Chancery, in which last case the patent is expressed to be "per breve de privato sigillo," "by writ of privy seal."[1]

In early times, the king used occasionally to deliver to the Chancellor several seals of different materials, as one of gold and one of silver, but with the same impression, to be used for the same purpose; and hence we still talk of "the *seals* being in commission," or of a particular individual being "a candidate for the *seals*," meaning the office of Lord Chancellor;—although, with the exception of the rival Great Seals used by the king and the parliament during the civil war in the time of Charles I., there has not been for many centuries more than one Great Seal in existence at the same time.[2]

When on a new reign, or on a change of the royal arms or style, an order is made by the sovereign in council for using a new Great Seal, the old one is publicly broken, and the fragments become the fee of the Chancellor.[3]

---

[1] See 2 Inst. 552, 555; 2 Bl. Com. 347.

[2] The French expression of "Garde des Sceaux" arose from the Chancellor in France always having the custody of a variety of seals applicable to different purposes. In England the same person has had the custody of the Great Seal and the Privy Seal: but this was contrary to law and usage, the one being a check upon the other.—1 Hale's Pleas of the Crown, ch. xvi.

[3] This being the general rule, an amicable contest, *honoris causâ*, arose upon the subject between two of the most distinguished men who have ever held the office. Lord Lyndhurst was Chancellor on the accession of William IV., when by an order in council a New Great Seal was ordered to be prepared by his Majesty's chief engraver;* but when it was finished and an order was made for using it,† Lord Brougham was Chancellor. Lord Lyndhurst claimed the old Great Seal on the ground that the transaction must be referred back to the date of the first order, and that the fruit must therefore be considered as having fallen in his time; while Lord Brougham insisted that the point of time to be regarded was the moment when the old Great Seal ceased to be the "*clavis regni*," and that there was no exception to the general rule. The matter being submitted to the King as supreme judge in such cases, his Majesty equitably adjudged that the old Great Seal should be divided between the two noble and learned litigants, and as it consisted of two parts for

---

* 4th August, 1830. † 31st August, 1831. Books of Privy Council.

The Close Roll abounds with curious details of the careful manner in which this Great Seal was kept in its "white leathern bag and silken purse" under the private seal of the Chancellor. There was a rule that he should not take it out of the realm; and this was observed by all Chancellors except Cardinal Wolsey, who, in 1521, carried it with him into the Low Countries, and sealed writs with it at Calais,—a supposed violation of duty which formed one of the articles of his impeachment. Indeed, the better opinion is that the Great Seal cannot be used out of the realm even by the sovereign. Edward I. having himself affixed the Great Seal at Ghent to a confirmation of the charters, the Earls of Norfolk and Hereford objected that this act in a foreign country was null, and the charters were again confirmed under the Great Seal on the King's return to England.[1]

Some readers may feel a curiosity to know whether there are any emoluments belonging to the office of Chancellor besides the fragments of the old Great Seal when a new one is adopted. I shall hereafter present copies of grants of salary, and tables of fees and allowances, showing the profits of this high officer in different reigns. In the meanwhile it must suffice to say, that, on account of his distinguished rank, his important duties, his great labors, and the precariousness of his tenure, he has generally received the largest remuneration of any servant of the crown. In early times this arose mainly from presents, and I am afraid from bribes. The deficiency was afterwards often supplied by grants of land from the crown, which continued down to the time of Lord Somers. Then came the system of providing for

---

making an impression on both sides of the wax appended to letters patent,—one representing the Sovereign on the throne, and the other on horseback,—the destiny of the two parts respectively should be determined by lot. His Majesty's judgment was much applauded, and he graciously ordered each part to be set in a splendid silver salver with appropriate devices and ornaments, which he presented to the late and present Keeper of his Conscience as a mark of his personal respect for them.—The ceremony of breaking or "damasking" the old Great Seal consists in the Sovereign giving it a gentle blow with a hammer, after which it is supposed to be broken, and has lost all its virtue. But to counterfeit the old Great Seal is treason. So held in the 9th of Edward IV. of counterfeiting the Great Seal of Henry VI., although this sovereign had been attainted as an usurper.—1 Hale's Pleas of the Crown, 177.

[1] A.D. 1298. See Black. Law Tracts, 345.

the Chancellor and his family by sinecure places in possession and in reversion. Now all these places are abolished, together with all fees; and parliament has provided a liberal, but not excessive, fixed salary for the holder of the Great Seal,—with a retired allowance when he has resigned it, to enable him to maintain his station, and still to exert himself in the public service as a judge in the House of Lords and in the Privy Council.[1]

I shall conclude this preliminary discourse with the notice of certain forms connected with the Great Seal, to which high importance has sometimes been attached, and which have given rise to serious controversies.

By a standing order of the House of Lords, the Lord Chancellor, when addressing their Lordships, is to be uncovered; but he is covered when he addresses others, including a deputation of the commons.

When he appears in his official capacity in the presence of the Sovereign, or receives messengers of the House of Commons at the bar of the House of Lords, he bears in his hand the purse containing (or supposed to contain) the Great Seal. On other occasions it is carried by his purse-bearer, or lies before him as the emblem of his authority. When he goes before a Committee of the House of Commons he wears his robes, and is attended by his mace-bearer and purse-bearer. Being seated, he puts on his hat to assert the dignity of the upper House; and then, having uncovered, gives his evidence.

Although the Lord Chancellor no longer addresses the two Houses at the opening or close of a session of parliament, he still is the bearer of the royal speech, which, kneeling, he delivers into the hand of the Sovereign.

When the Prince of Wales is to take the oaths for any purpose in the Court of Chancery, the Lord Chancellor meets him as he approaches Westminster Hall, and waits upon him into court. The Prince's Chancellor holds the book, and the oaths are read by the Master of the Rolls. The Lord Chancellor sits covered while the oaths are administered, the bar standing. The Lord Chancellor then waits on the Prince to the end of Westminster Hall.[2]

---

[1] Lord Loughborough was the first Chancellor who had a retired allowance by act of Parliament. The present arrangement was made by Lord Brougham See 2 & 3 W. 4, c. 122.

[2] Case of Prince of Wales, afterwards George II. Dickens, xxix.

DEGRADATION OF THE OFFICE.

When a younger son of the King is to take the oaths, the Lord Chancellor meets him at the steps leading from the Hall to the Court, and conducts him into court. The Master of the Rolls reads the oaths, the senior Master in Chancery holding the book. His Lordship sits covered, the bar standing. He then uncovers, takes the purse in his hand, and attends his royal highness down the steps into the Hall.[1]

When peers take the oaths before the Lord Chancellor, the deputy usher holds the book, while a deputy of the clerk of the crown reads the oaths. The Lord Chancellor sits covered during the time the peers are in court, except at their entrance and departure, when he rises and bows to them.[2]

When the Lord Mayor of London comes into the Court of Chancery on Lord Mayor's Day, and by the Recorder invites the Lord Chancellor to dinner at Guildhall, the Lord Chancellor remains covered, and does not return any answer to the invitation.[3]

I have only further to state respecting the privileges and disabilities of the office of the Lord Chancellor, that by stat. 24 Hen. 8, c. 13, he is entitled "to weare in his apparell velvet satene and other silkes of any colours *excepte purpure*, and any manner of furres *except cloke genettes*."

Let us now proceed to the Lives of the illustrious men who have held this office from the foundation of the monarchy.

NOTE TO FOURTH EDITION.—(*September*, 1856.)

I AM grieved to say that since the year 1845, when the above sketch of the office of Lord Chancellor was composed, it has been sadly shorn of its splendor.—
"Stat nominis umbra."

If the same course of proceedings to degrade the office should be much longer continued, instead of the Chan-

[1] Case of Duke of Cumberland, 16th June, 1755. Dickens, xxx.
[2] Dickens, xxxii.
[3] *Ex relatione* a Lord Chancellor who never would be wanting in any point of due courtesy to high or low—Lord Lyndhurst.

cellor answering the description of John of Salisbury in the reign of Henry II.—

" Hic est qui leges regni *cancellat* iniquas,
Et mandata pii Principis *æquat* facit."—

he may return to what Gibbon declares to have been his original functions as " door-keeper or usher of the court, who, by his *cancellæ* or *little bars*, kept off the multitude from intruding into the recess or *chancel* in which he sat."

The real importance of the Chancellor did not arise from "the seal and maces," which still " dance before him," but—1. From his being a leading member of the cabinet, originating and controlling all the measures of the government connected with the administration of justice; 2. From his presiding in the Court of Chancery and laying down doctrine to govern that all-absorbing department of our jurisprudence called EQUITY : and, 3. From his practically constituting in his own person the ultimate Court of Appeal for the United Kingdom, by giving judgment in the name of the House of Lords, according to his own notion of what was right.

Such powers having belonged to a Hardwicke, were transmitted by him to a line of distinguished successors, and, having been exercised to the great contentment and advantage of the realm, gave a *prestige* to the office of Chancellor,—which is already seriously, diminished, and ere long may be destroyed. 1. No act of parliament has as yet touched the first source of cancellarian greatness; but I must here reiterate the complaint which I have already made in vain, both publicly in my place in parliament, and by earnest representation in private, that the ancient subordination and co-operation of the legal functionaries under the Crown has ceased,—and that nothing is now certain with respect to measures for the improvement of our juridical institutions, except that a bill passed at the recommendation of the government in one house of parliament will be lost in the other—by the resistance, active or passive, of the members of the same government. 2. The stat. 14 & 15 Vic. c. 83, " To improve the administration of justice in the Court of Chancery," will soon banish the Lord Chancellor from his Court, and the Lords Justices will reign in his stead. By § 5, "all the jurisdiction of the Court of Chancery which is now possessed and exercised by the Lord Chancellor, and all powers, authorities, and duties, as well ministerial as judicial, incident to such jurisdiction, now exercised and performed by the Lord Chancellor, shall and may be had, exercised, and performed by the Lords Justices." The Lord Chancellor, if his taste so incline, may sit along with them, or he may sit in a separate court concurrently with them. But he will then be acting as a volunteer Judge; and practically and substantially the Lords Justices must be looked up as to the supreme authority in Equity. In time to come, the visits of the Lord Chancellor, "few and far between," will not, I am afraid, be regarded with the reverence generated by the unexpected appearance of an Angel. 3. Recent events have been still more unfortunate for the office of Lord Chancellor as connected with the appellate jurisdiction of the House of Lords, Without the slightest blame being imputable to the present excellent holder of the Great Seal, the judgments of the House of Lords in his time had not given entire satisfaction to the bar or to the public, and some change in the tribunal became necessary. The creation of a peerage for life was very inconsiderately resorted to. "Hoc fonte derivata clades—." The Lords, in the exercise of their undoubted privileges, having judicially determined that a peer for life cannot as such sit in parliament, a committee was appointed to consider what was fit to be done for improving the appellate jurisdiction of the House. This was eagerly embraced as an opportunity to bring forward charges which, though most offensive to former holders of the Great Seal, and, generally speaking, quite unfounded, were listened to without the smallest check by the committee. In consequence a sudden belief arose in the public mind, that the appellate jurisdiction of the House of Lords, which for centuries had commanded more respect than the jurisdiction of any tribunal in the kingdom, was usurped, and was liable to every charge which can be made against forensic proceedings except that of pecuniary corruption. Some new measure was necessary to satisfy the nation; and, instead of recurring to expedients which might have been rendered effective by their own authority, the Lords, following the unlucky advice of their leaders on both sides, preferred a scheme for which the sanction of the two houses as well as of the Crown was necessary, viz., having a certain number of salaried peers for life, with the title of "Deputy Speakers" to assist the Lord Chancellor. The Bill for this purpose being thrown out of the House of Commons, in what a state is the Lord Chancellor for the time being now left? "Single-seated justice," which was applauded in the time of Lord Hardwicke and Lord Eldon, will no longer be endured, nor the *divisum imperium* of the Lord Chancellor and a retired Common-law Judge, however distinguished. The probable experiment will now be a JUDICIAL COMMITTEE, consisting of peers, and of judges and privy councillors summoned to advise the House. There the Chancellor will have no official ascendency, and a Vice-Chancellor or a Puisne Judge may be selected to declare the judgment of this tribunal according to the applauded practice in the Judicial Committee of the Privy Council.

I care little about the reduced salary of the Lord Chancellor, although it is not now sufficient to enable him to keep a carriage, and to exercise becoming hospitality, much less to make any provision for his family. Against poverty a noble struggle may be made; but there seem to be causes in operation which, in spite of the most eminent learning and ability, must speedily reduce the office to insignificance and contempt. This is a sad prospect for the Biographer of the Chancellors.

> "May I lie cold before that dreadful day,
> Pressed with a load of monumental clay!"

"And yet" (in the beautiful language of my predecessor, Lord Chief Justice Crewe) "Time hath its revolutions; there must be a period and an end to all temporal things—*finis rerum*—an end of names and dignities, and whatever is *terrene*— for where is BOHUN? Where is MOWBRAY? Where is MORTIMER? Nay, which is more and most of all, Where is PLANTAGENET? They are entombed in the urns and sepulchres of mortality"!!!
—And why not the MARBLE CHAIR?

CHAPTER I.

OF THE CHANCELLORS UNDER THE ANGLO-SAXON KINGS.

IT has been too much the fashion to neglect our history and antiquities prior to the Norman conquest. But to our Anglo-Saxon ancestors not only are we indebted for our language and for the foundation of almost all the towns and villages in England, but for our political institutions; and to them we may trace the origin of whatever has most benefited and distinguished us as a nation.[1] It is a point of filial duty incumbent upon us, to commemorate and to honor the individuals among them who, in any department, attained to great eminence. Of those who filled the office of Chancellor under the Anglo-Saxon kings, little has been handed down to us; but that little ought not to be allowed to fall into oblivion.

According to Selden, Ethelbert, the first Christian king among the Saxons, had AUGMENDUS for his "Chancellor" or *Referendarius*, the officer who received petitions and supplications addressed to the sovereign, and made out writs and mandates as *Custos Legis*. There is great reason to believe that he was one of the benevolent ecclesiastics who accompanied Augustine from Rome on his holy mission, and that he assisted in drawing up the Code of Laws then published, which materially softened and improved many of the customs which have prevailed while the Scandinavian divinities were still worshipped in England.[2]

There are three others whose names are transmitted to us as having been Chancellors to Anglo-Saxon kings without any history attached to them, legendary or authentic,—CENWONA, under Offa, king of the Mercians; BOSA, under Withlofe; and SWITHULPHUS, under Berthulph.[3]

---

[1] The descendants of the Anglo-Saxons seemed destined to be by far the most numerous and powerful race of mankind,—occupying not only the British Isles in Europe, but the whole of America from Mexico to the Polar Seas, and the whole of Australia and Polynesia. The English language will soon be spoken by an infinitely greater number of civilized men than ever was the Greek, the Latin, or the French.

[2] Selden's Office of Chancellor, 2. Dugd. Or. Jur. 32. Philpot's Catalogue of Chancellors. Spel. Gloss. Cancellarius, p. 10.

[3] Selden's Office of Chancellor, 2. Dugd. Or. Jur. 32. Philpot's Catalogue of Chancellors. Spel. Gloss. Cancellarius, p. 109.

Next comes the Chancellor so celebrated for his *pluvious* propensity, St. SWITHIN, who held the office under two sovereigns, and of whom much that is true, as well as much that is fabulous, has been transmitted to us. We can trace his history as certainly as that of Bede or Alcuin, and he left, like them, among his countrymen, a bright reputation for learning and ability, which was rationally cherished till obscured by the miracles afterwards imputed to him.

Swithin was a native of Wessex, and was born at the very commencement of the ninth century. He was educated in a monastery at Winchester, then the capital of the kingdom. He prosecuted his studies with such ardor that he made wonderful proficiency in all the knowledge of the age, and having been ordained presbyter in 830 by the Bishop of Helmaston, was selected by King Egbert for his chaplain, and tutor to his son Ethelwulf.[1] He soon showed a capacity for state affairs, and was placed in the office of Chancellor, continuing, like his successor, à-Becket, while intrusted with the administration of justice, to superintend the education of the heir-apparent. He is said to have enjoyed the confidence of the King without interruption, and by his counsels to have contributed to the consolidation of the states of the Heptarchy into one great kingdom.

On the accession of his royal pupil to the throne, he retained his office of Chancellor, and was in still higher favor. So wise a minister was he esteemed, that William of Malmesbury, referring to his sway, says the ancient opinion of Plato was verified in this reign, that "a state would be happy when philosophers were kings, or kings were philosophers." Alstan, Bishop of Sherborne, took a more conspicuous lead, and several times in person conducted the army to battle against the Danes; but Swithin guided the counsels of the sovereign, as well as being personally beloved by him. He was now made Bishop of Winchester, being recorded as the 17th prelate who had filled that see. He proved a devoted friend to the

---

[1] William of Malmesbury represents that he was employed in affairs of state before he had the care of the King's son. 'Naturâ, industriâque laudabilis auditum Regis non effugit. Quocirca illum hactenus excoluit, ut et multa negotiorum ejus consilio transigeret, et filium Adulfum ejus magisterio locaret."— *W. Malm.* 242.

church, hitherto slenderly provided for among the Anglo-Saxons, and he procured a law to pass in the Wittenagemot for the universal and compulsory payment of tithes.

But the nation was most of all indebted to him for instilling the rudiments of science, heroism, and virtue into the infant mind of the most illustrious of our sovereigns. The son of Ethelwulf, afterwards Alfred the Great, was, from childhood, placed under the care of the Chancellor, who assisted his mother in teaching him to read and to learn the songs of the Scalds, and afterwards accompanied him on a pilgrimage to Rome, taking the opportunity of pointing out to him the remains of classical antiquity visible in the twilight of refinement which still lingered in Italy.

On Swithin's return to England, his last years were disturbed by the successes of the Danish invaders, and not having the military turn of some ecclesiastics and Chancellors, he shut himself up in his episcopal house, employing himself in acts of piety and charity. He died on the 2nd of July, 862, having directed that his body should be buried, not in the Cathedral, but in the churchyard among the poor.[1]

He was much admired by ecclesiastics at Rome, as well as in his own country, having first established in England, for the benefit of the Pope, the payment called "Peter's pence." In consequence, about fifty years after his death, he was canonized.

Now comes the legend of St. Swithin. It was thought that the body of the Saint ought to be translated from the churchyard to be deposited under the high altar, and the 15th of July was fixed for that ceremony,—when there were to be the most gorgeous processions ever seen in England. But he highly disapproved of this disregard of his dying injunction, and sent a tremendous rain, which continued without intermission for forty days, and until the project was abandoned. Ever since he regulates the weather for forty days from the day of his proposed translation, laying down this rule, that as that day is fair or foul, it will be fair or foul for forty days thereafter.

[1] " Jam vero vitæ præsenti valefacturus pontificali authoritate præcepit astantibus, ut extra ecclesiam cadaver suum humarent, ubi et pedibus prætereuntium et stillicidiis ex alto rorantibus esset obnoxium."—*Wm. of Malm.* 242.

The founders of the Reformation in England seem either to have believed in his miraculous powers, or to have entertained a very grateful recollection of his services to the Church, for they have preserved the 15th of July as a Saint's day dedicated to Lord Chancellor Swithin.

It must be admitted that there is great difficulty in distinguishing between what is authentic and what is fabulous in his history.[1]

TURKETEL is the first English Chancellor with whom we can be said to be really acqainted. He was of illustrious birth, being the eldest son of Ethelwald, and the grandson of Alfred. He was early distinguished for learning, piety, and courage. Taking priest's orders, his royal uncle, Edward the Elder, immediately offered him high ecclesiastical preferment. This he declined, thinking that it might interfere with the civil employments which, notwithstanding his tonsure, he preferred. Ingulphus informs us that the King thereupon made him his Chancellor and Prime Minister:—" Cancellarium suum eum constituit, ut quæcunque negotia temporalia vel spiritualia Regis judicium expectabant, illius consilio et decreto (nam tantæ fidei ettam profundi ingenii tenebatur) omnia tractaren tur, et tractata irrefragabilem sententiam sortirentur."[2]

He retained his office under his cousin Athelstan, who by his advice first took the title of " King of England."[3]

---

[1] Most of Lord Chancellor Swithin's decisions have perished, but I find one case reported which was brought judicially before him, and in which he gave specific relief, although seemingly the remedy was at common law by an action of trespass. An old woman came to complain to him that the eggs in her basket which she was carrying to market had all been wantonly broken. "Is ante se adductæ mulierculæ annis et pannis squalidæ querelam auscultat, damnum suspirat, misericordia mentis cunctantem miraculum excitat, *statimque porrecto crucis signo, fracturam omnium ovorum consolidat.*"—*Wm. of Malm.* 242.

There is much faith in the Ex-Chancellor, not only in England but in Scotland, where for many centuries there has been this proverb:—

"St. Swithin's day, gif ye do rain,
For forty days it will remain;
St. Swithin's day, an ye be fair,
For forty days 'twill rain na mair."

In some parts of Scotland, St. Martin (whose day is 4th of July) is the *raining* Saint.

[2] Ingulphi Hist. g. h. Dug. Or. Jur. 32.

[3] His father and grandfather had been styled kings of the Anglo-Saxons, and their predecessors merely kings of Wessex.

At the famous battle of Brunenburgh, so celebrated in the relics of Saxon and Scandinavian poetry, in which Athelstan had to fight for his crown against five confederated nations, Norwegians, Danes, Scots, Irish, and Britons, Chancellor Turketel rendered the most signal service to his sovereign and his country. The citizens of London marched under his banner, and supported by *Singin*, with the men of Worcestershire, he penetrated into the midst of the Scots, killed the son of their king, and compelled Constantine himself to seek safety in flight. Some historians relate that, although the Chancellor led his troops to the scene of action, he refused himself to mix in the fight, because the canons prohibited to clergymen the effusion of blood; but it was the doctrine of the age, that an exception was allowed in war undertaken for the protection of the country against a pagan invasion, and we shall find some of his ecclesiastical successors combating stoutly in the field even against Christian adversaries.[1]

Turketel still continued Chancellor under the two succeeding monarchs, Edmund and Edred, the brothers of Athelstan, and was likewise "Consilarius primus, præcipuus et a secretis familiarissimus."[2] As Edred was afflicted with a lingering and painful disease during the greater part of his reign, the sceptre was actually in the hands of the Chancellor, and he was obliged not only to superintend the administration of justice, and to conduct the civil government of the kingdom, but on several occasions to command the military force both against foreign and domestic enemies.

In a fit of religious enthusiasm, while still powerful and prosperous, he suddenly bade adieu to wordly greatness for the seclusion of a monastery. It is related that going on a message from the King to Archbishop Wolstan, it chanced that his road lay by the abbey of Croyland, which had been reduced to ruins in recent warfare, and now only afforded shelter to three aged monks. Touched by their piety and resignation, he believed himself divinely inspired with the design to enter into their society, and to restore their house to its ancient splendor. Having obtained permission to carry this design into effect,—before his civil extinction, in imitation of a

---

[1] See Lingard, i. 112.   [2] Ingul. g. h.

dying caliph, he sent the public crier through the streets of London, where, during four reigns he had exercised such authority, announcing to the citizens that the Chancellor, before quitting his office and entering into the monastic order, was anxious to discharge all his debts, and offered to make threefold reparation to any person he might have injured. Every demand upon him being liberally satisfied, he resigned the office of Chancellor into the King's hands, made a testamentary disposition of his great possessions, put on the monastic cowl, was blessed by the Bishop of Dorchester, recovered for the abbey all that it had lost in the Danish wars, endowed it with fresh wealth, was elected Abbot, and procured from the King and the Witan a confirmation of all the rights which his house had ever enjoyed, with the exception of the privilege of sanctuary, which he voluntarily renounced, on the ground that his experience as Chancellor made him consider it a violation of justice and an incentive to crime. He survived twenty-seven years, performing, in the most exemplary manner, the duties of his new station, and declaring that he was happier as Abbot of Croyland than Chancellor of England.[1] He died in 975.

The next Chancellor of whom any mention is made was ADULPHUS under King Edgar; but we are not told what part he took in the measures of this peaceful and prosperous reign.[2]

Ethelred, who mounted the throne in 978, had, for his first Chancellor, ALFRIC, the eleventh Abbot of St. Alban's, of whom nothing memorable has been transmitted to us. The King then made a whimsical disposition of the office, which he meant to be perpetual, "dividing it between the Abbots for the time being, of Ely, of St. Augustine in Canterbury, and of Glastonbury, who were to exercise it by turns; the Abbot of Ely, or some monk by him appointed, acting as Chancellor four months yearly from Candlemas, and the other two abbots each four months successively, making up the twelve."[3] Lord

---
[1] Ingul, 25–52. Ordine, 340.   [2] Or. Jur. 32.
[3] The words of an old monk of Ely: "Statuit atque concessit quatenus Ecclesia de Ely extunc et semper in Regis curia Cancellarii ageret dignitatem quod et aliis, Sancti, viz. Augustini et Glaconiæ Ecclesiis constituit, ut abbates istorum cœnobiorum vicissim a signatis succedendo temporibus, annum trifarie diviserint cum sanctuari et cæteris ornatibus altaris ministrando." See Drg. Off. Ch. § 1.

Coke commenting upon this arrangement says, "Albeit it was void in law to grant the Chancellorship of England in succession, yet it proveth that then there was a Court of Chancery."[1]

We are not informed how the three Abbots actually discharged their duties, or how long they enjoyed the office. If the grant was not revoked as illegal at the accession of Edmund Ironside, we need not doubt that it was violated on the conquest of the kingdom by Canute, who probably employed one of his own countrymen to assist him in administering justice to his new subjects.

We have no further notice of any Chancellor till the reign of Edward the Confessor. During his long exile in Normandy he had contracted a taste not only for the language, but also for the usages of that country; and among other Norman fashions, he introduced that of having a great seal to testify the royal will in the administration of justice, and in all matters of government. Sealing had been occasionally resorted to by his predecessors on solemn occasions,[2] but they then only used a private seal, like the prelates and nobles; and public documents were generally verified by the signature of the Chancellor, or by the King affixing to them the sign of the cross. A large state seal was now made, upon the model which has been followed ever since. It bore the representation of the King, in his imperial robes, sitting on his throne, holding a scepter in his right hand and a sword in his left, with the inscription "Sigillum Edwardi Anglorum Basilei."[3]

LEOFRIC was the Confessor's first Chancellor;[4] but it is doubtful whether this great seal had been adopted in

---

[1] 4 Inst. 78.

[2] Thus on inspecting an old Saxon charter of King Edgar to the abbey of Pershore, still extant, three labels are to be seen for seals to be appended by; and Godfric, Archdeacon of Worcester, writing to Pope Alexander III. of this very charter, says: "Noverit sanctitas vestra, verum esse quod conscripti hujus scriptum originale in virtute Sanctæ Trinitatis sigilla tria, trium personarum autenticarum, ad veritatem, triplici confirmatione commendat; Est autem sigillum primum illustris Regis Edgari; secundum Sancti Dunstani Cant. Arch.: tertii Alferi Ducis Merciorum, sicut ex diligenti literarum impressarum inspectione evidenter accepi." Dug. Off. Chan. § 3.

[3] See an engraving of it, Palgrave's History of England, i. 328, taken from the original in the British Museum. An admirable picture by words,—of the Chancellor sitting in the Wittenagemot,—will be found in the preface to the same valuable publication, p. xiv.

[4] Spel. Gloss. 109.

his time, as he is not recorded as having used it. We know that it was in the custody of WULWIUS, his successor. A royal charter to the church of Westminster, framed by him, thus concludes: "Ut hoc decretum a nobis promulgatum pleniorem obtineat vigorem, nostra manu subter apposito signo roboravimus, atque fidelibus nostris præsentibus roborandum tradidimus, nostræque imaginis sigillo insuper assignari jussimus," &c., with the attesting clause, "Wulwius, regiæ dignitatis Cancellarius, relegit et sigillavit," &c.[1]

The next Chancellor was REIMBALDUS, who likewise sealed with the royal seal, as we find by another charter of the Confessor to the Church of Westminster, thus authenticated:—"Ego, Reimbaldus, Regis Cancellarius, relegi et sigillavi," &c. When he was presented by absence or indisposition from acting, his duties were performed by SWARDUS, who appears to have been his Vice-Chancellor. Thus another charter of the Confessor, granting many manors to the church of Westminster, has this concluding clause:—" Ad ultimum, cartam istam sigillari jussi, et ipse manu mea propria signum crucis impressi, et idoneos testes annotari præcepi." Then follows:— "Swardus, notarius ad vicem REIMBALDI *regiæ dignitatis cancellarii*, hanc cartam scripsi et subscripsi."[2]

Lord Coke is justified in his contemptuous assertion that Polydor Virgil, in affirming that the office of Chancellor came in with the Conqueror, "perperam erravit:"[a] but he himself was very imperfectly acquainted with its history, and we are still left much in the dark respecting its duties, and the manner in which it was bestowed in the Saxon times. Then, as long after, the little learning that existed being confined to the clergy, we need not doubt that a post requiring the art of writing and some knowledge of law, was always filled by an ecclesiastic; and as it gave constant access to the person of the King and was the highway to preferment,—even if the precedence and emoluments belonging to it were not very high,—it must have been an object struggled for among the ambitious. Human nature being ever the same, we may safely believe that at that early period, as in succeeding ages, it was the prize sometimes of talents and virtue, and sometimes of intrigue and servility.

[1] Or. Jur. 34.   [2] 4 Inst. 78.

As we approach the era of the Conquest, we find distinct traces of the Masters in Chancery, who, though in sacred orders, were well trained in jurisprudence, and assisted the Chancellor in preparing writs and grants, as well as in the service of the royal Chapel. They formed a sort of college of Justice of which he was the head. They all sate in the Wittenagemot, and, as "Law Lords," are supposed to have had great weight in the deliberations of that assembly

CHAPTER II.

OF THE CHANCELLORS FROM THE CONQUEST TO THE REIGN OF HENRY II.

FROM the Conquest downwards we have, with very few interruptions, a complete series of Chancellors. Yet till we reach the reign of Richard I., when records begin which are still extant, containing entries of the transfer of the Great Seal, we can seldom fix the exact date of their appointment; and we glean what is known of them chiefly from the charters which they attested, from contemporary chroniclers, and from monkish histories of the sees to which they were promoted.

Few of those who held the office under the Norman monarchs before Henry II. took any prominent part in the conduct of public affairs, and they appear mostly to have confined themselves to their official duties, in making out writs, superintending royal grants, athenticating the acts of the sovereign by affixing the Great Seal to all instruments which ran in his name, and by sitting in a subordinate capacity, in the *Aula Regia*, to assist in the administration of justice.

The office of Chief Justiciar, introduced by William, long continued to confer great splendor on those who held it, while the highest functions of the Chancellor were considered those of being almoner and secretary to the King. Odo, Bishop of Bayeux,[1] William Fitzosborne,

---

[1] Or. Jur. chap. xvi. Palgrave's Hist. Eng. Preface.
[2] He was William's uterine brother, and, though an ecclesiastic, he was a distinguished military leader. In the famous Bayeux tapestry, giving a

and William de Warenne, successively Justiciars, were men of historical renown; they assisted William in his great military enterprise: they afterwards took an active part in imposing the yoke on the conquered, and they governed the realm as viceroys when he occasionally visited his native dominions. Till Thomas à-Becket arose to fix the attention of his own age and of posterity, the Chancellors were comparatively obscure.

They probably, however, were William's advisers in the great changes which he made in the laws and institutions of the country. English writers, with more nationality than discrimination or candor, have attempted to show that he was called *Conqueror*, merely because he obtained the crown by election instead of hereditary descent.[1] In all history there is not a more striking instance of subjugation. Not only did almost all the land in the kingdom change hands—the native English being reduced to be the thralls of the invaders—but legislative measures were brought forward, either in the sole name of the Sovereign, or through the form of a national council under his control, seeking to alter the language, the jurisprudence, and the manners of the people.[2] It would have been very interesting to have ascertained distinctly by whose suggestion and instrumentality the French was substituted for the English tongue in all schools and courts of justice; the intricate feudal law of Normandy superseded the simplicity of Saxon tenures; trial by battle was introduced in place of the joint judgment of the Bishop and the Earl in the county court; the separation was brought about between ecclesiastical and civil jurisdictions; and the great survey of the kingdom was planned and accomplished, of which we have the result in DOMESDAY, "the most valuable piece of antiquity possessed by any nation."[3] But while there is blazoned before us a roll of all the warlike chiefs who accompanied William in his memorable expedition, and we have a minute account of the

pictorial history of the Conquest, he makes the greatest figure next to William and Harold. The other Justiciars of this reign were hardly less eminent.

[1] As in the law of Scotland property acquired by an individual is called his *conquest*.

[2] The vitality of the Anglo-Saxon language and institutions at last prevailed, but there is hardly to be found such a striking instance of race tyrannizing over race, as in England during the reigns of the Conqueror and his immediate descendants. [3] Hume.

life and character of all those who took any prominent part in the battles, sieges, and insurrections which marked his reign, we are left to mere conjecture respecting the manner in which justice was administered under him,[1] and the measures of his civil government were planned and executed.[2]

But I must now proceed to give the names of William's Chancellors, with such scanty notices of their history as can be furnished from the imperfect materials which are preserved to us.

In 1067, the year after the battle of Hastings, when he had obtained the submission of a considerable part of England, although it was not till long after that he reduced the northern and western counties to his rule, he appointed as his first Chancellor, MAURICE, a Norman ecclesiastic, who had accompanied him as his chaplain when he sailed from St. Vallery for the coast of England.

We know little with certainty of the acts of this functionary beyond his perusing and sealing a charter by which the Conqueror, after the example of the Confessor, granted large possessions to the abbot and monks of Westminster.[3]

In the usual course of promotion, Maurice, being Chancellor, was made Bishop of London. Here we find him

[1] A very ample report of the *cause célèbre* between Odo, as Earl of Kent, and Lanfranc, Archbishop of Canterbury, at Penenden Heath, before Chief Justiciary Godfrey, has come down to us, but no notice of any other judicial proceeding in this reign can be traced.

[2] In classic antiquity lawgivers were honored not less than conquerors, and all the most celebrated laws of Rome bore the names of their authors; but in our own history (horresco referens) oblivion seems to await all those who devote themselves to legal reform. We do not know with any certainty who framed the statutes of Westminster in the time of Edward I., the Statutes of Fines, the Statutes of Uses, the Statute of Wills, or the Statute of Frauds, although they ought to have been commemorated for conferring lasting benefit on their country.

"—— Sed omnes illacrimabiles
Urguentur, ignotique longa
Nocte, carent quia vate sacro."

The Grenville Act for the trial of controverted elections was the first which conferred any *éclat* on the name of its author, and Fox's Libel Act is almost the only other down to our own times.

[3] The charter is thus attested: "Ego, Mauritius Cancellarius, favendo legi et sigillavi." 4 Inst. 78.—The words of the Conqueror's first charter are curious: "Ego Willielmus, Dei gratia, Rex Anglorum, Dux Normannorum, et Princeps Cenomannorum, hoc præceptum scribere præcepi, et scriptum hoc signo Dominico sic confirmado + stabilivi, nostræque imaginis sigillo insuper assignari curavi," &c.

highly celebrated for his exertions to rebuild St. Paul's. The year before his consecration the greatest part of the City of London, built of wood, had been consumed by fire, and the Cathedral where it now stands, on the site of an ancient temple of Diana, had been almost entirely destroyed. But by his pious exhortations, assisted by a royal grant, it rose from its ashes with new magnificence.[1]

Maurice enjoyed the dignity of Chancellor on his first appointment but for a short space of time, as it seems to have been the policy of William never to allow his great seal to remain long in the same hands. Spelman represents him as having been again Chancellor in 1077,[2] and there can be no doubt that he continued a person of considerable influence during the whole of this and the succeeding reign.

We have, however, no distinct account of the part which he again took in public affairs till Rufus was accidentally killed by Sir Walter Tyrrel while hunting in the New Forest. Henry, the king's younger brother, who was of the party, in violation of the superior claims of Robert, then absent in Normandy, hastened to London to claim the vacant throne. In those days anointment by a prelate was supposed to give a divine right to kings, and the commencement of a reign was calculated from the day of the coronation, not from the death of the predecessor. The privilege of crowning the kings of England has always been considered to belong to the Archbishop of Canterbury as Primate, but Anselm from his quarrel with the late King was now in exile. Henry in this extremity applied to Maurice, the Ex-Chancellor, and overcame his scruples respecting the law of primogeniture by a share of the royal treasure, which he had secured to himself as he passed through Winchester, and by which history records his usurpation was accomplished. On the third day from the tragical end of Rufus, Maurice placed the crown on the head of the new sovereign in the abbey of Westminster.

The Great Seal was now again within his reach, but he preferred the quiet use of his riches, and the hope eagerly cherished, though never realized, of succeeding to the primacy. He died in 1107, still Bishop of London, hav-

[1] W. Malmesb. De Gestis Pontificum, lib. ii.
[2] Gloss. Series Cancell. Angl.

ing seen a rapid succession of eight or nine Chancellors after his own resignation or dismissal.

The Conqueror's second Chancellor was OSMOND. Dugdale and Spelman leave the year of his appointment uncertain, and we might never have been informed of his having filled this office, had it not been that in 1078 he was promoted to the bishopric of Sarum, and we find some account of him in the annals of that see. He was, of course, a Norman; for now, and long after, no Saxon was promoted to any office, civil, military, or ecclesiastical. Having come over with William, and fought for him in the field, he was first made Earl of Dorset,—and now being girt with a sword, while he held the Great Seal in one hand, a crosier was put into the other.[1]

Of Osmond's conduct in his office of Chancellor few particulars are transmitted to us; but he is said to have been much in the confidence of the Conqueror, who consulted him about the most arduous and secret affairs of state, as well as confiding to him the superintendence of the administration of justice. William of Malmesbury is his chief panegyrist, celebrating his chastity, his disinterestedness, his deep learning, and, above all, his love of sacred music,—representing as the only shade on his character his great severity to penitents, which was caused by his own immaculate life. After his elevation to the episcopal dignity, he devoted himself entirely to his sacredotal duties.

He is the first Chancellor I have to mention as an author. His principal work was "A History of the Life and Miracles of Alden, a Saxon Saint, the first Bishop of Sherborne." He likewise composed the service "secundum usum Sarum," which remained in great repute, and was followed in the West of England till the Reformation.[2]

From a charter of the Conqueror, dated in 1069, confirming a grant of the Confessor to Leofric, who was the first Bishop of Exeter, and from another charter of the

---

[1] Such a combination long continued very common, and the Reformation even did not recognize the separation which now prevails between sacred and secular employments. James I. had a bishop for Lord Keeper of the Great Seal; Charles I. had a bishop for his Lord Treasurer; Queen Anne, with the loud approbation of Swift and the High Church party, had a bishop for her Lord Privy Seal and one of her ambassadors to negotiate the treaty of Utrecht. [2] De Gestis Pontificum, lib. i.

Conqueror, dated in 1073, granting lands to the Dean and Canons of St. Martin's, in the City of London, we know that the Great Seal was at those times held by ARFASTUS,[1] who is stated to have been Bishop of Helmstadt, in Germany. He is supposed to have been one of the ecclesiastical adventurers who ranged themselves under the standard which the Pope had blessed when William proclaimed his grand enterprise. As a reward for his services he was in 1070 appointed Bishop of Elmham, in Norfolk, a see established there as early as 673. In 1076 he removed the see to Thetford, where he died in 1084.[2]

Of his successor we know little but the name, there being no description added to it to tell us from what country he sprang, or what other office he ever filled; but a charter granted at this time by the Conqueror to the monks of St. Florentius of Andover is witnessed and authenticated by BALDRICK as King's Chancellor.[3] He was no doubt King's Chaplain, but does not seem to have reached any higher ecclesiastical dignity. Although the custody of the Great Seal was in those days considered a certain step to the bishopric, premature death or loss of power had disappointed the hopes of this aspirant.[4]

Next came HERMAN, with whose origin and history we are well acquainted. He was a Norman by birth, and before the coming in of William he had been promoted to the bishopric of Sherborne. It is a curious consideration that in the reign of the Confessor there was the most familiar intercourse between England and Normandy; the French language was spoken at his Court,[5] and many Normans were employed by him. Of these Herman was one

---

[1] He thus subscribes both charters:—
"+ EGO ARFASTUS CANCELLARIUS."

[2] Vide Spelm. Gloss. 109, where he is stated to have been twice Chancellor. The see was soon afterwards removed to Norwich, where it has ever since remained. Annal. Winton. Angl. Sax. I. 249. Waver, 827.

[3] Inspex. Pat. Ed. 2, p. 2, MS. Lold. Chron. Ser. 1.

[4] It is said that the poetical name for a belt or girdle was taken from this Chancellor, who is supposed to have worn one of uncommon magnificence.
"Athwart his breast, a BALDRICK brave he ware,
That shined like twinkling stars with stones most precious rare."—SPENCER.
"A radiant BALDRICK o'er his shoulders tied
Sustain'd the sword that glittered at his side."—POPE.
But this probably arose from the difficulty of finding any other etymology for the word.

[5] See Thierry's History of the Norman Conquest.

of the most favored, and he is supposed to have assisted in the artifices which his native prince resorted to for the purpose of being designated heir to the crown of England, in derogation of the rights of the true representative of the line of Cerdic and of the claims of Harold, who aspired to be the founder of a new Saxon dynasty. Immediately after the battle of Hastings he sent in his adhesion to William, and he steadily supported him in the protracted struggle which took place before the Norman yoke was imposed upon the whole of England. For reasons not explained to us, he wished to remove his episcopal see from Sherborne to Old Sarum, which has been so often talked of as a decayed borough, but which William of Malmesbury describes as being at this time such a wretched place, that "a miserable commerce was carried on there in water."[1] He was gratified in this whim, and his services were farther rewarded by the custody of the Great Seal.

He was succeeded by WILLIAM WELSON, who being appointed Bishop of Thetford, soon gave up the office of Chancellor, and retired to the discharge of his spiritual duties.[2]

The Conqueror's last Chancellor was WILLIAM GIFFARD, who, though promoted to the rich See of Winchester, eagerly retained the Great Seal. He was a very dexterous man, who could accommodate himself to the various tastes of persons and times. Though once deprived of office by an unexpected turn of affairs, and for a considerable interval baffled in his schemes for recovering it, he at last contrived to be reinstated; and he was Chancellor under three successive sovereigns.

He was not incapable of giving good advice, and of taking the liberal side when it suited his interest. Although he had heartily concurred in the oppression of the Saxons in the early part of William's reign, and had declared that they were to be considered aliens in their native land, and had assisted in the measures for upsetting English law and extirpating the English language, yet, when the two great Earls, Morcar and Edwin, appeared still formidable, and discontent among the natives had become so deep and general as to threaten a dangerous revolt, the Chancellor joined with several other prelates

[1] De Gest. Pont. lib. ii.   [2] Spel Gloss. 109.

in praying that the conquered people might be emancipated from some of the galling disabilities which had been inflicted upon them, and he induced the Conqueror to restore a few of the laws of the Confessor, which, though seemingly of no great importance for the protection of general liberty, gave extreme satisfaction by creating the hope of farther concessions. He was associated with Godfrey, Bishop of Constance, the Grand Justicier, in the government of the country, while the Conqueror was engaged in his last fatal campaign against the French King.

When Rufus suddenly presented himself in England, announcing his father's death and claiming the crown, Giffard at first cordially supported him, and gained him the good will of the native English by promises to them of good treatment and of enjoying the license of hunting in the royal forests. As a reward for his services he was confirmed in the office of Chancellor. This, however, he did not then long hold. It is suspected that, thinking he discovered in the public mind a strong feeling for the rights of primogeniture, and influenced by the promise of still higher promotion from Prince Robert, he was engaged in the abortive conspiracy among the Barons in favor of that unfortunate prince. Whatever might be the cause, the Great Seal was taken from him, and he was relegated to his see during the remainder of this reign. We take leave of him for the present.

He was succeeded by a man more unscrupulous than himself, ROBERT BLOET, a Norman who, with several brothers, had come over with the Conqueror.[1] He laughed at the conciliatory policy which had been lately adopted, and keenly abetted the king in all the arbitrary proceedings now resorted to for the purpose of breaking the spirit of the English. Although in high favor, he could not obtain a mitre till he had been Chancellor five years, and then he owed his promotion to a dangerous illness with which the king was visited. The sees of Canterbury and Lincoln had been kept long vacant, that their rich temporalities might swell the royal revenue. The Keeper of the King's Conscience had in vain pointed out to him the impiety of this practice, till his arguments were en-

---

[1] The family still subsists in Monmouthshire, the name being now spelt Bluet.

forced by a disease which left the royal spoliator little hope of recovery. Now, for the good of his soul, he bestowed the primacy on Anselm, who afterwards became so famous a champion of the church, and Lincoln was the prize of the Chancellor himself. But there was still much difficulty in getting possession of the see; for no sooner did the penitent monarch become convalescent than his appetite for ecclesiastical property returned in full force, and it was only on the condition of large pecuniary contributions that he would accept the homage of the new bishop.[1] The better to enable him to support these, Bloet himself set up as a wholesale dealer in church preferment, while he was guilty of great extortion in his office of Chancellor; and he became famous above all his predecessors for venality and oppression.

Authors differ as to the circumstances of his end. Some assert that for his crimes he was thrown into prison by the King, where he died; while others circumstantially state that he contrived to keep the King in good humor by large presents; that riding together near Woodstock, the Chancellor fell from his horse in an apoplectic fit; and that being carried into the palace, he presently died, the King lamenting over him. Lord Coke dryly observes of him, "that he lived without love and died without pity, save of those who thought it pity he lived so long." Yet he is not without admirers; he was of agreeable manners, and he softened censure by an ostentatious disclaimer of principle, so that the world, seeing that he was not so profligate as he pretended to be, gave him credit for some portion of latent honesty. By one writer he is characterized as "a handsome man, well spoken, and of a serene mind." His death happened in 1090.[2]

[1] "Afterwards repenting himself of such liberality in that he had not kept it longer in his hands towards the enriching off his coffers, he devised a shift how to wipe the bishop's nose of some of his gold, which he performed after this manner. He caused the bishop to be sued, quarelinglie charging him that he had wrongfullie usurped certeine possessions together with the citie of Lincoln, which apperteined to the see of Yorke. Which although it was but a forged cavillation and a shamefull untruth; yet could not the bishop be delivered out of that trouble till he paid to the king £5000."—*H. Hollinsh.* ii. 34.

[2] Anglia Sacra, vol. ii. 694. Hunt. De Contemptu Mundi, 698. Spel. Gloss. 109. Or. Jur. 1. Turner's History of England, i. 406. Lives of Chancellors, i. 4. Parkes, 22.

The odium which Bloet excited was much softened by his successor, Chancellor FLAMBARD,—a monster unredeemed from his vices by any virtue or agreeable quality. His original name was Ranulphus or Ralfe, but he afterwards acquired the nickname of *Flambard* or "devouring torch," which stuck to him, and by which he is known in history. Of the lowest origin, he reached high station by extreme subtlety and by a combination of all sorts of evil arts. I am sorry to say he is the first practicing advocate I read of who was made Chancellor. Having begun his career as a common informer, he took to the practice of the law, and being "a pleader never to be daunted,—as unrestrained in his words as in his actions, and equally furious against the meek as the turbulent,"[1] he rose to great eminence both in civil and ecclesiastical courts. Of course he was a priest.[2] Bred in Normandy, he was familiar with the language as well as the law, now introduced in England. He succeeded in making himself useful to the Ex-Chancellor Maurice, Bishop of London, who employed him and introduced him at Court. There he was found a ready and efficient instrument of extortion and tyranny, and he was rapidly promoted. He first acted as chaplain and private secretary to the King, and on the disgrace or death of Bloet, the Great Seal was delivered to him. His ingenuity was now sedulously employed in devising new methods of raising money for his rapacious employer. The liberty of hunting was circumscribed by additional penalties; new offenses were created to multiply fines; capital punishments were commuted by pecuniary mulcts; and a fresh survey of the kingdom was ordered to raise the renders to the Crown of those estates which were alleged to have been underrated in the record of Domesday, and to discover ancient encroachments on the royal domains.[3] Though a churchman, he openly advised the King to apply the revenues of the church to his own use. So greatly was Rufus delighted with these services, that he pronounced Chancellor Flambard to be the only man who, to please a mas-

---

[1] William of Malmesbury.
[2] The true maxim was "nullus causidicus nisi clericus."
[3] Hic juvenem fraudulentis stimulationibus inquietavit Regem, incitans ut totius Angliæ reviseret descriptionem, Anglicæque telluris comprobans iteraret-partitionem, subditisque reciderit, tam advenis quam indigenis quicquid inveneretur ultra certam dimensionem. Ord. Vital. 678.

ter, was willing to brave the vengeance of all the rest of mankind.[1]

In the midst of the ill-will and the envy which the Chancellor excited, a plot was laid to get rid of him,—very different from the intrigues of modern times resorted to for the same purpose. Gerold, a mariner who had formerly been in his service, set on by rival courtiers, one day pretended to come to him as a messenger from the Bishop of London, and prevailed on him to step into a boat on the margin of the Thames, that he might visit this venerable Prelate. represented to be lying at the point of death in a villa on the opposite bank. When the Chancellor had reached the middle of the river the boat was suddenly turned down the stream, and he was soon forcibly taken from it, put on board a ship, and carried out to sea. The intention was that he should be thrown overboard, but fortunately for him, before this was executed, a tremendous storm arose; a superstitious dread overtook some of those engaged to murder him; they quarreled among themselves; Gerold, the chief conspirator, was induced by entreaties and promises to put him ashore: and on the third day, to the amazement and terror of his enemies, he appeared in Court with the Great Seal in his hand, as if nothing extraordinary had happened.

He was now made Bishop of Durham, in consideration of a present of £1000 extracted from him by the King, who had been taught by him to keep ecclesiastical benefices long vacant, and then to sell them to the highest bidder.

According to some authorities Flambard was farther advanced to the offices of Treasurer and Grand Justiciar, but at all events he appears to have held the Great Seal along with his other employments (whatever they were) till the end of reign.

On Rufus coming to his untimely end, the indignation of the people broke out against his obnoxious minister; and to satisfy the public clamor, Flambard was committed to the Tower by the new government. Here he is said to have lived sumptuously on the allowance which he received from the Exchequer, and presents which were sent him, till, having lulled the vigilance of his keepers, he

[1] Malmes. 69, 158.

contrived to escape. In the bottom of a pitcher of wine sent to solace him was concealed a coil of rope. He invited the knights who guarded him to dine with him and partake of the wine; they remained drinking till late in the evening, and when they at last reclined on the floor to sleep, the ex-Chancellor, with the aid of this rope, let himself down from the window,[1] and was received by his friends, who conducted him to the sea-shore and safely landed him in Normandy. He was there kindly entertained by Duke Robert, and notwithstanding his many misdeeds, and the perils he had run, he was afterwards restored to his see, and he peaceably ended his days in his native land. A month before he died he caused himself to be carried from the castle to the high altar of the Cathedral of Durham, and there, in the presence of the clergy and laymen of rank in the county, he began with many groans to repent him of his conduct towards the church, confessing that his proceedings had been prompted not by necessity, but by the purest avarice. After this confession, he proceeded to make restitution; and the charter is preserved, sealed on the occasion with the episcopal seal, by which he restores to the monks the lands of which he had deprived them. The penitent language of this charter is very strong, and we may hope that it was sincere: —" Ea omnia quæ eis vol untate et cupiditate mea abstuleram, sciatis me eisdem in perpetuum possidenda, mali facti pœnitens, et misericordiam quærens, super altare Sancti Cuthberti per annulum reddidisse."[2] Nevertheless he was branded to all posterity as "the plunderer of the rich, exterminator of the poor, and the confiscator of other men's inheritances."[3]

Henry I. was no sooner placed on the throne by the means we have glanced at in the life of Lord Chancellor Maurice, now Bishop of London,[4] than he restored the Great Seal to WILLIAM GIFFARD, Bishop of Winchester, who, from the infamous conduct of the last two Chancellors, in spite of his inconsistencies and want of steady principle, had come to be regarded with some respect; and the new sovereign aimed at popularity by this appoint

---

[1] This window, with the mullion to which the rope was attached, may still be admired by antiquaries in the Tower.
[2] Communicated to me ny one of the present prebendaries.
[3] W. of Malmesbury.   [4] Ante, p. 43.

ment as well as by the commitment and threatened punishment of Flambard.

When Duke Robert returned from the taking of Jerusalem and invaded England, claiming the crown both as his birthright and under the agreement with Rufus, it was generally felt that, from his incapacity to govern, notwithstanding his personal bravery, he had not for a moment any chance of success, and Lord Chancellor Giffard adhered steadily to the youngest brother, to whom he had sworn allegiance. He continued to hold the Great Seal under him for six years, until, after the conquest of Normandy and the imprisonment of Robert, the formidable dispute broke out with Anselm respecting investitures. Giffard's feelings as a churchman outweighed his gratitude to the family of the Conqueror, and the leaning which, as Chancellor, he must have had in favor of the power of the Crown. He took a decided part with the Primate, and re-echoed the words of Pascal, the Pope: " Priests are called gods in Scripture, as being the vicars of God ; and will you, by your abominable pretensions to grant them their investiture, assume the right of creating them?"[1]

Henry dismissed him from the office of Chancellor, and banished him the kingdom. After the compromise with Anselm, he was allowed to return to his diocese, but he was never restored to favor. He lived some years in tranquillity, and dying at Winchester was buried in the cathedral there. He is famed for having built the palace in Southwark, near London Bridge, in which, for many centuries, the Bishops of Winchester resided when they visited the metropolis, and the site of which still belongs to the see. He likewise founded a convent for monks at Framley, and another for nuns at Taunton.[2]

On the dismissal of Giffard, Henry would have been glad to have appointed a layman for his Chancellor, but persons in orders only were then considered qualified to hold the office. He selected one who, though a priest, had not yet received much preferment, and who might be expected to be submissive to the royal will. This was ROGER, afterwards Bishop of Sarum, who was of obscure origin and of defective education, but who, from his parts

---

[1] Eadmer, p. 61.   [2] Or. Jur. 1. Spel. Gloss. 109. De Gestis Pont. lib. i.

and his pliancy, made a distinguished figure in this and the succeeding reign.

Roger began his career as a country parson,—the incumbent of a small parish in the neighborhood of Caen, in Normandy. The story goes, that Prince Henry, then in the employment of his brother Robert, accidently entered with some of his companions, the little church in which Roger was saying mass. The priest, recollecting that soldiers do not generally like long prayers, and being more anxious for favor on earth than in heaven, despatched the service with extraordinary rapidity. Whereat they were all so well pleased that the Prince jestingly said to him, " Follow my camp,"—which he did;—and this was the first step in the preferment of the man who was afterwards Lord Chancellor, Bishop of Salisbury, and Chief Justiciar, and who had great influence in disposing of the Crown of England.

Henry at first employed him only as chaplain, but as he kept up his reputation for short prayers and showed other courtier-like qualities, though he was rather illiterate, he was appointed private secretary, and gained the entire good will of the Prince. Since the commencement of the present reign he had been a sort of humble dependant at court,—generally liked, but not much respected,—and hardly considered fit to be promoted to any high station. Henry, afraid of clerical pride and obstinacy,—in his present difficulty to find a pliant priest, conferred the Great Seal upon him, with the title of Chancellor.

Roger's faculties always expanded with his good fortune. He now showed much dexterity in business, and executed all the duties of his office entirely to the satisfaction of the King, and even of the public. Without seeming to desert the interest of his order, he supported the royal prerogative, and he was mainly instrumental in bringing about the accommodation with Anselm, which suspended to a future time the collision between the crown and the mitre. Henry rewarded him with the Bishopric of Salisbury, and grants of many manors.

When he had filled the office of Chancellor for some years he resigned it for the still higher one of Chief Justiciar,[1] which he held till near the conclusion of this

---

[1] H. Hunt. lib. vii. p. 219.

reign. He was now really prime minister, although the title was not yet known in any European monarchy,—and during the King's residence in Normandy, sometimes for years together, he governed England as Regent.

He is much celebrated for his skill in conducting the negotiations respecting the succession to the Crown after the melancholy shipwreck in which the King's only son perished. Matilda, his daughter, married first to the Emperor Henry V., and then to Geoffry, Count of Anjou, was the great object of his affections; and his solicitude now was that she might succeed him in all his dominions. But the laws by which the Crown was to descend were then by no means ascertained. Although Queen Boadicea had ruled over the Britons,—among the Anglo-Saxons no female had mounted the throne: the Salic law was supposed to prevail in Normandy, and no one could say whether with the Norman dynasty it was to be considered as transferred into England. Supposing females to be excluded from the succession, it was doubtful whether the exclusion would extend to a male deriving his descent from the royal stock through a female. Roger, to suit his present purpose, now laid it down *ex cathedrâ* as incontrovertible doctrine, "that the Crown, like a private inheritance, should descend to the daughter and heiress of the person last seized;" and he was greatly instrumental in obtaining from the barons of England as well as Normandy a recognition of Matilda as successor to her father in both countries. He even succeeded in prevailing upon them to swear fealty to her—himself setting the example.

He continued in high favor with Henry for several years; but afterwards, from some dispute, the nature of which has not been explained to us, he was dismissed from the office of Chief Justiciar, which was given to De Vere, Earl of Oxford.

No sooner did a demise of the crown take place than Roger, forgetting what he owed to the late King, and his oath to Matilda, and listening to the offers of her rival Stephen, the grandson of the Conqueror by his daughter, married to the Count of Blois,—was active in persuading the Archbishop of Canterbury to give the royal unction to the usurper, and influenced many of the Barons to declare in his favor, on the new constitutional doctrine which he propounded, "that males only could mount the throne of England, but that a male might claim through a female." He defended his consistency,—asserting that circumstances only had changed, and that he still remained true to his principles.

Stephen getting possession of the government, Roger, the Ex-Chancellor, was rewarded for his bad law and his perfidy first with the Great Seal, and then with the office of Lord Treasurer. He was now in all things highly favored by the new king, and, under a license from him, erected at Devizes one of the largest and strongest castles in England, where he appears to have displayed a sort of sovereign state and independence.

Before long he quarreled with Stephen, who had convened a council at Oxford, to which the Bishops were all summoned. Roger refused to attend, and set at defiance all the threats held out to induce him to submit. A strong force being sent against his castle at Devizes, he showed a determination to hold out to the last extremity, and he would probably have made a long defense, and might have been rescued by the assistance of other turbulent and faithless Barons, if an expedient had not been resorted to which strongly marks the barbarous manners of the times. The Bishop had a natural son, to whom he was much attached. The King having got possession of this youth, threatened to hang him before the walls of the castle, in his father's sight, unless the castle were immediately delivered up. The menace had the desired effect, and the Bishop unconditionally surrendered. His sacred office protected him from personal violence, but he soon after fell ill of a quartan ague, and died on the 4th December, 1139.

We have the following graphic sketch of the career of this Chancellor from William of Malmesbury:—" On the 3rd of the ides of December, Roger Bishop of Salisbury, by the kindness of death, escaped the quartan ague which had long afflicted him. To me it appears that God exhibited him to the wealthy as an example of the mutability of fortune, that they should not trust in uncertain riches. He first ingratiated himself with Prince Henry by prudence in the management of domestic matters, and by restraining the excesses of his household. Roger had deserved so well of him in his time of need, that, coming to the throne, he denied him nothing; giving him estates, churches, prebends, and abbeys; committing the kingdom to his fidelity; making him Chancellor and Bishop of Salisbury. Roger decided causes, had the charge of the treasury, and regulated the expenditure of the kingdom. Such were his occupations when the King was in England; such, without an associate or inspector, when the King resided in Normandy. And not only the King, but the nobility—even those who were secretly stung with envy by his good fortune, and more especially the inferior ministers and the debtors of the King—gave him almost whatever he could fancy. Did he desire to add to his domain any contiguous possession,—he would soon lay hold of it by entreaty, or purchase, or force. He erected splendid mansions of unrivaled magnificence on all his estates. His cathedral he dignified to the utmost with matchless buildings and ornaments. In the beginning of Stephen's reign his power was undiminished, the King repeating often to his companions, ' By the birth of God, I would give him half England if he asked for it. Till the time be ripe, he shall tire of asking before I tire of giving.' But Fortune, who in former times had flattered him so long and so transcendently, at last cruelly pierced him with scorpion sting. The height of his calamity was, I think, a circumstance which even I cannot help commiserating;—that though in his fall he exhibited to the world a picture of such wretchedness, yet there were very few who pitied him;—so much envy and hatred had his excessive prosperity drawn on him from all classes, not excepting those very persons whom he had advanced to honor." [1]

The precise time when Roger gave up the custody of the Great Seal in exchange for the office of Chief Justiciar is not ascertained; and there is much obscurity with respect to the Chancellors after him during the remainder of the reign of Henry I. WALDRIC, GODFREY Bishop of Bath, HERBERT Bishop of Norwich, GEOFREY RUFUS Bishop of Durham, RANULPHUS, or ARNULPH, and REGINALD Prior of Montague, are enumerated in different lists of Chancellors, and are casually noticed by different writers as having held the Great Seal in this interval; [2]

[1] Gesta Reg. Angl. p. 637.   [2] Or. Inst. 1. Spel. Gloss. 109

but the superior splendor of Roger of Salisbury threw them all into obscurity; and little is known respecting any of them, with the exception of Geoffrey Rufus and Ranulphus, and it would have been well for the memory of these two if they had been as little known as all the rest.

GEOFFREY RUFUS is famous for being recorded as the first that openly bought the office of Chancellor for money. There was an ancient legal maxim, "Quod Cancellaria non emenda est,"[1] yet the Pipe Roll of 31 Henry I. states that Geoffrey Rufus, Bishop of Durham, purchased the Chancery from the king for £3006. 13s. 4d. a sum equivalent to £45,000 of present money;[2] and he must, no doubt, have been guilty of much extortion and oppression to indemnify himself for so great an outlay. From the fractional sum which the Great Seal then fetched, we might almost suppose that it had been put up to auction and sold to the highest bidder. In subsequent reigns we shall find other instances of its being disposed of for money; but we are never distinctly informed whether this was by public auction or private contract.[3]

Of RANULPHUS Henry of Huntingdon relates, that from the general hatred excited by his misdeeds, he was supposed to have come to his end by a special visitation of Divine Providence. The King having kept his Christmas at Dunstable, proceeded to Berkhamstead. "Here there was a manifestation of God worthy of himself. Ranulphus, the King's Chancellor, had labored under sickness for twenty years. Nevertheless, at court he was ever

---

[1] This probably arose from the semi-sacred nature of the office, including the care of the king's chapel and the keeping of his conscience, so that the purchase of it may be considered to savor of simony.

[2] Et idem Cancellarius, viz. "Gaufridus debet MMM et VI l. et xiijs. et iiijd. pro sigillo." This is the most ancient roll in the series, and for many years was supposed to belong to the 5th Stephen. But, first, Prynne discovered it had been wrongly assigned, and fixed it to the 18th Henry I.:—then Madox (though he always quotes it as 5 Steph. in the body of his "Exchequer"), in a learned Latin "disceptatio," following the "Dialogus de Scaccario," at the end of his work, clearly shows that it belongs to Henry's reign, but leaves the precise year uncertain:—lastly, Mr. Joseph Hunter, in his preface to the Roll itself, published by the Record Commission, proves, without the possibility of a doubt, that the Roll is that of 31 Henry I.

[3] The office of Common-law Judge was likewise venal. The same year Richard Fitz-Alured fined in fifteen marks of silver that he might sit with Ralph Basset at the King's Pleas. "Ricardus filius Aluredi dabat xv. marcus argenti ut sederet cum Radulfo Basset at Placita Regis."—*Madd. Ex.* iv. 4.

more eager than a young man after all manner of wickedness, oppressing the innocent and grasping many estates for his own use. It was his boast, that while his body languished his mind was still vigorous. As he was conducting the royal party to his castle, where the King proposed to stay some time as his guest, and he had reached the top of a hill from which the stately structure might be descried,—while he was pointing to it with great elation, he fell from his horse, and a monk rode over him. In consequence, he was so bruised that he breathed his last in a few days. *Ecce quanta superbia quam vilissime, Deo volente, deperiit,*" [1]

We shall not attempt giving any further details respecting the Chancellors of Henry I. It is to be regretted that the accounts of them which have descended to us are so very scanty. From the character of this Sovereign, who was not only a great warrior, but the brightest wit and most accomplished scholar of his age, we may believe that those who were selected by him to hold his great seal, and consequently to be in constant familiar intercourse with him, were distinguished by their talents, acquirements, and agreeable manners. We should be particularly glad to know which of them was the author of the Code which passes under the name of Henry I., but which must have been compiled by a jurist under his orders,—a work so useful to instruct us in the manners and customs of the times, and showing the broad distinction still made between the English and the Normans. But though the names of these functionaries are preserved as having filled the office of Chancellor, dark night envelops their history and their character.

When, on the usurpation of Stephen, Roger, Bishop of Salisbury, had, by his treachery to the family of Henry, his benefactor, acquired such influence with the new Sovereign,—after presiding as Chancellor at the Convention of Estates held at Oxford, when the charter was passed confirming the liberties of the church, the barons, and the people,—he bestowed the office on his nephew ALEXANDER, and made him Bishop of Lincoln.[2]

---

[1] Hen. Hunt. lib. vii. p. 382. The last reflection is too quaint for translation.

[2] Parl. Hist. 5. There is extant among the archives of the Dean and Chapter of Exeter the original of the famous "Charta Stephani Regis de Liber-

The new holder of the Great Seal was not without good qualities; but it is said that having been brought up in great luxury by his uncle, he had contracted an inordinate taste for expense, which soon brought him into difficulty and disgrace. Wishing to excel other chiefs by his splendor and his largesses, he tried to supply the deficiency of his own resources by preying upon others who were in his power. Still his extravagance exceeded all his means of supplying it. His vanity was gratified by being called "the Magnificent" at the Court of Rome. He went thither in 1142, and again in 1144, with a view to settle the disputes between the King and the Pope, and he had the singular good luck in these negotiations to please both parties. With the approbation of the King he was appointed legate by the Pope, with power to convene a Synod, at which several useful canons were made to repress the enormities of the times. He made a third journey to the Pope, then in the south of France, where, in the month of August, in the year 1147, growing sick, as was supposed from the heat of the climate, he returned home and died.

During his career he had been more than once in arms against his sovereign. Besides founding convents, he built three strong castles, Banbury, Sleaford, and Newark. These excited the jealousy of Stephen, who compelled him to surrender them, and after getting possession of Newark, this capricious tyrant for some time detained him in prison. However, he was speedily restored to favor, and at his death was denominated "Flos et Cacumen Regni et Regis."[1]

His successor as Chancellor was the natural son of his uncle "ROGER THE GREAT," Bishop of Salisbury. This promotion shows strongly the power and influence which the family had attained; for the new Chancellor displayed no personal good qualities to compensate for the stain on his birth. He is mentioned by the monkish historians under the name of "ROGER PAUPER." He seems neither to have possessed the wealth nor the pliancy of his father. Taking part with the Barons who held out their castles against the King, he was made prisoner. He

tatibus Ecclesiæ Angliæ et Regni;" dated at Oxford, Regni mei anno primo, A.D. 1136, and witnessed "ROGERO CANCELLARIO."

[1] Hen. Hunt. lib. vii. p. 290. Guil. Neib. l. i. c.

might have been set at liberty if he would have changed sides; but this he constantly refused to do, even when threatened with the penalties of treason. As a singular favor he was allowed to abjure the realm, and he is supposed to have died in exile.[1]

We ought here to mention the Chancellors of Queen Matilda. Though not enumerated by historians among the sovereigns of England, she was crowned Queen, and while Stephen was her prisoner,—by the prowess and fidelity of her natural brother, Robert Earl of Gloucester, she was in the enjoyment of supreme power throughout the greatest part of the kingdom. Making the city of Gloucester her metropolis, she filled up all the great offices of state with her adherents. She was the first sovereign that ever entrusted the Great Seal to the keeping of a layman. For her Chancellor she had WILLIAM FITZGILBERT, a knight who had gallantly fought for her; and she granted the office in reversion to Alberic de Vere, Earl of Oxford, to be held by William de Vere, his brother, when it should be rendered up by William Fitzgilbert.

But Stephen was released from prison, and after a protracted struggle, being successful in the field, this grant was nullified by the arrangement which allowed him to reign during his life,—the sceptre on his death to descend to the issue of Matilda.

There are three other Chancellors of this reign whose names have been discovered by antiquaries. PHILIP, ROBERT DE GANT, and REGINALD, Abbot of Walden; [2] but every thing respecting them is left in impenetrable obscurity. What part they took in the civil war, whether they mitigated or aggravated its horrors, and whether they were steady to their party, or changed sides as interest prompted, must remain for ever unknown. Of this disturbed period little can be learned respecting the administration of justice or change of laws. The contending parties were both exclusively Norman; the descendants of the conquered were equally oppressed by both, and no one had yet arisen to vindicate the reputation or to defend the rights of the Anglo-Saxon race. The darkest hour is immediately before break of day, and the next Chancellor we have to introduce to the

[1] Ord. Vit. pp. 919, 920.   [2] Spel. Gloss. 109.

reader was of Saxon origin; he was one of the most distinguished men of any race that this island has ever produced, and he is now invoked as a Saint by all the votaries of the Romish church. We have a full and minute biography of him by a contemporary who was his kinsman, and the various events of his life, which make a conspicuous figure in our national annals, are as well known and authenticated as if he had flourished in the eighteenth century.

CHAPTER III.

LIFE OF LORD CHANCELLOR THOMAS A BECKET.

KING STEPHEN having died in the year 1154, he was succeeded by the son of Matilda, the first of the Plantagenet line,—a prince for vigor and ability equal to any who ever filled the throne of England. From early youth he had given presage of his discrimination and talents for government, and one of the first acts of his reign after his arrival in England, was to appoint as his Chancellor the famous THOMAS A BECKET.[1]

Gilbert Beck or Becket, the father of this most extraordinary man, was of Saxon descent, a merchant in London, and though only of moderate wealth had served the office of sheriff of that city. His mother, whose name was Matilda, was certainly of the same race, and born in same condition of life as her husband; although, after her son had become chancellor and archbishop, a martyr and a saint,—a romantic story was invented that she was the daughter of an Emir in Palestine; that Gilbert, her future consort, having joined a crusade and being taken prisoner by her father, she fell in love with him; that when he escaped and returned to his native country, she followed him, knowing no words of any western tongue except "London" and Gilbert;" that by the use of these she at last found him in Cheapside; and that being converted to Christianity and baptized, she became his wife.[2]

[1] We are not informed in whose custody the Great Seal was between the king's accession and the appointment of Becket.
[2] That monkish chroniclers and old ballad-mongers should have repeated

Thomas, their only child, was born in London in the year 1119, in the reign of Henry I. Being destined for the Church, his education was begun at Merton Abbey in Surrey, and thence he was transferred to the schools of London, which (making ample allowance for exaggerated praise) seem then to have been very flourishing.[1] He was afterwards sent to finish his studies at Paris, where he not only became a proficient in philosophy and divinity, but likewise in all military exercises and polite acquirements, and was made an accomplished cavalier.

and credited this fable is not surprising: but I cannot conceal my astonishment to find it gravely narrated for truth by two recent, most discriminating and truthful historians. Sharon Turner and Thierry, who, while they were enlivening, one would have thought, must have had some suspicion that they were deluding their readers. Becket himself, in an epistle in which he gives an account of his origin, is entirely silent about his Syrian blood; and Fitzstephen, who describes himself as "his fellow-citizen, chaplain, and messmate, remembrancer in his chancery, and reader of papers in his court," says expressly that he was born of parents who were citizens of London. I should much sooner expect to find the statement believed, that his mother when with child of him dreamed that she carried Canterbury Cathedral in her womb, or that the midwife, when she first received him into the world, exclaimed, "Here comes an Archbishop!" for which there is uncontradicted authority: "Eum in lucem editum obstetrix in manibus tollens, ait Archiepiscopum quendam a terra elevavi." Fitzst. 10. The story of the Emir's daughter first appears in the compilation called *Quadrilogus*, not written till long after. Lib. i. c. 2. There has been a supposition equally unfounded recently started, that Becket was of the Norman race. See Ed. Rev. CLXXIII., July, 1847, p. 137. His Saxon pedigree appears from all contemporary authorities.

[1] "In Lundonia tres principales ecclesiæ scholas celebres habent de privilegio et antiqua dignitate. Disputant scholares, quidam demonstrative, dialectice alii; hii rotant enthymemata; hii perfectis melius utuntur syllogismis. Quidam ad ostentationem exercentur disputatione, quæ est inter colluctantes; alii ad veritatem, quæ est perspectionis gratia. Oratores aliqui quandoque orationibus rhetoricis aliquid dicunt apposite ad persuadendum, curantes artis præcepta servare et ex contingentibus nihil omittere. Pueri diversarum scholarum versibus inter se conrixantur; aut de principiis artis grammaticæ, vel regulis præteritorum vel supinorum, contendunt. Sunt alii qui in epigrammatibus, rythmis et metris utuntur vetere illa triviali dicacitate; licentia Fescennina socios, suppressis nominibus, liberius lacerant; lœdorias jaculantur et scommata; salibus Socraticis sociorum vel forte majorum, vitia tangunt; vol mordacius dento rodunt leonino audacibus dithyrambis. Auditores, multum ridere parati

Ingeminant tremulos naso crispante cachinnos."

—*Descriptio polulignamæ civitatis Lundoniæ*, 4. Fitzstephen is equally eloquent in describing the sports of the Londoners. "Plurimi civium delectantur, ludentes in avibus cœli, nisis, acci pitribus in sylvis. Habentque cives suum jus venandi in Middlesexia, Hertfordsira, et tota Chiltra, et in Cantia usque ad aquam Crayæ." p. 9. But he shakes our faith in all his narratives by asserting that, in the reign of Stephen, London was capable of sending into the field 20,000 cavalry and 60,000 infantry, p. 4.

One great object of his residence in Paris was to get rid of his English accent, which was then a mark of degradation and a bar to advancement. When he returned it might well have been supposed from his conversation and manners, that his ancestors had fought at Hastings under the banner of the Conqueror, and that his family had since assisted in continuing the subjugation of the conquered race.

Like Sir Thomas More, one of his most distinguished successors, he began his career of business by holding a situation in the office of the Sheriff of London; but this was not at all to his taste, and he soon contrived to insinuate himself into the good graces of a great baron of Norman blood resident in the neighborhood of the metropolis, with whom he gaily spent his time in racing, hunting, and hawking,—amusements forbidden to the Saxons.

His next patron was Theobald, Archbishop of Canterbury, who, finding him a youth of uncommon parts, and captivated with his grace and winning address, made him take deacon's orders, and conferred upon him the livings of St. Mary le Strand and Othford in Kent, with prebends in the cathedrals of London and Lincoln. His ambition for high preferment was now kindled; and he found himself deficient in a knowledge of the civil and canon law, then the great means of advancement both in church and state,—and he prevailed on his patron to send him to Bologna, which had been for some time the most famous university in the world for such studies. After residing there a year, attending the lectures of the celebrated Gratian, he went to Auxerre in Burgundy, where there was likewise a flourishing juridical school, and he returned to England fully qualified for any situation, however exalted, to which fortune might raise him.

He was now promoted to the archdeaconry of Canterbury, an office of considerable trust and profit, Displaying great talents for business, he gained the entire confidence of the primate, and was employed by him in two delicate negotiations with the court of Rome. The first was to recover for the see of Canterbury the legatine power which properly belonged to the primacy, and of which it had been stripped. This point he carried to the great delight of Theobald, who attached the highest importance to it.

The next was a matter of more national importance. Notwithstanding the solemn treaty between Stephen the reigning king, and Henry the son of Matilda, the right heir to the crown, intrigues were going on to defeat the succession of the Angevin line, and a plan was in contemplation to have Eustace, the son of Stephen, crowned King of England in his father's lifetime. Theobald and the majority of the prelates remaining true to their engagement, deputed Archdeacon Becket to obtain from Pope Eugenius a bull against any bishop officiating at the coronation of the son of Stephen. This mission was attended with considerable difficulty, for young Henry Plantagenet had already shown himself hostile to the encroachments of the papal see, and there was an apprehension of danger from the union of the crown of England with his immense continental possessions, extending from Picardy to the Pyrenees; and one of the cardinals who favored Eustace observed to Becket, that "it would be easier to hold a ram by the horns than a lion by the tail." But Becket's great abilities in negotiation proved successful, the intended coronation was prevented, and on the death of Stephen, Henry was peaceably proclaimed king.

The new Sovereign was then in Normandy. On his arrival in England he was informed by Archbishop Theobald, who crowned him, of the services of the Archdeacon of Canterbury; and à Becket, then the handsomest and most accomplished young man in the kingdom, was presented to him. Henry was at once captivated by his appearance and his agreeable acquirements, and soon admitted him to his familiarity and confidence. The future Saint, at this stage of his career, has incurred the suspicion of having forgotten what was due to the priestly character or to the strict rules of morality, for the purpose of securing an influence over the dissipated Sovereign. He not only joined him in military exercises and in the sports of the field, but in all sorts of court festivities, and it is to be feared in revelries, which could only be palliated by the habitual license of Norman manners; although some of his biographers stand up for his immaculate purity in the midst of the most alluring temptations.

Archbishop Theobald was at first the King's chief

favorite and adviser, but his health and his influence declining, Becket was found apt for business as well as amusement, and gradually became intrusted with the exercise of all the powers of the crown. He received the wardenship of the Tower of London, the custody of the castle of Berkhamstead, and a grant of the honor of Eyre, with the service of 140 knights.

The exact time of his appointment as Chancellor has not been ascertained, the records of the transfer of the Great Seal not beginning till a subsequent reign, and old biographers being always quite careless about dates.[1] But he certainly had this dignity soon after Henry's accession, and to him are ascribed by historians the restoration of the laws of Henry I., the resumption of the grants by which Stephen had impoverished the crown, the restoration of the English exiles who had fled to the Continent during the late troubles, and the other wise and liberal measures which characterized the commencement of this reign. While he continued Chancellor, the office of Grand Justiciar does not seem to have been filled up, and, except the King, he had no superior. Tall in stature, with a placid, handsome and commanding countenance, his figure pleased the eye; while his subtle reasonings, his polished elocution, and facetious gayety, won the heart. His loftiness of mind, that was proud and ceremonious with rank and power, softened into affability, gentleness, and liberality towards his inferiors and dependents. Popularity being his passion, he studied to be attractive, and he knew that the condescensions of greatness have still greater influence than its power.[2] He was the first to give the office of Chancellor the pre-eminence and splendor which have since belonged to it.

We may imagine the joy of the Saxon race in witnessing his elevation. For nearly a century they had been treated as aliens and serfs in their own country; no one of Saxon blood had been promoted to any office of distinction, civil, military, or ecclesiastical. The tradition was, that the Danish dynasty established by Canute had been overturned by too great leniency being shown to the native English: and William and his descendants were resolved to avoid a similar error. The Anglo-Saxon lan-

---

[1] Spelman makes him Chancellor in 1145, and Dugdale not till 1157.
[2] Gervase, 1688.

guage was proscribed at court: the Normans would at this time as little have condescended to learn it as the wild Irish whom they soon after conquered; and every opportunity was taken to show contempt for the dress, the habits, and the manners of the subjugated descendants of Hengist and Horsa.

Becket had risen by acquiring the dialect and accomplishments of the dominant caste, but he was too noble-minded now to be ashamed of his origin : he proclaimed his lineage, and professed himself a protector of the rights and liberties of all his countrymen.

It is doubtful whether at this time the Chancellor had any separate judicial duties; but we know that Becket sat as a member of the Supreme Court, or Aula Regis; that he sealed all the King's grants with the Great Seal; that he had the care of the royal chapel; and that he acted as secretary to the King in domestic affairs, and in all foreign negotiations.

Of his conduct, habits, and demeanor, while he continued Chancellor, we have a very graphic and trustworthy account from his secretary; and instead of diluting it, after the modern fashion, into a mixture from which all its pungency and raciness would evaporate, I think I shall much better convey an accurate notion of the character of the individual, and of the manners of the times, by a literal translation of a few of the most remarkable passages of this interesting work:

"The Chancellor's house and table were open to all of every degree about the court who wished to partake of his hospitality, and who were, or appeared to be, respectable. He hardly ever sat down to dinner without earls and barons whom he had invited. He ordered the rooms in which he entertained company to be daily covered during winter with clean straw and hay, and in summer with clean rushes and boughs,[1] for the gentlefolks to lie down upon, who on account of their numbers could not be accommodated at the tables, so that their fine clothes might not be soiled by a dirty floor. His house was splendidly furnished with gold and silver vessels, and was plentifully supplied with the most costly meats and wines.

"The prime nobility of England and the neighboring

---

[1] A custom which continued in England down to the time of Erasmus, and which he describes in nearly the same words.

kingdom sent their sons to be servants to the Chancellor. He gave these young men handsome entertainment and a liberal education, and when he had seen them duly admitted into the order of knighthood he returned them back to their fathers and relations. Some he retained near his own person. The King himself entrusted his own son, the heir apparent of the kingdom, to be brought up by him, and the Chancellor maintained the prince with all suitable honor, together with many sons of the nobility of the same age, and all their train, instructors, and servants.

" Many nobles and knights paid homage to the Chancellor, which he received with a saving of their allegiance to the King, and he then maintained and supported them as their patron.

" When he was going beyond sea he had a fleet of six or more vessels for his own use, and he carried over free of expense all who wished to cross at the same time. When he was landed he recompensed the masters of his ships and the sailors to their hearts' content. Hardly a day passed in which he did not give away magnificent presents, such as horses, hawks, apparel, gold or silver furniture. or sums of money. He was an example of the sacred proverb:—*Some bountifully give away what belongs to them, and still always abound; while others seize what does not belong to them, and are always in want.* So gracefully did the Chancellor confer his gifts, that he was reckoned the charm and the delight of the whole Latin world.

" The Chancellor was in high favor with the King, the clergy, the army, and the people, on account of his eminent virtues, his greatness of mind, and his good deeds, which seemed to spring spontaneously from his heart. Serious business being finished, the King and he consorted as young comrades of the same station, —whether in the palace, in church, in private society, or in excursions on horseback.

" One cold wintry day they were riding together through the streets of London when they observed an old beggar-man coming towards them, wearing a worn-out, tattered garment. Said the King to the Chancellor, ' Do you see that man?'—*Chancellor.* ' I see him.'—*King.* ' How poor! how wretched! how naked he is! Would it not be great

charity to give him a thick warm cloak?'—*Chancellor.*
'Great indeed; and you, as King, ought to have a disposition and an eye for such things.' Meanwhile the beggar comes up; the King stops, and the Chancellor along with him. The King in a mild tone addresses the beggar, and asks him 'if he would like to have a good cloak?' The beggar, not knowing who they were, thought it was all a joke. *The King to the Chancellor.*—'You indeed shall have the grace of this great charity:' and putting his hands on a very fine new cloak of scarlet and ermine which the Chancellor then wore, he struggled to pull it off, while the Chancellor did his best to retain it. A great scuffle and tumult arising, the rich men and knights who formed their train, in astonishment, hastened to find out what sudden cause of contest had sprung up, but could gain no information; both the contending parties were eagerly engaged with their hands, and seemed as if about to tumble to the ground. After a certain resistance the Chancellor allowed the King to be victorious,—to pull off his cloak,—and to give it to the beggar. The King then told the whole story to his attendants, who were all convulsed with laughter. There was no want of offers from them of cloaks and coats to the Chancellor. The old beggar-man walked off with the Chancellor's valuable cloak, enriched beyond his hopes, rejoicing and giving thanks to God.'

"Sometimes the King took his meals in the dining-hall of the Chancellor for the sake of amusement, and to hear the stories told at his table and in his house. While the Chancellor was sitting at table, the King would be admitted into the hall on horseback, sometimes with a dart in his hand, returning from the chase or riding to cover; sometimes he merely drank a cup of wine, and having saluted the Chancellor, retreated; sometimes, jumping over the table, he sat down and partook of the banquet. Never in any Christian age were two men more familiar or friendly."

Becket continued Chancellor till the year 1162, without any abatement in his favor with the King, or in the power

[1] It is impossible not to admire the finesse with which Fitzstephen tells this story, particularly the courtly acquiescence of the Chancellor after a proper resistance, and the profusion of offers of coats and cloaks to the Chancellor, then the favorite, and the distributor of the favors of the Crown.

which he possessed, or in the energy he displayed, or in the splendor of his career. He not only presided in the Aula Regis and superintended the domestic administration of the kingdom, but, when the necessities of the state so required, he himself went on foreign embassies, and led armies into the field.

The King's eldest son was still a boy and a pupil of the Chancellor, to whom it was thought that his education might be better intrusted than to any other, both for literature and chivalry. According to the custom of that time, which continued for centuries afterwards, it was usual to contract marriage between the children of sovereign princes long before they reached the age of puberty, and Henry, the son of a Count, thought it would add to the splendor of his family and to the stability of his throne, if his infant heir were affianced to a daughter of the King of France. To bring about this alliance, which was opposed by the Emperor of Germany, Henry proposed that the Chancellor should himself proceed to the French court, and he at once accepted the embassy.

"He prepared," says Fitzstephen, "to exhibit and pour out the opulence of English luxury, that among all persons and in all things the Sovereign might be honored in his representative, and the representative in himself. He took with him about two hundred mounted on horseback, of his own family, knights, priests, standard-bearers and squires,—sons of noblemen forming his body-guard—and all completely armed. All these, and all their followers, were festively arrayed in new attire, each according to his degree. He likewise took with him twenty-four changes of raiment, almost all to be given away, and left among the foreigners he was to visit. He carried along with him all kinds of dogs and birds for field sports used by kings and rich men. In his train he had eight wagons; each wagon was drawn by five horses equal to war horses, well matched, and with uniform harness; each horse was taken care of by a stout young man dressed in a new tunic. Two wagons carried nothing but ale made with water and malt,[1] in casks fastened with iron, to be given to

---

[1] I find no mention of *hops* in the text, and I suspect that the ale so boasted of was only the ancient Scandinavian drink described by Tacitus as "a corruption of barley," and still manufactured in Flanders under the name of "bierre blanche."—Some say that hops were unknown in England till the end of the

the French. The furniture of the Chancellor's chapel filled one wagon, his chamber another, his kitchen another; others were loaded with eatables and drink for the use of himself and his train. He had twelve *sumpter horses;* eight carried the Chancellor's gold and silver plate. Coffers and chests contained the Chancellor's money in good store, sufficient for his daily expenses, and the presents which he meditated, together with his clothes, books, and articles of the like nature. One horse, which preceded all the rest, carried the holy vessels of his chapel, the holy books, and the ornaments of the altar.

"Likewise each wagon had chained to it, either above or below, a large, strong, and fierce mastiff, which seemed able to contend with a bear or a lion, and on the top of every sumpter horse there was a monkey with a tail, or an ape, mimicking the human countenance. On entering the French towns and villages the procession was headed by about two hundred and fifty young men on foot, in groups of six, or ten, or more, singing some verses, in their own tongue, after the manner of their country. Then came at a little distance harriers and other dogs coupled, together with their keepers and whippers-in. Soon after the wagons, strengthed with iron and covered over with great skins of animals sewed together, rattled over the stones of the streets; at a short distance followed the sumpter horses, rode by their grooms, who sat upon their haunches. The Frenchmen running out from their houses at all this noise, inquired. '*Whose family can this be?*' Being answered, '*Behold the Chancellor of the King of England going on a mission to the King of France,*' they exclaimed, '*How wonderful must be the King of England himself, whose Chancellor travels in such state!*'

"After the sumpter horses followed esquires carrying the shields of the knights and leading the saddle horses;

---

reign of Henry VIII., when the liquor made bitter by them was called by the new name of "beer." Hence the popular lines—

"*Hops*, Reformation, Carp, and *Beer*,
Came to England all in one year,"

According to Virgil, the northern nations knew how to flavor their *wort* with acids:

——— " et pocula læti
Fermento atque *acidis* imitantur vitea sorbis."

then came other knights,—then pages,—then those who
bore hawks,—then the standard-bearers and the upper
and lower servants of the Chancellor's household,—then
soldiers and priests riding two and two;—last of all came
the Chancellor, surrounded by some of his friends.

"As soon as the Chancellor landed in France, he sent
forward a messenger to inform the French King of his
approach. The King appointed to meet him at Paris by
a certain day. It is the custom of the French Kings to
purvey for all persons coming to court, and while they remain there; and the King now wishing to purvey for the
Chancellor, by an edict published by him at Paris, prohibited all persons from selling any thing to the Chancellor or his people. This coming to the knowledge of
the Chancellor, he sent on his servants to St. Denis and
the neighboring town, that, changing their dress and concealing their names, they should buy for him bread, flesh,
fish, wine, and all eatables in abundance, and when he
entered the 'Hotel du Temple,' which he was to occupy
in Paris, they ran up and informed him that he would
find it supplied with provisions fully sufficient for the use
of a thousand men for three days.

"He gave away all his gold and silver plate and changes
of raiment,—to one a robe, to another a furred cloak, to
a third a pelisse;—to this man a palfrey, and to that a
war horse. Why should I enter into further particulars?
he won favor above all men. He successfully completed
his embassy; he gained his object: whatever he solicited
was granted to him.

"In returning, he apprehended and lodged in prison
Vedo de la Val, an enemy of the King of England, and
a notorious public robber."[1]

That this union might not afterwards be broken off,
and might cement a good understanding between the two
countries; according to the treaty which the Chancellor
had concluded, Margaret, the infant princess, was put
under the care of a Norman baron, who was to superintend her education; and her dower, consisting of a great
domain in the Vexin, was placed in the hands of the
Knights Templars till the celebration of the marriage.

It is said that the Chancellor continued zealously to
cultivate peace; but in spite of his efforts, war with

[1] Fitzstephen.

France became inevitable. The duchy of Toulouse had belonged to the father of Eleanor, who had been married to the King of France, and being divorced from him, was now Queen of England. Henry claiming this territory in her right,—under some pretense Louis insisted that he was entitled to dispose of it,—and both parties prepared to settle the dispute by an appeal to arms. The Chancellor, with his usual penetration, saw, that instead of the feudal militia, who were to fight without pay for forty days, it would be much better to commute personal service for a pecuniary contribution, by which a regular army might be equipped and maintained. He therefore introduced the pecuniary aid, called *scutage*, of £3 to be levied on every knight's fee ; and the number of 60,000 knights' fees established by the Conqueror, still remaining, he thus collected £180,000, and engaged a numerous force of mercenaries, whose attendance in the field was to be extended to three months. With them marched, from the love of glory, an illustrious host, consisting of English Barons, and many from Henry's continental dominions : a Prince of Wales, Malcolm King of Scotland, and Raymond King of Arragon, to whose infant daughter had been affianced the King's son, Richard, afterwards *Cœur de Lion*, then an infant in his nurse's arms. But of all who compose this great army, the bravest and most active warrior was Lord Chancellor à Becket, who had enlisted a body of 700 knights at his own expense, and, marching at their head, was the foremost in every enterprise.

Louis was shut up with a small force in the city of Toulouse, to which Henry laid siege. Becket represented that it might easily be taken by assault, offering to lead on the storming party himself, and it is generally allowed that this blow might at once have put a glorious termination to the war; but Henry, when congratulated on the prospect of having in his power such an illustrious captive, conceived conscientious scruples against offering violence to his liege lord, whom he had sworn to guard and protect. The Chancellor laid down for law that the King of France, by assuming the command there in person, had deliberately put himself in the situation of an enemy on equal terms with his opponent. During this discussion a great French army came to the rescue of their King; the golden opportunity was lost, and Henry was obliged to retreat with the bulk of his forces into Normandy. "The Chancellor, with his own followers and the single aid of Henry of Essex, the King's Constable, remained to preserve the English authority in that quarter, all the other leaders having refused to do so. Armed with helmet and coat of mail, he afterwards, with his own brave band, took three very strong castles which had been deemed impregnable. Nay, more, he crossed the Garonne with a military force, attacked the enemy, and having established the authority of the King in all that province, he returned triumphant and honored.[1]

In a subsequent campaign, the Chancellor, besides 700 knights of his own family, had under his command 1200 cavalry and 4000 infantry, whom he had taken into pay, for the space of forty days. "Each soldier serving on horseback received from him three shillings a day to provide horses and attendants, and was entertained at the Chancellor's table. He himself, although in holy orders, encountered Engleran de Trie, a valiant French knight, who, in full armor, rode furiously against him, his lance in the rest: the priest unhorsed the knight, and made a prize of his charger. Of the whole army of the King of England, the soldiers of the Chancellor were always the first, the most daring, and the most distinguished for their exploits, he himself instructing them, encouraging them, and leading them on."[1]

Peace being at last restored, the Chancellor unbuckled his sword, again put on his robes at Westminster, and returned to the discharge of his civil duties. His administration of justice was vigorous and impartial, no favor being shown to Saxon or Norman, to layman or ecclesiastic. Hitherto he preferred the interest of the Crown to those of his own order.

During the late war the rich prelates and abbots of the Norman race, whose military zeal had greatly subsided since they could no longer plunder a vanquished people, excused themselves from yielding to the summons to serve in the field, because, said they, *Holy Church forbade them to shed blood;* and farther, on the same pretense, they refused to pay the tax substituted for personal service, which, they said, was indirectly violating a divine precept. But the Chancellor overruled their scruples, and

[1] Fitzst.

compelled them to pay up the arrears. Upon this the heads of the Church uttered the most violent invectives against him. Foliot, Bishop of London, publicly accused him of plunging a sword into the bosom of his mother, the Church; and Archbishop Theobald, his former patron, threatened to excommunicate him. Becket still showed an entire indifference to ecclesiastical censures, and established Henry's right to personal service or scutage for all the lands held by the Church. One day, at a meeting of the clergy, some bishops affected to talk in high-flown terms of their *being independent of royal authority;* but the Chancellor, who was present, openly contradicted them, and, in a severe tone, reminded them that they were bound to the King by the same oath as men of the sword, "to be true and faithful to the King, and truth and faith to bear of life and limb and earthly honor."

Some have supposed that Becket all this time, while he held the office of Chancellor, was hypocritically acting a part to secure Henry's favor, that he might be elevated to the primacy, with the premeditated purpose of then quarreling with the King, and taking part against him in the controversies which had been going on between the civil and ecclesiastical authorities. But notwitstanding his conversation with the Abbot of Leicester, it is much more probable that his change of sentiments and policy was brought about by change of situation, and that hitherto he had served the King with sincerity and zeal, although it was foreseen by those well acquainted with his character, that he might become a very dangerous subject if placed in a high situation independent of the Crown.

It would appear that he himself, while Chancellor, and a devoted friend and servant of Henry, had a presentiment of his future destiny, and, we may believe, an earnest desire to avoid it. The age and infirmities of Theobald showing that the primacy must soon be vacant, the general expectation was that the Chancellor would succeed to it, not only from his extraordinary merits and success, but such being the usual course of promotion.[1]

---

[1] Fitzstephen in describing the nature of the office of Chancellor says "All ecclesiastical preferments are disposed of by his advice; so that, by God's grace and his own merits, he is almost sure to become an archbishop or bishop if he pleases."

In this state of things, Becket, residing at St. Gervas, near Rouen, fell dangerously ill; and such interest did his condition excite, that he had a visit from the King of England and the King of France on the same day. Afterwards, when the danger was over, and he was convalescent, he one day sat playing at chess dressed in a cloak with sleeves, like a young courtier—" Aschatinius, Prior of Leicester, coming from the King's Court, then in Gascony, entered to pay him a visit, and addressing him with familiarity, on account of their long intimacy, said: 'How is it that you wear a cloak with sleeves? This dress is fitter for those who go a-hawking; but you are an ecclesiastical character—one in *individuality*, but many in *dignity*—Archdeacon of Canterbury,—Dean of Hastings,—Provost of Beverley,—canon here and prebendary there,—nay, the proxy of the Archbishop, and (as the report goes at Court) archbishop soon to be.' To this speech the Chancellor made answer, among other things:—'Truly I know three poor priests in England, any one of whom I would rather wish to be promoted to the primacy than myself; for if by any chance I were appointed, knowing my Lord the King previously so well, I should be driven either to lose his favor, or (which Heaven forefend!) to sacrifice the service of God.' Nevertheless this afterwards fell out as he foretold."[1]

In April, 1161, Archbishop Theobald died. Henry declared that Becket should succeed,—no doubt counting upon his co-operation in carrying on the policy hitherto pursued in checking the encroachments of the clergy and of the see of Rome, and hoping that, his obsequious minister uniting supreme and ecclesiastical dignity, the remainder of his reign would be characterized by internal tranquillity and harmony, so that he might turn his undivided attention to schemes of foreign aggrandizement.

The same opinion of Becket's probable conduct was generally entertained, and a cry was raised that "the Church was in danger." The English bishops sent a representation to Henry against the appointment, and the electors long refused to obey his mandate, saying that "it was indecent that a man who was rather a soldier than a priest, and who had devoted himself to hunting and fal-

---

[1] Fitzst.

conry instead of the study of the Holy Scriptures, should be placed in the chair of St. Augustine."

Matilda, the King's mother, with more penetration into character, interfered to prevent the election on another ground, and warned her son that when once Becket was independent of him, being consecrated Archbishop, he would turn out a rival and an enemy, and would disturb the peace of the kingdom. Henry's eagerness for the appointment was only inflamed by opposition, and he resolved to carry it in spite of all obstacles.

Becket himself still pretended indifference or aversion, occupied himself with the duties of Chancellor, and continued his usual courtly life and secular habits. His rival, Gilbert Foliot, Bishop of Hereford, a prelate from his youth upwards, of rigid morals and severe demeanor, who was himself looking to the primacy, had been in the habit of asserting that the Chancellor was impatiently watching the demise of Theobald, and being in Normandy when he heard of that event, immediately hastened to England in the hope of succeeding him. The ecclesiastics with whom the election was, remaining obstinate, Becket with seeming unconcern attended to business at Harfleur, or hunted in the forests around Rouen.

At the end of a year the King, determined to be trifled with no longer, communicated to the Chancellor at Falaise that he must prepare for a voyage to England, and that in a few days he should certainly be Archbishop of Canterbury. It would be difficult to analyze the feelings of the future Martyr at this announcement. He probably experienced a glow of pleasure at the near prospect of greatness, yet was so far his own dupe as to persuade himself that he was unwilling to have it thrust upon him. His biographer informs us, that, casting a smile of irony on his dress, he replied,—" that he had not much the appearance of an archbishop, and that if the King was serious, he must still beg leave to decline the preferment, because it would be impossible for him to perform the duties of the situation and at the same time retain the favor of his benefactor."

The legate, Henry of Pisa, happening to be present, assisted in combating these scruples, and Becket, taking an affectionate leave of the King, sailed for England, agreeing to be consecrated as Primate if the election should fall upon him.

On the 3rd of June, 1162, the prior and monks of Canterbury, with the suffragan bishops, assembled at Westminster, and now, with one exception, concurred, after many prayers and masses, in electing Becket as Archbishop. The dissentient was Foliot, who observed, when the ceremony was over, that "the King had worked a miracle in having that day turned a layman into an archbishop, and a soldier into a saint." Many of the nobles who happened to be present testified their approbation by loud applause, and Prince Henry, under a commission from his father, gave the royal assent to the election.

Down to this time Becket, notwithstanding his many ecclesiastical benefices, was only in deacon's orders, which were then supposed to be consistent with most of the pursuits and habits of a layman; but he was now ordained priest by the Bishop of Rochester, and, proceeding to Canterbury, he was consecrated by the Bishop of Winchester, assisted by many other bishops. He was enthroned with extraordinary solemnity. The ceremony was almost as pompous as a coronation, all ranks being eager to gratify the King, and to pay court to the favorite.

The universal expectation was, that Becket would now attempt the part so successfully played by Cardinal Wolsey in a succeeding age; that, Chancellor and Archbishop, he would continue the minister and personal friend of the King; that he would study to support and extend all the prerogatives of the Crown, which he himself was to exercise; and that in the palaces of which he was now master he would live with increased magnificence and luxury. When we judge of his character, we must ever bear in mind that all this was easily within his reach, and that if he had been actuated by love of pleasure or mere vulgar ambition, such would have been his career.

Never was there so wonderful a transformation. Whether from a predetermined purpose, or from a sudden change of inclination, he immediately became in every respect an altered man. Instead of the stately and fastidious courtier, was seen the humble and squalid penitent. Next his skin he wore hair-cloth, populous with vermin; he lived upon roots, and his drink was water, rendered nauseous by an infusion of fennel. By way of further penance and mortification, he frequently inflicted stripes on his naked back. Daily on his bended knees he washed the feet of thirteen beggars, refreshed them with ample food, and gave each of them four pieces of silver. He wandered alone in his cloister, shedding many tears, from the thought of his past sins, and his great occupation was to pray and read the Scriptures. He wore the habit of a monk; and the monks, astonished at the sanctity he displayed, already talked of his conversion as a most evident miracle of Divine grace, poured out upon him at his consecration.

The wonder of mankind was still further excited by the next step, which he speedily took, without ever consulting the King or any previous notice of his intention; he sent the Great Seal to Henry, in Normandy, with this short message, "I desire that you will provide yourself with another Chancellor, as I find myself hardly sufficient for the duties of one office, and much less of two."

The fond patron, who had been so eager for his elevation, was now greviously disappointed and alarmed. He knew Becket too well to believe that this resignation proceeded from real humility and dislike of temporal power; he therefore looked upon it as an indication of a higher and more dangerous ambition, believing that the Archbishop would have continued his Chancellor if he had not aspired to become his competitor, and to exalt the mitre above the crown. He at once saw that he had been deceived in his choice, and that the worst predictions of his mother were likely to be speedily verified.

He resolved, however, to treat the Archbishop with patience and forbearance, though with firmness, and that, while he showed to the world that he would be master in his own dominions, he should not appear the aggressor in the controversy which he anticipated. He therefore still allowed Prince Henry to remain under the tuition of the Archbishop.

The two old friends first met at Southampton, on the King's return from Normandy. Becket went thither to do homage for the temporalities of his see, and was received courteously, though coldly. Having intimated his incapacity to fulfill the duties of two offices, he was required to resign that of Archdeacon of Canterbury, which was of great value, and which he wished to retain. Here the King had clearly the law on his side, and he succeeded. But Becket immediately resolved, by an appeal to the law, to be revenged. On the ground of vindicating the rights of his see, he demanded of the King the castle and town of Rochester with other possessions;—of the Earl of Clare, a favorite of the King, the castle of Tunbridge,—and of other noblemen various other properties, which he alleged had once belonged to the church of Canterbury, and to which no length of time could ever confer a title as lay fee.

How far he might have been able to establish these claims may be doubtful, but before they could be brought to a legal inquiry he set up others which he could not support, and the King being determined to curb ecclesiastical encroachments by new laws, which the Archbishop resolutely resisted, a fatal rupture took place between them.

William de Eynsford, a military tenant of the Crown, having ejected from a rectory in Kent, the advowson of which belonged to him, a priest presented to it by Becket, was immediately excommunicated by him, contrary to a well established law, which had been respected ever since the Conquest, that the tenants of the Crown should not be excommunicated without the King's knowledge and consent. Henry, by a messenger, sent him orders to absolve Eynsford, but received for answer that it belonged not to the King to inform him whom he should absolve and whom excommunicate. After many remonstrances and menaces, the royal mandate was at last obeyed. Henry had at this time great advantages in asserting the royal prerogative, for his reputation was high from the success of his government both at home and abroad; his barons all concurred in his policy; and the power of the Church was weakened from their being two rival popes; —each claiming to be the successor of St. Peter;—one under the title of Victor IV., residing at Rome, and patronized by the Emperor; and another under the title of Alexander III., who kept his court in France, protected by Louis VII. Henry had sent in his adhesion to the latter, but with significant doubts of his title. Alexander, who was only restrained by his peculiar situation from carrying the pretensions of the triple crown as high as any of his predecessors, looking on Becket as a great prop of his power, had received him with high distinction at Tours, and secretly abetted him in his designs.

The grand struggle which the Church was then making was, that all churchmen should be entirely exempted from the jurisdiction of the secular courts, whatever crime they might have committed. A priest in Worcestershire, having about this time debauched a gentleman's daughter, had proceeded to murder the father. On a demand that he should be delivered up and brought to trial before the King's judges, Becket insisted on the privileges of the Church,—confined the criminal in the bishop's prison lest he should be seized by the King's officers,—passed upon him merely sentence of degradation, and insisted that, when degraded, he could not again be brought to trial for the same offense.

Henry, thinking that he had a favorable opportunity for bringing the dispute to a crisis, summoned an assembly of all the prelates at Westminster, and himself put to them this plain question: "Whether they were willing to submit to the ancient laws and customs of the kingdom?" Their reply, framed by Becket, was: "We are willing, *saving our own order.*" There was only one dissenting bishop: he was willing to give an unqualified answer in the affirmative, but Becket sorely upbraided him for his servility. The King, seeing what was comprehended in the reservation, retired with evident marks of displeasure, deprived Becket of the government of Eye and Berkhamstead, and all the appointments which he held at the pleasure of the Crown, and uttered threats as to seizing the temporalities of all the bishops, since they would not acknowledge their allegiance to him as the head of the state. The legate of Pope Alexander, dreading a breach with so powerful a prince at so unseasonable a juncture, advised Becket to submit for the moment; and he with his brethren, retracting the saving clause, absolutely promised "to observe the laws and customs of the kingdom."

To avoid all future dispute, Henry resolved to follow up his victory by having these laws and customs, as far as the Church was concerned, reduced into a code, to be sanctioned by the legislature, and to be specifically acknowledged by all the bishops. This was the origin of the famous "Constitutions of Clarendon."

We Protestants must approve of the whole of them, for they in a great measure anticipate the measures which were taken when the yoke of the Church of Rome was thrown off at the Reformation; but, in justice to Becket, we must acknowledge that they were in various particulars an innovation upon the principles and practices which had long prevailed. Not only did they provide that clerks accused of any crime should be tried in the King's courts; that all suits concerning advowsons and presentations should be determined according to the course of the common law; and that the clergy should no longer pretend to the right of enforcing payment of debts contracted by oath or promise, whereby they were drawing all questions of contract and property before their trbunals; but that the appeal in all spiritual causes should be carried from the archdeacon to the bishop, from the bishop to the primate, and *from the primate to the king*, without whose consent it should go no farther; that no clergyman should leave the realm without the King's license; that, on a vacancy, the revenue of episcopal sees should belong to the Crown; that the members of each chapter, or such of them as the King might please to summon, should sit in the King's chapel till they made the new election with his consent; and that the bishop elect should do homage to the Crown.[1]

Under these conditions, Henry would have disposed of all ecclesiastical dignities by his own authority, would have prevented all appeals to Rome, and would have been himself "the Head of the Church." Being submitted to the great council called at Clarendon, they were unanimously and joyfully carried by the barons. The prelates were then called upon individually to set their seals to them, and to promise to observe them. No one

---

[1] One of the articles shows that the right of sitting in the House of Lords now belonging to bishops, and greatly prized by them, was originally forced upon them at a time when they thought it an indignity to sit in any assembly except by themselves, as a separate order: " That the archbishops, bishops, and other spiritual dignitaries should be regarded as barons of the realm, should possess the privileges and be subjected to the burthens belonging to that rank, and *should be bound to attend the king in his great councils*, and assist at all trials, till sentence either of death or loss of members be given against the criminal."

ventured to oppose the King's will, except Becket. He for some time resolutely refused his assent, though urged to compliance by prelates as well as barons of the greatest authority in the kingdom.

What follows subjects him to the imputation of occasional weakness or duplicity, and disregard of the sacred obligation of an oath. At a private meeting of the prelates, Richard de Hastings, Grand Prior of the Templars, throwing himself on his knees before him, and with many tears entreating him that if he paid any regard to his own safety or that of the Church, he should yield, he exclaimed, "It is my master's pleasure that I should forswear myself, which I resolve to do, and to repent afterwards as I may." He then marched at their head to the King, and took an oath "*with good faith, and without fraud or reserve*, to observe the Constitutions."

They were immediately sent over to Pope Alexander, and it was hoped he would ratify them, thinking only of his recent obligation to the Sovereign of England; but he plainly seeing that they went to establish the independency of England of the papacy, condemned them in the strongest terms, abrogated and annulled them, absolved all who had taken an oath to submit to them, and threatened with excommunication all who should presume to enforce them.

Becket, who had been overwhelmed with remorse from the moment of his weakness, followed Henry to Woodstock—some think with the intention of abdicating the primacy;—but, not being able to obtain an interview, and being encouraged by the spirited conduct of the Pope, he resolved to make ample atonement for the offense he had committed, and from this time to his death showed a fortitude, perseverance, and self-devotedness, which have never been surpassed. He refused to exercise any part of his archiepiscopal functions till he received the special pardon and absolution of the Pope, and proportioning his discipline to the enormity of his supposed offense, he redoubled his austerities to punish himself for his momentary consent.

Much less with a view to his own safety than in the hope of more effectually embarrassing the King by his absence from the realm, he twice attempted to cross the Channel; but was driven back by contrary winds, and being brought into the royal presence, he was asked by Henry, "if he thought that one island could not hold them both."

A great council was called at Northampton, where Henry planned to accomplish the utter destruction of his competitor. He was peremptorily summoned and compelled to attend. When seated among the peers, various charges were brought against him, and others sought to make him accountable for larger sums of money than it was possible for him to repay.

This is the earliest state trial of which there is any account extant; and we have a very minute and seemingly very accurate report of it.[1] It lasted a good many days, the court sitting on Sundays as well as week days. The judges were English prelates, and Norman as well as English barons. The high treason consisted in the Archbishop not having appeared when summoned in one of the King's courts, although he had sent four knights to appear for him. He was found guilty, and his person being admitted to be sacred, he was sentenced to forfeit all his goods and chattels,—a penalty commuted for a fine of £500.

Judgment was then prayed against him that he might refund £300 of the rents which he had received as warden of Eye and Berkhamstead. He coolly answered that he would pay it; for although he had expended a larger sum in repairs, money should never prove a cause of dissension between him and his Sovereign. The next item was £500 alleged to have been advanced to him when he was Chancellor, and lay before Toulouse. He maintained that it was a gift, but he was obliged to give sureties for the amount. Then followed a demand which testified a total disregard of justice, and a fixed determination to ruin him—44,000 marks alleged to have been received from vacant bishoprics and abbeys during his chancellorship. He pleaded that he had been publicly released of all such obligations under the King's authority, by the Earl of Leicester and the Prince when he was consecrated, and that it was well known that he had spent all these sums in the public service. His plea was overruled. The object was to force his resignation, and Foliot strongly (not disinterestedly)

---

[1] St. Tr. vol. I. p. I.

advised him to yield; but he would now sooner submit to martyrdom.

The following morning, having first celebrated the mass of St. Stephen with the office beginning " Princes sat and spake against me," he proceeded to Court, arrayed in his pontifical robes, and bearing in his hand the archiepiscopal cross. The King, astonished at this parade, retired with the barons into an inner apartment, and was soon after followed by the bishops. Becket remained alone with his attendants in calm and intrepid dignity. Henry used the most violent language against him, in which he was joined by his courtiers. Bloodshed being dreaded, the bishops came to him in a body, and Hilary of Chichester said to him in an upbraiding tone, "You *were* our primate, but by opposing the royal customs you have broken your oath of fealty to the King." "I have," was his only reply. The bishops seated themselves on the opposite side of the hall, and solemn silence long prevailed. At length the door opened, and the Earl of Leicester, at the head of the barons, desired him to listen to his sentence. "My sentence!" interrupted the Archbishop. "Son and Sir Earl, hear me first; you know with what fidelity I served the King,—how reluctantly, to please him, I accepted my present office, and in what manner I was declared by him free from all similar claims. For what happened before my consecration I ought not to answer, nor will I. Know, moreover, that ye are my children in God; neither law or reason allows you to judge your father. I therefore decline your tribunal, and refer my quarrel to the decision of the Pope. To him I appeal; and shall now, under the protection of the Catholic Church and the apostolic see, depart." As he slowly withdrew, some courtiers threw straw at him which they picked up from the floor, and the voice of one whom he recognized called out to him, "Traitor!" A feeling of his ancient knightly prowess was for a moment excited, and as soon suppressed. Turning round he rejoined, "Were it not that my order forbids me, that *coward* should repent of his insolence." At the gate the populace received him with acclamations, and he was conducted in triumph to his dwelling.

He then asked permission to go beyond the seas, and being told that he should have his answer next morning, concluded that a plan had been laid to assassinate him in the night. He pretended he was going to seek sanctuary, and he had a bed prepared for himself in a church; but this was only to further his escape, against which they had taken great precautions. By the help of a disguise he eluded the vigilance of the guards stationed at the north gate of the town, and assuming the name of "Brother Christian," and traveling as a pilgrim, after many adventures and perils he reached Sandwich, and was safely landed at Gravelines.

Forthwith he visited the King of France, who was delighted to receive and encourage him, as an instrument to disturb the government of the King of England. He next proceeded to Sens, the court of Pope Alexander, whose feelings were more divided, and who was obliged to act with more caution. The Pontiff, however, although he was unwilling to incur the direct hostility of Henry, behaved with generosity to the illustrious exile who had suffered so much for the cause of the Church. Becket having resigned his mitre, on the ground that there had been something uncanonical in his original election, was immediately reinstated by him with the archiepiscopal dignity, and a secure residence was assigned to him in the convent of Pontigny. Here he put on the habit of a Cistercian monk, and for some years found an asylum; but he lived in state, and received strangers with great magnificence, having ample funds from the voluntary contributions of his admirers. The prosecution he had undergone had caused all his errors to be forgotten, and he was now high in the favor of mankind. With general applause he compared himself to our blessed Saviour, who had been condemned by a lay tribunal, and who, he said, "was crucified anew in the present oppressions under which his church labored." He still pretended to be the spiritual Father of the King and all the people of England; propounded the doctrine that kings reigned solely by the authority of the Church, and threatened to pronounce sentence of excommunication against the King, whereby his subjects would be absolved from their allegiance.

Henry, on the other hand, sequestrated all Becket's property in England; banished his servants and dependants, to the number of 400; suspended the payment of

Peter's pence; made overtures for an alliance with the Emperor Frederic Barbarossa, the enemy of Alexander; and indicated an intention of recognizing the Antipope Pascal III. as the true successor of St. Peter.

The exiled Archbishop, being forced from his retreat at Pontigny by a threat of Henry to confiscate the possessions of all the Cistercian abbeys in England, took shelter some time at Sens, and afterwards removed to the city of Rome, of which Alexander had got possession on the death of Victor, the succeeding Antipope. In this interval he wrote many letters, which are still extant, to support his cause,—some addressed to the Pope, some to the English Bishops, and some to Henry himself, whose heart he attempted to touch by addressing him in a very different strain from that to which they had been accustomed when, as boon companions, they had both rather laughed at sacred things.[1]

The English nation, and even the English clergy, took part with their sovereign, and treated the primate as a factious and turbulent demagogue, who was looking only to gratify his own vanity and to aggrandise his own power;[2] but in the continental dominions of England there was a strong disposition to regard him as a martyr and a hero, and Henry trembled for the consequences of being put under the ban of the Church. Alexander now could afford to support Becket more openly, and conferred legatine powers upon him, which rendered him more formidable. Had England alone been concerned, Henry might probably, like his successor of his own

---

[1] Speaking of Henry's supposed persecution of the Church, he says, "the Daughter of Zion—the Spouse of the great King—is held captive in your hand."—*Ep. Beck.* lib. iv. ep. 63.

[2] This appears clearly from the letters addressed to him which are preserved. Thus writes the Bishop of Lisieux:—"Some think that your struggle does not proceed from virtue, but from pride; that still *the Chancellor in spirit*, you are striving that none should resist your will; that you seek to make the diadem subordinate to the Church, and that you hope that having overcome royalty, your power will be without limit or control."—L. i. ep. 85. So the clergy in an address to him, after ironically reciting his pretenses to piety, they advise him to continue in a course of humility and charity, and abstaining from injury and menaces, to advance his cause by patience, meekness, and dependence on Heaven. "Study with paternal care to feed the sheep committed to your charge, that they may have life, peace, and security."—Ibid. John of Salisbury wrote him a private letter in a still severer strain, concluding with the words, "Take it as you please,"—"vos accipiatis ut placet," and was excommunicated for his pains.—Ep. 31.

name, have entirely thrown off the yoke of Rome; but he was obliged to temporize; for the Pope and Louis, of whom he held his fair provinces in France as liege sovereign, were stirring up a most formidable resistance to his authority.

The crisis was hastened by the offense taken on account of the coronation of Henry, the King's son, by the Archbishop of York, in derogation of the rights of the see of Canterbury, and in the teeth of a papal bull enjoining that no English prelate except the primate should officiate at this ceremony.

Henry saw with alarm that the thunder which he had so long feared was about to burst upon him, and he was ready to resort to any expedient which should not permanently disable him from future resistance, for the purpose of now averting the storm. Negotiations were repeatedly attempted without effect;—the King in the terms proposed always insisting on a salvo to "his royal dignity,"—and the Archbishop on a salvo to "the honor of God,"—each of which was indignantly rejected as a cloak for treachery. Henry tried to gain over the King of France to his side by an appeal to their common interests, as sovereigns, saying, "There have been many Kings of England, some of greater, some of less authority than myself; there have also been many Archbishops of Canterbury, holy and good men and entitled to every sort of respect, Let Becket but act towards me with the same submission which the greatest of his predecessors have paid to the least of mine, and there shall be no controversy between us." Louis, struck with this mode of putting the case, professed to condemn the primate, but was soon again carried away by a common feeling of animosity to Henry.

At last it was agreed that the King of England and the Archbishop of Canterbury should have a personal interview in a spacious meadow near the town of Fereitville, on the borders of Touraine. Henry pretended to be desirous of a cordial and permanent reconciliation, but still fostered secret schemes of vengeance, and privately took an oath that he would stop short of giving the Archbishop "*the kiss of peace*," which, like eating salt with an enemy among Eastern nations, would have for ever prevented him from executing or being privy to any act of violence against him.¹

However, they met with apparent cordiality. As soon as Becket appeared, the King galloped up with his cap in his hand, and respectfully saluted him; and, as if there never had been any difference between them, addressed him with the easy familiarity which had distinguished their former friendship. Henry, carrying his politeness to an excess which might have excited the suspicion of the Archbishop, exclaimed, "As for the men who have betrayed both you and me, I will make them such return as the deserts of traitors require." The Archbishop, probably likewise dissembling his real feelings,—as if melted to submission and tenderness—alighted from his horse, and threw himself at the feet of his Sovereign. But the King immediately raised him, and, holding his stirrup, insisted that he should remount, saying, "In short, my Lord Archbishop, let us renew our ancient affection for each other." Then returning to his attendants, he observed, "I find the Archbishop in the best disposition towards me; were I otherwise toward him, I should be the worst of men." The articles agreed between the high contracting parties were,—That the King should restore to the Archbishop the possession of the see of Canterbury, taking him into his grace and favor,—and in mercy make amends to that Church for the injury it had sustained at the late coronation of his son:—in return for which the King was promised love, honor, and every service which an Archbishop could render in the Lord to his earthly sovereign;—that the Archbishop should return to England to resume the exercise of his sacred functions, and that the King should furnish him with a sum of money to discharge his debts, and defray the expenses of his journey.

Henry was then asked to seal the compact with "*the*

---

¹ We have a lively description from an eye-witness of the effect produced upon Henry by receiving a despatch disclosing a new machination of the archbishop, and we may conceive how much it must have cost him, even for a short time, to affect moderation. " He threw his cap from his head, unfastened his belt, cloak, and vest, scattered them to a distance, with his own hand tore off the silk covering from his bed, and began to gnaw pieces of straw." "Pileum de capite projecit,—belteum discussit, pallium et vestes longius abjecit,—stratum sericeum quod erat supra lectum manu propriâ removit—et cœpit straminis mast care festucas."—L. i. ep. 44.

kiss of peace," but he declined,—making this excuse:— "In my own country I will kiss his face, hands and feet a hundred times; but now let it be postponed. To salute him in England will be thought an act of favor and affection; it would look like compulsion here."

The French King construed this refusal as a proof of unextinguished resentment, and counseled Becket not to leave France; but the Archbishop said that "duty called him to England, whatever perils he might encounter." After some interval, during which *the kiss of peace* was studiously avoided by Henry, Becket took leave of him with a foreboding mind, emphatically telling him he was afraid he should see him no more. Henry exclaimed, "Do you take me for a traitor?" Becket added these pathetic words, which, however he may have feigned on other occasions, he probably spoke with sincerity: "Necessity obliges me, in the lowly state to which I am reduced, to revisit my afflicted Church. I go, sir, with your permission, perhaps to perish for its security, unless you protect me. But whether I live or die, yours I am, and yours I shall ever be, in the Lord. Whatever may befall me, may the blessing of God fall upon you and your children!"

Henry promised to meet him at the sea-coast, to supply him there with the stipulated pecuniary aid, and to accompany him to England; but failed in all these promises, and Becket was obliged to borrow £300 for the payment of his debts and expenses, from the Archbishop of Rouen, and to embark under the superintendence of John of Oxford, with whom he had had a personal feud, and who was set over him as a spy.

Finding the King still so hostile, he determined to make the most vigorous use of the weapons now in his own power, and to maintain his independence and ascendency to the last extremity. The Pope, before he heard of the peace of Fereitville, had issued letters of excommunication against the Archbishop of York and the Bishops of London and Salisbury for officiating at the coronation of the King's son, contrary to the papal bull. Becket having received these letters, at first, for the sake of peace, had wisely resolved to suppress them; but in a fit of irritation he now despatched them to England, before himself, by a trusty messenger, who had instructions to elude the search for bulls from Rome, now strictly made at all the outports, and who succeeded in publishing them at Canterbury, so as to give effect to them according to the canon law. The three excommunicated prelates inveighed against the Archbishop's implacable hatred of his opponents and unquenchable thirst for agitation; they denounced him to the young King as a person who was coming to tear the crown from his head; and they hastened to Normandy to inflame the resentment and to invoke the vengeance of Henry.

Becket being informed that it would be dangerous for him to land at Dover, where the castle was garrisoned by the King's troops, directed his ship to Sandwich, then a port belonging to his see, where he was sure of a good reception from his tenants. After he had disembarked he experienced some rudeness from the sheriff of Kent, who hastened to the spot with a band of soldiers, and without venturing to offer any violence to him, told him that he was entering the land with fire and sword, that he had excommunicated the Archbishop of York and two other prelates for merely doing their duty, and that unless he took better counsel it would be safer for him to remain in foreign parts. The Archbishop boldly asserted his right to punish the prelates for disobedience to their canonical superiors, and, denying all treasonable intentions, expressed his resolution to defend the liberties of the Church.

His march to Canterbury was a triumphal procession. There, to honor his return, banquets of unexampled splendor were prepared; the cathedral was hung with silks and precious vestments, and as he walked up to take possession of his throne, the notes of the organ were drowned by the sound of trumpets, the ringing of bells, and the shouts of the multitude, thrown into all the raptures of religious enthusiasm. Encouraged by this expression of public feeling, he made a progress to London, intimating that, under his archiepiscopal and legatine powers, he there meant to begin his visitations on those ecclesiastics whose conduct had been uncanonical in his absence. The dignitaries of the church who had taken part against him, now, under great apprehensions, expostulated with him for disturbing the public tranquillity. He answered, "that the peace of sinners was no peace;

that the Pope had sent a mandate ordering evil peace to be broken; that Jerusalem in her wealth and self-indulgence might think she was at peace, but that the Divine vengeance was hovering over her." He was everywhere greeted with the loudest acclamations of the multitude, who believed that he had been persecuted, and among whom a notion very generally prevailed that he had quarreled with the King in standing up for the Saxon race. As he approached Southwark the metropolis was emptied of its inhabitants—the clergy, the laity, men and women of all ranks and ages pouring forth to meet him, and celebrating with hymns of joy his triumphant entrance.

He was very desirous of seeing Prince Henry, over whom, as his pupil, he hoped to exercise great influence; but the King's ministers, who carried on the government in the Prince's name, became alarmed, and sent a peremptory order to the Archbishop immediately to return to Canterbury, and not to march through any towns or castles on his way back. He obeyed—traveling privately in company with a few knights, to protect him from insult. When he arrived at Canterbury, meeting with many indignities from those connected with the government, he had a presentiment of his fate; he told his clergy that the quarrel could not now end without effusion of blood, and he wrote to the Pope that the sword of death hung over him, but that he was ready to perish in the cause which, however, unworthy, he had been called by Providence to support.

On Christmas day, celebrating high mass himself, and preaching to the people, he took occasion to say that one of their Archbishops had been a martyr, and that it was possible they might have another, but he should never flinch from his duty; and he concluded the service of this sacred anniversary with pronouncing the excommunication of the three prelates, with all the energy and fierceness which could be engendered by religious fanaticism and personal resentment.

On the fourth day afterwards, about two in the afternoon, entered abruptly the Archbishop's apartment the four knights whose names have become so famous in the martyrdom of St. Thomas—Reginald Fitzurse, William Tracy, Hugh de Morville, and Richard Brito. They had been present at the court of Henry in Normandy when, on the arrival of the three excommunicated prelates and their account of Becket's insolent proceedings in England, the King had exclaimed—"Of the cowards who eat my bread, is there not one who will free me from this turbulent priest?"—Construing this expression into a royal license, or recommendation, or command, they bound themselves by oath to return to England and avenge their Sovereign. To avoid suspicion they traveled by separate routes; and they met at Saltwood, near Canterbury, the residence of Robert de Broc, a baron included in the excommunication, to arrange their operations. Henry was not aware of their departure, and sent other messengers to arrest Becket. The four knights, however, having collected a large military force from the neighboring castles, entered the city of Canterbury, and ordered the mayor to arm the citizens and have them ready for the King's service. He hesitated, suspecting their design, when he was commanded, as he valued his own safety, to keep all quiet within the walls, whatever might happen.

They were unarmed when they appeared before the Archbishop, and seating themselves without saluting him, they first tried to gain his submission by intimidations, and in the King's name ordered him forthwith to absolve the excommunicated prelates. With the greatest calmness and intrepidity he replied, that the Pope alone could decide the case of the Archbishop of York; but that he himself would absolve the others, on condition that they previously took the accustomed oath of submitting to the determination of the Church. "From whom had you your archbishopric?" demanded Reginald. "Its temporals from the King," said Becket, "its spirituals from God and the Pope." The barons murmured, and gnashed their teeth. Becket, still undaunted, said to them,—"In vain you menace me. If all the swords in England were brandishing over my head, your terrors could not move me. Foot to foot, you would find me fighting the battle of the Lord." It so happened that three of them had been in his service when he was Chancellor, and had sworn allegiance to him. Alluding to this circumstance, he added, in a tone of tenderness, "Knowing what has passed between you and me, I wonder that you should threaten me in my own house." "We will do more than threaten," cried Reginald, fiercely,—and with his accomplices left the apartment. They then rushed through the hall to the fore-court, where was stationed the band that had accompanied them, and called "To arms!" Reginald having put on his mail, seized an axe, and began to batter the gate which had been shut against them.

The Archbishop's attendants were in an agony of alarm; but he, neither in look, tone, nor gesture, betrayed the slightest symptom of apprehension. In this moment of suspense, the voices of the monks singing vespers in the adjoining choir were heard, and it being suggested that the church offered the best chance of safety, Becket agreed to join the worshipers there, thinking that, at all events, if he were murdered before the altar, his death would be more glorious, and his memory would be held in greater veneration by after ages. He then ordered the cross of Canterbury to be carried before him, and slowly followed his friends through the cloister. He entered the church by the north transept, and hearing the gates barred behind him, he ordered them to be reopened, saying, that the temple of God was not to be fortified like a castle. He was ascending the steps of the choir when the four knights, with twelve companions, all in complete armor, burst into the church, their leader calling out, "Hither, to me, ye servants of the King!"

As it was now dusk the Archbishop might have retreated and concealed himself, for a time at least, among the crypts and secret passages of the building, with which he was well acquainted; but, undismayed, he turned to meet the assassins, followed by his cross-bearer, the only one of his attendants who had not fled. A voice was heard—"Where is the traitor?" Silence for a moment prevailed; but when Fitzurse demanded—"Where is the Archbishop?" he replied, "Here I am; the Archbishop, but no traitor! Reginald, I have granted thee many favors. What is thy object now? If you seek my life, let that suffice; and I command you, in the name of God, not to touch one of my people."

Being again told that he must instantly absolve the prelates, he answered, "Till they make satisfaction I will not absolve them." "Then die," said Tracy. The blow aimed at his head only slightly wounded him, as it was warded off by the faithful cross-bearer, whose arm was broken by its force. The Archbishop, feeling the blood trickle down his face, joined his hands and bowed his head, saying, "In the name of Christ, and for the defense of his Church, I am ready to die." To mitigate the sacrilege, they wished to remove him from the church before they despatched him; but he declared he should there meet his fate, and retaining the same posture, desired them to execute their intentions or their orders, and, uttering his last words, he said, "I humbly commend my spirit to God, who gave it." He had hardly finished this prayer when a second stroke quickly threw him on his knees, and a third laid him prostrate on the floor, at the foot of the altar. There he received many blows from each of the conspirators, and his brains were strewed upon the pavement.

Thus perished, in the fifty-third year of his age, the man who, of all English Chancellors since the foundation of the monarchy, was of the loftiest ambition, of the greatest firmness of purpose, and the most capable of making every sacrifice to a sense of duty or for the acquisition of renown.

To the general historian it belongs to narrate the escape of the conspirators and their subsequent destiny,—the indignation and horror of the whole Christian world when the deed was made public,—the remorse of Henry, and the humiliations to which he submitted by way of penance and atonement,—together with the permanent consequences of this memorable controversy upon religion and the state. I must content myself with a short notice of subsequent occurrences connected personally with Becket, and an attempt at a fair estimation of his character.

The government tried to palliate or justify the murder. The Archbishop of York likened Thomas à Becket to Pharaoh, who died by the Divine vengeance, as a punishment for his hardness of heart; and a proclamation was issued, forbidding any one to speak of Thomas of Canterbury as a martyr: but the feelings of men were too strong to be checked by authority; pieces of linen which had been dipped in his blood were preserved as relics; from the time of his death it was believed that miracles were worked at his tomb; thither flocked hundreds of thousands, in spite of the most violent threats of punishment; at the end of three years he was canonized at Rome; and, till the breaking out of the Reformation, St. Thomas of Canterbury, for pilgrimages and prayers, was the most distinguished Saint in England.

Henry VIII., when he wished to throw off the authority of the Pope, thinking that as long as the name of St. Thomas should remain in the calendar men would be stimulated by his example to brave the ecclesiastical authority of the Sovereign, instructed his Attorney-General to file a *quo warranto* information against him for usurping the office of a Saint, and he was formally cited to appear in court to answer the charge. Judgment of *ouster* would have passed against him by default had not the King, to show his impartiality and great regard for the due administration of justice, assigned him counsel at the public expense. The cause being called, and the Attorney-General and the advocate for the accused being fully heard, with such proofs as were offered on both sides, sentence was pronounced, that "Thomas, sometime Archbishop of Canterbury, had been guilty of contumacy, treason, and rebellion; that his bones should be publicly burnt, to admonish the living of their duty by the punishment of the dead; and that the offerings made at his shrine should be forfeited to the Crown." A proclamation followed, stating, that "forasmuch as it now clearly appeared that Thomas Becket had been killed in a riot excited by his own obstinacy and intemperate language, and had been afterwards canonized by the Bishop of Rome as the champion of his usurped authority, the King's Majesty thought it expedient to declare to his loving subjects that he was no saint, but rather a rebel and traitor to his Prince, and therefore strictly charged and commanded that he should not be esteemed or called a saint; that all images and pictures of him should be destroyed, the festivals in his honor be abolished, and his name and remembrance be erased out of all books, under pain of his Majesty's indignation and imprisonment at his Grace's pleasure."[1]

But the permanent reputation of Becket must depend on the qualities he displayed, and the actions he performed in his lifetime; not on the decrees of popes or

[1] Walk. Con. iii. 385, 841. Burn. Ref. 152.

the proclamations of kings since his death. In considering his merits and defects, it is, above all, requisite to guard against religious prejudices, by which he has been elevated into a hero of almost spotless virtue, or degraded into a hypocrite, stained with the crimes of ingratitude and perjury.

The early part of his career, so brilliant and so successful, is not liable to any severe censure. His participation in the irregularities of his youthful Sovereign is denied, and when repented of might be forgiven. All the functions of the office of Chancellor he is allowed to have fulfilled most satisfactorily, and the measures which he recommended as minister were just and prudent. His military prowess and skill we cannot read of without being dazzled; and, with the exception of Ignatius Loyola, there is probably no such striking metamorphosis of a soldier into a saint. The grand dispute respecting his character and conduct begins from the time when, being consecrated Archbishop, he resigned the Great Seal. As he proved such a champion of the supremacy of the Pope, it is perhaps not surprising that in recent times his vituperators are bigoted Protestants, and his unqualified eulogists are intolerant Roman Catholics.

The former contend that Becket, being in reality little better than an infidel, had nothing in view but his own aggrandisement, which he thought he could most promote by exalting the power of the Church;—that he had long aimed at the primacy, with the intention, as soon as he had obtained it, to trample on the Crown; and that, to disarm the suspicion of the King, he pretended to conform to all his notions respecting ecclesiastical as well as secular affairs;—that from the moment of his elevation he threw off the mask, and did every thing in his power to annoy and injure his benefactor, as if animated by the most deadly spite against him;—that he proved his want of principle by swearing to observe the Constitutions of Clarendon, and immediately afterwards, regardless of his oath, infringing them himself, and stirring up others to resist them;—that during his banishment, though he displayed firmness worthy of a better cause, he continued, from selfish motives, to refuse all reasonable terms of accommodation, and to plot against his Sovereign and his country;—that when at last restored, he broke the engagements into which he had entered, persecuted his opponents with implacable resentment, and showed that, according to his long-fostered design, he was still determined to make priests in the West, like Brahmins in the East, the dominant caste, for the purpose of himself, as their leader, exercising absolute sway ;—that he provoked his tragical end ;—and that, although the deed of his assassins cannot be strictly defended, there is reason to rejoice in it, as the hazards and the evils of his daring enterprise were thus shown to be greater than the advantages to be attained by it,—ecclesiastical encroachment was effectually checked,—and no more Odos, Dunstans, Anselms, or Beckets appear in our annals.

On the other hand, say the undiscriminating worshipers of Papal supremacy,—Becket having had the primacy pressed upon him by the King for the purpose of subverting the authority of the Church, so necessary to the maintenance of true religion, then, for the first time, thought seriously of the duties and obligations of this new dignity, and his eyes were at once opened to the necessity of a new course of life, both for his own sake and for the good of others. Although, like Wolsey in a subsequent age, he might have joined in his own person all civil and spiritual power, enjoyed ease, wealth and pleasure, and reigned in the King's name, he saw that such a course, however agreeable, would be sinful ;—that great sacrifices were required from him, and that he must thenceforth exclusively dedicate himself to the discharge of his spiritual duties. He therefore afforded the single instance which has ever occurred of the Chancellorship being voluntarily resigned, either by layman or ecclesiastic. He meditated nothing beyond what belonged properly to his sacred office, when the King began the persecutions against him, which only ended with his murder. The Constitutions of Clarendon, however consonant to the doctrines of Wickliffe, afterwards adopted by Luther, were inconsistent with the clear precepts of the Gospel, and the privileges and immunities conferred upon the apostles and their successors, and, at all events, were inconsistent with established law and custom. In a moment of weakness Becket promised to observe them ; but this was to save himself from fatal violence which then threatened, and at last overtook him. A forced promise is not binding, and from this promise he was formally absolved by the Vicar of Christ. The unfounded charges brought against him at Northampton, and the unjust pecuniary demands then made upon him, with the threats of personal outrage, rendered it necessary for him to seek an asylum on the Continent, to appeal to foreign nations, and to put himself under the protection of the common Father of Christians. While at Pontigny, Sens, and at Rome, he was always willing to make any personal sacrifice for reconciliation, so that the cause of religion was safe; but the King, under pretense of guarding his royal dignity, was still bent on prosecuting his scheme for annihilating the influence of the clergy, which nothing but the heroic courage of one man hindered him from accomplishing. The conditions solemnly ratified at Fereitville the King was the first to violate. The excommunication of the three prelates was in strict accordance with the canon law, which was parcel of the law of the land; and Becket's only chance, either of personal safety or of preserving the liberties of the country, was then to enforce the rights which clearly belonged to his office and to his order. His martyrdom must be considered one of the most splendid that has occurred since the propagation of the Gospel to edify Christians, for, not ignorant of what was prepared for him, and being able at any time, by a slight concession, to avert his fate, he braved the assassins whom he could not withstand, and he received the deadly wounds they inflicted upon him with a constancy which could only have proceeded from a fervent faith in the promises of revelation, and the immediate aid of its divine Author.

Setting aside exaggeration, and miracle, and religious prejudice, I must confess I am inclined to think that this last view of Becket is not only the more merciful, but the more just. I cannot doubt his sincerity, and almost all will agree that he believed himself to be sincere. Let us consider the sudden effect of the touch of the mitre on men of honor in our own time. It must be remembered that by the same ardor and enthusiasm he was led to put on a coat of mail and engage in single combat with a stalwart knight, and afterwards to wear a shirt of hair and to submit to the discipline of the whip. If he bore implacable resentment, he showed inflexible resolution in the support of what he considered a good cause, willingly submitting to poverty, exile, and death itself.

Both sides concur in ascribing to him brilliant talents, great acquirements, and delightful manners, which captivated alike king and commonalty.

Some have lately thought they discovered in Becket a patriot who took up the cause of the Saxons, and quarreled with the Normans in trying to obtain justice for his countrymen; but although he is celebrated for his impartiality to both races while Chancellor, I can find nothing political in his subsequent disputes,—which appear to have been purely between the civil and spiritual authorities, and not between race and race.[1]

We can best judge him by the large collection of his letters which have come down to us. In these, although we should in vain look for the classical style and delicate raillery of Erasmus, we find a vigor, an earnestness, and a reach of thought quite unexampled in the productions of the age in which he lived. Making us familiar with him, they explain to us the extraordinary ascendency which he acquired over the minds of mankind.[2]

[1] Thierry, the great supporter of the notion that Becket's actions and his fate are to be explained from his being the champion of the Saxon race against Norman oppression, quotes (iii. 190) from a note in Hearne's edition of William of Newbury:—

"Willelmus Maltret percussit cum pede sanctum
Defunctum, dicens; Pereat nunc proditor ille,
Qui regem regnumque suum turbavit, et omnes
Angligenas adversus eum consurgere fecit."

But there was no insurrection in England during Henry's reign, and the poem from which these are taken giving an exaggerated account of the martyrdom of St. Thomas, is evidently the production of a later age.

[2] See Fitzstephen, Hoveden, Quadrologus, Lord Lyttelton's History of Henry II., Thierry's History of the Norman Conquest; Epist. Sanc. Thom.; Sanctus Thomas Cantuariensis, ed. J. A. Giles; and a Life of Becket in the "English Review" for September and December, 1846.

CHAPTER IV.

CHANCELLORS FROM THE RESIGNATION OF THOMAS A BECKET TO THE DEATH OF HENRY II.

THE history of the Great Seal during the reign of Henry II. is left in a state of much uncertainty from the time when it was resigned in 1162 by Thomas à Becket till it was delivered in 1181 to Geoffrey Plantagenet, the King's natural son. In this interval there were very powerful chief justiciars—Richard de Luci, and Robert Earl of Leicester; and they probably rendered the office of Chancellor for the time of little consequence. However, we find the names of several who are said to have held it.

First, "JOANNES Cancellarius"[1] occurs; but of this John we know not the surname, nor what other dignity he ever attained. Next comes RODOLPHUS de Warnavilla, of whom we only know that when he was appointed he was archdeacon of Rohan.[2] The third is WALTER de Constantiis, who was made Bishop of Ely. Although the last is supposed to have been at one time Chancellor to the King, it would appear that in the year 1175 he only held the Great Seal as a deputy, if we may judge from the account given us by Hoveden of an embassy to the Earl of Flanders, in which he was joined with the famous Ranulphus de Glanvil, afterwards Chief Justiciar, and the earliest writer on the Law of England. On this occasion he is described as "Vice-Cancellarius."[3] What share any of these Chancellors had in the stirring events of the time,—the framing of the Constitutions of Clarendon,—the deadly controversy with Becket,—the conquest of Ireland,—the war with Scotland,—the feudal subjection of that country on the capture of William the Scottish King, and the continued disputes and wars between Henry and his sons, we shall never learn.

It is the fashion of historians down to a much later era, to ascribe all the acts of government, even those con-

---
[1] Spel. Gloss. 109.
[2] Spel Gloss. 109. Or. Jur. 3.
[3] Et ad audiendum inde responsum comitis (Flandriæ) misit *Walterum de Constantiis*, VICE-CANCELLARIUM suum et Ranulphum de Glanvilla. Hoveden, P. ii. p. 561, n. 10.

nected with legislation and domestic administration, to the autocracy of the nominal chief of the state; but the most active sovereign could only in general have the merit of selecting good counselors and taking good advice; and if our kings would sometimes lose credit, they might as often be relieved from obloquy, by a disclosure of the share which each minister had in the measures of their reign.

We now come to another Chancellor, whose origin, career, and character are well known to history. In the year 1181 Henry delivered the Great Seal to GEOFFREY, his son by the fair Rosamond.[1] Of all his progeny, legitimate or illegitimate, this was his favorite. The boy was tenderly reared at Court, and as he displayed lively parts, great pains were taken with his education. He could not have a regular appanage, as if he had been a son of the Queen, but it was thought that an ample provision might be made for him in the Church. While yet a youth, he was appointed archdeacon of Lincoln, and while in the 20th year of his age, by royal mandate he was elected bishop of that see. For a considerable time, under favor of a papal dispensation, he enjoyed the temporalities, without having been consecrated bishop, or even admitted into holy orders. A rebellion breaking out in 1174, he raised a large military force, took several castles, displayed great personal prowess, and was of essential service in reducing the insurgent Barons to subjection.

When Henry was raising an army to repel an invasion of the Scots, Geoffrey joined him, and brought, under his own banner, 140 knights raised in his bishopric, with many more men-at-arms, well mounted and accoutred. The King received him with much joy, and said in the hearing of a great multitude of persons who were present at their meeting,—" My other sons, by their conduct, have proved themselves bastards, but this alone has shown himself to be really my true and legitimate son."

Though as a soldier Geoffrey obtained reputation, he was very deficient in his duty as a churchman, and after being seven years a bishop, he still refused to become a priest. At last, in the year 1181, Pope Alexander III. sent a mandate to Richard, Archbishop of Canterbury, requiring the Primate to compel him by ecclesiastical

---

[1] Orig. Jur. I. Spel. Gloss. 109.

censures no longer to defer what could not without scandal be any longer dispensed with, or renounce his election to the bishopric of Lincoln.

The slender restraints then imposed on ecclesiastical dignitaries weighed with him little, but to priestly tonsure and tunics he would not submit; and as in spite of all remonstrance he persisted in sincerely saying, "Nolo episcopari,"—so the see was declared vacant and bestowed on another. This was not from any levity of character or love of idleness, for Geoffrey had applied himself diligently to study, and had made considerable progress in the civil and canon law. By way of indemnity for his loss, the office of Chancellor was conferred upon him.

Even in those days such an appointment must have been considered a very glaring job, the young man, notwithstanding his talents and acquirements, being entirely without experience, and the custody of the Great Seal having important judicial duties annexed to it. Nevertheless, he is said to have dedicated himself to business in a very exemplary manner, and to have given considerable satisfaction to the public.

A doubt exists how long he remained in the office. Some accounts represent him as holding it during the remaining eight years of his father's reign,[1] while there are notices of three others having during this interval been in possession of the Great Seal,—NIGEL, Bishop of Ely,[2] WALTER de Bidun,[3] and the before-mentioned WALTER de Constantiis. Perhaps the authorities may be reconciled by supposing that these merely assisted as Vice-Chancellors, while Geoffrey remained Chancellor, enjoying the dignity and emoluments of the office till his father's death. Ranulphus de Glanvil was now Chief Justiciar, and he must have thrown into the shade all others connected with the administration of the law. A skillful military commander, he quelled a dangerous rebellion and gained a brilliant victory over the Scots, taking their King prisoner; he presided with distinguished lustre in the *Aula Regia ;* and he wrote a book on the law and constitution of England, which is now read by all who

[1] The opinion is espoused by Lord Lyttelton in his History of Henry II.
[2] Cart. 5 Ed. 3, m. 1.
[3] Lel. Coll. vol. i. p. 38.

wish to acquire a critical knowledge of them as they stood in the first century after the Conquest, before they were modified by the great charter of King John.[1]

Whatever might be the qualifications of Geoffrey Plantagenet for his office of Chancellor, all authors are loud in his praise for his steady fidelity and attachment to the King, while his brothers were constantly thwarting and annoying him, and were often in arms against him. In 1189, near the close of this reign, the pious Chancellor fought valiantly by his father's side in a hard-contested battle near Frenelles in Normandy, and the English army being obliged to retreat in some disorder, he offered to keep watch at an outpost, fatigued and spent as he was, while his father should enjoy some repose; but Henry would not suffer him to be his guard with so much danger to himself.

Soon after, hearing of his father's dangerous illness at Chinon, he hastened thither, and finding him so much oppressed by fever that he could not sit up in his bed, he gently raised his head and supported it on his own bosom. Henry fetched a deep sigh, and turning his languid eyes upon him, said: "My dearest son, as you have in all changes of fortune behaved yourself most dutifully and affectionately to me, doing all that the best of sons could do, so will I, if the mercy of God shall permit me to recover from this sickness, make such returns to you as the fondest of fathers can make, and place you among the greatest and most powerful subjects in all my dominions. But if death should prevent my fulfilling this intention, may God, to whom the recompense of goodness belongs, reward you for me." "I have no solicitude," replied Geoffrey, "but that you may recover and may be happy."

The king with his last breath expressed a wish that this pious son should be provided for by his suc-

---

[1] Glanvil not having been Chancellor, I do not feel myself at liberty to give any detailed account of his life; but I may be excused transcribing in a note a character of him to be found in the preface to the eighth part of Lord Coke's Reports. "Et nota quod præfatus Raunlph' de Glanvilla fuit vir præclarissimus genere utpote de nobili sanguine, vir insuper strenuissimus corpore, qui provectiori ætate ad Terram Sanctam properavit et ibidem contra inamicos crucis Christi strenuissime usque ad necem dimicavit." Coke seems to envy the glory of the crusader; for though he himself had "written learnedly and profoundly," his own exploits as ex-chief justice when sheriff of Buckinghamshire could not compare with those of ex-chief justice Glanvil

cessor,—a wish that was held sacred by the penitent Richard.

Geoffrey, dutiful to the last, attended the corpse to the nunnery of Fontevrault,—where blood running from its mouth at the approach of Richard, that generous though violent spirit, in a fit of remorse, reproached himself as the murderer of his father.

During the latter part of the reign of Henry II., while his son Geoffrey was Chancellor, all things being reduced to peace, our legal polity is supposed to have made greater advances than it had done from the Conquest downwards. The great regularity in the order of proceeding, and the refinement with which questions respecting property were treated, show that if the age was barbarous, it produced individuals of enlarged minds and well skilled in the principles of jurisprudence.

Very able men followed as Chancellors in the succeeding reigns, but from foreign war and domestic strife little improvement was affected by any of them for near a century afterwards.

Although there be as yet no traces of the Chancellor having a separate court of his own, either for common law or equitable jurisdiction, it is certain that in the time of Henry II. he was looked up to as a high judicial authority, and he occasionally went the circuit as a justice in eyre or of assize.[1]

CHAPTER V.

CHANCELLORS DURING THE REIGN OF RICHARD I.

RICHARD, as soon as he had attended his father's funeral, was impatient to join the Crusade. From the arrangements he had made for the government of the realm in his absence, it was not convenient that Geoffrey should be continued in the office of Chancellor, but an offer was made to him of ecclesiastical preferment which he could not resist. He was appointed Archbishop of York, and being now in France, he suffered himself to be consecrated to the holy office by the Archbishop of

[1] Madd. Ex. p. 61. See Lord Lyttelton's Hist. iii. 479. 4 Inst. 159.

Tours, metropolitan of Anjou. He agreed not to take possession of his see for three years, during which time he swore that he would not set foot on English ground, —an oath required of him by Richard, who had some suspicions as to his fidelity. How he observed the oath we shall see as we proceed with the life of his celebrated successor.

Richard's Chancellor was WILLIAM LONGCHAMP, Bishop of Ely,[1] one of the most eminent men who have ever held the Great Seal. He was a native of Beauvais in France, and of mean extraction, but he gave early proof of extraordinary ability and address. He first came into notice in the service of the Chancellor Geoffrey, the son of Rosamond. Being afterwards introduced to Prince Richard, he contrived to insinuate himself into his good graces without incurring the suspicion of the old King, and through successive promotions in the Church he was made Bishop of Ely—always displaying great vigor of character and capacity for business, and hitherto concealing his inordinate ambition and rapacity. Although he had now resided many years in England, he did not understand one word of the English language; but such was still the depression of everything Anglo-Saxon, that neither in parliament, nor in courts of justice, nor in the society of the great, did he experience any inconvenience from this deficiency. The King, about to set off upon his memorable expedition to the Holy Land, not only conferred upon him the office of Chancellor, but made him Grand Justiciar and guardian of the realm jointly with Hugh, Bishop of Durham;[2] and that he might better insure the public tranquillity, procured for him the authority of legate from the Pope. Richard's great object was to deprive his brother John of all power and influence, —being apprehensive that this Prince, who had early displayed his faithless character and turbulent disposition, would, in his absence, according to various prior examples in the Norman line, enter into cabals with discontented Barons, and aim at the Crown. But he fell into a mistake in appointing the Bishop of Durham as a check on the power of Longchamp. The one would bear no equal, and the other no superior.

[1] Or, Jur. Hoved. 375. Spel. Gloss. 109.
[2] Hoved. 378. M. Par. in ann. 1189.

No sooner had Richard left England on his voyage to the Mediterranean than their animosities burst forth, and threw the kingdom into combustion. Longchamp,[1] presumptious in his nature, elated by the favor which he enjoyed with his master, holding the Great Seal, and armed with the legatine commission, refused to share the executive power of the state with his colleague, treated him with contumely, and, upon some show of resistance, went so far as to arrest him, and, as the price of his liberty, extorted from him a resignation of the earldom of Northumberland, and his other dignities. The King, informed of these dissensions, ordered, by his letters from Marseilles, that the Bishop should be reinstated in his offices; but the Chancellor had still the boldness to refuse compliance, on pretense that he himself was better acquainted with the King's secret intentions. He proceeded to govern the kingdom by his sole authority, to treat all the nobility with arrogance, and to display his power and riches with the most invidious ostentation. A numerous guard was stationed at his door. He never traveled without a body of 1500 foreign soldiers, notorious for their rapine and licentiousness. Nobles and knights were proud of being admitted into his train. He sealed public acts with his own signet seal instead of the Great Seal of England. His retinue wore the aspect of royal magnificence; and when in his progress through the kingdom he lodged in any monastery, his attendants, it is said, were sufficient to devour in one night the revenue of several years. To drown the curses of the natives, he brought over from France, at a great expense, singers and jesters, who sang verses in places of public resort, declaring that the Chancellor never had his equal in the world.

In the meanwhile he abused his power to enrich himself and his family; he placed his relations and friends of foreign birth in all posts of profit or honor, and gave them the government of castles and cities, of which, under various pretexts, he deprived men of the pure Norman race, spoiling them and the descendants of the Saxon thanes with indiscriminate violence. Contemporary

---

[1] In the following account of the administration of Longchamp, his flight and his subsequent career, I have chiefly followed " the History of the Norman Conquest" by Thierry, who cites authorities, most of which I have examined, and which fully support his statement. See vol. iv. 40-52, 64-75.

authors say, that "by reason of his rapines a knight could not preserve his silver belt, nor a noble his gold ring, nor a lady her necklace, nor a Jew his merchandise." He showed himself, besides, haughty and insolent, and he enforced submission to his will by the severity and promptitude of his vengeance. The King, who was obliged to winter in Sicily, and was detained in Europe longer than the Chancellor expected, being informed of the arbitrary and tyrannical conduct of his minister, made a fresh attempt to restrain his power, and sent orders appointing Walter, Archbishop of Rouen, William Marshal, Earl of Strigul, Geoffrey Fitz-Peter, William Briewere, and Hugh Bardolph, councillors to Longchamp, and commanding him to take no measure of importance without their concurrence and approbation. But such general terror had he created by his violent conduct, that for a long while they did not venture to produce the King's mandate. When it was produced the Chancellor insisted that it was a forgery, and he still exercised an uncontrolled authority over the nation.

Prince John, aware of the general discontent, and seeing with envy the usurpation of the Chancellor, at last took courage to make head against him; and all those who were smarting under his exactions, or who hoped to better their condition by change, actively engaged in the party formed for his overthrow. An open rupture broke out between those rivals for power, on the occasion of the Chancellor's attempt to deprive Gerard de Camville, a Norman by race, of the office of sheriff of the county of Lincoln, which the King had made over to him for a sum of money. The Chancellor, who wished to bestow this office on one of his friends, summoned Camville to deliver up to him the keys of the castle of Lincoln; but he resisted the demand, saying that he was a liege man to Prince John, and that he would not surrender his fief till tried and condemned in the court of his liege lord. On this refusal the Chancellor came with an army to beseige the castle at Lincoln, and took it. Camville demanded justice from his superior and protector. By way of reprisals, John took possession of the royal castles of Nottingham and Tickhill—there raised his flag, and stationed his men, declaring, according to Hoveden, that if the Chancellor did not do speedy justice to Camville his vassal, he would visit him with a rod of iron. The Chancellor quailed under his threat, and entered into a treaty, by which John remained in possession of the two castles he had taken.

The next assault upon the authority of the Chancellor proceeded from his predecessor in office, Geoffrey, now Archbishop of York. Regardless of his oath not to enter the realm of England for three years, and of a solemn warning he received when about to embark, he resolved to take possession of his see, and to enjoy the benefit of any chances of farther preferment which might open to him. The Chancellor sent armed men to seize him upon his landing. He escaped their pursuit in disguise, and gained a monastery in the city of Canterbury, where the monks hospitably received him. A report, however, getting abroad that he had taken refuge there, the convent was surrounded by soldiers, and the Archbishop being seized in the church, when he was returning from celebrating mass, was shut up in the castle of the city under the keeping of the Constable de Clare.

The violent arrest and imprisonment of an Archbishop made a great noise all over England, and John, thinking this a favorable occasion for extending his own power, openly took the part of his captive brother. Although he had hitherto regarded Geoffrey as an enemy, he now pretended to feel for him the most tender affection, and with menaces he insisted on the Chancellor setting the Archbishop at liberty. Longchamp, on account of the sacred character of his prisoner, did not venture to resist. John then wrote to all the Bishops and Barons to assemble at Reading; while the Chancellor by other letters, forbade them to accept the invitation of a prince whose object it was to disinherit his Sovereign. The assembly, however, was held: John and Geoffrey met, wept, and embraced, and the latter on his knees besought his fellow-peers to avenge the insult which had been offered in his person to the immunities of the Church and the right of sanctuary.

John, becoming bolder and bolder, repaired to London, there convoked the great council of the Barons and Bishops, and accused the Chancellor before them of having grossly abused the authority with which the King had entrusted him. The accused had injured and offended so many of those who were to decide his case, that the accuser was sure of a favorable hearing.

The Chancellor was cited to appear before the Barons by a certain day. He refused, and assembling a military force, marched from Windsor, where he kept his Court, upon London, to anticipate the re-assembling of the body who presumed to act as his judges. But John's men-at-arms came upon him at the gates of the city, attacked and dispersed his followers, and compelled him in great haste to throw himself into the Tower of London, where he shut himself up, while the Barons and Bishops assembled in Parliament and deliberated on his fate.

The majority of them had resolved to strike a great blow, and to depose by their authority the man who, holding the royal commission, could not regularly be deprived of office without the express order of the Sovereign. In this daring enterprise, they, being themselves Normans, were desirous of having the assistance of the Saxon inhabitants of London, constituting the great mass of the population. In the morning of the day appointed for their meeting, they caused the great alarm-bell to be rung, and as the citizens issued from their houses, persons stationed for the purpose directed them to repair to St. Paul's Cathedral. The merchants and trades-people going thither to see what was the matter, were surprised to find assembled the grandees of the country, the descendants of those who had conquered at Hastings,—with whom hitherto they had had no other relation than that of lord and villain. Contrary to the custom, the Barons and Prelates gave a gracious reception to the citizens, and a temporary equality was established among all present. The English guessed as well as they could the meaning of the speeches addressed to them in French, and there was read and explained to them a pretended letter of the King, intimating that if the Chancellor should be guilty of malversation in his office, he might be deposed. A vote was then taken of the whole assembly, without distinction of race, and the Norman heralds proclaimed "that it pleased John, the King's brother, and all the Bishops, Earls, and Barons of the kingdom, and the citizens of London, that the Chancellor should be deposed."

It was at first thought that he would have stood a siege

in the Tower, but he was without courage at the approach of real danger, and he immediately offered to capitulate. He was freely allowed to depart on condition of delivering up the keys of all the King's castles. He was made to swear that he would not leave England till he had done so, and two of his brothers were detained as hostages for his good faith.

He withdrew to Canterbury, under pretense of fulfilling his oath; but when he had remained there a few days, he formed the resolution to fly, liking better to expose his brothers to death than to deliver up the castles, by the possession of which he hoped to recover what he had lost. He left the city on foot and in disguise, having over his own clothes a gown with great sleeves and a petticoat,—his face being covered by a thick vail,—carrying under his arm a pack of linen, and in his hand an ell measure.[1] In this attire, which was that of an English female pedlar of the time, the Chancellor made for the sea-shore, and was obliged to wait for the ship in which he was to embark. He seated himself quietly on a stone with his *pack* on his knees, and some fishermen's wives, who were passing by, accosted him and asked him the price of his wares;—but, not knowing a single word of English, the Chancellor made no reply, and shook his head,—to the great surprise of those who wished to become his customers. They walked on; but other women coming up, and examining the quality of the linen, made the same demand as the first. The pretended female pedlar still preserved silence, and the women repeated their questions. At length, at his wit's end, the Chancellor raised a loud laugh, hoping so to escape from his embarrassment. At this laugh without a jest, they believed they saw before them a female out of her mind, and raising her vail to ascertain who she was, discovered the face of a man of a swarthy complexion, lately shaved.[2] Their cries of surprise attracted the workmen of the port, who, glad to find an object of sport, seized hold of the person in masquerade, drawing him by his garments,[3] causing him to tumble on the

---

[1] "Tunicâ fœmineâ virid....cappam habens ejusdem coloris....manica am ...peplum in capite....pannum lineum in manu sinistrâ....virgam venditoris in dextrâ."—Hoveden.

[2] "Viderunt faciem hominis nigram et noviter rasam."—Hoveden.

[3] "Et facta est statim multitudo virorum ac mulierum extrahentium de

ground, and making merry with his vain efforts to escape
from them and to enable them to comprehend who he
was. After dragging him a long way over stones and
through mud, the sailors and fishermen concluded by
shutting him up in a dark cellar.[1] Here he remained till
he contrived to communicate his misadventure to the
agents of the government. He was then forced to deliver
up the keys of all the royal castles, according to his engagement, and was permitted freely to leave England.

On arriving in France, he immediately wrote to the
King that Prince John, having got possession of his
fortresses, was about to usurp the throne, and pressing
him immediately to return from the Holy Land. He
seems to have convinced Richard that he himself had
acted as a good and loyal subject, and that his struggle
with the Barons was only in the support of the Royal
authority. To his honor it is recorded that, hearing of
Richard's captivity in Germany, he repaired thither, and
obtained permission to visit, in prison, that generous
master, whom the universe seemed to have abandoned.[2]
Richard received him as a personal friend persecuted in
his service, and employed him in repelling the unfounded
charge brought against him as a pretext for his detention,
and in conducting the negotiations for his liberation.

As soon as Longchamp had been subdued and exiled
by John and the Barons, the office of Chancellor was restored to Geoffrey Plantagenet, now fully installed in his
bishopric, and he held it till Richard's return to England,
when he was finally deprived of it. He experienced
clemency to which he was not much entitled, considering
his perfidy and breach of oath, and he seems to have employed himself in the discharge of his ecclesiastical
duties during the remainder of his reign.

It will be convenient that I should here relate what
further is known of him as Ex-Chancellor. After the

---

capite peplum et trahentium eum prostratum in terram per manicas et
capucium."—Ibid.
  [1] Pluribusque modis turpiter tractavit per totam villam et....in quodam
cellario tenebroso....inclusit."—Hoveden.
  [2] Thus the Chancellor is supposed to have serenaded the King:—

"O Richard, mon Roy,
  L'univers t'abandonne,
Mais pour moy je garde ma foy,
  Toujours fidèle à ta personne."

death of Richard he was no longer suffered to live in tranquillity. John seized all his goods, and the profits of his bishopric, and Geoffrey raised a strong party against him. A truce was established between them; but this was of short duration. John requiring for his wars, without the consent of the great council of the nation, the tenth shilling of what every body was worth, this tax was resisted as illegal by Geoffrey, who pronounced sentence of excommunication on all within his diocese who should pay it. John vowed a bitter revenge, and was proceeding to such extremities against him that he went into voluntary exile, and died at a distance from his native land, before the memorable era when the Barons at Runnymede obtained security against unlawful taxation, and the tyranny of John was effectually restrained.

But we must now return back to Longchamp. No sooner was Richard again in possession of the Royal sceptre, than, disregarding the charges which were brought against his vice-gerent, he re-instated him in the office of Chancellor, and restored to him all his authority.

In 1194 a parliament was called at Nottingham. When it was opened, Hubert, Archbishop of Canterbury, sat on the King's right hand, and Geoffrey, Archbishop of York, on his left. But Longchamp, the Chancellor, was present, and although only ranking according to the precedence of his see, he guided all their deliberations. The session was about the usual length, viz. four days. On the first day sentence was passed on several rebellious Barons and sheriffs, who were deprived of their castles and jurisdictions. On the second day the King pronounced judgment against his brother John, who was absent, for having, contrary to his oath of fealty, usurped his castles, and entered into a conspiracy with the King of France against him—when he was ordered to appear by a certain day under pain of banishment. On the third day a supply of two shillings on every plow-land was voted to the King; and the last day was spent in hearing and redressing grievances, and resolving that to nullify the King's submission to the Emperor when in captivity, he should be crowned again. This ceremony was actually performed at Winchester.

But Longchamp, the Chancellor, had soon to extricate the King from a new perplexity. A calumny was propagated, and generally believed, that while in the East he had murdered the Marquis of Montferrat.[1] This charge was invented by Phillip, King of France, Richard's great rival, with whom he was now at open war, and it much damped the zeal of his supporters, both in England and on the Continent. All protestations and reasonable proofs of innocence being vain, the Chancellor forged a supposed autograph letter, professing to have been written by "The Old Man of the Mountain," to the the Duke of Austria, in Hebrew, Greek, and Latin characters,—of which the following is a translation:—

"To Leopold, Duke of Austria, and to all princes and people of the Christian faith, greeting. Whereas, many Kings in countries beyond the seas impute to Richard, King and Lord of England, the death of the Marquis, I swear by the God who reigns eternally, and by the law which we follow, that King Richard had no participation in this murder. Done at our castle at Messina, and sealed with our seal, Mid-September, in the year 1503 after Alexander."

This extraordinary missive was formally communicated by the Chancellor to foreign sovereigns, and he likewise sent copies of it to the monks who were known to be employed in compiling the chronicles of the time. Its manifest falsity was not remarked in an age when criticism and a knowledge of eastern manners had made little progress in the north of Europe. It had a sensible effect in weakening the imputations of the King of France among his own subjects, and it greatly encouraged those of the King of England to fight for a master whose character was thus proved to be immaculate.

Longchamp soon after resigned the Great Seal; but Richard made as much use of his counsel as ever to the day of his death. He was, in 1197, together with the Bishop of Durham, sent on an embassy to the Pope, and while still in the public employment, he died at Poictiers in the beginning of the following year. He certainly was a man of great energy and ability, and tried by the standard of honor and morality which prevailed in the 12th century, he probably is not to be very severely condemned either as a Chancellor or a Bishop.[2]

[1] See the tale of the "Talisman" by Sir Walter Scott.—Sir Roger Comyn's "History of the Western Empire," ii. 265.   [2] See 1 Parl. Hist. 7.

1—8

Richard appointed as his successor, EUSTACE, Bishop of Ely,[1] who had previously been Vice-Chancellor.

In this reign we have the earliest distinct evidence of the existence of the officer connected with the Great Seal, called indifferently "Custos Sigilli," "Sigillifer," and "Vice-Cancellarius;" but in all probability the office was long before well known. It has been usual to consider the Great Seal as inseparable from the person of an existing Chancellor, and that the Keeper of the Great Seal, from the remotest antiquity, exercised all the functions of the Chancellor under another title; but, as we shall see, for many ages to come there were often concurrently a Chancellor and Keeper of the Great Seal. When the King went abroad, sometimes the Chancellor accompanied him with the Great Seal, another seal being delivered to a Vice-Chancellor, to be used for the sealing of writs and despatch of ordinary business. At other times the Chancellor remained at home, with the custody of the Great Seal, and a Vice-Chancellor attended the King with another seal while he was abroad, and acted as Secretary of State. While the King remained in England, if the Chancellor went abroad, a Vice-Chancellor was always appointed to hold the Seal in his absence; and while the King and the Chancellor were both in England, it often happened that, from the sickness of the Chancellor, or his absence from Court on public or private business, or from his being ignorant of law or absorbed in politics, a Vice-Chancellor was appointed, who, as deputy, transacted all affairs connected with the Great Seal, the patronage and profits still belonging to the Chancellor.

Longchamp, while he held the office of Chancellor, always had Vice-Chancellors acting under him, who were intrusted with the custody of the Great Seal. The first of these was John de Alençon, Archdeacon of Lisieux. Then came Roger Malus Catulus, or Malchien. Hoveden relates, that while Longchamp, the Chancellor, remained in England to administer the government, Malchien, as Vice-Chancellor, attended Richard in Sicily, on his way to Palestine, and was afterwards drowned near Cyprus, having the Great Seal suspended round his neck.[2] It is

---

[1] According to Spelman, Eustace was made Chancellor in 1190, Gloss, 100; and according to Dugdale, in 1198.—Or. Jur. 5.

[2] This occurrence induced Lord Coke to say, that the form of conferring

said that the King, on his return, ordered all charters that had been sealed with it to be resealed with another seal, bearing a different impression, made to replace it,—upon the suggestion that the lost seal might have been misapplied, and therefore would not properly authenticate the royal grants,—this being in reality a device to draw money to his exhausted exchequer.

Subsequently, one "Master Bennet" was Vice-Chancellor; but he must have been appointed in England by John and the rebellious Barons, or by their Chancellor, for we find him anathematized by Longchamp, who, as Bishop of Ely and Pope's legate, could call in the censures of the Church, to aid his temporal authority. In a list of those excommunicated for disobedience to the Chancellor, who represented the King, we find "Etiam denunciamus excommunicatum Magistrum Benedictum, qui sigillum Domini Regis contra statuta Regis et Regni, et contra prohibitionem nostram, ferre præsumpsit."[1]

When Longchamp was again Chancellor, he had for his Vice-Chancellor one Eustace, styled "Sigillifer," Dean of Salisbury, who succeeded him as Chancellor, and as Bishop of Ely. Eustace likewise had a Vice-Chancellor, Warine, Prior of Loches.

Eustace and Warine remained in their respective offices without anything memorable occurring to them, till the Lion-hearted Richard, who had gained such renown by his prodigies of valor in the East, fell ingloriously before the little castle of Chalus; and, as might have been expected, they were immediately dismissed by his successor, who had been at constant enmity with him during his life, and even hated his memory.

We have one remarkable juridical monument of this reign—the Laws of Oleron, the foundation of the maritime jurisprudence of modern Europe, and cited as authority at the present day on both sides of the Atlantic. The Code is said to have been framed by Richard himself, when on a visit to his continental dominions, but was probably the work of Vice-Chancellor Malchien, or some lawyer who had accompanied him.[2]

---

the office of Chancellor was by suspending the Great Seal round the neck of the person appointed.—4 Inst. 87.

[1] Hoved. p. ii. p. 707, n. 30.
[2] Some are now disposed to ascribe the Laws of Oleron to a different

CHAPTER VI.

OF THE CHANCELLORS DURING THE REIGN OF KING JOHN.

WE have now materials for an exact history of the Great Seal. From the beginning of the reign of King John to the present time, it has seldom been placed in the custody of any person, even for a single day, without a memorandum of the transfer being entered in records still extant.

This, the most worthless of English sovereigns, having usurped the throne in derogation of the rights of Arthur, the unfortunate son of Geoffrey his elder brother, was anxious to prop up his defective title by the support of the Church; and, with that view, he appointed as his Chancellor WALTER HUBERT, Archbishop of Canterbury, who had been for a short time Chief Justiciar, during the stormy period of the preceding reign.[1] While he held this office, the monks of Canterbury had complained to the Pope that, contrary to the canons of the church, their archbishop was a judge in causes of blood, and that, being involved in secular affairs, he neglected his ecclesiastical duties. The Pope, therefore, sent a paternal remonstrance to the King, requiring him to remove the Archbishop from all lay employments, and, for the future, not to admit him, or any priest, into a secular office.

Hubert, however, without hesitation, accepted the offer of the Chancellorship from John, and was in the habit of boasting of its powers and emoluments. It is related that, when he was stating how much this office was to be preferred to any other, he was thus rebuked by Hugh Bardolfe, an unlettered Baron:—"My Lord, with your good leave, if you would well consider the great power and dignity of your spiritual function, you would not undertake the yoke of lay servitude."[2] The office was too lucrative to be abandoned for such a gibe, and the Arch-

---

author and to a later age. *Luder's Essays; Hallam's Middle Ages; Penny Cyclopædia, tit. Oleron, Laws of.* But I do not think that their arguments outweigh the record in the Tower of London, and the authority of Coke, Selden, Hale, Prynne, and Blackstone. No doubt the Code is a collection of rules and customs which had gradually sprung up, but I see no sufficient reason to doubt that it was compiled and published to the world under the authority of Richard.   [1] Spel. Gloss. 100. Or. Jur. 5.   [2] Hoveden, 451.

bishop, on the contrary, immediately obtained a charter from the King which, under pretense of regulating, increased the fees to be taken by him and his officers.[1]

[1] The reader may be amused by a translation of this curious document.

"*Ordinance of the King concerning the Fees of the Great Seal of England.*

"John, by the grace of God, King of England, Lord of Ireland, Duke of Normandy, Acquitain, and Earl of Anjou, to his archbishops, bishops, abbots, earls, barons, justiciaries, sheriffs, provosts, and all bailiffs and faithful people, greeting. Forasmuch as divine mercy has called us to the government of the kingdom of England, which belongs to us of hereditary right, and, under the unanimous assent and favor of the clergy and people, has most mercifully exalted us to be king; we desire with great desire, as indeed we ought, to provide fully for the liberty and freedom of the clergy and people ; and for the honor of God and the holy church, and the peace and tranquillity of the clergy and people, to entirely abolish bad and wicked customs which have arisen either from covetousness, bad counsel, or evil disposition of the mind.

"And forasmuch as the Seal of Richard, our illustrious brother, formerly King of England, of good memory, in his days had fallen into that state, that for certain acts pertaining to the Seal some things were received out of the usual ancient course, more from inclination than reason, to the prejudice of the regal dignity and the liberty of the kingdom ; to wit, for letters patent of protection eighteen shillings and fourpence were given, for which only two shillings ought to have been given, and for simple confirmations in which nothing new is inserted, twelve marks and five shillings were given, for which only eighteen shillings and fourpence ought to have been given ; we, for the health of the souls of ourself, of Henry, formerly king of England, our father, of happy memory, and of the said King Richard, our brother, and all our ancestors and successors, will and grant, and at the instance of the venerable father Hubert, Archbishop of Canterbury, our Chancellor, do ordain, that in future times nothing shall be received by the Seal of us or our successors, for acts, beyond what was anciently ordained to be received for the Seal of the Kings of England, and which was received for the Seal of Henry, our father, formerly King of England, of good memory, to wit, for a charter of new infeoffment of lands, tenements, or liberties, shall be taken *one mark of gold or ten marks of silver for the use of the Chancellor*, and one mark of silver for the use of the Vice-Chancellor, and one mark of silver for the use of the prothonotary, five shillings for wax. For a simple confirmation, in which nothing new is added, shall be *given one mark of silver for the use of the Chancellor*, one besant for the use of the Vice-Chancellor, and one besant for the use of the prothronotary, and twelve pence for wax. For a simple protection two shillings shall be given.

"If any one shall presume to act contrary to this our ordinance, he shall incur the anger of Almighty God, and of us, and every curse by which an annointed and consecrated king can curse. Moreover, the aforesaid Archbishop of Canterbury, our Chancellor, and all bishops who at our consecration laid hands on us, have with our consent promulgated sentence of general excommunication against all who shall presume to act contrary to this our ordinance. To this our ordinance which we have made concerning our Seal, we have put that Seal in witness and perpetual confirmation. Witness, &c.

"Given under the hand of Hubert, Archbishop of Canterbury, our Chancellor, at Northampton, on the 7th day of June, in the first year of our reign."
—*Fœd.* 75. Beyond these fees, it appears in an ancient memorial concerning the constitution of the king's house, registered in the Red Book of the Ex-

Hubert retained the office of Chancellor till his death in 1205, but does not seem to have attended much to its duties, as he constantly had the assistance of Vice-Chancellors; first of Simon Fitz-Robert, Archdeacon of Wells, and John de Gray, Archdeacon of Cleveland, jointly; then of John de Brancestre, Archdeacon of Worcester; next of Hugh Wallys, Bishop of Lincoln; and, lastly, of Josceline de Wells, afterwards Bishop of Bath and Wells.

This is the most disgraceful period in the annals of England. Arthur, the right heir to the throne, was murdered by the King, and the English were expelled from Normandy, and almost the whole of the possessions in France which had been united to the Crown since the accession of the house of Anjou.

John, upon his return after these disasters, attempted to throw the blame of them upon the Chancellor and his other ministers in England, whom he accused of remissness in not sending him proper supplies; and, under pretense of a new expedition to recover his Continental dominions, he, in the most arbitrary manner, extorted taxes from his subjects, which he wasted in wanton prodigality.

On the death of Hubert, the Archbishop, the office of Chancellor came into the King's hands,[1] and then the Great Seal remained some time in the custody of JOHN DE BRANCESTRE, who had before acted as Vice-Chancellor, while the King considered how he should dispose of it. To raise money for his necessities, he at last put it up for sale. The purchaser was one WALTER DE GRAY, who paid down 5000 marks (equal to £61,245 of present money) for it during the term of his natural life, and the grant was made out to him in due form. Under this he actually held the Chancellorship, without interruption or dispute, for six years. He began by doing the duties of the office himself,[2] but he afterwards had for Keepers of

chequer by Alexander de Swereford, that the Chancellor at this time had five shillings a day, besides an allowance of Simnel's bread, salt, wine, candles, &c. Lib. Rab. fol. xxx. col. 2. The Chancellor had also in the next reign "ad sustentationem suam et clericorum Cancellariæ Regis D. marcarum per annum."

[1] Hic devenit Cancellaria in manum Domini Regis post mortem H. Cantaruensis Archiepiscopi.—Chart. 7 John, m. 8.

[2] Hic recepit Dominus W. de Gray Cancellariam. And of the first charter

the Seal, or Vice-Chancellors, Hugh Wallys, and Richard de Marisco, Archdeacon of Richmond, who afterwards was himself Chancellor.

Walter de Gray, having become, by purchase, "Keeper of the King's conscience," appears to have been much in his confidence, and to have abetted him in those fatal measures which brought the Crown of England under feudal subjection to the see of Rome. But Hugh Wallys, the Vice-Chancellor, who had expressed great zeal on the King's side, went over to the opposite faction on receiving a favor which was intended as a reward for his fidelity.

The grand dispute had arisen respecting the appointment to the see of Canterbury, the Pope having consecrated Langton archbishop, without the King's authority or privity. Langton was not allowed to take possession of his archiepiscopal throne, and was obliged to reside abroad. In the mean time the see of Lincoln became vacant, and Wallys was elected to it by the King's recommendation, on the condition that he should not recognize Langton as archbishop. The Bishop elect desired leave to go abroad in order to receive consecration from the Archbishop of Rouen; but he no sooner reached France than he hastened to Pontigny, where Langton then resided, and paid homage to him as his primate.[1] It has happened in all ages of the church that ecclesiastics, on reaching the dignity of the mitre, have preferred the interest of their order to the ties of gratitude or the reputation of consistency, and have speedily forgotten the express or implied undertaking which was the condition of their elevation. The pliant Archdeacon, become Bishop of Lincoln, showed himself a rigid supporter of papal supremacy, and received consecration from Langton, whom John still disowned. By way of punishment for his contumacy, he was for five years deprived of the temporalities of his bishopric. He afterwards took an active part in obtaining *Magna Charta*, acting, it is to be feared, rather from revenge than from patriotism.

Walter de Gray was still Chancellor when the most

next following it is said, "Data *per manum Walteri de Gray*, iij die Octobris, anno vii."—Chart. 7 J. n. 51.

[1] Hume calls this person "Hugh Wells," and describes him as "Chancellor," but *Wallys* was his true name, and he never held the Great Seal as Chancellor.—Vol. ii. 60.

ignominious charter passed to which the Great Seal of England has ever been appended. Pandulph, the Pope's legate, not being satisfied with John's promise that he would acknowledge Langton for primate,—that he would restore all the exiled clergy and laity who had been banished on account of the contest,—that he would make them full restitution of their goods and compensation for all damages,—and that every one outlawed or imprisoned for his adherence to the Pope should immediately be received into favor,—required John to resign his kingdom to the Church,—to put himself under the immediate protection of the Apostolic See,—to acknowlege the Pope as his liege lord, and to authenticate the act by an instrument under the Great Seal, which should be confirmed by the national council. Accordingly, with the King's concurrence, a charter was framed in his name, in which he declared that, "not constrained by fear, but of his own free will, and by the common consent and advice of his barons, he had, for the remission of his own sins and those of his family, resigned England and Ireland to God, St. Peter and St. Paul, and to Pope Innocent and his successors in the apostolic chair; he agreed to hold these states, as feudatory of the church of Rome, by the annual payment of 1000 marks—700 for England, 300 for Ireland; and he stipulated, that if he or his successors should ever presume to infringe this charter, they should instantly, except upon admonition they repented of their offense, forfeit all right to their dominions."

To the honor of the memory of Walter de Gray and his deputies, and to the credit of the nation, there is reason to believe that the King could not find a subject in his dominion sufficiently base to put the Great Seal to this charter, although, owing to the presence of a French army, and the deplorable condition to which public affairs had been reduced, it could not be successfully resisted. From an entry in the Patent Roll it appears that about this time the Seal was in the King's own keeping, and we may reasonably suppose that he affixed it to the charter with his own hand.[1]

---

[1] English historians, when they would infer the feudal dependence of Scotland on England from the homage done by William while a prisoner of war to Henry II., notwithstanding the release of Richard I. of any such claim, utterly forget that, according to their reasoning, there is much more ground for con-

Lord Chancellor de Gray now bartered his office for preferment in the Church. He was first elected Bishop of Lichfield and Coventry, but some obstacle arising about his consecration, he never was in possession of this see. In 1214, however, he became Bishop of Worcester. He finally reached the dignity of Archbishop of York,— not without difficulty, for the Chapter long refused to elect him on the ground that he was "*minus sufficiens in literaturâ*," notwithstanding that he had studied at the University of Oxford, and for some years filled the office of Lord Chancellor. His election being at last carried, he could not for some time obtain consecration from the Pope, who again urged the objection of "*crassa ignorantia.*" This was hardly denied; but the topic relied upon in answer was his virgin chastity amidst the general profligacy of churchmen. Still the scruples of His Holiness could not be overcome without an exacted present of £10,000 sterling. This is said to have compelled the Archbishop to lead, for some time, a very mean and penurious life, and unjustly to incur the censure of covetousness; but having reached extreme old age, and been Archbishop forty years, he not only contributed much to the ornamenting of the cathedral, but he annexed the manor of Thorpe, in Yorkshire, to the archiepiscopal see, and bought York Place, in Westminster, of the Dominicans, which remained the town residence of his successors till it was made over by Cardinal Wolsey to Henry VIII.

The next Chancellor after Walter de Gray was RICHARD DE MARISCO,[1] Dean of Salisbury, Archdeacon of Northumberland, and afterwards Bishop of Durham, who twice held the office. His first Chancellorship ceased in about a year, when the King going into Poitou, Peter de Rupibus, Bishop of Winchester, was appointed Chief Justiciar and Regent, and the Great Seal was delivered to be held under him to Ralph de Neville.[2]

tending that England is now subject to the Pope of Rome as superior; for this superiority was solemnly yielded by the king and the legislature; not only King John, but King Henry III. did homage to the Pope as liege lord; the stipulated tribute or render as the badge of dependence was paid for ages, even by such a prince as Edward I.,—and there has never at any time been a renunciation of the claim by the court of Rome.

[1] Rot. Cart. 16 John, m. 7.
[2] Nono die Octobris anno regni Domini Regis quinto decimo liberavit

The King soon returned to England, and continuing his tyrannical and oppressive measures, the insurrection of the Barons took place, which ended in their obtaining Magna Charta. No one witnesses it as Chancellor, and it does not clearly appear in whose keeping the Great Seal then was, there being no farther entry in the records on the subject during the rest of this reign; but there is great reason to believe that it remained in the hands of Ralph de Neville,—the Nevilles, already a powerful family, taking part with the King, and Hugh de Neville being mentioned among the barons who appeared on his side at Runnymede.[1]

Whoever might then be Chancellor or Keeper of the Great Seal, he had nothing to do with the framing of Magna Charta. There was no negotiation as to terms. Archbishop Langton and the insurgent barons dictated whatever clauses they deemed desirable; and it is considered a great proof of their moderation and wisdom, that they merely guarded against abuses, and introduced useful reforms, without touching on the essential prerogatives of the Crown. The Bishop of Winchester and the Bishop of Worcester, who had been the King's Chief Justiciar and Chancellor, certainly were with him at Runnymede, and one of them might have acted as Chancellor on this occasion. At all events, the Great Seal was in due form affixed by the King personally, or by some one under his authority, not only to the original, but to various copies of the Great Charter, sent to archbishops, bishops, and priors, to be safely kept *in perpetuam rei memoriam*.[2]

From this time till his death, John could scarcely have had any counselors near him, and he seems merely to have acted according to the impulses of his own capricious mind; all regular government must have been at an end, and the administration of justice entirely suspended. We may therefore consider the office of Chancellor as in

---

Magister Ricardus de Marisco, Archidiaconus Richemundiæ et Northumbriæ Domino Regi sigillum apud Ospreng. Vicesimo secundo die Decembris liberatum fuit sigillum apud Windlesor Radulpho de Nevill sub Domino Wintoniensi Episcopo deferendum.—*Pat.* 15 J. m. 8, n. 28, m. 6, n. 18.

[1] This was after the famous fine paid by his wife to the king, of 200 hens, that she might be allowed to sleep with Ralph one night.—*Madd. Exch.* 326.

[2] 4 Inst. Proeme. Some of them are still extant. See Bl. Ed. of Charters, p. 303.

abeyance till the autumn of the following year, when John, after a long agony of body and spirit, closed his wicked and disgraceful career.

The Chancellors during this reign did nothing to be entitled to the gratitude of posterity, and were not unworthy of the master whom they served. The guardians of law were the feudal barons, assisted by some enlightened churchmen, and by their efforts the doctrine of resistance to lawless tyranny was fully established in England, and the rights of all classes of the people were defined and consolidated.

We here reach a remarkable era in our constitutional history. National councils had met from the most remote times; but to the end of this reign their acts, not being preserved on record, are supposed to form a part of the *lex non scripta*, or common law.[1] Now begins the distinction between common and statute law, and henceforth we can distinctly trace the changes which our juridical system has undergone. These changes were generally introduced by the Chancellor for the time being; and I shall hereafter consider it my duty to notice them in each successive reign.

CHAPTER VII.

CHANCELLORS DURING THE REIGN OF HENRY III. TILL THE APPOINTMENT OF QUEEN ELEANOR AS LADY KEEPER OF THE GREAT SEAL.

HENRY III. on his accession being still a child, the valiant Earl of Pembroke, who had held the office of Mareschal at the conclusion of the late reign, was elected Protector with royal authority, and he appointed RICHARD DE MARISCO Chancellor.[2] The conduct of these two men was wise and conciliatory. They immediately summoned a parliament, in which the Great

---

[1] It was in the interval between the Conquest and the end of the reign of King John, that what we call the Common Law of England, which differs essentially from the Anglo-Saxon law, must have been framed.—See Hallam's Middle Ages, ii. 122.

[2] Pat. Rol. 3 H. 3, m. 14. Spel. Gloss. 100. Or. Jur. 8.

Charter, with a few alterations, was confirmed in the name of the infant sovereign.

For three years all grants passed under the seal of the Protector, although in the King's name.[1] A new Great Seal was then made,[2] but that it might not be abused to the King's disherison, an act was passed that "no charter or letters patent of confirmation, alienation, sale, or grant of anything in perpetuity, should be sealed with the King's Great Seal until his full age; and that if any such were sealed with that seal they should be void." In the ninth year of his reign the Great Charter was again confirmed, as it now appears at the head of the statute law of England.

De Marisco had for his Vice-Chancellor Ralph de Neville, an ambitious and unprincipled man, who was constantly intriguing against him, and finally supplanted him.

In the year 1226 a national council was held at Oxford, at which, contrary to the advice of the Chancellor, and by the instigation of Hubert de Burgh and De Neville, the King, after declaring himself, resolved to take the management of public affairs into his own hands, canceled and annulled the Great Charter and the Charter of the Forest, which he had previously confirmed and directed to be observed throughout the kingdom—now alleging that they were invalid, having been granted during his minority, when there was no power in his own person or his seal to infringe the prerogatives of the Crown.

This was followed up by another arbitrary act, with a view to fill the treasury, for which a precedent in Richard's reign was cited. All persons enjoying liberties and privileges were required to take a fresh grant under the Great Seal, the King being now of age, and they were compelled to pay for these renewals according to the extortionate discretion of the Justiciar and the Vice-Chancellor, who were the authors of the measure.

The insolence of Vice-Chancellor Neville, backed by Hubert de Burgh, who was now rising rapidly to the uncontrolled power he afterwards possessed, grew to such a

---

[1] "In cujus rei testimonium has literas nostras sigillo comitis mariscalli rectoris nostri sigillatas, quia nondum sigillum habuimus, vobis mittimus, teste WILLIELMO comite Mariscallo."—1 Hale's Pleas of the Crown, ch. xvi.

[2] Claus. 3 H. 3, m. 14, *hic incepit sigillum regis currere.*

pitch, that he entirely superseded De Marisco in all his functions, and in writing to him styled him merely "Bishop of Durham," without deigning to give him his title of "Chancellor."

This conduct drew forth the following reprimand:—

"Richard, by the grace of God, Bishop of Durham, Chancellor of our Lord the King, to his beloved Ralph de Neville, Dean of Lichfield, greeting. It is marvelous in our eyes, and it must be a subject of general astonishment, that in your letters you have omitted to address us by the title of 'Chancellor,' since you must be well aware that we were solemnly appointed to that office, and that by God's grace we are still resolved to enjoy its powers and pre-eminence, the attempts of our enemies recoiling upon themselves, and in no respect shaking our constancy. However much they may strive to partition me, I am resolved to remain entire.

"Know, that in letters with which I have been lately favored from our Lord the Pope, and several of his cardinals, they have all saluted me by the title which you suppress, and you are bound to follow, or rather to worship their footsteps.

"Be advised then by me for the future to act a discreeter part, and having a proper respect for others when you write to them, give them the appellations of honor to which they are entitled. Reverence for the law requires that every one should be called by the name of his dignity. Accius, the poet, being addressed at supper by his own proper name, brought his action of damages.[1]

"We might consider this suppression of our title by you as a premeditated injury, and act accordingly; but we are contented with this remonstrance for the present, in the hope of your amendment. Farewell."[2]

---

[1] See "Retoricorum ad Herennium," lib. i. 14, were the case being put that "the fact is admitted and the law is disputed," Cicero, or whoever the author may be, gives this illustration: "Mimus quidam nominatim Accium poetam compellavit in *scena : cum eo* Accias injuriarum agit: hic nihil aliud defendit, nisi licere nominari eum, cujus nomine scripta dentur agenda." The Chancellor has changed "scena" into "cœnaculo." "Scena cum eo" had, probably, been first turned into "scœnaculo." This is a specimen of the perils to which manuscript literature is exposed. However, the familiarity of the Mediæval writers, from Bede downwards, with the Latin classics is often very striking.

[2] "Ricardus Dei gratia Dunelmensis Episcopus Domini Regis Cancellarius dilecto suo Radulpho de Neville Decano Lichefeldensi Salutem. Mirabile

If any such hope was really entertained it was disappointed. De Neville not only did all the duties of Chancellor, but took every opportunity of insulting his superior, and refused to give him any account of fees received. De Marisco, finding that he could obtain no redress, sent in the long-wished resignation, and retired to his diocese, where he soon after died.[1]

The title of Chancellor was conferred on DE NEVILLE, who had for some time enjoyed the powers and the profits of the office.[2]

This ambitious man was now also Bishop of Chichester, and was bent upon engrossing the highest civil and ecclesiastical dignities. That he might be secure in the office of Chancellor against such acts as he himself had practiced, he obtained a charter from the King, dated the 12th of February, in the 11th year of his reign, " granting and confirming to him the King's Chancery, to hold during his whole life, with all the issues, liberties and other things thereto belonging, as freely, quietly, entirely and honorably as the Chancellors of former Kings, his predecessors, held the same."

Four years after, he received a renewal and confirmation

fuit in oculis nostris et satis admirari dignum vos nomen Cancellarii in literis vestris nobis destinatis suppressisse; cum experientiam vestram non lateat nec conscientiam vestram latere debeat, nos dictæ dignitatis officio fuisse et esse sollempniter assignatos, ejusdem prærogativæ preeminentia gratia Dei ulterius gavisuros, oblatrantium morsibus in se ipsos redeuntibus, et nostri constantiam in nullo contaminantibus. Quia quid me dimidiant integer esse volo. Dominus autem Papa, et Cardinales sui quamplures, nos pridie literarum suarum beneficiis memoratæ dignitatis appellatione minus suppressa gratia sui visitarunt, et vos eorum non solum sequi sed potius adorare vestigia tenemini. Et de consilio nostro de cætero non intercepto discretiori judicio teneamini, reverencia locum suum decenter etiam sortita inter cætera attributa personæ de jure, et ratione convenientia nequaquam in literis vestiis exterminata. Legis enim reverencia est quemvis nomine dignitatis nuncupare, et Accium Poetam in cœnaculo proprio nomine compellatum injuriarum egisse. Et nos sepedictæ suppressionis occasione licet condigna et consimili ratione injuriarum agere possimus in præsentiam dignum duximus sub expectatione melioris subticere. Valete."—Ex orig. in Turr. Lond.

[1] He was interred in his own cathedral, where a monument was erected to his memory with the following curious epitaph:—

Culminis qui cupi		laudes pompasque sui	
Et sedata si		si me pensare veli	
Qui populos regi	tis	memore super omnia si	tis
Quod mors immi		non parcit honore poti	
Vobis præposi		similis fueram benesci	
Quod sum vos eri		ad me currendo veni	

[2] Rot. Cart. 11 Hen. 3.

of this grant, "with power that he might bear and keep the Seal, either by himself in person as long as he pleased, or by some other discreet, sufficient and fit assignee; which assignee should be sworn to the King for his faithful service for the true and faithful keeping of the said Seal, in the room of the said Ralph, before receiving it into his custody; and if such assignee died, or became professed in religion, or should be put out for any reasonable cause, either by the King or the Chancellor, or if the assignee refused to keep the Seal any longer, then the Chancellor, in the room of such assignee, was to substitute some other discreet, sufficient and fit person, who should be sworn to the King for his faithful service, in like manner as the first assignee was before he received the Seal into his keeping."[1] For some reason, which we do not understand, this grant was twice renewed, nearly in the same words. According to Matthew Paris, these grants were confirmed in Parliament, so that the Chancellor was not to be deposed from the custody of the Seal unless it were so ordained by the consent and advice of the whole realm.[2]

De Neville's cupidity was not yet satisfied, and in the eighteenth year of the reign, the King "granted and confirmed for himself and his heirs to Ralph, Bishop of Chichester, then his Chancellor of England, the Chancellorship of Ireland, to hold during the life of the Chancellor, with all the appurtenances, liberties, and free customs to the said Chancellorship of Ireland belonging." And the King sent a writ patent, dated at Gloucester the 21st May, in the eighteenth year of his reign, to Maurice Fitzgerald, his Justiciar of Ireland, reciting the said grant of the Chancellorship of Ireland, and "that G. de Turville, Archdeacon of Dublin, should be admitted Vice-Chancellor, the Chancellor having deputed him thereto."[3] This, I believe, is the only instance of the office of Chancellor of England and Chancellor of Ireland being held at the same time by the same individual.

---

[1] This is an exact translation of the clause giving a power to appoint a deputy, which shows that the multiplication of words in legal instruments is not a very modern invention.

[2] Itaque scilicet ut non deponeretur ab ejus sigilli custodia nisi totius regni ordinante consensu et concilio.

[3] Rot. Cart. 17 Hen. 3, m. 8.

Neville for a while enjoyed the additional dignity of Guardian of the realm. The King, going into Gascony with Hubert de Burgh, and taking the Great Seal with him, appointed the Chancellor and Stephen de Segrave to govern the kingdom during his absence, directing all writs and grants to be sealed with another seal, which he gave into the Chancellor's keeping.[1]

This insatiable lover of perferment still longed for higher ecclesiastical dignity, and had nearly reached the summit of his ambition, for, upon a vacancy in the see of Canterbury, he was elected Archbishop; but the Pope thought him too much attached to the Crown by his civil offices, and assumed to himself the power of annulling the election. In the hope of better success by bribery another time, the Chancellor went on amassing immense wealth by the plunder of England and Ireland.

Hubert de Burgh was no check on his rapacity, for the Chief Justiciar had obtained a similar grant for life of his own office, although it had hitherto been always held during pleasure. His grant likewise was confirmed in Parliament; and, to support these corrupt jobs, the plausible maxim was relied upon, that judges ought to be independent of the Crown.

But little respect was paid to charters or acts of parliament making judges for life when the opposite faction prevailed, and *Peter de Rupibus* or *des Roches*, Bishop of Winchester, at the head of it, succeeded to absolute power in the name of the feeble Henry.

As soon as this revolution was accomplished, an attempt was made to remove De Neville from his office, and the Great Seal was demanded from him in the King's name; but he refused to deliver it up, alleging, that as he had received it from the common council of the realm, he could not resign it without their authority.[2]

Some time after this the Chancellor was elected by the monks of Winchester bishop of that see, in preference to the King's half-brother, who was a candidate for it on the court interest. Hereupon, the King's indignation being beyond control, he bitterly reproached both the Chancellor and the monks; he banished the Chancellor from court, and forcibly taking the possession of the Great Seal, delivered it into the custody of GEOFFREY, a

[1] Pat. 14 Hen. 3, m. 3.   [2] M. Par. 294, 319.

Templar, and JOHN DE LEXINGTON.[1] De Neville, residing in his diocese, retained the title of Chancellor, and the emoluments of the office.

He was then summoned to return to court and to perform his official duties; but he refused, as his enemies had a complete ascendency there, and he felt that, although he might as a priest be safe from personal violence, he must be exposed to perpetual mortification and insult. For this contumacy he was superseded.

He was succeeded, if not by a very learned or able, by a very honest man, "SIMON THE NORMAN," who is celebrated among the few who have lost the office of Chancellor by refusing to comply with the royal will, and to do an unconstitutional act. He was a great favorite at court, and seemed likely to have a long official career, but is said to have incurred the King's displeasure (more probably Queen Eleanor's) because he would not put the Great Seal to a grant of four pence on every sack of wool to the Earl of Flanders, the Queen's uncle. He was too good for the times in which he lived, and we hear no more of him, except that he was "expelled from court."[2]

The Great Seal was then sent into the temporary keeping of Richard Abbot of Evesham; but before a new Chancellor was appointed a sudden counter-revolution took place at court. Hubert de Burgh, who, on his disgrace, had been obliged to take sanctuary in a church, and, being dragged thence by the King's orders, had been confined in the castle of Devizes,—contrived to make his escape,—immediately found himself at the head of a great confederation,—put all his enemies to flight, and was once more lord of the ascendant,—although he declined to resume his own office, thinking that he could irregularly enjoy more power without it. By his influence, the Great Seal was restored to De Neville, who continued in the undisturbed possession of the office of Chancellor till his

---

[1] "Cum autem videret Rex, iterum instantiam precum suarum effectu caruisse, justæ postulationi monachorum adversando, multa convitia congessit in eundem Episcopum; dicens eum impetuosum, iracundum, perversum; vocans omnes fatuos, qui eum in Episcopum postularunt. Insuper sigillum suum quod idem Episcopus universitatem regni receperat custodiendum Rex violenter abstulit et fratri Galfrido Templario, et Johanni de Lexirsbuna commisit bajulandum; emolumentis tamen ad Cancellariam spectantibus Episcopo quasi Cancellario redditis et assignatis."—M. Paris, 320.

[2] Spel. Gloss. 100. M. Par. 320.

death. Notwithstanding increasing infirmities, he was afraid to employ a Vice-Chancellor, lest he should be the victim of the same policy which he had practiced against his predecessor De Marisco. He expired in November, 1244, in his episcopal palace, which he had built in Chancery Lane, now the site of Lincoln's Inn.[1]

Notwithstanding the unscrupulous means he employed to advance himself, and the rapacity of which he was guilty, he is said to have made a good judge. Matthew Paris, in relating the manner in which the Great Seal was forcibly taken from him, speaks of him as one "who long irreproachably discharged the duties of his office,"[2] and afterwards warmly praises him for his speedy and impartial administration of justice to all ranks, and more especially to the poor.[3]

Under the presidency of De Neville, in the twentieth year of the King's reign, was held the famous parliament at Merton Abbey, in Surrey, where he was overruled upon a proposal brought forward, "that children born out of wedlock should be rendered legitimate by the subsequent marriage of their parents." All the prelates present were in support of the measure; but all the earls and barons with one voice answered, "We will not change the laws of England hitherto used and approved."[4]

Shortly before De Neville's death, a national assembly had been summoned to meet at Westminster for the purpose of obtaining a pecuniary aid. But the bishops and

---

[1] "Venerabilis Pater Episcopus Cicestrensis Radulphus de Neville, Cancellarius Angliæ, vir per omnia laudabilis, et immota columna in regni negotiis, fidelitatis, Londini in nobili palicio suo, quod a fundamentis non procul a Novo Templo construxerat vitam temporalem terminavit, perpetuam adepturus."—M. Par. A.D. 1244. Dug. Or. Jur. 230.

[2] "Qui irreprehensibiliter officium diu ante administraverat."—M. Par. 328.

[3] "Radulphus de Neville qui erat Regis fidelissimus Cancellarius et inconcussa columna veritatis, singulis sua jura, precipue pauperibus, singulis juste reddens et indilate."—M. Par. p. 312.

[4] We have not a list of the lords spiritual and temporal at this parliament, to ascertain their comparative numbers; but we have such a list of those summoned to and present at various subsequent parliaments, showing that the spiritual peers sometimes considerably outnumbered the temporal; and the difficulty arises, why, upon matters, respecting the church and churchmen, on which they always acted together, the prelates did not succeed in carrying whatever measures they wished. But I suspect that although the two bodies sat in the came chamber, they were long considered as separate orders, the consent of each being necessary to the making of laws, so that although the bishops and mitred abbots might be more numerous, they could not carry a law against the will of the earls and barons.

the barons took time to consider, and the result of their deliberations was to give to the King a statement of grievances, which if he would redress, the aid required should be granted to him. The chief grievance was, that by the King's interference with the Great Seal the course of justice had been interrupted, and they therefore desired that both the Chancellor and Justices should be elected "*per solemnem et universalem omnium convocationem et liberum assensum*," and that if upon any occasion the King should take his Seal away from the Chancellor, whatever might be sealed with it should be considered void and of none effect till it should be re-delivered to the Chancellor.

The King negatived the petition, and would go no further than to promise that he would amend any thing he might find amiss. This refusal raised such a storm, that, to quiet it, he was obliged to grant a charter, by which he agreed that the Chancellor should be elected by the common consent of the great council. But this was soon disregarded; for popular election was found quite as bad as appointment by court favor or corruption, and the complaints against the venality and extortion of the Chancery were louder than before.[1]

A rapid succession of Chancellors followed during the remainder of his reign, few of them much distinguished for learning or ability; and the personal contests in which they were engaged were of no permanent interest. We shall therefore do little more than enumerate the names. "History," says Hume, "being a collection of facts which are multiplying without end, is obliged to adopt arts of abridgment,—to retain the more material events, and to drop all the minute circumstances, which are only interesting during the time, or to the persons engaged in the transactions. This truth is no where more evident than with regard to the reign of Henry III. What mortal could have patience to write or read a long detail of such frivolous events as those with which it is filled, or attend to a tedious narrative which would follow, through a series of fifty-six years, the caprices and weaknesses of so mean a prince?" We must be consoled by the reflection that we are now approaching the period when our representative constitution was formed, and the adminis-

M. Par. 564. Madd. Ex.

tration of justice was established, on the basis of which they remained through nearly six centuries to our own time.

The next Chancellor was RANULPH BRITON, Bishop of Bath and Wells, of whom we know little, except that almost immediately after he received the Great Seal, he is said to have died of apoplexy,—without any insinuation that his days were shortened by remorse at having deserted his party in agreeing to accept it. He is represented likewise as having been Chancellor to the Queen, an office I do not find mentioned elsewhere, the Queen Consort being considered sufficiently protected by being privileged as a feme sole, and having a right to sue by her attorney-general.[1]

He was succeeded by SILVESTER DE EVERDON,[2] who had been the King's chaplain and Vice-Chancellor, and who very soon retired from state affairs against the wishes of the King, being elected Bishop of Carlisle, and choosing to devote himself to the superintendence of this remote see.

Next came JOHN MAUNSEL,[3] who held the office of Lord Chancellor for nearly two years. He had gained some distinction as an ecclesiastical judge while Chancellor to the Bishop of London. While he held the Great Seal, he was promoted to be provost of Beverley; but he does not seem to have obtained any farther preferment. This could not have arisen from the want of courtly compliance; for it was in his time that the dispensing power was first practiced by a King of England since the Conquest, and he introduced the *non obstante* clause into grants and patents. The Chancellor might have urged by way of extenuation, that till this reign the prerogative could hardly be said to be under the restraint of law. The novelty being objected to, the defense actually made was, "that the Pope exercised a dispensing power, and why might not the King imitate his example?" —which made Thurkesley, one of the King's justices, exclaim, " Alas, what times are we fallen into? Behold, the civil Court is corrupted in imitation of the ecclesiastical,

---

[1] "Ranulfus Brito Regi et Reginæ Cancellarius lethali apoplexiâ corruit." M. Paris, p. 719, n. 40. Spelman doubts whether he was more than Keeper of the Great Seal under De Neville.—Gloss. 110.

[2] Rot. Pat. 29 Hen. 3, m. 20.   [3] Rot. Pat. 31 Hen. 3, m. 2.

and the river is poisoned from that fountain." These irregularities becoming more grievous, they were made the subject of solemn remonstrance to the King by the great men assembled in Parliament, who, complaining of the conduct of the Chancellor, desired "that such a Chancellor might be chosen as should fix the state of the kingdom on its old basis." The King promised "that he would amend what he had heard was amiss," but did not farther attend to the remonstrance.

If Maunsel did not reach the mitre, he was a considerable pluralist, as he is computed to have held at once 700 ecclesiastical livings, having, I presume, presented himself to all that fell vacant, and were in the gift of the Crown, while he was Chancellor. Matthew Paris observes of him, that "it may be doubted whether he was a wise or a good man who could burthen his conscience with the care of so many souls."[1]

JOHN DE LEXINGTON, who had been entrusted with the custody of the Great Seal during his absence on an embassy, succeeded him as Chancellor,[2] and continued in the office for four years, having for his keepers of the Seal Peter de Rivallis and William de Kilkenny, Archdeacon of Coventry.

Great disputes now arose respecting the King's partiality to foreigners, and the national discontents were loud and deep. Yet the Chancellor at first was not blamed as author of the bad measures of the government; and, on the contrary, regret was expressed that he was not more consulted. In an answer by the Parliament to a demand of the King for supplies, they complained, among many other grievances, "that he had neither Chancellor, Chief Justiciar, nor Treasurer in his council as he ought to have, and as his most noble predecessors had before him."—"The King, when he heard all this, was much confounded within himself, and ashamed," says M. Paris, "because he knew it all to be true."

The Parliament obtaining no redress, afterwards petitioned for the removal of the present Chancellor, Chief Justiciar, and Treasurer, and the appointment of others deserving to be employed and trusted.

This roused the indignation of the King, who said, "The servant is not above his lord, nor the disciple

[1] M. Paris. 856. [2] Rot. Claus. 33 Hen. 3, m. 2.

above his master; and what is your King more than your servant, if he is to obey your commands? Therefore my resolution is neither to remove the Chancellor, Justiciar, nor the Treasurer at your pleasure, nor will I appoint any other." The Barons unanimously replied, that their petition being refused, they would no longer impoverish themselves to enrich foreigners, and the Parliament being dissolved without any supply, the King was obliged to raise money by the sale of his plate and jewels.[1]

Lexington continued Chancellor till he was succeeded by a Lady Keeper.

CHAPTER VIII.

LIFE OF QUEEN ELEANOR, LADY KEEPER OF THE GREAT SEAL.

IN the summer of the year 1253 King Henry, being about to lead an expedition into Gascony to quell an insurrection in that province, appointed QUEEN ELEANOR Lady Keeper of the Great Seal during his absence, with this declaration—"that if anything which might turn to the detriment of the Crown or realm was sealed in the King's name, whilst he continued out of the realm, with any other seal, it should be utterly void." The Queen was to act with the advice of Richard Earl of Cornwall, the King's brother, and others of his council.[2]

She accordingly held the office nearly a whole year, performing all its duties, as well judicial as ministerial. I am thus bound to include her in the list of "Chancellors and Keepers of the Great Seal," whose lives I have undertaken to delineate.

[1] 1 Parl. Hist. 23, 25.
[2] The commission to her as "LADY KEEPER" is extant and curious. "De Magno Sigillo commissio. Rex omnibus, &c., salutem. Noverit universitas vestra quod nos in Vasconiam proficiscentes dimisimus Magnum Sigillum nostrum in custodia dilectæ Reginæ nostræ sub sigillo nostro privato et sigillis dilecti fratris et fidelis nostri Ricardi Comitis Cornubiæ et quorundam aliorum de consilio nostro ; tali conditione adjecta quod si aliquid signatum fuerit nomine nostro, dum extra regnum Angliæ fuerimus, alio sigillo quam illo, quod vergere poterit in coronæ nostræ vel regni nostri detrimentum vel diminutionem, nullius sit momenti et viribus careat omnino."—T. &c. pat 37 H. 3, m. 8.

Eleanor was the second daughter of Berenger, Count of Provence, and his wife Beatrice of Savoy. From infancy she was celebrated for her wit and her beauty. While only thirteen years old she had written an heroic poem in the Provençal tongue, and it was sung by troubabours, who added verses of their own, praising the unparalleled charms of "*Alienora la bella.*"

In the year 1235 Henry III. had agreed to marry Johanna, a daughter of the Count de Ponthieu, but broke off the match on hearing so much of the attractions of Eleanor of Provence, and sent an embassy to solicit her to share his throne. He would trust no layman on such a delicate mission, but chose for his ambassadors four sober priests—the Bishops of Ely and Lincoln, the Master of the Temple, and the Prior of Harle. After some difficulties about dower had been surmounted, the contract was joyfully signed, although Henry was more than double the age of the "Infanta;"—and she was delivered, with all due solemnity, to the very reverend plenipotentiaries.

The royal bride began her journey to England, attended by all the chivalry and beauty of the South of France, "and followed by a stately train of nobles and demoiselles, and jongleurs." Having been feasted with great distinction by Theobald King of Navarre, himself a poet, and welcomed, on crossing the French frontier, by her elder sister, Queen of St. Louis, she landed safely at Dover, and, on the 4th of January, 1236, she was united to Henry, by the Archbishop of Canterbury, before she had completed her fourteenth year.[1]

We have the following description of her from Piers of Langtoft:—

> "Henry owre Kynge at Westmonster tuke to wyfe
> Th' Earle's daughter of Provence, the fayrest Maye in lyfe,
> Her name Elinore of gentle nurture;
> Beyonde the sea there was no suche creature."

The contemporary chronicles are filled with accounts of the festivities with which she was received in the city of London, and the jewels and rich dresses which she wore at her coronation—particularly of the wedding present of her sister, the Queen of France—a large silver peacock whose train was set with sapphires and pearls,

[1] Matthew of Westminster, p. 295.

and other precious stones, wrought with silver and gold, used as a reservoir for sweet waters, which were forced out of its beak into a chased silver basin for the use of the guests at the banquet.

Although Eleanor conducted herself with great personal propriety at the English court, her popularity was short-lived. Unfortunately she was accompanied by an immense number of relations and countrymen,—and the King's half-brothers, sprung from his mother's second marriage with the Count de la Marche, coming over soon after and obtaining great preferment, it was said that "no one could prosper in England but a Provençal or a Poictevien."

She enriched one uncle, Peter of Savoy, by a large grant of land between London and Westminster, a part of which still bears his name; and for Boniface, another uncle, she obtained the Archbishopric of Canterbury by writing with her own hand, a very elegant epistle in his behalf, "taking upon herself," indignantly says Matthew of Westminster, "for no other reason than his being of kin to her, to urge the suit of this unfit candidate in the warmest manner; and so my lord the Pope named to the primacy this man who had been chosen by a woman!"

She likewise soon commenced an unextinguishable feud with the citizens of London, by requiring that all vessels freighted with corn, wool, or any valuable cargo navigating the Thames, should unlade at her hithe or quay called "Queenhithe," where she levied an excessive tax upon them, which she claimed to be due to the Queen-consort of England.

In spite of such extortions, so poor were she and her husband by their largesses to foreigners,[1] that they ceased to put on their royal robes, and unable to bear the expense of keeping a table, they daily invited themselves, with a chosen number of their kindred favorites, to dine with the rich merchants of the city of London, or the great men of the court, and manifested much discontent unless presented with costly gifts at their departure, which they took, not as obligations and proofs of loyal affection to their persons, but as matters of right.

[1] Her finances had likewise been very much deranged by a large bribe she had found it necessary to give to the Pope for his decree declaring null the precontract of Henry with Johanna of Ponthieu, on account of which the validity of her own marriage had been questioned.

Eleanor never made any attempt to acquire the slighest knowledge of English, the use of which was still confined to the lowest rank,—Norman-French or Provençal being spoken at Court,[1] and Latin being the language of the Church.

There were great rejoicings when she gave birth to an heir to the throne, afterwards Edward I., one of the bravest and wisest of our sovereigns; and we ought to honor her memory for the skillful manner in which she conducted his education, notwithstanding the indiscreet interference of her imbecile husband.

But while Henry was generally liked, her manners was so haughty and overbearing, that she quarreled with Hubert de Burgh, Peter des Roches, Simon Montfort, and the leaders of all parties,—as well as being odious to the populace from her ill-concealed contempt for English barbarism. She acquired, however, a great ascendant over the mind of the King, who had sufficient sense to value her superior understanding and accomplishments.

In the prospect of his going into Gascony in 1253, having intrusted her with the custody of the Great Seal, on the 6th of August he sailed from Portsmouth to Bordeaux to take command in person of an army there assembled, and the Queen was left in the full exercise of her authority as Lady Keeper.

The sealing of writs and common instruments was left, under her direction, to Kilkenny, Archdeacon of Coventry; but the more important duties of the office she executed in person. She sat as judge in the *Aula regia*, beginning her sittings on the morrow of the nativity of the blessed Virgin Mary.[2]

These sitting were interrupted by the *accouchement* of the judge. The Lady Keeper had been left by her husband in a state of pregnancy, and on the 25th of November, 1253, she was delivered of a princess, to whom the Archbishop of Canterbury, her uncle, stood godfather, and baptized by the name of Catherine, being born on St. Catherine's day.[3]

[1] Proclamations to preserve the peace were read in three languages, French, Latin, and Saxon. We still have the commencement in the first, Oyez! Oyez! Oyez! corrupted into O yes! O yes! O yes!

[2] "Placita coram Domina Regina et consilio Domini Regis in Crastino Nativitatis Beat. Mariæ."—Rot. Thes. 37 Hen. 3.

[3] "Et Nomen aptante et baptizante infantulam Archiepiscopo, vocata est

The Lady Keeper had a favorable recovery, and being churched,¹ resumed her place in the *Aula Regia*.

She now availed herself of the King's absence, not only to enforce rigorously her dues at Queenhithe, but by demanding from the city of London a large sum which she insisted they owed her for " aurum reginæ" or " Queen gold,"—being a claim by the Queens of England on every tenth mark paid to the King on the renewal of leases on crown lands or the granting of charters,—matters of grace supposed to be obtained from the powerful intercession of the Queen.² Eleanor in this instance demanded her " queen gold" on various enormous fines that had been unrighteously extorted by the King from the plundered citizens. For the non-payment of this unjust demand, the Lady Keeper, in a very summary manner, committed the Sheriffs of London, Richard Picard and John de Northampton, to the Marshalsea prison, and she soon after sent Richard Hardell, the Lord Mayor, to keep them company there, for the arrears of an aid unlawfully imposed towards the war in Gascony.

These arbitrary proceedings caused the greatest alarm and consternation; for the city of London had hitherto been a sort of free republic in a despotic kingdom, and its privileges had been respected in times of general oppression.

In the beginning of 1254 a parliament was called, and the Queen being present and making a speech, pressed for a supply; but on account of her great unpopularity it was peremptorily refused.

A new arrangement was then made for carrying on the government; the Great Seal was transferred into other hands, and on the 16th of May she sailed from Portsmouth, with a courtly retinue of ladies, nobles, and knights, and joined the King at Bordeaux. They then visited Paris, where Queen Eleanor had the happiness of meeting her three sisters, all splendidly married,³ and

Catherina, eo quod die Sanctæ Catherinæ nata, aera hauserat primitivum."—M. Paris.

¹ One of the grandest scenes ever seen in England was the queen's *churching* after the birth of her eldest son,—all the great ladies of the land being summoned to attend the queen to church: but the ceremony on this occasion was conducted very privately.

² 1 Bl. Com. 221.

³ Dante, in celebrating RAMONDO BERLINGHIERI, seems to have been most of all struck with the elevation of his daughters :—

"Quattro figlie ebbe, e ciascuna reina."—*Parad.* c. vi.

where a banquet was given, much celebrated by the chroniclers, at which the kings of France, of England, and of Navarre, with all their prime nobility, were present, trying to outvie each other in courtesy as well as splendor.

Eleanor and her husband landed at Dover on the 5th of January, 1255, and on the 27th of the same month made their public entry into London with extraordinary pomp; but notwithstanding the display of banners and tapestry by the different companies, it was evident that hatred of the Queen was still rankling in the hearts of the citizens.

She disdained to take any step to mitigate their resentment. All the violations of Magna Charta were imputed to her, and she was charged with instilling her own political opinions into her eldest son.

The following is a specimen of the ballads published upon her:—

> "The queen went beyond the sea, the king's brethren also,
> And ever they strove the charter to undo;
> They purchased that the pope should assoil I wis
> Of the oath and the charter, and the king and all his.
>
> "It was ever the queen's thought, as much as she could think,
> To break the charter by some woman's wrencke;[1]
> And though Sir Edward[2] was proved a hardy knight and good,
> Yet the same charter was little to his mood."[3]

In the following year, while residing in the Tower, she was threatened with violent treatment by the citizens of London, and she resolved for her safety to proceed by water to the Castle of Windsor; but as she approached London Bridge the populace assembled to insult her. The cry ran, "*Drown the Witch!*" and besides abusing her with the most opprobrious language, and pelting her with dirt and rotten eggs, they had prepared great stones to sink her barge when she should attempt to shoot the principal arch. She was so frightened that she returned to the Tower. Not considering herself safe in this fortress, she took sanctuary at night in the Bishop of London's palace, within the precincts of St. Paul's. She was thence privately removed to Windsor Castle, where Prince Edward was at the head of a military force. He never forgave the Londoners the insult they had offered to his mother.

[1] Wrenching or perverting the meaning of the charter.
[2] Prince Edward.   [3] Robert of Gloucester.

In the civil war that took place at the close of her husband's reign, Eleanor often showed great determination and courage, and after repeated disasters still made head against the impetuous Earl of Leicester. At last, when the confederated barons were triumphant, and Henry was made a prisoner, she took refuge with her younger children in France; but after the battle of Evesham she returned to England and had her revenge upon the citizens of London, who for their ill-behavior to her were fined 20,000 marks to her use. She continued to act a conspicuous part during the remainder of this reign.

Soon after the accession of her son to the crown, she renounced the world and retired to the monastery of Ambresbury, where, in the year 1284, she actually took the vail. She had the satisfaction of hearing of the brilliant career of her son, and she died in 1292, when he was at the height of his glory, having subdued Wales, pacified Ireland, reduced Scotland to feudal subjection, and made England more prosperous and happy than at any former period.

Although the temper and haughty demeanor of Eleanor were very freely censured in her own time, I believe no imputation was cast upon her virtue till the usurper Henry IV., assuming to be the right heir of Edmund her second son, found it convenient to question the legitimacy of Edward her first born, and to represent him as the fruit of an adulterous intercourse between her and the Earl Marshal. Then was written the popular ballad representing her as confessing her frailty to the King her husband, who, in the garb of friar of France, has come to shrive her in her sickness, accompanied by the Earl Marshal in the same disguise.

> "Oh, do you see yon fair-haired boy
> That's playing with the ball?
> He is, he is the Earl Marshal's son,
> And I love him the best of all.
>
> "Oh, do you see yon pale-faced boy [2]
> That's catching at the ball?
> He is King Henry's only son,
> And I love him the least of all."

But she was a very different person from her successor, Isabella of France, Queen of Edward II., and there is no

---

[1] Prince Edward.   [2] Prince Edmund.

reason to doubt that she was ever a faithful wife and a loving mother to all her children.

Although none of her judicial decisions, while she held the Great Seal, have been transmitted to us, we have very full and accurate information respecting her person, her career, and her character, for which we are chiefly indebted to Matthew Paris, who often dined at table with her and her husband, and composed his history of those times with their privity and assistance.[1]

CHAPTER IX.

LORD CHANCELLORS FROM THE RESIGNATION OF LADY KEEPER QUEEN ELEANOR TILL DEATH OF HENY III.

ON Queen Eleanor's resignation of the office of Lady Keeper, WILLIAM DE KILKENNY, who had been employed by her to seal writs while she held the Great Seal,[2] was promoted to the office of Chancellor.

He did not continue in it long, and in his time nothing memorable occurred, except the representation from the clergy respecting alleged encroachments by the Crown upon their order. A deputation, consisting of the Primate and the Bishops of Winchester, Salisbury, and Carlisle, came to the King with an address on the frequent violation of their privileges, the oppressions with which he had loaded them and all his subjects, and the uncanonical and forced elections which were made to vacant ecclesiastical dignities. Lord Chancellor Kilkenny is said to have written the King's celebrated answer: —" It is true I have been faulty in this particular: I obtruded you, my Lord of Canterbury, on your see: I was obliged to employ both entreaties and menaces, my Lord of Winchester, to have you elected. My proceedings, I confess, were very irregular, my Lords Salisbury and

---

[1] Mat. Par. 562, 654, 719, 799, 884, 989, 1172. 1200, 1202. Miss Strickland's Lives of the Queen's of England—tit. "ELEANOR."

[2] Rex dilectæ consorti suæ A, eadem gratia Reginæ salutem. Mandamus vobis quod cum delectus clericus noster W. de Kilkenni. Archidiaconus Coventrensis ad vos venerit, liberatis ei sigillum scaccarii nostri bajulandum et custodiendum usque ad reditum nostrum de partibus Wasconiæ, &c.— Pat. 37 H. 3, m. 5.

Carlisle, when I raised you from the lowest stations to your present dignities. I am determined henceforth to correct these abuses: and it will also become you, in order to make a thorough reformation, to resign your present benefices, and try again to become successors of the Apostles in a more regular and canonical manner.[1]

On St. Edward's day, in the year 1255, William de Kilkenny[2] resigned his office of Chancellor, but he was still in such favor, that, though suspected of having misapplied funds that came officially into his hands, the King granted him letters patent, whereby he declared that William, having long served him diligently and acceptably, should be quit of all reckonings and demands for the whole time that he had been Keeper of the King's Seal in England. He was afterwards sent on an embassy to Spain, where he died on the 21st of September, 1256. He is said to have been a very handsome person, eloquent, prudent, and well skilled in the municipal laws of the realm, as well as in the civil and canon law.

On the day of his resignation, the Great Seal was delivered to HENRY DE WENGHAM, afterwards Bishop of London,—and, with Walter de Merton, for his deputy, he remained Chancellor till he was removed by the mutinous Barons who for some time established an oligarchy in England.[3]

The ill-humor of the nation was manifested at a General Council called to meet in London at Easter, 1255, when the attempt was renewed that the Chancellor and other great officers should be appointed by the Prelates and Barons, as was said anciently to have been the custom, and that those officers might not be removed, except upon notorious faults, without the common assent. The King refusing these demands, a resolution was carried to postpone the further consideration of supply till Michaelmas.[4]

Simon de Montfort was now taking advantage of the unpopularity of the government for his own aggrandisement, and attempting successfully to wrest the sceptre from the feeble hand which held it. In June, 1258, met "the Mad Parliament," where, notwithstanding the resistance of the Chancellor and the King's other ministers, were

[1] Mat. Par. A.D. 1253.   [2] Rot. Pat. 39 H. 3, m. 16.   [3] 1 Parl. Hist. 29.
[4] M. Paris, 904.   1 Parl. Hist. 27.

passed the famous "Provisions of Oxford," by which twenty-four Barons were appointed, with unlimited power, to reform the Commonwealth, and annually to choose the Chancellor and other great officers of state.[1] The King for the time submitted, and even Prince Edward was obliged to take an oath to obey their authority.

De Wengham was for some time permitted by them to retain the office of Chancellor, having made oath that he would duly keep the King's Seal under their control.[2]

However, to give a full proof of their prerogative, they subsequently removed him, and elected in his place NICHOLAS DE ELY, Archdeacon of Ely,[3] a mere creature of their own. The old Great Seal, surrendered up by De Wengham, was broken in pieces, and a new one was delivered to the Chancellor of the Barons. We have a very circumstantial acconnt of this ceremony, showing that the King was present as a mere puppet of the twenty-four. After relating the oath of the new Chancellor, and that he forthwith sealed with the new seal, it says that "the King delivered the pieces of the old broken seal to Robert Wallerand, to be presented to some poor religious house of the King's gift."[4]

But the nation was soon disgusted by the arbitrary and capricious acts of Montfort and his associates: there was a strong reaction in favor of the King, and for a time he recovered his authority. Before proceeding to resume the full exercise of his royal functions, he applied to Rome for a dispensation from "the Provisions of Oxford" which he had very solemnly sworn to observe. This was readily promised him; but, unluckily, Alexander the Pope died before the dispensation was sealed, and considerable delay was likely to arise before a successor could be elected.

Henry or his advisers, to take advantage of the present

---

[1] Rot. Pot. 39 H. 3, m. 16.

[2] The oath made to the Chancellor was to this effect:—"That he would not seal writs without the command of the King and his Council, and in the presence of some of them, nor seal the grant of any great wardship, great marriage or escheat, without the assent of the Council or the major part of it, nor would seal any thing contrary to the ordinances made or to be made by the twenty-four, or the greater part of them, nor would take any reward but only such as other Chancellors have formerly received; and if he should appoint a deputy, it should only be according to the power to be provided by the council."—*Annal. Burton*, 413.

[3] Rot. Pat. 44 H. 3, m. 2.

[4] Pat. 44 H. 3, n. 2. Claus. Rol. 44 H. 3, n. 2.

favorable state of the public mind, called a Parliament to meet in the castle of Winchester. There he openly declared that he would no longer be bound by "the Provisions of Oxford," which had rendered him more of a slave than a King. He then called before him the Chancellor and Justiciar appointed by the Barons, and demanded from them the seals and the rolls of their respective offices. They answered that they could not lawfully obey him without the consent of the Council of twenty-four. The baronial officers were, however, in his power: they were obliged to submit, and the Great Seal was delivered up to Henry.

He appointed WALTER DE MERTON as Chancellor.[1] At the same time, to put on an appearance of moderation, the following Letters Patent were passed under the Great Seal, in compliment to the Ex-Chancellor thus forcibly displaced:

"The King to all whom, &c. Know ye that our beloved clerk, Master Nicholas, Archdeacon of Ely, did, on the day of St. Luke the Evangelist, in the 44th year of our reign, receive from us our Great Seal to be kept, which said seal we received from him on Tuesday next after the Feast of the Translation of St. Thomas the Martyr, in the 45th year of our reign. We have therefore specially to recommend him for his good services to us. In witness, &c. Witness the King, at the Tower of London, on the 14th day of July."[2]

De Wengham would probably have been restored to the office; but he had fallen into bad health, and he died soon after. De Merton's appointment was by patent with an express declaration that it was "*without the consent of the Barons.*" At the same time a grant was made to him of 400 marks a year for support of himself and the Chancery, so long as he should remain in office.[3]

---

[1] Rot. Pat. 43 Hen. 3, m. 8.
[2] Pat. 45 H. 3, m. 7. Liberata 45 H. 3, m. 3. Pat. 49 H. 3, m. 18.
[3] This sum would be equal to about £4000 of present money. An addition of 100 marks was made to the salary of his successor Out of this the Chancellor had to pay the Chancery Clerks or Masters in Chancery, and to defray other expenses of the Chancery; but he had besides, as we have seen, high fees on grants from the crown, and he generally held large ecclesiastical benefices, so that he must have had a revenue and maintained a state equal to the great hereditary Barons. In the reign of Henry II. the Chancellor was allowed "five shillings a day, two demean and seasoned simnels, one sextary of clear wine, one sextary of *vinum expansabile*, one pound of wax and forty

Walter de Merton is the most considerable man we have found in the office during the present reign. He gained great distinction as a student at Oxford, where he afterwards founded Merton College. He had been appointed to act as Vice-Chancellor from his knowlege of law and capacity for business. He was twice Lord Chancellor, and being appointed to the see of Rochester, he was distinguished as a prelate for his sanctity and good works.

In 1262 the King went abroad, and was accompanied by John de Mansel, his secretary, appointed Keeper of the Seal, while Walter de Merton, remaining at home, was continued in the office of Chancellor.[1] Henry returned to England in a few months, and Walter de Merton continued for some time to act as his minister, under the title of Chancellor, employing Keepers of the Seal to do the laborious duties of the office. Of these the only distinguished man was John de Chishull, who was afterwards Chancellor.

Not only "the Provisions of Oxford," but the Great Charter, and the Charter of the Forest, were now disregarded, and the doctrine was promulgated, which had abettors among lawyers down to the Revolution of 1688, that no royal grants or acts of the legislature are binding on the Sovereign if they infringe his essential prerogatives, the nature and extent of which are to be judged of by him and his ministers.

The bold and artful Montfort, in exile, hearing of the discontents occasioned by these arbitrary measures, came over secretly from France, again collected the forces of his party, and commenced an open rebellion. He seized and imprisoned John de Mansel, the Ex-Keeper of the Great Seal, because he had published the bull at last obtained from Rome, absolving the King and kingdom from their oaths to observe "the Provisions of Oxford;" and he threatened the utmost vengeance against Walter de

pieces of candle." The five shillings per diem would have been then equal to about £1400 per annum, but it is impossible to estimate the value of the other items. From a schedule found in the chamber of accounts at Paris, it appears that Philippe d'Antoigni, Chancellor to St. Louis, a contemporary sovereign, received for himself and his horses seven shillings a day; and another schedule states that the same Chancellor received seven shillings a day for himself, his horses, his grooms (valets à cheval), and for all others except his clerk and his valet-de-chambre, who sat at the king's tables.

[1] Rot. Claus. 47 H. 3, m. 6. The Chancellor, during the King's absence, was only to seal instruments attested by H. le Despenser, the Justiciar.

Merton, and the other adherents of the King, as soon as they should fall into his power. Deserted by all ranks, they found it prudent to set on foot a treaty of peace, and to make an accommodation with him on terms the most disadvantageous. "The Provisions of Oxford" were confirmed,—even those which entirely annihilated the royal authority, and the Barons were again reinstated in the sovereignty of the kingdom. Their first step was to remove Walter de Merton from the office of Chancellor, and to restore it to their partisan, Nicholas de Ely.[1]

He continued to hold the Great Seal as Chancellor till the famous parliament assembled by Simon Montfort, in the 49th of Henry III., which was summoned by writs in the form now used,—which was attended by representatives from counties, cities, and boroughs, and which was the model of all succeeding parliaments in England.

Under this last settlement an interval of quiet arose, during which Henry crossed the Channel, to confer with the French monarch, who was then holding a meeting of his states at Boulogne. The Great Seal remained in the custody of Archdeacon Nicholas, who, during the King's absence, put it only to instruments of course.[2]

Henry returned to celebrate the feast of the Translation of St. Edward, and to hold a Parliament at Westminster. Here a party sprung up for the King, and an attempt was made to repeal "the Provisions of Oxford," and to restore to the Crown the power of appointing the Chancellor; but the Earl of Leicester still had a majority of spiritual and lay Peers. Several treaties were attempted between the moderate men of both parties, and, according to the custom of the age, it was at last agreed to refer "the Provisions of Oxford," and all other matters in difference, to the arbitration of the French King.

[1] The entries in the Close Roll are still worded as if the government had been regularly proceeding under the royal authority. "Here W. de Merton departed from court, and on Thursday next before the feast of St. Margaret the Virgin, in the presence of Simon de Montfort, Earl of Leicester, and of the other nobles of England, Master Nicholas, Archdeacon of Ely, took at Westminster the custody of the King's Seal, and he immediately sealed with it."—Rot. Cl. 47 H. 3.

[2] Memorandum, that on the 18th September the Lord the King departed from Westminster to foreign parts, and the King's Great Seal remained in the custody of Nicholas, Archdeacon of Ely, who acted during the King's stay beyond the sea. He however sealed nothing but writs which were attested by H. le Despenser, Justiciar of England, &c.—Pat. 47 H. 3, m. 1.

The royal arbitrator, having taken upon himself the burden of the reference, and having patiently heard both sides in full assembly of his nobility, gave judgment in favor of the King of England, by declaring "the Provisions of Oxford" null and void, and adjudging that the King might nominate his Chancellor and the other great officers of the kingdom according to his own pleasure.

The King was proceeding to act upon the award; but the Barons refused to be bound by it, alleging that it was contradictory on the face of it, and that the arbitrator had exceeded his authority.

Both parties again flew to arms, and soon after was fought the " Mise" or "battle of Lewes," which ended in the captivity of Henry, of his brother the King of the Romans, of Prince Edward his son, and of Comyn, Bruce, and of the chief opponents of Montfort who survived the perils of that bloody field.

The parliament was called in the King's name, the King being apparently on the throne, the Lords spiritual and temporal attending, and the commonalty of the realm fully represented by the knights, citizens, and burgesses who had been elected under the new-fashioned writs which Montfort or his Chancellor had framed. This assembly, however, had merely to register the decrees of the usurper. An Act was passed (the first professing to have the sanction of the third estate), according to the following tenor:—
"This is the form of the peace unanimously approved of by our Lord the King, and the Lord Edward his son, and all the Prelates and Barons, *together with the whole community of the kingdom of England,*"—the leading enactment being, that, for the reformation of the state of the kingdom, there should be chosen three discreet and faithful men who should have power and authority from the King of choosing nine counselors, out of whom three at least, by turns, should always be present at Court, and the King, by the advice of those nine, should make his Justiciar, Chancellor, Treasurer, and all the other great and small officers connected with the government of the kingdom.[1]

For some reason not explained, Nicholas de Ely was removed by De Montford from the office of Chancellor. He was probably suspected of having temporized between the two parties, and of having countenanced the reference to

[1] 1 Parl. Hist. 31.

the King of France. He is to be had in remembrance as the first Chancellor who ever sealed writs for the election of knights, citizens, and burgesses to Parliament.¹ Whether he, as an Englishman, suggested the measure—foreseeing the benefits it might confer upon his native land—or De Montfort, who had been born and educated abroad, introduced it from some country in which the third estate was admitted to grant supplies and have a share in legislation,—or whether the two thought of nothing but a present expedient for enlarging and confirming their power, by taking advantage of the popularity they then enjoyed with the classes on whom the elective franchise was bestowed, without looking to precedent or regarding distant consequences, it would now be vain to conjecture. Although there was much of accident with respect to the time when the institution first appeared among us, yet it could not have continued to flourish if it had not been suited to the state of society and the wants of the nation. In spite of violence and opposition, in spite of continued foreign or domestic war, commerce made advances, wealth increased among the middling orders, the feudal system began gradually to decline, and both the King and the people favored a new power which was more submissive than the Barons to the regular authority of the Crown, and at the same time afforded protection against their insolence to the inferior classes of the community.

Nicholas de Ely seems, after Montfort's fall, to have reconciled himself to the Court, for though he did not again hold any civil office, he was made Bishop of Worcester in 1268, and before the end of that year translated to the see of Winchester, which he held till his death in 1280.

The new Chancellor appointed by the twenty-four Barons now vested with supreme power, was THOMAS DE CANTILUPE.² He was of noble extraction, being son of

---

¹ Some writers have attempted to give a much earlier date to the popular representation in England, but I think without success; for not only are there no earlier writs for the election of representatives extant, but there is no trace of the existence of such a body in accounts of parliamentary proceedings, where, if it had existed, it must have been mentioned —as the trial of Thomas à Becket, which is as minutely reported as the impeachment of Warren Hastings. The great council of the nation hitherto consisted of the prelates and barons, assisted by the officers of state and the judges.

² The entry on the record, however, shows that the government was still decently carried on in the King's name. "On Wednesday next after the feast of St. Peter in cathedra, Master John de Chishull, Archdeacon of Lon-

William Baron de Cantilupe, of an illustrious Norman family. Being destined for the church, he studied at Oxford, where he made great proficiency in the Canon Law: he took the degree of Doctor of Laws, and became Chancellor of that University, then an annual office; but he had not yet reached any higher ecclesiastical dignity than that of Archdeacon of Stafford.

Lord Chancellor Cantilupe had a grant of 500 marks a year, payable at the Exchequer at four terms in the year, for the support of himself and the clerks of the King's Chancery,[1] so long as he should continue Archdeacon of Stafford.

He had a very short and troubled possession of his new office. Prince Edward had escaped from imprisonment, and was again in the field at the head of a numerous and well appointed army. Cantilupe's services were wanted to assist in opposing him at a distance from London, and the Great Seal was temporarily transferred to Ralph de Sandwich, Keeper of the Wardrobe, to be kept by him till Thomas de Cantilupe should return, under the superintendence, and to be used with the concurrence, of Peter de Montfort, Roger St. John, and Giles de Argentine.[2]

don (who had been sigillifer), restored to the King his Seal, and he on the same day committed the custody of it to Master Thomas de Cantilupe, who immediately sealed with it."—Claus. 49 H. 3, m. 9.

[1] This document is still extant, and is curious as recognizing the election of the Chancellor by parliament, and showing the form observed when a grant was to pass under the Great Seal in favor of the Chancellor himself. "Rex omnibus, &c., salutem. Cum dilectus nobis in Christo Magister Thomas de Cantilupo, per nos et magnates nostros qui sunt de Concilio nostro, electus sit in Cancellariam Regni nostri, et nos ipsum ad officium illud gratanter admiserimus, nos sustentationi suæ et clericorum Cancellariæ nostræ providere volentes, concessimus ei quingentas marcas, singulis annis percipiendas ad Scaccarium nostrum, &c., ad sustentationem suam et Clericorum Cancellariæ nostræ predictæ quamdiu steterit in officio. In cujus, &c. Teste Rege apud Westmon. xxvj° die Marcii. Et sciendum quod Dominus Rex manu sua fecit consignari, presentibus similiter H. le Dispenser, Justiciario Angliæ," &c.—Pat. 49 H. 3, m. 18. This grant was continued to his successors, as we several times find credit given to sheriffs for payments made to the Chancellor by the King's order in discharge of the allowance of 500 marks for the sustentation of himself and the clerks of the Chancery.—Mag. Rot. 52 H. 3. 50 H. 3.

[2] The following memorandum of this transfer is to be found in the Patent Roll:—"That on Thursday next after St. John Port Latin Master Thomas de Cantilupe, the King's Chancellor, delivered the King's Seal to Ralph de Sandwich, the Keeper of the wardrobe, in the presence of the King and of Hugh le Despenser, Justiciar of England, and Peter de Montfort, to be kept by him until Thomas should return;—to be used in this manner—Ralph to keep it in the wardrobe under the seal of Peter de Montfort, Roger de St. John, and

Ralph de Sandwich was probably a personal attendant on the King in whom no confidence was reposed. The three superintendents were devoted adherents of the party who now kept the King prisoner, and ruled in his name.

Before Thomas de Cantilupe did return, the battle of Evesham was fought,—Simon de Montfort was slain, and his party was for ever extinguished.

Prince Edward is celebrated for the merciful disposition he now displayed. No blood was shed on the scaffold, and all who submitted were pardoned. Cantilupe, though removed from his office, was afterwards taken into favor, made Bishop of Hereford, and employed in an embassy to Italy, where he died in 1282. Notwithstanding the political factions in which he was engaged, he acquired a character for extraordinary sanctity; miracles were said to be wrought by his dead body. He was canonized by Pope John XXII.; and all his successors, the Bishops of Hereford, out of respect to his memory, have used his family arms as the heraldic bearings of their see.

The victory of Evesham having fully re-established the royal authority during the remainder of his reign, WALTER GIFFARD, who had always steadily adhered to the court party, was appointed to the office of Chancellor.[1]

He was of a good family, and of great abilities. Having mastered all that was to be learned in England, he completed his education in Italy, where he was ordained priest and made private chaplain to the Pope. On his return to his own country, mixing in secular affairs, he rose to be Lord Treasurer, an office which he lost by a sudden revolution in the state. In 1264 he reached the secure elevation of the prelacy, being made Bishop of Bath and Wells. This dignity he held when he received the Great Seal. In about a year after, the Archbishopric of York falling vacant, he aspired to it, and had the court interest; but William de Langton, Dean of York, was

---

Giles de Argentein, or one of them—when taken out, Ralph to seal the writs of course in the presence of the person under whose seal it had then been inclosed, or in his absence if he was not minded to be there, but mandatory writs only in the presence of such person and with his assent; and when the writs either of course or mandatory were sealed, then the King's seal was to be sealed up under the seal of one of the three persons above named, and to be carried by Ralph into the wardrobe, to be there kept in form aforesaid, until Thomas de Cantilupe should return."—Rot. Pat. 49 H. 3, m. 16.

[1] Rot. Pat. 48 H. 3. m. 10.

elected by the Chapter. Both parties appealed to the Pope, and, after a keen struggle, Giffard succeeded through his superior interest. As soon as he was installed Archbishop, he voluntarily resigned the Great Seal, and devoted himself to the government of his new see, which he held above ten years. He left behind him the reputation of great learning, as well as of integrity and piety.

He was succeeded in the office of Chancellor by GODFREY GIFFARD, Archdeacon of Wells,[1] another member of the same family, who, through his mother, was related to the King, and seems to have owed his promotion entirely to court favor. He was removed from the office after he had held it a very short time, without any turn in politics, and without any advancement in the church,—whence it is inferred that he was found wholly incompetent for secular duties. Nevertheless he was afterwards considered sufficiently qualified for high ecclesiastical preferment, and in 1269 he was appointed to the see of Worcester, which he held without reproach for 24 years. While he was Chancellor, in the 52nd year of the King's reign, a parliament assembled at Marlbridge, where many useful laws were passed for restraining the abuse of Distresses, regulating the incidents of tenure, and improving civil and criminal procedure. Several of these display great discrimination, and an acquaintance with the general principles of Jurisprudence greatly above the comprehension of the Chancellor; and if he introduced them, they must have been framed by superior men whom he had the wit to employ.[2]

The next Chancellor was a man of much renown in his day, JOHN DE CHISHULL, Dean of St. Paul's. He had risen from an obscure origin by his own powers, and being well skilled in the civil and common law, with a great readiness for business, he had been found very useful to Lord Chancellor de Merton, who made him his Vice Chancellor.[3] Having always taken the royalist side, he was persecuted by the Barons; but they being now crushed, his fidelity was rewarded with the office of

[1] Rot. Pat. 51 H. 3, m. 22. 52 H. 3, m. 30. Rot. Claus. 52 H. 3, m. 10.
[2] See Stat. Marlb. 52 H. 3.
[3] There is an entry in the Charter Roll, 49 H. 3, which has induced some to support that Chishull was Chancellor before Cantilupe; but though he delivered the Great Seal to the King, he had not before held it as Chancellor.

Chancellor, which he filled with great applause till the year 1270, when he exchanged it for that of Treasurer. In 1274 he was made Bishop of London, and he spent the remainder of his days in works of charity, and in seeking to expiate the sins he had committed in his political career.[1]

His successor in the office of Chancellor was RICHARD DE MIDDLETON, of whom so little is known that it has been questioned whether he was a layman or an ecclesiastic; but there can be little doubt that he was one of the active, aspiring priests who, in those troublous times, were employed as secretaries to the King, and were intrusted with the Great Seal as a step to high promotion in the church. While he was Chancellor he certainly provided for the expenses of the King's chapel out of the profits of his office, and no doubt officiated in it as chaplain.[2] He died while Chancellor, on Sunday before the Feast of St. Lawrence, in the year 1272, before any other provision had been made for him,[3] and the Great Seal

---

[1] *Matthew of Westminster.*—The family of De Chishull was settled for several centuries at Little Bardfield in Essex; and in the parish register of that place there is the following entry respecting him, which seems to have been written about the year 1539: "John de Chishull, archdeacon of London, and treasurer of England, was made Keeper of the Great Seale in the yeare of our redemption one thousande two hundred sixtie and four, being the eight and fortie yeare of the raigne of King Henry the Third. This man was consecrated Bishopp of London in the yeare of Christ one thousand two hundred seventie and foure, the third kalendes of May. He died in the yeare that the word of the father became one thousand two hundred seventie and nine, the fourth ides of February, in the seventh yeare of the scourge of the Scotts and Welshmen."—*Extracted from the parish register by my son Hallyburton.*

[2] In the fifty-fifth year of King Henry III., John le Fauconer, receiver of the fees of the Great Seal, rendered to De Middleton his account, which is still extant, and in which he is allowed certain disbursements for the King's chapel, among other expenses to be defrayed by the Chancellor. "Compotus Johannis le Fauconer Receptoris denariorum proveniencium de exitibus Sigilli Regis, a festo Apostolorum Simonis et Judæ, anno Liiij usq; ad idem festum anno Lvj incipiente, videlicet per duos annos.—Summa summarum, DCCCCLxxiij l. xvj s. In thesauro nichil." Among the credits, "Et Johanni Partejoye custodi summarum Regis Cancellarii pro vadiis suis per CCCxxx dies vj l. iij s. ix d. per idem breve [Regis]. Et in percameno ad opus clericorum Cancellariæ predictæ, et aliis minutis expensis ejusdem Cancellariæ et Campellæ Regis xiij l. ij s. vi d. per idem breve." Mag. Rot. 55 H. 3. Rot. 1 a, in Rot. Compotor. The amount of these fees is considerable, regard being had to the value of money in those times.

[3] "Die Dominica proxima ante festum Sancti Laurentii obiit Ricardus de Middleton quondam Cancellarius Regis et Sigillum Regis liberatum fuit in Garderobam Regis.—Chart. 56 H. 3, m. 2.

was deposited in the King's wardrobe to abide the disposal of the Council who now governed the kingdom.

Prince Edward, having crushed De Montfort and the associated Barons,—seduced by his avidity for glory, and by the passion of the age for crusades, had undertaken an expedition, in conjunction with St. Louis, to recover the Holy Sepulchre, and, after the death of that pious and romantic sovereign, was now signalizing himself by acts of valor in Palestine, and reviving the splendor of the English name among the nations of the East. King Henry, overcome by the cares of government and the infirmities of the age, was visibly declining, and could no longer even appear to take a part in the government. Letters were written in his name to the Prince, urging his immediate return, and pointing out the dangers to which the state was exposed from the mutinous Barons, who were again commencing their machinations and disorders. In the mean time the Council did not venture to appoint a new Chancellor, but delivered the Great Seal to John de Kirby, with the title of Vice-Chancellor, that he might seal writs with it, and do what was requisite for the ordinary routine of government till the Prince's arrival.

Kirby was a churchman, eager for promotion;—as yet only Dean of Winbury and Archdeacon of Coventry, but active, cunning, and unscrupulous. His conduct in this emergency gave such satisfaction, that in the ensuing reign he was made Bishop of Ely and Lord Treasurer. But he is accused by contemporary writers of having neglected his spiritual for his temporal duties, and of having taken little notice of the flocks committed to his charge, except when he was to shear them.

He held the Great Seal from the 7th of August, 1272, to the 16th of November following, the day that closed the inglorious reign of Henry III. The moment that the King had breathed his last, Kirby surrendered it to Walter Archbishop of York, and the rest of the Council assembled to take measures for securing the accession of the new Sovereign.[1]

During this reign there were sixteen Chancellors, and many Keepers[2] of the Great Seal besides; but none of

---

[1] Rot. Claus. and Pat. 57 H. 3, m. 1.
[2] In the longer reign of George III. there were only eight.

them of much historical importance. Learning was very low, and was confined entirely to the clergy. Not only were the Chancellors of this order, but many dignitaries of the Church were Justices in the Courts at Westminster and in the Eyre. Nay, the advocates in the secular courts were ecclesiastics, and from them only could any competent Judges be selected. There was a canon published about this time, " Nec advocati sint clerici vel sacerdotes, in foro seculari, *nisi vel proprias causas vel miserabilium prosequantur.*" The exception excused their appearance in Westminster Hall, and their violation of the rule was, from necessity, connived at.[1]

After the Great Charter and the Charter of the Forest had been confirmed, the King's ministers were too much occupied in counteracting the plots and resisting the violence of the mutinous Barons to have much leisure for legal reform, and the only attempts at it by legislation were the statutes of Merton[2] and Marlbridge.[3] Several provincial and legatine constitutions were passed by convocations of the clergy, at the instigation or with the concurrence of clerical Chancellors, for exempting ecclesiastics from all secular jurisdiction, and effecting those objects which had been defeated by the Constitutions of Clarendon and the vigorous administration of Henry II.

It is curious that, in the most disturbed period of this turbulent reign, when ignorance seemed to be thickening and the human intellect to decline, there was written and given to the world the best treatise upon law of which England could boast till the publication of Blackstone's Commentaries, in the middle of the eighteenth century.[4] It would have been very gratifying to me if this work could have been ascribed, with certainty, to any of the Chancellors whose lives have been noticed. The author, usually styled Henry de Bracton, has gone by the names of Brycton, Britton, Briton, Breton, and Brets; and some

---

[1] But the inns of court for education in the common law were about this time established, and a separate order of laymen learned in the common law sprung up and flourished.

[2] 20 H. 3, the chief enactment of which was to encourage the enclosure of waste land.

[3] 52 H. 3, for regulating the right of distress.

[4] The book must have been written between the years 1262 and 1267, for it cites a case decided in the 47th of H. 3, and takes no notice whatever of the Statute of Marlbridge, which passed in the 52nd of H. 3.

have doubted whether all these names are not imaginary. From the elegance of his style and the familiar knowledge he displays of the Roman law, I cannot doubt that he was an ecclesiastic who had addicted himself to the study of jurisprudence; and as he was likely to gain advancement from his extraordinary proficiency, he may have been one of those whom I have commemorated,—although I must confess that he rather speaks the language likely to come from a disappointed practitioner than of a Chancellor who had been himself in the habit of making Judges.[1] For comprehensiveness, for lucid arrangement, for logical precision, this author was unrivalled during many ages. Littleton's work on Tenures, which illustrated the reign of Edward IV., approaches Bracton; but how barbarous, in comparison, are the Commentaries of Lord Coke, and the Law treatises of Hale and of Hawkins![2]

Towards the end of this reign the office of Chief Justiciar, which had often been found so dangerous to the Crown, fell into disuse. Hugh le Despenser, in the 49th of Henry III., was the last who bore the title.[3] The hearing of common actions being fixed at Westminster by Magna Charta, the *Aula Regia* was gradually subdivided, and certain Judges were assigned to hear criminal cases before the King himself, wheresoever he might be, in England. These formed the Court of King's Bench. They were called "Justitiarii ad placita coram Rege," and the one who was to preside "Capitalis Justiciarius." He was inferior in rank to the Chancellor, and had a salary of only 100 marks a year,[4] while the Chancellor had generally 500.

[1] Describing the judges of his time, he calls them "Incipientes et minus docti, qui cathedram judicandi ascendunt antequam leges dedicerint."

[2] It must be admitted that juridical writing is a department of literature in which the English have been very defective, and in which they are greatly excelled by the French, the Germans, and even by the Scotch. The present state of the common law may now probably be best learned from "the notes of Patteson and Williams on Sergeant Williams's notes on Saunder's Reports of Cases decided in the reign of Charles II.," and written in Norman-French.

[3] Dugdale, in his Chronica Series, when he comes to 55 H. 3, A. D. 1271, changes the heading of his column of justices from "Justiciariorum Angliæ" to "Justic. ad Plac. coram Rege."

[4] Dugd. Or. Jur. p. 104. The puisnes had only forty pounds a year. The chief Justice of Common Pleas had one hundred marks, the chief baron forty marks, and the puisne barons twenty. 2 Reeve's Hist. of Law, 91. This is certainly poor pay, and I am afraid may have induced the judges to be guilty of the corrupt conduct for which they were punished in the following reign.

Henceforth the Chancellor, in rank, power, and emolument, was the first magistrate under the Crown, and looked up to as the great head of the profession of the law.

There are some cases decided in this reign which are still quoted as authority in Legal Digests;—the writs and summonses to Simon de Montfort's parliament are now given in evidence on questions of peerage,—and the England in which we live might then be descried.

CHAPTER X.

CHANCELLORS AND KEEPERS OF THE GREAT SEAL DURING THE REIGN OF EDWARD I. TILL THE DEATH OF LORD CHANCELLOR BURNEL.

EDWARD being proclaimed King, while still absent from England, the Council, as an act of power authorized by the urgency of the case, resolved to appoint a Chancellor. After nine days' deliberation they selected WALTER DE MERTON, who had filled the office in the preceding reign, and who, having always been a zealous royalist, they had every reason to believe would be agreeable to the new Sovereign.

The letters addressed to the Prince requiring his presence had produced the desired effect, and he had reached Sicily on his return from the Holy Land, when he received intelligence of the death of his father. Learning the quiet settlement of the kingdom, he was in no hurry to take possession of the throne; but from France he wrote a letter dated the 9th of August, in the first year of his reign—"To his beloved Clerk and Chancellor, Walter de Merton," confirming his appointment, and requesting him to continue to discharge the duties of the Chancellorship.[1]

The work was, however, very light till the times when salaries were so much increased. In the reign of Henry VI. the judges never sat more than three hours in the day, from eight in the morning till eleven, employing the rest of their time in reflection, reading, and contemplation, while the councillors and sergeants went to the parvise at Paul's to meet their clients.—Fort de Laud.

[1] "EDWARD, by the grace of God King of England, Lord of Ireland, and

The nobles assembled at the " New Temple" in London, had ordered a new Great Seal to be made, having the name and style of Edward inscribed upon it, and in the attestation of public documents by the guardians of the realm during the King's absence the words occur,— " In cujus, &c., has literas sigillo Domini Regis quo utimur in agendis, eodem absente, fecimus consignari."—De Merton displayed extraordinary ability as Chancellor, and materially contributed to the auspicious commencement of the new reign.

To the great joy of the people the King at last arrived, was crowned, and took the Government into his own hands. He ordered another Great Seal, under which he confirmed the grants made in his absence, by "inspeximus"—according to the following form:—" Is erat tenor prædictarum literarum quas prædicto sigillo nostro fecimus quo prædicti locum nostrum tenentes utebantur, quod quia postmodum mutatum est, tenorem literarum prædictarum acceptantes præsenti sigillo nostro fecimus consignari."[1]

De Merton was now removed from the office,—not because his conduct was at all censured, but the King wished to promote to it a personal friend who had followed him in all his fortunes, and for whose abilities and character he had the highest respect. The bishopric of

Duke of Aquitaine, to his beloved Clerk and Chancellor, Walter de Merton, greeting.

"We give you special thanks for the diligence you have applied to our affairs and those of our kingdom, beseeching that what you have so laudably begun you will happily take care to continue, causing justice to be done to every one in matters which belong to your office, inducing others also to do the same, not sparing the condition or rank of any person, so that the rigor of justice may control those whom the sense of equity cannot restrain from injuries. Those things which you have rightly done in this matter we, God willing, will cause to be fully confirmed.

"Given at Mellune on Seine, 9th of August, in the first year of our reign."

This letter shows that the king clearly conceived he had a right to remove the Chancellor if he had thought fit, though he had been appointed by the council. This appointment is adduced by Prynne in his "Opening of the Great Seal," as a proof that the Chancellor was the officer of the parliament, not of the king; but the appointment of De Merton was an act of power exercised in the king's name, and demanded by necessity, as at the decease of Henry III. there was no Chancellor, and the Seal was deposited in the wardrobe. Unless some one had been appointed Chancellor, writs could not have been sealed, and the government of the country could not have been conducted till the king should return or manifest his pleasure upon the subject.

' Mat. West. 401.   ² Pat. Rot. 1 Ed. 1.

Rochester was bestowed on the Ex-Chancellor, and he employed his time in building, endowing, and making statutes for Merton College, Oxford, where his memory is still revered. He died in 1277.[1]

On the day of St. Matthew the Apostle,[2] 1274, the office of Chancellor was conferred on ROBERT BURNEL, and he continued to hold it with great applause for eighteen years, during all which time he enjoyed the favor and confidence of Edward, and was his chief adviser in all public affairs. He is a striking example of the unequal measure with which historical fame has been meted out to English statesmen. Although intimately connected with the conquest and settlement of Wales;—although he conducted Edward's claim to the superiority over Scotland, and pronounced the sentence by which the crown of that country was disposed of to be held under an English liege Lord;—although he devised a system for the government of Ireland upon liberal and enlightened principles;—although he took the chief part in the greatest reforms of the law of England recorded in her annals, —and there can be no doubt that he occupied a considerable space in the public eye during his own age,—his name has since been known only to a few dry antiquaries incapable of appreciating his merits.[3]

Robert Burnel was the yonnger son of Robert de Burnel, of a powerful family settled from time immemorial at Acton Burnel, in the county of Salop.[4] Here the future Chancellor was born;[5] here, he afterwards, by the King's license, erected a fortified castle; and here, to

---

[1] In the reign of Queen Elizabeth, his tomb being much dilapidated, it was repaired by the Warden and Scholars of Merton, who supplied an epitaph giving a minute account of the life and dignities of their Founder, and concluding with these lines:

"Magne senex titulis Musarum sede sacrata,
Major Mertonidum maxime progenie.
Hæc tibi gratantes post secula sera nepotes,
Et votiva locant Marmora, Sancte Parens."

[2] Sept. 21.
[3] In Hume's very superficial history of the reign of Edward I., Lord Chancellor Burnel is not once named or alluded to.
[4] The little village of Acton Burnel, picturesquely placed near the foot of the northernmost Caer Caradoc in Shropshire, and contiguous to a Roman road originally connecting Wroxeter with Church Stretton, is remarkable both for its early history and its architectual remains."—*Hartshorne.*
[5] Rot. Pat. 12 Ed. 1, m, 7, m. 18.

illustrate his native place, he prevailed on the King to hold a parliament at which was passed the famous law, "DE MERCATORIBUS," called "the Statute of Acton Burnel."

As his elder brother, Hugh, was to inherit the paternal estate, and was, of course, to do military service as a knight and baron, Robert was destined to rise in the state by civil and ecclesiastical employments, which were then generally combined. He early distinguished himself by his proficiency not only in the civil and canon law, but in the common law of England; and there is reason to think that after he had taken holy orders, he practiced as an advocate in the Courts at Westminster. During the Barons' wars, while still a young man, he was introduced to Prince Edward, who was about his own age, and was much pleased with his address and social qualities, as well as his learning and ability. He became chaplain and private secretary to the heir apparent, suggested to him the counsels which enabled him to triumph over Simon de Montfort, and attended him in his expedition to the Holy Land.[1]

When appointed Chancellor he had reached no higher ecclesiastical dignity than that of Archdeacon of York. He was soon after raised to the see of Bath and Wells,— with which he remained contented, devoting the whole of his energies to affairs of state.

He presided at the Parliament which met in May, 1275, and passed "the STATUTE OF WESTMINSTER THE FIRST," deserving the name of a CODE rather than *an Act of Parliament*. From this chiefly, Edward I. has obtained the name of "the English Justinian"—absurdly enough, as the Roman emperor merely caused a compilation to be made of existing laws,—whereas the object now was to correct abuses, to supply defects, and to remodel the administration of justice. Edward deserves infinite praise for the sanction he gave to the undertaking; and from the observations he had made in France, Sicily, and the East, he may, like Napoleon, have been personally useful in the consultations for the formation of the new Code,—but the execution of the plan must have been left to others professionally skilled in jurisprudence, and the

---

[1] Rot. Claus. 2 Ed. 1, m. 4. Rot. Pat. 50 H. 3, m. 3.

chief merit of it may safely be ascribed to Lord Chancellor Burnel, who brought it forward in parliament.

The statute is methodically divided into fifty-one chapters. Without extending the exemption of churchmen from civil jurisdiction, it protects the property of the Church from the violence and spoliation of the King and the nobles, to which it had been exposed. It provides for freedom of popular elections, then a matter of much moment, as sheriffs, coroners, and conservators of the peace were still chosen by the freeholders in the county court, and attempts had been made unduly to influence the election of knights of the shire, almost from the time when the order was instituted. It contains a strong declaration to enforce the enactment of MAGNA CHARTA against excessive fines which might operate as perpetual imprisonment. It enumerates and corrects the great abuses of tenures,—particularly with regard to the marriage of wards. It regulates the levying of tolls, which were imposed in an arbitrary manner, not only by the Barons, but by cities and boroughs. It corrects and restrains the powers of the King's escheator and other officers under the Crown. It amends the criminal law, putting rape on the footing to which it has been lately restored, as a most grievous but not a capital offense. It embraces the subject of "*Procedure*," both in civil and criminal matters, introducing many regulations with a view to render it cheaper, more simple, and more expeditious.

Having gone so far, we are astonished that it did not go farther. It does not abolish trial by battle in civil suits,—only releasing the demandant's champion from the oath (which was always false) that he had seen seizin given of the land, or that his father, when dying, had exhorted him to defend the title to it. But if total and immediate abolition of this absurd and impious practice had been proposed, there would have been sincere and respectable men who would have stood up for ancestral wisdom, —asserting that England owed all her glory and prosperity to trial by battle in civil suits, and that to abolish it would be impiously interfering with the prerogative of Heaven to award victory to the just cause.

Lord Chancellor Burnel was soon to appear in a very different capacity. Llewellyn, Prince of Wales, had given great assistance to the Montfort faction, and though he was included in the general amnesty published after the battle of Evesham, there was a lurking resentment against him for his past misdeeds, and a strong desire to curb and curtail his power, that he might be less dangerous in future. By the Chancellor's advice he was summoned to this parliament to do homage for his principality, which he admitted that he held of the British Crown. The Welsh Prince neglected the summons and sent for excuse,—" that the King having shown on many occasions an extreme animosity against him, he would not trust his person with his declared enemy." Nevertheless, he offered to come, provided Edward would give him his eldest son in hostage, with the Earl of Gloucester and *the Lord Chancellor*. We may believe that Burnel, known to be very unfriendly to the Welsh, would not have been very willing to trust himself among these savage men in the recesses of Snowdon.

The Prince was peremptorily summoned to appear at a parliament held in 1276,—and, making default,—after a solemn hearing of the matter in his absence, he was adjudged by the mouth of the Chancellor to be guilty of felony, and war was immediately proclaimed against him. Llewellyn being soon after slain in battle, the principality of Wales was completely subjugated, and Burnel was employed to devise measures for its pacification and future government. He was stationed at Bristol, where he held courts of justice for the southern counties, and gave general directions for the introduction of English institutions among the natives, who, notwithstanding their boast of ancient independence and love of poetry, had made very little advance in civilization or the common arts of life. He then prepared a Code under which Wales was governed till the reign of Henry VIII., when it was allowed to send members to Parliament, and was fully included within the pale of the English constitution. This was first in the form of a charter, to which the Great Seal was affixed, but being confirmed in a parliament held at Ruthlan Castle, it is generally called "Statutum Walliæ," or "the Statute of Rutland;"[1] reciting that Wales, with its inhabitants, had hitherto been subject to the King *jure feudali*, but had now by Divine providence

[1] 10 Ed. I.

fallen *in proprietatis dominum*,—it introduces the English law of inheritance,—regulates the jurisdiction of the "*Justiciarius de Snaudon*,"—establishes sheriffs and coroners,—and provides for the administration of civil and criminal justice. Seconded by the immense castles erected by Edward, which now give us such a notion of his wealth as well as of his wisdom, this Code had the effect of preserving tranquillity, and gradually preparing the way for greater improvements.

In May, 1282, the King paid his Chancellor a visit of three days at Acton Burnel, and the following year spent six weeks with him there, from the 29th of September to the 12th of November, during the trial of Prince David for high treason before the Parliament at Shrewsbury, from which, as an affair of blood, all prelates were absent. After the disgraceful sentence passed on the last of a princely line,—that for bravely defending his own rights and the independence of his country, he should be dragged at horses' heels through the streets of Shrewsbury, hanged, beheaded, and divided into four quarters, to be distributed through the four chief towns of England;[1] the King, to gratify his host, adjourned the parliament to Acton Burnel, and it is said that the prelates, barons, knights, citizens, and burgesses assembled in the great hall of the strong castle, which, by royal license, the Chancellor had built in his native place.[2] Here was passed the most admirable

[1] There was a keen controversy between York and Winchester for his right shoulder, which was awarded to the capital of Wessex.

[2] Pro Roberto Burnel Bathon' et Well ⟩ Rex omnibus ad quos etc. salutem. Episcopo de manso Kernellando. ⟨ Sciatis quod concessimus pro nobis et heredibus nostris venerabili patri Roberto Burnel Bathoniensi et Wellensi Episcopo Cancellario nostro quod ipse et heredes sui mansum suum de Acton Burnel muro de petra et calce firmare et Carnellare possint quandocumque voluerint, et mansum illud sic firmatum et carnellatum tenere sibi et heredibus suis in perpetuum ; sine occasione vel impedimento nostri et heredum nostrorum Justiciariorum et ministrorum nostrorum quorumcunque. In cujus etc. T. R. apud Lincolniam, xxviii die Januarii. Pat. 12 Ed. I.

The remains of the castle still attract the curious in mediæval architecture. It is a quadrangular structure, enclosing an area of 70 feet by 47, with engaged square towers at each angle. The interior has been much disturbed, and is now so choked up with modern erections, that the dimensions and uses of the original chambers can no longer be ascertained. However, there had certainly been a spacious hall on the first floor, lighted by three large windows to the south, in which, probably, the parliament assembled. There seems to be no doubt that the three estates of the realm were not then separated as has been supposed into two chambers, but deliberated together, and formed one

statute, "De Mercatoribus,"[1] for the recovery of debts,—showing that this subject was fully as well understood in the time of Chancellor Burnel as in the time of Chancellor Eldon or Chancellor Lyndhurst. The grievance (which was peculiar to England) of being obliged to bring an action and have a debt established by the judgment of a court of law before enforcing payment of it, where there is not the smallest doubt of the validity of the instrument by which it is constituted, has always been a reproach to the administration of justice in this country. To mitigate the evil, the Statute of Acton Burnel enacts, that where a debt has been acknowledged before the Mayor of a town,—immediately after default of payment, there shall be execution upon it, and that by an application to the Chancellor the creditor may obtain satisfaction by sale of the debtor's goods and alienable lands in any part of England.[2]

As long as Burnel continued in office, the improvement of the law rapidly advanced,—there having been passed in the sixth year of the King's reign the "Statute of Gloucester;" in the seventh year of the King's reign the "Statute of Mortmain;" in the thirteenth year of the King's reign the "Statute of Westminster the Second," the "Statute of Winchester," and the "Statute of Circumspecte agatis;" and in the eigteenth year of the King's reign the "Statute of *Quo Warranto*," and the "Statute of *Quia Emptores*." With the exception of the establishment of estates tail, which proved such an obstacle to the alienation of land till defeated by the fiction of Fines and Common Recoveries,—these laws were in a spirit of enlightened legislation, and admirably accommodated the law to the changed circumstances of the social system,—which ought to be the object of every wise legislator. The provisions for checking the accumulation of property in the possession of ecclesiastical corporations, for defining the jurisdiction of the ecclesiastical courts, for preventing subinfeudation by enacting that on

legislative assembly.—See *Rymer*, vol. ii. 247, and preamble of statute. *Hartshorne* on ancient Parliament, and Castle of Acton Burnel."

[1] 11 Ed. 1.
[2] I have repeatedly, but ineffectually, attempted to extend the principle of this measure to the modern securities,—bonds and bills of exchange,—and to assimilate our law in this respect to that of Scotland, of France, and of every other civilized country.

every transfer of land it shall be held of the chief lord of the fee, and for the appointment of the circuits of the judges, such as we now have them, deserve particular commendation. But we must not conclude the brief notice of the legislation of this period, under the auspices of the Chancellor, without mentioning the " Ordinatio pro Statu Hiberniæ,"[1] for effectually introducing the English law into Ireland, and for the protection of the natives from the rapacity and oppression of King's officers:—a statute framed in the spirit of justice and wisdom, which, if steadily enforced, would have saved Ireland from much suffering, and England from much disgrace.

The Chancellor, being so deeply engaged in state affairs, was often unable to attend to his judicial duties, and he was obliged from time to time to intrust the Great Seal to the custody of a Keeper, who acted under him. This was generally John de Kirby, who had been in possession of the Great Seal, as Keeper, without any Chancellor over him, at the conclusion of the last reign. In 1278 there is an entry that, on the Chancellor going abroad, he delivered the King's seal into the King's wardrobe, to be kept under the seal of Kirby, whom the Chancellor had appointed to expedite the business of the Chancery.[2] There is an original letter extant in the Tower, written in the following year by the King to Kirby, in which he is desired to come to the King, and to leave the Seal, sealed up under his own seal, in the custody of Thomas Bek. From the 25th of May to the 19th of June the Chancellor was with the King in France. During this time the Seal was in the joint keeping of Kirby and Bek, and it was restored to Burnel on his return.[3] There are likewise several entries of the Seal being delivered to Kirby when the Chancellor was about to visit his diocese, or to retire to his country house (*ad partes proprias*).[4] Kirby, for his good services, was in 1287 made Bishop of Ely. The subsequent Keepers of the Seal, under Burnel,

---

[1] 17 Ed. I.   [2] Rot. Claus. 6 Ed. I, m. 12.
[3] Rot. Vasc. 7 Ed. I. Rot. Claus. 7 Ed. I, m. 6. Rot. Pat. 7 Ed. I, m. 15.
[4] Rot. Pat. 4 Ed. I, m. 16. Rot. Pat. 10 Ed. I, m. 18, m. 14. Rot. Claus 10 Ed. I, m. 6. 11 Ed. I, m. 8. Rot. Pat. 12 Ed. I, m. 7, 18. Madd. Exch. 49. Rot. Claus. 12 Ed. I, m. 4.

were Hugh de Hendel, Walter de Odiham,[1] and William de Marchia.

However, the Chancellor himself, as head of the law, exercised a vigilant superintendence over the administration of justice, and in the parliament held at Westminster, in the beginning of the year 1290, brought forward very serious charges against the judges for taking bribes and altering the records,—upon which they were all convicted except two, whose names ought to be held in honorable remembrance,—John de Matingham and Elias de Bekingham. Sir T. Wayland, Chief Justice of the Common Pleas, being found the greatest delinquent, had all his goods and estates confiscated by the King, and was banished for life out of the kingdom. Sir A. T. Stratton, Chief Baron of the Exchequer, was fined 34,000 marks. Sir R. de Hengham, Chief Justice of the King's Bench, was let off with a fine of 7000 marks; for although he had improperly altered a record, it was not supposed to have been from corrupt motives. The taint had spread into the Court of Chancery, and R. Lithebury, Master of the Rolls, was fined 1000 marks. These sentences, pronounced in parliament by the Chancellor, had upon the whole a very salutary effect, but are supposed, for some ages, to have induced the Judges to adhere too rigorously to forms and the letter of the law.

The Chancellor was now engaged in assisting the King in the most memorable transaction of his reign, the settlement of the dispute respecting the succession to the Crown of Scotland, which arose on the death of Alexander III. The ambitious scheme of getting possession of Scotland by a claim of feudal superiority when the hope of accomplishing the object by marriage had failed, is, no doubt, to be ascribed to Edward himself; but the manner in which it was conducted was chiefly devised by Burnel. He accompanied the King to Norham, and there addressed the Scottish Parliament, assisted by Roger de Brabaçon, the Chief Justice.

It is remarkable that the English Chancellor spoke to them in French;[2] but this was then the court language,

---

[1] He on one occasion delivered the Seal to these two as early as 1284 at Aberconway, when he was going to Acton Burnel. Rot. Claus. 12 Ed. 1, m. 47.
[2] Rymer, vol. ii. 643. It is hardly possible that, like Chancellor Long-

not only of England, but of Scotland, where almost the whole of the nobility were of Norman extraction,—superior knowledge and address having established the illustrious descendants of Rollo in the northern part of the island, as superior bravery had in the southern.

Nothing can exceed the dexterity with which the competitors for the crown were induced to submit themselves to the arbitrament of Edward, and the whole Scottish nation to put themselves in his power. These results were chiefly ascribed to the management of the Chancellor. The Prelates, Barons, and Knights of Scotland, representing the whole community of that kingdom, having met in a green plain on the left of the Tweed, directly opposite to the castle of Norham, in pursuance of the leave given them to deliberate in their own country,—Burnel went to them in his master's name, and asked them "whether they would say anything that could or ought to exclude the King of England from the right and exercise of the superiority and direct dominion over the kingdom of Scotland which belonged to him, and they would there and then exhibit it if they believed it was expedient for them;—protesting that he would favorably hear them,—allow what was just,—or report what was said to the King and his council, that what justice required might be done." Upon repeated demands, the Scots answered nothing; whereupon the Chancellor recapitulated all that had been said at the last meeting relative to the King's claim; and a public notary being present, the right of deciding the controversy between the several competitors for the crown of Scotland was entered in form for the King of England. After which the Chancellor, beginning with Robert Bruce, Lord of Annandale, asked him in the presence of all the Bishops, Earls, Barons, &c., "whether, in demanding his right, he would answer and receive justice from the King of England as superior and direct Lord over the kingdom of Scotland?" Bruce in the presence of them all, and of the public notary, none contradicting or gainsaying, answered "that he did acknowledge the King of England superior and direct Lord of the Kingdom of Scotland,

champ, he knew no other language than French, the vernacular tongue, springing from the Anglo-Saxon, being now generally spoken in England and in the lowlands of Scotland.

and that he would before him, as such, demand answer and receive justice." The same question was successively put to all the other competitors, who returned the like response. Not contented with this, Burnel required that they should sign and seal a solemn instrument to the same effect, — which they according did,— quickened by hints thrown out that the candidate who was the most complying would have the best chance of success.[1]

Eighty commissioners were appointed from both nations to assist in taking evidence, and hearing the arguments of all who were interested. Their meetings were held at Berwick, and the English Chancellor presided over their deliberations.

Edward being obliged to return to the south to attend the funeral of his mother, Queen Eleanor (Ex-Lady-Keeper of the Great Seal), left Burnel behind at Berwick to watch over the grand controversy, which was now drawing to a close. The claims of all the competitors, except two, were speedily disposed of; and as between these the doctrine of representation prevailed over proximity of blood. The judgment was accordingly in favor of Baliol, the grandson of the elder sister, against Bruce, the son of the younger, the judge being probably influenced as much by a consideration of the personal qualities of the competitors as by the opinion of the great jurists in different parts of Europe who were consulted. Baliol had already exhibited that mixture of subserviency and obstinacy, of rashness and irresoluteness, which made him such a desirable vassal for a Lord, resolved by all expedients, as soon as a show of decency would permit, to get the feud, by pretended forfeiture, into his own hands.

Lord Chancellor Burnel died at Berwick on the 25th day of October, 1292, and was buried in his own cathedral at Wells. He surely well deserves a niche in a gallery of English statesmen.

He was censured for the great wealth he amassed;[2] but

---

[1] 1 Parl. Hist. 4.
[2] It appears from the inquisition held in the year after his death (21 Ed. 1), that the extent of his temporal possessions was commensurate with his dignities, as he held more than thirty manors, besides other vast estates in nineteen different counties.—Cal. Lug. p. m. I. p. 115.

he employed it nobly, for he not only erected for his family the castellated dwelling in which he received the King and parliament, but also a splendid episcopal palace at Wells, long the boast of his successors. Nepotism was another charge against him, from his having done so much to put forward two brothers and other kindred. This however must be regarded as a venial failing in churchmen, whose memory could not be preserved in their own posterity.[1] If he was rather remiss in the discharge of his episcopal duties, he is to be honored for the rational and moderate system he pursued in ecclesiastical affairs,—neither encroaching on the rights of the clergy, nor trying to exalt them above the control of the law. As a statesman and a legislator, he is worthy of the highest commendation. He ably seconded the ambitious project of reducing the whole of the British Isles to subjection under the crown of England. With respect to Wales he succeeded, and Scotland retained her independence only by the unrivaled gallantry of her poor and scattered population. His measures for the improvement of Ireland were

[1] The whole of the family possessions centered in the Chancellor's nephew, Philip, who was summoned to parliament as a Baron by writ in 1311. The male line of the family soon after failed: but in the reign of Edward III. the Chancellor was represented, through a female, by Nicholas Lord Burnel, who gained great renown in the French wars, and had a keen controversy respecting the Burnel arms with the renowned warrior Robert de Morley. It happened that they were both at the seige of Calais, under Edward III., in 1346, arrayed in the same arms. Nicholas Lord Burnel challenged the shield as belonging to the Burnels only, he having at that time under his command 100 men, on whose banners were his proper arms. Sir Peter Corbet, then in his retinue, offered to combat with Robert de Morley in support of the right which his master had to the arms, but the duel never took place, probably because the king denied his assent. The suit was then referred to the court of chivalry, held on the sands at Calais, before William Bohun, Earl of Northampton, high constable of England, and Thomas Beauchamp, Earl of Warwick, earl marshal. The trial lasted several days, when Robert, apprehending that the cause would go against him, took an opportunity, in presence of the king, to swear by God's flesh, that if the arms in question were adjudged from him, he never more would arm himself in the king's service. On this the king, out of personal regard for the signal services he had performed in those arms, and considering the right of Nicholas Lord Burnel, was desirous to put an end to the contest with as little offense as possible. He therefore sent the Earl of Lancaster, and other lords, to Nicholas, to request that he would permit Robert de Morley to bear the arms in dispute for the term of his life only, to which Nicholas, out of respect to the king, assented. The king then directed the high constable and earl marshal to give judgment accordingly. This they performed in the church of St. Peter, near Calais, and their sentence was immediately proclaimed by a herald in the presence of the whole army there assembled.—*Pennant's North Wales.*

frustrated by the incurable pride and prejudices of his countrymen. But England continued to enjoy the highest prosperity under the wise laws which he introduced.[1]

CHAPTER XI.

CHANCELLORS AND KEEPERS OF THE GREAT SEAL FROM THE DEATH OF LORD CHANCELLOR BURNEL DURING THE REMAINDER OF THE REIGN OF EDWARD I.

ON the death of Burnel the Great Seal was for a short time in the keeping of William de Hamilton,[2] a man of business and of moderate abilities, who subsequently became Chancellor. But if he expected to succeed to the envied office on this occasion, he was disappointed; for soon after the King heard of the loss he had sustained he named as the new Chancellor JOHN DE LANGTON, a person who, though much inferior to his predecessor, acted a considerable part in this and the succeeding reign. He was of an ancient family in Lincolnshire, which produced Cardinal Stephen Langton, Archbishop of Canterbury, so illustriously connected with Magna Charta, and of which Bennet Langton, the friend of Dr. Johnson, was the representative in the reign of George III. He early distinguished himself by his talents and industry, and rendered himself useful to Lord Chancellor Burnel. Being introduced into the Chancery as a

---

[1] Edward I., returning from the Holy Land, at Bologna, engaged in his service Franciscus Accursii, a very learned civilian, who he employed as his ambassador to France and to Pope Nicholas III.—but, as far as I can trace. not in his law reforms, or in any part of his domestic administration. A hall at Oxford was appropriated to the use of this Italian, from which some have supposed that he there gave lectures on the civil law. When he left England in 1281, he received from the king 400 marcs, and the promise of an annuity of 40 marcs.—See Palg. on council note L, p. 134, Duck. xxii.

[2] There is an entry in the Close Roll. 20 Ed. 1, stating that the Great Seal was in the keeping of Walter de Langton, keeper of the wardrobe, under the seal of William de Hamilton; but it is certain that Hamilton sealed the writs, and did the business of the Great Seal, which was probably ordered to be kept in the King's wardrobe under the superintendence of the keeper of the wardrobe.

clerk, he rose to be Master of the Rolls, and showed qualities fitting him for the highest offices in the state.¹

He continued Chancellor for ten years, to the entire satisfaction of his royal master, who required no ordinary zeal and activity in his ministers.

Immediately upon his appointment he published an ordinance in the King's name for the more regular despatch of business, " that in all future parliaments all petitions shall be carefully examined, and those which concern the Chancery shall be put in one bundle, and those which concern the Justices in another, and those which are to be before the King and his Council in another, and those which are to be answered in another."²

A parliament was called at Westminster soon after, when the new Chancellor had to begin the session with disposing of a very novel appeal, which was entered by the Earl of Fife against Baliol King of Scotland as vassal of Edward King of England;—and the question arose, whether the appeal lay? This was immediately decided by Lord Chancellor Langton, with the unanimous concurrence of the Lords, in the affirmative; and the respondent was ordered to appear. Formerly in the English parliaments there had always been placed on the right hand of the throne, and on the same level with it, a chair for the King of Scotland, who came to do homage for Cumberland and his other possessions in England,—as the Kings

¹ The following is a true copy of a letter of congratulation to him on his appointment as Chancellor, lately discovered in the Tower:—

"Domino suo reverendo suus devotus in omnibus si quid melius sit salutem. Immensa Dei clementia quæ suæ virtutis gratia gratis interdum occurrit homini non quæsita vos ad regni gubernaculum in regiæ Cancellariæ officio feliciter promovit non est diu. Super quo Ei regratior a quo fons emanat indeficiens totius sapientiæ salutaris. Sed ecce Domine vos qui in parochia de Langeton originem duxistis sicut placuit Altissimo et ibidem refocillati fuistis maternis sinibus nutritivis. Quæ immenso gaudio vos post doloris aculeos pariendi refocillavit ad honorem Dei et Regni gubernaculum quo præestis in quo ipse placeat qui vos ad culmen honoris hujusmodi evocare dignatus est ut ei primo secundario domino Regi et populo complacere possiti; ad honorem Jesu Christi, ut autem ei fiducialius obsequamini qui vos sic promovit de gratia sua speciali ut ei visceralius obsequamini cum vacare poteritis affectione pleniori portitorium quoddam non extra septa portarum portantem vobis mitto rogans quatenus exilitatem tanti munusculi exemplo Catonis placide admittentes servitium divinum in eodem exercere et discere vobis placeat in honorem illius qui omnia creavit ex nichilo et retributor est universalis bonitatis."—*Royal and other Letters, temp. Edward I.* 65, xx. S.

² Claus. 21 Ed. 1, m. 7. This shows the Aula Regia to have become familiar.

of England did homage to the Kings of France for Normandy and Guienne. Baliol now claimed the place and precedence of his royal predecessors; but the Chancellor in the name of the House, announced the resolution of their Lordships, "that he should stand at the bar as a private person amenable to their jurisdiction, and that having been guilty by his contumacy of a breach of feudal allegiance, three of his principal estates should be seized into the King's hands till he gave satisfaction.[1]

Baliol, seeing the degradation to which he had reduced himself and his country, soon after renounced his allegiance as unlawfully extorted from him, and in the vain hope of effectual assistance from France, set Edward at defiance. "And now," says Daniel, "began the contests between the two nations which spilt more Christian blood, did more mischief, and continued longer, than any wars that we read of between any two people in the world."[2]

Lord Chancellor Langton had the proud satisfaction of presiding at a parliament held at Berwick in 1296, after Edward had overrun, and for the time subjugated Scotland. There he administered the oaths of allegiance to all the Scottish nobility, who were reduced to the sad necessity of swearing fealty to the haughty conqueror, and of binding themselves to come to his assistance at any time and place he might prescribe. But Wallace soon arose; Robert Bruce was to follow;—and amid the general gloom the Highland seers could descry on the distant horizon shadows of the glories of Bannockburn.

We must confine ourselves to events in which Lord Chancellor Langton was more immediately concerned. The following year Edward, thinking that he had conquered Scotland, determined to carry on war against France, that he might take vengeance for the perfidy of the monarch of that country, by which he asserted he had been tricked out of Guienne. Having assembled his fleet and army at Winchelsea, then the great port of embarkation for the Continent, he hastened thither himself to meet them, accompanied by the Chancellor, who on board the ship "Edward" delivered the Great Seal into his own hand as he was setting sail for Flanders.[3] The King carried it abroad with him, having appointed John

[1] 1 Parl. Hist. 41. [2] Dan. Hist. p. 111.
[3] Rot. Pat. 25 Ed. 1, n. 2, m. 7. Rot. Claus. m. 7.

de Burstide, who attended him as his secretary, to keep it. But Langton still remained Chancellor, and on his way back to London, at Tonbridge Castle, another seal was delivered to him by Prince Edward, appointed guardian of the realm in the King's absence.

A parliament was soon after held while the King remained abroad, nominally under the young Prince, but actually under Langton. Here broke out a spirit of liberty which could not be repressed, and the Chancellor was obliged to allow the statute to pass both Houses, called "The Confirmation of the Charters," whereby not only MAGNA CHARTA and CHARTA DE FORESTA were confirmed, but it was enacted that any judgment contrary to them should be void; that copies of them should be sent to the cathedral churches throughout the realm, and read before the people twice every year;[1] that sentence of excommunication should be pronounced on all who should infringe them;[2] and that no aids should be taken without the consent of parliament.[3]

The statute was in the form of a charter, but the Chancellor conceived that he had no power to give the royal assent by putting the seal to it, and it was sent to Flanders by messengers from both Houses, to be submitted to Edward himself. After much evasion and reluctance, he ordered De Burstide to seal it with the Great Seal which he had brought along with him.

The King, baffled in his military operations against France, and alarmed by the news of an insurrection in Scotland under Wallace, found it prudent to return to his own dominions, and (according to the Close Roll) on Friday, the 14th of March, 1298, he landed at Sandwich from Flanders, and the next day, about one o'clock, John de Langton, the Chancellor, came to the King's bedchamber at Sandwich, and there, in the presence of divers noble persons, by the King's bed-side, he delivered up to the King the seal that had been used in England during his absence, and the King immediately after, with his own hand, delivered to the Chancellor the Great Seal which he had taken with him to Flanders.[4]

Edward, having obtained (it is to be feared by the advice of the Keeper of his conscience) a dispensation from

---
[1] 25 Ed. 1, c. 2.   [2] C. 3.   [3] C. 4, C. 5 and 6.   2 Inst. 525.
[4] Rot. Pat. 26 Ed. 1, mm. 23, 12, in dorso. 26 Ed. 1. Rot. 57, a.

the Pope from the observance of "the confirmation of the Charters" to which he had given his assent when out of the realm, the Parliament the following year passed the statute of "Articuli super Chartas," which introduced the new enactment, "that the commonalty should choose three persons in every county to be authorized by the King's letters patent under the Great Seal, to hear and determine such complaints as should be made of those who offended in any point against the Charters, as well the King's officers as others, and to punish them by imprisonment, ransom, or amercement, according to the trespass." To this statute the King gave his royal assent in person from the throne, "the Chancellor and the Judges sitting on the woolsacks," and from this time no sovereign of England has denied that the Charters are law, however in practice they may have been violated."[2]

The Chancellor was now involved in a dispute in which he was personally interested, and which caused him great trouble and anxiety for some years. He had not had the good luck to be promoted to the episcopal bench,—when the see of Ely becoming vacant, he thought he was secure of it. But while some of the monks voted for him according to the wishes of the government, others gave their voices for their own Prior, who, they said, would have much more leisure to attend to the duties of a faithful overseer of the church of Christ.

The court then lay at York, the Chancellor, as usual, attending the King. He posted off to Lambeth to consult the Archbishop of Canterbury, leaving the Seal with three persons, John de Crancombe, John de Caen, and William de Birlay, to be kept by them in their joint custody on the King's behalf until he should return.[1] The Archbishop advised him to proceed in person to Rome, the Prior of Ely having already appealed to the Pope. Langton, without resigning his office of Chancellor, had leave of absence to prosecute his suit, and on the 14th of February, 1299, delivered up the Great Seal, to be held, during his stay abroad, by John de Burstide as Keeper. He landed at Dover on his return, on the 11th of June following, and on the 16th of the same month the Seal was re-delivered to him by the King.[3]

[1] 28 Ed. 1, stat. 3.   [2] 1 Parl. Hist. 43.
[3] Rot. Pat. 26 Ed. 1 m. 27, and Rot. Claus. 26 Ed. 1, m. 10.

He had not succeeded at the Vatican, notwithstanding all the influence exerted in his favor. The Holy Father, taking this opportunity to show the plenitude of his power, entirely set aside the election of the monks, consecrated the Bishop of Norwich to the see of Ely, bestowed Norwich on the Prior of Ely, and, by way of consolation to the English Chancellor, made him Archdeacon of Canterbury.

On the 12th day of August, 1302, Langton resigned his office of Chancellor, for some reason not explained to us. This occurrence certainly did not proceed from a desire to sacrifice him to a rival, for the King was much perplexed in the appointment of a successor. The Close Roll gives a very circumstantial account of the ceremony of the resignation:—

"Be it remembered that in the 30th year of King Edward, on Monday after the Assumption of the Blessed Virgin, about the hour of vespers, in the chamber wherein the King then lodged, in the Hostel of the Archbishop of York, near Westminster, immediately after the King rose from council, Lord John de Langton, the Chancellor of England, restored to the King his Great Seal, and the King, in the presence of Amadio Earl of Savoy, John de Bretagne, and divers others of his council, delivered the same to the Lord John de Drakensford, then Keeper of his Wardrobe, to be kept there."[1]

After a lapse of ten days, the King had not yet made up his mind who should be Chancellor; but there being a necessity that the judicial business connected with the office should proceed, the Great Seal was given under certain restrictions into the keeping of Adam de Osgodebey, Master of the Rolls, of which we have the following entry:—

"On the 23rd of August, in the 30th year of the King, in the King's chamber at Kensington, in the presence of Otho de Grandison, Amadio Earl of Savoy, John de Bretagne, and others of the King's council, the King's Great Seal was delivered by the King's order by the hand of Lord John de Drakensford, Keeper of the Wardrobe, to Lord Adam de Osgodebey, Keeper of the Rolls of the Chancery, who was enjoined to keep it under the seal of Master John de Caen, and the Lords William de Birlay

[1] Rot. Cl. 27 Ed. I, m. 11   [2] Cl. Rol. 30 Ed. I, m. 8

and Robert de Bardeley, *until the King should provide himself with a Chancellor*.[1] The Seal being so disposed of, the King set forward on his journey to Dover by the way of Chichester."

At last, on the 30th of September following, a new Chancellor was declared in the person of WILLIAM DE GRENEFIELD, Dean of Chichester. The reader may be gratified by the record of the appointment and installation:—

"On Sunday the morrow of St. Michael, in the same year, in the King's Chapel, at St. Redegund, immediately after mass, in the presence of Lord John de Drakensford and others, chaplains and clerks of the said chapel of the King, Lord Adam de Osgodebey delivered the Great Seal to our Lord the King, who then received it into his own proper hands, and straightway delivered it to Master Willlam de Grenefield, Dean of Chichester, whom he had chosen for his Chancellor, to keep, and the said Chancellor delivered the said Seal again to the said Adam, to be carried with him the said Chancellor to Dover; and on the same day at Dover, the Chancellor received it back from the said Adam, and the next day sealed writs with it in the House of God there."[2]

Langton, the Ex-Chancellor, remained some years without any promotion; but in 1305 he was made Bishop of Chichester, and he obtained quiet possession of that see, which he continued to govern with great credit till he was again restored to the office of Chancellor in the succeeding reign.

William de Grenefield (sometimes called *Grenevill*), now his successor, was descended from an ancient family in the West of England, represented by the present Duke of Buckingham. He entered the church when very young, and was a Canon of York before he was Dean of Chichester. He frequented the court of Edward I., and had shown qualities which induced the belief that he would make a useful servant to the Crown. When raised to his new dignity he is said to have been "eminent in counsel, and very eloquent."

He and Edward's other ministers were excessively unpopular, insomuch that at a parliament called soon after

---

[1] —quousque Dominus Rex sibi de Cancellario providisset. Cl. 30 Ed. I, m. 6   [2] Cl. Rol. 30 Ed. I, m. 5.

his appointment, an attempt was made to carry a favorite scheme several times brought forward in weak reigns about this period of English History, but which we should not have expected to find proposed to him who had conquered Wales, and led his victorious armies to the extremity of Scotland,—" that the Chancellor, Chief Justice, and Treasurer should be chosen or appointed by the community of the kingdom." The King, by the Chancellor's advice, returned for answer,—" I perceive you would at your pleasure make your King truckle to you and bring him under subjection. Why have you not asked the Crown of me also? whilst at the same time you look upon that as very fit and necessary for yourselves which you grudge me that am your King; for it is lawful for every one of you, as master of his own family, to take in or turn out what servant he pleases; but if I may not appoint my Chancellor, Chief Justice, and Treasurer, I will be no longer your King: yet if they or any other officers shall do you any wrong or injustice, and complaint be made of it to me, you shall then have some reason to grumble if you are not righted." This firmness had such an effect, that the Barons humbly begged the King's pardon for their presumption.[1]

The only other public matter in which Lord Chancellor Grenefield was concerned, was in framing an answer to a letter which the Pope had written to Edward, remonstrating with him upon his invasion of Scotland, and claiming that kingdom as a right belonging to the see of Rome; but his Holiness was gravely assured that " ever since the coming of Brute and his Trojans into this island, Scotland had been under feudal subjection to the King of England, who had frequently made gift of it to one of their subjects, and resumed the gift at their pleasure." The Barons of England, to the number of 112, unanimously concurred in "an address to the Pope, devoutly kissing his blessed feet," in which they told him " that he had no right to interfere in the affairs of Scotland, which belonged exclusively to the Crown of England." It is curious that although this address was voted in Parliament and appears on the Parliament Roll, subscribed by all the Barons, it is not subscribed by the Chancellor or any spiritual Peer.

De Grenefield had great reason to avoid appearing too

[1] 1 Parl. Hist. 48, 48.

openly in this controversy, and notwithstanding his caution, he seems to have given offense to the Roman Pontiff. On the 4th of December, 1303, he was elected Archbishop of York, and on the 24th of the same month the royal assent was given to his election; but although he was not liable to any reasonable objection, the Pope refused to allow his consecration. Letters and proxies being ineffectual, the Archbishop elect resolved to go in person to Rome; and to show his devotedness to his spiritual duties, he absolutely resigned the office of Chancellor before his departure.

The journey of the Ex-Chancellor to Rome must have been very rapid, and the energy of his personal application extraordinary; for, having delivered up the Great Seal at Westminster on the 29th of December, 1304, he was consecrated there on the 30th of January following,—his representations on the equity of his case being fortified by a present to the Pope of 9500 marks. He was admitted to the temporalities of the see on the 31st of March, 1305; but he is said to have been reduced to such poverty by the exactions of the Court of Rome, that he was twice forced to have recourse to the clergy of his diocese for subsistence, first by way of "benevolence," and the second time of "subsidy." He is celebrated for his support of the Knights Templars, then persecuted by the Pope and Philip of France. In the year 1311 he sat in the Council of Vienna, called to quiet the disputes which then agitated the church, and representing the clergy of England he was allowed precedence next after the Prince, Archbishop of Treves. He died in 1315.[1]

During the temporary absence of De Grenefield, when he had been sent on an embassy, Osgodebey, the Master of the Rolls, had acted as keeper of the Seal; but on his resignation a new Chancellor was appointed,—WILLIAM DE HAMILTON, Dean of York.[2]

[1] While he was Chancellor the practice was established of members of the House of Commons being allowed their wages. At the end of the session, writs out of Chancery under the Great Seal were delivered to them, certifying their attendance, and requiring the sheriff by assessment to raise the necessary sum for paying them.—Rolls of Parliament, 33 Edward 1.

[2] Rot. Claus. 33 Ed. 1, m. 22. "Master William de Grenefield, Canon of York and the king's Chancellor, being elected Archbishop of York, did in the king's chamber at Lincoln, on Tuesday next after the feast of the Lord's Nativity, to wit, on the feast of St. Thomas the Martyr, in the thirty-third year of the king's reign, say to the king before his council, that it behoved

At the time of his nomination, being absent from court, the great Seal was delivered into the King's wardrobe to be kept by John de Burstide; and on the 16th of January following it was delivered to the new Chancellor, who continued to hold it above two years. Soon after he was appointed there was an admonition given to him in full parliament (probably in consequence of a petition from the Commons) against granting letters of protection from suits to persons absent in Ireland.[1]

In 1306 the Chancellor put the Great Seal to the famous statute "De Tallagio non concedendo,"[2] framed in the form of a charter, which had become necessary from the King, of his own authority, having taken a talliage of all cities, boroughs, and towns, and which finally put an end to the direct claim of the kings of England to impose any tax, and drove those who, in future, wished to rule without a parliament, to resort to such subterfuges as "benevolences," and "ship-money."

Any credit which De Hamilton might have had in inducing the King to agree to this concession was outweighed by the disgrace which he allowed to be brought upon the King and the nation from the mock trial and murder of Sir William Wallace, who, owing no allegiance to the King of England, was tried at Westminster under a commission sealed by an English Chancellor, and was executed on Tower Hill as a traitor, for having defended, against a public and oppressive enemy, the liberties of his native land with signal conduct, intrepidity and per-

him to go to Rome on the Thursday following relative to the business of the said election, and begged the king to ordain what was to be done with the Great Seal; and the king then nominated and elected William de Hamilton, Dean of York, Chancellor and Keeper of the Seal, and commanded the Archbishop elect to deliver the Seal the next day into the wardrobe to Sir John de Burstide, to remain there under the seals of Sir Adam de Osgodebey, &c., until the arrival of the new Chancellor; and the Archbishop elect the next day, at the sealing time, delivered the Seal to the king in bed." On the 16th of January following, by virtue of a writ of privy seal, the Great Seal was delivered to Sir William de Hamilton, so chosen Chancellor, and the same day after dinner he sealed a writ for Master William de Grenefield, elect of York, the Ex-Chancellor.—Rot. Pat. 33 Ed. 1, p. 1, m. 29.

[1] Rot. Parl. 38 Ed. 1. Memorandum quod vj die April. a. 33, Dominus Rex in pleno parliamento suo apud Westm. inhibuit Wilhilmo de Hamelton, Cancellario suo ne de cetero concedat alicui literas Regis de protectione in Hibn.

[2] 34 Ed. 1. 2 Inst. 531 Its genuineness has been questioned, without sufficient reason.

severance, entitling him to be placed in the highest class of heroes and patriots.

De Hamilton did not live to see the effect of this barbarous policy in the rising of the Scottish nation, headed by Robert Bruce,—all ready again to brave every danger in the hope of freedom and vengeance. He died in the possession of the office of Chancellor on the 20th of April, 1307, while in attendance on the King near the Scottish border,—not having reached any higher dignity in the church than that of Dean of York.

The Great Seal was found in a purse sealed up under the private seal of the deceased Chancellor. The King immediately declared his resolution to bestow the vacant office on Ralph de Baldock, Bishop of London, then in the South; and the following day, as the Great Seal could not be personally delivered to him, his appointment was made out in the following form:—

"Edward, by the grace of God King of England, Lord of Ireland, and Duke of Aquitaine, to the Treasurer or his deputy, and to the Barons of our Exchequer, health. Forasmuch as William de Hamilton who was our Chancellor is now with God, we command and ordain that the Bishop of London be our Chancellor, and that he come without delay to London to our said Exchequer to receive in your presence our Great Seal, which we now send thither by our dear clerks Adam de Osgodebey, Master John de Caen, and Robert de Bardeley. We command you that you cause the said Seal to be delivered to the said Bishop, and that you receive from him the oath of office belonging to the said office. Given under our Privy Seal at Cornhill the 21st day of April, in the 35th year of our reign."[1]

"Hereupon on the vigil of the ascension next following, RALPH DE BALDOCK, in the Court of Exchequer at Westminster, before William de Carleton, Baron of the Exchequer, Deputy of the Bishop of Lichfield and Coventry, the King's Treasurer, then with the King in the Marches of Scotland, before the other Barons, and also Roger de Barbançon, the King's Justiciary of the Bench, took the oath well and faithfully to demean himself in the office of Chancellor, and the impressions of the private seals with which the purse containing the Great

[1] Pas. Commun. 35 Ed. 1. Rot. 46.

Seal was guarded, being broken, it was taken therefrom and delivered to the said Ralph de Baldock, to be kept by him as Chancellor."[1]

De Baldock, by industry and ability, had reached his present high station from an obscure origin. He studied at Merton College, Oxford, and made himself master of all the learning of the times. He wrote in Latin "Annals of the English Nation," a work which was praised in his lifetime, although it has not come down to us. When appointed Bishop of London, he gained great fame by the splendid repair of St. Paul's Cathedral at his own cost, and it was on this occasion that the immense collection of ox skulls were dug up, which fortified the tradition that here had stood a great temple of Diana.

Having received the Great Seal, he remained stationary, devoting himself to his official duties, till news reached London of the death of the King. Edward, at the head of a mighty army, was marching for Scotland to take vengeance for the defeat which his General, Aymer de Valence, had sustained from Robert Bruce, and (as he hoped) finally to subjugate the Scottish nation; but he sickened and died at Burgh on Sands, near Carlisle, on the 7th of July, 1307, in the 69th year of his age, and the 35th year of his reign.

At the present time such an event as the demise of the Crown would be known in a few hours all over the kingdom; but for a period of eighteen days the news of the death of Edward I. did not reach the Chancellor in London, who, down to the 25th of July, continued to seal writs as usual, unconscious that a new reign had commenced. Letters of Privy Seal were then received from the new King, ordering that his father's seal should be sent to him under the seal of the Chancellor, and accordingly he received it into his own hands at Carlisle, on the 2nd of August.[2]

His eagerness to change the Chancellor in whom his father had confided, showed that the influence of personal favorites was already felt, and was a prelude to his own misfortunes and the disgrace which he brought upon the country.

De Baldock, freed from the cares of office, spent the

[1] Rot. Fin. 35 Ed. 1, m. 1.   Rot. Pat. 35 Ed. 1, m. 1.
[2] Rot. Fin. 1 Ed. 2, m. 11.

remainder of his days in the pursuit of literature and the services of religion. He died on the 24th of July, 1313.

Although we have no trace of the decisions of the Chancellors of Edward I., we know, from recent discoveries in the Tower of London, that they exercised important judicial functions, both in the King's council and in their own court, where they sometimes had the assistance of others, and sometimes sat alone. No case of importance was heard in the Council when the Chancellor was absent; and cases were referred by the Council for his consideration in Chancery, either by himself, or with the advice of specified persons whom he was to summon to assist him. Sometimes the subject of these suits was such as would now only be taken cognizance of in courts of law,—as disturbance of right of pasture;—but others were of a nature that would now be properly considered in a court of equity,—as assignment of dower, a discovery of facts by the examination of the defendant, and the exercise of the visitatorial power of the Chancellor representing the Sovereign.

All writers who have touched upon our juridical history have highly extolled the legal improvements which distinguished the reign of Edward I., without giving the slightest credit for them to any one except the King himself; but if he is to be denominated the English Justinian, it should be made known who were the Tribonians who were employed by him: and the English nation owes a debt of gratitude to the Chancellors, who must have framed and revised the statutes which are the foundation of our judicial system,—who must, by explanation and argument, have obtained for them the sanction of parliament,—and who must have watched over their construction and operation when they first passed into law. I shall rejoice if I succeed in doing tardy justice to the memory of Robert Burnel, decidedly the first in this class, and if I attract notice to his successors, who walked in his footsteps. To them, too, we are probably indebted for the treatises entitled "Fleta,"[1] and "Britton,"[2] which are

---

[1] "Fleta" must have been written after the thirteenth year of the King, and not much later; for it frequently quotes the Statute of Westminster the Second, without referring to the later statutes of the reign. The title is taken from its having been written in the Fleet Prison.

[2] "Britton" has been attributed to John Breton, Bishop of Hereford but

said to have been written at the request of the King, and which, though inferior in style and arrangement to Bracton, are wonderful performances for such an age, and make the practitioners of the present day, who are bewildered in the midst of an immense legal library, envy the good fortune of their predecessors, who, in a few manuscript volumes, copied by their own hand, and constantly accompanying them, could speedily and clearly discover all that was known on every point that might arise.

We now approach a period when civil strife and national misfortune suspended all improvement, and when a career of faction and violence terminated in the deposition and murder of the Sovereign.

CHAPTER XII.

CHANCELLORS DURING THE REIGN OF EDWARD II.

IT is not certainly known from records or otherwise, how the young King disposed of the Great Seal from the time when he received it at Carlisle till his return to London in the autumn of the year 1307. He probably carried it with him into Scotland in the short and inglorious campaign which he then made in that country,—forgetting alike what the exigencies of justice required in his own dominions, and the dying injunctions of his father to lead on the expedition with the utmost energy, and never to desist till he had reduced the Scottish nation to complete subjection. From the hour of his accession to the throne, he betrayed an utter incapacity for government, and an unconquerable aversion to all serious business. He seems for a long time to have appointed neither Chancellor nor Keeper of the Seal. He retreated without striking a blow,—disbanded his army, and thought of nothing but conferring power and places on his favorite, Piers Gaveston.[1]

this cannot be correct, for he died in the third year of the King, and the Treatise quotes the statutes of the thirteenth. It set the example of writing law books in French, which was followed for four centuries.

[1] A charge was afterwards brought against Gaveston of having about this time put the Great Seal to blank charters, which he filled up according to his fancy.

JOHN DE LANGTON.

Whilst the Barons, from the beginning, showed the utmost indignation at the advancement of this upstart, John de Langton, Bishop of Chichester, who had been Chancellor in the late reign, formed a coalition with him, and in recompense was restored to his former office. It was thought, even by the Gascon youth himself, that it would have been too great an outrage at once to have made him Chancellor, although, as we shall see, he was ere long entrusted with the Seal as Keeper.

The two years during which John de Langton was now Chancellor, were chiefly occupied with the disputes between the King and the Barons on account of the preference shown to the foreign favorite.

Edward continued occasionally to find a respite beyond sea from the factious proceedings of his native subjects. In the beginning of 1308, going to Aquitaine, he left the Chancellor guardian of the realm, and delivered to him a new seal to be used for certain necessary purposes. The Great Seal was intrusted to the keeping of William Melton, the King's secretary, who accompanied him. On Edward's return, the Chancellor delivered to him the Seal which had been in use during his absence, and the King delivered back to the Chancellor the Great Seal which he had carried with him abroad.[1]

Soon after, the King paid a short visit to Boulogne, when the Chancellor seems to have accompanied him, for Piers Gaveston was left with a seal to be used for the sealing of writs and other necessary business. In the Close Roll we have a very circumstantial account of the manner in which this seal was dealt with in the Court of Exchequer on the King's return.[2]

Edward was in the habit of occasionally taking the

---

[1] Rot. Cal. 1 Ed. 2, m. 7.

[2] "Whereupon William de Melton, controller of the King's wardrobe, came and brought into the Exchequer the King's Seal used in England at the time when the King was in foreign parts; which Seal was used for sealing the writs that issued out of the King's Chancery in England, at that time under the teste of Peter de Gaveston, Earl of Cornwall, then the King's lieutenant in England, and the said Seal being in a bag or purse of white leather, sealed with the Privy Seal of John de Langton, Bishop of Chichester, Chancellor of England, was by him delivered in at the Exchequer in the presence of the Chancellor of the same Exchequer, and the Barons and the Remembrancer. And straightway the said Seal, being in the purse so sealed up, was delivered to the Chamberlain of the Exchequer to be kept in the King's treasury," &c.—Hil. Com. 1 Ed. 2. Rot. 40, b. Madd. Exch. 51 52.

Seal into his own custody, and using it without any responsible adviser. Thus, on the 13th of June, 1308, at the New Temple in London, the Bishop elect of Worcester, the Treasurer, ordered the Chancellor, pursuant, he said, to the verbal commands he had received from the King, to send the Great Seal to Windsor by Adam de Osgodebey,—which was accordingly done,—and it remained with the King till the 20th of the same month, when it was again restored to the Chancellor in London. In this interval, by the personal command of the King, was sealed the patent appointing Gaveston Lieutenant of Ireland, contrary to the sentence pronounced against him in Parliament.[1]

In May, 1310, John de Langton was obliged to yield to the storm raging against him and the favorite. A petition was presented in Parliament, which, being backed by an armed force, was equivalent to a command, praying that Edward would dismiss his ministers, and devolve on a junto the whole authority of the Crown, with power, for a limited time, to enact ordinances for the government of the kingdom and the regulation of the royal household.

Gaveston was banished, and Langton, resigning the Great Seal, retired to his bishopric.[2] He did not again mix with the factious disputes which long continued to convulse the kingdom. He seems to have been a man unscrupulous as to the means by which he reached power, but, as far he thought consistent with the safety of his tenure of it, disposed to promote beneficial measures, and to restrain irregularities and excesses in the government. Having assisted the zeal of the first Edward for the public good, he continued, while he remained in office, to mitigate the son's evil propensities, which at last produced consequences so tragical. Lord Coke relates the following anecdote, to show that "this Lord Chancellor of England was of a great spirit, and feared not the face of great men in that dangerous time to do that which he ought. Earl Warren, though married to the King's niece, carried off the Countess of Lancaster from her husband to his castle

---

[1] See Mem. in Cl. R. 1 Ed. 2, which the Chancellor is supposed to have entered to show that he was not to be considered answerable for Gaveston's appointment.
[2] May 11, 1310.

of Ryegate, in Surrey, and there lived with her in open advoutry. Langton, as Bishop of Chichester, according to his office and duty, called the said Earle Warren in question for the said shameful offense, and by ecclesiastical censure excommunicated him for the same; in revenge whereof, the Earle adding a new offense to the old, came with many of his followers, weaponed for the purpose, towards the Bishop to lay violent hands upon him; but the Bishop being well attended with gentlemen and other his household servants issued out, and not only manfully defended himself against that barbarous attempt, but valiantly overcame the Earle, and laid him and his gallants in prison: *armaque in armatos sumere jura sinunt.*"[1]

For some time after Langton's resignation of the Great Seal there was great difficulty as to the disposal of it. As the person holding it necessarily came so much into the royal presence, even the Barons felt a delicacy in putting it into the hands of any one personally obnoxious to the King. For about two months it remained in the custody of Ingelard de Warlegh,[2] with power merely to seal writs with it in the presence and with the concurreuce of three persons specified; and then Osgodebey, the Master of the Rolls, held it for a short time under similar restrictions.[3]

At last, on the 6th of July, a compromise took place, and WALTER REYNOLDS was declared Chancellor,[4] he having on the occasion advanced £1000, said to have been lent to the King, but probably divided between the King and the Barons.

Reynolds, by his parts and address, had gained the favor of that discerning prince, Edward I., who made him tutor to his son, a Privy Councillor, and Bishop of Worcester. He cannot be held accountable for the defective character or conduct of his royal pupil, who, though he might have been expected to have inherited great talents from both his parents, was by nature of an understanding narrow, frivolous, and incapable of cultivation or correction. Edward was nevertheless attached to his preceptor, in spite

---

[1] 2 Inst 574. He died 9th July, 1337, and he was buried in the cathedral of Chichester, under the great south window, which remains to this day a monument of his taste as well as of his magnificence.

[2] Rot. Cl. 4 Ed. 2, m. 6.

[3] Rot. Cl. 4 Ed. 2, m. 26.

[4] Ibid.

of profiting so little by his tuition, and was much gratified by the forbearance of the Barons in allowing one he loved to hold the office which was substantially in their gift.

Reynolds continued Chancellor till the 28th of September, 1311, having twice during that time given the Seal to be kept by Osgodebey, the Master of the Rolls; once when he attended the King to Berwick-upon-Tweed, and the second time when he went to assist at a general council of the Western church held at Vienne, in Dauphiny. Soon after his return he resigned the office of Chancellor, or, more properly, he was driven from it by the dispute between the Kings and the Barons, which now raged with more violence than ever. Edward had the indiscretion to recall Gaveston, and again to load him with favors at court. This proceeding excited such general disgust, that the King was compelled to agree to an act, to confer permanently upon a committee of Parliament the power of appointing to all the great offices of state;—and Gaveston being taken prisoner, his head was struck off by the hand of the executioner.

While these things were going on, the Barons, for expediting judicial business, arranged that the Great Seal should remain with the Master of the Rolls. Twice the King got possession of it; but he was obliged to return it to the same custody.

The unpopular favorite being put to death, the Barons became more moderate, and there was a reaction in the nation against a parliamentary commission for carrying on the government, which, in experience, had always been found to aggravate the confusion whence it had arisen.

A settlement accordingly took place, upon the understanding that there should not, for the present, be a Chancellor, but that the King should appoint a Keeper to do all the duties of the office, under the superintendence of three persons, to be named by the Barons.

Walter Reynolds was the new Keeper,[1] and he is a singular instance of a person holding the Great Seal with this title after having held it as "Chancellor," while there are very many instances of a person holding it as "Chancellor" after having held it as "Keeper."

Reynolds was translated from Worcester to the see of Canterbury, by Papal permission, on the 1st of October,

[1] Rot. Cl. 6 Ed. 2, m. 26.

1313;[1] but he had a keen controversy for this dignity with Thomas Cobham, Dean of Salisbury. He at last prevailed, and, in April, 1314, he was installed in the archbishopric with extraordinary magnificence. He still continued Keeper, with the same restrictions; the Great Seal being deposited in a purse, under the seals of the superintendents, and, after each day's sealing, restored to the purse in their presence.

Intestine feuds now ceased for a time, that the nation might take vengeance on the Scots, who not only had reconquered their own country, but, under Robert Bruce, had made successful inroads into England, enriching themselves by the plunder of the northern counties. The Barons, forgetting their paltry differences about the appointment of the Chancellor, rallied round Edward, and he marched to the frontier with a well-equipped army, amounting to a hundred thousand men. It is well known that this expedition ended in the fatal battle of Bannockburn, the greatest defeat which England had sustained since the Norman conquest.

According to the English authorities, which I think may be relied upon, no one had attended the King to the North as Chancellor or Keeper; but Hume of Goldscroft, in his "History of Scotland and of the House of Douglas," relates that the Lord Keeper was among the slain, and that the Great Seal being taken as a trophy of the victory, was restored to the English by Robert Bruce.[2] Reynolds, who had probably remained, with the Great

[1] In December, 1313, Edward went on a pilgrimage to a statue of Our Lady at Boulogne, still famous. During his absence the Great Seal remained in the custody of the Archbishop elect.—R. Cl. 7 Ed. 2.

[2] "The English king did bring into the field all that he was able to make, not only of English, but of his beyond-sea dominions; neither of those that were his own subjects only, but he was also aided and assisted by his friends and confederates in Flanders, Holland, Zealand, Brabant, Picardy, Gascony, Normandy, Guienne, Bullonois, and Bourdeaux; of these and of his own countrymen he had in all 150,000, intending to have exterminated the whole nation of Scots, with so confident a presumption of victory, that he brought with him a Carmelite friar (a poet according to the time) to commit his triumph to writing. He was defeated by 30,000, or 35,000 at the most (as all agree), and that in a plain and open field, where there was slain of his men 50,000." "The Carmelite also changed his note, singing their victory whose overthrow he came to set forth, and chanting their discomfiture whose praises he was hired to proclaim. He thus began his ditty :—

'De planctu cudo metrum cum carmine nudo,
Risum detrudo, dum tali themate ludo.'"

Seal, in London, went to York to be present at the Parliament, or rather Council of the prelates and nobility, which Edward called on his arrival there, after his precipitate flight. However, the nation was in such consternation from their late calamity, that no business was conducted at this assembly except the exchange of the wife of Robert Bruce against some English prisoners of war.

Reynolds did not long retain the Great Seal after his return to the South, having finally resigned it on the 26th of September, 1314.

He is much blamed for his subsequent conduct. He now took part with the court of Rome in its encroachments on the prerogatives of the Crown, and he obtained no fewer than eight bulls from the Pope, conferring upon himself privileges and jurisdictions of a novel and invidious nature. But what was much worse, he took part against the King, his former pupil, who had treated him with so much personal kindness, and had exalted him to his present height of greatness. By abetting the profligate Queen and her associates, he was supposed to have hurried the unhappy Edward to a prison and a grave.

The Ex-Chancellor became more superstitious as he became more unprincipled, and he is said to have died of fear, because the Pope had threatened him with spiritual censures for having somewhat irregularly consecrated Berkeley, Bishop of Exeter, with a view to please the Queen and her favorite.

While he was Chancellor there was published an ordinance by the King relating to the Chapel at Windsor, which shows that the Chancellor for the time being was still considered chief of the Chapel Royal, and bound to see that it was provided with proper ornaments.[1]

On his resignation of the Great Seal he was succeeded by JOHN DE SANDALE, then Treasurer of the Exchequer,

---

Among the slain he enumerates "Sir Robert Northbrooke (Lord Keeper of the Broad Seal) and Sir Ralph Mortimer, who had married the king's sister." He adds, " Mortimer was dimitted ransome free, and obtained the King's Broad Seal at Bruce's hands."—pp. 32-35.

[1] "Et le Chaunceler de Roy, qui quil soit, pur coe quil est chef de la Chapele nostre Seignour le Roy face chescun an un tour illoeges sil puit, pur congie de nostre Seignour le Roy pur veer que la dite Chapele (i.e. de Wyndesor) soit servie des ornementz," &c.—Ryl. Append. ad Plac, P. p. 535. Anno 6 Ed. 2.

who was declared Chancellor,[1] and held the office near four years. He had the good luck to be speedily promoted to the Bishopric of Winchester.

He was present at the parliament held at Lincoln on the 28th of January, 1315, and superintended the judicial business there transacted—when the Justices of both Benches brought in briefs of such matters as were properly determinable in parliament;[2] but the King himself declared the cause of the summons to be for advice and assistance against the Scots.

During almost the whole time he was Chancellor, there were concurrently Keepers of the Great Seal, whether to assist or control him may be doubtful. In the entries in the Rolls, a reason is generally assigned for the appointment of these Keepers,—as that the Chancellor was going to the Earl of Lancaster at Kenilworth on the King's business,—or was absent from Court about his election to his diocese,—or was employed on a foreign mission for the King.

De Sandale at last incurred the displeasure of Hugh le Despenser, the new favorite, and was removed from the office of Chancellor on the 11th of June, 1318. He lived in obscurity about two years, and fortunately died before the transactions occurred which brought such a reproach on the memory of his predecessor.

Little is to be found respecting his character, conduct, or tastes, except that he appears to have been somewhat of an epicure. In the 10th year of the King's reign (1316), he sent two famous poulterers, Adam Fitz-Rupert and Thomas de Duston, into divers parts of the realm to pur-

[1] Rot. Cl. 7 Ed. 2, m. 7.
[2] An order was made by the Lords that the Chancellor and the other judges should lay before parliament the cases pending in their courts, which they cannot decide without parliament.—Rolls, i. 350. By another order made at this parliament, we have great light thrown upon the history of proxies in the House of Lords. "Et injunctum fuit Johi. de Sandale, Cancellar. quod ipse reciperet procuratoria et excusationes Prelatorum et aliorum summonitorum ad dictum parliamentum et non venientium et quod ipse ac alii quos Dns. Rex sibi associaret, ea examinaret et excusationes sufficientes allocarent, dum tamen, excusantes Procuratores herent sufficientes: et quod nomina non venientium nec se excusantium nec·procuratores destinantium Dno. Regi referrent, ita quod ipse inde posset pcipere quod deberet."—Rolls, v. 2, p. 350. Other entries show that the attendance of peers in early times was very strictly enforced, and that all who were absent without the king's license were fined. But the king gave such as he favored leave to attend by a proxy, who was at first a stranger, and afterwards another peer.

chase delicate poultry for his table, and he fortified them
with letters patent of intendance and safe conduct under
the Great Seal, for which he obtained a warrant under
the King's sign-manual.[1]

His successor was JOHN DE HOTHAM, who rose to the
dignity of Chancellor by the successive steps of King's
Chaplain, Provost of Queen's College, Oxford, Chancellor
of that University, Chancellor of the Exchequer, and
Bishop of Ely. He is said to have been a prudent and
pious man, but of no learning; yet he now held the office
of Chancellor till the beginning of the year 1320, and
he was restored to it at the commencement of the succeeding reign.

During his first Chancellorship he presided at a parliament held at York, where the Earl of Lancaster, at the
head of a military force, dictated all the laws that were
passed. One of these was, "that the Chancellor should
make a charter under the Great Seal, absolute and without condition, pardoning the Earl of Lancaster himself,
and all such as he should by his letters name to the Chancellor, of all treasons against the King, and other crimes
of which they might at any time hitherto have been
guilty." Here likewise a parliamentary sanction was
given to an indenture which the King had been forced to
sign, providing that two Bishops, one Earl, one Baron,
named by parliament, and one Baron or Banneret of the
family of the Earl of Lancaster, acting in his name,
should be present and remain with the King, to deliberate with and advise him in due manner,—and it was
ordered that this indenture should be carried by the
Chancellor to the Chancery, and enrolled there.[2]

While De Hotham continued Chancellor, it is difficult
to say whether he was to be considered the minister of
the King or of the Earl of Lancaster. There are three
different entries in the Close Roll of his going from court,

---

[1] Adam filius Roberti et Thomas de Duston, Prelatarii venerabilis Patris
J. Wyntoniensis Episcopi Cancellarii Regis, quos idem Cancellarius ad pre-
letriam pro sustentatione ipsius Cancellarii et Clericorum Regis de eadem
Cancellaria pro denariis ipsius Cancellarii emendam et providendam ad
diversas partes regni mittat, habent literas Regis omnibus ballivis et fidelibus
suis, quod eisdem preletariis in præmissis intendentes sint et respondentes
quociens et quando, &c., per unum annum duraturas. T. R. apud Westm
primo die Junii,—Pat. 10 Ed. 2, part ii. m. 10.

[2] 1 Parl. Hist. 65.

being sent by the King to the Earl of Lancaster, and of the appointment of Keepers of the Great Seal in his absence; but the object of these missions must have been to receive the commands of the haughty Baron, who was now master of the kingdom.

A new parliament was held in the beginning of 1320, the Earl of Lancaster still maintaining his ascendency,— when De Hotham, disgusted with the irksomeness of his position, or frightened by the perils that were thickening round all who were connected with the Court, resigned his office of Chancellor,[1] and withdrew from secular affairs till Edward III. was placed on the throne.

The new Chancellor was JOHN DE SALMON, Bishop of Norwich,[2] who is stated in the Close Roll to have been "made in full parliament," meaning, I presume, by the body of Barons, on the recommendation of the Earl of Lancaster,— the authority of the committee, which he ruled by his proxy, being suspended while parliament was sitting,—although in ordinary times a creation in "full parliament" only means an exercise of the royal pregogative in the presence of the three estates of the realm, for the sake of greater solemnity, and to do honor to the object of the royal favor.

There was now an interval of tranquillity in England, and the Chancellor went to France with the King, who was summoned to do homage for the duchy of Aquitaine. The Great Seal was not carried abroad with the King, as had been usual, but was ordered to be kept close in some secure place during his absence, and the little seal which had been before used when the King was absent in France, was to be again used in England while he remained abroad. The Chancellor sealed up the Great Seal and delivered it to the King, and gave the little seal to the Master of the Rolls, to be assisted by Robert de Bardeley

---

[1] 23 Jan. 1320.
[2] Rot. Claus. 13 Ed. 2, m. 9. It is there stated that the King had commanded Hotham not to execute any mandate under the Great Seal, in consequence of the messages of any person of whatever rank who might come to him in his Majesty's name, unless he had verbally, or under the Privy Seal, declared to him his pleasure thereupon; that on the 23rd of January, 1320, the Chancellor delivered the Great Seal to the King at York, who with his own hands placed it at the head of his bed, but subsequently intrusted it to three clerks in Chancery, and on the following day the Bishop of Norwich, who had been appointed Chancellor, in full parliament received it from the King.

and William de Clyff. He returned to England in about two months, when the Great Seal was restored to him.

He was soon after absent from court visiting his diocese, and he made a journey to the marshes of Scotland on a public embassy, on which occasions, by his appointment, the Master of the Rolls held the Great Seal and acted for him; but in the end of July, 1321, being grievously indisposed, he surrendered the Great Seal to the King, that his Majesty might dispose of it as to him should seem good. The King forthwith sent it by Richard Camel, his Chamberlain, to the Queen, with directions that it should remain in her custody, and that she should deliver it daily to the Master of the Rolls, who should return it to her after each day's sealing. Immedietely on the Queen's receiving it, she delivered it to the Lady Elizabeth de Montibus, lady of her bed-chamber, to be enclosed in a casket; and every day on which the seal was required for use, the Master of the Rolls had it from the hands of the Queen, or the Lady Elizabeth, and returned it to them to be placed in the casket when the sealing was finished.[1] But I cannot fairly include Queen Isabella more than the Lady Elizabeth de Montibus in my list of "Keepers," whose lives are to be written, as, unlike Queen Eleanor's, her functions were merely ministerial; she had no commission, and she was not intrusted with any portion of judicial power. I am not permitted, therefore, to attempt to enliven my tedious narrative by entering into the details of her character or her actions—her spirit, her enterprise, her deadly antipathies, her guilty loves, her share in her husband's murder, or her punishment by her heroic son.

On the 5th of November the Queen restored the Great Seal to the King, and it remained a considerable time in his own keeping; his Majesty entrusting it daily to persons who were to use it, and receiving it back from them after each day's sealing. At the end of some months De Salmon, who was still considered Chancellor, having recovered his health, returned to Court and resumed the discharge of his duties.

He now took a decided part against the Earl of Lancaster, who, become generally odious by his violent and arbitrary conduct, had raised the standard of revolt.

[1] Cl. Roll. 15 Ed. 2.

The King, acting by the Chancellor's advice, displayed more energy and conduct at this juncture than during any other part of his reign. Suddenly collecting an army, he marched against the rebels, took their castles, dispersed their forces, got possession of the person of Lancaster, tried him by a court-martial, and ordered him to be led to instant execution.

But the Chancellor in vain attempted to prevail on Edward to begin a new plan of government, on the principle of an impartial administration of justice to all his subjects. The banished Spensers were recalled and loaded with new favors. Not only were the forfeitures of the Lancastrian party bestowed upon these minions, but to enrich them, royalist barons were stripped of manors inherited from a long line of ancestors, and the insolence of the younger Spenser was inflamed by success to a pitch insupportable to all who approached him.

The Chancellor, although he had not opposed the recall of the Spensers, whose banishment had taken place under an arbitrary ordinance of the Barons, in which neither the Prelates nor the Commons had concurred, strenuously resisted the influence they were now acquiring, and their illegal acts in the King's name. Finding his resistance ineffectual, he resolved to retire from political life, and his resignation was hastened by a severe recurrence of his former malady. He finally resigned the Great Seal on the 5th of June, 1323.[1] He died on the 6th of July, 1325, without having violated his purpose to spend the rest of his days in retirement. He is chiefly celebrated by his biographers for having built the hall and chapel of the episcopal palace at Norwich, and for having settled a maintenance for four priests there to pray for the pardon of his sins.

The Spensers now for a long time carried everything their own way without the slightest check to their authority, and they appointed for Chancellor one on whose fidelity, pliancy, and zeal they entirely relied, ROBERT DE BALDOCK, Archdeacon of Middlesex.

Dreadful storms were impending, but such tranquillity prevailed for a brief space as allowed the usual amusements of the King to proceed. It is related that the Court being at Windsor, and field sports going on in

[1] Rot. Cl. 17 Ed. 2, m. 39.

which the new Chancellor did not take much delight, he obtained leave from the King to return home for more suitable recreation. Impatient to escape, he delivered the Great Seal to the King, while his Majesty was engaged in hunting; and when the chase was over, it was placed in the custody of William de Ayremynne, then Keeper of the Privy Seal.[1] From the 16th of November till the 12th of December the Chancellor was absent on a journey to York to treat with the Scots, during which time the Great Seal was in the keeping of Richard de Ayremynne, who had succeeded his brother William as Master of the Rolls.[2]

Soon after his return the troubles began which terminated fatally for him as well as his royal master. Those troubles were mainly caused by the misconduct of Lord Chancellor Baldock, who seems to have been a very profligate man, and to have been unscrupulous in perverting the rules of justice, regardless of public opinion, and reckless as to consequences, so long as he gratified the royal favorites. It was his maladministration which made the nation blind to the enormity of the conduct of the Queen, now combined with Mortimer, her paramour, against the King her husband.

When she landed in Suffolk with her small army from Holland, three princes of the blood, the Earls of Kent, Norfolk, and Leicester, joined her, with all their followers. Three Prelates, the Bishops of Ely, Lincoln, and Hereford, brought her both the force of their vassals, and the authority of their character. She rallied all ranks round her standard by the declaration "that the sole purpose of her enterprise was to free the King and kingdom from the tyranny of the Spensers, and above all of their creature Lord Chancellor Baldock!"

Edward, after ineffectually trying to rouse the citizens of London to some sense of duty, having departed for the West, where he vainly hoped to meet with a better reception, the rage of the populace broke out without control against him and his ministers. Having seized the Bishop of Exeter, a loyal prelate, as he was passing through the streets,—beheaded him, and thrown his body into the river Thames,—they made themselves masters of the Tower, in the hope of there finding the Chancellor,

[1] Rot. Cl. 18 Ed. 2, m. 38.   [2] Rot. Cl. 18 Ed. 2, m. 26.

whom they threatened with a similar fate; but he had fled to the King, carrying the Great Seal along with him.

Before long Edward was a prisoner in Kenilworth Castle, and the two Spensers and Lord Chancellor Baldock fell into the hands of the insurgents. Spenser, the father, without form of trial, was immediately condemned to death by the rebellious Barons, and hanged on a gibbet, his head being afterwards set on a pole, and exposed to the insults of the populace. The younger Spenser, the great favorite of the King and patron of Baldock, was arraigned before Sir William Trussel, a special Justiciar, and without witness or proof of any sort, sentence of death was instantly pronounced upon him. The learned Judge's address to this prisoner is equally bitter against the Chancellor, and shows how he would have been dealt with had he been a layman:—

"Hugh, your father, Robert Baldock, and other false traitors your adherents, taking upon you royal power, you caused the King to withdraw himself, and carried him out of the realm, to the danger of his body and dishonor to him and his people, feloniously taking with you the treasure of the realm, contrary to the Great Charter. Hugh, all the good people of the kingdom, great and small, rich and poor, by common consent do award that you are found as a thief, and therefore shall be hanged, and are found as a traitor, and therefore shall be drawn and quartered; and for that you have been outlawed by the King and by common consent, and returned to the Court without warrant, you shall be beheaded; and for that you abetted and procured discord between King and Queen, and others of the realm, you shall be embowelled and your bowels burnt; and so go to your judgment, attainted, wicked traitor."[1]

Baldock being a priest, he could not with safety be so suddenly despatched; but he was sent to the Bishop of Hereford's palace in London, and the populace were informed of his arrival, and reminded of his misdeeds. As his relentless enemies foresaw, the palace was broken open by a riotous mob,—he was seized, and, after many indignities, thrown into Newgate,—where he soon after expired from the cruel usage he had sustained. There seems a considerable resemblance between his fate and that of his

[1] 1 St. Tr. 36.

successor, Lord Chancellor Jeffreys, at a distance of 360 years; but, though not chargeable with the same degree of cruelty, his systematic perversion of justice had excited a still greater degree of resentment against him, or the rage of the people would have given way to their reverence for the sacerdotal character. He had reached no higher dignity in the Church than Archdeacon of Middlesex. When he received the Great Seal a few months before, he no doubt confidently expected that he should long hold it, and that it would lead to the primacy,

On the 20th of October, 1326, the King having gone away with Hugh le Despenser to Ireland, and left the realm without any government, the prelates, earls, barons, and knights assembled at Bristol, and chose Edward, the King's son, Custos of the kingdom whilst his father continued absent. On the same day the Prince assumed the government, and issued the necessary legal proceeedings under his privy seal, "because he had no other seal for the purpose."

When the King returned from Ireland he found himself already dethroned. The Queen was now in the enjoyment of supreme power. She kept her husband in close confinement, hypocritically pretending to lament his misfortunes. She pretended to associate the Prince her son with herself in the government; and she contrived to get the Great Seal into her possession,—which considerably facilitated her proceedings, for less respect was paid by the multitude to the privy seal, which she had hitherto used.

The Bishop of Hereford was sent to the King at Kenilworth, with a deceitful message, to request that he would give such directions respecting the Great Seal as were necessary for the conservation of the peace, and the due administration of justice. The King, without friend or adviser, said he would send the Seal to his Queen and son, not only for these purposes, but likewise for matters of grace. He then handed the Great Seal to Sir William le Blount, who on the 30th of November, delivered it to the Queen and the Prince; but the Queen had the uncontrolled dominion over it. She pretended to hand it over to Ayremynne, the Master of the Rolls, as Keeper, and she employed it to summon a parliament at Westminster, in her husband's name, for the purpose of deposing him.

According to the tenor of the writs under the Great Seal, the parliament was to be held before the King, if he should be present; and if not, before Isabel, the Queen-consort, and Edward, the King's son.

The sympathies of the people beginning to be excited in favor of the King, and her scandalous commerce with Mortimer being published to the world, she was under some apprehension of a counter-revolution; but she uttered a proclamation setting forth the misgovernment of the Spensers and the late Lord Chancellor Baldock, to the great injury of Holy Church and the dishonor of the King and his heirs, and she gathered a strong army around her to overawe the metropolis.

At the parliament which met on the 7th of January, 1327, no Chancellor was present. Adam de Orleton, Bishop of Hereford, acted as Prolocutor, and put the memorable question to the assembled Lords and Commons,—"Whether King Edward the father, or his son Edward, should reign over them?"

The articles against the King contained no specific charge of misrule to give any color to the proposed deposition, and no proof was adduced in support of them. Nevertheless, no one ventured to raise a voice in his behalf; and a deputation sent to Kenilworth extorted from him a resignation of the Crown. Then Sir William Trussel, of whose oratory we have had a specimen, in the name of the whole Parliament, renounced their allegiance in the following form:

"I, William Trussel, procurator of the prelates, earls, and barons, and other people in my procuracy named, having for this full and sufficient power, do surrender and deliver up to you, Edward, heretofore King of England, the homage and fealty of the persons in my procuracy named, &c.; and do make this protestation in the name of all those that will not, for the future, be in your fealty or allegiance, nor claim to hold any thing of you as King, but account you as a private person, without any manner of royal dignity."

On the 20th of January, 1327, the deposition of Edward II. being completed, Edward III., then a youth of fourteen years of age, was proclaimed King, and was supposed to begin his reign, although it was not till the 21st of September following that in Berkeley Castle, were heard the agonizing shrieks caused by the horrid deed of Gournay and Montravers.

Without any formal appointment as Chancellor, after the death of Baldock, ADAM DE ORLETON, Bishop of Hereford, must be considered as having acted in that capacity under the Queen. He is famous not only for having conducted the proceedings in parliament on the deposition of Edward, but for being supposed to have counseled his murder by the equivocal line which he composed and sent to his keepers,

"Edwardum occidere nolite timere ;—bonum est,"

although he contended that his words, by a proper punctuation or pause, conveyed a strong injunction against regicide.[1]

No important change was introduced into the law during the reign of Edward II., but the institutions of his father were steadily maintained by his successive Chancellors, and, having stood the shock of such convulsions, might now be considered permanently established for the administration of justice in England. It has been suggested that the office of Master of the Rolls, so nearly connected with that of Chancellor, was now created, and that William de Ayremynne was the first who bore that title;[2] but John de Langton had been called "Custos Rotulorum Cancellariæ Domini Regis."[3] Adam de Osgodebey is expressly stated to have filled the office in the same reign; and as there were clerks in the Chancery from the most remote antiquity to assist the Chancellor, who were afterwards denominated "Masters in Chancery," I have little doubt that the senior or chief of them had for ages before had the particular care of the records of the Court, and being so often intrusted with the custody of the Seal in the Chancellor's absence, had gradually been permitted to act as his deputy.

Towards the conclusion of this reign, under Lord Chancellor Baldock, there were heavy complaints in parliament of the delays of justice, and that when petitions for redress were presented to parliament, they were sometimes referred to the King and sometimes to the Chancellor, without any thing being ever done upon them

[1] Edwardum occidere nolite ;—timere bonum est.
[2] Reeve's Hist. of the Law, vol. ii. p. 362.
[3] See Discourse on Office of M. R.
[4] Et auxint Sire firent vos liges gentz que par la ou ils ont hote leur avant

From petitions and answers lately discovered, it appears that during this reign the jurisdiction of the Court of Chancery was considerably extended, and the "Consuetudo Cancellariæ" is often familiarly mentioned. We find petitions referred to the Chancellor in his Court, either separately or in conjunction with the King's Justices or the King's Sergeants—on disputes respecting the wardship of infants, partition, dower, rent-charges, tithes, and goods of felons. The Chancellor was in full possession of his jurisdiction over charities, and he superintended the conduct of coroners. Mere wrongs, such as malicious prosecutions and trespasses to personal property, are sometimes the subject of proceedings before him; but I apprehend that those were cases where, from powerful combinations and confederacies, redress could not be obtained in the courts of common law.

There was now and during some succeeding reigns the exercise of a prerogative of the Crown vested in the Court of Chancery, which we should have expected to find reserved for the King's executive government, viz., the power of granting letters of marque and reprisals against the subjects of a foreign state that refused to render justice to the subjects of the Crown of England.[1] Thus, in 2 Edward II., certain English merchants plundered by Flemish pirates, not obtaining redress from the Earl of Flanders, they petitioned the King, and they were referred by him the Court of Chancery, there to pursue their remedy as was accustomed in in similar cases.[2] Again, in the 8th year of this reign, Adam le Clerk, having complained that his ship and merchandise had been captured and carried into the town of Perth in Scotland, it is ordered that he should apply to the Chancellor, and that justice should be done to him according to the custom of the Chancery.[3]

lour petitions au diverses parliamentz des diverses grievances et les unes sont ajournes devant le Roi, et les autres devant le Chancellier dount nul issue n'est fait q'il plaise a vautre haute seignurie comander remedie. Resp. Il plest au Roi.—Par. Rol. 19 Ed. 2, i. 430.

[1] It appears from Grotius and Puffendorf, that down to their time letters of reprisal were considered rather in the nature of a private remedy, and did not by any means amount to war between two nations. The capture was rather in the nature of a security to obtain justice.

[2] Resp. "Adeant Cancellarium et perquirant remedium sicut consuevit fieri in consimilibus casibus, secundum formam petitionis."

[3] Resp. "Sequatur in Cancell. et ostendat processum inde habitum et literas testimon. si quas habeat de defen. exhibitionis justitiæ et tunc sequx'ur

Now begins the series of reports of cases decided in the superior courts, the grand repertory of law in England; but the "Year Books" are now rather curious for their antiquity than valuable for their contents, being chiefly the notes taken by the reporters in Court, without being properly digested or revised.

In the 9th year of the King, while Sandale was Chancellor, was passed a statute, still yearly acted upon, by which it was enacted that Sheriffs who were formerly chosen by the freeholders, should be proposed by the Chancellor and Judges on the morrow of St. Martin, and the power of appointing them was vested in the Crown.[1]

At the close of the reign, at the Parliament held under Lord Chancellor Baldock, the statute "De Prerogativa Regis" was passed, giving to the King the profits of the lands of idiots,[2] the probable foundation of the Lord Chancellor's jurisdiction in lunacy under the royal sign-manual.

The only law book imputed to this reign is the "Mirror of Justices," which, though often quoted by Lord Coke, is a wretched compilation, and shows an increasing degeneracy among English juridical writers.

The Chancellors were still all churchmen, and from this order only could good lawyers hitherto be selected; but there was now rising up a class of laymen who, devoting themselves to the study of the municipal law of England, and educated at the Hostels or Inns of Court (of which Lincoln's Inn then was, and ever has continued to be, the most eminent,[3]) were attracting public consideration and confidence, and from among whom, in the succeeding reign, Chancellors were chosen, to the great content of the nation.

secundum processum, &c., et fiat ei justitia secundum consuetudinem Cancellariæ."

[1] 9 Ed. 2, stat. 2.
[2] 17 Ed. 2, c. 8.
[3] The Society of Lincoln's Inn was founded in the commencement of this reign, under the patronage of William Earl of Lincoln, who, for the accommodation of the members, gave up to them his hostel, which he held under the Bishops of Chichester.

CHAPTER XIII.

CHANCELLORS AND KEEPERS OF THE GREAT SEAL FROM THE COMMENCEMENT OF THE REIGN OF EDWARD III. TILL THE APPOINTMENT OF SIR ROBERT BOURCHIER, THE FIRST LAY LORD CHANCELLOR.

THE Parliament which continued irregularly to sit under writs issued in the name of Edward II., commenced the new reign by the appointment of a council of regency, consisting of twelve persons—five prelates and seven temporal peers—with the Earl of Lancaster as President or Protector;—and John de Hotham, Bishop of Ely, was called from his retreat to be made Chancellor. But he only consented to hold the office till a settlement of the kingdom should take place; and he finally resigned it on the 1st of March following.

In this interval acts of parliament were passed indemnifying the Queen and her partisans for all they had done, and enabling them to carry on the government in the name of the young King. As yet all went smoothly, for he was not of competent age to understand the wrongs done to his father, his mother's shame, or the usurpation of his own rights.

Hotham joyfully returned to his diocese, where he occupied himself in repairing and ornamenting the cathedral, till he was struck with the palsy. After being bedridden two years, he died in 1336. He is said to have been pious, and naturally shrewd, though with little knowledge acquired from books. He is gratefully remembered by his successors in the see of Ely for the princely munificence with which he enriched it.

Till the 12th of May the Great Seal remained in the keeping of Henry de Clyff, Master of the Rolls; and on that day it was delivered to HENRY DE BURGHERSH, or BURWASH, as Chancellor.[1] He was of noble birth, and nephew of Bartholomew de Badislimer, Baron of Leeds, a man of great power and fame in the reign of Edward II. Having been educated at Oxford,—in 1320, while yet a young man, he obtained, through his uncle's in-

[1] Rot. Cl. 2 Ed. 3. m. 26.

terest, the rich bishopric of Lincoln. He soon after quarreled with the King, and the temporalities of his see were sequestered. They were restored in 1324, and he was again taken into favor at court. But he subsequently took the Queen's part against her husband, and was active in bringing about the ruin of this unhappy prince. Along with the other chief conspirators, he was promoted at the commencement of the new reign, and enjoyed power till the young King discovered their plots and avenged the memory of his father.

The Great Seal of Edward II., which had likewise been that of Edward I., continued to be used till the 5th day of October, 1327, when a new Great Seal, with the effigies and style of Edward III., was put into the hands of the Chancellor.[1]

The business of the parliament being finished, he accompanied the Queen-mother to Berwick. During his absence the Seal was left with the Master of the Rolls, and it was restored to him on his return to court. He went abroad with the King on the 26th of May, 1329, and returned on the 11th of June following, still confident of continuing prosperity.

But the termination of his official carreer was at hand. Mortimer, the paramour of Isabella, had quarreled with the Earl of Lancaster and the princes of the blood, and had made a victim of the Earl of Kent, the King's uncle. For a short time Mortimer enjoyed a sort of dictatorship. He threw the Earl of Lancaster into prison, and prosecuted many of the prelates and nobility. The immense fortunes of the Spensers and their adherents were mostly converted to his own use. He affected a state and dignity not inferior to the royal. His power became formidable

---

[1] Rot. Cl. 1 Ed. 3, m. 11. "When the King dies, the Great Seal of the lost King continues the Great Seal of England till another be made and delivered. Edward III., who began his reign 25th of January, on the 3rd of October following directed a proclamation to all the sheriffs of England, signifying that he had made a new Great Seal, sent them an impression of the new Seal in wax, and commanded them, after the 4th of October, to receive no writs but under the new Seal. On the 4th of October, being Sunday, the Bishop of Ely, Chancellor, producing the new Seal, declares the King's pleasure that it should be from thenceforth used. The Monday after the old Seal is broken, *præcipiente rege*, and the pieces delivered to the SPIGURNEL."— 1 *Hale's Pleas of the Crown*, 176. The *Spigurnal* was an officer whose place was to seal the King's writs.—*Camb. Rem.* 26.

to every one, and all parties, forgetting past animosities, conspired in a wish for his overthrow.

Edward, now in his 18th year, feeling himself capable of governing, repined at his insignificance, and resolved to free himself from the fetters of this insolent minister. By an extraordinary combination of courage and dexterity on the part of Mortimer's enemies, the minion was seized in the castle of Nottingham, in an apartment adjoining the Queen-dowager's, at a moment when he thought himself absolute and permanent master of the kingdom.

A parliament was immediately summoned, before which he was accused of having procured the death of the late King, and of various other crimes, and upon the supposed notoriety of the facts,—without hearing his answer, or examining a witness, he was convicted and executed.

Instead of the Chancellor, the young King himself is said to have made a speech at the opening of this parliament, complaining much of the conduct of the Queen and Mortimer, and intimating that, with the consent of his subjects, he designed to take the reins of government into his own hands.[1]

Burghersh being an ecclesiastic, was safe from corporal punishment, but he was deprived of the Great Seal,[2] and on the day before Mortimer's execution it was intrusted to JOHN DE STRATFORD,[3] Bishop of Winchester, by whose advice the young King had acted in bringing about this revolution. The Ex-Chancellor died in exile at Ghent about ten years after. It is said "that he was a covetous man, and easily abused his power to the oppressing of his neighbors."[4]

The new Chancellor was a native of Stratford in Essex, from which place he took his name, according to the custom of the age. He and his brother Robert, of whom we shall have to speak very soon, were instances then not

---

[1] Parl. Hist. 83.
[2] One of the charges against him was the abuse of his ecclesiastical patronage. It seems the livings in the Chancellor's gift were intended as a provision for the clerks of the different courts of Justice, who were then all in orders, and that Burghersh had been in the habit of selling them or giving them to favorites; whereupon an order was made by parliament, that "the Chancellor should give the livings in his gift, rated at twenty marks and under, to the King's clerks in Chancery, the Exchequer, and the two Benches, according to usage, and to none others."—Rolls, 4 Ed. 3, vol. ii. 136.
[3] Rot. Cl. 4 Ed. 3, m. 20.   [4] See L. C. 26.

uncommon of persons of talents, enterprise, and perseverance, raising themselves from obscurity to the highest offices in the state. He studied at Oxford, and there acquired great reputation for his proficiency in the civil and canon law. It is curious to observe that the law in those times, not less than in the present, was the great avenue for new men to political advancement. In the struggle for power which was ever going on, those who were distinguished for their learning and their subtlety were found useful to the Crown, to the barons, and to the great ecclesiastics—were confidentially employed by them on occasions of difficulty, and were rewarded with ecclesiastical and temporal offices in which they had often more influence than the great hereditary nobles.[1] John de Stratford was early promoted to the deanery of Lincoln, and giving earnest of the talents which he afterwards displayed, he was promoted to the judicial office of Dean of the Arches, which has continued down to our own times to be filled by men of the greatest learning and ability. Here he showed such knowledge of the laws, and such judgment and prudence in deciding causes, that he made a Privy Councillor to Edward II., and was admitted to an important share in the government of the kingdom.

In 1323 he was sent ambassador to the Pope, then established at Avignon, to settle various points of controversy, of great delicacy, which had arisen between the Crown of England and his Holiness. It happened that at that time the Bishop of Winchester died, and the Pope, at the earnest request of the Archbishop of Canterbury, without the sanction of the King, somewhat irregularly consecrated his Excellency the English minister Bishop of the vacant see.

Baldock, then Lord Chancellor, having intended this preferment for himself, was mortally offended, and took violent steps to prevent the new Bishop from deriving any benefit from the elevation. A very severe proclamation was issued against Stratford in the name of the King, "so that none should harbor or relieve him," and the fruits of the bishopric were confiscated to the Crown.

[1] The two Stratfords, who successively held the office of Lord Chancellor in the 14th century, may aptly be compared to the two Scotts, Lord Eldon and Lord Stowell, in the 19th.

The Pope and the Archbishop, however, still befriended him, and Baldock's influence declining, he was again taken into favor and employed in several important embassies. In the last year of Edward II. he was made Lord Treasurer, and he adhered with great constancy and zeal to his unhappy master. Probably this was the reason why, when the regicides were punished and the youthful Sovereign took upon himself the government of the realm, Stratford was appointed to the office of Chancellor.

Under his advice the Queen-mother was confined to her own house at Castle-Rising; and to prevent her from again forming a party which might be formidable to the Sovereign, her revenue was reduced to £4,000 a year, so that she was never able to reinstate herself in any credit or authority.

Effective measures were taken to restore order and tranquillity throughout the realm. Writs under the Great Seal were directed to the Judges, enjoining them to administer justice without paying any regard to the arbitrary orders they might receive from any great men or officers of state. As robbers, thieves, murderers, and criminals of all kinds, had during the late convulsions multiplied to an enormous degree, and they sometimes enjoyed high protection, a promise was exacted from the Peers in parliament that they would break off all connection with such malefactors; and the ministers of justice were urged to employ the utmost diligence in discovering, pursuing, and punishing them.

There was likewise introduced about this time a great improvement in the administration of justice, by rendering the Court of Chancery stationary at Westminster. The ancient Kings of England were constantly migrating,—one principal reason for which was, that the same part of the country, even with the aid of purveyance and pre-emption, could not long support the Court and all the royal retainers, and the render in kind due to the King could be best consumed on the spot. Therefore, if he kept Christmas at Westminster, he would keep Easter at Winchester, and Pentecost at Gloucester, visiting his many palaces and manors in rotation. The Aula Regis, and afterwards the courts into which it was partitioned, were ambulatory along with him—to the great vexation of suitors. This grievance was partly corrected by MAGNA

CHARTA, which enacted that the Court of Common Pleas should be held "in a certain place,"—a corner of Westminster Hall being fixed upon for that purpose. In point of law, the Court of King's Bench and the Court of Chancery may still be held in any county of England,—"wheresoever in England the King or the Chancellor may be." Down to the commencement of the reign of Edward III., the King's Bench and the Chancery actually had continued to follow the King's person, the Chancellor and his officers being entitled to part of the purveyance made for the royal household. By 28 Edw. I., c. 5, the Lord Chancellor and the Justices of the King's Bench were ordered to follow the King, so that he might have at all times near him sages of the law able to advise him. But the two Courts were now by the King's command fixed in the places where, unless on a few extraordinary occasions, they continued to be held down to our own times, at the upper end of Westminster Hall, the King's Bench on the left hand, and the Chancery on the right, both remaining open to the Hall, and a bar being erected to keep off the multitude from pressing on the Judges.

The Chancellor, on account of his superior dignity, had placed for him a great marble table, to which there was an ascent by five or six steps, with a marble chair by the side of it. On this table writs and letters patent were sealed in the presence of the Chancellor sitting in the marble chair. Here he received and examined the petitions addressed to him. On the appointment of a new Chancellor, he was inaugurated by being placed in this chair.[1]

John de Stratford continued Chancellor under his first appointment nearly four years, during which time he appears to have been almost constantly absorbed in political business, and to have hardly ever attended personally to

---

[1] The marble table and chair are said to have been displaced when the Court was covered in from the Hall. But till the Courts were finally removed out of Westminster Hall, there were easy means of communication between the Chancery and King's Bench, which enabled Sir Thomas More to ask his father's blessing in the one Court before he took his seat in the other; and I myself remember, when a student of law, that if the Chancellor rose while the King's Bench was sitting, a curtain was drawn and the Judges saluted him.—*Orig. Jurid.*, tit. "*Chancery*." In the "Lives of Lord Clarendon, &c." published in 1712, it is said, "This marble table is *now* covered with the Courts there erected, to which there are four or five steps to go up."

the judicial duties of his office. From the 4th to the 20th of April, 1331, he was in Normandy with the King.

In the year 1331, a parliament met at Westminster, the day after Michaelmas-day. The Chancellor declared the cause of the summons, and applied himself to the prelates, earls, and barons for their advice, whether they thought it best for the King to proceed by war or by an amicable treaty with the King of France for the restitution of Aquitaine?[1] The parliament agreed to the latter as the least dangerous process, and the Chancellor, accompanied by the Bishops of Worcester and Norwich, and others, went on an embassy to the court of France for this purpose. They set sail on the 21st of November, and succeeded in preserving for a time the relations of amity between the two nations.

The Chancellor's return is not recorded, but it must have been before the 12th of March in the following year, for on that day a new parliament was opened at Westminster by a speech from him, in which he intimated that the King wished for the advice of the parliament "whether he should comply with a request from the King of France and many other kings and princes to accompany them to the Holy Land against the common enemy of Christendom?"[2] A subject of greater urgency on which the advice of parliament was asked was, "whether the King might go over to the French court to settle in person the differences between the two crowns?" Edward had begun to talk of his preposterous claim to the throne of France through his mother Isabella, and Philip de Valois had threatened to declare forfeited all the fiefs which Edward held in France, because Edward, questioning his title, had declined to do homage to him as his liege lord. It is remarkable that after the Chancellor's oration, Sir Jeffrey Scroop, by the King's command and in his presence, harangued the parliament, and enforced the topics on which the Chancellor had dwelt.[3]

The Lords and Commons objected to the expedition to the Holy Land, but consented to the proposed meeting with the French King. It is remarkable that the knights, citizens, and burgesses withdrew to a separate chamber to deliberate, and that this is the first instance of their doing so. There seemed then a probability that there might

[1] 1 Parl. Hist. 85.   [2] Ibid. 89.   [3] Ibid. 90.

have been three houses of parliament, one for each of the three estates of the realm, as there always had been in France till the memorable meeting of the States General at Versailles in 1789,—for the Lords spiritual likewise on this occasion retired to a separate chamber, and came in the first instance to a separate vote, although all the branches of the legislature were finally unanimous in the advice they gave.[1]

We may remark as we pass, that notwithstanding the jealousy afterwards displayed by the Tudor sovereigns of parliament ever interfering with the functions of the executive government, in the time of the Plantagenets nothing was more common than for the King expressly and specifically to consult parliament on questions of peace and war, and even as to the manner in which war was to be carried on. It was probably found that 10ths and 15ths were more readily voted from this seeming cordiality and confidence, and privilege had not yet acquired any independent sway by which it seemed likely ever to become formidable to prerogative.

Edward called another parliament to meet on the 9th of September, 1332, where Lord Chancellor Stratford declared, "that the cause of their meeting was about the affairs of France and the King's expedition thither, and to put an end to the success his enemies gained in those parts."[2] The Lords and Commons did each by their several petitions advise the King not then to go into France, but to use all his efforts to bring to a conclusion the war that had broke out with Scotland after the death of Robert Bruce, and the attempt of Edward Baliol on the Scottish crown. This war lasted till after the termination of John de Stratford's first Chancellorship. Such satisfaction had he given to the King up to this time, that in the beginning of 1334 he was raised to the metropolitan see of Canterbury.

Being so much occupied with political and ecclesiastical affairs while he retained the office of Chancellor, he intrusted the custody of the Great Seal successively to Robert de Stratford, his brother, to Henry de Clyff, M R., to William de Melton, Archbishop of York, and for a short time jointly to Henry de Edenstowe, Thomas de Baumburgh, and John de St. Paul, probably Masters in

[1] 1 Parl. Hist. 91.   [2] Ibid.

Chancery, and these persons sealed writs and charters, and despatched the other business of the Court. The fees of the office, as was usual when the custody of the Great Seal was thus deputed, were brought to the credit of the absent Chancellor.[1]

On the 28th of September, 1334, Archbishop Stratford ceased to be Chancellor (whether from any quarrel with the King we are not informed), and the office was conferred on RICHARD DE BURY, Bishop of Durham,[2] one of the most eminent scholars and wits who cast a lustre on the reign of Edward III., and made it distinguished for literature as well as for military glory. From a most interesting book written by this estimable man, which is a sort of autobiography, his "PHILOBIBLON," we are made familiarly acquainted with his history, his habits, and his character.

He was born in the year 1287, in the house of his father, near Bury St. Edmunds.[3] Although the son of Sir Richard de Angraville, of an ancient knightly family, he, according to the custom of the age, took his name from the place of his birth. Having lost his father when very young, he was educated by his maternal uncle, a priest descended from the noble house of Willoughby. He studied at Oxford, where he gained great distinction from his proficiency both in philosophy and divinity, and was eminent at once for the brilliancy of his conversation and the sanctity of his life.

In the work referred to, which was the amusement of his old age, he gives a delightful picture of his college days, showing the enthusiasm with which he had sought improvement.[4] "From an early age we attached ourselves with most exquisite solicitude to the society of

---

[1] Among these was a very liberal supply of wine from the King's vineyards in Gascony. In the Close Roll, 3 Ed. 3, we find that the following memorandum respecting what was to be done by the customer of Southampton:—
"Quod de vino blanco Regis liberan, sex dolia et quatuor pipæ." The few bottles of Constantia till very lately given by the Crown to the Chancellor and the other great officers of state may be considered the last remnant of such gratuities.

While Stratford was Chancellor, it was resolved in parliament "that the Chancellor is the Ordinary of the free chapels of the King, and that it belongs to him to visit them by virtue of his office."—Rolls, 8 Ed. 3, vol. ii. p. 77.

[2] Rot. Cl. 8 Ed. 3, m. 10.

[3] In quadam villula." Angl. Sax. vol. ii. p. 765.

[4] It is written in a very indifferent Latin. I have chiefly followed an Eng-

masters, scholars, and professors of various arts, whom wit and learning had rendered most conspicuous;—encouraged by whose agreeable conversation, we were most deliciously nourished, sometimes with explanatory examination of arguments, at others with recitations of treatises on the progress of physics—as it were with multiplied and successive dishes of learning. Such were the comrades we chose in our boyhood; such we entertained as the inmates of our chambers and the companions of our journeys; such the messmates of our board, and such our associates in all our fortunes."[1]

Being considered a very accomplished scholar, he was selected as tutor for Edward III. when Prince of Wales, and to him may be traced the love for literature and the arts displayed by his pupil when on the throne. He was rewarded with the lucrative appointment of treasurer of Gascony.

When the civil disturbances arose towards the end of the reign of Edward II., he took part with the Queen, and supplied her with money out of the royal revenue, which she made use of to the prejudice of her husband. He was questioned for this during the ascendency of the opposite faction, and having fled to Paris, and being demanded from the French government, it is said that he was glad to hide himself for several days in the belfry of a church there.

Edward III., on coming to the throne, with his own hand wrote a letter to the Pope, praying that the stalls in the cathedrals of Hereford, London, and Chichester, lately held by Gilbert de Middleton, might be conferred on his tutor, whom he says he loves beyond all the clerks in his realm: "Eo quod nostro assidue lateri assistendo, novimus ipsum virum in consiliis providum, conversationis et vitæ munditia decorum, literarum scientia præditum, et in agendis quibuslibet circumspectum." His Holiness complied, and De Bury was now rapidly promoted in the state as well as in the church, being appointed cofferer to the King, then treasurer of the wardrobe, and soon after Keeper of the Privy Seal. This office he held five years, during which time he twice visited Italy, made the ac-

lish translation published anonymously in the year 1832; printed for that very learned and worthy bookseller, my friend, "Thomas Rodd, Great Newport Street." [1] Phil. ch. viii.

quaintance of Petrarch, and was treated with great honor and distinction by the Supreme Pontiff, John XXII., who nominated him chaplain to his principal chapel, and took upon himself to appoint him, by a special bull, to the first see which should become vacant in England.

From the offices and preferments he already enjoyed, he was enabled to display great magnificence and splendor; and when he appeared in the presence of the Pope or Cardinals, he was attended by twenty clerks and thirty-six esquires attired in the most expensive and sumptuons garments.[1]

Soon afterwards the see of Durham became vacant, and the Prior and Chapter elected as bishop, Robert de Greystones, a monk and sub-prior of Durham, who was actually consecrated by the Archbishop of York. But at the request of the King the election was set aside by the Pope, De Bury was substituted, and on the 19th of December, 1333, the ceremony of his consecration was performed by the Archbishop of Canterbury. The following year he was personally installed at Durham. On this occasion he gave a magnificent entertainment to the King and Queen, her mother, and the King of Scotland, at which were present two archbishops, five bishops, seven earls and their countesses, and all the nobility north of Trent, besides a great number of knights and esquires, and also many abbots and other ecclesiastics.

Soon after this he was raised to the dignity of Chancellor. We have no account of his procession to Westminster, or of the festivities on his being seated in the "Marble Chair" at the upper end of the hall, but we need not doubt that they were distinguished by their taste and sumptuousness.

De Bury filled the office of Chancellor only from the 28th of September, 1334, to the 5th of June, 1335, when he exchanged it for that Treasurer. During this interval he held the Great Seal himself, and did all the duties belonging to it, without the assistance of any Vice-Chancellor, and he seems to have given satisfaction to the public.

A parliament met at Whitsuntide, and he presided at it; but we cannot celebrate him as a legislator, for at this parliament only one act passed, which was "to regulate

---

[1] His last journey to Rome is said to have cost him 5000 marks.

the herring fishery at Yarmouth;" and the time was occupied in obtaining a supply to enable the King to carry on war against the Scots. Edward having gained the battle of Hallidown Hill, in which Douglass the Scottish leader fell, was sanguine in the hope of being able to reduce the whole of Scotland to subjection; but he was soon driven back by the spirit which had baffled all the efforts of his father and grandfather, and he came to the conclusion that he must look out for an easier field in which he might gain distinction as a conqueror.

De Bury went thrice to Paris as ambassador from Edward to the King of France respecting his claim to the crown of that country, and afterwards visited Antwerp and Brabant, with a view of forming alliances for the coming contest. But before the French war had made much progress he resigned the Great Seal, and retired from public life.

He now shut himself up in his palace at Bishop's Auckland among his books, which he preferred to all other human enjoyments,—still, however, exercising a most splendid hospitality.[1] He employed himself ardently in the extension of his library, which, whether out of compliment to him, or as a satire on his brother ecclesiastics, was said to "contain more volumes than those of all the other bishops in the kingdom put together." By the favor of Edward he gained access to the libraries of all the great monasteries, where he shook off the dust from volumes preserved in chests and presses, which had not been opened for many ages. Not satisfied with this privilege, he extended his researches by employing stationers and booksellers, not only in England, but also in France, Germany, and Italy, regardless both of expense and labor.[2]

To solace his declining years, he wrote the "Philobiblon," in praise of books; a treatise which may now be perused with great pleasure, as it shows that the author had a most intimate acquaintance with the classics, and not only a passion for books exceeding that of any modern

[1] This appears from the roll of his domestic expenses, preserved among the muniments of the bishopric.
[2] "Pecuniam læto corde dispersimus, nec eos (sc. librarios et stationarios) ullatenus impedivit distantia, neque furor maris abstersuit, nec eis aut æs pro expenso deficit, quin ad nos optatos libros transmitterent vel afferrent. Sciebant enim pro certo, quod spes eorum in sinu nostro reposita defraudario non poterat, sed restabat apud nos copiosa redemptis cum usuris."

collector, but a rich vein of native humor, which must have made him a most delightful companion.

An extract from chapter viii., entitled "Of the numerous Opportunities of the Author of collecting Books from all Quarters," may bring some suspicion upon his judicial purity: but the open avowal of the manner in which his library was accumulated proves that he had done nothing that would not be sanctioned by the public opinion of the age:

"While we performed the duties of Chancellor of the most invincible and ever magnificently triumphant King of England, Edward III. (whose days may the Most High long and tranquilly deign to preserve!), after first inquiring into the things that concerned his Court, and then the public affairs of his kingdom, an easy opening was afforded us, under the countenance of royal favor, for freely searching the hiding-places of books. For the flying fame of our love had already spread in all directions, and it was reported not only that we had a longing desire for books, and especially for old ones, but that any body could more easily obtain our favor by quartos than by money. Wherefore, when supported by the bounty of the aforesaid Prince of worthy memory, we were enabled to oppose or advance, to appoint or discharge; crazy quartos and tottering folios, precious however in our sight as well as in our affections, flowed in most rapidly from the great and the small, instead of new-year's gifts and remunerations, and instead of presents and jewels. Then the cabinets of the most noble monasteries were opened; cases were unlocked; caskets were unclasped; and astonished volumes which had slumbered for long ages in their sepulchres were roused up, and those that lay hid in dark places were overwhelmed with the rays of a new light. Books heretofore most delicate, now become corrupted and nauseous, lay lifeless, covered indeed with the excrements of mice, and pierced through with the gnawing of worms; and those that were formerly clothed with purple and fine linen, were now seen reposing in dust and ashes, given over to oblivion, the abodes of moths. Amongst these nevertheless, as time served, we sat down more voluptuously than the delicate physician could do amidst his stores of aromatics; and we found an object of love, we found also full enjoyment

Thus the sacred vessels of science came into our power—some being given, some sold, and not a few lent for a time.[1]

"Without doubt, many who perceived us to be contented with gifts of this kind, studied to contribute those things freely to our use. We took care, however, to conduct the business of such so favorably, that the profit might accrue to them: justice therefore suffered no detriment.

"Moreover, if we would have amassed cups of gold and silver, excellent horses, or no mean sums of money, we could in those days have laid up abundance of wealth for ourselves; but indeed we wished for books, not bags; we delighted more in folios than florins, and preferred paltry pamphlets to pampered palfreys.

"In addition to this, we were charged with the frequent embassies of the said Prince, of everlasting memory, and, owing to the multiplicity of state affairs, were sent first to the Roman Chair, then to the Court of France, then to various other kingdoms of the world, on tedious embassies and in perilous times, carrying about with us, however, that fondness for books which many waters could not extinguish; for this, like a certain drug, sweetened the wormwood of peregrination; this, after the perplexing intricacies, scrupulous circumlocutions of debate, and almost inextricable labyrinths of public business, left an opening for a little while to breathe the temperature of a milder atmosphere. O blessed God of gods in Sion! what a rush of the flood of pleasure rejoiced our heart as often as we visited Paris, the paradise of the world! There we longed to remain, where, on account of the greatness of our love, the days ever appeared to us to be few. In that city are delightful libraries in cells redolent of aromatics; there flourishing green-houses of all sorts of volumes; there academic meads trembling with the earthquake of Athenian paripatetics pacing up and down; there the promonotories of Parnassus, and the porticos of

---

[1] A modern deceased Lord Chancellor was said to have collected a very complete law library by borrowing books from the bar which he forgot to return. If so, he only acted on the maxims of his predecessor De Bury:
"Quisquis theologus, quisquis legista peritus
　Vis fieri; multos semper habeto libros.
　Non in mente manet quicquid non vidimus ipsi.
　Quisque sibi libros vendicet ergo. Vale."—p. 151.

the Stoics. There, in very deed, with an open treasury and untied purse-strings, we scattered money with a light heart, and redeemed inestimable books from dirt and dust.

"Again. We will add a most compendious way by which a great multitude of books, as well old as new, came into our hands. Never indeed having disdained the poverty of religious devotees, assumed for Christ, we never held them in abhorrence, but admitted them from all parts of the world into the kind embraces of our compassion; we allured them with most familiar affability into a devotion to our person, and, having allured, cherished them for the love of God with munificent liberality, as if we were the common benefactor of them all, but nevertheless with a certain propriety of patronage, that we might not appear to have given preference to any,—to these under all circumstances we became a refuge; to these we never closed the bosom of our favor. Wherefore we deserved to have those as the most peculiar and zealous promoters of our wishes, as well by their personal as their mental labors, who, going about by sea and land, surveying the whole compass of the earth, and also inquiring into the general studies of the Universities of the provinces, were anxious to administer to our wants, under a most certain hope of reward.

"Amongst so many of the keenest hunters, what leveret could lie hid? What fry could evade the hook, the net, or the trawl of these men? From the body of divine law, down to the latest controversial tract of the day, nothing could escape the notice of these scrutinizers. If a devout sermon resounded at the fount of Christian faith, the most holy Roman court, or if an extraneous question were to be sifted on account of some new pretext; if the dullness of Paris, which now attends more to studying antiquities than to subtly producing truth; if English perspicacity overspread with ancient lights, always emitted new rays of truth—whatsoever it promulgated, either for the increase of knowledge or in declaration of the faith—this, while recent, was poured into our ears, not mystified by imperfect narration nor corrupted by absurdity, but from the press of the purest presser it passed, dregless, into the vat of our memory."

[1] Pp. 50–56.

He does not himself seem to have been much acquainted with Grecian lore, but he was fully convinced of its value, and he says, that "ignorance of the Greek language is at this day highly injurious to the study of Latin authors; without it, neither Gentile nor Christian writings can be fully comprehended. Wherefore, we have taken care to provide for our scholars a Greek as well as a Hebrew grammar, with certain adjuncts, by the help of which, studious readers may be instructed in writing, reading, and understanding those languages, although hearing them spoken can alone give a perfect knowledge of their idiom."

He is nowhere more entertaining than in describing and reprobating the ill-usage to which the clasp-books of his time were liable: "You will perhaps see a stiff-necked youth, lounging sluggishly in his study: while the frost pinches him in winter time, oppressed with colds, his watery nose drops,—nor does he take the trouble to wipe it with his handkerchief till it has moistened the book beneath it with its vile dew. For such a one I could substitute a cobbler's apron in the place of his book. He has a nail like a giant's, perfumed with stinking ordure, with which he points out the place of any pleasant subject. He distributes innumerable straws in various places, with the ends in sight, that he may recall by the mark what his memory cannot retain. These straws, which the stomach of the book never digests, and which nobody takes out, at first distend the book from its accustomed closure, and being carelessly left to oblivion, at last become putrid. He is not ashamed to eat fruit and cheese over an open book, and to transfer his empty cup from side to side upon it: and because he has not his alms-bag at hand, he leaves the rest of the fragments in his books. He never ceases to chatter with eternal garrulity to his companions; and while he adduces a multitude of reasons void of physical meaning, he waters the book, spread out upon his lap, with the sputtering of his saliva. What is worse, he next reclines with his elbows on the book, and by a short study invites a long nap; and by way of repairing the wrinkles, he twists back the margins of the leaves, to the no small detriment of the volume. He goes out in the rain, and returns, and now flowers make their appearance upon our soil. Then the scholar we are describing, the neglecter rather than the inspector of books, stuffs his volume with firstling violets, roses, and quadrifoils. He will next apply his wet hands, oozing with sweat, to turning over the volumes, then beat the white parchment all over with his dusty gloves, or hunt over the page, line by line, with his fore-finger covered with dirty leather. Then, as the flea bites, the holy book is thrown aside, which, however, is scarcely closed once in a month, and is so swelled with the dust that has fallen into it, that it will not yield to the efforts of the closer."[1]

I can only venture on one other extract, which goes to show why the Chancellors in those days were ecclesiastics, and exposes the gross ignorance which prevailed among laymen, who, being unable to read, did not know how to hold a book, and are coupled with "dirty scullions:" "Farthermore, laymen, to whom it matters not whether they look at a book turned wrong side upwards or spread before them in its natural order, are altogether unworthy of any communion with books. Let the clerk also take order that the *dirty scullions*, stinking from the pots, do not touch the leaves of books, unwashed."[2]

Like a Bishop and an Ex-Chancellor, he properly concludes by supporting his doctrine with the highest authorities. "The most meek Moses instructs us about making cases for books in the neatest manner, wherein they may be safely preserved from all damage. *Take this book*, says he, *and put it in the side of the ark of the covenant of the Lord your God*. O befitting place, made of imperishable Shittim wood, and covered all over, inside and out, with gold! But our Saviour also, by his own example, precludes all unseemly negligence in the treatment of books, as may be read in Luke iv. For when he had read over the Scriptural prophecy written about himself, in a book delivered to him, he did not return it till he had first closed it with his most holy hands; by which act students are most clearly taught that they ought not, in the smallest degree whatever, to be negligent about the custody of books."[3] He might well say of himself— "ecstatico quodam librorum amore potenter se abreptum."[4]

[1] Pp. 97, 98.   [2] P. 100.
[3] P. 101. Luke iv. 20: "And he closed the book, and he gave it again to the minister, and sat down."
[4] As it was said that Garth did not write his own "Dispensary," the

From his book-buying propensity, then much more costly than in our time, he got into pecuniary difficulties, and he was obliged to pledge to Lord Neville of Raby, for £100, a set of gorgeous church vestments, of red velvet, embroidered with gold, and pearls, and imagery.[1]

He died at Bishop's Auckland on the 14th of April, 1345, full of years and of honors. Fourteen days after his death he was buried " quodammodo honorifice, non tamen cum honore satis congruo," says Chambre, before the altar of the blessed Mary Magdalene, in his own cathedral. But the exalted situation he occupied in the opinion and esteem of Petrarch and other eminent literary men of the fourteenth century, shed brighter lustre on his memory than it could have derived from funeral processions, or from monuments and epitaphs. " What can be more delightful to a lover of his country's intellectual reputation, than to find such a character as De Bury in such an age of war and bloodshed, uniting the calm and mild conduct of a legislator with the sagacity of a philosopher and the elegant mind of a scholar?"[2]

On De Bury's resignation of the Great Seal in 1335, it was restored to Archbishop Stratford, whose second Chancellorship extended to 1337.[3]

From the groundless claim set up by the Plantagenets to the crown of France against the house of Valois, now began the bloody wars which lasted above a century, and which laid the foundation of that jealousy and hostile rivalry between the two nations, which unfortunately has never since entirely subsided. While the great bulk of the people of England eagerly supported the warlike

---

Philobiblon has been attributed to *Holcot*, a Dominican friar. who was the author's amanuensis,*—but without any reason, for it bears the strongest internal evidence of being the composition of the Chancellor De Bury himself: it was attributed to him by his contemporaries, and a notice on an early copy of it says :—" Quod opus (Philobiblon) Auclandiæ in habitatione suâ complevit 24 die Januarii, anno a communis salutis origine 1344, ætatis suæ 58, et 11 sui pontificatus."

[1] After his death, Lord Neville being informed of his intention to leave these vestments to his successors, generously restored them, and they remained the boast of the see of Durham till the reformation.

[2] Dibdin, *Bibliomania;* p. 247.—I am rather surprised that a " De Bury Club " has not yet been established by Philobiblists, as he was undoubtedly the founder of the order in England.

[3] Rot. Cl. 9 Ed. 3, m. 28.

* See " Bibliographical and retrospective Miscellany," Art. *De Bury*.

measures of the King, it ought to be recorded to the immortal honor of this Chancellor, that he dissuaded the enterprise in its commencement, and always strove for the restoration of peace at the hazard of offending the King, and with the certainty of incurring the public odium by combating the popular delusion.

It must be confessed that on this occasion we not only were the aggressors, but that there was not even any plausible or colorable pretense for going to war. No national grievance could be urged, for the French had merely assisted the Scotch in fulfillment of ancient treaties. Then, as to the family dispute,—by the Salic law which had regulated the descent of the crown of France from the foundation of the monarchy, no female could wear the crown, so that no claim to the crown could be made through a female, and the title of Philip de Valois, which Edward himself had, though reluctantly, recognized by doing homage to him as his liege Lord, was unquestionable, both by hereditary right and the general consent of the French people. But the glaring absurdity in the claim was, that if the Salic law were entirely disregarded, and female descent were admitted in France, as in England, there were females in existence, and males descended through females, whose title was clearly preferable to that of Edward.[1]

Archbishop Stratford resigned the Great Seal the second time just before Edward assumed the title of King of France with the armorial bearings of that crown, and set out on his first expedition to support his title. There is great reason to think that it was the Chancellor's pacific policy which led to his retreat. Still, however, he was on good terms with the King, and his brother was appointed to succeed him.[2]

ROBERT DE STRATFORD appears to have been almost as much distinguished for ability, and to have had a career almost as brilliant as John, and they exhibit the single instance of two brothers holding successively the office

---

[1] This was the sensible view of the question taken by the Chancellor, who gave very different advice to Edward III. from that which, according to Shakspeare, was given by Archbishop Chicheley to Henry V.

K. Hen.—" May I with right and conscience make this claim ?"

Archb.—" The sin upon my head, dread Sovereign."

Rot. Cl. 11 Ed. 3, m. 29.

of Lord Chancellor. He, too, had studied at Oxford, and had gained the highest honors of the University. When the Great Seal was delivered to him, his rank in the Church was only that of Archdeacon of Canterbury, but he was soon after raised to the see of Chichester; and he was elected Chancellor of the University of Oxford, probably as much from hopes excited by his present power as from the recollection of his academical proficiency. He had several times previously been entrusted with the custody of the Great Seal as Vice Chancellor, and he must have been familiar with the duties of the office; but, on account of his many avocations, soon after his elevation he delivered the Great Seal into the keeping of St. Paul, the Master of the Rolls, who was to act as his deputy.[1]

He continued Chancellor till the 6th of July, 1338, when he retired for a time, and was succeeded by RICHARD DE BYNTEWORTH, or BENTWORTH, or WENTWORTH,[2] Bishop elect of London. What was the reason of this change I have not been able to discover. The Stratfords do not seem then to have lost the favor of the King, and while he was engaged in preparing to prosecute the French war, they still assisted him with their counsels, however much they might disapprove of his measures.

I find little respecting the history of the new Chancellor except that he had been a prebendary of St. Paul's. He enjoyed for a very short time his new dignities. Having received the Great Seal and been sworn in as Chancellor at Walton, he immediately returned the Seal to the King, being obliged to go to London to be consecrated. It was then given in charge to St. Paul and Baumburgh, to keep until the Chancellor should be returned to court. The King left England for France on the 11th of July, having sent them a new Great Seal, which he wished to be used in England during his absence, he taking abroad with him the Great Seal before in use. The temporary Seal was delivered to the Chancellor on the 19th of July,[3]

---

[1] Rot. Cl. 11 Ed. 3.
[2] Rot. Cl. 12 Ed. 3. This is an instance of B. and W. being interchangeable, of which we have another in the *Bicestre* at Paris, built by the Bishop of Winchester, Vincester—Vincester—Bincester, Bicestre. So in some parts of England walnuts are called *balnuts* or *bannets*. In the Spanish language every *v* is convertible into *b*. Hence the felicitous pun:—" Beati quibus *v*ivere est *b*ibere."
[3] Rot. Cl. 12 Ed. 3, m. 12.

and continued in his possession till the 7th of December in the following year,—when he suddenly died.

The Seal was delivered the next morning, by two of the officers of the deceased Chancellor, to the Archbishop of Canterbury, who immediately sent it to the Council appointed by the King to administer the government in his absence. They handed it over to three persons to be used for sealing necessary writs, and on the 16th of February following it was placed in the sole custody of the Master of the Rolls, by virtue of a letter of Prince Edward, Guardian of the realm.

The King having returned to England in about a fortnight after, he delivered to the Master of the Rolls a new Seal, which he had brought with him from France, with the *fleur-de-lys* engraved upon it,—impressions of which were sent into every county in England for the purpose of making it generally known.[1]

On the 28th of April, 1340, John de Stratford, Archbishop of Canterbury, was made Lord Chancellor for the third time. The King was again to pass beyond the seas, and he placed this old public servant at the head of the Council to govern in his absence, in the belief that he was the fittest man that could be selected to obtain supplies from Parliament, to levy the subsidies that might be voted, and to raise men for the war now carrying on to win the crown of France.

While Edward lay at the siege of Tournay a parliament was held by commission at Westminster, and the Chancellor, on the 7th of July, the first day of the session, declared that it had been summoned "to consult what farther course was best for the King and his allies to take against France."[2] Liberal supplies in money and provisions were voted, and notwithstanding the charge of treachery or remissness afterwards brought against the Archbishop, he seems to have exerted himself to the utmost to render them available to the public service.

On account of his infirmity of body he again resigned the office of Chancellor, and the King again appointed Robert de Stratford, Bishop of Chichester, as his successor.[3]

[1] Rot. Cl. 14 Ed. 3, m. 42.   [2] Parl. Hist. 99.
[3] Rot. Cl. 14 Ed. 3, m. 13. Upon this occasion the Great Seal was broken on account of a change in the King's armorial bearings, and another Seal, with

The two brothers continued jointly to manage the King's affairs in England without the slightest suspicion of any change in his sentiments towards them till his sudden and wrathful return, when they were dismissed from their employments, and, but for their sacred character as ecclesiastics, would have been in great danger of losing their heads.

Edward had derived no fruits from the great naval victory he had lately gained on the coast of Flanders, and though he had commanded a more numerous army than ever before or since served under the banner of an English sovereign, he had been able to make no progress in his romantic enterprise. He had incurred immense debts with the Flemings, for which he had even pawned his own person. The remittances from England came in much slower than he expected, and he found it convenient to throw the blame on those he had left in authority at home.

He escaped from his creditors, and after encountering a violent tempest, arrived at the Tower of London in the middle of the night of the 30th of November. He began by committing to prison and treating with unusual rigor the constable and others who had charge of the Tower, on pretense that it was negligently guarded. His vengeance then fell on the Lord Chancellor, whom next day he deprived of his office, and ventured for some time to detain in prison.

Nay more, he inveighed against the whole order of the priesthood, as unfit for any secular employment, and he astonished the kingdom by the bold innovation of appointing a layman as Chancellor. Considering how ecclesiastics in those ages had entrenched themselves in privileges and immunities, so that no civil penalty could regularly be inflicted upon them for any public malversation, and that they were so much in the habit, when once elevated to high station by royal favor, of preferring the extension of priestly domination to gratitude or respect for temporal authority, it seems at first sight wonderful that the great offices of state were ever bestowed upon them. On the other hand, there were peculiar causes

an improved emblazonment of the *fleur-de-lys*, was delivered by the King, when embarking for France, to St. Paul, the Master of the Rolls, to be carried to the new Chancellor.

which favored their promotion. Being the only educated class, they were best qualified for civil employments requiring knowledge and address; when raised to the prelacy they enjoyed equal dignity with the greatest barons, and gave weight by their personal authority to the official powers intrusted to them, while at the same time they did not excite the envy, jealousy, and factious combinations which always arose when laymen of obscure birth were elevated to power. They did not endanger the Crown by accumulating wealth or influence in their families, and they were restrained by the decency of their character from that open rapine and violence so often practiced by the nobles.[1] These motives had hitherto induced Edward to follow the example of his predecessors, and to employ ecclesiastics as his ministers, at the risk of their turning against him and setting him at defiance. But, finding that by the Clementine Constitutions he was obliged immediately to release the dismissed Chancellor from prison, and that the Archbishop, whom he likewise wished to call to account, fulminated an excommunication against him, he resolved in future to employ only men whom he could control and punish.

CHAPTER XIV.

CHANCELLORS AND KEEPERS OF THE GREAT SEAL FROM THE APPOINTMENT OF SIR ROBERT BOURCHIER TILL THE APPOINTMENT OF WILLIAM DE WICKHAM.

THE first lay Lord Chancellor appointed by an English King was Sir ROBERT BOURCHIER, Knight'[2]—a distinguished soldier.

He was the eldest son of Sir John Bourchier, a Judge of the Court of Common Pleas,—the representative of a family long seated at Halstead, in Essex. His education was very slender, being engaged in military adventures from early youth; but he showed great capacity as well as courage in the field, and was a particular favorite of King Edward III., whom he accompanied in all his cam-

[1] Hume's Hist. vol. ii. p. 408.   [2] Rot. Cl. 14 Ed. 3, m. 10.

paigns. In 1337 he was at the battle of Cadsant, and had lately before Tournay witnessed the discomfiture of all Edward's mighty preparations for the conquest of France. He joined in the loud complaints against the ministers who had been appointed to superintend the supplies and levies at home, and in the advice that the Stratfords should be punished for their supposed misconduct.

The resolution being taken to put down the ascendency of ecclesiastics,—from the shrewdness and energy of this stout knight, he was thought a fit instrument to carry it into effect, and not only was the Great Seal delivered to him, but he was regarded as the King's chief councillor.

After Robert de Stratford, the late Chancellor, had been released from prison, he made submission, and it was agreed to take no farther steps against him. He appears now to have retired from politics, and we read no more of him except that he acquired great applause for the prudence with which he suppressed a mighty sedition in the University of Oxford, arising from the opposite factions of the northern and southern scholars,—the former, by reason of the many grievances they complained of, having retired for a time to Stamford in Lincolnshire. He afterwards resided entirely in his diocese. His life was prolonged to the 9th of April, 1392.

But it was determined to take ample vengeance on Ex-Chancellor John de Stratford, to whose mismanagement was imputed the bad success of the war, and who continued to defy the power of the Crown.

First came a proclamation under the Great Seal, framed by Lord Chancellor Bourchier, and ordered to be read in all churches and chapels,—charging the Ex-Chancellor with having intercepted the supplies granted to the King, and either with having appropriated them to himself, or having diverted them from their legitimate objects. To this Stratford opposed a pastoral letter, victoriously refuting the accusation.

But parliament was always considered the ready engine of vengeance in the hands of the dominant party, and one was summoned to meet at Westminster, in April, 1341. Still some apprehensions were entertained from the sacred character of the party to be accused, and from his eloquence and influence if he were regularly heard in his own defense. The King and his military Chancellor therefore resorted to the unconstitutional step of withholding from him a writ of summons, thinking that he might thus be prevented from appearing in the Upper House. The Ex-Chancellor, nothing appalled, sent a remonstrance to the King, stating (among other things), "that there were two powers by which the world was governed, the holy, pontifical, apostolic dignity, and the royal subordinate authority; that of these two powers the clerical was evidently the supreme, since priests were to answer at the tribunal of the Divine judgment for the conduct of Kings themselves; that the clergy were the spiritual fathers of all the faithful, and therefore of Kings and Princes, and were entitled by a heavenly charter to direct their wills and actions, and to censure their transgressions; and that Prelates had heretofore cited Emperors before their tribunal, had sat in judgment on their life and behavior, and had anathematized them for their obstinate offenses."[1]

On the day when parliament met, the Archbishop showed himself before the gates of Westminster Hall,—arrayed in his pontifical robes,—holding the crosier in his hand, and attended by a pompous train of priests. This ceremony being finished, he was proceeding to the chamber where the Peers were assembled, but he was forbid by the captain of the guard to enter. While demanding admittance, he was seized by officers and carried to the bar of the Court of Exchequer, where he was called upon to plead to an information which had been filed against him by the Attorney General, and which treated him as a great pecuniary defaulter to the Crown. He then stationed himself in Palace Yard, and solemnly protested that he would not stir from that place till the King gave him leave to come into parliament, or a sufficient reason why he should not. Standing there in this manner, with the emblems of his holy office, some that were by began to revile him, saying to him, "Thou art a traitor: thou hast deceived the King and betrayed the realm." He answered them, "The curse of the Almighty God and of his blessed Mother, and of St. Thomas, and mine also, be upon the heads of them that inform the King so. Amen, amen."

During two days the King rejected his application; but

[1] St. Tr. 57.

he petitioned the Peers against the injury thus offered to
the first Peer in the realm, and the House took it up as a
matter of privilege. The King agreed to a personal conference with him in the Painted Chamber, and after some
discussion, consented to his taking his seat in the House;
but his Majesty then abruptly withdrew, and employed
Sir John Darcy and Sir William Killesby to accuse him
before the citizens of London and the House of Commons.

The Lords, alarmed for the rights and honor of their
body, prayed the King to acknowledge, that when a Peer
was impeached by the Crown for high crimes and misdemeanors, he could not be compelled to plead before
any other tribunal than the House of Peers; and when
Edward objected that such an acknowledgment would be
prejudicial to the public interests, and derogatory to the
royal prerogatives, they requested his permission to refer
the matter to a committee of four prelates, four
earls, and four barons. The committee reported, as an
undeniable principle, "that no Peer could be arraigned or
brought to judgment, except in parliament and by his
peers." This was unanimously approved of by the House,
and embodied in an address to the King.[1]

The apprehension of serious consequences from this
rupture, and the necessity of securing a supply, induced
Edward to declare that he was willing that the charge
should drop. The triumph of the Primate was complete,
for he now desired that, "whereas he had been publicly
defamed through the realm, he might be arraigned in
open parliament before his peers;" but the King adjourned the matter to the next parliament, and then he
ordered all the proceedings against him to be annulled

[1] St. Tr. 65. They further insisted that no Peer who had been employed
in the great offices of the Crown should, in respect of his office, be called before any other court of justice: and that in such a case he ought not to be
arraigned at the prosecution of the King, nor lose his temporalities, lands,
tenements, goods, or chattels, nor be arrested, imprisoned or outlawed, nor
plead nor receive judgment, except in full parliament and before his peers,
although they admitted that a peer in receipt of the King's moneys ought to
account in the Exchequer, and also that a Peer if he pleased might plead
before another court, but without prejudice to the rights of the peerage, as
far as regarded others or himself, on future occasions. This early case of
privilege by no means settled the law on the subject, for it is only in cases of
treason and felony that a Peer is entitled to be tried by his peers, and this
immunity is restricted to Peers noble by blood, so that the prelates are triable
in all cases by a jury. See 1 St. Tr. 57.

and vacated. In truth, the Ex-Chancellor's crime consisted in expostulating with the King about his profuseness, and in persuading him to make peace with France.

He lived seven years afterwards, universally honored and beloved; and at his death, after founding and endowing a college at his native place, he left all his estate to his servants and domestics. He is said to have been " a man of a mild and gentle nature, more inclinable to pardon the guilty than to punish them with severity, and very charitable to the poor."[1]

Bourchier, during his short Chancellorship, was entirely occupied with the King's political business, particularly in the management of his diplomacy,—the duties of foreign secretary of state, which were transacted by the Chancellor, being at this time very onerous. He transferred the Great Seal almost always into the custody of the Master of the Rolls or the King's Chamberlain, who sealed writs, and ordinarily sat in the Court of Chancery, —although, on great occasions, the Lord Chancellor himself, notwithstanding his inexperience, attended in person, and decided according to his own notions of law and equity.

The King sometimes took the Seal into his own keeping, without meaning to make any change in the office of Chancellor. On the 7th of August in this year, Bourchier having experienced no loss of favor, and not meaning to resign his office, under an order he received to that effect, sent the seal to the palace by Ralph Lord Stafford and Philip de Weston. The King kept it in his own possession till the next day, and having sealed some grants with it, he returned it to the Chancellor.[1]

If there had been complaints of ecclesiastical Chancellors, this experiment of conferring the office on an illiterate layman, who neglected its duties, caused unprecedented dissatisfaction; and there was an agitation in favor of the plan for restraining the prerogative of the Crown in the appointment of its officers, which had distracted the weak reigns of Henry III. and Edward II.

The matter was taken up by the legislature, and the Commons, by petition to the King, prayed (tantamount to passing a bill) " that the Chancellor, together with the other great officers, might be chosen in open parliament,

[1] See 1 Parl. Hist. 101.   [2] Rot. Cl. 15 Ed. 3, m. 34.

and that, at the same time, they should be openly sworn to obey the laws of the land and Magna Charta."

The ferment in the public mind was so great, and such was the necessity for soothing the Commons with a view to a supply, that the King did not venture to put a direct veto upon this proposal, and he yielded this much, "that if any such office, by the death or other failure of the incumbent, become void, the choice to remain solely with the King, he taking therein the assent of his Council, but that every such officer shall be sworn at the next parliament, according to the petition; and that every parliament following, the King shall resume into his hands all such offices, so as the said officers shall be left liable to answer all objections."[1]

The Commons expressed themselves satisfied with this concession, and the Prelates and Barons approving of the arrangement for the periodical resumption of offices with a view to facilitate charges against those who had filled them, the three estates made a request to the King, that the petition and answer might be reduced into the form of a statute. This being done, the statute was read aloud in the King's presence, and he assented to it, having secretly entered a protest against it.

His officers who were present were then called upon to swear to observe the statute; and to render the oath more binding, it was required to be taken on the cross of Canterbury, then in attendance on the Archbishop. Several took the oath without hesitation; but when it came to the turn of Lord Chancellor Bourchier he refused it, as contrary to his former oath of allegiance and to the laws of the realm. Nevertheless, he exemplified the statute under the Great Seal, and delivered it to the Lords and Commons.[2] This was only to delude them; for no sooner was the parliament dissolved than, by his advice, the King attempted to revoke the concession by a proceeding more extraordinary than that by which he had submitted to it. An order in council was made, abrogating the obnoxious statute—on the ground that the King by force had suffered it to pass into law; and special writs were directed to all the peers and to all sheriffs of England, declaring it to be null and void, and ordering proclamation to be made

---

[1] Rot. Parl. 15 Ed. 3. See also stat. 15 Ed. 3. H. 1, cc. 3 & 4.
[2] 1 Parl. Hist. 104.

to that effect. The preamble of these writs (no doubt the composition of the gallant Lord Chancellor) must be allowed to be very simple and plain-spoken: " Whereas some time since, in our parliament at Westminster, there was a certain petition made contrary to the laws and customs of England, and not only very prejudicial but reproachful also to our royal dignity, which, if we had not permitted to be drawn into a statute, the said parliament had been without success, and dissolved in discord, and so our wars with France and Scotland had very likely (which God forbid) been in ruin; and we, to avoid such dangers, permitting protestations of revoking those things, when we could conveniently, that had been so extorted from us against our will, yet permitted them to be sealed with our seal at that time, and afterwards, by the advice and assent of certain earls, barons, and other wise men" (meaning the privy council), " for lawful causes, because we never consented to the making of the statute, but as it then behoved us, we dissembled in the premises, we have declared it null, and that it ought not to have the name and force of a statute, we willing, &c."

The Ex-Chancellor John de Stratford showed great zeal on the opposite side, and considering that an oath had been taken on his cross of Canterbury to observe the statute, he summoned a provincial council for the purpose of hurling excommunication against all who should dare to infringe it.

Lord Chancellor Bourchier then sent him a writ of prohibition under the Great Seal in the King's name, in these words:—

" We understand you have summoned a provincial council to meet at London on the morrow of St. Luke next coming, in which you intend to excite the bishops of your province against us, and to ordain and declare some things prejudicial to us about confirming the said pretended statute, and for the enervation, depression and diminution of our royal jurisdiction, rights, and prorogatives for the preservation whereof we are bound by oath; and that you intend to promulge grievous censures concerning these things; we, willing to prevent so great mischief, do strictly forbid that in that council you dare to propound, or any way attempt, or cause to be attempted, any thing in derogation or diminution of our royal dignity, power, or rights, or of the laws and customs of our kingdom, or in confirmation of the pretended statute, or otherwise in contumely of our name and honor, or to the grievance and disadvantage of our counselors or servants; and know ye, that if ye do these things, we will prosecute you as our enemy and violator of our rights with as much severity as lawfully we may."

A violent crisis seemed now at hand, and men speculated differently upon the probable triumph of the mitre or the crown; but Edward dextrously avoided the danger by sacrificing the Chancellor whose unpopularity and imprudence had involved him in such difficulties, and by appointing a successor who must unite the suffrages of the whole kingdom in his favor.

On the 28th of October, 1341, Bourchier was dismissed from the office of Chancellor, and on the following day, to the great joy of the people, it was conferred on a man who had been regularly bred to the bar, who had already filled judicial offices with great credit, and who enjoyed the highest reputation for integrity as well as for learning and ability.[1] This excellent appointment operated instantly to allay the storm.[2] All discontents were appeased; the Archbishop's power was gone, and the obnoxious statute was no more thought of till two years afterwards, when it was in due form repealed by the parliament, then in good humor from the admirable conduct of the new Chancellor.[3]

John de Stratford died soon after. He must have had extraordinary talents and tact to raise himself from low degree first to be the favorite and friend, and then the rival for sway, of his heroic sovereign.

We need not wonder that the elevation of Bourchier had been so unfortunate, notwithstanding his prior reputation. Most of his predecessors had been regularly trained in the civil and canon law, and had risen in the gradual progress of official advancement, while he was taken from camps in which he had spent his life to be placed in the marble chair in Chancery, and on the woolsack in the House of Lords. In this assembly likewise he was under a great disadvantage, as he sat there without being, like the Prelates who had preceded him, a member

---

[1] Rot. Cl. 16 Ed. 3, m. 19
Cott. Abr. 38. 39

[2] —— "Simul alba nautis
Stella refulsit,
Defluit saxis agitatue humor."

of the House,—and being merely permitted to put the question as prolocutor,—so that the office which he filled was shorn of its dignity and influence.

Being restored to his proper sphere, he soon recovered and increased his reputation. He was with Edward the Black Prince in the heat of the battle of Cressy, and was afterwards one of the ambassadors to treat with France for a peace. As a reward for his services he was summoned as a Peer to parliament, and his family thus ennobled was long very flourishing, and became allied to the Crown. He died of the plague in the year 1349, leaving as his heir and successor in the peerage, John his son, by his wife Margaret, daughter and heir of Sir Thomas de Preyers.

He obtained from Edward III., in 1330, a grant of free warren in his twenty-one lordships in Essex,—in 1336, a license to impark his woods at Halstead,—and in 1341, while he was Chancellor, a warrant to convert his house there into a battlemented castle.

Sir ROBERT PARNYNGE, who now held the Great Seal, was the first regularly bred common lawyer who was ever appointed to the office of Chancellor in England. I do not find any account of his parentage or early education. He was probably of obscure origin, owing his rise to his talents and his industry. Having distinguished himself greatly for his proficiency in the study of the common law as a member of the inns of court, and as an utter barrister, he took the degree of the coif in the 8th of Edward III., and was soon made a King's Sergeant.[1] "For his profound and excellent knowledge of the laws," he was, in Trinity term, 14 Ed. 3, created Chief Justice of England. On the 15th of December following he was made Lord Treasurer of England, and he remained in that office till he was constituted Lord Chancellor.[2]

The Equitable jurisdiction of Chancery had been greatly extended, and to the duties of his own Court the new Chancellor sedulously devoted himself. But he thought, as did Lord Eldon and the most celebrated of his successors, that the best qualification for an Equity Judge is not the mere drudgery of drawing bills and answers, but a scientific knowledge of the common law; and he further thought it essential that his knowledge of the common law should be steadily kept up by him when Chancellor,

[1] Orig. Jur. p. 43.   [2] 4 Inst. 79.

"This man," says Lord Coke, "knowing that he that knew not the common law, could never well judge in Equity (which is a just correction of law in some cases), did usually sit in the Court of Common Pleas (which court is the lock and key of the Common Law), and heard matters in law there debated, and many times would argue himself, as in the Report, 17 Ed. 3, it appears."[1]

It was only once, and for a very short time, that the Great Seal was out of his own custody while he was Chancellor. On the 16th of May, 1342, it was delivered to two great Barons, Henry de Lancaster, Earl of Derby, and William de Bohun, Earl of Northampton, not, as may well be supposed, for any judicial purpose, but to give effect to a proceeding which the Chancellor probably condemned and resisted. The Close Roll, 16 Ed. 3, states, that "immediately after the Earls above named had obtained possession of the Seal, they caused divers letters of pardon, 'sectæ pacis regis,' for homicide to be sealed, and ordered the same charters to be enrolled in Chancery without the payment of any fee, and afterwards the King re-delivered the Seal to the Chancellor."

On the 4th of October, 1342, when the King was on board the George, at Sandwich, bound for Brittany, Lord Chancellor Parnynge delivered the Great Seal into his Majesty's hands, and another seal was delivered to him to be used in England during the King's absence.[2] On the 4th of March following the King being returned delivered to the Chancellor the Great Seal which he had taken with him into Brittany, and at the same time received back the seal which had been used in the interval.[3]

There was only one parliament held while Parnynge was Chancellor, in which he presided with dignity, although the inconvenience was still felt of the Speaker not being a member of the House of Peers. The Commons, not from any dissatisfaction with him, but rather, I presume, with a view that he might be raised to the peerage, petitioned the King "that the Chancellor may be a peer of the realm, and that no stranger be appointed thereunto, and that he attend not to any other office." Edward, much nettled, chose to consider this a wanton interference with his prerogative, and returned for answer: "Le Roi

[1] 4 Inst. 79. [2] Rot. Cl. 16 Ed. 3, m. 32. [3] Ibid.

poet faire ses ministres come lui plaira, et come lui et ses ancestres ont fait en tut temps passez."[1]

However, with the exception of this little breeze, there was great tranquillity during the session, and the Chancellor, by order of the House, having examined before them some of the King's officers respecting the war and the negotiation with France, the three estates concurred in advising the King to adhere to the truce which had been concluded with Philip, and to try to convert it into a permanent peace, though, if this should be unattainable, they would maintain his quarrel with all their power.[2]

Parnynge's last appearance in public was in the august ceremony of the King creating his eldest son Prince of Wales in full parliament,—investing him with a coronet, a gold ring, and a silver rod.

It was now generally expected that he himself would be made a peer; but on the 26th of August, 1343, he suddenly died while enjoying the full favor of his Prince and the entire confidence of his fellow-subjects.

I cannot find any trace of his decisions while Chancellor; but we know that he is to be honored as the first person who held the office with the requisite qualifications for the proper discharge of its important duties, and he must have laid the foundation-stone of that temple to justice, afterwards reared in such fair proportions by an Ellesmere, a Nottingham, and a Harwicke.

The Great Seal was now for a short time (according to modern phraseology) "*in commission*," that is to say,—without the appointment of a Chancellor, it was intrusted to the Master of the Rolls and two others, jointly, for the despatch of all business connected with it,[3] and they held it till Michaelmas-day following. On that day the Earl of Warwick, by the King's command, sealed five charters

---

[1] 1 Parl. Hist. 105. Rol. P. vol. ii. 140ᵇ.   [2] 1 Parl. Hist. 106.

[3] The entry of this commission on the Close Roll is curious, as almost the only one not in Latin. "Le Roi a ses chers Clercs Maistre de Thoresby, Johan de St. Paul, et Thomas de Brayton, salutz. Come Mons. Robert Parnyng votre Chanceller soit a Dieu, mandez nous assurantz de vos sens et loialtez, nous mandons que vous receivez notre Grand Seal en la presence de notre conseil a Londres, et facez ceo que a l'office du dit Seal appeint come gardeins dicel tanque nous eut eoms autremont ordeinez. Done souz notre secre seal a West. le xxvj. jour d'Augst, l'an de notre regne d'Engleterre dis-septisme et de France quartrieine."—17 Ed. 3. m. 24.

of pardon with it, and it was then delivered by the King to ROBERT DE SADYNGTON as Chancellor.[1]

He was descended from a family of great eminence in the law, the members of which had been successively Justices in Eyre to Henry III., Edward I., and Edward II. I do not find any account of his early career, except that he studied at the inns of court, and was regularly bred to the bar. He was appointed Chief Baron of the Exchequer 20th of March, 11 Edward III.; Vice-Treasurer of England 25th of June, 13 Edward III.; and Lord Treasurer 2nd of May, 14 Edward III.

He seems to have turned out a very indifferent Equity judge, and to have disappointed public expectation. Lord Coke, eager to praise Chancellors taken from the common law, while he celebrates the merits of Parnynge and Knyvet, the contemporaries of Lord Chancellor Sadyngton, has not a word to say in his praise; and he performed so indifferently as to reconcile the nation to the old practice of making ecclesiastical Chancellors.

He presided at a parliament which met on the 7th of June, 1344, in the presence of the King and the Prince of Wales, declared the cause of this summons to be "concerning the late truce with France, and the breach of it by the French King, of which he gave seven particular instances; and he desired the three estates of the realm to consider of those things, and that they would give him such advice and assistance as was necessary for the saving of his and their own rights and honors."[2] They answered, by the mouth of the Chancellor, that they "prayed him to make a speedy end of the war, either by battle or a proper peace, if such might be had; and that when he had embarked to cross the seas he should not, for the letters or command of the Pope, or any other, lay aside his voyage until he had made an end one way or another."

While Sadyngton was Chancellor, the King several times took the Great Seal from him for the purpose of sealing a charter of pardon (which seems to have been considered as the direct act of the Sovereign), and then restored it to him.

When the King was sailing on his expedition to France, Sadyngton delivered the Great Seal to him at Sandwich, and received it back on Edward's return to England

[1] Rot. Cl. 17 Ed. 3, m. 20.   [2] 1 Parl. Hist. 109.

The entry on the record of this ceremony is curious, as showing that the Chancellor now regularly sat in his court in Westminster Hall, surrounded by the Masters in Chancery as his assessors.[1]

Sadyngton was soon after obliged to give up the Great Seal altogether, having been found inefficient both in parliament and in the Court of Chancery, and the complaints against him becoming so loud that the King was afraid the Commons might renew their efforts to wrest from the Crown the appointment to the office of Chancellor. But a job was done for the Ex-Chancellor, who had exerted himself to please his party. Chief Baron Stenford being induced to resign, Sadyngton was reinstated as head of the Court of Exchequer, where he continued to preside till his death.[2]

The last experiment of a legal Chancellor had succeeded so indifferently that the King resolved, for his next choice, to return to the Church. There had been murmurs from the prelates, who considered the office of Chancellor as belonging to their order; and it was perhaps thought that the causes of summoning a parliament, and the topics for a liberal supply, would come with more effect from the holy lips of a mitred occupant of the woolsack than from a profane lawyer known to have practiced as a retained advocate in Westminster Hall.

On the 26th of October, 1345, in the room called "the Cage Chamber," in the palace at Westminster, the King delivered the Great Seal to JOHN DE OFFORD, Dean of Lincoln, to be held by him as Chancellor, and, having taken the oaths, on the following day he sealed writs and letters patent with it in the Court of Chancery in Westminster Hall.[3]

He was of noble extraction, being a younger son of Robert Earl of Suffolk. He was early dedicated to the church, and, as usual with those who hoped to rise in it, applying himself diligently to the study of the civil and canon law, he took the degree of Doctor *utroque jure*.

[1] "Quod quidem sigillum idem Dominus Rex a Roberto de Sadyngton Cancellario suo super passagio suo versus dictas partes Flandriæ prius recessit eidemque Cancellario in quadam bursa inclusum in Magna Aula Regis apud Westmonasterium in loco ubi idem Cancellarius communiter sedet inter Clericos Cancellariæ pro officio suo exercendo in præsentia eorundem clericorum liberavit."—Rot. Cl. 19 Ed. 3, p. 2.
[2] Or. Jur. 47.
[3] Rot. Cl. m. 10.

From family interest, as well as personal merit, he soon got preferment, and being Dean of Lincoln, while still a young man he had a promise of the next vacant bishopric.

He held the office of Chancellor with great credit for five years, and would probably have been continued in it much longer but for his untimely death.

At the parliament held in the beginning of the year 1347 he had the satisfaction of announcing the victory of Cressy, and of obtaining supplies larger than ever before voted, to enable the King to push on the seige of Calais.[1]

The Commons, finding no fault with him as an equity judge, made an effort to reduce the fees payable upon writs out of Chancery, which were represented to be contrary to the words of Magna Charta, "Nulli *vendemus justitiam*;" but these constituted a branch of the royal revenue, which the King would not suffer to be touched, and he returned for answer, "Unto the poor it shall be given *for God's sake*, and it is reasonable that those who can afford to pay should pay, as they have been accustomed."[2]

Offord remained in great favor with the King, and in September, 1348, while Chancellor, he was promoted to the see of Canterbury. He had both the royal commendation and the Papal provision for his consecration, and in all proceedings during the latter part of his time, he is designated "Archbishop of Canterbury elect, and Chancellor."[3]

[1] 1 Parl. Hist. III.   [2] Rot. Parl. 21 Ed. 3.
[3] One of the most curious of these is a writ which he sent in the King's name to the sheriffs of London, commanding them to make proclamation to different classes of suitors how respectively they were to obtain justice, and is supposed to show that the distinction between common law and equity was then fully established, and that the latter was not exclusively administered by the Chancellor, but by him or the Keeper of the Privy Seal, subject to the control of the King in Council. "Rex Vicecomit. *London*, salutem. Quia circa diversa negotia nos et statum regni nostri Angl. concernantia sumus indies multipliciter occupati, volumus quod quælibet negotia tam communem legem regni nostri Angl. quam gratiam nostram specialem concernantia penes nosmetipsos hab' prosequend' eadem negotia, videlicet negotia ad communem legem penes venerab' virum elect' Cantuar' confirmat' Cancellarium nostrum per ipsum expediend. et alia negotia de gratia nostra concedenda penes eundem Cancellarium seu dilectum clericum nostrum Custodem sigilli nostri privati prosequantur. Ita quod ipsi vel unus eorum petitiones, negotiorum quæ per eos nobis inconsultis expediri non poterunt, una cum advisamentis suis inde ad nos transmittant vel transmittat, absque alia prosecutione penes nos inde faciend' ut his inspectis ulterius præfato Cancellario, seu

Lord Chancellor Offord seems to have had the Great Seal always in his own keeping, unless when he parted with it for some temporary purpose. On the 28th of October, 1348, he delivered it to the Master of the Rolls to take to the King at Sandwich, then about to sail for the Continent. As soon as the King received it, he ordered certain commissions to be sealed with it, and then gave it to Andrew de Offord to carry to his brother the Chancellor,[1] who did not afterwards part with it.

He had got possession of the temporalities of his see, and was making great preparations for his inauguration, when he was suddenly struck with a disease of which he died on the 26th of August, 1348.

He was more a statesman than a lawyer or a divine; but he left behind him a considerable reputation for assiduity and discretion in the discharge of his official duties.

On his death, the Great Seal remained in the custody of the Master of the Rolls and three others for about a month, while the King deliberated about a successor, and things having gone on so smoothly under a clerical Chancellor, he at last appointed to the office JOHN DE THORESBY, Bishop of St. David's,[2] who held it for seven years.

This man, very eminent in his own time, had studied at Oxford, where he not only became a deep divine, but very knowing in the civil and canon law. While still young, he wrote many tracts both in Latin and in English, now beginning to be cultivated by men of learning.

Custod inde significamus velle nostrum, et quod nullus alius hujusmodi negotia penes nosmetipsos de cætero prosequantur, vobis præcipimus quod statim visis præsentibus præmissa omnia et singula in civitate prædicta in locis ubi expediri videritis public proclamari faciatis in forma prædicta et hoc nullatenus omittatis. Teste Rege apud Langley, 13 die Januar. Anno regni 22 Ed. 3. Claus. p. 2, m. 2, in dorso per ipsum Regem."—Where it is said that common law business was to be prosecuted before the Chancellor, I presume this can only mean that application should be made for original writs out of Chancery. Or may "matters concerning the common law" mean disputes between subject and subject to be decided judicially by the Chancellor, and "matters concerning our special grace cognizable before us" mean grants and matters of favor depending on the pleasure of the Crown?

[1] The learned and accurate Hardy represents Andrew de Offord to have been a keeper of the Great Seal; but, with great deference he was not intrusted to use it, and was merely a messenger to convey it to London.—Hardy's *Chancellors*, 78. Rot. Cl. 22 Ed. 3, m. 8.

[2] Rot. Cl. 22 Ed. 3, m. 8.

His most popular was a "A Commentary on the Lord's Prayer, the Decalogue, and the Creed;" but none of them were considered to be of sufficient value to be preserved and printed. He early took orders, and was made a Master in Chancery. On the 21st of February, 15 Ed. 3, he was appointed Master of the Rolls. He rose into high favor with the King, and, showing an aptitude for state affairs, was intrusted with the Privy Seal, and sworn a member of the council.[1] He was elected Bishop of St. David's in September, 1347, and was translated to Worcester in November, 1349.

Although considered the most learned man of his time, he was very deficient as an orator, and while he held the Great Seal, as often as parliament met, the causes of the summons were declared by the Chief Justice of the King's Bench, supported by the King's Chamberlain or some other courtier.

The most memorable proceeding in parliament while he presided there, was the passing of the famous Statute of Treasons.[2] For the first time in any European monarchy, the law gave a definition of the acts against the state which should amount to *lese-majesty* and subject the offender to the high penalties which must be enacted against those who aim at the life of the Sovereign, or who attempt by violence to bring about a revolution in the established government of the country. This statute, which did more for the liberties of England than Magna Charta itself, continues in force to the present day. It has been considerably extended by judicial construction beyond its original terms. Where the King's life is not directly aimed at, no act of public nature, short of levying war against the King in his realm, being expressly declared to be treason, the judges have been driven to decide that any revolutionary movement or plot is constructively a compassing of the King's death. It would have been better if the deficiency had been supplied by the legislature; but it would be too late now to resort to a strict interpretation of the statute, although the judges of the present day would hardly hold with some of their

---

[1] In the Rolls, in which he is mentioned about this time, he is sometimes styled "Magister," and sometimes "Dominus," but the one title seems to have been considered quite as high as the other.
[2] 25 Ed. 3, c. 2.

predecessors, that an insurrection to destroy all dissenting meeting-houses, or all inclosures, or all brothels, would be a compassing of the death of our Lady the Queen.[1]

Lord Chancellor Thoresby, if he did not bring forward, must have acquiesced in the passing of this memorable reform of the law, for which we owe some respect to his memory; for he has had successors who not only originated no good measure, but have zealously supported every legal abuse.

While Thoresby was Chancellor, the Commons renewed their attempt to reduce the fees payable on writs out of Chancery,—the King returning to their petition this soft and evasive answer: "It pleases the King, that the Chancellor shall be as moderate as he can touching fees on writs, having regard to the condition of the persons who purchase them."

The Commons then made an attack on the equitable jurisdiction of the Council and the Chancellor, but in such general terms that their petition could not be negatived. Citing Magna Charta, that "no man shall be prejudged of his freehold or franchises save by the law of the land," they prayed that no one might be put to answer for such matters but by due process at the common law, and that anything to the contrary should be held null and void. The answer was, "It pleases our Lord the King that the petition be granted."[2]

He appears to have interfered very little with the judicial duties of the office, for during almost the whole of his time the Great Seal was in the hands of Keepers,— either of several jointly, or of one under the seals of two others,—in whose presence alone it could be used. The necessity for the Chancellor's attendance in his diocese is several times the reason assigned in the Close Roll for the King giving him leave of absence from London and the appointment of Keepers till his return.

In November, 1356, Thoresby, being promoted to the

---

[1] "Constructive Treason" is practically abolished by 11 and 12 Vic. c. 12, a statute which I myself originated, drew, and carried through parliament while a member of the Cabinet; whereby the seditious proceedings formerly denominated *constructive treason* are made *felony*, punishable by transportation for life or by imprisonment.

[2] "Il plest a nre. Seigr le Roi, q. la petition soit *ottroié*."—Rot. Parl. 25 Ed. 3. "Ottroyer," or "Octroyer," was the proper French word to designate a royal grant. Hence the "Octroi" or municipal tax granted by the King.

Archiepiscopal see of York, resigned the Great Seal. We have many instances of Archbishops of Canterbury holding the office of Chancellor, as they had only to cross the Thames in their state barge from Lambeth to Westminster Hall; but the duties of the northern metropolitan were generally considered incompatible with a continued residence in London, although Wolsey, and a few others, unscrupulously sacrificed them to gain their ambitious ends.

Thoresby died on the 6th of November, 1373, leaving behind him a great reputation for piety and charity as well as learning. While he was Archbishop of York, the precedency of the two archbishops which hitherto had been contested was settled, and the title of "Primate of all England," since borne by the Archbishop of Canterbury, was invented.

On Archbishop Thoresby's resignation, the Great Seal was delivered to WILLIAM DE EDINGTON, Bishop of Winchester, as Chancellor, and he held it above six years.

This individual, highly distinguished in his own time, though so little known in ours, took his name from the place of his birth, *Edington*, in Wiltshire, where he afterwards founded the priory of " Bons Hommes." He studied at Oxford, and there acquired great reputation for his skill in law and divinity.

He was warmly patronized by Adam de Orleton, Bishop of Winchester, who presented him to the living of Cheriton, in Hampshire, and introduced him at Court. Gaining the good-will of Edward III., he was appointed to the see of Winchester on the death of his patron, and was the first of four prelates who, being all Chancellors, successively held it for near 150 years.[1]

While Edington remained Chancellor, he himself did all the duties of the office without the assistance of any Keeper or Vice-Chancellor. According to the accustomed form, the Great Seal was twice surrendered up by him to the King on his going beyond seas, and on his Majesty's return exchanged for the seal used during his absence.

In his time England was at the height of military glory, the Black Prince having gained the battle of Poictiers, and John King of France and David King of Scots being fellow-prisoners in London. Nevertheless he

[1] Edington, Wm. of Wickham, Cardinal Beaufort, and Waynflete.

had to set the Great Seal to the treaty of Bretigni in 1360, by which Edward, after all his victories, renounced his claim to the Crown of France, in consideration of being allowed to hold certain provinces in that kingdom in full sovereignty.

There was now an interval of repose for domestic improvement, and in 1362 the Chancellor carried through parliament the famous statute whereby it was enacted that all pleadings and judgments in the Courts of Westminster should for the future be in English,[1] whereas they had been in French ever since the Conquest;—and that all schoolmasters should teach their scholars to construe in English, and not in French as they had hitherto been accustomed. Although the French language no longer enjoyed any legal sanction, it had such a hold of legal practitioners, that it continued to be voluntarily used by them down to the middle of the eighteenth century. Their reports, and treatises, and abridgments are in French; and if we would find anything in Chief Baron Comyn's Digest composed in the reign of George II. about "Highways," "Tithes," or "Husband and Wife," we must look to the titles "Chemin," "Dismes," and "Baron & Feme."[2]

[1] 36 Ed. 3, c. 15.
[2] The Law, having spoken French in her infancy, had great difficulty in changing her dialect. It is curious that acts of parliament long continued to be framed in French, and that French is still employed by the different branches of the legislature in their intercourse with each other. Not only is the royal assent given to the bills by the words "La Reyne le veult," but when either House passes a bill there is an indorsement written upon it, "Soit bailé aux Seigneurs," or "aux communes;" and at the beginning of every parliament the Lords make an entry in their Journals, in French, of the appointment of the Receivers and Tiers of Petitions, not only for England, but for *Gascony*. E. g.: Extract from Lords' Journal, 24th August, 1841:—

"Les Recevours des Petitions de Gascoigne et des autres terres et pays de par la mer et des isles.

 "Le Baron Abinger, Chief Baron de l'Exchequer de la Reyne,
 "Messire James Parke, Chevalier.
 "Messire John Edmund Dowdeswell, Ecuyer.

"Et ceux qui veulent delivre leur Petitions les baillent dedans six jours procheinment ensuivant.

"Les Triours des Petitions de Gascoigne et des autres terres et pays de par la mer et des isles.

 "Le Duc de Somerset.
 "Le Marquis d'Anglesey,
 "Le Count de Tankerville.
 "Le Viscount Torrington.
 "Le Baron Campbell.

Edington might have been raised to the primacy if he had pleased,—but he refused the preferment, saying, "*That indeed the rack of Canterbury was higher, but the manger of Winchester was larger.*"

When Lord Treasurer, in 1350, he had incurred great odium by debasing the coin; but he seems to have passed through the office of Chancellor without reproach. He concurred in passing several very salutory statutes for correcting the oppressive abuses of purveyance, whereby it was enacted, that "if any man that feeleth himself aggrieved contrary to any thing contained in these statutes will come into the Chancery, and thereof make his complaint, he shall there have remedy." The process, no doubt, was by petition, on which the Chancellor, in a summary manner, inquired and gave judgment.

He resigned the Great Seal in Feburary, 1363, and died at Winchester on the 8th of October, 1366. He acquired great reputation for piety by the monastic institution which he founded in his native place; but perhaps his best claim to the gratitude of posterity was, his patronage of William of Wickham,—the architect of Windsor Castle, —his successor in the see of Winchester,—twice Lord Chancellor, and founder of Winchester School and New College, Oxford.

The next Chancellor was SIMON DE LANGHAM, Bishop of Ely.[1] I cannot find out the origin of this aspiring and unamiable man. He first appears as a monk in the Abbey of Westminster; but under his cowl he concealed unbounded ambition and very considerable talents. He is one of the few instances of the regular clergy attaining to great eminence in England. He was always rising in the world. From a great reputation for piety he was eagerly resorted to as a Confessor, and he acquired much influence over his penitents, which he turned skillfully to his own account. He could adapt his manners to all classes and characters, and the monk who recommended himself to some by fasting and penance gained the favor of Edward III. by his courtly manners, and the aptitude he displayed

---

"Tout eux ensemble, ou quatre des seigneurs avant-ditz, appellant aut eux les Serjeants de la Reyne, quant sera besoigne, tiendront leur place en la chambre du Chambellan.

"Recevours et Triours des Petitions de la Grande Bretagne et d'Ireland" were appointed the same day.

[1] Rot. Cl. 37 Ed. 3, m. 39.

for civil business. Though generally somewhat stern, and rather unpopular with those who depended upon him, he courted his superiors so assiduously and so successfully, that he was successively Treasurer of Wells, Archdeacon of Taunton, Prior and Abbot of Westminister, Bishop of Ely, and Treasurer of England. He had been elected Bishop of London; but Ely falling vacant before his consecration, he preferred it as being richer, though inferior in rank.

Being now Chancellor, he was, in 1366, translated to the see of Canterbury, uniting in his own person the two offices of highest civil and ecclesiastical dignity. But if we may credit a waggish distich which was then penned upon him, this translation caused equal joy in one quarter and consternation in another:—

> "Lætantur cœli,—quia Simon transit ab Ely,
> Cujus in adventum—flent in Kent millia centum."

Among those with whom he quarreled at Canterbury was the famous John Wickliffe, then a student at the College there erected by Islip, his predecessor. This ardent youth being unjustly expelled, and finding no redress for the wrong he suffered, turned his mind to clerical usurpation and oppression, and prepared the way for that reformation in religion which blessed an after age.

Langham was installed in his office of Chancellor with extraordinary pomp and magnificence. Being appointed on Sunday, 19th February, the record says that on Tuesday next following, taking the Great Seal with him to Westminster, " et in sede marmorea, ubi Cancellarii sedere sunt assueti, sedens, &c., literas patents, &c., consignari fecit."[1]

All the parliaments called in his time were opened by an oration from him. We may give as a specimen his performance on the 4th of December, 1364. He set the example, long followed on such occasions by ecclesiastical Chancellors,[2] of beginning with a text from the Holy

---

[1] Rot. Cl. 37 Ed. 3, m. 39. See Dugd. Or. Jur. 37. He adds that the marble chair remained to this day, being fixed in the wall over against the middle of the marble table.

[2] "When a bishop was Lord Chancellor, he took a text of Scripture, which he repeated in Latin and discoursed upon the same. But when a judge was Lord Chancellor, he took no text, but in manner of an oration showed summarily the causes of the parliament."—4 Inst. 8.

Scriptures as a theme. He now selected the saying of the Royal Prophet—" Faithful judgment doth adorn the King's seat;"—whence he took occasion to extol the great valor of the King, his master, and the many victories which, by God's assistance, he had gained in his youth; not forgetting the constant dutiful goodwill and ready concurrence of the King's loyal subjects towards the furtherance of those his important undertakings: "For all which, as the King did now by him return them his hearty thanks, so he let them know that for his part he was resolved to seek the common peace and tranquillity of all his people, especially by enforcing a due observance of all good and wholesome laws, and amending such of them as should be thought defective; as also by establishing new ones as necessity should require."

Notwithstanding these smooth words there were heavy complaints against the Chancellor for increasing the fines in Chancery payable to the King; and the Commons prayed that these fines should not be higher than they were in the time of the King's father, or at the King's first coronation. It would appear that the new practice was agreeable as well as profitable to the King, who was determined to continue it by returning this answer:—" The King wills that fines be reasonable to the ease and quiet of his people."

In the beginning of 1367 Langham's ambition was further gratified, as he was made a Cardinal by Pope Urban V.; and there being nothing further in England which he could covet, he aspired to the triple crown itself. It was probably with this view that he soon after resigned the office of Chancellor, and went to Avignon to intrigue among the Cardinals. There he lived eight years in great credit and splendor. In 1371 he came to London as a legate from the Pope to negotiate a peace between France and England. But while speculating at Avignon about a vacancy in the papacy, all his ambitious schemes were for ever terminated by an attack of palsy, of which he immediately died. He is celebrated more for his liberality to to the abbey and monks of Westminster, than for his just administration of the law, or any improvements in legislation.

CHAPTER XV.

CHANCELLORS AND KEEPERS OF THE GREAT SEAL FROM THE APPOINTMENT OF WILLIAM OF WICKHAM TILL THE DEATH OF EDWARD III.

THE successor of Langham is still regarded with high respect by the English nation,—the famous WILLIAM OF WICKHAM.

This distinguished man,—twice Lord Chancellor,—was born in the year 1324 at the village in Hampshire from which he took his name,—of poor but honest parents,—being the son of John Lang and Sibyl his wife.[1] He probably never would have been known to the world had he not, when quite a child, attracted the notice of Nicholas Uvedale, Lord of the Manor of Wickham, and governor of Winchester, who put him to school in that city. He is likewise said to have been sent to study at Oxford; but there is great reason to doubt whether he ever was at any university, and his splendid foundations for the education of youth probably proceeded less from gratitude, than from a desire to rescue others from the disadvantages under which he had himself labored, for he never possessed scholastic learning, and he owed his advancement to the native fervor of his genius and the energy which enabled him to surmount all difficulties. While still a youth, he became private secretary to his patron, and was lodged in a high turret in

---

[1] It has been lately asserted that Wickham, or Wykeham, was his *family* name, because it is said to have belonged to several relations born elsewhere; but all the earliest accounts of him concur in the statement I have adopted. For example :—

> " Qua capit australes comitatu Hamptona Britannos,
>   Wichamia est vicus, nec nisi parvus ager.
> Vixit Iohannes illic cognomine Longus,
>   Cui fuit in casti parte Sibylla thori.
> Hanc habuit patriam GULIELMUS et hosce parentes.
>   Wichamus, augurio nec tamen absque bono ;
> Namque loci ut nomen, sic vim matrisque patrisque
>   Haud dubie in vitam transtulit ille suam,
> *Longus* enim ut *longo* duraret tempore, caute
>   Et bene *prospiceret* cuncta, *Sibylla* dedit."
>
> *Ortus et Vita Gul. de Wicham.*

Winchester Castle, of which Uvedale was constable. Here he imbibed that enthusiastic admiration of Gothic architecture which was the foundation of his fortune. Ere long there was no cathedral, ancient church, baronial hall, or Norman castle many miles round that he had not visited and studied; and he set to work to consider scientifically how such stately structures were erected, and to figure in his imagination others grander and of finer proportions. He was first noticed by Edington, the Bishop of Winchester, then Lord Chancellor,—little thinking that he was himself to be Bishop of Winchester and Lord Chancellor. But from him he had only fair words and good cheer.

Uvedale afterwards happened to mention to the King the remarkable young man he had for his secretary, and Edward, ever ready to avail himself of efficient service and to encourage merit in every department, desired that he might be presented to him. He was accordingly brought to Court, and he instantly made a most favorable impression by his modest and insinuating manners, and his great knowledge of the subject to which he had devoted himself. First he was made "Clerk of all the King's works in his manors of Henle and Yelhampsted,"[1] and then "Surveyor of the King's works in the castle and park of Windsor."[2]

Edward, after his great victories, now meditated the erection of a palace where, according to the taste of the age, he might entertain the flower of European chivalry, of which he was the acknowledged head,—affording his brother knights a full opportunity to display their prowess in the tournament, and to lead the dance with their lady-loves in the brilliant hall at night. Windsor, the destined site, had been occasionally the residence of our sovereigns since the Conquest; but what was then called "the Castle," consisted of a few irregular buildings, with pepper-boxes at the corners of them.

Wickham furnished the designs for the new Castle such nearly as we now behold it—suitable to its noble position, and for simplicity and grandeur superior to any royal residence in the world. He showed corresponding vigor in carrying the plan into execution. By a stretch of prerogative every county in England was obliged to send a

[1] Patent dated 10th May, 1356.   [2] Patent, 30th Oct. 1356.

contingent of masons and other workmen, and in a surprisingly short period the structure was completed.

The King, to celebrate the event, founded the illustrious order of the Garter, which now adds to the patronage of the Prime Minister, and furnishes the object of highest ambition to our greatest nobles.

It is said that the architect gave deep offense to his royal master by placing on one of the gates the inscription, "*This made Wichem*," which was construed into an arrogant appropriation to himself of all the glory of the edifice. But he insisted that the words were to be read as a translation of "Wichamum fecit hoc"[1]—not of "Hoc fecit Wichamus,"—that according to the usual idiom of the English language, "Wichem" was here the accusative case, instead of the nominative—and that he only wished posterity to know that his superintendence of the work had gained him the royal favor, and thus had raised him from low degree to exalted fortune. Edward was appeased, and ever afterwards delighted to honor him.

Except the common law, the only road to wealth and power open to a *non-combatant* in those days—was the church. It was now too late for William to begin the study of Bracton, Fleta, and the Year Books, and to try to obtain practice in Westminster Hall; but he was prevailed upon to take orders, and ecclesiastical preferments were showered upon him. It has been supposed that he had early taken deacon's orders, because in 1352 he was styled "clericus" or *clerk*, but this designation was given to men in civil employments,[2] although not in the church; and hitherto he had no ecclesiastical function or benefice. On the 5th of December, 1361, he was admitted to the order of "*acolyte;*"—he was ordained subdeacon on the 12th of March, 1362, and priest on the 12th of June following. He was now inducted into the rectory of Palham in Norfolk,—he was presented to a prebend in the cathe-

[1] This use of "facere," *to make a man*, rather strengthens the presumption that he did not study at Oxford.

[2] Thus in the contemporary poem of the "Wife of Bath's Prologue" by Chaucer—

"My fifthe husbande, God his soule blesse!
Which that I toke for love and no richesse,
He sometimes was a CLERK of Oxenforde,
And had left scole and went at home at borde.

Of course the *clerk* had not taken orders, or he could not have entered into this matrimonial alliance.

dral at Lichfield, and he received the King's grant of the deanery of the royal free chapel or collegiate church of St. Martin's-le-Grand, London,—with other pluralities. His *secular* preferment likewise still proceeded, as he was appointed "chief warden and surveyor of the King's castles of Old and New Windsor, and sundry others, with the parks belonging to them," for which he had, besides many fees and perquisites, an assignment of 20s. a day out of the Exchequer.

He now likewise entered the field of politics; on the 11th of May, 1364, he was made Keeper of the Privy Seal, and soon after he is styled "Secretary to the King," performing the functions of the officer afterwards designated "Principal Secretary of State." In May, 1365, he was commissioned along with others to treat of the ransom of David II. King of Scotland, taken prisoner at Neville's Cross, and the prolonging of the truce with the Scots.

Under the bull of Pope Urban V. against pluralities, he was reluctantly compelled to make a return of his ecclesiastical benefices, in which he calls himself "Sir William of Wykeham, clerk, Archdeacon of Lincoln, and secretary of our lord the illustrious King of England, and keeper of his Privy Seal,—and in which he reduces the total amount of annual produce to £873 6s. 8d.

He did not attend much to his spiritual duties, but he showed great dexterity in civil business, and a natural aptitude for every situation in which he was placed,—so that he escaped the envy that might have been expected to attend his elevation, and was a general favorite. Conscious how much he owed to his delicate attention to the feelings of others, when he had from the Heralds a grant of arms, he took for his motto, "Manners makyth man."[1]

At last, on the death of Ex-Chancellor Edington, Bishop of Winchester, in 1366, at the earnest recommendation of the King, he was elected by the prior and convent to succeed him in that see. This promotion in

---

[1] We must not infer defective education from the seeming ungrammatical structure of this motto, for our ancestors, like the Greeks, put a singular verb to a plural neuter substantive, as

"—— cragges and stones
Maketh pilgrims weary bones."

his native county must have been particularly gratifying to him, and as he was only in his forty-second year, we may hope that his parents were still alive, and walked from the village of Wickham to Winchester to see him enthroned.

The resignation of the Great Seal by Archbishop Lang ham in pursuit of the triple crown, threw the King into considerable perplexity, there being neither lawyer nor churchman whom he considered perfectly well qualified for the office of Chancellor. He yielded to personal inclination, and appointed to it his favorite, William of Wickham, whose installation he graced by delivering to him a new Great Seal, with the lilies engraved upon it, in consequence of a resolution of parliament that he should resume the title of King of France.[1]

This appointment, in spite of William's abilities and popularity, must have been generally condemned, and shows that while the King was all-powerful from the success of his arms abroad, he disregarded public opinion in the acts of his domestic government. The jurisdiction of the Court of Chancery had been greatly extended during the last forty years, and Parnynge while presiding there must have given something like system to its practice. The result soon showed that no one who was an entire stranger to legal pursuits and habits, could decently discharge the duties even of an equity judge, discretionary as they were then deemed to be.[2]

The Chancellor no doubt invited those who practiced in his court to sumptuous banquets at his place in Southwark;—made himself very agreeable in society;—availed himself discreetly of the talents and experience of those

[1] Rot. Cl. 43 Ed. 3, m. 18.
[2] His promotion to be judge was ascribed to his skill as an architect.

"Windesora fuit pagus celeberrimus, illic
 Rex statuit castri mœnia magna sui,
Wicamus huic operi præponitur : inde probatum est
 Ingenio quantum polluit, arte, fide.
Ergo fit Edwardo charus CUSTOSQUE SIGILLI
 . Non ita post multos incipit esse dies."
Ort. et Vit. Gul. de Wick.

The analogous case would be, if Sir C. Barry, as a recompense for his excellent plan for the new houses of Parliament, were now to be made Lord Chancellor. Wickliffe, in revenge for being questioned by Wickham as a heretic, complained that promotion fell " only on kitchen clerks and *men wise in building castles.*"

around him;—and, that he might not give unnecessary trouble to himself nor offense to others, *affirmed* in all cases brought before him on appeal;—but the suitors complained bitterly of his delays and inefficiency, and, as their wrongs gradually excited the sympathy of the public, at last parliament interfered. In 1371, when William had been Chancellor four years, the "Earls, Barons, and Commons of England," (the Lords spiritual, as might have been expected, not joining in the vote), petitioned the King, "that thenceforth none but laymen should be appointed Chancellor or other great officer or governor of the realm, for the state had been too long governed by churchmen *queux ne sont mye justiciables en touz cas*." [1]

The altered posture of the King's affairs rendered it impossible for him to stand out against the wishes of parliament and the people. All the efforts of his younger son to gain the crown of Castile had failed; and the treaty of Bretigni being broken, new expeditions against France were to be undertaken, and fresh supplies were indispensable. Accordingly, on the 24th of March, the Great Seal was taken from William of Wickham, and two days after, it was delivered to the man universally considered the best qualified to perform the duties belonging to it,—Sir ROBERT THORPE, who had been regularly bred to the bar, and for some time had, with great applause, filled the office of Chief Justice of the Common Pleas.

He was of obscure origin, and took his name from Thorpe, in Norfolk, the place of his birth. He was bred at Pembroke Hall, Cambridge, then lately founded, of which he became the second master. He laid the foundation of the divinity schools at Cambridge, with the chapel over them, which were afterwards completed by his brother Sir William.

Instead of going into orders, he transferred himself to the inns of court, and became a very diligent student of the common law. We do not exactly know when he began to practice at the bar, but as early as 1330 we find him employed as a Justice Itinerant.[2] In 1344 he was appointed a King's Sergeant, and he was summoned with the judges to attend in the House of Lords. For ten years he continued at the head of the bar in Westminster Hall, taking precedence of the Attorney and Solicitor

---

[1] Rot. Parl. 45 Ed. 3.   [2] Rot. Cl. 4 Ed. 3. m. 32.

General, and having the chief practice in all the courts. On the 27th of June, 30 Ed. III., he was raised to the office of Chief Justice of the Common Pleas, which he held with the highest character for learning, industry, and integrity, till, to gratify the Commons, who had petitioned that none but a layman should be Chancellor, and to soothe the growing discontents of the people, the Great Seal was delivered to him.

His elevation was universally hailed with joy, and even William of Wickham, his predecessor, gracefully assisted not only at the ceremony of his being sworn in before the King, but at his public installation in Westminster Hall.[1] Thorpe, as Chancellor, fully equalled public expectation, and introduced some very useful reforms into the Court of Chancery; but unfortunately, when he had held the office little more than a year, he fell into a mortal distemper, and he died on the 29th of June, 1372.

There is not preserved any report of his equitable decisions, and no parliament met during the short time he held the office of Chancellor; but from his addresses to the Lords and Commons, while Chief Justice during the Chancellorship of Bishop Thoresby, he seems to have been eloquent, and Lord Coke pronounces him "a man of singular judgment in the laws of this realm," and dwells with great complacency on his elevation to the woolsack, evidently much sympathising with "the complaint of the Lords and Commons, that the realme had bin of long time goverened by men of the Church in disherison of the Crown."[2] It is to be deeply deplored of a virtuous magistrate, like Thorpe, such slender memorials remain, as it is so much more agreeable to relate what is honorable than what is disgraceful to human nature—to praise rather than to condemn; but I find from my laborious researches, that while a Chancellor is going on in the equal and satisfactory discharge of his duty, little notice is taken of him, and that he is only made promi-

---

[1] In Magna Aula Westmonasterii ubi Placea Cancellariæ habetur præsentibus præfato Episcopo Wyntoniensi Clericos Cancellariæ dictam bursam aperire," &c.—Rot. Cl. 45 Ed .3, m. 35. There is a curious en ry on the 28th March, intimating that on that day the late Chancellor in the preience of Chancellor Thorpe, surrendered up to the King two other Great Seals and two Privy Seals lately in use, which the King had placed in the Bishop's custody, and which were then delivered to the Lord Treasurer.—Ibid.

[2] 4 Inst. "Chancery."

nent by biographers and historians when he takes bribes, perverts the law, violates the constitution, oppresses the innocent, and brings ruin on his country:—

> The evil that men do lives after them:
> The good is oft interr'd with their bones."

Thorpe, approaching his end, while he lay in the palace of the Bishop of Sarum, in Fleet Street, "languens in extremis, videns se circa ea quæ ad officium Cancellarii pertinent, ulterius laborare non posse prout moris est," says the Close Roll,—enclosed the Great Seal in a bag under his own private seal and that of Chief Justice Knyvet. There it was found when he expired, and the following day it was delivered by his servants to Sir William Latymer the Chamberlain, Sir Richard le Scrope the Treasurer and Sir Nicholas de Carew, Keeper of the Privy Purse, who carried it to the King at Westminster, and on the 5th of July following he sent it by his son, John of Gaunt, then styled "King of Castile and Leon, and Duke of Lancaster," to Chief Justice KNYVET, as Chancellor, with power to administer the oaths to him—a ceremony which was performed with great solemnity in the King's Chapel.[1]

Sir John Knyvet seems to have been the first important member of his family. Camden, speaking of it in a subsequent generation, calls it "an ancient house ever since Sir John Knyvet was Lord Chancellor under Edward III." In 1347 he was called to the degree of Sergeant-at-law; he was soon after appointed a Justice of the Common Pleas, and he so continued till 1357, when he was advanced to the Chief Justiceship of the King's Bench, which he held with high credit.

Lord Coke calls him "a famous man in his profession," and during four years and a half he presided in the Court of Chancery to the general contentment of the people, Lord Coke, speaking of him and his predecessor, says with honest pride;—"In perusing the rolls of parliament in the times of these Lord Chancellors, we find no complaint at all of any proceeding before them. But soon after, when a Chancellor was no professor of the law, we find a grievous complaint by the whole body of the realm, and a petition that the most wise and able men within the realm might be chosen Chancellors, and that

[1] Rot. Cl. 46 Ed. 3, m. 20.

the King seek to redress the enormities of the Chancery."[1]

In November, after Knyvet's appointment, a parliament was held at Westminster, but for some reason not explained to us the Chancellor did not preside at the opening of it, and by the King's command the causes of the summons were declared by Sir Henry Bryan, one of the King's council.[2] No business of importance was transacted except the grant of a supply, and this being done, the Lords and Commons met the King in the White Chamber, when the Chancellor declared to the King,— " how kind the parliament had been to him in granting him such a supply," and " the King very humbly thanked them for their great aid." The petitions of the Commons were then read and answered according to custom. A proceeding then occurred, which shows that the House of Commons had not yet with any certainty taken its place in the constitution with defined powers and privileges. The Knights of shires had leave to depart, and writs for their wages and expenses were made out for them by the Chancellor's order; but he commanded the citizens and burgesses to stay, and they, being again assembled before the Prince, Prelates, and Lords, granted for the safe conveying of their ships and goods, two shillings on every tun of wine imported or exported out of the kingdom, and sixpence in the pound on all their goods and merchandise for one year.[3]

Another parliament was summoned to meet at Westminster in November, 1373. It is amusing to observe the required qualifications of the members to be returned to the House of Commons by the new-fangled writs which the Chancellor framed. The sheriff of every county was ordered " to cause to be chosen two dubbed knights, or the most honest, worthy, and discreet esquires of that county, *the most expert in feats of arms, and no others*, and of every city two citizens, and of every borough two burgesses, discreet and sufficient, and such as had the greatest skill in shipping and merchandising."[4] There was no express exclusion of lawyers any more than of non-combatant country gentlemen, but no individual of either class could well be brought within either category in the writ.

[1] 4 Inst. 78. [2] 1 Parl. Hist. 136. [3] Rot. Parl. 46 Ed. 3. [4] 1 Parl. Hist. 137.

The Lords and Commons being assembled in the Painted Chamber, Lord Chancellor Knyvet, in the presence of the King, declared the causes of the summons. Being a layman, he did not take a text of Scripture, as the theme of his discourse, but he spoke with great eloquence of the negotiations with France,—of the military exploits of the King's son, "King of Castile and Leon,"—and of the duty of refreshing and comforting with force and aid the lords and others who had ventured their lives and fortunes to defend the nation from their enemies. "Wherefore the King charged and besought them, considering the dangers that might happen to the kingdom for these causes, that they would speedily consult on the matter, and give the King such advice as might be for the safety of him, the nation, and themselves."[1]

The required supply was granted, a favorable answer was returned to the petitions of the Commons, and all separated in good humor.

But a very different scene was presented at the next parliament, which met in April, 1376, and was long known among the people by the name of "the Good Parliament."

The King's fair fortune had begun to fail, and, no longer surrounded by the splendor of victory, those who had formerly cheerfully yielded to his wishes and liberally supplied his wants, now sharply criticised the measures of his government, blamed his ministers, and for every grant of money wrung from him some new concession. Much scandal had likewise been excited by the ascendency of Alice Pearce, the King's mistress, who, though said to be of great wit as well as beauty, had been so indiscreet as openly to interfere in the disposal of offices civil and ecclesiastical, and even to appear and sit in the courts of justice, and publicly to favor those suitors who had bribed her for her support. On one occasion, at a tournament in Cheapside, to the great consternation of the citizens of London, she came among them on a white palfrey, in splendid attire, as "lady of the sun and sovereign of the day."

The Chancellor escaping personally any suspicion of being influenced by her, was well aware of the deep discontent which now universally prevailed. Nevertheless, he opened the session in a speech framed as if nothing

[1] 1 Parl. Hist. 138.

were to be expected but submission and gratitude. In declaring the causes of the summons, he said, "the first and principal was to advise about the good government and peace of the realm;—for the defense and safety of the King, as well by sea as land;—to take order for the maintenance of the war with France and elsewhere;—and how and in what manner it might be done for the best profit, quickest dispatch, and greatest honor of the King and kingdom." He then expressly told them, that what the King had hitherto done was always with their advice and assistance, for which his Majesty entirely thanked them, and desired that they would diligently consult about these matters,—"the Prelates and Lords by themselves, and the Commons by themselves,—and give in their answers as soon as they conveniently could."

The Commons, in answer to the Chancellor's harangue, after they had voted a supply, not contented, in the modern courtly style, to praise all the ministerial measures of the session, enumerated the plentiful aids which the King had obtained from his people, and asserted their firm conviction, that if the royal revenue had been faithfully administered, there could have been no necessity for laying additional burdens on the nation. They intimated a want of confidence in the King's present ministers; they impeached several of his favorites of extortion, of selling illegal grants, and raising loans for their own profit; and they requested that ten or twelve new members might be added to the council.[1]

It was admitted that the conduct of the Chancellor was without reproach; but a charge was brought against an Ex-Chancellor, William of Wickham, who, laboring under a strong suspicion of being protected by Alice Pearce, was accused of several misdemeanors in his office of Chancellor. Contrary to the claim of privilege so lately asserted, he was handed over to common-law process, and, without being heard, was condemned to forfeit his temporalities, and to keep himself at the distance of twenty miles from the King's person.

Knyvet, the Chancellor, attempted in vain to allay the storm. Lord Neville, Lord Latimer, and several other of his colleagues were dismissed, and the Commons insisted on an ordinance, or act, being passed "forbidding women

[1] Parl. Hist. 140.

to pursue causes and actions in the King's Courts, by way of maintenance, for hire and reward, and particularly Alice Pearce, under the penalty of forfeiting all that she can forfeit, and of being banished out of the realm-" This ordinance, to which the Chancellor intimated the royal assent, runs in the King's name, and, considering the relation which subsisted between him and the object of it, must be considered a very curious specimen of the legislation of the age.

During all these storms, Knyvet continued in his high office, but his health was so severely injured by his application to business that he was obliged to retire, carrying with him the respect of all classes of the community. He resigned the Great Seal into the King's hands on the 11th of January, 1377, and died soon after.[1]

As he and his predecessor, taken from the common-law courts, had given such satisfaction, we may wonder that the Great Seal should ever have been delivered to men of any other class; yet the next regularly bred lawyer appointed Chancellor was Sir Thomas More, in the middle of the reign of Henry VIII., an interval of above 150 years.

England had been advancing with unexampled celerity in wealth and refinement, but a long period of adversity was at hand. All the glories of the third Edward's long reign had passed away, and it was concluding in misfortune and sorrow. "The sable warrior was fled;" the foreign conquests which had so much gratified the national pride were lost; and deep discontents and misery prevailed at home. Alice Pearce, the King's mistress, as soon as "the Good Parliament" was dissolved, again had the chief disposal of places and preferment, and through her interest a clerical Chancellor was now announced, to the great disgust of the public. This was ADAM DE HOUGHTON, Bishop of St. David's.[2]

One feels little disappointment in not being able to trace the origin or education of this individual, although he accidentally filled the office of Chancellor during two reigns, for he was neither eminent for his virtues nor his vices, and he must have been promoted for his mediocrity, to exclude abler men whose superiority might have created jealousy and alarm.

[1] Rot. Cl. 50 Ed. 3, m. 7. [2] Rot. Cl. 51 Ed. 3, m. 7.

He was educated at Oxford, where he took the degree of doctor of laws. By Papal mandate he was placed in the see of St. David in 1361, and the purchased patronage of Alice Pearce is the only solution of the mystery, that he who for sixteen years had been a Welsh bishop suddenly became Lord Chancellor of England.

A parliament was held at Westminster on the 27th of January, 1377, which was opened by Lord Chancellor Houghton with a speech from this text, "Ye suffer fools gladly, seeing that you yourselves are wise." The application of his subject was, "that they, being wise, desired to hear who was the contrary." From thence he took occasion to argue, that God loved the King and the realm;— the King because "*quos diligit castigat;*"—"*Uxor tua sicut vitis abundans in lateribus,*" "*ut videas filios filiorum,*" —which the King now had the pleasure to see. That God loved the realm, he proved from the recovery of so renowned a prince, the said recovery happening in the fiftieth year of his reign.[1]

The Commons now made another attempt to abolish fines to the King on writs out of Chancery, as a sale of justice contrary to Magna Charta; but the answer was "Let it be in this case in the discretion of the Chancellor for the time being, as it has been hitherto used."[2]

The Chancellor soon after went abroad on an embassy to France, and Burstall, the Master of the Rolls, and two others, were constituted Keepers of the Great Seal till his return.[3] While the Chancellor was still abroad, Edward expired, on the 21st of June, 1377, in the sixty-fifth year of his age, and the fifty-first year of his reign.

Hume observes, that "the domestic government of this prince is really more admirable than his foreign victories," and he certainly deserves to be celebrated for his vigorous and impartial administration of justice. While he wisely adhered to the laws and system of tribunals framed by his grandfather, he conferred an unspeakable benefit on the suitors by making the Chancery and the King's Bench stationary at Westminster, instead of following the person of the Sovereign "wheresoever in England," as they had before practically done,[4] and are still

---

[1] 1 Parl. Hist. 142. [2] Rot. Par. 51 Ed. 3.
[3] Rot. Cl. 51 Ed. 3, m. 7.
[4] The officers of the Chancery lived or lodged together in an Inn or *hospitium*,

by fiction of law supposed to do,—and his appointment of Chancellors, upon the whole, did great credit to his good intentions and his discernment.

The jurisdiction of the Court of Chancery was now established in all matters where its own officers were concerned,[1] on petitions of right, where an injury was alleged to be done to a subject by the King or his officers,[2] in re-

---

which, when the King resided at Westminster, was near the palace, and from very early times the marble table at the upper end of the great hall of the palace was appropriated for the sealing of writs and letters patent. When the King traveled, he was followed by the Chancellor, masters, clerks, and records. On these occasions it was usual to require a strong horse, able to carry the rolls, from some religious house bound to furnish the animal, and at the towns where the King stopped during his progress an hospitium was assigned to the Chancery. In the 20 Ed. 1, the Abbot of Kingswood paid forty shillings to buy a horse to carry the rolls of Chancery, but the money, by order of the Chancellor, was paid over to William le Marchant, of Dover, in part discharge of certain debts due to him from the King.* In 3 Ed. 2, the Abbot of Beaulieu was commanded to provide a strong pack horse to carry the rolls of Chancery to Stamford, where the parliament was about to assemble, the King stating in the mandate that he was in great need of such an animal.†

[1] 18 Ed. 3, ii. 154. The Clerks in Chancery petitioned the King and Council, that whereas the Chancellor and Keepers of the Great Seal for the time being ought to have the cognizance of all pleas of trespass done by the said Clerks or their servants, in cities, towns, or elsewhere where the Chancery is; yet notwithstanding the sheriffs of London had attached Gilbert de Chishull, one of the Clerks of the said Chancery, at the suit of Thomas de Theslingbury, a draper, upon a bill of trespass, whereupon Gilbert brought a supersedeas of privilege to the sheriffs, but which they would not allow, and drove him to find sureties. The Clerks therefore pray remedy and maintenance of their liberties.

This petition was answered with the assent of the parliament, The claim was allowed, and writs were ordered to be sent to the Mayor of London to attach the sheriffs and others who were parties and maintainers of the quarrel, to appear before the King in Chancery at a day certain, to answer as well to the contempt of the process as to the breach of the liberty and damage of the party.

[2] Thomas de Berkelei petitions the King that he may have a writ to the Abbey of St. Austin, Bristol, to have deliverance of his monuments, &c., which were arrested by Richard Lovel and others of the King's Officers.

Let a writ be issued out of Chancery to those who have arrested the things mentioned in the petition, and let them certify in Chancery the cause of the arrest, and upon their certificate let right be done.—Temp. Ed. 3, ii. 385.

---

* Memorandum quod decimo octavo die mensis Januarii, quadraginta solidi, quos Abbas de Kingeswode liberavit in Cancellaria in subvencionem cujusdam equi emendi ad portandum rotulos Cancellariæ, liberati fuerunt per præceptum Cancellarii, per manus Domini Johannis de Langeton, Willielmo le Marchaunt de Dovorr', in partem solucionis debitorum in quibus Rex ei tenetur."—Rot. Claus. 21 Ed. 1, m. 11, a.

† Par. Writs, II. part i. p. 20, No. 2, 3.

lieving against judgments of the courts of law,[1] and generally in cases of fraud, accident, and trust.

The qualifications of the Chancellor now became of great importance to the due administration of justice, not only from the increase of his separate jurisdiction, but from the practice for the common-law judges, when any question of difficulty arose before them in their several courts, to take the advice of Parliament upon it before giving judgment. In a case which occurred in the King's Bench, in the 39th of Edward III., Thorpe, the Chief Justice, says, "Go to the Parliament, and as they will have us do we will, and otherwise not." The following year Thorpe himself, accompanied by Sir Hugh Green, a brother judge, went to the House of Lords, where there were assembled twenty-four bishops, earls, and barons, and asked them, as they had lately passed a statute of joefails, what they intended thereby. Such questions, which were frequent in this reign, must have been answered by the Chancellor.[2]

In the forty-second year of this reign, while William of Wickham was Chancellor, occurred the first instance of a parliamentary impeachment. Criminal jurisdiction had been before exercised by the Lords, but not on the prosecution of the Commons. Sir John Lee was now impeached by the Lower House for malpractices while steward of the household, and the punishment not extending to life or member, the Chancellor, though a priest, was not disqualified from presiding. Before the close of the reign the Commons preferred impeachments against many de-

[1] Margaret de Jonehill complains of a judgment in the Court of Common Pleas.

Let this petition be referred to the Chancery, and let the Chancellor cause to be summoned before the counsel of Madame to appear in Chancery on a certain day, and also the king's sergeants and some of the justices, and if nothing is shown or said which may reasonably disturb the judgment, or if the counsel of Madame do not choose to appear, then let a writ issue to the justices where the plea was depending before judgment, to proceed according to the law and usages of the land.—21 & 22 Ed. 3, ii. 206.

Geoffrey de Lacer complains of a judgment at law.

Let the petition be referred to the Chancery, and there let the evidence which the said Geoffrey says he hath to manifest the loss of the aforesaid commodities be received, and that justice was not done him in his suit for recovery of losses in these parts, and therefore let speedy remedy be ordained him according to the law used in such cases. Temp. Ed. 3, ii. 437.

[2] Y. B. 29 Ed. 3. Y. B. 40 Ed. 3. If the Lords were still liable to be so interrogated, they would not unfrequently be puzzled, and the revival of the practice might be a check to hasty legislation.

linquents for political and other offenses, and the practice of impeachment, according to the present forms of proceed·ng, was fully established.

In this reign the Chancellor acquired that most important and delicate function of appointing Justices of the Peace,—a magistracy peculiar to the British Isles, the judges having a most extensive criminal jurisdiction, being generally without legal education, and serving without any remuneration except the power and consequence which they derive from their office.

The Chancellors in the latter part of this reign, following the example of the distinguished philobiblist De Bury, prided themselves on their attainments in literature, and their protection of literary men, and they must have had a powerful influence in directing the pursuits and developing the genius of Chaucer and Gower. They encouraged the use of the English language, not only by the statute against the use of French in the courts of law, but by their own example on the most public occasions. In the 36 Edward III. we find the earliest record of the use of English in any parliamentary proceeding. The roll of that year is found in French, as usual, but it expressly states that the causes of summoning parliament were declared "*en Englois.*"[1] The precedent then set by Lord Chancellor Edington was followed in the two succeeding years by Lord Chancellor Langham,[2] and from this time *viva voce* proceedings in parliament were generally in English, with the exception of giving the royal assent to bills, although the entry of some of these proceedings in the reign of Queen Victoria is still in Norman French.[3]

[1] Rot. Parl, 36 Ed. 3. [2] Rot. Parl. 37 and 38 Ed. 3. [3] Ante, p. 241.

CHAPTER XVI.

CHANCELLORS AND KEEPERS OF THE GREAT SEAL FROM THE COMMENCEMENT OF THE REIGN OF RICHARD II. TILL THE SECOND CHANCELLORSHIP OF WILLIAM OF WICKHAM.

RICHARD was a boy, only eleven years old, when, on the death of his grandfather, he was proclaimed King. The Keepers of the Great Seal, who had been appointed during the absence of the Chancellor abroad, nevertheless surrendered it into the royal stripling's own hand when he was seated on the throne, and surrounded by his nobility and great officers of state. The Duke of Lancaster, acting as Regent, although formally no Regent or Protector had been appointed, then took it from him, and handed it to Nicholas Bonde, a knight of the King's chamber, for safe custody. De Houghton, the Bishop of St. David's, returned to England in a few days after, and on his arrival at Westminster the King, by his uncle's direction, delivered the great Seal to him, and he again took the oath of office as Chancellor.[1] There was no intention of continuing him in the office beyond the time when a satisfactory arrangement could be made for the appointment of a successor.

Richard being crowned on the 4th of August, writs were issued for the calling of a parliament to meet fifteen days after the feast of St. Michael. On the appointed day, the cause of summons was declared by the Chancellor in a speech founded on the text, "*Rex tuus venit tibi.*" The language introduced at the Conquest was still used on most public occasions, and he thus began: "Seigneurs et Sires, ces paroles vue j'ay dit, sont tant a dire en Franceys, *Vostre Roy vient a toy.*"[2] He then divided the subject into three parts, showing the causes of joy for the King's accession, with his usual quaintness. But he raised a great laugh by an unlucky quotation from Scripture—observing that a *man's* heart leaps for joy when he hears good tidings, like Elizabeth, the mother of John the Baptist :—"*Et exultavit infans in utero ejus.*"[3]

This harangue does not appear to have given perfect

[1] Rot. Cl. 1 Ric. 2, m. 46.   [2] Rolls of Parl. iii. 3.   [3] 1 Parl. Hist. 158.

satisfaction; for the next day Sir Richard Scrope, steward of the King's household, who was rising rapidly into favor, made another speech on behalf of the King, asking the Commons "to advise him which way his and the kingdom's enemies might be resisted, and how the expenses of such resistance were to be borne with the greatest ease by the people, and profit and honor to the kingdom?"

The Commons having, for the first time, chosen a Speaker, set about reforming the abuses of the state in good earnest, and tried to provide for the proper conduct of the government during the King's minority. They obtained the banishment of Alice Pearce, and the removal of the late King's evil councillors. They then proposed, "that, till the King was of age, the Chancellor, High Treasurer, Chief Justice of one bench and the other, the Chief Baron of the Exchequer and other officers, might be made by parliament." This the Lords modified to their own aggrandisement by an amendment "that while the King was under age, the Councillors, Chancellor, Steward of the Household, and Chamberlain, should be chosen by the Upper House, and that the King should make the other officers with the assent of the Council." The Commons acquiesced in this arrangement."[1]

At the parliament which met in the Abbey of Gloucester on the 20th of October, 1378, the young King being seated on the throne, attended by his three uncles, Lancaster, Cambridge, and Buckingham—the Lord Chancellor de Houghton, in a long speech, explained to the Lords and Commons the causes of their being summoned, entering with some prolixity into the subsisting relations of England with France and Scotland. But he gave no satisfaction; and Sir Richard le Scrope the next morning again addressed the two Houses on the same topics, and by way of urging a supply, pointed out the enormous expense which the crown incurred in keeping up garrisons in Brest, Cherbourg, Calais, Bourdeaux, and Bayonne. While the parliament sat, which was only a few days, Sir Richard le Scrope seems to have taken the entire lead, and by his good management the desired subsidy was voted.[2]

[1] 1 Parl. Hist. 162.
[2] The Close Roll contains a very minute account of this transfer of the Great Seal in the house of the Abbot of Gloucester.—2 R. 2, m. 25.

On the 28th of October, as a reward for his services, he was actually made Lord Chancellor on the resignation of the Bishop of St. David's, who seems to have been much hurt at the disrespectful treatment he had experienced.[1] The Ex-Chancellor retired to his see, and there peaceably ended his days at a distance from the strife which marked this unhappy reign. He survived till April, 1389.

RICHARD LE SCROPE, the new Chancellor, was the third son of Sir Henry le Scrope, Chief Justice of the King's Bench, and Chief Baron of the Exchequer in the reign of Edward II. and Edward III., and was born in the year 1328. Instead of being trained in the university, the inns of court, and Westminster Hall, he was a soldier from his early youth, and served during the whole course of the late wars with France. He was at the Battle of Cressy in 1346, and serving under Lord Percy, he was knighted on the field for his gallantry in the Battle of Durham, fought in the same year, where the Scots were signally defeated. In the following year he served at the siege of Calais, where he was obliged to maintain his right to his crest— a crab issuing from a ducal coronet. He was in the memorable sea-fight of Winchelsea in August, 1350, when Edward III. and the Black Prince defeated a greatly superior fleet under Don Carlos de la Cerda. He was with Edward III. at the rescue of Berwick in 1356. In October, 1359, he served under John of Gaunt in the army which invaded France, and in the April following approached close to the walls of Paris, where he was engaged against the family of Grosvenor in another heraldic dispute about his right to certain bearings in his shield. In the parliament which met in 1364, he was elected representative for the county of York. In 1366 he accompanied the Duke of Lancaster into Spain, and the following year was in the decisive battle of Najarre in that country, where the Black Prince commanded in person.

On the renewal of the war with France, in 1369, he again went to France with the Duke of Lancaster, and continued in that country till near the conclusion of the reign of Edward III. In 1371 he was appointed Treasurer of the King's Exchequer. On the accession of Richard II. he was promoted to be Steward of the King's Household, and it was in this capacity that he was em

[1] 1 Parl. Hist. 163.

ployed to address the two Houses, and that he so much distinguished himself in the last two parliaments. Although with little book-learning, he had so much natural talent, and had seen so much of the world, and had such a quick insight into character, that he was reckoned a consummate practical statesman, as well as a distinguished military commander; and his appointment to the office of Chancellor, if it astonished, did not much offend, the public.

The Close Roll tells us that the following day he held a Seal in the church of St. Mary le Crypt at Gloucester, and I read no more of his judicial exploits.[1] That he might more effectually assist the government in the House of Lords, he was raised to the peerage by the title of Baron Scrope of Bolton, in the county of York. Here he had a large domain, and, under a license from the Crown, he erected a strong castle, which stood several seiges, and was afterwards more illustrated by being one of the prisons of Mary Queen of Scots.

In the parliament which met at Westminster on the 14th of January, 1379, he very ably expounded the causes of the summons, was much applauded for his eloquence, and obtained a large supply for the King. The Commons prayed that there might not be another parliament till a year after that time, and that the Chancellor, the Treasurer, Keeper of the Privy Seal, Chief Chamberlain, and Steward of the Household might not be changed in the meanwhile.[2] At the same time they made a complaint of the interference of the Court of Chancery and of the Council with the course of the common law. The answer was, "that parties should be sent to the proper court to answer according to due course of law; provided always, that where the King and his council should be credibly informed that by maintenance, oppression, and other outrages, the common law could not have due course, the Council in such case might send for the party against whom the complaint is made, and put him to answer for the misprision."[3]

We are not informed of the particulars of the intrigue which, on the 2nd of July, 1379, put an end to the first Chancellorship of Lord Scrope; and we only know, from the Close Roll, that on that day he surrendered the Great Seal, and that on the 4th of July the King delivered it to

[1] Rot. Cl. 2 Rich. 2, m. 25. [2] 1 Parl. Hist. 169, 170. [3] Rot. Parl. 2 Rich 2.

SIMON DE SUDBURY, Archbishop of Canterbury,—who, having taken the oaths, was the following day installed as Chancellor in Westminster Hall.¹

Simon de Sudbury assumed that name from the town in Suffolk where he happened to be born. Yet was he of noble extraction, being the son of Nigel Theobald, of a baronial family whose founder had come over with the Conqueror. Having been carefully educated in England, he was sent by his father beyond sea to study the civil law, of which he became a Doctor after disputations in several Continental universities. Such was his fame as a wrangler, that he was admitted of the Counsel to Innocent VI. and Auditor of the Rota in the court of Rome. On the recommendation of the Pope, he had great promotion when he returned home to his own country, being made Chancellor of Sarum, then bishop of London, and, in 1375, translated to the see of Canterbury.

He called forth some censure by accepting the Great Seal; for, though there were many precedents of a Chancellor becoming Archbishop of Canterbury, it was not thought consistent with the dignity of the church that an Archbishop of Canterbury should become Chancellor. It would have been well if he had confined himself to the discharge of his ecclesiastical duties, as, by engaging in politics, he was brought to an untimely and violent end.

He opened the parliament, which met at Northampton, at the feast of All Saints, 1380, and, after much difficulty and management, prevailed upon the Commons to grant the fatal "capitation tax," which was to be "three groats of every person of the kingdom, male or female, of the age of fifteen, of what state or condition soever." This was denounced as "a new and strange subsidy," and Hollingshead writes, that "great grudging and many a bitter curse followed on the levying of this money, and that much mischief rose thereof, as after did appear." If the insult had not been offered by the tax-gatherer to the daughter of Wat Tyler, some other accidental spark would probably have thrown the whole country into a flame.

The Chancellor being the author of the abhorred tax, in the rebellion which it excited he was the first victim. John Ball, the famous seditious preacher, inveighed bit-

¹ Rot. Cl. 3 Rich. 2, m. 22.

terly against him by name; and, in reference to his aristocratic birth, the often-quoted lines were made which, Hume says, "in spite of prejudice, we cannot but regard with some degree of approbation:"

> "When Adam delv'd and Eve span,
> Where was then the gentleman?"

The army, or rather mob, 100,000 strong, under Tyler and Straw, having taken post at Blackheath, and threatening general destruction—more especially to lawyers,[1] and all who were supposed to have been instrumental in imposing the tax, or who resisted the demands for its repeal, the Chancellor took refuge in the Tower of London. They pursued him thither, attacked his fortress, and it being feebly defended, they soon stormed it. They instantly seized him, and dragged him to Tower Hill, with the declared intention of executing him there as a traitor.

In this extremity he displayed great courage and constancy, and, addressing the multitude, reminded them of his sacred character, and tried to rouse them to some sense of justice and humanity.[2] All these appeals were ineffectual; after many blows his head was struck off, and his dead body was treated with barbarous indignity.

---

[1] Walsingham, in his interesting relation of Wat Tyler's rebellion, says:— "Voluit namque ad alia commissionem pro se et suis obtinuisse, ad decollandum omnes juridicos et universos qui vel in lege docti fuere vel cum jure ratione officii communicavere. Mente nempe conceperat, doctis in lege necatis, universa juxta communis plebis scitum de cætero ordinari, et nullam omnino legem fore futuram vel si futura foret, esse pro suorum arbitrio statuenda."—*Walsingham,* p. 361. So in Cade's rebellion, temp. Hen. 6:—

"*Dick.* The first thing we do, let's kill all the lawyers.
Cade. Nay, that I mean to do." (And proceeds to give his reasons.)
Shak. Second Part Hen. VI. a. iv. s. 2.

In the riots of 1780, a similar spirit was displayed, and siege was laid to the inns of court, with the intention of exterminating the whole race of lawyers, that "the skin of an innocent lamb might no longer be converted into an indictment." I have heard Judge Burrough relate that siege being laid to the Temple, he and many other lawyers armed themselves, and headed by a sergeant of the Guards took post in Inner Temple Lane; there they stood valiantly till a pannel of the gate was forced in from Fleet Street: they then became rather nervous, but the sergeant having hallooed out, "Take care no gentleman fires from behind!" they all burst into a loud laugh; whereupon the mob, fearing there was a stratagem, suddenly made off, and the Temple was saved.

[2] "Quid est charissimi filii, quid est quod proponitis facere? Quod est peccatum meum quod in vos commisi, propter quod me vultis occidere? Cavendum est ne me interfecto, qui pastor, prælatus et archiepiscopus vester sum, veniat super vos indignatio justi vindicis, vel certe pro ta!l facto, tota supponatur Anglia interdicto." Wals. 262.

But it was believed that miracles were worked to punish his murderers, and to show that he had been received in heaven as a Saint. It is gravely related, that the executioner who had committed the horrid sacrilege went mad, and was struck with blindness; that a man, blind for many years, on praying to be cured for his sake, was immediately restored to sight ; and (as we may well believe) that a woman who had been long in difficult labor, having prayed for his intercession, was the same day delivered of three fine boys,—all received into the church by baptism.[1] The same historian, who was his contemporary, and speaks from personal knowledge, gives him the character of being "very eloquent, and incomparably wise above all the great men of the kingdom."

The rebellion having been quelled by the gallantry of Sir William Walworth and the presence of mind and address of the youthful King, which raised a disappointed expectation of his qualifications for government,—the Great Seal was given into the temporary custody, first of Richard Earl of Arundel, and then of Hugh de Segrave "till the King could conveniently provide a Chancellor."[2] On the 10th of August, Segrave restored the Seal to the King, who immediately delivered it with the title of Chancellor to WILLIAM COURTENAY, Bishop of London.

The office of Chancellor appears, in this age, to have been an object of ambition to men of the most illustrious descent. William was a younger son of Hugh Courtenay, Earl of Devon, having in his veins the blood of French kings and of Emperors of the East, as well as of the Plantagenets.[3] While yet a youth, he had made great proficiency in the civil and canon law, and taking orders, he rose rapidly in the church from personal merit and family interest.

After holding almost innumerable prebends and livings he was made Bishop of Hereford, and then translated to London. He was very popular with the Londoners, who stood by him in a dispute with John of Gaunt, and could hardly be restrained by him from pulling down the

[1] "Mulier quædam quæ impregnata fuerat et parere nullo modo poterat, postulato ejus auxilio, eodem die deliberata est de tribus puerulis, qui omnes baptizati sunt."—p. 263.
[2] Rot. Cl. 5 Ric. 2, m. 25.
[3] His mother, Margaret de Bohun, was a granddaughter of Edward I.

Duke's house. He was made a Cardinal, and he succeeded De Sudbury as Archbishop of Canterbury as well as Lord Chancellor.

He sat in Chancery himself, without the assistance of the Master of the Rolls, or any other Keeper; but he appears to have excited great dissatisfaction as a judge, and the cry against delays and corruption in his court soon became very loud and general.

A parliament met in September, and it was opened by the Chancellor in a speech from this text, "Rex convenire fecit concilium."[1] He declared the chief cause of the summons to be to punish the authors of the late horrible tumults, and to do away with the charters of liberty and manumission which the King had been forced to grant to bond-tenants and villains under the great seal of England.[2] But the parliament immediately proceeded to inquire into the abuses in the government of the country, and the Commons petitioned for the appointment of a new Chancellor and other judges. In consequence of these proceedings, Archbishop Courtenay was removed from the office of Chancellor, and Lord le Scrope, who had been leader of the oppositon, was placed in it the second time. The Ex-Chancellor devoted the rest of his days to his ecclesiastical duties. He held a celebrated synod at London, in which the doctrines of Wickliffe were solemnly condemned. A little before his death he obtained a grant by a papal bull of the sixtieth part of the income of all the clergy within his province; but the Bishop of London refusing to pay, and appealing to the Pope, the Archbishop died while the matter was depending, July 31, 1396.

During this last transfer of the Great Seal, the King had it a short time in his own possession, and himself sealed a commission by which he appointed John de Holland, his brother by the mother's side, John de Montague, Steward of his household, and Simon de Burle, his

[1] In the Parliament Roll the Chancellor is said to have made *un bone collacion et Engleys.*—Rot. Parl. 5 Ric. 2. Although the formal written proceedings in parliament were, and are still, in French, I conceive that from the time when representatives from cities and boroughs were admitted, a liberty must have been allowed to speak in English, and the use of the French in debate must have been gradually laid aside.

[2] It appears by the Close Roll that the Great Seat had been a short time in the king's own keeping, and I presume these charters were then sealed

Chamberlain, to proceed to Germany, there to receive the Lady Ann, the sister of the Emperor, as his future Queen, and to conduct her to his presence. This might be excusable, as matter personally relating to himself; but he at the same time sealed several other commissions and important charters with his own hand, which gave him a taste for acting without any responsible adviser and contrary to the opinions expressed by his ministers.

The Commons now made another effort to abolish all fines on writs out of Chancery as contrary to the Great Charter; but the King answered, "that such fines had always been received in Chancery as well since as before the Great Charter, by all his noble progenitors, Kings of England."[1]

As soon as parliament was dissolved, the King quareled with Lord le Scrope, the new Chancellor, who resisted the gross job of conferring upon some worthless favorites the lands which, on the death of the Earl of March, had fallen to the Crown. Richard became incensed by his behavior, and sent messenger after messenger to demand the Great Seal from him; but he refused to deliver it except to the King himself. At length the King got possession of it on the 11th of July, and gave it into the keeping of Hugh de Segrave and others, to be used by them for the sealing of writs and charters till a new Chancellor should be found.[2]

On the 20th of September, ROBERT DE BRAYBROKE was made Chancellor. He was of a noble family, the Braybrokes, of Braybroke Castle, in the county of Northampton. Having studied at Cambridge, and becoming a licentiate in laws, he entered the Church, was made canon of Lichfield, and in 1381 was consecrated Bishop of London. At this time he was high in favor with John of Gaunt, who was the means of his being made Chancellor from the capacity for political intrigue which he was supposed to have displayed. He was not created in the usual manner by the King delivering the Seal to him, but by writ addressed to those who had it in their keeping.[3]

---

[1] Rot. Par. 5 Ric. 2.   [2] Rot. Cl. 6 Ric. 2, m. 24.
[3] De par le Roy.

"Treschers et foialx, nous avons ordinez et volons que le Reverent Pere en Dieu, et notre trescher Cosin, levesque de Londres, serra notra Chanceller Denglitere, pur le grand, affiance que nous avons en luy. Si vous mandons et chargeons que veues cestes, vouz facez delivrer a luy notre Grand Seal

During his short tenure of office, two parliaments were called and opened by speeches from the Chancellor, but they were chiefly occupied with measures to put down the heresy of Wickliffe, and no civil business of any importance was transacted at them.[1]

This Chancellor is celebrated for having resorted to a pious fraud for what he considered the good of the church. In the parliament held in the 5 Richard II., he introduced a bill authorizing the Lord Chancellor to issue commissions to sheriffs to arrest and imprison such as should be certified into Chancery to be heretics. This was approved of by the Lords, but thrown out by the Commons. Nevertheless the Chancellor at the end of the session caused it to be inscribed on the parliament roll, and it was vigorously acted upon—to the great vexation of the subject. When parliament again met, the Commons in a fury passed a bill to which the Lords agreed, declaring the former act to be null. "But in the parliamentary proclamation of the acts passed *in anno* 6 Richard II., the said act of 6 Richard II., whereby the said supposed act of 5 Richard II. was declared to be be null, is omitted, and afterwards the said supposed act of 5 Richard II. was continually printed, and the said act of 6 Richard II. hath, by *the craft of the prelates*, been ever from time to time kept from the print."[2]

Robert de Vere, Earl of Oxford, the favorite of Richard II., being raised to the title of Duke of Ireland, was now engrossing all power into his own hands, and he resolved to intrust the Great Seal to a layman who, if from his education unfit for its judicial duties, was eminent for talents, address and suppleness—qualities sometimes as much considered in filling up the office of Chancellor.

On the 13th of March, 1383, the Great Seal was taken from Robert de Braybroke, and given to MICHAEL DE LA POLE. The Close Roll says, that the Bishop earnestly

esteant ore en votre garde, over le trouble de son cherge et toutes autres a ly appurtienantz come a notre Chanceller. Et cette lettre vous ent serra garrant. Donnez, &c."—Rot. Cl. 6 R. 2.

[1] 1 Parl. Hist. 176.
[2] Lord Coke's Reports, part xii. 58. 4 Inst. 51. The sham act is still to be found in the Statute Book as 5 Ric. 2, stat. 2, c. 5. Lord Coke adds, that "by color of the supposed act certain persons that held that images were not to be worshiped were holden in strong prison until they, to redeem their vexation, miserably yielded to take an oath, and did swear to worship images, which was against the moral and eternal law of Almighty God."

desired to be relieved from the office of Chancellor;[1] but there can be no doubt that he parted with it very unwillingly, and thought himself very ill used in being deprived of it. He lived more than twenty years afterwards, but never had more than this taste of political power. He died in 1404, having seen the family of Lancaster seated on the throne.

Michael de la Pole was the son of Sir William de la Pole, a merchant, and Mayor of Kingston-upon-Hull.[2] He had served Edward III. both as a civilian and a soldier, and had acquired the friendship of that monarch. In the troubles of the present reign his support was coveted by both parties, and he was esteemed the person of great experience and capacity among those who were attached to the Duke of Ireland. He was sworn in Chancellor on the 13th of March, 1383.[3]

He did not at first resort to the expedient of handing over the Seal to a legal Keeper to act as his judicial deputy; and as he is said to have performed well in the Court of Chancery, he must have been like some of the military Chancellors in our West India Islands, who, by discretion, natural good sense, taking hints from the clerks in court, and giving no reasons for their decrees,[4] have very creditably performed the duties of their office.

On the 1st of November in the same year, he made his first appearance on the woolsack, when he had to open parliament by an oration in the presence of the King and both Houses.[5] He began with great modesty, excusing his own unfitness for the place he held, and declaring that he was forced to accept it, though he had pleaded his incapacity. He then presented a very able exposition of

---

[1] " Desiderans cum magna instantia de officio Cancellarii exonerari."—Rot. Cl. 6 Ric. 2.

[2] The founder of this illustrious family was the Chancellor's father, who, when Edward III. was lying at Antwerp very destitute of money, lent him £1000 in gold, in recompense whereof (26th Sept. 13 Ed. 3) he was constituted second Baron of the Exchequer, and advanced to the degree of a banneret, with an allowance, for the better support of that dignity, payable out of the customs at Hull. He died, 40 Ed. 3, seised of large estates, which descended to the Chancellor.—*Dugdale.*

[3] Rot. Cl. 6 Ric. 2, m. 12.

[4] According to the advice of Lord Mansfield to a military man going to sit as Chancellor of Jamaica: " Your decision may be right, but your reasons must be wrong."

[5] 1 Parl. Hist. 176.

the King's wars with Scotland and with France, and pressed for a subsidy, which was readily granted.[1]

While this parliament sat, an unjust charge was brought against him of taking a bribe. He was acquitted, and John Cavendish, his accuser, was fined 1000 marks for defamation.

At the parliament held in November in the following year, he was considerably bolder, and he ventured to give good advice to the two chambers, telling them, "there were four ways or means which would greatly speed their consultations. First, to be early in the house; next, to repel all melancholy passions; the third, to begin always on the most needful inquiries, and to proceed without mixture of any orders; and, lastly, to avoid all maintaining and partaking."[2]

The Commons made a complaint to the King for commissions issued by the Chancellor, but they could not obtain a more favorable answer than that "those who felt themselves aggrieved should show their special grievance to the Chancellor, who would provide a remedy."[3]

On the 6th of August, 1386, Michael de la Pole was

---

[1] I give from the Rolls of Parliament a specimen of this modest oration :—
"Mons. Michel de la Pole, Chivaler, Chanceller d'Engleterre, par commandement nre. Sr. le Roi avoit les paroles de la pronunciation des causes de la somonce de cest present parlimit, y dist. Vous Mess. Prelatz et Seignrs. Temporalx, et vous mes compaignons les chivalers et autres de la noble Coe. d'Engleterre cy presentz, deinez entendre, Qe combn. q. je ne soie digne, mes insufficient de seu de tout autre Cre., toutes voies pleust a nre. Sr. le Roi nalgairs de moy creer son Chanceller, et sur ce ore moy ad commandez, q'ore en vos honorables presences je vous soie de par luy exposer les causes de la somonce de son present Parlement. Et partant purra clerement apparoir q. si haute busoigne come ce est de pler si chargeante matire devant tantes et tielles si nobles et sages persones q. vous estez, je ne ferroie myc per presumption ou sur guiderie de moy mesmes, einz soulement par deux enchesons resonable. L'une est q. longement et coement. ad este accustumee deinz mesme le Roialme q. les Chancellers d'Angleterre devant moy si ont fait chescun en son temps pronunciation de par le Roy de semblabes parlimentz devaunt ore tenuz; et ne vorroie, si pleust a Dieu q. en mon temps defaute de mon dit office, si avaunt come je le purroie maintenir en tout bien et honour. La seconde cause est purquoy je assume de present si grant charge sur moy devant touz les autres sages cy presentez: gar le Roy nre. Sr. lige ycy present m' ad commandez de l'faire, a qi me faut a fyn force en ce et en touz autres ses commandementz q. purroiunt tournir au pfit. de lui et de son roialme obeire. Et issint ne ferroie ceste chargeante busoigne en aucun manere, sinon constreint par reson de mon office, et commandement de mon Sr. lige come dist est."—Roll. Parl. 7 Ric. 2, vol. iii. 148.

[2] 1 Parl. Hist. 180. "*Maintenance* and *champerty*," the corruption of those days, when "*railroad shares*" were unknown.

[3] 1 Parl. Hist. 185.

created Earl of Suffolk, the first instance of a Lord Chancellor, while in office, being raised to this rank in the peerage. He had, at the same time, a grant of 1000 marks a year from the public revenue to support his new dignity.

A parliament was held soon after. We have an account from Speed, of a debate which took place in the House of Lords at the opening of the session—the earl est which I find reported, and giving us a lively picture of the eloquence and manners of the age. The Bishop of Norwich, the famous "Fighting Prelate," had led an army into Flanders; being obliged to return with discomfiture, he had been charged with breach of the conditions on which a sum of money was granted to him, and the temporalities of his see were sequestered. A motion was now made by Thomas de Arundel, Bishop of Ely, then rising into notice, and afterwards five times Lord Chancellor, that the temporalities should be restored to him, which he said—"would be a small matter for the King." This was warmly opposed by the new Earl of Suffolk, Lord Chancellor, who rose up and thus addressed the Bishop of Ely: "What is that, my Lord, which you ask of the King? Seems it to you a small matter for him to part with that Bishop's temporalities, when they yield to his coffers above £1000 a year? Little need hath the King of such councillors, or such friends as advise him to acts so greatly to his disadvantage." To which the Bishop of Ely replied, "What says your lordship, my Lord Michael? Know that I ask not from the King what is his own, but that which he, drawn thereunto by you, or such as you are, withholds from other men, upon none of the justest titles,—which, as I think, will never do him any good. As for yourself, if the King's advantage be the the thing you drive at, why did you so greedily accept of 1000 marks a year at the time he created you Earl of Suffolk." "The Chancellor," adds our authority, "was hit so home by this round retor, that he offered no farther to cross the restitution of the Bishop's temporalities."[1]

This year the Earl of Suffolk went abroad upon an embassy, and the Great Seal was given into the custody of John de Waltham, Master of the Rolls,[2] celebrated for his invention of the writ of subpœna, on which the Equitable jurisdiction of the Court of Chancery has been supposed

[1] Speed, in ann. 1386. [2] Rol. Cl. 9 Ric. 2, m. 12.

to be founded. The faction of the favorite, De Vere, had now become very odious, and there were loud complaints among the people against misgovernment. What was more formidable, there was a strong combination among the Barons, who were resolved upon a change. The King's necessities, however, required the summoning of a new parliament. The two Houses met on the 1st of October, 1386.[1] The session was opened as usual by a speech from the Lord Chancellor, in which he said that the principal cause of calling them together at that time was "to acquaint them that it had been determined the King should cross the seas in person with an army royal, and that they were to debate in what manner and how it was to be done." But the Commons, instead of intimating any intention of granting a supply, expressed in the royal presence their resolution to impeach the Lord Chancellor for divers crimes and misdemeanors. We are informed that the King thereupon retired, lest he might seem to countenance their proceedings. He went to his palace at Eltham, where he spent his time in vain amusements, while transactions were going on which before long led to his dethronement. Both Houses, with joint consent, thought proper to send this message to him: "That the Chancellor and Treasurer ought to be removed from offices, because those men were not for the advantage of himself and kingdom." Adding, "that they had matters to treat of relating to the Lord Michael de la Pole, which could not safely be done while he remained in the office of Chancellor." The King admonished them to proceed forthwith to the business for which they were summoned, and told them "that he would not for them, or at their instance, remove the meanest scullion in his kitchen." The Lords and Commons were not to be so daunted, and they returned their joint answer to the King, "That they neither could, nor by any means would, proceed in any business of parliament, or despatch so much as the least article of it till the King should come and show himself among them, and remove the said Michael de la Pole from his office." Remonstrances and refusals of redress being some time continued, the King threatened to call in the advice of the King of France, to whom he would sooner submit than truckle to his own subjects. In their

[1] 1 Parl. Hist. 185.

address in answer, the two Houses said, "We have an ancient Constitution, and it was not many ages experimented[1] (it grieves us that we must mention it), that if the King through any evil counsel, or weak obstinacy, or contempt of his people, or out of a perverse and froward willfulness, or by any other irregular courses, shall alienate himself from his people, and refuse to govern by the laws and statutes of the realm, but will throw himself headlong into wild designs, and stubbornly exercise his own singular arbitrary will,—from that time it shall be lawful for his people, by their full and free assent and consent, to depose that King from his throne, and in his stead to establish some other of the royal race upon the same."[2]

Richard was obliged to yield; and laying aside his passion, he promised that after three days he would come to the parliament, and with mature advice willingly acquiesce in their petitions. Accordingly he came at the time appointed, and consented to an entire change of ministers. The Earl of Suffolk was removed, and his enemy THOMAS DE ARUNDEL, Bishop of Ely, made Chancellor in his stead.

Not contented with his dismissal, the Commons prayed that all manner of charters and letters made in the time of the late Chamcellor, contrary to law, be annulled and repealed in the present parliament, to which the answer was, "Le Roi le voet par advys de son conseil."[3]

They then proceeded to impeach him; but his official integrity was established by the frivolous nature of the offenses which his enemies in the present plenitude of their power, thought proper to object against him.[4]

This is the first instance of the impeachment of a Chancellor, and it created great interest from the elevated rank and distinguished personal character of the accused. The bill of impeachment was divided into seven heads, charging the Earl, while Chancellor, with having enriched himself by defrauding the Crown, and with having put the Great Seal to illegal charters and pardons. He had intrusted his defense to his brother-in-law, Lord le Scrope, an Ex-Chancellor: but the Lords observed it would be more to his honor if he should conduct it him-

[1] Referring to the deposition of Edward II.
[2] Rot. Par. 10 Ric 2.
[3] 1 Parl. Hist. 186.
[4] 1 Parl. Hist. 189.

self. He thereupon went through the different charges in order, contending that those which were fit ground of impeachment were unfounded in fact, and that the others did not amount to any legal offense. "As to his deserts he would be silent, but hoped that what he had suffered for the King would not be forgotten." Here Scrope was allowed to interpose. "The individual now accused of misconduct as Chancellor," he remarked, "had served in war thirty years as a knight banneret without disgrace or reproof, had thrice been a captive in the hands of the enemy, and had been governor of Calais, Admiral of the fleet, and oftentimes Ambassador from the King to foreign states,—in all which capacities he had conducted himself with the purest honor as well as with the highest ability."

The managers for the Commons were heard in reply, and chiefly dwelt upon the charge, that, being Chancellor, and obliged by his oath to consult the King's profit, he had purchased lands from the King below their true value. He proved that he had made no purchase from the Crown while he was Chancellor, and that all the bargains referred to had been concluded before he was raised to that office. Nevertheless he was found guilty of having defrauded the Crown, and adjudged to forfeit several large sums of money, and to be imprisoned during the King's pleasure. He was accordingly committed to the custody of the High Lord Constable, and sent close prisoner to Windsor Castle, where he remained till this parliament was dissolved,—when he was taken into favor, and was able again to make head against his enemies.

This prosecution is memorable as it confirmed to the Commons their new claim of impeaching the ministers of the Crown, and showed how the power might be abused to the purposes of faction.

De la Pole, the Ex-Chancellor, was actively engaged in the struggle which soon arose from the attempt to subject Richard, like Henry III. and Edward II., to a council of Barons, armed with the powers of royalty. Upon the defeat of the party who resisted these proceedings he was obliged to go into exile. He was kindly received by the King of France, but died soon after of a broken heart, said to have been produced less by his private misfortunes than by the calamities he saw impending over his country. That he was fit for the office of Chancellor, which had been held by Parnynge and Knyvet, it impossible to assert; but he seems to have filled it with unspotted integrity, and he certainly displayed high qualities as a statesman as well as a soldier. His descendants were nearly allied to the throne, and several of them are among the most distinguished characters in English history.

The new Chancellor, THOMAS DE ARUNDEL, was of illustrious descent, being the son of Robert Earl of Arundel and Warren. He very early displayed great talents, and he had a respectable share of the learning of the times. Taking orders, he was made Archdeacon of Taunton when scarce twenty-two years of age, and it was not long before he entered parliament as a prelate, where we have seen he was the antagonist of De la Pole the Chancellor, with whom he had a long-continued rivalry. Supported by Gloucester, the King's uncle, he was now completely in the ascendant; for the two houses were willingly ruled by him, and the King could make no resistance. He used his power with no moderation: for, not contented with crushing his predecessor, he attempted permanently to make himself master of the King and the kingdom. An Act was passed, to which the royal assent was nominally given, appointing a council of fourteen persons, to whom the sovereign power was transferred for a twelvemonth,—and the King was in reality dethroned. The Chancellor was the first named in the commission.

But although Richard had taken an oath never to infringe it, at the end of the session he publicly entered a protest that the prerogatives of the Crown, notwithstanding his late concession, should still be deemed entire and unimpaired. The Commissioners, disregarding this declaration, took possession of the government,—but they were not long allowed to exercise their authority without disturbance. Richard was sensible of the contempt into which he had fallen, and, instigated by the Earl of Suffolk, whom he restored to liberty, he made a bold effort to recover his authority. He assembled Tressilian, the Chief Justice of England, and the other Judges, at Nottingham, and obtained an opinion from them that those who procured the late commission, or advised the King to consent to it, were punishable with death, and that those who should persevere in maintaining it were guilty of treason; and that the House of Commons cannot, without the King's consent, impeach any of his Ministers or Judges.

Gloucester and the Chancellor flew to arms as soon as they heard of this consultation, and met Richard near Highgate with a force which he and his adherents could not resist. They accused the Earl of Suffolk, the Duke of Ireland, Sir Robert Tressilian, and others who impugned the commission, as public and dangerous enemies to the state.

A new parliament was called in February, 1388,[1] which was opened by a speech from the Bishop of Ely, the Chancellor, inveighing against the opposite faction. An appeal of treason, consisting of many articles, was preferred against the discomfited leaders of it, and, as a matter of course, they were found guilty. Tressilian, the Chief Justice, being discovered in an apothecary's shop in Palace Yard, where he had some time lain concealed, was hanged at Tyburn, and his fate seems to have excited little compassion, for he had shown himself ready to mete out like injustice to others, and he had extra-judicially pronounced opinions which, if acted upon, would have been for ever fatal to public liberty.

It seems as if those now in power never could be deprived of it. Thomas of Arundel, the Chancellor, had been made Bishop of York, and he no doubt expected to hold the Great Seal without interruption for many years. But in the beginning of May, 1389, Richard unexpectedly and peaceably recovered his authority, and all those who had been concerned in the late plots against him were dismissed from their employments. This change seems to have been brought about merely by a reaction in public opinion, and a dislike in the English nation to power remaining long in the same hands.

Richard, on this occasion, conducted himself with great moderation, and he confirmed by proclamation the general pardon which the parliament had passed for all offenses.

[1] 1 Parl. Hist. 196. 1 St. Tr. 89.

CHAPTER XVII.

CHANCELLORS AND KEEPERS OF THE GREAT SEAL FROM THE SECOND CHANCELLORSHIP OF WILLIAM OF WICKHAM TILL THE END OF THE REIGN OF RICHARD II.

WILLIAM OF WICKHAM, Bishop of Winchester, after a retirement from office of eighteen years, was again made Chancellor, as a person likely to be generally acceptable.

After his resignation of the Great Seal in 1371, he had employed himself in repairing the twelve castles, or manorial residences, belonging to him as Bishop, on which he spent 20,000 marks;—in rebuilding the cathedral at Winchester;—and in reforming abuses in the monasteries and religious houses within his diocese, particularly the ancient hospital of St. Cross, founded by the famous Bishop Henry de Blois, brother of King Stephen.[1] Having been appointed by "the Good Parliament," which met in 1376, one of the council established to superintend the conduct of public affairs, he had the misfortune to incur the displeasure of the Duke of Lancaster, who then wished to engross all power into his own hands. By his contrivance, eight informations were filed against the Bishop in the beginning of the next Michaelmas term, charging him with various acts of pecuniary defalcation, oppression, and perversion of the law while he was Keeper of the Privy Seal and Lord Chancellor. The cause was tried before a partial commission of Bishops, Peers, and Privy Councillors, and although convicted only on one charge, which amounted at most to an irregularity, he was heavily fined, an order was issued for sequestering the revenues of his bishopric, and he was forbidden to come within twenty miles of the Court. When, on the petition of the Commons, the general pardon was issued by the King in consideration of its being the year of his jubilee, the Bishop of Winchester alone was exempted from its benefit. His enemies contrived to throw an imputation upon him that

[1] Under a regulation then made, every traveler who visits the hospital is now presented with a cup of ale and a small loaf,—*ut gustavi*.

he was patronized by Alice Pearce, and that he instigated her to withstand the parliament. In spite of this scandal, his brethren of the clergy now assembled in convocation, manfully took up his cause, and his temporalities were restored to him on condition of his fitting out three ships of war for the defense of the kingdom. The mulct was remitted on the accession of Richard II.; but the prosecution subjected him to a loss of 10,000 marks.

During the minority of Richard, the Ex-Chancellor had not interfered with politics, except that after the suppression of Wat Tyler's rebellion he was one of the seventeen persons appointed by the Commons to confer with them on the condition of the kingdom, and that in 1386 he was one of the fourteen appointed by the parliament, at the instigation of the King's uncle, the Duke of Gloucester, to be a council to the King for one year, and to exercise all the powers of government. In this capacity he conducted himself with so much mildness and moderation, that when Richard recovered his authority he still wished to have him near his person.

His restoration to the office of Chancellor under the present circumstances was generally approved of; for if his judicial qualifications for it were slender, the people were pleased to see it once more filled by a man of moderate opinions and unsullied integrity.

In January, 1390, a parliament met, which he opened with a speech, "declaring the King to be of full age, and that he intended to govern his people in peace and quiet, and to do justice and right to all men."¹

The Chancellor then, to gain popularity, went through a ceremony prescribed by a repealed statute of Edward III. ;—he surrendered the Great Seal to the King before both houses of parliament;—the Bishop of St. David's, the Lord Treasurer, at the same time delivered up the keys of the Exchequer; and they prayed that they might be discharged,—" complaining of the great labor and costs to which they were continually put in their said offices, and praying that other good and sufficient persons might be appointed in their stead." After this resignation, it was openly proclaimed in full parliament, "that if any person could justly complain of any illegal action or anything done amiss by them in their several offices, he

1 Parl. Hist. 216.

should come forth and he should be heard, for they now stood upon their deliverance." Both the Lords and Commons answered "that they knew nothing amiss against them, and that they had behaved themselves well in their respective offices." Whereupon the King reinstated the Bishop of Winchester in the office of Chancellor, and re-delivered to him the Great Seal, and the Bishop of St. David's in the office of Treasurer, and re-delivered to him the keys of the Treasury.

Nevertheless the Commons showed suspicion and jealousy of the future proceedings of the Chancellor, for they prayed the King "that neither the Chancellor nor the King's Council, after the parliament is ended, may make any ordinance against the common law nor the ancient customs of the land, nor against the statutes heretofore passed in the present parliament, and that no judgment rendered be annulled without due process of law." An evasive answer being given, the Commons returned to the attack, and prayed "that if the Chancellor should compel the King's lieges to appear before him to answer any thing that may be recovered at common law, he shall be liable to a penalty of £100;" but the answer still was —"The King willeth, as his progenitors have done, saving his regality."[1]

William of Wickham remained Chancellor, the second time, till the 27th of September, 1391,—when he was succeeded by Thomas Arundel, Archbishop of York, who had been his immediate predecessor.[2] This change took place without any convulsion, and seems to have been the result of an amicable compromise between the contending parties. The Duke of Gloucester was restored to his place in the council, and, for a short time, there was a prospect of public tranquillity.

Here we must take leave of Lord Chancellor Wickham. From this date he seems to have interfered little in public affairs. He was in some danger in 1397, when the Duke of Gloucester was put to death, and several of his associates were attainted for their former resistance to the royal authority; but, at the intercession of the Commons, it was declared by the King, from the throne, that the Bishop of Winchester had not been implicated in what his fellow-commissioners had then done. He was

[1] Rot. Par. 13 Ric. 2.   [2] Rot. Cl. 15 Ric. 2, m. 34.

present in the parliament held the 30th of September, 1399, when Richard was deposed, and in the first parliament of Henry IV., summoned a few days after; but this was the last which he attended. He now devoted himself to his episcopal duties, and the superintendence of his two noble foundations at Winchester and Oxford, which have contributed so much to the cause of sound education in England, and have rendered his name so illustrious.[1]

He expired on the 27th of September, 1404, in the eighty-first year of his age, having presided over the see of Winchester above thirty-eight years.

None of his decisions as Chancellor have come down to us, but he left a greater name to posterity than many of his successors of much higher judicial authority. We are to admire in him not only his unrivaled skill in one of the fine arts, but his extraordinary aptitude for all civil business, his equal and benevolent temper, his enlightened munificence, and his devout love of learning.[2]

We are now in the tranquil period of Richard's reign, in which he was permitted to give free scope to his love of indolence, low pleasure, and frivolous company. Thomas de Arundel's second Chancellorship lasted about five years, without being marked by any striking events till the close of it. Parties continued pretty equally balanced, and what has since been called a *juste milieu* government prevailed.

During this time the jurisdiction of the Court of Chancery was greatly extended, and the famous writ of subpœna came into use as invented or improved by John de Waltham, who was Master of the Rolls, and several times intrusted with the custody of the Great Seal as deputy to the Chancellor, though he never held it in his own right.[3]

[1] The bull of Pope Urbanus VI. for founding Winchester School, was granted 1st June, 1378. The building of the college at Oxford, which he called "St. Mary College of Winchester, at Oxford," afterwards "New College," was begun in 1380 and finished in 1386; the papal bull confirming its statutes is dated 19th July, 1398.—I have a great kindness for the memory of William of Wickham, when I think of his having produced such Wickhamists as my friends Baron Rolfe and Professor Empson.

"Hactenus ire libet, tu major laudibus istis
Suscipe conatus, Wicame Dive, meos."

[2] See Hist. Descrip. Gul. Wick. Life by Lowth.

[3] Blackstone is entirely mistaken in asserting that John de Waltham was

These innovations were highly unpopular, and vigorous attempts were made to check them; but nothing more Chancellor to Richard II.*, and as he never was Chancellor, nor held the Great Seal as Keeper in his own right, he does not properly come into the list of those whose lives I have undertaken to write. Yet, as his name is so distinguished in the history of the Equitable jurisdiction of the Court of Chancery, the reader may be desirous of being informed of what is known concerning him.

His birth and place of education have not been traced. He was an ecclesiastic who devoted himself to the study of the civil and canon law, in which he made great proficiency. He was early introduced as a clerk in Chancery, and soon rose to be a Master. Rendering himself useful to Lord Chancellor Courtenay, he was by his interest appointed one of the Receivers of Petitions for England, Ireland, Wales, and Scotland, in the parliament which met in 5 Ric. 2, and in the same year was created Master of the Rolls.† The following year, under Lord Chancellor Scrope, he was a Keeper of the Great Seal along with Hugh de Segrave, the Treasurer of England, and William de Dighton, Keeper of the Privy Seal, and he was a joint Keeper of the Great Seal ‡ likewise, under the two succeeding Chancellors. But in April, 1386, he was appointed sole Keeper of the Great Seal under Lord Chancellor de la Pole §, and again in September, 1394, under Lord Chancellor Arundel,‖ He was afterwards consecrated Bishop of Salisbury, and finally was made Lord Treasurer of England.¶

But the great disgrace or glory imputed to him, was the invention of the writ of SUBPŒNA in Chancery, and some have represented him by the sale of his new writ, and his extension of the jurisdiction of the Chancellor, in derogation of the common law, to merit the denunciation,

"Vendidit hic auro patriam, dominumque potentem.
Imposuit, fixit leges pretio atque refixit;"

while others would inscribe his name among those

" Inventas—qui vitam excoluere per artes,
Quique sui memores alios fecere merendo."

In censuring and extolling him there has been much exaggeration. While obscurity veils the honor due to the first happy discoverers of the *latitat* and *quo minus*, the indignant complaint of the Commons " that the subpœna in Chancery had never been known before the time of Sir John de Waltham," has fixed upon him the responsibility of being the author of this writ. In reality, he first framed it in its present form, when a clerk in Chancery, in the latter end of the reign of Edward III.; but the invention consisted in merely adding to the old clause *Quibusdam certis de causis*, the words " Et hoc sub pœna centum librarum nullatenus omittas;"** and I am at a loss to conceive how such importance was attached to it, or how it was supposed to have brought about so complete a revolution in equitable proceedings; for the penalty never was enforced, and if the party failed to appear, his default was treated (according to the practice prevailing to our own time) as a contempt of court, and made the foundation of compulsory process.

John de Waltham continued to hold the office of Lord Treasurer till his death in September, 1395. By the command of Richard II. he was buried in the chapel royal of Westminster Abbey, among the Kings of England.

---

* Bl. Com. iii. 52.   † Rot. Pat. 5 Ric. 2, m. 22.   Rot. Parl. 3 Hen. 5, m. 2.
‡ Rot. Cl. 6 Ric. 2, m. 12.   Rot. Cl. 9 Ric. 2.   § Rot. Cl. 9 Ric. 2, m. 5.
‖ Rot. Cl. 18 Ric. 2, m. 31.   ¶ 14 Ric. 2. Or. Jur. 54.
** See Rot. Pat. 39 Ed. 3, p. i. m. 15.   Rot. Claus. 20 Ed. 3, p. ii. m. d. 4

could be effected in this reign than passing stat. 17 Ric. 2, c. 6, entitled, "Upon an untrue suggestion in the Chancery, Damages may be awarded," whereby, after reciting "that forasmuch as people be compelled to come before the King's counsel or in the Chancery by writs grounded on untrue suggestions," it is enacted, "that the Chancellor for the time being, presently after that such suggestions be duly found and proved untrue, shall have power to ordain and award damages, according to his discretion, to him which is so troubled unduly, as aforesaid."

This remedy, which was referred to the discretion of the Chancellor himself, whose jurisdiction was to be controlled, proved, as might have been expected, wholly ineffectual; but it was used as a parliamentary recognition of his jurisdiction, and a pretense for refusing to establish any other check to it.

In the month of September, 1394, the Chancellor attended the King into Ireland, when the Great Seal was committed to the custody of John de Waltham, who had now risen to the dignity of Bishop of Salisbury and Treasurer of England; but when *he* likewise went to Ireland, it was handed over to John Searle, who had succeeded him as Master of the Rolls. It was thrice again in the keeping of the same person before the next revolution of the government, on occasions when the Chancellor, now translated to the see of Canterbury, was too much occupied with his other avocations to attend to his judicial duties.[1]

The Duke of Gloucester, to whose party Arundel had attached himself, was making a struggle to grasp the whole power of the state, and, according to Froissart, aimed at the crown itself, although Richard had declared in parliament that, in case of his decease without issue, the house of March, descended from the Duke of Clarence, the second son of Edward III., were his true heirs.

Richard for a short time showed some energy in defense of his rights. Arundel, the Chancellor, was removed from his office, and replaced by EDMUND STAFFORD, Bishop of Exeter, who had sided with Gloucester's enemies, and Gloucester himself was arrested and sent over to Calais as a state prisoner. The Dukes of Lancaster and York, the King's other uncles, concurred in these meas-

[1] Rot, Cl. 18 Ric. 2, m. 12. 20 Ric. 2, m. 28.

ures, and all who had opposed them were now at the mercy of the ruling faction.

As usual on such occasions, a parliament was called to register decrees of vengeance, and acted with the expected vigor and unanimity. Some objection might safely be made to a particular measure which did not excite the passions of men as it passed through either House; but a regular parliamentary opposition was unknown, and no division ever took place on a bill of attainder or forfeiture, —for this plain reason, that the names of the minority would have been immediately introduced into the bill, and they would forthwith have found themselves entering through the Traitor's Gate into the Tower, shortly to tread the scaffold on Tower Hill, if not assassinated before the day fixed for their execution.

Lord Chancellor Stafford opened the session with a speech from the words of Ezekiel, " Rex unit erit omnibus." He prepared men for a little wholesome severity, by saying, " That laws ought to be executed, appears by the common example of a good father who uses to strike as well as stroke his child; for the better execution of them, the King has appointed new judges and officers through the realm."[1]

The first step of the Commons was to impeach the Ex-Chancellor Arundel for treason, in respect of what he had done when Bishop of Ely, in procuring the commission in the tenth year of the King's reign. Knowing that defense was useless, and that being a churchman his life was safe, he confessed the charge. Upon this the King and the Lords temporal and (strange to say) the Prelates by a lay commoner who held their proxy, " adjudged and declared the said article which the Archbishop had confessed to be treason, and that it touched the King himself; for which they also adjudged and declared him a traitor, and it was awarded that he should be banished out of the kingdom, have his temporalities seized, and forfeit all his lands and goods to the King." However he had six weeks allowed him to pass by the port of Dover into France.[2]

The Earl of Arundel, his brother, to the same charge pleaded the pardon granted by act of Parliament as well as by proclamation; but the plea was overruled, and he was convicted and executed.

[1] 1 Parl. Hist. 221.   [2] 1 St. Tr. 123.

The new Chancellor the Bishop of Exeter, who presided over these atrocities, was of illustrious descent, being of the family of the STAFFORDS, which from the conquest till the reign of Henry VIII. flourished at the head of the English nobility. He was a younger brother of the present Earl. The men of obscure origin, however great their talents, generally worked their way slowly up to the high ecclesiastical dignities, which were often bestowed on youths of high birth, almost before they were of canonical age to take orders. Edmund Stafford was consecrated Bishop of Exeter, possessing little theological learning, and was now made Lord Chancellor without any knowledge of the law. But he was a daring and reckless politician.

It is to be hoped that he did not counsel the murder of the Duke of Gloucester at Calais, although Hume rather justifies this *coup de 'état*, on the ground that a person of such influence, could not have safely been brought to trial in England;[1] but the Chancellor openly sanctioned the banishment of Henry Bolingbroke and the Duke of Norfolk, together with the other hasty and tyrannical measures which were precipitating the fate of the unhappy Richard.

On the death of John of Gaunt, Duke of Lancaster, the King, with the concurrence of the Chancellor, seized all the possessions and jurisdictions of this powerful family as forfeited to the Crown, although the sentence against Henry of Bolingbroke had only been banishment for ten years, and it had been expressly stipulated that he should be entitled by his attorney to enter into possession of any succession that might fall to him in the mean time. This act of injustice made Henry desperate, and led to his invasion of England and his claim of the Crown.

Edmund Stafford, the Chancellor, did not accompany Richard in his ill-judged expedition to Ireland, and he seems to have remained in possession of the Great Seal in London till after Henry had landed at Ravenspurg,—had been joined by the Duke of York at St. Albans,—had taken Bristol,—had put to death the Earl of Wiltshire and others of the King's ministers whom he found there,—had got possession of Richard's person on

---

[1] Vol. iii. 32.

his return from Ireland,—and was *de facto* master of the kingdom.

As might be expected, the records at the conclusion of this reign are very defective, and historians and antiquaries have been much puzzled respecting the manner in which the office of Chancellor was then disposed of. There is no entry to be found of any transfer of the Great Seal under Richard after the time when Stafford, Bishop of Exeter, was first sworn in; but from Privy Seal bills still extant, it is certain that before Richard's formal deposition, and the elevation of Henry to the throne, Thomas de Arundel, Archbishop of Canterbury, and JOHN SEARLE, who had been made Master of the Rolls in 1394, were successively invested with the office of Chancellor.

The transfer of the Seal to Arundel must have been between the 15th of July and the 23d of August, the former being the last date of the Privy Seal bills addressed to the Bishop of Exeter, and the other the earliest date of those addressed to the Archbishop of Canterbury; and on the like evidence Searle's appointment must have been between the 3d and 5th of September.

The learned and acute Mr. Duffus Hardy conjectures that Richard had recalled the Archbishop from banishment, and again made him Chancellor:[1] but with the greatest respect for this high authority, I think it certain that the change was made, though in Richard's name, yet without his privity, and by those who were about to dethrone him.

When Bolingbroke and the Duke of Norfolk were banished, it was prescribed that they should have no intercourse with Archbishop Arundel, then in exile, and considered a very dangerous man; but as soon as Bolingbroke had renounced all thoughts of reconciliation with Richard, he entered into a close alliance with the Archbishop, and they jointly planned the invasion of England during Richard's absence in Ireland. The Archbishop, with his nephew the young Earl of Arundel, embarked with Henry at Nantes, landed with him in Yorkshire, advised and supported him in all his proceedings, and actually placed the crown upon his head. From the time when Richard surrendered himself to the Earl of Northumberland at Conway, which was on the 18th of August, he was a prisoner

[1] Hardy's Chancellors, 46.

and having been forced to issue writs for the calling of a parliament to depose him, he was carried to London and kept in close custody in the Tower. We may conjecture that an order was extorted at the same time for delivering the Seal to the Archbishop, and that by him the writs were sealed.

It seems at first sight more difficult to account for Arundel's parting with the office so suddenly; for Searle was certainly Chancellor by the 5th of September, and Richard's reign nominally continued till the 30th of the same month, when parliament met, and his deposition was pronounced. Searle was in the interest of Henry, and was continued by him in office.

The probability is, that the Archbishop, who cast all the parts in the drama of the revolution, intending that he himself, as metropolitan and first in precedence in the realm, should lead Henry to the vacant throne in Westminster Hall, and crown him in Westminster Abbey, conceived that it would have a better effect if he should appear only in his sacred character, and the civil office of Chancellor should for the time be filled by another. He, therefore, may have handed it over to Searle, his creature, in the belief that he should be able to resume it at pleasure.

I do not find Searle's name mentioned as taking any active part in the parliamentary proceedings on this change of dynasty, and he was probably only permitted to sit on the woolsack in the House of Lords, and to put the question as Speaker.

On Michaelmas-day, the Archbishop accompanied Henry to the Tower, Richard, while a prisoner there, having said that "he was willing to resign as he promised, but that he desired to have some discourse with his cousin the Duke of Lancaster and the Archbishop of Canterbury before he fulfilled such his promise." The record of the deposition on the Parliament Roll relates that "the King, having had discourse with the said Duke and Archbishop, exhibiting a merry countenance as appeared to those that stood round about, holding the schedule of renunciation in his hand, very willingly read the same and subscribed it, and absolved all his subjects from their allegiance to him." When this instrument, supposed to have been so freely and cheerfully executed, was read in parliament next day, "it was demanded by the Chancellor of the estates and people then present,—to wit, first, the Archbishop of Canterbury, to whom, by reason of the dignity and prerogative of his metropolitan church, it belongs in this behalf to have the first voice amongst the rest of the prelates and nobles of the realm, *whether for their interest, and the utility of the kingdom, they would be willing to admit such renunciation and cession?*" This being carried with great applause, the Archbishop thought it it would be well to have another string to his bow, lest hereafter the free agency of the act of resignation should be doubted by some suspicious persons, and he caused articles to be exhibited against Richard for misgovernment, and a solemn sentence of deposition to be pronounced against him.[1]

The throne thus being declared vacant, Henry of Bolingbroke, who had taken his seat at the head of the temporal lords, rose and made his memorable claim, "in the name of Fader, Son, and Holy Ghost," having humbly fortified himself with the sign of the cross on his forehead and on his breast.

The states, with the whole people, having consented that the said Duke should reign over them, the Archbishop, taking him by the right hand, led him to the royal chair of state, which had been placed at the upper end of the hall; and when the new King, kneeling down before it, had prayed a little while, the Archbishop caused him to sit in the royal seat, and delivered an oration from the text, *Vir dominabitur populo,* "A man shall reign over my people," 1 Sam. ix. 17; in which he pointed out the evils of the rule of children, and the abuses of the late reign, and the blessings to be expected from the mature wisdom of him who was now to wield the sceptre; concluding with these words—"And so, in the stead of a child wantoning in foolish stubborn humors, a man shall reign —and such a man, that it shall be said of him, *A king shall reign in wisdom, and he shall execute judgment and do justice in the earth.*"[2]

On the 6th of October following, a new parliament met under writs of summons issued under Henry's Great Seal to ratify these proceedings.

Lord Chancellor Searle was still silent, and the session was opened by a speech from the Archbishop, who took

[1] St. Tr. 135. 1 Parl. Hist. 242.   [2] 1 Parl. Hist. 249.

for his text these words out of Maccabees, "*Incumbit nobis ordinare pro regno*,"—propounding the constitutional doctrine, "that a King is not to rule by his own will or humor, but to be governed by the honorable, discreet, and sage men of the realm."[1]

His motion for confirming what had been done in the deposition of Richard and the elevation of Henry, was passed with the dissentient voice of one, who strenuously resisted it, and earned the bright testimony "that he was the only honest man in this parliament, scorning life and fortune in respect to his Sovereign's right and his own allegiance." The noble speech of the Bishop of Carlisle on this occasion, as given by Sir John Hayward, greatly exceeds, not only in boldness, but in lucid arrangement, close reasoning, and touching eloquence, any thing that could be expected from that age.[2] The oration was listened to; but as soon as soon as the orator had concluded it, he was attached of high treason, and sent prisoner to the Abbey of St. Alban's. Though his life was safe, he was deprived of his bishopric. The Pope, as a testimony to his integrity, made him titular Bishop of Samos.

The Archbishop then moved that the King should be prayed to create his eldest son Prince of Wales, Duke of Cornwall, and Earl of Chester, which was carried unanimously; and thereupon the King, sitting in his royal seat in full parliament, put a coronet on the head of Prince Henry, and a ring of gold on his finger, and gave him a golden rod in his hand, and kissed him.[3]

The Archbishop had next to manage a very delicate matter—"the disposal of Richard's person in order to his keeping in safe custody, for the King would have his life saved." Twenty-two spiritual and thirty-six lay lords, being all who were present, were severally asked their opinion, and they all assented to the resolution, "that he should be put under a safe and secret guard, and that no person who had been familiar with him should be about his person, and that it should be done in the most secret manner that could be devised."[4]

[1] 1 Parl. Hist. 285.
[2] Ibid. 274. See a beautiful abstract of it at the conclusion of Hume's History of Richard II., vol. iii. 43, and see Shak., Richard II., act iv. scene 1.   [3] 1 Parl. Hist. 273.   [4] Ibid. 274.

We must not enter into the controversy how the unhappy Richard came to his end,—whether by violence or famine;—and before passing on to the Chancellors of his successor, we can only make a few observations on the Equitable jurisdiction of the Court of Chancery during his reign.

The practice of referring matters by parliament to the Chancellor still occasionally prevailed. Thus in 15 Rich. II. two petitions were addressed to the King and the Peers, and the answer to each was the same,—" that the petition be sent to the Chancery,—the Chancellor to hear both parties,—and further let there be done by authority of parliament that which right and reason and good faith and good conscience demand."[1]

But the circuity of a petition to parliament or to the Council was now seldom resorted to. I have shown the opinion to be unfounded, that the Equitable jurisdiction of the Court of Chancery was not of earlier date; but there can be no doubt that, about this time, it was very much extended. The petition of the Commons in the 13th of Richard II., "that the Chancellor might make no order against the common law, and that no one should appear before the Chancellor where recovery was given by the common law," carry in them an admission that a power of judicature did reside in the Chancellor, so long as he did not determine against the common law, nor interpose where the common law furnished a remedy. The King's answer, "that it should continue as the usage had been heretofore," clearly demonstrates that such an authority, restrained within due bounds, was recognized by the constitution of the country.

The use of the writ of subpœna to compel an appearance by the defendant, gave new vigor to the process of the Court, and the necessity for previously filing a written statement of the grievance alleged to require relief in equity, introduced the formal proceeding by "Bill and Answer," instead of a mere loose petition to be heard in a summary way, *ore tenus*. In fact, the practice of addressing bills directly to the Chancellor had become quite common, and many of them are still extant.

The greatest indignation broke forth in this reign against the Masters in Chancery, who were considered

[1] Rot. Parl. vol. iii. 297.

overgrown and oppressive sinecurists. In 5 R. II. a complaint was exhibited against them in parliament, "that they were over fatt both in body and purse, and over well furred in their benefices, and put the Kinge to veiry great cost more than needed,"[1]—yet nothing effectual was done to reform them.

The execution of Tressilian, and the punishment of the other common-law judges under Lord Chancellor Arundel, was attended with much violence, but had a powerful influence in creating a respect for parliamentary privilege, which they had attempted utterly to subvert.

Upon the whole, down to the accession of the House of Lancaster, our juridical institutions, including the Court of Chancery, had gone on with a steady improvement, but they remained nearly stationary from this time till the union of the Roses in the reign of Henry VII.[2]

CHAPTER XVIII.

CHANCELLORS AND KEEPERS OF THE GREAT SEAL DURING THE REIGN OF HENRY IV.

JOHN SEARLE, who had nominally been Chancellor to Richard II., and presided on the woolsack as a tool of Archbishop Arundel, was for a short time continued in office by the new Sovereign.

Little is known respecting his origin or prior history. He is supposed to have been a mere clerk in the Chancery brought forward for a temporary purpose to play the part of Chancellor. Having strutted and fretted his hour upon the stage, he was heard of no more. It proved convenient for the Staffords, the Beauforts, and the Arundels, that he should be thus suddenly elevated and depressed.

Henry began his reign by summoning a parliament to meet at Westminster on the 21st of January, 1401. On that day the knights and burgesses were called into the Court of Chancery in Westminster Hall before the Chancellor, and by the King's authority he put off the meeting of the parliament till the morrow.[3] The Lords and Com-

[1] Harg. Law Tracts, 314.
[2] See Cooper on Public Records, ii. pp. 359, 360, 377.   [3] 1 Parl. Hist. 285.

mons then met the King in the Painted Chamber, but on account of incapacity for public speaking the Chancellor was silent, and the speech explaining the causes of calling parliament, was, by the King's command, delivered by Sir William Thyrning, Chief Justice of the King's Bench.

On the 9th of March following Lord Chancellor Searle surrendered the Great Seal to the King in full parliament, and his Majesty immediately delivered it to Edmund Stafford, Bishop of Exeter, who had held it towards the end of the preceding reign, and had been a special favorite of Richard, but had joined in the vote for deposing him.

We are left entirely ignorant as to the fate of Ex-Chancellor Searle. Had he been a prelate, we should have traced him in the chronicles of his diocese; but we have no means of discovering the retreat of a layman, unconnected with any considerable family, and of no personal eminence. He was probably fed in the buttery of some of the great barons whom he had served, hardly distinguished while he lived or when he died from their other idle retainers. He may enjoy the celebrity of being the most inconsiderable man who ever held the office of Chancellor in England.[1]

Edmund Stafford, restored to the office of Chancellor, now found his situation very irksome, and very different from what it had been under the feeble Richard. Henry looked with jealousy and distrust even on those who had helped him to the crown, and confined all whom he employed strictly to their official duties. The Chancellor's disgust was increased by an attack which the Commons now made on the jurisdiction of his Court. They complained by petition to the King of the new writ of subpœna, and prayed "that people might be only treated according to the right laws of the land anciently used;" but the King's answer tended to confirm the jurisdiction complained of: "Such writs ought not to issue except in necessary cases, and then by the discretion of the Chancellor or King's Council for the time being."

A considerable improvement, however, was effected in the mode of proceeding when issues were joined upon

[1] His name appears in the new House of Lords among the Chancellors, but it has baffled the research of the most learned antiquaries to discover his armorial bearings. Doubts are entertained even whether his name was "Searle" or "Scarle."

controverted facts in the Court of Chancery. The custom seems to have been for the Chancellor himself to try them, calling in common-law judges to his assistance; but the Commons now prayed "that because great mischiefs happen in the Court of Chancery by the discussion of all pleas in matters traversed in the said Court, and by the judges of the two benches being taken out of their Courts to assist in the discussion of such matters, to the great delay of the law and to the damage of the people, the King would ordain that traverses in the Court of Chancery be sent and returned either into the King's Bench or Common Pleas, and there discussed and determined according to law." The King's answer was, "The Chancellor, by virtue of his office, may grant the same, and let it be, as it has been before these times, at the discretion of the Chancellor for the time being."[1] Ever since, when an issue of fact is joined on the common-law side of the Court, the Chancellor hands it over to be tried in the Court of King's Bench, and controverted facts in equity proceedings he directs to be tried by a jury in any of the common-law Courts at his discretion.

Stafford held the Great Seal only till the end of February, 1403. The office stripped of its power had lost its attraction for him, and he, who differed very little from the warlike baron his elder brother, had no inclination to sit day by day as a judge in the Court of Chancery, for which he felt himself so unfit,—under the vigilant superintendence of the unmannerly Commons. He therefore willingly resigned the Great Seal into the King's hands, and retired to his diocese to exercise baronial hospitality, and to enjoy hunting and the other sports of the field, in the vain hope that some revolution in politics would again enable him to mix in the factious strife which still more delighted him. But he continued to languish in tranquillity, and before the war of the Roses began, which would so much have suited his taste, he was gathered to his fathers.

Upon this vacancy the Great Seal was given to the King's half-brother, HENRY BEAUFORT,[2] who was four times Lord Chancellor, who was created a Cardinal, and who made a distinguished figure as a statesman during three reigns.

[1] Rot. Par. 2 Hen. 4.   [2] Privy Seal Bills, 4 Hen. 4.

He was the second son of John of Gaunt, by his mistress Catherine Swinford, afterwards his wife, and with the other issue of this connection, he had been legitimated by act of parliament in the 20th of Richard II., under the condition of not being entitled to succeed to the Crown. He studied both at Oxford, at Cambridge, and at Aix la Chapelle. Taking orders, he rose rapidly in the church, and while still a young man, he was, in 1397, made Bishop of Lincoln by his royal cousin. He gained great celebrity by assisting at the Council of Constance, and by making a pilgrimage to Jerusalem. When he first obtained the Great Seal he still remained Bishop of Lincoln.

The following year he was translated to Winchester, where he succeeded the famous William of Wickham, and he continued till his death to hold this see, then considered the best in England to accumulate wealth,—which was through life his ruling passion, great as was his love of power.

During this reign the King was his own minister, and neither the present nor any of his other Chancellors had much influence in the affairs of government. They were in the habit of delivering a speech at the opening of every parliament; but it was rather considered the speech of the King, which could not be censured without disloyalty.

Three parliaments met in Henry Beaufort's first Chancellorship, at which nothing very memorable was effected; but at the last of them an attempt was made by the Commons (probably at the instigation of the King), which, if it had succeeded, would have greatly altered both the ecclesiastical and civil history of the country. All who are friendly to a well-endowed church ought to exclaim, "Thank God we have had a House of Lords." The Chancellor, in a speech from the text, "Rex vocavit seniores terræ," having pressed most urgently for supplies, the Commons came in a body, and the King being on the throne proposed, "That without burthening his people, he might supply his occasions by seizing on the revenues of the clergy; that the clergy possessed a third part of the riches of the realm, which evidently made them negligent in their duty; and that the lessening of their excessive incomes would be a double advantage both to the church and the state."

Archbishop Arundel, being now free from the trammels of office, said to the King, who seems to have been addressed as the president of the assembly, "That though the ecclesiastics served him not in person, it could not be inferred that they were unserviceable; that the stripping the clergy of their estates would put a stop to their prayers night and day for the welfare of the state; and there was no expecting God's protection of the kingdom if the prayers of the church were so little valued." The Speaker of the Commons standing at the bar, smiled, and said openly, "that he thought the prayers of the church a very slender supply." To which the Archbishop answered, with some emotion, "that if the prayers of the church were so slighted, it would be found difficult to deprive them of their estates without exposing the kingdom to great danger; and so long as he were Archbishop of Canterbury, he would oppose the injustice to the utmost in his power." Then suddenly falling on his knees before the King, "he strongly pressed him in point of conscience, and endeavored to make him sensible that of all the crimes a Prince could commit, none was so heinous as an invasion of the church's patrimony." The King, seeing the impression made upon the Peers, declared "that he had made a firm resolution to support the church with all his power, and hoped by God's assistance to leave her in a better state than he found her." The Archbishop, construing this as a peremptory veto on the proposal of the Commons, turned to them and made them a most insulting speech, telling them their demand was built wholly on irreligion and avarice; "and verily," added he, "I will sooner have my head cut off than that the church should be deprived of the least right pertaining to it." Such a scene is very inconsistent with our notions of parliamentary decorum. The Commons, not convinced,—on their return to their own chamber passed a bill to carry their scheme into effect; but the solicitations of the Archbishop and the other Prelates were so powerful with the Lords that they threw it out.[1]

The recklessness of the Commons may have arisen from their not having had a single lawyer among them. Lord Chancellor Beaufort, in framing the writs of summons, illegally inserted a prohibition, "that no appren-

[1] 1 Parl. Hist. 294.

tice or other man of the law should be elected,"—grounded on a most unconstitutional ordinance of the Lords in the 46th of Edward III., to which the Commons had never assented, and which had not been acted upon. In return for such a slight, our law books and historians have branded this parliament with the name of "parliamentum indoctum," or the "lack-learning parliament;" and Sir Edward Coke observes with some spleen, that "there never was a good law made thereat;"—adding that as these writs were against law, lawyers ever since (FOR THE GREAT AND GOOD SERVICE OF THE COMMONWEALTH) have been eligible.[1]

At the end of two years Henry Beaufort appears to have lost his royal brother's favor, for he was removed from his office, and he did not recover it during the remainder of his reign.

He was now succeeded by an ecclesiastic, THOMAS LONGLEY, who then having high church preferment, was likewise keeper of the Privy Seal,—was soon raised to the see of Durham,[2]—was afterwards made a Cardinal,[3]—and had the fortune to be made Chancellor under three successive Sovereigns.

This minion of fortune was of obscure origin, being the son of a yeoman, who lived at Longley, in the county of York. We first hear of him as chaplain in the family of John of Gaunt, who by a will made in 1386, appointed him his executor. In the course of three years he became canon of York, and he soon rose rapidly in the church. He then recommended himself to Cardinal Beaufort, by whose interest he was made Keeper of the Privy Seal.

Longley's first Chancellorship lasted little more than a year. During that time he presided at a parliament called by the King, chiefly for the purpose of introducing the Salic law into England, whereby, although the Crown had come to the house of Plantagenet through a female, it was to descend only to males,—with a view of superseding the claim of the descendants of the daughter of Lionel, Duke of Clarence, one of whom, according to the doctrine of legitimacy, was now entitled to occupy the

---

[1] 1 Bl. Com. 177. 4 Inst. 48. Some writers say that the prohibition was contained in letters written by the King himself to the Sheriffs.
[2] May, 1406.
[3] By Pope John XXIII. in 1411.

throne. The Chancellor, to prepare the minds of the members of both Houses of Parliament for this measure, opened the session with a very learned and conciliatory speech from the text, " Multorum consilia requiruntur in magnis," and he compared the King to Ahasuerus, *Qui interrogavit sapientes et illorum cauta jaciebat consilia.*

An act was accordingly passed in due form for entailing the Crown on the present King and the heirs male of his body, tacitly excluding females; but this act was so much disliked by the nation, who, during the foreign wars arising out of the claim of Edward III. to the Crown of France, had fought for the contrary doctrine, and who dreaded future civil wars from any change in the law of succession, that it was almost immediately after repealed, and the Crown was settled on the King and his descendants according to the ancient rules of inheritance.[1]

The House of Commons took the opportunity to inquire diligently into all abuses, particularly in the administration of justice, and complained of the encroachments and delays in the Court of Chancery, which was denounced as a great public grievance. There had been heavy complaints of abuses both with respect to the Great and Privy Seal, and " it was agreed by the King and Parliament, that for the preservation of the laws of the kingdom the Chancellor and the Keeper of the Privy Seal should not allow any warrant, grant by patent, judgment, or any other thing to pass under the seals in their custody, which by law and right ought not to pass, and that they should not unduly delay such as ought to pass.[2]

The Commons then presented articles to the King, " That worthy councillors and officers be appointed, and not to be removed without good proof of their ill-management. That two certain days in the week be appointed for all suitors to present their petitions to the King. That none of the Council hold pleas of matters determinable at common law, and that all the King's great officers of every Court shall maintain the common law." There is added an article which seems to us a strange mode of preserving the independence and purity of the judges: " That no official officer in any of the Courts enjoy any office but at will." This was probably aimed at the sale of these offices, whereby it was thought

[1] 1 Parl. Hist. 298.   Rot. Parl. vol. iii. p. 586.

by reason of a supposed vested right in the purchaser, they were placed beyond the control of parliament. The King, who, on account of the infirmity of his title, was obliged to court popularity, not only agreed to all these articles himself, but after a stout resistance from the Upper House, prevailed on the Archbishop of Canterbury, and all the Lords spiritual and temporal, to swear to observe them, " whereby they became statutes binding in law and conscience."[1]

Archbishop Arundel's compliance was quickened by the prospect of recovering the Great Seal, and in the beginning of 1407 he became Chancellor the fourth time.[2]

The first proceeding before him was the trial of William Thorpe, a priest, for heresy, of which we have a very interesting report by the defendant himself. He says: " Being brought before Thomas Arundel, Archbyshope of Canterbury, and Chancellor of Ingland, when that I came before hym he stoode in a great chamber and moche people aboute hym; and when that he sawe me he went faste into a closett, bydding all secular men that followed hym to go forth from hym." There is then a long account of the heresies imputed to the defendant, with his answers, filling many pages, in which he gives himself greatly the advantage over his judge. At last, allusion being made to the Archbishop's banishment, his Grace said, " I shall assaye if I can make thee as sorrowfull, as it was tolde me thou waste gladde, of my laste going out of Ingland; by Seynt Thomas I shall tourne thy joye into sorrowe." The narrative continues—" And I sayde, ' There can no body proue lawfully that I ioyed ever of the manner of your goynge out of this land. But, Sir, to say the sothe, I was joyfull when ye were gone.'—The Archbishoppe said to me, ' Be this thinge well known to the, that God (as I wot well) hath called me agayne, and brought me into this lande for to destroye the, and the false secte that thou arte of, as, by God, I shall persue you so narroulye that I shall not leave a steppe of you in thys lande.'—And I said to the Archebishoppe, ' Sir, the holy prophete Jeremy saide to the false prophete Anany, *Whan the worde that is the prophecye of a prophete is knowen or fulfilled, than it shall be knowen that the Lorde sente the prophete in treuth!* '—And the Archebishoppe,

[1] 1 Parl. Hist. 290.   Rot. Cl. 8 Hen 4, m. 23.

as if he hadde not been pleased with my sayinge, turned him awaye ward hyther and thyther, and sayde, 'By God, I shall sette upon thy shynnes a pair of perlis, and thou shalt be gladde to chaunge thy voice.'"[1] This keen encounter ended in Thorpe being "led forth and brought into a foul unhonest prison,"—where he is supposed to have died; for he was no more heard of.[2]

The Chancellor now remained in high favor with the King for three years. On one occasion during this period, His Majesty bestowed his bounty upon him in a manner that at first caused him much alarm. The Great Seal was abruptly demanded from him; the King kept it only a few hours, while he caused a charter to be sealed granting the lordship of Queenbury to the Chancellor for life, and immediately after the Seal was restored to him.[3]

However it was taken from him in good earnest on the 21st of December, 1409,[4] when he must have had some serious difference with the King concerning the business to be brought forward at the parliament then about to assemble. Henry kept it in his own hands till the 19th of January following, during which time several charters, letters patent, and writs were sealed by himself. It was then delivered to John Wakering, Master of the Rolls, as Keeper, for the despatch of judicial business.[5]

In the mean time the parliment met, and, there being no Chancellor, the session was opened by a speech from Ex-Chancellor Henry Beaufort, the King's brother, from the text "Decet nos implere omnem justitiam," in which he reminded the parliament of Aristotle's answer to Alexander when asked the best mode of defending a city—"that the strongest walls were the hearty goodwill of his subjects;" but gave them a strong hint that a supply was expected, by reminding them that *benevolence* was due from subjects to a Sovereign as well as *reverence*.[6]

The Commons now eagerly pressed their expedient of seizing the property of the church, which they estimated at 485,000 marks a year, and which they proposed to divide among 15 earls, 1500 knights, 6000 esquires, and 100 hospitals, besides £20,000 a year which the King might

---

[1] It appears also by the report of Lord Cobham's trial, that his Grace was much given to swearing, even when acting judicially in a capital case. His favorite oath on that occasion was, "By our Lady."—2 St. Tr. 219.
[2] 2 St. Tr. 175.   [3] Rot. Cl. 10 Hen. 4, m. 18.
[4] Rot. Cl. 11 Hen. 4 m. 8.   [5] Ibid.   [6] 1 Parl. Hist. 312.

take for his own use; and they insited that the clerical functions would be better performed than at present by 15,000 parish priests paid at the rate of 7 marks apiece of yearly stipend.

The King was violently suspected of secretly favoring this project; but finding that it could not be carried, he threw all the blame upon the poor Lollards, and, to satisfy the church, ordered a Lollard to be burnt while the parliament was still sitting.[1]

We have now a lay Chancellor, but not a lawyer,—another half-brother of the King, Sir THOMAS BEAUFORT, who could not have been very fit for the office, but who reached the highest dignity in the peerage of any man who ever held the Great Seal. He was bred a soldier, and in the reign of Richard II. had gained considerable credit by opposing his bad counsels. He was created successively Earl of Dorset and Duke of Exeter.

He continued Chancellor two years, during which time he must often have sat in the marble chair at the marble table; but he seems to have been much engaged in political business, and he had the assistance of Sir John Wakering, the Master of the Rolls. On one occasion he declared that he was so much occupied with other business, that he had no time to attend to the duties of his office (*Quod circa alia negotia adeo occupatus erat ut sigillatoni vacare non posset*). Political Chancellors have not always been so plain-spoken.

After his surrender of the Great Seal, he remained inactive till the end of this reign; but he afterwards made a most distinguished figure in the wars of Henry V., and upon the untimely death of that Sovereign he was constituted guardian of the person of his infant successor, then crowned King of France as well as of England. Although he comes in the list of Chancellors, he had little to do with the duties of the office or the profession of the law, and I should not be justified in narrating his campaigns or entering more circumstantially into his history. He died at Greenwich in 1425, without issue, leaving his immense wealth to his royal ward.

We have no certain explanation of the reason why he

[1] 1 Parl. Hist. 308. This was the beginning of burning heretics in England, a practice which became more common till after the violent struggle excited by the Reformation had subsided.

ceased to be Chancellor any more than why he was first appointed. Henry, though now only forty-five years of age, had fallen into a mortal distemper, and felt serious compunction for the manner in which he had acquired the Crown, as well as for some of his acts in the exercise of royal authority. Perhaps, as his strength declined, he wished to have a spiritual "keeper of his conscience" who had been his chief councillor and accomplice, and who might be expected to be a lenient and absolving confessor.

On the 5th of January, 1412, the Great Seal was transferred to the aged Archbishop Arundel,[1] who became Chancellor for the fifth time. While Henry languished under his malady, nothing memorable occurred. He had long expected death, and in one of his fits was supposed to be dead. At last, on the 20th of March, 1413, he expired, in the Jerusalem Chamber, at Westminster, having been taught to believe that he had made a full atonement for all his transgressions, by vowing that, if he recovered, he would lead an army to the East and reconquer the Holy Land, and that his death under these circumstances was tantamount to a fulfillment of his vow.

He had appointed all his Chancellors merely from political convenience, without any regard to their fitness for the judicial duties of the office, and our jurisprudence is under no obligation to them. They showed great vigor, however, in enforcing the due administration of justice. While Cardinal Beaufort was Chancellor, the Archbishop of York had been guilty of an overt act of high treason, by joining in open rebellion and levying war against the King. Being taken prisoner, he claimed to be set at liberty on account of his sacerdotal character, but the government ordered him to be brought to trial. Sir William Gascoigne, Chief Justice of the King's Bench, who had courage to commit the Prince of Wales to prison for a contempt, was afraid to try an archbishop. Thereupon, a commission passed the Great Seal for his trial before another judge, Sir William Falthorpe, and he was convicted and executed, to the great horror of all churchmer and many of the laity, although clerical exemptions and privileges were now regarded with much less respect than at any prior era.[2]

[1] Rot. Cl. 13 Hen. 4, m. 1.
[2] As civilization advanced, it was desirable that the power and exclusive

The Chancellors at this time successfully resisted an attempt by the Commons to participate in the appellate jurisdiction of parliament, and obliged them to be contented with a resolution that their consent was necessary to all legislative acts.[1]

CHAPTER XIX.

CHANCELLORS DURING THE REIGN OF HENRY V.

WE now come to a reign for military exploits, one of the most brilliant in our annals, but by no means distinguished for juridical improvement, although during the course of it the office of Chancellor was filled by very eminent men.

Henry V. being proclaimed King, to the great joy of the people,—the first act of his reign was to take the Great Seal from Archbishop Arundel, and deliver it to his uncle, Henry Beaufort, Bishop of Winchester, the Cardinal, who now entered on his second Chancellorship. The young King was not actuated by any desire to change his father's ministers. Contrary to the expectations of his dissolute companions, and of the nation generally, his plan was to continue in their offices all who had faithfully served the Crown.[2] Perhaps he was induced to make an exception in the case of the Archbishop, on account of the active

privileges of the clergy should be curtailed: but their ascendency during the dark ages had been highly beneficial to the community. Not only were they the sole depositaries of learning, but they were often the protectors of the people against the tyranny of the King and the nobles. The enlightened reformers at Runnymede therefore made it the first article of Magna Charta, "quod Ecclesia Anglicana libera sit, et habeat omnia jura sua integra, et libertates suas illesas."

[1] See *Hale's Jurisd. House of Lords*. There is a curious entry in the Parliamentary Roll, showing the hours when the two Houses now met for the despatch of business. At the parliament which assembled in 1406, after the choice of the Speaker had been confirmed, "Et sur ceo le Chanceller d'Engleterre dona en charge de par le Roi as ditz Communes, q. pur l'esploit du dit parlement ils soient assemblez en lour maison accoustemez deinz l'Abbeie de Westm' chescun jour durant le parlement a *sept* del clocke; et semblable charge il dona as seignrs. du parlement, qu'ils de lour partie pur mesme l'esploit se assemblent, en lour lieu accustume a *noef* del clocke.—Roll. Par. iii. 568.

[2] We might have expected to see the Great Seal now delivered to Sir John

part which this Prelate had taken in the dethronement of Richard II. Young Henry expressed the deepest sorrow for the fate of that unhappy Prince, did justice to his good qualities, performed his funeral obsequies with pomp and solemnity, and cherished all those who had distinguished themselves by their loyalty and attachment to him. The Archbishop, while in exile, and on his return to England, had devised and prosecuted the plans which led Richard to his grave, and he might now be an object of personal dislike to the new King, who did not go so far as to resign his Crown to the true heir, but affected much to favor the doctrine of legitimacy.

We must now take final leave of Ex-Chancellor Arundel. Relieved from official duties, he occupied himself in carrying on a violent prosecution against the Lollards, whom the King was rather disposed to screen, and he presided on the trial and condemnation of Sir John Oldcastle, Lord Cobham, their leader, who had incurred the peculiar hatred of the clergy by actively supporting the proposal to encroach on the revenues of the church. This intriguing Prelate and Chancellor does not fill so great a space in the eye of history as might have been expected from the important part he acted in the revolutions of his age; but such was his reputation for ability with his contemporaries, that when impeached for high treason in 1397, the Commons having finished their case,—as he began to answer for himself, Sir John Busby, the Speaker, entreated the King that this might not be allowed him, "lest he might, by his subtlety and great wit, bring persons over to believe him innocent,"—so that he was forced to remain silent.[1] Of his judicial character no author makes mention. He died in January, 1413.

Cardinal Beaufort, two days after his appointment, sealed writs for a new parliament to meet at Easter; and when the time came, opened the session with a speech from the text, "Ante omne actum consilium stabilire."[2] The Commons made an attempt to reform the Ecclesiastical Courts and other abuses, but exhausted themselves in attacks on Falstaff, that he might play the part of "King;" but instead of this, the stern order was given:—

"Go, carry Sir John Falstaff to the Fleet:
Take all his company along with him."

[1] 1 St. Tr. 226.   [2] 1 Parl. Hist. 319.

the Lollards. These were renewed in a parliament which met the following year, when laws were passed at the suggestion of the Chancellor and other Prelates against reading Wickliffe's translation of the Bible, and against other such enormities.[1] But the Church was alarmed by the Commons again urgently pressing that the revenues of the clergy should be applied to the purposes of the State, and passing a bill which, says Hall, "made the fat abbots to sweat, the proud priors to frown, the poor monks to curse, the silly nuns to weep, and indeed all to fear that Babel would fall down."

It is said by some historians, that it was to divert this storm from the church, that Chicheley, the new Archbishop of Canterbury, strongly advised the King to claim the crown of France, and to lead an army across the seas in support of his pretended right. Certainly there is extant a long and very extraordinary speech of his addressed to the King in the House of Lords, making out the title of Edward III., notwithstanding the Salic law, and insisting that whatever title that Sovereign had was now vested in his present Majesty. He thus concluded, " Consider the just title you have to this crown, devolved on you by Queen Isabella your great-grandmother, sister and heir to three successive kings of France, who died without children, and take up noble arms to assist so just a cause. Advance your standard into France, and with assured hopes of victory march to conquer these dominions which are your own by inheritance. There is no true Englishman but is ready to devote his life and fortune to so glorious a service of his King. And in full persuasion of the justness of the war, we, the clergy, have given such a sum of money to maintain it as was never granted to any of your predecessors, and will join all our prayers for the success of your arms." His grace found it convenient to forget not only the objections to the claim of Edward III., but the awkward fact, that supposing this monarch to have been entitled to the crown of France,—if the succession to it was not regulated by the Salic law, the true heir was the Earl of March, descended from his second son, the Duke of Clarence, and not Henry V., descended from his third son, the Duke of Lancaster;—and if the parliament of England could

[1] Parl. Hist. 324.

change the descent of the English crown, transferring it to a younger branch of the royal family, it could have no such power over the crown of another country, which could not be considered, like the Isle of Man, as appurtenant to the crown of England.[1] But the Primate was warmly supported by the Ex-Chancellor, Thomas Beaufort, then Earl of Dorset, afterwards Duke of Exeter, and his arguments prevailed with the King and the royal brothers, who, being young and thirsting for glory, were impatient to signalize their courage against the old enemies of their native land. The same gallant spirit diffusing itself through the minds of the other nobles, they all declared for a war with France. The Ecclesiastical Revenues Bill was allowed to drop, and as soon as a supply was voted, the parliament was prorogued. The successive ecclesiastical Chancellors who presided in the House of Lords from this time till the quarrel with Rome in the reign of Henry VIII., contrived to prevent the subject being again brought forward again in parliament.

But the clamors against the abuses of the Court of Chancery could not be silenced. Cardinal Beaufort was now extending his jurisdiction in a manner that greatly alarmed the common lawyers, and caused the most lively remonstrances from the House of Commons. As soon as the King returned to England, after his glorious campaign, commenced by the capture of Harfleur, and crowned by the battle of Agincourt,—a parliament was called, and the Chancellor, in his speech with which the session was opened, tried to divert attention from all domestic grievances by a glowing description of the martial glory the nation had won. He strongly urged them to be content with nothing less than the conquest of France, endeavoring to demonstrate "that a thing well begun, and continued with diligence, must have a prosperous event, according to the saying, *Dimidium facti qui bene cœpit habet.*"[2]

There were, of course, warm congratulations on account of the splendid success of the royal arms; but the first real business was a petition from the Commons to the

---

[1] After the Revolution of 1688, William III. and our constitutional kings of the House of Hanover called themselves kings of France, and bore the lilies in their shield till the year 1801;—but to make out their title would have required the eloquence of the Archbishop. [2] 1 Parl. Hist. 331.

King (the usual mode of legislating in that age) against the recent encroachment of Courts of Equity,—praying that no causes should be drawn thither which might be determined in the Courts of common law. The petition is curious, as containing a full exposition of the opinion of the great body of the nation upon the subject of equitable jurisdiction.[1]

The royal veto was put upon the measure, the response being, "Le Roy s'avisera."[2] The chief grievance now complained of was afterwards remedied in practice, by the plaintiff being obliged to put upon the file of the Court a bill specifying his cause of suit before the subpœna issued.

In the following year, the Commons renewed the complaint against arbitrary proceedings contrary to the course of the common law, although the Chancellor had tried to tranquillize them by an opening speech from the text, "Operam detis ut quieti situs."[3] There had, as we have seen, been an early practice of presenting petitions to parliament complaining of private grievances. After the separation of the two Houses, these were reserved for the consideration of the Lords, and were first submitted to

[1] "Also the Commons pray, that inasmuch as many persons of your kingdom feel themselves greatly aggrieved in this, that your writs, called writs of subpœna and certiorari, are made and sued out of your Chancery and Exchequer for matters determinable by your common law, which never were granted or used before the time of the late King Richard; when John Waltham, heretofore Bishop of Salisbury, of his craft, invented, made, and commenced such innovations against the form of the common law of your realm, &c.: And whereas, by reason of your justices of either Bench, when they ought to attend in their places, to enter pleas and take inquests for the deliverance of your people, are occupied upon examinations upon such writs, to the great vexation, loss, and cost of your liege subjects, who are long time delayed in the sealing of their writs, sued in your Chancery, by reason of the great occupations upon the said examinations, which things are not profitable to you, most Sovereign Lord, nor to your liege subjects, on which examinations there is great clamor and noise by divers persons not aware of the law, without any record thereupon entered in your said places: That it please our most Sovereign Lord to ordain in this present parliament, that every person who shall sue such writs shall put all the cause and matter of his suit in the said writs, and that all such writs, in the Courts out of which they shall issue, shall be enrolled in the said Courts, and made patent, and shall remain for the defendants therein, without being returned in the said Courts, &c. And if any such writs, called subpœna and certiorari, and informations shall be sued out of your said courts, against this ordinance, in time to come, that the said writs, and all the proceedings depending thereupon, shall be wholly void and holden for nothing."* [2] Rot. Parl. 3 Hen. 5. [3] 1 Parl. Hist, 333.

* Rot. Parl. 3 Hen. 5, part ii. vol. iv. p. 84.

the triers of petitions, who were appointed at the commencement of every session. Such of them as disclosed matters only fit for the ordinary tribunals of the country were in regular manner referred to those tribunals, and some were not improperly allotted to the Chancellor, or the Privy Council. But this course was resorted to chiefly by suitors who knew they had no chance of success in the Courts of common law;—and, as an expedient for securing themselves a hearing before those by whom the rules of the common law were disregarded, they presented petitions to parliament, and themselves indorsed upon them a supposed reference to the Council or the Chancellor,— which was considered as giving the Council or Chancellor jurisdiction, although the subject-matter was properly cognizable at common law.

The House of Commons now prayed the King " that if any man shall indorse his bill or petition with these words, *by authority of parliament, let this bill or petition be sent to the Council of the King, or to the Chancellor of England, to execute and determine what is contained therein,* by which the said bill or petition be not by the Commons of the Parliament inquired into, affirmed, or assented unto, (WHICH NO ONE CAN INDORSE ON ANY SUCH BILL OR PETITION, WITHOUT THE ASSENT AND REQUEST OF THE COMMONS OF PARLIAMENT,) let him be sent to answer for disobeying the laws of the kingdom of England."

The King's answer still was, " Le Roy s'avisera,"[1]— which I can only account for from the parenthetical claim of privilege set up by the Commons, that they were to join in hearing and disposing of petitions to parliament respecting the administration of justice, and that, without their concurrence, the Lords could neither themselves determine the matter nor refer it to another tribunal. The simple condemnation and prohibition of the unauthorized practice of individuals so indorsing their petitions without the sanction of either House, could not have been refused; but a great jealousy has always been manifested of an encroachment by the Commons on the judicial powers of the Upper House.

The Chancellor had now a very delicate matter to negotiate ; and he had to encounter a very formidable struggle

[1] Rot. Par. 4 Hen. 5.

between his avarice and his love of power. The King was reduced to the greatest necessity for money to carry on the war with France. Tenths and fifteenths were voted to him, but a long time was required to collect them; and cash to pay the mutinous troops was indispensable. A sum was raised upon the personal responsibility of the Dukes of Clarence, Bedford, and Gloucester, who made themselves liable if the King should die; but this was quite insufficient for the present exigency, and there was no hope except in the Lord Chancellor. He had amassed immense riches from the profits of his see and of his office; but he refused to make any gift, and even to lend on the security with which others had been satisfied. At last the King offered to pawn to him the Crown itself. Thereupon, taking the pledge into his custody, the Chancellor advanced a very large loan, and the war was vigorously prosecuted.

At the last parliament over which Cardinal Beaufort presided during the present reign, an act was passed with his concurrence, and probably with the great applause of the English nation,—who for many centuries hated, and despised, and oppressed their Irish fellow subjects,—"That none of the Irish nation should be elected an Archbishop, Bishop, Abbot, or Prior; and that whoever promoted such to those ecclesiastical preferments, or brought any such Irish rebels to parliaments, councils, or other assemblies among the English, should have all their temporal estates seized into the King's hands till they have paid the fines due for such offenses."

On the last day of the session, the King, sitting on his throne in full parliament, created Thomas Beaufort, who was Earl of Dorset and Ex-Chancellor, Duke of Exeter, with a pension of £1000 a year. The Lords, with a proper respect for Ex-Chancellors, so much approved of the King's liberality, that they said no objection could be made, but only that it was too little, and not proportionable to the merits and services of that noble person.[1]

Cardinal Beaufort, in this Chancallorship, never parted with the custody of the Great Seal, except from the 5th of September to the 12th of October, 1416, during which time he was absent with the King of France, and the Great Seal was intrusted by him to the keeping of Simon

[1] Parl. Rol. 4 & 5 Hen. 5. 1 Parl. Hist. 335.

Gaunstede, Master of the Rolls, to be re-delivered to him on his return.[1] We have slender means of knowing how he performed his judicial duties; but we may, from his general disposition, not uncharitably believe that he was assiduous in business, and encouraged suitors that he might multiply fees. He resembled the fallen angel, whose

> ——"looks and thoughts
> Were always downward bent, admiring more
> The riches of Heaven's pavement, trodden gold,
> Than aught divine or holy."

His avarice, however, was now to receive a heavy and unexpected blow. From the hard bargain he made when he advanced money for the public service, or his importunity to be repaid, he disgusted the King. The Close Roll, 5 Hen. V., records that, "On the 23rd of July, 1417, Henry Beaufort, Bishop of Winchester, delivered up the Great Seal of gold to the King, on which day it was given to Thomas Longley, Bishop of Durham, who became Chancellor the second time."[2] but no writer gives us the particulars of the intrigue which brought about this change.

The Ex-Chancellor now visited the Council of Basil, and contrived to get himself named by Pope Martin V. Cardinal and Apostolic Legate in England and Ireland; but, upon the remonstrance of Archbishop Chicheley, the King forbade him to accept these dignities, and he was not gratified with wearing the red hat till after he had finally resigned the Great Seal in the succeeding reign.

A parliament was soon after called, which was opened by the new Chancellor with a speech from the text *Comfortamini et viriliter agite et gloriosi eritis*.[3] The most remarkable transaction during this parliament, throwing particular discredit on the Chancellor, was the order by the Lords that Sir John Oldcastle, Lord Cobham, should be burnt under the sentence passed against him as a heretic. He was the first English peer who ever suffered death for religion.[4]

About the same time the Ex-Chancellor Beaufort, Bishop of Winchester, managed to get a private bill of

---

[1] Rot. Cl. 4 Hen. 5, m. 13. [2] Rot. Cl. 5 Hen. 5, m. 15.
[3] 1 Parl. Hist. 335. [4] Ibid. 337.

his smuggled through both Houses, that a security given to him for a loan on the customs of Southampton, should be confirmed by parliament.[1]

Nothing memorable connected with the office of Chancellor occurred till 1421, when Henry's victories having led to the treaty of Troyes, by which he was to marry the Princess Catharine, and was declared regent of France and heir to that kingdom, he called a parliament to ratify the treaty.[2] This parliament was opened by a speech from the King's own mouth, the first instance I have found of of the Sovereign himself declaring the causes of summoning his great council. Henry represented to them the state of affairs,—" what conquests he had made in France, and what supplies were necessary to continue the war;—assuring them that the Dauphin and his party, who maintained some cities and provinces, being subdued, that kingdom might be entirely united to the English crown."

The Lord Chancellor, by order of the King, read the articles of the treaty of Troyes, which had been sworn to by the two Kings of England and France, and ratified also by the three estates of France; whereupon both Houses of Parliament avowed that they approved and accepted it as most conducive to the good of both nations, and of all Christendom; and every one promised for himself, his heirs, and successors, that they would inviolably observe it.[3] It is marvelous that such men as Longley and the spiritual Peers, whose blood was not heated by being personally engaged in the conflict, should have sanctioned a treaty which nothing but the power of the sword could carry into execution, and which, if it had taken effect, must have proved equally pernicious to England and to France.

At this parliament the Commons made another unsuccessful attempt to put an entire stop to the writ of subpœna in Chancery, as well as to Privy Seals bringing matters of private right before the Council; but they had a limited and temporary triumph by carrying an act to endure until the next parliament, "that the exception how that the partie hath sufficient remedy at the common law, shall discharge any matter in Chancery."[4] The act was never renewed, so that the concurrent jurisdiction of

[1] 1 Parl. Hist. 337.   [2] Ibid. 339.   [3] Ibid.   [4] Rot. Parl, 9 Hen. 5.

the Courts of equity and the Courts of common law in partition, dower, account, and many such matters, has continued.

Henry, leaving the government in the hands of his brother, the Duke of Bedford, and of the Chancellor, returned to France,—espoused Catherine,—got possession of Paris,—had his infant son proclaimed heir of both kingdoms, and died at Vincennes in the thirty-fourth year of his age.

His last parliament had been held in his absence, the Chancellor opening the session with a formal speech. After voting a supply, the chief business was regulating the coinage, which had fallen into great disorder from the short-sighted fraud of adulteration, first begun in the reign of Edward III.;—and it was enacted, "that the Chancellor of England should deliver to those who would have them good and just weights of the noble, half-noble, and farthing of gold, to prevent the people being abused by such as were counterfeit."[1]

During this reign the equity jurisdiction of the Chancellor was so actively enforced, that some have ascribed its origin to the Chancellorship of Cardinal Beaufort. He first exercised a control over the marriage of infants, and along with uses and trusts he took cognizance of many miscellaneous matters, which would now be referred to courts of common law, either civil or criminal.[2]

It may be remarked, that at this period of our history there was an unusual ferment in men's minds, and the Commons showed a strong spirit of innovation both in church and state, so that there seemed a great probability that important changes would be introduced with respect to the maintenance of the clergy and the administration of justice; but the absorbing foreign war in which the country was engaged preserved all our institutions untouched by legislation during the whole reign of Henry V.

[1] 1 Parl. Hist. 340.   [2] See 2 Cooper on Records, 361.

CHAPTER XX.

CHANCELLORS FROM THE COMMENCEMENT OF THE REIGN OF HENRY VI. TILL THE DEATH OF CARDINAL BEAUFORT.

HENRY VI. was, at his father's death, an infant of nine months old. The Duke of Gloucester, his uncle, having been named Regent of England by the late King, was at first allowed to assume the government under that title. At the end of the month a council was held at Windsor, at which the baby monarch in his nurse's arms was present, and was supposed to preside. Longley, Lord Chancellor to the late King, put the Great Seal into the royal lap, and placed upon it the hands of the child, who was too young even to be amused with it as a toy. The Regent, then, in the King's name, delivered it to Simon Gaunstede, the Master of the Rolls, for the despatch of necessary business.[1]

But the Regent soon found that he could not exercise his authority without the sanction of the legislature, and a commission passed the Great Seal for a new parliament to be held before him.

The session was opened, by his command, with a speech from Chicheley, Archbishop of Canterbury. Business being begun, it is stated in the Parliamentary History, that the two bishops of Durham and London, the former having been Chancellor of England in the late reign, and the other Chancellor of the Duchy of Normandy, who had both delivered up the several seals of their offices, prayed to be discharged by act of parliament, and that the same might be enrolled,—which was granted. It was then also enacted, that the King's style and titles should be changed, and that upon all his seals should be engraven, " Henricus Rex Franciæ et Angliæ, et Dominus Hiberniæ." At the request of the Commons, the Duke of Gloucester declared that the King had appointed the Bishop of Durham to be

---

[1] "Præfatus Dominus Rex nunc sigillum illud per manna præfati Ducis prædicto Simoni liberavit custodiendum." &c. Rot. Cl. 1 Hen. 6. m. 15.— This was the precedent chiefly relied upon for the fictitious use of the Great Seal during the insanity of George III.

his Chancellor, which appointment was confirmed by Parliament.[1]

In reality, the whole administration was arranged by the Lords and Commons, who had been gradually extending their influence during the reigns of the Lancastrian Princes. Disregarding the will of the late King, they declined altogether the name of "Regent" for England. They appointed the Duke of Bedford "Protector" of that kingdom, a title which they thought implied less authority they invested the Duke of Gloucester with the same dignity during the absence of his eldest brother—with a council of nine, by whose advice he must act; and the guardianship of the person of the infant King was given to the two Ex-Chancellors, the Bishop of Winchester and the Duke of Exeter, with whom it was thought he must be safe, as, from the stain on their birth, they themselves could never aspire to the crown.[2]

In this parliament, a vigorous effort was made to limit the jurisdiction of the Court of Chancery. The Commons presented a petition to the King, which, if agreed to, would very effectually have preserved the supremacy of the common law, but would have deprived the country of many benefits derived from equitable interference. They proposed, that to prevent persons being called upon to answer in Chancery for any matter for which there is remedy provided by the common law, no one should be allowed to sue any process before the Chancellor till the complainant had sent a bill, containing all the matter of his plaint or grievance, to be approved of by two judges of the King's Bench, or Common Pleas, and they should have certified that for such matter he could not have any action or remedy by the common law. But the answer returned in the King's name, by the advice of the Council of Regency, was, "Let the statute on this subject, made in the 17th year of the reign of King Richard II., be observed and put in due execution,"[3] which was, in fact,

---

[1] 1 Parl. Hist. 345. Rot. Parl. Hen. 6, vol. xv. 170.

[2] In Nov. 1422, a new Great Seal was made, because the King's style in the inscription on the former seals was not suited to the reigning monarch. The order in council recited, that "great peril might ensue to the King if the said seals were not immediately altered," and required the keepers of all the King's seals to cause them to be altered forthwith.—Rot. Parl. 1 Hen. 6.

[3] Rot. Parl. 1 Hen. 6.

a *veto*, and left the Chancellor without control to determine the limits of his own jurisdiction.

Lord Chancellor Longley opened another parliament in October, 1423, with a speech from the text, "Deum, timete, Regem honorificate," showing that peculiar honor ought to be rendered to the present King, notwithstanding his tender years, since now this realm had attained their wish, which was that the King of England might also be King of France, and that the love due to the father was due to the son, for *omnis qui diligit eum qui genuit diligit eum qui genitus est.*[1]

The petition or bill against the Court of Chancery, which had for some time been nearly annual, was now dropped; and nothing more memorable was transacted at this parliament than passing an act, " to secure those persons who had only the late King's jewels in pawn, and that the Bishop of Winchester, who had lent the King 20,000 marks on the crown, should have letters patent to receive the said sum out of the customs."[2]

The great struggle for power between Humphry, Duke of Gloucester, the Protector, and the Bishop of Winchester, his uncle, which produced such calamities, and which ended so fatally to both, was now begun, and the Bishop, from his superior shrewdness and vigor, was gaining the ascendant, although his rival, as Protector, claimed to exercise all the prerogatives of the crown.

Beaufort, by intriguing with the Council, contrived to resume the office of Chancellor, which added both to his wealth and his authority. On the 6th of July, 1424, the Great Seal was delivered to him for the third time.[3]

Longley, who was then forced to resign it, retired to the duties of his diocese, which he fulfilled very reputably till 1437, when he died. He was buried in that beautiful structure at the west end of Durham Cathedral, called the Galilee, on the restoration of which he had expended a

---

[1] 1 Parl. Hist. 347.   [2] Ibid. 348.
[3] The Close Roll states with much gravity that the Bishop of Durham surrendered the Great Seal into the hands of the King (not then two years old), and that the King delivered it to the Bishop of Winchester "cujus sacramentum de officio Cancellarii bene et fideliter faciendo præfatus Dominus Rex recepit." We are told that the Bishop then took it with him to his hospitium of St. Mary Overy, in Southwark, and on the following Monday sat for the despatch of business "in domo capitulari Fratrum Predicatorum infra Ludgate Londoniæ."—Rot. Cl. 2 Hen. 6, m. 2.

large sum of money. As an ecclesiastic, he is said to have possessed a love of learning, which he testified by princely donations of books to both the universities, and by legacies to establish public libraries in Durham, Leicester, and Manchester; but he never gave much proof of ability for civil affairs, and his promotion, like that of many others, was probably owing to his mediocrity and his pliancy.

The Bishop of Winchester, as Chancellor, opened a new parliament in the spring of the following year, under very extraordinary circumstances. With a view probably of throwing into the shade the lustre of the office of Protector, he on this occasion produced the King himself, a child of three years old, as ruler of the realm. On the day of meeting, the royal infant was carried on a great horse from the Tower of London through the city to Westminster. Having taken some pap at the palace, he was thence conducted to the House of Lords, and sat on his mother's knee on the throne. " It was a strange sight," says Speed, " and the first time it ever was seen in England, an infant sitting in his mother's lap, and before it could tell what English meant, to exercise the place of sovereign direction in open parliament."

The Chancellor took for his text, " Gloria, honor, et pax, omni operanti bonum." He slyly threw out various sarcasms on his opponents in the Council, under pretense of inculcating the duty of the people to obey those who are set over them, although not good in themselves. " But a real good councillor" (meaning himself) " he compared to an elephant for three properties; the one in that he wanted a gall, the second that he was inflexible and could not bow, and the third that he was of a most sound and perfect memory."[1]

The following day the King was again placed on the throne, when the Commons presented Sir Thomas Nanton as their elected Speaker, who, as usual, disqualified himself. But the Chancellor, in the King's name, would not allow of his objections, confirmed the choice of the Commons, and granted to them all their ancient privileges.

At this parliament an act was passed throwing upon the Chancellor a duty very alien from its judicial functions. The exportation of butter and cheese being generally prohibited —" for the encouragement of husbandry the Chan-

[1] 1 Parl. Hist. 351.

cellor of England was empowered, at his discretion, to grant licenses to such persons as should desire to vend the said articles in foreign parts, as well as at the great staple at Calais."[1] While it was acted upon, it must have considerably increased the fees and emoluments of the office, and must have been highly agreeable to the present Chancellor.

The rivalry between him and the Protector now became dangerous to the public tranquillity, and each mustering his adherents and dependents, a civil war was apprehended. The former had added to his power and insolence by obtaining for himself the appointment of legate to the Pope in England, and on many occasions he asserted his superiority to the Protector, who though vested with that high title, he contended had no authority beyond others of the Council. The Protector, on the contrary, affected royal pomp, assumed much on his prospect of succeeding to the crown, and insisted that, during the minority of his nephew, he was entitled to exercise all the royal prerogatives under the control of parliament.

The citizens of London were of the party of the Protector. To overawe them, the Chancellor strengthened the garrison of the Tower, which had been intrusted to a creature of his own. The Protector was refused admission into this fortress, and the gates of the city were shut against the Chancellor. The next morning, the retainers of the Chancellor attempted to force the gates at London Bridge. The citizens flew to arms, and bloodshed was with difficulty averted by the Archbishop of Canterbury and the Prince of Portugal, who, it is said, were obliged to travel eight times in one day between Lambeth and the City of London to act as peace-makers. By their interposition, the rival parties were prevailed upon to suspend their feuds till the arrival of the Duke of Bedford, the Regent of France, who was coming over in the hope of establishing a reconciliation between them. There is extant a letter then written by the Chancellor to the Duke, for the purpose of unfairly gaining his favor:

"I recommend me unto you with all my heart; and as you desire the welfare of the King our Sovereign Lord, and of his realms of England and France, and your own health and ours also, so haste you hither; for, by my

---

[1] 1 Parl. Hist. 353.

troth, if you tarry, we shall put this land in jeopardy with a field—such a brother you have here. God make him a good man. For your wisdom knoweth that the profit of France standeth in the welfare of England. Writen in great haste on Allhallow even, by your true servant to my lives end. HEN. WINTON."

Bedford hastened over from Paris, and called an assembly of the chief nobility at St. Alban's; but the time was spent in hot contests between the hostile factions, and nothing was concluded. The assembly was adjourned to Northampton, but to as little purpose;—till at last the resolution was formed to refer the whole matter to a full parliament, to meet at Leicester on the 18th of February.[1]

Much care was taken to prevent tumults between the great trains of the Protector and the Chancellor, by strictly prohibiting any person whatever to come thither with sword, or any other warlike weapon. The order was *literally* obeyed; but the Lords and their attendants came armed with *bats* or great clubs on their shoulders, from which this meeting got the name of "The Parliament of Bats."

These weapons, as soon as they were observed, were forbidden also; and the Lords and Commons being peaceably seated in the great hall of the Castle of Leicester, the young King, now in his fifth year, was placed upon the throne. "His Majesty, from a little previous drilling, having graciously returned the salute of the Lords and Commons, was decorously quiet, and the Lord Chancellor declared the cause of the summons in a very short manner."[2] It had been probably stipulated that, on this occasion he should abstain from all party and personal reflections. His text was, "Sic facite ut salvi sitis;" and without any particular allusion to the existing differences, he recommended the protection of the church, the giving of good counsel, and the granting of needful subsidies.

But as soon as a speaker had been chosen, and business had begun, articles were regularly exhibited by the Protector against the Chancellor, which were answered with recrimination. We may take as a specimen the manner in which a charge of the crime of assassination was bandied between them. Article II.:—

"That the Chancellor laid wait for the Protector by

[1] 1 Parl. Hist. 354.   [2] Ibid. 355.

placing armed men at the end of London Bridge, and in the windows of the chambers and cellars of Southwark, to have killed him if he had passed that way."

Answer—

"True, indeed, it is, that he did provide a certain number of armed men, and set them at the foot of London Bridge and other places, without any intention to do any bodily harm to the Duke of Gloucester, but merely for his own safety and defense, being informed by several creditable persons that the Duke had proposed bodily harm to him, and gathered together a company of citizens for that end."[1]

The Commons having expressed their "much dislike" to the dissensions between these great men, and moved, for their their reconcilement, the farther examination of the charges and answers was devolved by the two Houses upon a select committee of peers and bishops,—both parties having agreed, by formal instruments, to submit to what should be awarded. The Duke of Bedford, who presided in the court of arbitration, reported in open parliament "that the Chancellor was innocent of the charge alleged again him, of having procured a person to murder the late King when he was Prince, and having advised the Prince to depose Henry IV., his father; but pronounced judgment, that in respect of the incivilities that had passed betwnen them, he should, in a submissive manner, ask pardon of the Duke of Gloucester; that the Duke of Gloucester should freely forgive him; and, in token of a thorough reconciliation, each should take the other by the hand, so that they should be firm friends for the future." They accordingly shook hands, and parted with all outward signs of perfect love and concord, "which yielded a mighty satisfaction to all people, both of the clergy and laity;" and by the advice of the Council, a magnificent feast was given, in the name of the King, in honor of this supposed reconciliation.

It is not stated by historians that it was part of this arrangement that Beaufort should give up his office of Chancellor, the better to preserve the equilibrium between him and his rival; but it may be fairly presumed that he would not have voluntarily parted with such a source of power and of profit. However this may be, we find him

[1] 1 Parl. Hist. 357.

immediately petitioning parliament to be discharged of the Great Seal, which, by common consent, was granted.[1] He delivered it to the Duke of Bedford,—who himself sealed some letters patent with it in the presence of the King's Council, but soon went through the form of putting it into the hands of the infant King,—and, on the 18th of March, it was given, in full parliament, to JOHN KEMPE, Bishop of London, as Lord Chancellor.[2]

Beaufort never resumed the Great Seal, and we can only give a slight sketch of his subsequent history. On his resignation he went abroad, and was declared Cardinal priest of St. Eusebius. Then he was first regularly raised to the purple;—although we have occasionally called him Cardinal, the title by which he is best known. At the same time he was appointed by the Pope Captain-General of the Crusaders, destined to oppose the Hussites, in Bohemia. On his return to England, he obtained leave to raise an army of 500 lancers and 5000 archers for the expedition; but for a bribe of 1000 marks, he consented that the men whom he had raised for the crusade should be led against the King's enemies in France.

He was constantly on the watch for an opportunity to regain his political influence, and in 1429 he succeeded in humbling Gloucester, by having the young king crowned, and inducing the parliament to declare on the occasion that the office of Protector was at an end. Gloucester was thus reduced to his rank as a peer, and the Cardinal from this time to his death bore chief sway.

In 1431 he again went abroad, and at Rouen he assisted at the trial of Joan of Arc, the Maid of Orleans, and joined in the sentence that she should be burnt alive for heresy and witchcraft. He was the only Englishman who was concerned in this atrocity, and our neighbors the French, when they so eagerly impute it to us as a national disgrace, should remember that the Bishop of Beauvais and all her other judges were Frenchmen: and that she was brought to trial under an arrest of the parliament of Paris.

The Duke of Gloucester, though no longer Protector, was still formidable, and from time to time seemed on the

---

[1] " The Bishop of Winton, for sundry causes, prayed to be discharged from the office of the Great Seal, and he was consequently discharged."—Rot. Parl. 4 Hen. 6. Rot. Cl. 4 Hen 6, m. 8   [2] Rot. Cl. 4 Hen. 6. m. 8.

point of recovering his authority. He accused the Cardinal of having incurred the penalties of a præmunire, by accepting papal bulls,—of having amassed immense wealth by dishonest means,—of having usurped the functions of sovereignty by appointing embassies and releasing prisoners of his own authority,—and of estranging all but his own creatures from the person of the young King. The Cardinal caused an accusation to be brought against the Duke's wife, to whom he was much attached, that she was guilty of witchcraft, by melting, in a magical manner, before a slow fire, a waxen figure of the King, with the intention of making the King's force and vigor waste away by like insensible degrees. The Duchess was condemned to do public penance, and to suffer perpetual imprisonment. But this proceeding was ascribed solely to the malice of the Duke's enemies, and the people increased their esteem and affection towards a Prince who was thus exposed without protection to such mortal injuries. The manifestation of these sentiments made the Cardinal sensible that it was necessary to destroy a man whose popularity might soon become dangerous, and from whose resentment everything was to be apprehended, if he should ever be in a situation to gratify it.

To effect this purpose, a parliament was called to assemble,—not at London, which was supposed to be too well affected to the Duke,—but at Bury St. Edmund's, where he would be helpless. As soon as he appeared, he was thrown into prison on a charge of treason. Soon after, he was found dead in his bed; and though it was pretended that his death was natural, no one doubted that he had fallen a victim to the vengeance of his arch-enemy.

The Cardinal himself died six weeks after the murder of his nephew, which, it is said, gave him more remorse in his last moments than could naturally have been expected to be felt by a man hardened, during the course of a long life of violence, in falsehood and in religious hypocrisy. His death-bed is described in harrowing terms by our great dramatic bard :—

> "Lord Cardinal, if thou think'st on Heaven's bliss,
> Hold up thy hand, make signal of thy hope !
> — He dies and makes no sign."

And the agony of his despair is, if possible, made more

dreadful by the lofty conception and successful execution of the scene in the masterpiece of Reynolds.

But volumes have been written to prove that his life was innocent and his end pious, by arguments which may carry conviction to the mind of those who believe that Richard III. was a remarkably straight and handsome man, with a very tender heart. The Cardinal's enormous wealth was applied, according to his will, in founding oratories for priests to pray for his soul, and these may account for the attempts which have been made to vindicate his memory.[1]

CHAPTER XXI.

CHANCELLORS DURING THE REIGN OF HENRY VI. FROM THE APPOINTMENT OF CARDINAL KEMPE TILL THE DEATH OF LORD CHANCELLOR WAYNFLETE.

WE have had a succession of Chancellors of high birth, some of them nearly allied to the Crown. Cardinal Beaufort's successor was one of that other class who had won their way in this country to high distinction from an obscure origin. He was born in Kent, of parents in a very low condition of life,[2] and educated as a poor scholar at Merton College in Oxford.

[1] Cardinal Beaufort is not only a favorite with ignorant chroniclers, but with the enlightened Dr. Lingard, who say that we owe to the imagination of Shakspeare the fiction of his dying agonies. But it is well known that Shakspeare, in his historical plays, most strictly followed history or tradition, and embodied the belief of his time. Dr. Lingard himself quotes a passage from Hall, stating "that the Cardinal lamented on his death-bed that money could not purchase life, and that death should cut him off when he hoped, now his nephew Gloucester was gone, to procure the purple tiara,"—which the historian tries to dicredit merely on the ground of improbability, because the Cardinal was so old and infirm, and had his funeral rehearsed while he was yet alive. Dr. Lingard even denies his avarice, because he did not receive interest on his loans to the crown, and only looked to be benefited by the forfeiture of the pledges which he took by way of security, and being paid back in gold coin the sums he seems to have advanced in silver. He thus demanded " that paement be maad in golde of the coigne of England of just weighte, elles I not to be bounde to delyver ayene the seide weddes (pledges), though the seide paiement were offered to be maad in silver." A usurer stipulating for ten per cent. interest would not show a more intense love of money.—Acts of Coun. iv. 234, 248. Ling. v. 124.

[2] I have since ascertained that at the time of his birth his father and mother were living in the parish of St. Gregory, in Wye, where he founded a college

Here amid all the evils·of penury, he applied himself with ardor to study, and made particular proficiency in the civil and canon law. In due time he took the degree of Doctor in both faculties, after disputations which attracted the notice of the whole university, and were talked of all over England.

After practising for some time as an advocate in the ecclesiastical courts,—on account of his high reputation as a jurist he was made Dean of the Arches and Vicar-general to the Archbishop of Canterbury. Rising rapidly in the church, he was consecrated Bishop of Rochester; whence he was translated to Chichester, and thence to London, the see he filled when appointed Lord Chancellor; finally he was appointed to the Archbishopric of York, and a cardinal's hat was bestowed upon him.

Soon after his high civil appointment, he was called upon to take a decisive part in checking the arrogance of the Duke of Gloucester, who having for a time got rid of Cardinal Beaufort, avowed his purpose to rule in an arbitrary manner, although the Duke of Bedford had not yet returned into France, exclaiming "Let my brother govern as him lusteth, whiles he is in this land; after his going over to France, I woll govern as me seemeth good." The Chancellor and the other members of the Council made a representation on the subject to the Duke of Bedford, and both brothers being present, the Chancellor delivered an address, stating "that the young Prince was the rightful King of England, and entitled to the obedience of all his subjects, of whatever rank they might be; that young as he was, he yet possessed by the law all the authority which would belong to him at a more mature age; that as, during his infancy, he could not exercise such authority, it was vested in the Lords spiritual and temporal assembled in parliament, or in the great council, and at other times in the Lords appointed to form *the continual council.*" and that this council, representing the King's person, had a right to exercise the powers of government, "*withouten that any one person may or ought to ascribe to himself the said rule of government.*"[1]

KEMPE'S first Chancellorship lasted six years. During

of secular priests, to attend divine service and instruct youth in grammar and other learning.—*Note to 3rd Edition.*

[1] Rot. Par. v. 409, 411. Acts of Coun. iii. 231, 242.

this time several parliaments were held, which he opened with suitable speeches, except that held in January, 1431, when on account of his sickness, the Duke of Gloucester, sitting in the chair of state in the Painted Chamber, commanded William Linewood, Doctor of Laws, to explain the cause of the summons,[1] which was done with infinite divisions and subdivisions; but the only important business transacted at these parliaments, was passing the famous statute which regulates county elections, and enacts that no freeholder shall vote who cannot spend from his freehold at least 40s. a year,[2]—all freeholders having before voted for knights of the shire as they still may for coroners.

A change in the office of Chancellor now took place, the reasons for which have not been explained to us, and all we know of it we learn from the Close Roll, which records:

"That the Lord Cardinal, Archbishop Kempe, on the 25th of February, 1432, delivered up to the King the gold and silver Seals, and the Duke of Gloucester immediately took them and kept them till the 4th of March, on which day he gave them back to the King, and they were delivered by his Majesty to JOHN STAFFORD, Bishop of Bath and Wells, who took the oath of office, and used the silver Seal for the dispatch of business."[3]

The new Chancellor was of illustrious descent, being the son of the Earl of Stafford by the Lady Anne Plantagenet, daughter and heiress of Thomas of Woodstock, sixth son of Edward III.,—and he was equally distinguished for his learning and industry. Having with great reputation taken the degree of Doctor of Civil Law at Oxford, he practiced for some time as an advocate in

---

[1] There is a curious entry of this in the Parliament Roll, showing a great anxiety to preserve the Chancellor's right to address the two Houses on the opening of parliament. After stating the meeting of Lords and Commons under the Duke of Gloucester, Custos Angliæ, it proceeds, " Pro eo quod Venerabilis Pater Johannes Archiepiscopus Ebor. Cancellarius Anglie, *cui ratione officii sui secundum consuetudinem laudabilem in Regno Anglie antiquitus usitatum pertinuit causam summonitionis parliamenti predicti pronunciare et declarare*, tali et tanta detenebatur infirmitate quod circa declarationem et pronunciationem predictas adtunc intendere non valebat, Reverendus vir Magister Willielmus Lynwoode, Legum Doctor, causam summonitionis ejusdem parliamenti de mandato prefati custodis egregie declaravit." —Vol. iv. 367. So in 31 and 32 Hen. 6, the Bishop of Lincoln stated causes of summons. "Johanne Arch. Cant. Cancellarie Angliæ tunc absento."— Roll. v. 227. [2] 10 Hen. 6. [3] Rot. Cl. 10 Hen. 6, m. 8.

Doctors' Commons, and rose into considerable business when Chicheley, Archbishop of Canterbury, elevated him to be Dean of the Arches, and obtained for him the deanery of St. Martin, and a prebend in Lincoln Cathedral. He then became a favorite of Henry V., who made him successively Dean of Wells, Prebendary of Sarum, Keeper of the Privy Seal, and Treasurer of England. He attached himself to the party of Cardinal Beaufort, by whose interest, in 1425, he was appointed Bishop of Bath and Wells.

He filled the office of Chancellor till, 1450, a longer period than any one since the Conquest had continuously held the Great Seal.

From the 22nd of April to the 23rd of May, 1433, he was absent on an embassy to Calais, and the silver Seal was in the custody of John French, Master of the Rolls, for the sealing of writs and the despatch of necessary business; but it was restored to the Chancellor on his return without any re-appointment, or new oath of office, the Master of the Rolls, as upon similar occasions, being merely considered as his deputy.

In 1436 an act was passed with the concurrence of the Chancellor, to check the wanton filing of bills in Chancery in disturbance of common law process. The Commons, after reciting the prevailing grievances, prayed " that every person from this time forward vexed in Chancery for matter determinable by the common law, have action against him that so vexed him, and recover his damages." The King answered, " that no writ of subpœna be granted hereafter till security be found to satisfy the party so vexed and grieved for his damages and expenses, if it so be that the matter may not be made good which is contained in the bill."[1]

We find few subsequent complaints against Lord Chancellor Stafford, and he seems to have diligently and quietly applied himself to the duties of office, not aiming at political ascendency himself, and bending submissively to the varying pressure of the times. In opening parliaments, and urging supplies, he had no victories to announce; but he had to tell of the raising of the siege of Orleans by the sorceress Joan of Arc, and of disasters rapidly succeeding each other, till, after the defection of

[1] From the petition and answer was framed stat. 15 Hen. 6, c. 4.

the Duke of Burgundy, and the death of the Duke of Bedford, the English were driven from Paris;—Guienne and Normandy were lost, and there was not left to the English a remnant of the conquests of Henry V. in France.

The Parliament Roll and the contemporary chroniclers give us a very slender account of this Chancellor's harangues in parliament: but from the specimen we have of them, they seem to have been very dull and quaint. His maiden exhibition was on the 12th of March, 1432, when the infant King being on the throne, he took for his text, "Deum timete, Regum honorificate:" on which words he remarked two points:—1. A general Counsel to Princes, that they might learn knowledge.—2. A Commandment to subjects to learn to obey and honor the Prince. Which points he learnedly enlarged upon, and endeavored to prove by many quotations, examples, and similitudes, that the King and realm of England might easily attain to the height of peace and prosperity, if true fear of God and honor to the Prince were in the hearts of the subjects.[1]

He had a more delicate task to perform the following day. The Duke of Gloucester rose in his place and declared for the contentment of the Commons, who, he was informed, had expressed some uneasiness on the subject, that although he was Chief President of the Council, yet he would act nothing without the consent of the majority of them. This declaration was communicated to the Commons by the Chancellor when they produced John Russell as their Speaker for the King's approbation; and it so much pleased them, that they immediately granted tonnage and poundage, with a new subsidy on wools.[2]

The Chancellor's text the following year was *Suscipiant montes pacem populo et colles justiciam.* "This subject he divided," we are told, "into three parts, according to the three estates of the realm; by *mountains*, he understood bishops, lords, and magistrates; by the *lesser hills*, he meant knights, esquires, and merchants; by the *people*, he meant husbandmen, artificers and laborers. To which three estates, he endeavored to prove, by many examples and authorities, that a triple political virtue ought to belong: to the first—unity, peace, and concord, without dis-

[1] 1 Parl. Hist. 365. [2] Ibid. 366.

simulations; to the second—equity, consideration, and upright justice, without partiality; to the third—a due obedience to the King, his laws and magistrates, without grudging."[1]

During the same session he seems gracefully to have expressed to the Duke of Bedford the confidence which all felt in his gallantry and honor, notwithstanding the reverses of the English arms in France. The Duke having said " that he had come over to clear himself from some slanders which were cast upon him, as that he had been the occasion of the late great losses by his default and negligence, and offered to take his trial for the same,"— the Chancellor, by the King's command, declared " That his Majesty took him for his true and faithful subject and most dear uncle, and for his coming at that time gave him most hearty thanks." This was followed up by a compliment from the other house, communicated in a way rather different from our present forms. The Commons came before the King and Lords, and by their Speaker praised the Duke of Bedford for his warlike behavior and notable deeds done in France, and particularly for his conduct in the battle of Verneuil.[2]

In 1435, the King sitting in his chair in the Painted Chamber, the Chancellor delivered a most violent invective against the defection of the Duke of Burgundy, his text being "*Soliciti sitis servare unitatem spiritus in vinculo pacis.*" This performance is plain, forcible, and eloquent. But he probably piqued himself much more on his speech the next year from the words *Corona Regni in manu Dei*:—

" On which he demonstrated that three sorts of men are crowned, viz., all Christians in their baptism, in token whereof they are anointed; all clerks in their orders, in token whereof they are shaven; and all kings in their coronation, who in token thereof wear a crown of gold set about with flowers and precious stones. The erecting and standing of the flowers in the upper part of the crown denoteth the King's pre-eminency over his subjects, which ought to be garnished with four cardinal virtues, that is to say, in the fore part ought to be wisdom, adorned with three precious stones, viz., memory of things past, circumspection of things present, and prudence in things

[1] 1 Parl. Hist. 368.   [2] Ibid. 369.

to come. On the right hand ought to be fortitude—accompanied with courage in attempting,—patience in suffering,—and perseverance in well-meaning. On the left side ought to be justice distributing her arms three ways, to the best, mean, and lowest. On the hinder part ought to be temperance, with her trinity, viz., restraint of sensuality in fear, silence in speech, and mortification in will; all which proceeding from God fully proved that the crown was in the hand of God."[1]

In 1439, the Chancellor, being a friend to free trade, passed an act lessening his duties and his emoluments,—"that cheese and butter might be exported to foreign parts without the Chancellor's license."

After an interval of some years, in which we have no account of any parliamentary proceeding, in February, 1445, the parliament met which was to sanction the King's marriage with Margaret of Anjou, daughter of the titular King of Sicily and Jerusalem, and the Chancellor put forth all his strength in painting the felicity of this happy union, selecting for his text, "Justitia et Pax osculatæ sunt."[2]

But a great difficulty arose respecting the peace with France, which had been negotiated at the same time with the marriage, and the conditions of which were so humbling to England. An act had been passed in the late King's time forbidding any treaty with the Dauphin of France, now Charles VII., without the assent of the three estates of both realms, and the Chancellor was afraid that, the peace being unpopular, he might be impeached for an infraction of this statute. To evade the danger,—in the presence of the King and the whole parliament, Stafford made a protestation "That the peace about to be made with France was merely of the King's own motion and will, and that he was not instigated thereto by any one whatsoever." This protest was enrolled, and thereupon the statute referred to was repealed, and it was declared, "that no person whatsoever should be impeached at any time to come for giving counsel to bring about this peace with France."[3]

It should be stated to the honor of the Chancellor, who cordially seconded the liberal intentions of the King, that

---

[1] 1 Parl. Hist. 374. [2] Ibid. 378. [3] Ibid. 379.

in this parliament he proposed and carried an act to confirm the foundation of Eton College, where—

"Grateful Science still adores
Her Henry's holy shade."

By concealing an article in the treaty with France, that the province of Maine, which was still in the possession of the English, should be delivered up, ministers contrived to obtain a vote of thanks from both Houses for concluding the treaty ; and for some time the Chancellor's tenure of office seemed more secure than ever. But after the murder of Gloucester and the death of Cardinal Beaufort, when the stipulated cession of Maine was made known, and France insisted on the strict performance of the treaty, there was a general burst of indignation throughout the country, and the greatest impatience was testified to bring to punishment the Duke of Suffolk, the Queen's favorite, who had negotiated the treaty, together with the Lord Chancellor, and all who were concerned in it.

The assembling of a parliament was delayed as long as possible. The Queen, who had gained a complete ascendant over her husband, apprehensive of danger to Suffolk, long prevented the writs from issuing, and under pretense of the plague, contrived to have the opening of the session several times adjourned.

At length both Houses met, in the beginning of the year 1450. Lord Chancellor Stafford, who had been lately made Archbishop of Canterbury, appeared on the woolsack, and tried to brave the storm, but soon found himself obliged to yield to it. Although he was the organ of announcing several prorogations, he was not permitted to deliver the usual address explaining the reasons for summoning parliament ; and the two Houses seem to have insisted, before beginning any business, that he should be dismissed from his office.

On the 31st of January, 1450, the day that parliament met pursuant to the last adjournment, " the Archbishop of Canterbury was discharged from the office of Chancellor, and John Kempe, Cardinal and Archbishop of York, was put in his place."[1] I conjecture that, to appease the two Houses, this transfer actually took place in their presence. From the entry in the Close Roll, it appears

[1] 1 Parl. Hist. 386.

that there were three seals delivered to the new Chancellor, all which, it is said, he took with him to his country-house at Charing Cross.¹

Ex-Chancellor Stafford was not further molested. He retired from politics, and died at Maidstone, in Kent, on the 6th of July, 1452. He was *par negotiis neque supra*, one of those sensible, moderate, plodding, safe men, who are often much relished by the leaders of political parties, as they can fill an office not discreditably, without any danger of gaining too much éclat, and with a certainty of continued subserviency.

Cardinal Kempe succeeded him likewise as Archbishop of Canterbury, and continued Chancellor till he died in the office on the 2nd of March, 1454. Any knowledge of the law he had acquired when he before held the Great Seal had utterly evaporated during his eighteen years' retirement from the office, and he must no doubt have now been very unfit for its judicial duties; but civil war was at hand, and the interests of justice were little regarded in the struggles of the different factions who were preparing for hostilities.

He had first to preside on the impeachment of the Duke of Suffolk, who, declaring " that he was as innocent as the child still in the mother's womb," instead of claiming to be tried by his peers threw himself without reserve on the will of his Sovereign. *Chancellor.*—" Sir, since you do not put yourself on your peerage for trial, the King will not hold you either guilty or innocent of the treasons with which you have been charged, but as one to whose control you have voluntarily submitted (not as a judge advised by the Lords),—he commands you to quit this land before the 1st of May, and forbids you ever to set your foot during the five next years on his dominions either in this kingdom or beyond the sea."² It is well known how the unfortunate Suffolk, who the cunning man in calculating his nativity had prophesied was to die by " Water," had his head struck off by " Walter " Whitmore, as he was crossing the sea under this illegal sentence.³

Then broke out Jack Cade's rebellion, which was specially aimed against the Chancellor and all concerned with the profession of the law. The measures at first taken

¹ Rot. Cl. 28 Hen. 6, m. 7.   ² Rot. Par. vol. v. 182.
³ Shaks. Hen. VI. Part II. act iv. sc. 1.

to suppress it were most inefficient, and the King and his court were obliged to seek protection in Kenilworth Castle, London opening its gates to the insurgents. The Chancellor took the chief management of affairs, and the rebels having received a repulse, he succeeded in dispersing them by offering a general pardon and setting a price on Cade's head, which was earned by Iden of Kent.[1]

Many supposed that Cade had been set on to try the disposition of the people towards the right heir to the crown. He pretended to be a son of Mortimer, who had married the daughter of the Duke of Clarence, elder brother of John of Gaunt; and in this belief thousands flocked to his standard. The Duke of York, the real heir through a daughter of Mortimer, at last openly set up his claim—for which there was now a very favorable opportunity from the intellectual weakness of the King;—from the extreme unpopularity of the Queen, whose private character was open to great suspicion, and who was considered a devoted partisan of France;—from the loss of the foreign possessions which had so much flattered the pride of the English nation;—from the death and discomfiture of the ablest supporters of the reigning dynasty;—from the energy and popularity of the pretender himself;—and from the courage, the talents, and the resources of his numerous adherents.

The claims of the rival houses being debated in the Temple Gardens, the red and the white roses there plucked became the opposing emblems,[2] and men took different sides according to their judgment, their prejudice, or their interest.

When the next parliament met at Reading in the spring of 1453, it was found that the Duke of York had a powerful party in both Houses, although many who preferred his title were very reluctant to take active measures to support it, on account of the mild virtues of the reigning Sovereign. The Chancellor being unable to attend,

[1] Shaks. Hen. VI. Part II.
[2] "*Plantagenet.* Let him that is a true born gentleman
And stands upon the honor of his birth,
If he suppose that I have pleaded true,
From off this brier pluck a *white rose* with me.

"*Somerset.* Let him that is no coward nor no flatterer,
But dare maintain the party of the truth,
Pluck a *red rose* from off this thorn with me."

the session was opened by a speech from the Bishop of Lincoln, who contented himself with declaring "the cause of summoning the parliament to be chiefly for the good government of the realm and safe defense of the same; to which end he bid the Commons choose their Speaker and present him at the bar."[1] The Speaker chosen was Thomas Thorpe, Chief Baron of the Exchequer, whose imprisonment gave rise to the famous case of parliamentary privilege, in which the Judges declared that such questions did not belong to them to consider. On the 22nd of July the Chancellor prorogued the parliament to the 7th of November, to meet at Reading, and it was farther prorogued to the 11th of February following, to meet at Westminster.

Before this day arrived, public affairs had fallen into a state of the greatest confusion. The King had been attacked by an illness which affected his mind and made him unfit for business, and his ministers seem to have been wholly at a loss what course they should adopt. The Duke of York did not yet venture formally to claim the crown; but he contrived to get almost all the power of the executive government into his own hands. A commission under the Great Seal was produced, appointing him to hold the parliament in the King's absence. Thorpe the Speaker being of the opposite party, and being imprisoned for damages recovered against him by the Duke of York, the Commons were prevailed upon to choose another Speaker, and the Chancellor announced to them the royal approbation of the choice.

This was the last act of Lord Chancellor Kempe; while still in possession of his office he suddenly sickened, and died on the 22nd of March, 1454. He had showed himself always ready to go with the ruling power, and recently even to join the Yorkists if necessary, a disposition which may account for the continued stream of promotion which flowed upon him through life. Besides being twice Lord Chancellor, he had held three bishoprics and two archbishoprics. He was first created cardinal by the title of *St. Albinus*, which afterwards, when he came to be Archbishop of Canterbury, he changed by the authority of the Pope for that of *St. Rufinus*. A barbarous line has been

---

[1] 1 Parl Hist. 381.

handed down to us describing his ecclesiastical preferments—

"Bis primas, ter præses, et bis cardinale functus."

Amidst the difficulties which arose in carrying on the government on the Chancellor's death, a committee of the Lords was appointed to go to the King, lying sick at Windsor, to learn his pleasure touching two articles: the first, to know who should be Archbishop of Canterbury, and who Chancellor of England in the place of John Kempe, by whose death they lay in the King's disposal;[1] the second to know whether certain Lords there named to be of the Privy Council were agreeable to him or not. On the 25th of March, the said committee reported to the whole House, "that they had been to wait upon the King at Windsor, and after three several repairs thither, and earnest solicitations to speak with the King, they could by no means have answer, or token of answer, being only told the King was sick." Two days afterward the Lords appointed the Duke of York Protector of the realm, so long as the same shall please the King. The Duke still hesitating about the assertion of his own right, with a view to the pains of treason to which he might afterwards be subjected, obtained a declaration of the House, "that he took upon him the said office by the particular appointment of the Lords, and not of his own seeking or desire." Letters patent to which the Duke must himself have affixed the Great Seal, were read in the House, appointing him Protector during the King's pleasure, or until such time as Edward the Prince, then an infant, a few months old, should come to the age of discretion.

---

[1] The entry in the Parliament Roll affords a curious specimen of the English language in the middle of the fifteenth century.

"Memorand' that on the xxiii day of Marche, forasmuche as God hath called to his mercy and shewed his will upon Maister John Kempe, late Cardinall Archebishop of Canterbury, and Chaunceler of Englond, whoos soule God assoile, and by whoos deth th' office of Chauncelor of Englond stondeth now voide, the which office, of force and necessite for the ease of the people and processe of the lawe, must be occupied; it was advised, ordeigned, assented, and thurroughly agreed by the Duke of York, the Kinges lieutenaunt in this present parlement, and all the Lordes spiritualx and temporalx assembled in the parlement chambre at Westr., that certain Lordes, that is to seie, &c., shoulde ride to Wyndesore to the Kynges high presence, to shewe and declare to his Highnesse the seid materes," &c. The instructions are then set out, and there is a long account of the whole transaction.—v. 244.

The Duke, in full parliament, then swore faithfully to perform the duties of his high office.[1]

His first judicial appointment must have caused considerable astonishment in Westminster Hall. The Close Roll of the year informs us, that "on the 2d of April, the King's three Great Seals, one of gold and two of silver, were brought into parliament; and the Duke of York, Lieutenant of the kingdom, delivered them to RICHARD NEVILLE, Earl of Salisbury, as Chancellor.[2]

He was the most powerful Peer who has ever been Chancellor of England; and if military prowess was the great requisite for the office, none could be better qualified to fill it. He was one of the chiefs of the family of Neville, "which," says Hume, "was perhaps at this time the most potent, both from their opulent possessions and from the characters of the men, that has ever appeared in England." This Earl of Salisbury was the son of the Earl of Westmoreland, and inherited by his wife, daughter and heir of Montacute Earl of Salisbury, killed before Orleans, the estates and title of that great house. In the 11th of Hen. VI. he was made warden both of the east and west marches, and gained great distinction in repressing incursions of the Scotch. He then served with gallantry in France, having under his own pennant 7 knights, 49 men at arms, and 1046 archers. He early espoused the interest of Richard, Duke of York. Having contributed his assistance to make him Protector, he was now rewarded with the office of Lord Chancellor, and seemed in the possession of permanent power and felicity, though actually destined to finish his career by the hands of the common executioner,—his head being stuck upon a pole erected over one of the gates of the city of York.

[1] 1 Parl. Hist. 393.—Historians are at a loss to account for Richard's reluctance to throw off his allegiance, even when his party had all the power of the state in their hands. The reason may be, that while the King was childless he would not run the risk of civil war, as he hoped that his family would succeed to the throne without any dispute, on failure of the line of Henry IV The war of the Roses may perhaps be ascribed to the birth of the Prince of Wales, which was considered so auspicious. There can be no doubt that had it not been for the birth of another Prince of Wales, the son of James II., William and Mary would have waited to claim the crown by right of blood.

[2] Another account states, that on the 2nd of April the coffer containing the Seals was brought into the parliament chamber, placed on the bench where the Duke of York sat as Lieutenant, and after an interval opened by the Earl of Salisbury himself, who took possession of them, and assumed the office of Chancellor.—Rymer, t. ii. p. 344.

He retained the office exactly one year. During this time the King so far recovered from his distemper as to be able to carry the appearance of exercising the royal prerogative; and the Duke of York not having boldly seized the Crown as his right, Margaret, in her husband's name, resumed the royal authority, annulled the protectorship, released the Duke of Somerset, the principal leader of the Lancastrians, from the Tower, and committed the administration into the hands of that nobleman. The Duke of York, and his Chancellor, saw that if they submitted to this revolution, they would soon be brought to trial for treason. They flew to arms, and employed themselves in levying forces in the counties where they were most potent.

On the 7th of March, 1455, THOMAS BOURCHIER, Archbishop of Canterbury, was made Lord Chancellor by the Queen's new government. There is an entry in the Close Roll of the surrender of the Seals;[1] but in reality, the same seals were not used by the different Chancellors of the opposing parties, and it was objected to the Earl of Salisbury that the true Great Seal had never been in his custody.

The new Chancellor holds a distinguished place in English history, having been Archbishop of Canterbury under five successive reigns, and having exercised a considerable influence upon the events of his time. He was of high lineage, being a descendant of Lord Chancellor Bourchier, and son of William Bourchier, Count of Eu in Normandy, by Anne, daughter of Thomas of Woodstock, sixth son of Edward III., and relict of Edmund Earl of Stafford. He early discovered that love of letters for which he was noted through life, and which induced him to take an active part in introducing the art of printing into England. In 1434, while he was still a young man, he was elected Chancellor of the University of Oxford, where he had been educated. He filled successively the sees of Worcester and Ely. In April, 1454, on the death of Cardinal Kempe, he was promoted to the Archbishopric of Canterbury; and in December following he received the red hat from Rome, being created Cardinal-priest of St. Cyriacus in Thermis.

Soon after his appointment as Chancellor was fought

[1] Rot. Cl. 33 Hen. 6, m. 9.

the great battle at St. Alban's, in which his predecessor had a leading command, and in which the Yorkists were superior, having, without any material loss on their part, slain 5000 of their enemies. Among these were the Duke of Somerset and several other of the most distinguished Lancastrian leaders, so that Margaret's party seemed almost annihilated.

The Duke of York still thought it the most politic course to exercise power in the name of the King, who had been taken prisoner, and for whom all outward respect was testified. As a proof of moderation, the Archbishop of Canterbury was allowed to retain the office of Chancellor, and a parliament, which met in July at Westminster, was opened by a speech from him. There was some mistrust, however, as to what he might say if left to himself to declare the causes of the summons, and his speech was settled at a conference between the two parties. It is related that "the Chancellor caused certain articles to be read before the Houses containing the causes of the summons, which were divided as follows—to take order for the expenses of the King's household; for the due payment of the garrison at Calais; for keeping the seas against any invasion of the French; to guard against the Scots, who had besieged Berwick; to procure a perfect accord and unity among the Lords," &c.[1]

The Earl of Salisbury, the late Chancellor, was present at this parliament, and produced a charter of pardon, under the Great Seal, to himself and his confederates for having taken arms and fought at St. Alban's, and all other acts which could be construed into treason. This charter was confirmed by both Houses, but was found a very feeble protection when the opposite party regained their superiority.

On the 31st of July the Archbishop of Canterbury, as Chancellor, in the King's presence and in his name, prorogued the parliament to the 12th of November.

In the interval he seems to have been entirely gained over by the Yorkists; for, when the parliament again met, he concurred with them in measures for utterly subverting the royal authority. A deputation from the Commons prayed the Lords that a Protector might be again appointed. The Lords consequently held a consultation,

[1] 1 Parl. Hist. 395.

when it was resolved that the Duke of York was the most worthy for the office, and a request was made to him by the whole House, that he would assume the Protectorship. The Duke excused himself, and desired time to consider of it. The deputation from the Commons expressed some impatience; to which the Lord Chancellor answered, that the King, with the assent of the Lords, had requested the Duke of York to be Protector. At the proper moment the Duke relented, but he accepted the office with the like protestation as on a former occasion—that it had been forced upon him by the King and the two Houses.[1]

This farce must have been somewhat disgusting to the people, who probably would have been better pleased had the right heir boldly seated himself on the throne under the title of Richard III. The Queen watched her opportunity; and, thinking that the Yorkists had incurred unpopularity, availed herself of the Duke's absence from London, produced her husband before the House of Lords, and made him declare his intention of resuming the government, and putting an end to the Protectorship. The manœuvre, being unexpected, was not resisted by the opposite party, and the House of Lords, who had unanimously appointed the Protector, unanimously assented to the immediate termination of his authority. Bourchier the Chancellor rejoined his old friends, and a writ under the Great Seal was addressed to Richard Duke of York, in the King's name, superseding him as Protector, and at the same time the King, by proclamation, committed the whole estate and governance of the realm to the Lords of his council—meaning the Lancastrian leaders with whom the Chancellor co-operated. The King's son was now created Prince of Wales, with a splendid provision for his maintenance during his minority.

The Parliament was prorogued by Archbishop Bourchier, which seems to have been the last act which he did as Chancellor. He rather affected neutrality in the struggle that was going forward, and he was always desirous of preserving peace between the contending parties. Maintaining his allegiance to the King, he refused to enter into the plots that were laid for the destruction of the Yorkists. The Great Seal was therefore now taken from

[1] 1 Parl. Hist. 398. [2] 1 Parl. Hist. 399.

him, and transferred to WILLIAM WAYNFLETE,[1] Bishop of Winchester, a most determined and uncompromising Lancastrian.

The Record states that the Court being at Coventry, in the Priory there, on the 11th of October, the Lord Chancellor Bourchier, in the presence of the Duke of York, who, with the Earls of Salisbury and Warwick had been invited to attend, and of many Lords spiritual and temporal, produced to the King in his chamber the three royal seals which had been intrusted to him, two of gold and one of silver, in three leather bags under his own seal, and caused them to be opened; that the King received them from his hands, and immediately delivered them to the Bishop of Winchester, whom he declared Chancellor; and that Waynflete, after taking the oath of office and setting the silver seal to a pardon to the late Chancellor for all offenses which could be alleged against him, ordered the seals to be replaced, and the bags to be sealed with his own signet by a clerk in Chancery, and was thus fully installed in his new dignity.[2]

Waynflete was the son of Richard Patten,[3] a gentleman of respectable family residing at Waynflete, in Lincolnshire. His biographers are at great pains to refute an imputation upon him that he was a foundling, and relate with much exultation that not only was his father "worshipfully descended," but that his mother, Margery Brenton, was the daughter of a renowned military leader, who for his gallantry in the French wars had been made governor of Caen. Young Patten was educated in the noble seminaries established by William of Wickham,—first at Winchester, and then at Oxford, and acquired very great reputation for his proficiency in classical learning.

He was ordained priest at an early age, and according to a very usual custom, even with those of good birth, he then exchanged his family name for that of the place where he was born. In 1429 he was made head master of Winchester School. Here he acquired high fame as a teacher, and in consequence gained the favor of Cardinal

---

[1] Dugdale calls him Wickham; but this is a mistake, as he certainly always went by the name of Waynflete, although he may be considered as spiritually a son of William of Wickham.—Rot. Cl. 35 Hen. 6, m. 10.

[2] Rot. Cl. 35 Hen. 6, m. 10.

[3] His father was sometimes called Bardon. At this time the surnames of families were very uncertain.

Beaufort, then bishop of the diocese, who introduced him to the King. "Holy Henry" was now employed in founding his illustrious establishment for education at Eton, and prevailed on Waynflete to consent to be named in the charter one of the original Fellows for three years; he was promoted to the office of Provost, and he not only superintended the studies of the place with unwearied industry, but largely contributed to the expense of the buildings from his private means.

On the death of Cardinal Beaufort, by the unanimous election of the Chapter and the royal consent, he was appointed Bishop of Winchester. In compliance with the fashion of the times he protested often, and with tears, against the appointment, till he was found about sunset in the church of St. Mary,—when he consented, saying, he would no longer resist the Divine will. He repeated often that verse of the *Magnificat*, "Qui potens est fecit pro me magna; et sanctum nomen ejus;"[1] which also he added to his arms as his motto.

He showed great energy in assisting in the suppression of Jack Cade's rebellion. He had a personal conference with Cade, and advised the publication of the general pardon, which drew off many of his followers.

The war of the Roses beginning, he took a most decided part in favor of the Lancastrians. The two armies being first arrayed against each other on Blackheath, the King sent Waynflete to the Duke of York to inquire the cause of the commotion; and the Lancastrians being indifferently prepared, a temporary reconciliation was brought about by his efforts.

He was selected to baptize the young Prince, who, to the great joy of the Lancastrian party, was born on St. Edward's day, 1453; and he so won the King's heart by framing statutes for Eton and King's College, Cambridge, that his Majesty added a clause with his own hand, ordaining that both colleges should yearly, within twelve days preceeding the feast of the Nativity, for ever after Waynflete's decease, celebrate solemn obsequies for his soul, "with commendations and a morrow mass;" a distinction not conferred on any other person besides Henry V. and Queen Katherine, the father and mother of the founder; and Queen Margaret, his own wife, for whom

---

[1] St. Luke, i. 49.

yearly obits are decreed, with one quarterly for the founder.

The prudence of the Bishop was now to be "made eminent, in warilie wielding the weight of his office"[1] of Lord Chancellor. For its judicial duties he must have been very unfit; and as he had not the assistance of a Vice-Chancellor, the defective administration of justice must have given great cause of complaint; but in such troublous times, these considerations were little attended to. His first act was to bring to trial, on a charge for publishing Lollardism, Peacock, Bishop of Chichester, inclined to Yorkism, if not to heterodoxy,—who was sentenced to sit in his pontificals, and to see his books delivered to the flames in St. Paul's churchyard, and then to retire to an abbey on a pension.

While the Yorkists renewed their efforts to shake the Lancastrian power, and the two parties continued to display mutual animosity, the peaceful King found consolation in his Chancellor. He sometimes, it is related, would bid the other Lords attend the council, but detain him to be the companion of his private devotion; to offer up with him in his closet prayers for the common weal.[2] However, the Chancellor, in reality, exerted himself to the utmost to depress the Yorkists, although he was sometimes obliged to dissemble, and to make the King assume a tone of moderation, and almost of neutrality.[3]

By the mediation of Archbishop Bourchier, a seeming reconciliation was brought about, and a formal treaty concluded, consisting of eight articles, to which the new Chancellor, with no very sincere intentions, affixed the Great Seal. In order to notify this accord to the whole people, a solemn procession to St. Paul's was appointed, where the Duke of York led Queen Margaret, and the chiefs of the opposite parties marched hand in hand. Chancellor Waynflete, I presume, had for his partner Ex-Chancellor the Earl of Salisbury. The less that real cordiality prevailed, the more were the exterior demonstrations of amity redoubled on both sides.[4]

[1] Hollinsh. vol. ii. p. 628.
[2] "Sæpius ob eximiam sanctimoniam in penetrale regium adhibitus, cæteroque senatu super arduis regni negotiis consilium inituro, *Quin abite* (inquit Princeps) *Ego interim et Cancellarius meus pro salute reipublicæ vota Deo nuncupabimus.*"—Budden, p. 86.
[3] Chandler's Life of Waynflete, c. iv. v.   [4] 1 Parl. Hist. 401.

Had the intention of the leaders been ever so amicable, they would have found it impossible to restrain the animosity of their followers; and a trifling quarrel between one of the royal retinue and a retainer of the Earl of Warwick, the son of the Earl of Salisbury, and soon famous under the title of "the King-maker," renewed the flames of civil war. The battle of Blore Heath was fought, in which the Earl of Salisbury acquired the most brilliant renown for his generalship; but this was soon followed by a heavy disaster to the Yorkists, arising from the sudden desertion of a body of veterans the night before an expected engagement, so that they were obliged to disperse; and the leaders flying beyond sea, for a time abandoned the kingdom to their enemies.

The Queen, under the advice of the Chancellor, took this opportunity of holding a parliament to attaint the Duke of York and his adherents. Both Houses met at Coventry on the 20th of November, 1459. No temporal Peers were summoned, except staunch supporters of the House of Lancaster. On the day of meeting, the King sitting in his chair of state in the Chapter House belonging to the Priory of our Lady of Coventry, the Lords and Commons being present, it is said that "William, Bishop of Winchester, then Chancellor, made a notable declaration why this parliament was called." But we have no account either of his text or his topics; and we are only told that he willed the Commons to choose their Speaker, and present him the next day to the King.[1]

The desired attainders were quickly passed; the members of both houses were sworn to support the measures taken to extinguish the Yorkists; and the Chancellor, in the presence of the King and of the three estates, and by his Majesty's command, after giving thanks to the whole body, dissolved the parliament.[2]

But in a short time the Yorkists again made head; and the youthful Earl of March, afterwards Edward IV., gained the battle of Northampton, in which above 10,000 of the Queen's forces were slain. The King was again taken prisoner, and a Yorkist parliament was held at Westminster.

Preparatory to this, the Great Seal was demanded in the King's name from Bishop Waynflete, and he resigned it

[1] 1 Parl. Hist. 401.   [2] Ibid. 473.

on the 7th of July, 1460, having held it three years and nine months.¹ He took the precaution of carrying away with him a pardon, under the Great Seal which he might plead if afterwards questioned for any part of his conduct. He likewise induced the King to write an autograph letter to the Pope, to defend him from the calumnies now propagated against him.²

William, Bishop of Sidon, a monk of the order of St. Austin, had acted for him as his suffragan while he was Chancellor, but he now returned to the personal discharge of his episcopal duties, and occupied himself for the rest of his days in founding Magdalen College, Oxford, that splendid monument of his munificence.

Although always at heart an affectionate partisan of the House of Lancaster, when Edward IV. had been firmly established on the throne, he submitted to the new dynasty; but he was allowed frequently to visit his ancient master, who, while a prisoner in the tower, being indulged freely in his devotions, hardly regretted the splendor of royalty. During Henry's short restoration, Waynflete assisted in re-crowning him; but after he and his son had been murdered, and Edward was restored, and re-crowned, the Ex-Chancellor again submitted, swore allegiance to the young Prince, who had been born in the sanctuary at Westminster, and accepted the office of Prelate to the Order of the Garter.

He was famed for the hospitable reception he gave to Richard III. in his new College. This sovereign, who seems not to have been by any means unpopular while on the throne, having intimated an intention of visiting the university of Oxford, Waynflete invited him to lodge at Magdalen, and went thither to entertain him. On his approach from Windsor on the 24th of July, 1483, he was honorably received and conducted in procession into the newly erected College by the founder, the presi-

---

¹ Rot. Cl. 38 Hen. 6, m. 5.

² This curious epistle is of considerable length, and I shall content myself with extracting one sentence as a specimen. "An:mo nobis est, vehementer et cordi, clarissimo viro fortasse per emulos tracto in infamiam, nostro testimonio quantum in nobis est omnem adimere culpam, huic presertim quem plurimum carum habemus Reverendo in Christo patri Willelmo Winton Episcopo; cujus cum opera et obsequiis, in regni negotiis gerendis non parum usi sumus, in nichilo tamen eum excessisse testamur quo juste denigrari possit aut debeat tanti fama Prelati, quam hactenus omnium ore constat intemeratam extitisse."—MS. C. C. C. Cambridge, Budden, p. 80.

dent, and scholars, and there passed the night with his retinue, consisting of many prelates, nobles and officers of state.¹

Next day two solemn disputations were held by the King's order in the College hall, the first in moral philosophy, the other in divinity,—the disputants receiving from the King a buck, and a present in money. He bestowed likewise on the president and scholars two bucks, with five marcs for wine. Such good will was created by his condescension and generosity, that the entry in the college register, made under the superintendence of Waynflete, ends with "Vivat rex in eternum."

The Ex-Chancellor lived to see the union of the Red and White Roses, and died on the 11th of August, 1486.²

His character and conduct are not liable to any considerable reproach, and his love of learning must ever make his memory respected in England.³

CHAPTER XXII.

CHANCELLORS DURING THE REIGN OF HENRY VI. FROM THE APPOINTMENT OF GEORGE NEVILLE, BISHOP OF EXETER, TILL THE DEATH OF LORD CHANCELLOR FORTESCUE.

WHEN the Great Seal was taken from Waynflete in 1460, from the 7th to the 27th of July it was in the custody of Archbishop Bourchier, but only till it could be entrusted to one in whom the Yorkists could place entire confidence. This prelate had

---

¹ It puzzles us much to understand how not only the King and his court, but the King and both Houses of Parliament, were anciently accommodated when assembled in a small town ; but it appeared that a great many truckle beds were spread out in any apartment, and with a share of one of these a luxurious baron was contented,—the less refined not aspiring above straw in a barn. Both Charles I. and Cromwell slept in the same bed with their officers. By Waynflete's statutes for Magdalen College, each chamber on the first floor in ordinary times was to contain two truckle beds.

² It is remarked as a curious fact that three prelates in succession held the bishopric of Winchester for 119 years, the time between the consecration of William of Wickham and the death of Waynflete.

³ Budden's Life of Waynflete. Chandler's Life of Waynflete.

lately much favored the Yorkists, but still they recollected his former vacillation.

On the 25th of July a new Chancellor was installed, about whose fidelity and zeal no doubt could be entertained;—GEORGE NEVILLE, Bishop of Exeter, the son of the Earl of Salisbury, and brother of the Earl of Warwick.[1] He had studied at Baliol College, Oxford, and taking orders, had such rapid preferment, that he was consecrated a bishop before he had completed his thirtieth year.

The parliament met on the 7th of October. We are told that, in the presence of the King sitting in his chair of state, in the Painted Chamber at Westminster, and of the Lords and Commons, George Bishop of Exeter, then Chancellor of England, made a notable declaration, taking for his theme, " Congregate populum et sanctificate ecclesiam." But we are not informed how he prepared the two Houses for the solemn claim to the crown now to be made by his leader, to which he was undoubtedly privy.[2]

The Duke of York, on his return from Ireland, having entered the House of Lords, he advanced towards the throne, and being asked by Bishop Bourchier whether he had yet paid his respects to the King, he replied, " he knew none to whom he owed that title." Then, addressing the Peers from the step under the throne, he asserted his right to sit there, giving a long deduction of his pedigree, and exhorting them to return into the right path by doing justice to the lineal successor. It might have been expected that he would have concluded the ceremony by taking his seat on the throne, which stood empty behind him; but he immediately left the House, and the Peers took the matter into consideration with as much tranquillity as if it had been a claim to a dormant barony. They resolved that the Duke's title to the crown should be argued by counsel at the bar, and they ordered that notice should be given to the King that he likewise might be heard. The King recommended that the Judges, the King's Sergeants, and the Attorney General should be called in and consulted. They were summoned, and attended accordingly; but the question being propounded to them, they well considering the danger in meddling with this high affair, utterly refused to be concerned in it.

[1] Rot. Cl. 38 Hen. 6, m. 7.   [2] 1 Parl. Hist. 404.

Nevertheless counsel were heard at the bar for the Duke; the matter was debated several successive days, and an order was made that every Peer might freely and indifferently speak his mind without dread of impeachment. Objections to the claim were started by several Lords, founded on former entails of the crown by parliament, and on the oaths of fealty sworn to the House of Lancaster; while answers were given derived from the indefeasibility of hereditary right, and the violence by which the House of Lancaster had obtained and kept possession of the crown.[1]

The Chancellor, by order of the House, pronounced judgment, "that Richard Plantagenet had made out his claim, and that his title was certain and indefeasible; but that in consideration that Henry had enjoyed the crown without dispute or controversy during the course of thirty-eight years, he should continue to possess the title and dignity during the remainder of his life; that the administration of the government, meanwhile, should remain with Richard, and that he should be acknowledged the true and lawful heir of the monarchy." This sentence was, by order of the House, communicated to the King by the Chancellor, who explained to him the Duke's pedigree and title; and thereupon the King acquiesced in the sentence. All this was confirmed by the full consent of parliament, and an act was published declaring the Duke of York to be right heir on a demise of the crown.[2]

---

[1] 1 Parl. Hist. 405.

[2] The entry of this proceeding on the Parliament Roll is very curious.

"Memorand' that on the xvi day of Octobr', the ixth daye of this present parlement, the counseill of the right high and mighty Prynce Richard Duc of York brought into the Parlement chambre a wryting conteignyng the clayme and title of the right that the said Duc pretended unto the corones of Englond and of Fraunce, and lordship of Irelond, and the same wryting delyvered to the right Reverent Fader in God, George Bishop of Excestre, Chanceller of Englond, desiryng hym that the same wryting might be opened to the Lordes spiritualx and temporalx assembled in this present parlement, and that the seid Duc myght have brief and expedient answere thereof: Whereupon the seid Chaunceller opened and shewed the seid desire to the Lords spiritualx and temporalx, askyng the question of theym, whither they wold the seid writyng shuld be openly radde before theym or noo. To the which question it was answered and agreed by all the seid Lords: Inasmuch as every persone high and lowe suying to this high court of Parlement, of right must be herd, and his desire and petition understaude. that the seid writyng shuld be radde and herd, not to be answered without the Kyng's commaundment, for so moche as the matter is so high and of soo grete wyght

But Margaret refused to be a party to this treaty, and was again at the head of a formidable army. The battle of Wakefield was fought, in which Richard Plantagenet fell, without ever having been seated on that throne to which he was entitled by his birth, and which had repeatedly seemed within his reach. Here bravely fighting by the side of his leader was taken prisoner, overpowered by numbers, the Ex-Chancellor, the Earl of Salisbury. He was immediately tried by martial law and beheaded. His head remained stuck over one of the gates of York till it was replaced by that of a Lancastrian leader after the battle of Mortimer's Cross.

For the dignity of the Great Seal I ought to give some account of the illustrious progeny of Lord Chancellor Salisbury. His sons were Richard Earl of Warwick, "the King-maker," John Marquis of Montagu, Sir Thomas, a great military leader, and George, the Bishop, made Chancellor in his father's lifetime. His daughters were, Joan, married to the Earl of Arundel; Cicily, to Henry Beauchamp, Earl of Warwick; Alice, to Henry Lord Fitzhugh of Ravenfroth; Eleanor, to Thomas Stanley, the first Earl of Derby of that name; and Katherine, to John de Vere Earl of Oxford, and afterwards to Lord Hastings, chamberlain to King Edward IV.

There is no entry in the Records respecting the Great Seal from the 25th of July, 1460, when George Neville was created Chancellor nominally to Henry VI., but really under the house of York, till the 10th of March, 1461, when he took the oaths to the new King, and, according to Dugdale, he continued Chancellor all the while; but it is impossible that he should have been allowed to exercise the duties of the office during the whole of this stormy interval; during a portion of it Margaret and the Lancastrians were in possession of the metropolis, and had a complete ascendency over the whole kingdom, although it does not appear by the Rolls or by any contemporary writer that any other Chancellor was appoinred.

If the celebrated Sir John Fortescue, author of the admirable treatise—" De Laudibus Legum Angliæ," ever

and poyse. Which writyng there than was radde the tenour whereof foloweth in these wordes," &c.

Then follow all the proceedings down to the King's confirmation of the *Concord.*

was *de facto* Chancellor of England, and in the exercise of the duties of the office, it must have been now, after the second battle of St. Alban's, and at the very conclusion of the reign of Henry VI.

Fortescue is generally by his biographers mentioned as having been Chancellor to this Sovereign. In the introduction to his great work, after describing the imprisonment of Henry VI., and the exile of Prince Edward his son, he says, " Miles quidam grandævus, PRÆDICTI REGIS ANGLIÆ CANCELLARIUS, qui etiam sub hac clade exulabat, principem sic affatur ;" and throughout the dialogue he always denominates himself " Cancellarius."

I suspect that he only had the titular office of Chancellor *in partibus*—when he accompanied the young Prince his pupil as an exile to foreign climes, and that he never exercised the duties of the office in England ;[1] but under these circumstances I am called upon to offer a sketch of his history,—and it is delightful, amidst intriguing Churchmen and warlike Barons who held the Great Seal in this age, to present to the reader a lawyer, not only of deep professional learning, but cultivated by the study of classical antiquity, and not only of brilliant talents, but the ardent and enlightened lover of liberty,—to whose explanation and praises of our free constitution we are in no small degree indebted for the resistance to oppressive rule which has distinguished the people of England.

Sir JOHN FORTESCUE was of an ancient and distinguished family, being descended in the direct male line from Richard Fortescue, who came over with the Conqueror. The family was seated first at Winston, and then at Wear Giffard in Devonshire, which still belongs to them.[2]
'He was educated at Exeter College, Oxford, and called to

---

[1] Spelman in his list of Chief Justices, under head *Jo. Fortescu*, writes, " Notior in ore omnium nomine Cancellarii quam Justiciarii, diu tamen functus est hoc munere ; illo vix aliquando. Constitui enim videtur Cancellarius, non nisi a victo et exulante apud Scotos Rege, Hen. 6. nec referri igitur in archiva regia ejus institutio, sed cognosci maxime e libelli sui ipsius inscriptione."— Glossarium Justiciarius. And under Spelman's Series Cancellariorum, he says, " Jo. Fortescue Justiciarius Banci Regii exulante Hen. 6 in Scotiâ videtur ejus consitui Cancellarius eoque usus titulo ; sed nulla de eo mentio in Rott. patentibus. Quidam vero contendunt eum non fuisse Cancellarium Regis sed filii ejus primogeniti ; contrarium vero manifestè patet lib. suo de L. L. Ang in introductione, ubi sic de se ait, Quidem Miles grandævus," &c.

[2] I have been favored with a sight of the pedigree by Earl Fortescue, and it is perfect in all its links.

the bar at Lincoln's Inn. Unfortunately there is no further memorial of his early career, and we are not informed of the course of study by which he acquired so much professional and general knowledge, and reached such eminence.

In 1441 he was called to the degree of the coif, and was made a King's Sergeant, and the year following he was raised to the office of Chief Justice of the King's Bench, the duties of which he discharged with extraordinary ability. In the struggle for the Crown he steadily adhered to the House of Lancaster while any hope seemed to remain for that cause,—being of opinion that Richard II. was properly dethroned for his misgovernment; that parliament then having the power to confer the crown upon another branch of the royal family, hereditary right was superseded by the will of the nation,—and that the parliamentary title to the House of Lancaster was to be preferred to the legitimist claim of the House of York.

Although advanced in years, and long clothed with the ermine, he seems, according to the fashion of the age, to have accompanied his party in their headlong campaigns, and to have mixed in the moody fight. By the side of Morton, afterwards Archbishop of Canterbury and Lord Chancellor, he displayed undaunted valor at Towton, where a great part of his associates were put to the sword, and the crown was fixed on the brow of Edward IV. Still he refused to send in his adhesion to the new Sovereign, and having vainly tried to strike another blow in the county of Durham, he was attainted for treason by act of parliament with other Lancastrian leaders.

After the fatal adventures which reduced the Queen and her son to the society of robbers in a forest, he accompanied the exiled family into Scotland, where it is said by some that the title of Chancellor was conferred upon him. While there he wrote a treatise to support, on principles of constitutional law, the claim of the House of Lancaster to the crown. Edward being firmly seated on the throne, and King Henry a prisoner in the Tower, he embarked with Margaret and her son for Holland, and continued several years in exile with them, intrusted with the education of the young Prince. He conceived that he was pursuing a judicious course for securing the future happiness of the English nation in forming the character of the heir apparent to the throne, and acquainting him with the duties of a patriot king—a task which in later times even Hampden did not look upon as derogatory to his talents or incompatible with his independence.[1]

With this view Fortescue now employed himself in the composition of his book "De Laudibus," for the instruction of his royal pupil, in which he fully explains the principles of the English constitution and English jurisprudence, and points out the amendments to be introducen into them by the Prince on recovering the throne.[2]

He afterwards accompanied the Queen back to England, but the cause of the House of Lancaster appearing at last utterly desperate, and parliament and the nation having recognized the title of the new dynasty, he expressed his willingness to submit himself to the reigning monarch.

Edward, with some malice, required that as a condition of his pardon he must write another treatise upon the disputed question of the succession, in support of the claim of the House of York against the House of Lancaster. The old lawyer complied, showing that he could support either side with equal ability; and afterwards, in a new petition, assured the King "that he had so clearly disproved all the arguments that had been made against his right and title, that now there remained no color or show of reason to the hurt thereof, and that the same stood the more clear and open on occasion of the writings hitherto made against them."[3]

The pardon was then agreed to, and expedited in due form. As he had been attainted by act of parliament, it was necessary that the attainder should be reversed by the same authority. He accordingly presented a petition for his restoration in blood, to which the Commons, the Lords, and the King assented, and which, according to the forms then prevailing, thus became a statute.[4]

[1] Preface to Amos's translation of the "De Laudibus."
[2] So minute is he in his law reforms, that he even recommends new ornaments for the robes of the judges.—Ch. 51.
[3] Rot. Parl. vi. 26, 69. He tried to ride off on a point of fact. In his first work he maintained that Philippa, daughter of Lionel Duke of Clarence, through whom the House of York claimed, had never been acknowledged by her father; in the second, that her legitimacy had been cleared up beyond all controversy.—See Ling. v. 217, n.
[4] By the favor of Earl Fortescue, his lineal representative, an exemplification of it under the Great Seal of Edward IV. now lies before me, and I copy it for the curious in historical antiquities.
"Edwardus dei gra. Rex Anglie, Francie, et Dominus Hibnie Omibz ad

He retired to Ebrington, in Gloucestershire, an estate which he had purchased before his exile, and which now gives the title of viscount to his descendants.

quos psentes lre prvint, saltm. Inspeximz quandam petioem in parliamento nro apud Westm. sexto die Octobr. Anno regni nri duodecimo sumonito et tento et p. diusas progacoes vsqz ad et in sextum diem Octobr. Anno regni nri tciodeoimo continuato et tunc tento nob. in eodem parliamento dco sexto die Octobr. dco Anno regni nri triodecimo p Johem Fortescu Militem exhibitam in hec vba : To the kyng oure soureyne lord, In the moost humble wise sheweth vnto yor most noble grace, your humble subget and true liegeman, John Fortescue, knyght, which is and eid. shalbe during his lyf yor true and feithfull subget and liegeman, soureigne lord by the gce of God. Howe be it the same John is not of power, ne hauoir to doo your highnes so goode suice as he hert and wille wold doo, for so moche as in your parlement holden at Westm. the iiijth day of Novembr, the first yere of your moost noble reigne, it was ordeyned, demed, and delared by auctorite of the same parlement, that the seid John, by the name of John Fortescu, knyght, among other psones shuld stond and be conuicted and attaynted of high treason, and forfeit to you, soureyn lord and your heires, all the castelles, manes, lordshippes, londes, tentes, rentes, suices, fees, advousons, hereditamentes and possessions, with their appurtenances, which he had of estate of inheritance, or any other to his vse had the xxx day of Decembr. next afore the first yere of your moost noble reigne, or into which he or any other psone or psones, feoffes to the vse or behofe of the same John, had the same xxx day lawfull cause of entre within Englond, Irelond, Wales, or Cales, or the marches thereof, as more at large is conteyned within the same acte or actes, pleas it your highnes, forasmoch as your seid suppliaunt is as repentaunt and sorowfull as any creature may be, of all that which he hath doon and committed to the displeasure of your highnes, contrie to his duetie and leigeaunce, and is and pseuantly shalbe to you, soueigne lord, true, feithfull, and humble subget ana liegeman, in wille, worde, and dede, of your moost habuudant grce, by thaduis and assent of the lordes spiell and temporell, and the coens in this pour psent parlement assembled, and by auctorite of the same to enact, ordeyne, and stablish the seid acte and all actes of atteyndre or forfeiture made ayenst the same John and his feoffes, to the vse of the same John, in your seid parlement holden at Westm. the said iiijth day of Novembr as ayenst them and euery of them, by what name or names the same John be named or called in the same acte or actes, of, in, or by reason of the pmisses, be vtterly voide and of noon effecte ne force: And that the same John nor his heires in no wise be purdiced or hurte by the same acte or actes made ayenst the same John: and that by the same auctorite your seid suppliaunt and his heires have possede, joy, and inherite all man^r of possessions and hereditamentes in like man^r and fourme, and in as ample and large wise as the seid John shuld haue done if the the same acte or actes neu^r had be made ayenst the same John : And that the seid John and his heires haue, hold, joy, and inherit all castelles, manes, lorshippes, londes, tentes, rentes, suices, fees, advousons, and all other hereditaments and possessions, with their appurtenances, which come or ought to haue come to yor handes by reason of the same acte or actes madeayenst the same John and feoffes to his vse : And vnto theym and euy of theym to entre, and theym to haue, joy, and possede in like man^r fourme, and condicion, as the same John shuld have had or doon if the same acte or actes neu^r had been made ayenst the seid John and his seid feoffes, to his vse, withoute suying theym or any of theym oute of your handes by peticion, lyne, or otherwise, by the course of your lawes. And that all lres, pattentes made by your highnes to the seid John, or to any psone or psones, of any of the

Here he quietly spent the remainder of his days, and here he died, leaving a great and venerable name to his posterity and his country.

He was buried in the parish church at Ebrington, where a monument, with the following inscription, was erected to his memory:—

> "In felicem et immortalem memoriam
> Clarissimi viri Dni Johannis Fortiscuti militis grandævi,
> Angliæ Judicis primarii et processu temporis sub Henrico VI.
> Rege et Edwardo principi summi Cancellarii Consiliarii Regis
> Prudentissimi, Legum Angliæ peritissimi, necnon earundem
> Hyperaspistis fortissimi, qui corporis exuvias lætam
> Resurrectionem expectantes hic deposuit."

In 1677 this monument was repaired by Robert Fortes-

---

pmisses be void and of noon effecte, sauing to euy persone such title, right, and lawfull entre as they or any of theym had at the tyme of the seid acte or actes made ayenst the same John, or any tyme sith other then by means and vtue of oure lres patentes made sith the iiijth day of March, the first yere of your reigne, or any tyme sith : And that no psone or psones be empeched nor hurt of or for takyng of any issues or pfittes, nor of any offenses doon in or of any of the pmisses afore the iiijth of the moneth of April, the xiij yere of your reigne, or at any tyme sith the seid iiijth day of Marche by the seid John or any feoffes to his vse by wey of accion or otherwise. Provided alway, that no psone or psones, atteynted, nor their heires, take, haue, or enjoy any advantage by this psent acte, but oonly the seid John and his hieres in the pmises. And also the feoffes to the use of the seid John, oonly for and in the pmisses which the same feoffes had to the vse of the seid John, the seid xxx day or any tyme sith. And your seid suppliaunt shall pray to God for the pseruacion of your moost roiall astate, consideryng soueigne lord that your seid suppiaunt louyth so and tendrith the goode of your moost noble estate, that he late by large and clere writyng dlyued vnto your highness hath so declared all the matrs which were written in Scotland and elles where ayen your right or title, which writynges haue in any wise comen vnto his knowl- edge, or that he at any tyme hath be pryue vnto theym : *And also hath so clerely disproued all the argumentes that haue be made ayen the same right and title, that nowe there remayneth no colour no matr of argument to the hurt or infayme of the same right and title by reason of any such writyng, but the same right and title stonden nowe the more clere and open by that any such writynges haue be made ayen hem.* Inspeximus eciam quendam assensum eidem peticoi p coitates regni nri Angl. in dco parliamento existen scm. et in dca peticoe specificat. in hec verba A CEST BILLE LES COENZ SONT ESSENTUZ. Inspeximus insup. quandam responsionem eidem peticoi p nos de acusamento et assessu dnoq. spualiu. et temporaliu. in dco parliamento simitil. existen. ac Coitates pdce necnon auctoritate eiusdem parliamenti ftam et inderso eiusdem peticois insertam in hec verba SOIT FAIT COME IL EST DESIRE. Nos autem tenores peticois assensus et responsionis predic. ad requisicoem pfate Johis duximus exemplificand. p psentes. In cuius rei testimoniu. has lras nras fieri fecimus patentes. Teste me ipo apud Westm. quartodecimo die Februaij Anno regni nri quarto decimo.   GUNTHORP.

Exᵃ p. { JOHN GUNTHORP, THOMAM JVO. } Cticos

cue, Esq., the then representative of the family, who added to it these quaint verses :—

> "Angligenas intra cancellos Juris et Equi
> Qui tenuit, cineres jam tenet urna viri.
> Lux viva ille fuit patriæ, lux splendida legis
> Forte bonis Scutum, sontibus et scutica.
> Clarus erat titulis, clarus majoribus, arte
> Clarus, virtute ast clarior emicuit.
> Jam micat in tenebris, veluti carbunculus orbis,
> Nam virtus radios non dare tanta nequit.
> Vivit adhuc Fortescutus laudatus in ævum
> Vivet et in legum laudibus ille suis."[1]

As a common-law judge he is highly extolled by Lord Coke, and he seems to have been one of the most learned and upright men who ever sat in the Court of King's Bench.

He laid the foundation of parliamentary privilege, to which our liberties are mainly to be ascribed. He had the sagacity to see, that if questions concerning the privileges

---

[1] I insert the following re-lease of the manor of Ebrington as a curious specimen of conveyancing, and of the English language in the reign of Henry VI.

"To alle men to whom this wrytvng shal come, Robt. Corbet, knyght, sende gretyng in oure Lord. For asmuch as I have solde to Sir John Fortescu, knyght, in fee symple, the reuersion of the Manour of Ebryghton, in the Counte of Gloucestre, with the apptenaunces, to be had after the decesse of Joyes, late the Wif of John Grevyle, Esquier, for Cli pounds, to be payed to me in certayn fourme betwene vs accorded, by reason of which sale I have by my dede enrolled and subscribed with myne owne hande, graunted the same reuersion to the said Sir John, and other named with hym, to his vse in fee by vertu of which the said Joyes hath attourned to the said Sir John ; and also I have delyuered to the same Sir John alle the evydences whiche euer come to myne handes concernyng the said Manour ; I wol and desire as welle the foresaid Joyes the abbot of Wynchecombe, and alle other personnes in whos handes the said Sir John or his heyres can wete or aspye any of the forsaid evydences to be kepte, to delyuer the same evydences to ham, for the right and title of the reuersion of the said Manour is now clerely, trewly, and lawefully in the said Sir John, his cofeoffees and theyre heyres, and from me and myne heyres for euer moore, and the said Mancur, nor the reuersion thereof, was neuer tayled to me, nor none of myne Auncestres, but alway in vs hathe he possessed in fee symple, as far as euer I coude knowe, by any evydene or by any manner, sayyng by my trouthe. Wherfore I charge Robt. my sone and myne heyre, his issue, and alle thos that shal be myne heyres herafter, vppon my blessyng, that they neuer vexe, implede, ne greve the forsaid Sir John, his said cofeoffees, theyre heyres, nor assignees, for the forsaid Manour ; and if they do, knowyng this my prohibicion, I wote wel they shal haue the curse of God, for theyre wronge and owr trouthe, and als) they shal haue my curse. Witnysyng this my wrytyng vnder my seale, and subscribed with myne owne hande, Wreten the v day of decembr, the yere of the reigne of Kyng Herry vi[to] after the conquest xxxv[ti]."

(L.S.)   Sir ROBERD CORBET, Knyth.

of parliament were to be determined by the common-law judges appointed and removable by the Crown, these privileges must soon be extinguished, and pure despotism must be established. He perceived that the House of Parliament alone were competent to decide upon their own privileges, and that this power must be conceded to them, even in analogy to the practice of the Court of Chancery and other inferior tribunals. Accordingly in Thorpe's case, he expressed an opinion, which from the end of the reign of King Henry VI. till the commencement of the reign of Queen Victoria, was received with profound deference and veneration.

Thorpe, a Baron of the Exchequer, and Speaker of the House of Commons, being a Lancastrian, had seized some harness and military accoutrements which belonged to the Duke of York, who brought an action of trespass against him in the Court of Exchequer to recover their value. The plaintiff had a verdict, with large damages, for which the defendant, during a recess of parliament, was arrested and imprisoned in the Fleet. When parliament reassembled, the Commons were without a Speaker; and the question arose whether Thorpe, as a member of the Lower House and Speaker, was not now entitled to be discharged.

The Commons had a conference on the subject with the Lords, who called in the Judges, and asked their opinion. "The said Lords, spiritual and temporal, not intending to impeach or hurt the liberties and privileges of them that were coming for the commerce of this land to this present parliament, but legally after the course of law to administer justice, and to have knowledge what the law will weigh in that behalf, opened and declared to the Justices the premises, and asked of them whether the said Thomas Thorpe ought to be delivered from prison by, for, and in virtue of the privileges of parliament or no?" "To the whole question," says the report "the Chief Justice Fortescue, in the name of all the Justices, after sad communication and mature deliberation had amongst them, answered and said: that they ought not to answer to that question; for it hath not been used aforetime that the Justices should in anywise determine the privilege of this high court of parliament; for it is so high and so mighty in its nature, that it may make law; and that that is law, it may make no law; and the determination and knowledge of that privilege belongeth to the Lords of the parliament and not to the Justices."[1]

In consequence of this decision the two Houses of parliament were for many ages allowed to be the exclusive judges of their own privileges; liberty of speech and freedom of inquiry were vindicated by them; the prerogatives of the Crown were retained and defined; and England was saved from sharing the fate of the monarchies on the Continent of Europe, in which popular assemblies were crushed by the unresisted encroachments of the executive government.

What acquaintance Fortescue had with equity we have no means of knowing; but it is clear that he was not a mere technical lawyer, and that he was familiar with the general principles of jurisprudence.

As a writer, his style is not inelegant, though not free from the barbarisms of the schools; and he displays sentiments upon liberty and good government which are very remarkable, considering the fierce and lawless period when he flourished. His principal treatise has been celebrated, not only by lawyers, but by such writers as Sir Walter Raleigh, and not only by Englishmen, but by foreign nations. "We cannot," says Chancellor Kent, in commenting upon it, "but pause and admire a system of jurisprudence which in so uncultivated a period of society contained such singular and invaluable provisions in favor of life, liberty, and property, as those to which Fortescue referred. They were unprecedented in all Greek and Roman antiquity, and being preserved in some tolerable degree of freshness and vigor amidst the profound ignorance and licentious spirit of the feudal ages, they justly entitle the common law to a share of that constant and usual eulogy which the English lawyers have always liberally bestowed upon their municipal institutions."[2]

Notwithstanding his tardy submission to the House of York, he is to be praised for his consistency as a politician. Unlike the Earl of Warwick and others, who were constantly changing sides according to interest or caprice, he steadily adhered to the House of Lancaster till it had no true representative, and the national will had been strongly

---

[1] Thorpe's Case, 31 Hen. 6, A.D. 1452. 13 Rep. 63. 1 Hatsell, 29. Lord Campbell's Speeches, 225. [2] Kent's Commentaries.

expressed in favor of the legitimate heir. We must, indeed, regret the tyranny of Edward, who would not generously pardon him on account of his fidelity to his former master; but his compliance with the arbitrary condition imposed upon should be treated with lenity by those who have never been exposed to such perils.

Lord Coke rejoiced that his descendants were flourishing in the reign of Queen Elizabeth; and I, rejoicing that they still flourish in the reign of Queen Victoria, may be permitted to express a confident hope that they will ever continue, as now, to support those liberal principles which, in the time of the Plantagenets, were so powerfully inculcated by their illustrious ancestor.

We must here take a short review of the law under Henry VI.; for although, after languishing ten years as a prisoner in the Tower, he was again, for a short time, placed as a puppet on the throne, we may consider that his reign really closed when, upon the military disasters of his party, his Queen and son went into exile, all his supporters were either slain or submitted, and a rival sovereign was proclaimed and recognized.

After the marriage of the King's mother, Catherine of France, with a Welsh gentleman, Owen ap Tudor, whereby the royal family was supposed to be much disparaged, a statute was passed[1] enacting, that to marry a Queen Dowager without the license of the King, should be an offense punishable by forfeiture of lands and goods. Some doubted whether this statute had the full force of law, because the prelates, asserting a doctrine still cherished by some of their successors, that "it belongs to the Church alone to regulate all matters respecting marriage," assented to it "only as far forth as the same swerved not from the law of God and of the Church, and so as the same imported no deadly sin;" but Lord Coke clearly holds it to be an act of parliament,[2] and it continues law to the present day.[3]

The only other statute of permanent importance, passed under Henry VI., was that for regulating the qualification of the electors of knights of the shire.[4]

[1] A.D. 1418, 6 Hen. 6.   [2] 4 Inst. 34.
[3] A vain attempt was made (as was supposed by the clergy) to do away with it by cutting off and stealing the membrane of the parliamentry roll on which it was inscribed. See 5 Ling. 105.   [4] 8 Hen. 6, c. 7.

The Chancellors of this reign, particularly Cardinal Beaufort, the Earl of Salisbury, Archbishop Bourchier and Bishop Waynflete, were men of great note, and had much influence upon the historical events of their age. Under them, assisted by John Frank, Master of the Rolls, the Court of Chancery grew into new consideration. The doctrine of uses was now established, and it was determined that they might be enforced without going to parliament. So low down as the 7th of Henry VI., this kind of property was so little regarded, that we find it stated by one of the judges as "a thing not allowed by law, and entirely void, if a man make a feoffment with a proviso that he himself should take the profits;"[1] but in the 37th year of the same reign, in the time of Lord Chancellor Waynflete, a feoffer "to such uses as he should direct," having sold the land and directed the feoffees to convey to the purchaser, it was agreed to by all the judges in the Exchequer, when consulted upon the subject, that the intention of the feoffor being declared in writing, the feoffees were bound to fulfill it; and they intimated an opinion, that where a testator devised that his feoffees should make an estate for life to one, remainder to another, the remainder-man should have a remedy in Chancery, to compel a conveyance to himself, even during the continuance of the life interest.[2] Very soon after, the distinction between the legal and equitable estate was fully settled on the principles and in the language which ever since have been appiied to it.[3]

On other points, Equity remained rather in a rude plight. For example,—in a subsequent case which came before Lord Chancellor Waynflete, the plaintiff having given a bond in payment of certain debts which he had purchased, filed his bill to be relieved from it, on the ground that there was no consideration for the bond, as he could not maintain an action to recover the debts in his own name. This case being adjourned into the Exchequer Chamber, the Judges, instead of suggesting that an action might be brought for the benefit of the purchaser, in the name of the original creditor, held, that the bond was without consideration, and advised a decree that it should be cancelled, which the Chancellor pronounced. An action was, nevertheless, brought upon the bond in

[1] Y. B. 7 Hen. 6, 436. [2] Bro. Ab. Garde, 5. [3] See Y. B. 4 Ed. 4, 3.

the Common Pleas, which prevailed,—that Court holding that the only power the Chancellor had of enforcing his decrees, was by inflicting imprisonment on the contumacious party, who might still prosecute his legal right in a court of law, notwithstanding the determination in Chancery, that the bond was unconscionable.[1] To remedy this defect, injunctions were speedily introduced, raising a warfare between the two sides of Westminster Hall, which was not allayed till after the famous battle between Lord Coke and Lord Ellesmere, in the reign of James I. Bills were now filed for perpetuation of testimony, the examination being taken by commissioners, and certified into Chancery. Possession was quieted by the authority of the Court, and its jurisdiction was greatly extended for the purpose of affording relief against fraud, deceit, and force.

CHAPTER XXIII.

CHANCELLORS IN THE REIGN OF EDWARD IV.

EDWARD IV. having been proclaimed King on the 6th of March, 1461, on the 10th of the same month George Neville, Bishop of Exeter, was declared Chancellor.[2] He had been an active leader in the tumultuary proceedings which took place in the metropolis during the late crisis. Without calling a parliament,—first by a great public meeting in St. John's Fields, and then by an assemblage of Bishops, peers, and other persons of distinction at Baynard's Castle, he had contrived to give a semblance of national consent to the change of dynasty.

The new King, after the decisive battle of Towton, in which 36,000 Englishmen were computed to have fallen, having leisure to hold a parliament, it met at Westminster in November, and was opened in a notable oration by Lord

[1] Y. B. 36 Hen. 6, 13.
[2] Fœd. xi. 473. A difficulty arose about having a Great Seal to deliver to him. At the commencement of a new reign, the Great Seal of the preceding Sovereign is used for a time, but that of Henry VI. was not forthcoming, and he had been declared an usurper. A new Great Seal, with the effigies of Edward IV., was speedily manufactured, though in a rude fashion.—1 Hale's Pleas of the Crown, 177.

Chancellor Neville, who took for his theme "Bonas facite vias;" but we are not informed whether he exhorted them to make provision for the highways, greatly neglected during the civil war, or to find out ways and means to restore the dilapidated finances of the country, or what other topics he dwelt upon. A Speaker having been chosen by the Commons, who addressed the King, commending him for his extraordinary courage and conduct against his enemies,—the Chancellor read a long declaration of the King's title to the crown,—to which was added a recapitulation of the tyrannous reign of Henry IV., and his heinous murdering of Richard II.[1]

The required acts of attainder and restitution were passed against Lancastrians and in favor of Yorkists, and the King, according to modern fashion, closed the session with a gracious speech, delivered by himself from the throne.[2] After his Majesty had ended his speech, the record tells us that "the Lord Chancellor stood up and declared, that since the whole business of the parliament was not yet concluded, and the approaching festival of Christmas would obstruct it, he therefore, by the King's command, prorogued the parliament to the 6th of May next ensuing." At the same time he told them of certain proclamations which the King had issued against badges, liveries, robberies, and murders, and which "the Bishops, Lords, and Commons promised to obey."[3]

Neville was made Archbishop of York, and continued to hold the office of Chancellor till the 8th of June, 1467; but I do not find any transaction of much consequence in which he was afterwards engaged. The parliaments called were chiefly employed in reforming the extravagant fashion prevailing among the people of adorning their feet by wearing pikes to their shoes, so long as to incumber them in their walking, unless tied up to the knee with chains of gold, silver or silk. There was a loud outcry against these enormities, and this appears to have operated as a diversion in favor of the Court of Chancery, which now enjoyed a long respite from parliamentary attack.

[1] 1 Parl. Hist. 419.
[2] A little specimen of the language and style may be interesting. "James Stranways and ye that be comyn for the common of this my lond, for the true hertes and tender consideracions that ye have had unto the coronne of this reame, the which from us have been long time withholde."—1 Parl. Hist. 419.
[3] 1 Parl. Hist. 422.

Several statutes were passed, regulating the length of pikes of shoes, under very severe penalties; but the fame of reformers is generally short-lived, and I cannot affirm that the Lord Chancellor gained any distinction by bringing forward or supporting these measures.

In 1463 the pleasing and novel task was assigned to Lord Chancellor Neville, of announcing to the Commons that, from the flourishing state of the royal revenue, the King released to them parcel of the grant of a former session.

For several months in the autumn of this year he was abroad, on an embassy to remonstrate against the countenance given to Lancastrians at foreign courts; and during his absence the Great Seal was in the custody of Kirkham, the Master of the Rolls.[1]

On the 10th of April, 1464, the Chancellor being about to leave London for Newcastle on public business, the Great Seal was again intrusted to the Master of the Rolls. who was directed by writ of privy seal to keep it until the 14th of May, and on that day to deliver it to Richard Fryston and William Moreland, to be conveyed to the Chancellor. They accordingly delivered it back to the Chancellor at York, on his return to London.

Things went on very smoothly for several years, till the quarrel of Edward IV. with the house of Neville, arising out of his marriage with the fair widow, the Lady Elizabeth Gray, while the Earl of Warwick, by his authority, was employed in negotiating an alliance between him and the Lady Bona of Savoy. The rupture was soon widened by the new Queen, who, regarding the Nevilles as her mortal enemies, was eager to depress them, and to aggrandise her own kindred.

In consequence, George Neville was dismissed from the office of Lord Chancellor. On the 8th of June, 1467, the King abruptly demanded the Great Seal from him, and gave it to John de Audley to carry to the palace. The next day it was delivered to the Master of the Rolls, without any Chancellor over him, but with a declaration, "that he was not to use it except in the presence of the Earl of Essex, Lord Hastings, Sir John Fagge, and Sir John Scotte, or one of them; and after each day's sealing, it was to be put into a bag, which was to be sealed

[1] Rot. Cl. 4 Ed. 4.

with those who were present at the sealing and the Master of the Rolls was every day, before night, to deliver the seal so enclosed to one of the perons above mentioned, and to receive it again the next morning, to be used in the manner here recited."[1]

The ruling party had not determined who should be the new Chancellor when Neville was dismissed, and an interval of ten days elapsed before the choice was made—employed, no doubt, in intrigues among the Queen's friends, from whom he was to be selected. At last, on 20th of June, it was announced that ROBERT STILLINGTON, Bishop of Bath and Wells, was appointed Chancellor, and the Great Seal was delivered to him.[2]

But before entering on his history, we must take a final leave of Ex-Chancellor Neville. He now harbored the deepest resentment against Edward, and entered into all the cabals of his brother the "King-maker," who was secretly leagued with Queen Margaret and the Lancastrians, and wished to unmake the king he had made.

Both brothers, however, attempted to conceal their wishes and designs, and at times pretended great devotion to the reigning Sovereign. In 1469, Edward, in a progress passing through York, was invited by the Archbishop, his Ex-Chancellor, to a great feast at the archiepiscopal palace. He accepted the invitation; but as he sat at the table, he perceived symptoms which suddenly induced him to suspect that the Archbishop's retainers intended to seize his person, or to murder him. He abruptly left the entertainment, called for his guards, and retreated.

When in the following year the civil war was openly renewed, and the Earl of Warwick, by one of the most sudden revolutions in history, was complete master of the kingdom, it is said that Edward was for a time in the custody of the Archbishop, who, however used him with great respect, not restraining him from the diversions of hunting and walking abroad, by which means Edward made his escape, and soon after recovered his crown. Upon the counter-revolution, the Archbishop was sur-

[1] Rot. Cl. 7 Ed. 4, m. 12. It had not been unusual to impose such restrictions on persons holding the seal without being Chancellor, but the Chancellor always had the unlimited use of it, upon his responsibility to the King and to Parliament.   [2] Rot. Cl. 7 Ed. 4, m. 12.

prised in his palace at Whitehall, and sent to the Tower; but on account of his sacred character was soon after set at liberty, although he had been repeatedly guilty of high treason, by imagining the King's death, and levying war against him in his realm. Being detected in new plots, about a year after his enlargement, the King again caused him to be arrested on a charge of high treason, seized his plate, money, and furniture, to the value of £20,000, and sent him over to Calais, then often used as a state prison. There he was kept in strict confinement till the year 1476, when on the score of his declining health he was liberated, and he died soon after. During the seven years he held the Great Seal, I do not find any charge against him of partiality or corruption; and his sudden changes in politics, and the violence with which he acted against his opponents must be considered rather as characteristic of the age in which he lived, than bringing any great reproach upon his personal character.

Robert Stillington, his successor, had the rare merit of being always true to the party which he originally espoused. He appears to have been of humble origin, but he gained a great name at Oxford, where with much applause he took the degree of Doctor of Laws. He was a zealous legitimist, and on the accession of Edward IV. he was a special favorite with that Prince, who successively made him Archdeacon of Taunton, Bishop of Bath and Wells, Keeper of the Privy Seal, and finally Lord Chancellor. He held this office for six years, with the exception of the few months when Edward was obliged to fly the kingdom, and the sceptre was again put into the feeble hand of Henry VI.

He had been appointed during a session of parliament. This was brought to a close on the 5th of July, when it is stated, that having in the presence of the King, Lords, and Commons, first answered certain petitions from the lower House, he thanked them in the King's name for the Statute of Resumption which they had passed,—told them that the King had provided for Calais, and had taken care for Ireland and Wales,—and assured them that his Majesty desired there might be a due execution of the laws in all his dominions. After which in the King's name he prorogued the parliament.[1]

[1] 1 Parl. Hist. 426.

At the opening of the following session, in May, 1468, Lord Chancellor Stillington, departing from the custom of inflicting upon King, Lords, and Commons a quaint discourse from a text of Scripture, with infinite divisions and subdivisions,—delivered a very eloquent and statesmanlike speech, which gave great satisfaction, if we may judge from the liberal supplies which were voted. After some observations in praise of the constitutional government of England:

"He put them in mind in what poor estate the King found the crown; despoiled of the due inheritance; wasted in its treasures; the laws wrecked; and the whole by the usurpation in a manner subverted. Add to this the loss of the crown of France; the Duchies of Normandy, Gascoigny, and Guienne, the ancient patrimony of the crown of England, lost also; and further he found it involved in a war with Denmark, Spain, Scotland, Brittany, and other parts, and even with their old enemy of France. Then, descending, he told them that the King had appeased all tumults within the realm, and planted such inward peace that law and justice might be extended. That the King had made peace with Scotland; that the Lord Wenters was negotiating a league with Spain and Denmark, so as to open a free commerce with those countries. But what was still the greatest, he had allied himself to the Dukes of Burgundy and Brittany, two most powerful princes, in such sort as they had given the King the strongest assurance of acting vigorously against France for the recovering of that kingdom and other the King's patrimonies; of which, since they made little doubt, the King thought fit not to omit such an opportunity, and such a one has never happened before. And that his Majesty might see this kingdom as glorious as any of his predecessors did, he was ready to adventure his own person in so just a cause. Lastly, he told them that the King had called this parliament to make them acquainted with these matters, and to desire their advice and assistance."[1]

The announcement of a French war was a certain mode of opening the purse-strings of the nation; a large subsidy of two tenths and two fifteenths was immediately

---

[1] 1 Parl. Hist. 427.

granted and a renewal of the glories of Cressy, Poictiers, and Agincourt was confidently anticipated.

But these visions were soon dispelled by the landing of the Earl of Warwick, now the leader of the Lancastrians, with the avowed object of rescuing Henry from the Tower, where he himself had imprisoned him, and replacing him on the throne from which he had pulled him down as an usurper. "The scene which ensues," says Hume, "resembles more the fiction of a poem or romance than an event in true history." It may be compared to nothing more aptly than the return of Napoleon from Elba. In eleven days from Warwick's landing at Dartmouth,—without fighting a battle, Henry was again set at liberty and proclaimed king, and Edward was flying in disguise to find a refuge beyond the seas.

The Lord Chancellor Stillington certainly did not submit to the new government; but I cannot find whether he followed Edward into exile, or where he resided during "the hundred days."[1] Most of the leading Yorkists fled to the Continent, or took to sanctuary, like the Queen,—who, shut up in Westminster Abbey, while assailed by the cries of the Lancastrians, was delivered of her son, afterwards Edward V., murdered by his inhuman uncle. Stillington probably relied for safety on his sacred character, and retired to his see.

A new Chancellor must have been appointed, as a parliament was called and the government was regularly conducted in Henry's name, this being now styled " the 49th year" of his reign ; but there is no trace of the name of any one who was intrusted with the Great Seal till after the restoration of Edward IV.

It is chiefly on the public records that we ought to rely for the events of those times, and as soon as Edward was again on the throne, the records of all the transactions which had taken place during his exile were vacated and destroyed. "There is no part of English history since the Conquest so uncertain, so little authentic or consistent, as that of the wars between the two Roses; and it is remarkable that this profound darkness falls upon us just on the eve of the restoration of letters, and when the art of printing was already known in Europe. All that

---

[1] Expression first used to describe the period which elapsed between the return of the great Napoleon from Elba and the battle of Waterloo.

we can distinguish with certainty through the deep cloud which covers that period, is a scene of horror and bloodshed, savage manners, arbitrary executions, and treacherous, dishonorable conduct in all parties."[1]

Thus we shall never know who was the Chancellor that stated the causes for calling, in the name of Henry VI., the parliament which met at Westminster on the 26th of November, 1470, — when Edward IV. was declared a traitor, and usurper of the Crown,—all his lands and goods were confiscated,—all the statutes made by him were repealed,—all his principal adherents were attainted,—and sentence of death was passed on the accomplished Tiptoft, Earl of Worcester, though, struck with the first rays of true science, he had been zealous by his exhortation and example to propagate the love of polite learning among his unpolished countrymen.[2] The strong probability is, that George Neville, King-maker Warwick's brother, at this time had the Great Seal restored to him, and took the oaths as Chancellor to King Henry VI.

But Edward soon returned to recover his lost authority, and to wreak vengeance on his enemies; the battles of Barnet and Tewkesbury were fought; the Earl of Warwick fell; Edward the Prince of Wales was assassinated; and the unhappy Henry, "after life's fitful fever slept well,"—whether relieved from his sufferings by the pitying hand of nature, or by the "weeping sword" of the inhuman Gloucester.

When King Edward had gone through the ceremony of being re-crowned, we find Stillington in possession of the Seal as Chancellor. There is no entry in the records of its being again delivered to him, and he was probably considered as holding it under his original appointment.

A parliament was soon afterwards called, which was opened and prorogued by a speech from the Chancellor, but at which nothing memorable occurred. The late parliament held in the name of Henry VI. was not then even recognized so far as that its acts were repealed, and the course was adopted as preferable of obliterating all rolls recording its proceedings. Had things so remained, it would have been difficult for lawyers to determine whether a statute then passed is now law.

I find nothing more related respecting Stillington while

[1] Hume. [2] 1 Parl. Hist. 428.

he continued Chancellor. He ceased to hold the office, not from having lost the favor of his master, but from having fallen into ill health, which incapacitated him from performing his duties. Being very unwell, on the 20th of September, 1472, John Alcock, Bishop of Rochester, himself afterwards Chancellor in the reign of Henry VII., was appointed to keep the Seal until the Chancellor should become convalescent; and on the 8th of June, 1473, being still unable to attend to business, he resigned his office.[1]

Leisure and freedom from anxiety soon restored his health. He would not again resume judicial duties, but he was still zealous to serve his royal patron, and he went upon an embassy to the Duke of Brittany, to persuade that Prince to give up the Earl of Richmond, who was considered heir of the Lancastrian family, and was afterwards King of England under the title of Henry VII. Stillington left nothing unessayed to accomplish his object, but was obliged to return without success.

A stain has been cast upon his memory by the imputation that he was privy to the crimes by which Richard III. mounted the throne. To show the invalidity of his brother's marriage with the Lady Elizabeth Gray, Richard asserted that Edward, before espousing her, had paid court to the Lady Eleanor Talbot, daughter of the Earl of Shrewsbury, and being repulsed by the virtue of that lady, he was obliged, before he could gratify his passion, to consent to a private marriage, which was celebrated by Stillington, Bishop of Bath and Wells; but the Bishop never confirmed this story, and although he was one of the supporters of the usurper at his coronation, there is no proof that he assisted in bastardizing the issue of the benefactor, much less in their murder.[2]

Henry VII. being crowned King, Stillington showed

[1] Rot. Cl. 12 Ed. 4, m. 11.
[2] See Horace Walpole's Historic Doubts. It is curious to observe that the precontract with the daughter of another nobleman was the only ground for contending that the issue of Edward's marriage were not entitled to inherit the throne, and that the continental doctrine of *royal mésalliance* never sprung up in England, that proud monarch, Henry VIII., having four wives who were without royal blood, and two of their descendants succeeding him. England differed from the continent in a more important particular, to which her greatness may be chiefly traced—the absence among us of *castes*—or the custom by which the younger sons of a peer were commoners, and the son of a peasant might rise to the highest rank of nobility.

his never-dying enmity to the House of Lancaster by taking up the cause of Lambert Simnel, the pretended heir of the House of York. Being detected in this conspiracy, the King, who had naturally a particular spite against him, resolved to show him no mercy. The Ex-Chancellor endeavored to conceal himself at Oxford, but the University agreed that he should be delivered up on an understanding that his life should be spared. He was conducted to Windsor, where he remained a prisoner till his death, in June, 1491.

On Stillington's resignation of the Great Seal, it was placed in the hands of the Master of the Rolls, who kept it till the 23d of June, on which day, by the King's command, he delivered it to HENRY BOURCHIER, Earl of Essex. This stout Earl was Lord Keeper only for one month, but as he held the Great Seal during Trinity Term in his own right for all purposes, and must for a time, though short, have transacted all the business belonging to the office, judicial as well as political,—according to the plan of this work some account ought to be given of him.

He was a brother of Archbishop Bourchier, and so descended from the Earl of Eu, in Normandy, and nearly related to the royal family.

He had been bred a soldier, and like many others, he had changed sides in the late wars as suited his interest. He was now high in the confidence of Edward IV., and at mortal enmity with all Lancastrians.

We have no information respecting his performances as Lord Keeper, but he must have found his seat in the marble chair very uncomfortable, for without any difference with the King, he resigned on the 27th of July, and was then made a Knight of the Garter. He died in 1483.

On his resignation, the Great Seal was delivered to LAWRENCE BOOTH, Bishop of Durham, with the title of Chancellor.[1]

Booth had risen by merit from obscurity. He studied at Cambridge, where he gained high distinction for his proficiency in literature, law, and divinity. While still a young man, he was elected head of his house and Chancellor of the University. In 1457 he was made Bishop of Durham, while Henry VI. was nominally King, but

[1] Rot. Cl. 15 Ed. 4.

under the influence of the Yorkists, to whom he continued steadily attached. It seems strange to us that an individual who for sixteen years had been occupied superintending a remote diocese, should in his old age be selected to fill the office of Lord Chancellor, now become one of great importance in the administration of justice; but there were, no doubt, political reasons for the appointment, and the interests of the suitors were not much regarded. It is possible that the Bishop might have been thought capable of silencing a noisy opponent in parliament, or that he was of that moderate, decent, unalarming character, which so often leads to promotion.

His appointment turned out a great failure. He was equally inefficient in the Court of Chancery and in parliament. Except that he did not take bribes, he had every bad quality of a judge, and heavy complaints arose from his vacillation and delays. While he presided on the woolsack in the House of Lords, he never ventured to open his mouth, unless in the formal addresses which he delivered by the King's command, at the commencement and close of the session, and these were so bad as to cause general dissatisfaction. On the 1st of February, 1474, he summoned the Commons to the Upper House, and told them "that they were assembled to consult which way the King might proceed in the wars; but because his majesty had yet heard nothing from his brother, the Duke of Burgundy, relating to that affair, whereon much depended, it was the King's command that this parliament should be prorogued to the 9th of May ensuing.[1]

When the two Houses again met, his incompetency became more glaring, and it was found that he had not the requisite skill, by eloquence or management, to carry the measures of the Court, or to obtain the supplies. He was accordingly dismissed from the office of Chancellor. To console him, he was soon after translated from Durham to York. He died after having quietly presided over this province between three and four years, during which time, abandoning politics, he exclusively confined himself to his spiritual duties.[2]

There is no record of the delivery of the Great Seal to ROTHERAM, his distinguished successor; but we know from the Privy Seal Bills extant, that he was Chancellor in

[1] 1 Parl. Hist. 432.   [2] Privy Seal Bills, 14 Ed. 4.

the end of February, 1475.¹ Although he held the Great Seal only for a short time on this occasion, it was afterwards restored to him, and he acted a most conspicuous part in the troubles which ensued on the death of Edward IV.

He owed his elevation to his own merits. His family name was Scot, unillustrated in England at that time, and instead of it, he assumed the name of the town in the West Riding of Yorkshire, in which he was born.² He studied at King's College, Cambridge, and was one of the earliest fellows on this royal foundation which has since produced so many distinguished men.³ He was afterwards Master of Pembroke Hall, and Chancellor of this University. For his learning and piety he was at an early age selected to be chaplain to Vere, thirteenth Earl of Oxford, and he was then taken into the service of Edward IV. Being a steady Yorkist, he was made Bishop of Rochester in 1467, and translated to Lincoln in 1471. To finish the notice of his ecclesiastical dignities, I may mention here that, in 1480, he became Archbishop of York, and that he received a red hat from the Pope with the title of Cardinal SCTÆ CICILIÆ.⁴

Soon after his elevation to the office of Chancellor he was called to open a session of parliament after a prorogation, and by holding out the prospect of a French war he contrived to obtain supplies of unexampled amount. In the beginning of the following year he passed a great number of bills of attainder and restitution, with a view to the permanent depression of the Lancastrians. On the 14th of March, by the King's command, he returned thanks to the three estates and dissolved the parliament, which had lasted near two years and a half.⁵ Since the

¹ L. C. 46.
² We are not to suppose from this that he was ashamed of his descent. Edward I., to introduce surnames, still rare, and to give variety to them, had directed that people might take as a name the place of their birth. Even princes of the blood were called by the place of their birth, as "Harry of Monmouth," "John of Gaunt," "Thomas of Woodstock," &c. Priests being *mortui sæculo*, very frequently relinquished their family names on their ordination.
³ Three Chancellors,—Rotherham, Goodrich, and Camden, and many most eminent lawyers,—as Chief Justice Sir James Mansfield, Chief Justice Sir Vicary Gibbs, Mr. Justice Patteson, Mr. Justice Dampier, and Mr. Justice Coleridge.
⁴ Fuller's Worthies, 214. Godwin Willis, 42. Wood's Ath. i. 147.
⁵ 1 Parl. Hist. 433.

beginning of parliaments no one had enjoyed an existence nearly so long. Formerly there was a new parliament every session, and the session did not last many days. But as the power of the House of Commons increased, it was found of great importance to have a majority attached to the ruling faction, and disposed to grant liberal supplies. When such a House was elected there was a reluctance to part with it, and prorogations were gradually subsituted for dissolutions; but the keeping of the same parliament in existence above a year was considered a great innovation. At common law, however, the demise of the Crown was the only limit to the duration of parliaments,—which accounts for the first parliament of Charles II. having lasted eighteen years, and there being sometimes no dissolution of the Irish parliament during a long reign.

The History of Croyland points it out as something very remarkable, that during this parliament of Edward IV. no less than three several Lord Chancellors presided. "The first," adds that authority, "was Robert Stillington, Bishop of Bath, who did nothing but by the advice of his disciple, John Alcock, Bishop of Worcester; the next was Lawrence Booth, Bishop of Durham, who tired himself with doing just nothing at all; and the third was Thomas Rotheram, Bishop of Lincoln, who did all, and brought every thing to a happy conclusion."

Although Rotheram had given such satisfaction as Chancellor,—on the 27th of April, 1476, JOHN ALCOCK, who had been formerly keeper of the Great Seal under Stillington, was sworn in Chancellor, and held the office till the 28th of September following, when Rotheram was reinstated in it.[1] We have no certain information respecting the cause of this discontinuance, or how he employed himself in the interval; but there is a strong probability that he accompanied the King in his inglorious expedition to claim the crown of France, which ended in the peace of Pecquigni, and that the negotiations with the Duke of Burgundy and Louis XI. were chiefly intrusted to him.

He continued Chancellor and chief adviser of the Crown during the remainder of this reign. Edward, immersed in pleasure and indulging in indolence, unless excited by

[1] Privy Seal Bills, 15 Ed. 4.

some great peril, when he could display signal energy as well as courage,—threw upon his minister all the common cares of government.

A parliament met at Westminster in January, 1477, when Lord Chancellor Rotheram, in the presence of the King, Lords, and Commons, in the Painted Chamber, declared the cause of the summons from this text, " Dominus regit me et nihil mihi deerit ;" upon which he largely treated of the obedience which subjects owe to their Prince, and showed, by many examples out of the Old and New Testament, what grievous plagues had happened to the rebellious and disobedient, particularly that saying of St. Paul, *Non sine causâ Rex gladium portat*. He added, that "the Majesty of the King was upheld by the hand and counsel of God, by which he was advanced to the throne of his ancestors."[1]

Lord Chancellor Rotheram now found it convenient to pass an act repealing all the statutes and nullifying all the proceedings of the parliament which sat during the 100 days, "alleged to have been held in the 49th year of Hen. VI., but which," it was said, "was truly the 9th of Ed. IV." He then obtained great popularity by an act showing the dislike to Irishmen, which still lingers in England, and which, with little mitigation, was long handed down from generation to generation,—"to oblige all Irishmen born, *or coming of Irish parents*, who reside in England, either to repair to and remain in Ireland, or else to pay yearly a certain sum there rated for the defense of the same." We fear this was not meant as an absentee tax for the benefit of Ireland, but was, in reality, an oppressive levy on obnoxious *aliens*, such as was imposed on the Jews till they were finally banished from the realm.

Now began the fatal dissensions in the royal family which led to the destruction of the House of York, and the extinction of the name of Plantagenet. There is no reason to think that the Chancellor did all that was possible to heal the dispute between the King and his brother, the Duke of Clarence. When the trial for treason came on in the House of Lords, the Duke of Buckingham presided as Lord Steward, and the King appearing personally as accuser, the field was left to the two brothers; "no one charging Clarence but the King, and no one answer-

[1] 1 Parl. Hist. 434.

ing the King but Clarence."[1] According to the universal usage, the Bill of Attainder passed both Houses unanimously; but the Chancellor, as a churchman, could not vote in this affair of blood. We may suppose that it was at the merciful suggestion of "the Keeper of his conscience," that the King was so far softened as to give his brother the choice of the mode of dying, and consented to his being drowned in a butt of his favorite malmsey.

On the 20th of January, 1482, the Chancellor opened Edward's last parliament with a discourse from the text, *Dominus illuminatio mea et salus mea;* but we are not told on what topics he enlarged; and nothing was brought forward during the session except a code or consolidation of the laws touching "excess of apparel," with a new enactment, "that none *under the degree of a Lord* shall wear any mantle, unless it be of such a length that a man standing upright, *il lui voilera la queue ;*"[2]—so that, instead of appearing in flowing robes, and with a long train, the privilege of the nobility now was to show the contour of their person to the multitude.

In "Cotton's Abridgment" is to be found a list of the peers summoned to attend another parliament at Westminster in the beginning of the following year; but there are no proceedings of such a parliament on record, and, if summoned, it was probably prevented from meeting by the last sickness and death of the King, which happened on the 9th of April, 1483, in the forty-second year of his age and the twenty-third of his reign.

There are to be found in the Year Books and Abridgments various cases decided by the Chancellors of Edward IV., showing that their equitable jurisdiction still required much to be improved and strengthened. Lord Chancellor Rotheram was considered the greatest equity lawyer of the age. While he held the Great Seal, a bill was filed by a person who had entered into a statute merchant (that is, had acknowledged before the mayor of a town that he owed a sum of money), who had paid the debt without taking a written discharge, and who was afterwards sued at law for the amount. The question was, whether he should have relief? The Chancellor, having great doubt,

---

[1] 1 Parl. Hist. 435.
[2] Translated in the Statute-book, "it shall cover his buttocks." 22 Ed. 4, c. 1.

called in the assistance of the Judges in the Exchequer Chamber,—where, after much argument, he pronounced that, a statute merchant being matter of record, no relief could be given, though it would have been otherwise in the case of a bond. And he decreed accordingly.[1]

But it is not to be wondered at that he proceeded warily, and that he stood in awe of the common-law Judges; for they appear to have formed a combination against him. In the same year in which the last case was decided, he had granted an injunction after verdict in a case depending in the Court of King's Bench, on the ground that the verdict had been fraudulently obtained. Hussey, the Lord Chief Justice, who had probably presided at the trial, was very indignant, and asked the counsel for the plaintiff "if they would pray judgment according to the verdict?" and they declared their dread of infringing the injunction. One of the puisne Judges argued, that "though the party himself against whom the injunction was directed might be bound by it, his counsel or attorney might pray judgment with safety." But this distinction being overruled, the Lord Chief Justice said "they had talked over the matter among themselves, and they saw no mischief that could ensue to the party if he prayed judgment, for the pecuniary penalty mentioned in the injunction was not leviable by law, so that there remained nothing but imprisonment;" and as to that he said, "If the Chancellor commits any one to the Fleet, apply to us for a *habeas corpus*, and upon the return to it we will discharge the prisoner, and we will do all to assist you." To avoid the impending collision, another puisne Judge said "he would go to the Chancellor, and ask him to dissolve the injunction;" but they all stoutly declared that "if the injunction were continued, they would nothingtheless give judgment and award execution,"—taking much credit to themselves for their moderation in refusing damages for the loss occasioned by the proceedings in Chancery.[2]

Yet the equitable jurisdiction of the Court of Chancery may be considered as making its greatest advance in this reign. The point was now settled that there being a feoffment to uses, the *cestui que use*, or person beneficially entitled, could maintain no action at law, the

[1] Y. B. 22 Ed. 4, 6. [2] Y. B. 22 Ed. 4, 37.

Judges saying that he had neither *jus in re* nor *jus ad rem*, and that their forms could not be moulded so as to afford him any effectual relief, either as to the land or the profits. The Chancellors therefore, with general applause, declared that they would proceed by *subpœna* aganst the feoffee to compel him to perform a duty which in conscience was binding upon him, and gradually extended the remedy against his heir and against his alienee with notice of the trust, although they held, as their successors have done, that the purchaser of the legal estate for valuable consideration without notice might retain the land for his own benefit.[1] They therefore now freely made decrees requiring the trustee to convey according to the directions of the person beneficially interested; and the most important branch of the equitable jurisdiction of the Court over *trusts* was firmly and irrevocably established.

A written statement of the supposed grievance being required to be filed before the issuing of the *subpœna*, with security to pay damages and costs,—bills now acquired form, and the distinction arose between the proceeding by bill and by petition. The same regularity was observed in the subsequent stages of the suit. Whereas formerly the defendant was generally examined *viva voce* when he appeared in obedience to the *subpœna*, the practice now was to put in a written answer, commencing with a protestation against the truth or sufficiency of the matters contained in the bill, stating the facts relied upon by the defendant, and concluding with a prayer that he may be dismissed with his costs.

There were likewise, for the purpose of introducing new facts, special replications and rejoinders, which continued to the reign of Elizabeth, but which have been rendered unnecessary by the more modern practice of amending the bill and answer. Pleas and demurrers now appear. Although the pleadings were in English, the decrees on the bill continued to be in Latin down to the reign of Henry VIII.[2] Bills to perpetuate testimony, to set out metes and bounds, and for injunctions against proceedings at law, and to stay waste, became frequent.[3]

[1] See Bro. Feoff. al Uses, pl. 45. Saunders on Uses. p. 20.

[2] They were now sometimes expressed to be "habita deliberatione cum justiciariis et aliis de dicti Domini Regis concilio peritis ad hoc evocatis et ibidem tunc præsentibus."

[3] See Calendar, and Reports of Record Commissioners, temp. Ed. 4.

The common-law Judges at this time were very bold men, having of their own authority repealed the statute DE BONIS, passed in the reign of Edward I., which authorized the perpetual entail of land,—by deciding in Taltarum's case,[1] that the entail might be barred through a fictitious proceeding in the Court of Common Pleas, called a "Common Recovery;"—the estate being adjudged to a sham claimant,—a sham equivalent being given to those who ought to succeed to it,—and the tenant in tail being enabled to dispose of it as he pleased, in spite of the will of the donor. One of these judges was Littleton, the author of the Treatise on Tenures, a work of higher authority than any other in the law of England. Fortescue is the only individual in the list of Chancellors who wrote in this reign, and his Dialogue "De Laudibus" was not published till long after.

In the old "Abridgments of the Law" there are various decisions of Edward IV.'s Chancellors, referred to under the head of "Conscience," "Subpœna," and "Injunctions," —the only prior ones being a few in the time of Henry VI.; but they show equity to have been still in the rudest state, without systematic rules or principles.

CHAPTER XXIV.

CHANCELLORS DURING THE REIGNS OF EDWARD V. AND RICHARD III.

BEFORE Edward IV. was laid in his grave, disputes began between the Queen's family and the Duke of Gloucester, her brother-in-law, who from the first claimed the office of Protector, and soon resolved at all hazards to seize the crown. Lord Chancellor Rotheram sided with the Queen, and when with her daughters and her younger son she had taken sanctuary within the precincts of the Abbey at Westminster, where on a former distress during the short restoration of Henry VI. she had been delivered of the Prince of Wales, he interfered in his sacred character of Archbishop to prevent her and the objects of her affection from being

[1] 12 Ed. 4.

forcibly laid hold of by Richard, who contended that the ecclesiastical privilege of sanctuary did not apply to them, as it was originally intended only to give protection to unhappy men persecuted for their debts or crimes. A messenger came from Richard to Rotheram, to assure him "that there was no sort of danger to the Queen, the young King, or the royal issue, and that all should be well;" to which he replied,—" Be it as well as it will, I assure him it will never be as well as we have seen it." Being at loss how to dispose of the Great Seal, which he no longer had a right to use, he went to the Queen and unadvisedly delivered it up to her, who certainly could have no right to receive it;—but repenting his mistake, he soon sent for it back, and it was restored to him.

Rotheram has escaped all suspicion of being knowingly implicated in the criminal projects of Richard; but he was unfortunately made the instrument of materially aiding them. The Queen still resisted all the importunities and threats used to get possession from her of the infant Duke of York, observing "that, by living in sanctuary, he was not only secure himself, but gave security to his brother, the King, whose life no one would dare to aim at, while his successor and avenger remained in safety."

Richard, with his usual art and deceit, applied himself to Rotheram and another Ex-Chancellor, Archbishop Bourchier, and contrived to persuade them that his intentions were fair, and that his only object in obtaining the release of the young Prince was, that he might keep the King, his brother, company, and walk at his coronation. These holy men at last prevailed with the Queen to give a most reluctant assent. Taking the child by the hand, and addressing Rotheram, she said:—" My Lord Archbishop, here he is; for my own part I can never deliver him; but if you will needs have him, take him; I will require him at your hands." She was here struck with a kind of presage of his future fate; she tenderly embraced him, she bedewed him with her tears, and bade him an eternal adieu.

Rotheram appears soon after to have surrendered the Great Seal into the hands of the Protector. There is no record of the transfer or delivery of it during the reign of Edward V. But we know that while the young King still lived and his name was used as sovereign, JOHN

RUSSELL was appointed to the office, and must have sworn fidelity to that Sovereign. Sir Thomas More, after giving an account of Richard taking upon himself the office of Protector, says: "at whiche counsayle also the Archebishoppe of York, Chauncellore of Englande, whiche had delivered uppe the Greate Seale to the Queene, was therefore greatly reproved, and the Seale taken from hyme, and delivered to Doctour Russell, Byschoppe of Lincolne."[1] Moreover there is an original letter extant in the Tower of London, addressed in the name of Edward V. to "John, Bishop of Lincoln, our Chancellor," and dated "the seconde daie of Juyn, in the furst yere of oure reigne." And Spelman[2] says, though without citing his authority,—" Hic mortuo rege Edwardo IV. sigillum tradidit (Thomas Rotheram) Reginæ Matri, de qua receptum Io. Russell datur, vivente adhuc Edward V."

But before entering on the life of the new Chancellor, we must conclude our account of the two Archbishops, who for the rest of their days confined themselves to the discharge of their ecclesiastical functions. Bourchier performed the marriage ceremony between Henry VII. and Elizabeth of York, by which the red and white roses were united; but his great glory is, that he was one of the chief persons by whose means the art of printing was introduced into England, and that he was a zealous and enlightened patron of reviving learning. He died at his palace of Knowle, near Sevenoaks, on the 30th of March, 1486, and was buried at Canterbury, where his tomb still remains on the north side of the choir, near the high altar.

Rotherham did not take any active part in the struggles which ensued, but he was so strongly suspected by Richard III. that he was detained in prison, till near the end of this reign, when the Lady Anne had been made away with. He was then liberated on account of his great influence over the Queen Dowager, that he might persuade her to agree to a marriage between her daughter Elizabeth and the murderer of her sons—which would have taken place if Richmond had been repulsed. After the battle of Bosworth, the Ex-Chancellor quietly submitted to the new government, but he was looked upon with no favor by Henry VII., who to the last retained his Lancastrian prejudices, and was desirous to depress

[1] Sir T. More's Hist. Ric. III. p. 46.   [2] Gloss. III.

all the partisans of the House of York. He died of the plague at Cawood, in the year 1500, aged 76, and was buried in his own cathedral.[1] He was founder of Lincoln College, Oxford, and showed his affection to the place of his nativity by building a college there, with three schools for grammar, writing, and music.

The Protector was wading through slaughter to a throne when he appointed John Russell to the office of Chancellor to the young King whom he had doomed to destruction. Yet this Prelate, though he did not altogether escape suspicion, appears to have been unstained by the crimes of his patron; and he is celebrated by most of the chroniclers of that period for uncommon learning, piety and wisdom. He was probably selected by Richard as a man who, from his mild disposition, would not be dangerous to him, and whose character might bring some credit to his cause.

I do not find any distinct account of this John Russell's parentage. He was most likely of the Bedford family, who, having held a respectable but not brilliant position in the West of England since the Conquest, was now rising into eminence.[2] He was born in the parish of St. Peter, in the suburbs of the city of Winchester, in the beginning of the reign of Henry VI.[3] Having studied some years at the school recently established by William of Wickham in the place of his birth, he was removed to the University of Oxford. Here he made particular proficiency in the canon law, and took the degree of Doctor in this faculty. In 1449 he was elected a fellow of New College, and residing there he still increased his academical reputation.[4] He was made a prebendary of Salisbury, and Archdeacon of Berkshire,—when he removed to Court, and was much noticed by Edward IV. In 1476 he was consecrated Bishop of Rochester, and in 1480 he was translated to the see of Lincoln. He was a man of very bland manners, and as he rose in the world, made himself still very

[1] In 1735 his vault was opened, and a head of good sculpture in wood was found, supposed to be a resemblance of him.—Will. York. 156, 180.
[2] John Russell, a lineal ancestor of the present Duke, was Speaker of the House of Commons in the second parliament of Hen. VI., which met in 1432. Wiffen, in his "History of the House of Russell," does not mention the Chancellor,—perhaps from a shyness to acknowledge him on account of his connection with Richard III., and the suspicion under which he unjustly labored of having betrayed two sovereigns to whom he had sworn allegiance.
[3] Wood, Hist. et Ant. Oxon. 413.   [4] Ibid. 413, 414.

acceptable to those above him, and popular with all ranks. He was left by Edward IV. one of his executors, and his appointment as Chancellor to the infant Sovereign was generally approved of.

We are not informed how the new Chancellor employed himself in the short interval during which the government was allowed to be carried on in the name of Edward V.; but as he is not mentioned in connection with the scenes of open violence which ensued, and no serious charge of treachery was urged against him when the Lancastrians triumphed, we are bound to believe that the usurpation was planned and effected without his privity, though, like most others in the kingdom, he was not unwilling to recognize the usurper. We must remember that the revolution proceeded on the ground that Richard was the right heir;—that the two young Princes, though set aside, still survived when he gave in his adhesion;—and that there is great reason to think that Edward actually walked at the coronation of his cruel uncle.[1]

Two days after the ridiculous farce acted at Guildhall, under the management of Buckingham, which Shakspeare has made so familiar to us, John Russell had the Great Seal again delivered to him, as Chancellor to Richard III., and he swore allegiance to the new King. The ceremony took place at Baynard's Castle in Thames Street, the residence of the Duchess of York, where the usurper first kept his Court. The record tells us, "that the Chancellor having there received the Great Seal from the King, carried it to his inn called the Old Temple, in the parish of St. Andrew, Holborn, and that on the 20th of June following he sat here, assisted by Morton the Master of the Rolls, and three Masters in Chancery."[2] We have no further account of the exercise of his judicial functions.

Richard was soon obliged to take the field that he might put down the insurrection of the Duke of Buckingham. The Chancellor was then confined to his bed in London by a severe fit of sickness. When Richard reached Lincoln at the head of his army, he sent to the Chancellor the following letter, the original of which is still preserved in the Tower:—

[1] So far Horace Walpole, I think, succeeds, although he fails egregiously in making Richard both handsome and virtuous.
[2] Rot. Cl. 1 Ric. 3, n. 100.

"By the King,

"Right Reverend Fadre in God, and right trusty and well-beloved, We grete you well, and in our hertiest wyse thank you for the many-fold Presents that your servantes in your behalve have presented unto us at this oure being here: which we assure you we toke and accepted with good herte: and so we have cause. And whereas we, by Goddes grace, intend briefly to avaunce us towards our rebel and traitor, the Duc of Buckingham, to resist and withstand his malicious purpose, as lately by oure other letters We certifyed you oure mynde more at large: For which cause it behoveth us to have our Grete Sele here, We being enfourmed that for such infirmities and diseases as ye susteyne ne may in your person to your ease conveniently come unto us with the same: Wherefore we wil, and natheless charge you that forthwith upon the sight of thies, ye saufly do the same oure Grete Sele to be sent unto us; and such of the office of our Cauncery as by your wisedome shall be thought necessary, receiving these oure letters for youre sufficient discharge in that behalve. Geven undre oure signet at oure cite of Lincolne the xii day of Octobre."

The letter, so far, is in the handwriting of a secretary. Then follows this most curious postscript in the handwriting of Richard himself:—

"We wolde most gladly ye came your selff, yf that you may, and yf ye may not, we pray you not to fayle, but to accomplyshe in al dillygence our sayde commaundemente, to send oure Seale incontinent upon the syght hereof as we truste you with such as ye truste and the officers parteyning to attende with hyt; praying you to ascerteyn us of your News ther, Here, loved be God, is al wel and trewly determyned, and for to resiste the malyse of him that had best cause to be trew, the Duc of Bokyngam, the most untrew creature lyvynge. Whom, with God's grace, we shall not be long til that we wyll be in that parties and subdew his malys. Wee assure you there was never falsre traitor purvayde for, as this Berrerr *Gloucestre* shall show you."[1]

The Great Seal was accordingly sent to the King, who retained it in his own custody till the 26th of November,

---

[1] See Kennet, i. 522 n.

when having returned in triumph to London, he restored it to Lord Chancellor Russell.[1]

There had as yet been no parliament since the death of Edward IV., but one was now summoned by writs under the Great Seal. The two Houses met in January, 1484, and the King being seated on the throne, the Lord Chancellor addressed them, and as soon as a Speaker was chosen, proposed a bill, whereby it was " declared, pronounced, decreed, confirmed, and established, that our Lord Richard III. is the true and undoubted King of this realm, as well by right of consanguinity and heritage, as by lawful election and coronation."

The issue of Edward IV. being bastardized, and the Earl of Richmond and all the Lancastrian leaders attainted, the parliament, at the suggestion of the government, set to work in good earnest to reform the law and to improve the institutions of the country. This policy, prompted by the King's consciousness of his bad title to the crown and his desire to obtain popularity, was warmly promoted by the Chancellor.

From the destruction and obliteration of records which followed upon the change of dynasty, we have very imperfect details of the proceedings of this parliament; but looking to the result of its deliberations as exhibited in the Statute Book, we have no difficulty in pronouncing it the most meritorious national council for protecting the liberty of the subject and putting down abuses in the administration of justice, which had sat since the time of Edward I.

I will fondly believe, though I can produce no direct evidence to prove the fact, that to " JOHN RUSSELL" the nation was indebted for the Act entitled—" The Subjects of this Realm not to be charged with Benevolence," the object of which was to put down the practice introduced in some late reigns of levying taxes under the name of " Benevolence," without the authority of parliament. The language employed would not be unworthy of that statesman bearing the same name, who in our own time framed and introduced Bills " to abolish the Test Act," and " to reform the Representation of the People of Parliament:"

" Remembering how the Commons, by new and unlaw-

[1] Rot. Cl. 1 Ric. 3, n. 101.

ful innovations against the laws of this realm, have been put to great thraldom and exactions, and in especial by a new imposition called *Benevolence*, be it ordained that the Commonalty of this realm from henceforth in no wise be charged therewith, and that such exactions aforetime taken shall be for no example to make the like hereafter, but shall be damned and annulled for ever."[1]

When the session of parliament was over, the Chancellor was employed to negotiate a peace with Scotland. At Nottingham he met commissioners from the Scottish King, and it was agreed, that to consolidate the amity between the two countries, Anne de la Pole, the niece of King Richard and sister of the Earl of Lincoln, declared to be heir presumptive to the crown, should be married to the eldest son of James III. The parties were then infants, and this marriage did not take place; but afterwards another English princess, eldest daughter of Henry VII., did become the bride of James IV., and was the means of uniting the whole island under one sovereign.

The Chancellor was next employed in a negotiation of a more difficult and delicate nature. Jane Shore, celebrated for her beauty, her frailties, and her amiable qualities,—after the death of her lover, Edward IV., having tried to support the title of his children to the throne, and having put herself under the protection of Hastings —on the fall of that nobleman, Richard was resolved to be revenged of her, and, complaining that she had conspired against him, caused her to be prosecuted in the ecclesiastical court for adultery and witchcraft,—her husband, the goldsmith of Lombard Street, being induced to join in the prosecution and to sue for a divorce. She had been found guilty, sentenced to penance, and imprisoned in Ludgate. While there she was considered a state prisoner, and, according to a custom which was acted upon in many succeeding reigns, the law officers of the Crown were sent to interrogate her, for the purpose of obtaining information respecting the movements of the Lancastrians, with whom she was now suspected to be in correspondence. It so happened that Sir Thomas Lynom, the Solicitor General, after two or three private interviews, was so smitten with her " pretty foot, cherry lip, bonny eye, and passing pleasing tongue," that he ac-

[1] Stat. 1 Ric. 3, c. 2.

tually offerered her his hand. Richard hearing of this extraordinary courtship, and thinking it indecent that his Solicitor General should marry a woman whose immodesty had been made so notorious, wrote the following letter to the Lord Chancellor, for the purpose of breaking off the match, yet (good naturedly, so as to furnish an argument for Horace Walpole to prove that the supposed bloody tyrant was a very worthy fellow)—with the intention that, if Mr. Solicitor was incurable, he might be put in the way of making Mrs. Shore Lady Lynom with as little discredit as possible:

" By the King.

" Right reverend fadre in God, &c. Signifying unto you, that it is shewed unto us, that our servaunt and sollicitor, Thomas Lynom, merveillously blinded and abused with the late (wife) of William Shore, now living in Ludgate by oure commandment, hath made contract of matrymony with hir (as it is said) and intendith, to our full grate marveile, to proceed to th' effect of the same. We for many causes wold be sorry that hee soo shulde be disposed. Pray you therefore to send for him, and in that ye goodly may, exhorte and stirre hym to the contrarye. And if ye finde him utterly set for to marye hur, and noon otherwise will be aduertised, then if it stand with the law of the churche,[1] We be content (the tyme of marriage deferred to our comyng next to London) that upon sufficient suertie founde of hure good abering, ye doo send for hure Keeper and discharge him of our said commandment by warrant of these, committing her to the rule and guiding of hure fadre or any othre by your discretion in the mene season. Geven, &c.

" To the right reverend fadre in God &c. the Bishop of Lincoln our Chauncellour."[2]

The particulars of the conference between the two legal dignitaries are no where mentioned; but the Chancellor must have succeeded in persuading the Solicitor General of the imprudence of a match which the world would censure, and which might hurt his advancement; for we know that the unfortunate lady never was married again,

[1] The doubt was whether, notwithstanding the divorce, a second valid marriage could be contracted.
[2] Harl. MS. Brit. Mus. 433, fol. 340, b. Walpole's Hist. Doubts, 118, where there is a wrong reference to the King's letter, which I have corrected after examining the MS.

and that she died in the reign of Henry VIII., still bearing the name of Jane Shore.¹

John Russell continued Chancellor till the 29th of July, 1485, having the Great Seal alwas in his own custody, except from the 19th of October to the 26th of November, 1483, on the occasion I have referred to.

We have no information as to the cause of the good Bishop's dismissal from the office of Chancellor. There was no party crisis or change of measures at the time, and there was no rival for the office who was to be preferred to him. It is possible that Richard, marching to meet the Earl of Richmond, acted as he had done in his expedition against Buckingham, and desired to take the Great Seal into the field with him, intending to restore it to the former keeper of his conscience when he returned victorious; but, on the other hand, it has been supposed that Richard suspected the Chancellor of being in correspondence with the Earl of Richmond, and that he meditated a dreadful revenge upon him when he had vanquished his enemy.

Ex-Chancellor Russell retired to his palace at Buckden, where he heard of the battle of Bosworth and the accession of Henry VII. He mixed no more in politics, and spent the remainder of his days in the care of his diocese and superintending the discipline of the University of Oxford.

He is celebrated as the first perpetual Chancellor of that learned body. Hitherto the office had been held only for a year, and frequently by some resident member of no very high rank. In 1483, when Russell was appointed Chancellor of England,—on account of the inconvenience arising from annual elections, and the great confidence reposed in him, he was elected Chancellor of the University for life.

Tired of the dignity, he resigned it in 1487; but great confusion being likely to arise from this step, " the Academicians earnestly desired him to take upon him the office again, which he promising they proceeded to election."² A keen contest took place, Peter Courtenay,

---

¹ She was seen by Sir Thomas More, poor, decrepit, and shriveled, without the least traces of that beauty which once commanded the admiration of a king and all his court. The story of her dying of hunger in a ditch, supposed after her, to be called *Shcre*ditch, is a fable.

² Fast. Ox. 64.

Bishop of Winchester, being put up against him; but he was re-elected, and held the office till his death, when he was succeeded by Lord Chancellor Cardinal MORTON. In 1488 he published certain "Aulary Statutes for the Government of the University," which were supposed to have made it a model for all universities.

He died January 30, 1494, and was buried in his cathedral, at the upper end on the south side, in a chapel where he had founded a chantry, under an altar tomb, with this inscription:—

> "Qui sum quæ mihi Sors fuerat narrabo. Johannes
> Russell sum dictus, servans nomen genitoris.
> Urbs Ventana parit, studium fuit Oxoniense:
> Doctorem juris, me Sarisburia donat
> Archidiacono; legatum mittit in orbem
> Rex, et privatum mandat deferre Sigillum;
> Cancellarii Regni tunc denique functus
> Officio, cupii dissolvi, vivere Christo.
> Ecclesiasque duas suscepi Pontificales
> Roffa Sacrum primo, Lincolnia condit in unum
> Anno milleno; C. quater quater atque viceno
> Bis septem junctis vitalia Lumina claudo." [1]

But the most valuable memorial to his fame is the character given of him by Sir Thomas More,—" A wyse mane & a good, & of much experyence, & one of the best learned menne undoubtedly that Englande hadde in hys time."[2]

He left behind him considerable reputation as an author, his two greatest works being "A Commentary on the Canticles," and a treatise " De Potestate summi Pontificis et Imperatoris." Had they been written a few years later, we should have been able to pass judgment upon them; but they never were printed, and they have not come down to us. He appears to have been a great encourager of reviving learning,[2] but he is more loudly extolled for his " re-edification of the episcopal palace at Buckden."[4]

---

[1] Willis's Cathedrals, Bishops of Lincoln, vol. iii. pp. 7, 59.

[2] Life of Ric. III., p. 529.

[3] On a manuscript of Matthew Paris (Royal MSS. 14, C. vii.) now in the British Museum, there is an inscription in Latin, dated June 1, 1488, in the handwriting and with the signature of *John Russell*, Bishop of Lincoln, in which whosoever shall obliterate or destroy the Bishop's memorandum respecting the ownership of the volume is solemnly declared to be accursed.— Warton's *Dissertation on Introduction of Learning into England*, p. 111. It appears, from an inscription in the author's own hand, to have been a presentation copy from himself, probably to some church or monastery.— *Sketches of the History of Literature and Learning in England*, vol. ii. 168. Knight's *Weekly Volume*, No. XVIII.

[3] God de præs. Linc. Although Lord Chancellor Russell has considerable

No other Chancellor was appointed by Richard during the short remainder of his reign. The invasion of the Earl of Richmond was now impending. To him the discontented were flocking as a deliverer, from all parts of the kingdom; and there was a general feeling among the people, that the man stained with so many crimes ought not longer to be permitted to occupy the throne which he had usurped. The Great Seal was given by Richard into the temporary keeping of Thomas Barrowe, Master of the Rolls,[1] for the despatch of necessary business, and it probably remainded with him till the conclusion of the reign, although some accounts represent that Richard carried it with him when he marched against Richmond, and had it in his tent at Bosworth Field,—in which case it must have at once have fallen into the hands of the victor, and next to the crown worn by Richard in the fight, have been his earliest emblem of royalty.[2]

We do not find any equity decisions in these two short reigns, although, amidst arms, the laws seem to have been regularly adminstered, and there have been handed down to us reports in the Year Books, beginning "De Termino Trinitatis Anno primo Edwardi Quinti." Lord Chancellor Russell appears to have been perplexed by the cases which came before him respecting uses; and to obviate the necessity for a Bill in Chancery, it was enacted that the person entitled to direct the trustee to convey should himself be entitled to execute a conveyance to carry the estate;[3] but this new expedient to remedy the inconvenience of uses only produced the additional confusion which must necessarily follow when two persons have an equal legal right to dispose of the same land, and the deduction of title, by tracing the legal estate, on which the security of tenure in England depends, became impossible.

historical interest, he is not mentioned by modern historians, and many of my well-informed readers may never have heard of his existence. I consider him one of the "Chancellarian mummies" I have dug up and exhibited to the public. [1] Rot. Cl. 3 Ric. 3, n. 1. Rym. F. xii. 272.

[2] See Nicholls' Lit. Anec. vi. 47. Walpole's Hist. Doubts. Antiq. Bish. Rochester. Harl. MSS. No. 2578. Buck's Life of Richard III. in Kennet, vol. i.

[3] 1 Ric. 3, c. 1. It is remarkable that this is the first statute in the English language, the statutes hitherto having been all in Latin or French, and it was taken as a precedent, for all statutes afterwards are in English. It is curious that in this reign, which we regard with so much horror, laws were given to

CHAPTER XXV.

CHANCELLORS AND LORD KEEPERS FROM THE ACCESSION OF HENRY VII. TILL THE APPOINTMENT OF ARCHBISHOP WARHAM AS LORD KEEPER.

KING Henry VII., returning from Bosworth Field, appointed for his first Chancellor John Alcock, now Bishop of Worcester,[1] who for a few months while Bishop of Rochester, had filled the office under Edward IV., and an account of whom I have reserved for this place. He was born at Beverley in the county of York, of no distinguished family, and raised himself entirely by his own merits. He studied at Cambridge, where he obtained great distinction, particularly for his great knowledge of the civil and canon law. He was patronized by Lord Chancellor Stillington,—was extremely useful to him,—and as his deputy, performed most of the duties belonging to the Great Seal. In 1471, as a reward for his services he was made Bishop of Rochester and Master of the Rolls. He contrived to ingratiate himself equally with Lord Chancellor Rotheram, through whose interest he was translated to Worcester, and intrusted, for a short time, with the Great Seal, under the title of Chancellor.

Now was the triumph of his powers of insinuation and versatility; having been brought forward and employed by the House of York, and never having had any open rupture with Richard, he at once gained the confidence of Henry, who hardly ever favored any one who had neither fought with the Lancastrians ih the field, nor been engaged in plots to promote their ascendency.

There is no record of the day of the delivery of the Seal to him; but in the Parliament Roll of the 1st of Henry VII. it is stated, that "on the 7th of November, in the first year of the King's reign, the Reverend Lord

---

the people of England, for the first time since the Conquest, in their own language, and acts of parliament were for the first time printed.—Macpherson's *Annals of Commerce*, i. 704. But it would appear that they were still entered on the parliament roll in French.—*Tomlin's Ed. of Statutes*, 638.

[1] Rot. Pat. 1 Hen. 7, p. 1.

and Father in God John Alcock, Bishop of Worcester, CANCELLARIUS MAGNUS ANGLIÆ, declared the cause of summoning parliament."

Great reliance must have been placed on his learning and experience for settling the delicate points which were to be brought forward. One of these was the effect of the attainder, by a parliament of Richard, of a great number of the temporal Peers now summoned. Could they, at the commencement of the session, take their seats in the House of Lords? The Chancellor asked the opinion of the Judges, who held that they ought not to sit till their attainder had been reversed,—thereby recognizing the principle that "any statute passed by a parliament under a King *de facto* is ever after to be taken for law till repealed." But a more puzzling question arose as to the effect of the attainder of Henry himself, as Earl of Richmond; for how could this be reversed without an exercise of the prerogative in giving the royal assent? and could the royal assent be given till the outlawry was reversed? The Chancellor again consulted the Judges, and they cut the knot by unanimously resolving, "that the descent of the Crown itself takes away all defects, and stops in blood by reason of attainder," which has ever since been received as a maxim of constitutional law; and no doubt was relied upon by the Jacobites, who attempted to restore the Princes of the House of Stuart, attainted under King William, Queen Anne, and George I.

The Chancellor gave great satisfaction to his wary master by the dexterity with which he met such difficulties, and he was translated to the rich see of Ely as a reward for his services; but there does not seem to have been any intention to employ him after the new government was fairly started; and the King reserved his real confidence for JOHN MORTON, who had been in exile with him, who had been attainted for adhering to him, who had mainly contributed to his elevation, and whom he resolved to make his chief adviser for the rest of his reign. The exact date of the transfer of the Great Seal to him is unknown, as it is not recorded in the Close Roll; but it is supposed to have happened in August, 1487, and was certainly before November in that year, when there were

[1] Parl. Roll. 1 Hen, 7. 1 Parl. Hist. 450.

bills addressed to him as Chancellor, which are still extant.¹

Bishop Alcock, the Ex-Chancellor, lived in the enjoyment of his new diocese till the first of October, 1500; when, according to a quaint authority I have consulted, " he was translated from this to another life." He had in his latter days a great character for piety, abstinence, and other religious mortifications. He built a chapel at Beverly, founded a chantry to pray for the souls of his parents, and turned St. Rudegunda's old nunnery at Cambridge, founded by Malcolm, King of Scots, into the flourishing foundation of Jesus College.

In the two first reigns of the House of Tudor, the Great Seal may be considered in its greatest splendor; for the Chancellor was generally the first minister of the Crown, and by his advice the Lord Treasurer, and the other high officers of state, were appointed. Henry, whose darling object was to depress the powerful barons hitherto so formidable to his predecessors, was determined to rule by men more dependent on him than the nobility, who enjoyed, by hereditary right, possessions and jurisdictions dangerous to royal authority. The new Chancellor was, in all respects, such a man as the King wished for his minister.

JOHN MORTON was born in the year 1410, as Bere, in Dorsetshire, of a private gentleman's family. He received his earliest education at the Abbey of Cerne, whence he was removed to Baliol College, Oxford, where he devoted himself to the study of the civil and canon law, and took with great distinction the degree of LL.D. He then went to London, at all times the best field for talents and energy, and practiced as an advocate in Doctors' Commons. In the Court of Arches, and the other ecclesiastical Courts, there was then much business, producing both fame and profit; and success at the civil law bar frequently led to promotion both in church and state. Morton was soon the decided leader; and he rose to such distinction by his learning and eloquence, that he gained the good opinion of Cardinal Bourchier, Archbishop of Canterbury, who recommended him to Henry VI. He was sworn of the Privy Council by that Sovereign, was made

---

¹ See Philpot, p. 68. Rot. Parl. 3 Hen. 7.

Prebendary of Salisbury, and had the valuable living of Blakesworth bestowed upon him.

In the struggles which ensued between the rival families, he adhered with the most unshaken fidelity and unbounded zeal to the Lancastrian cause,—till Edward IV. was firmly seated on the throne,—when he thought it not inconsistent with the duties of a good citizen to submit to the ruling powers, without renouncing his former attachments. He petitioned for pardon at the same time as Fortescue. Edward was so much struck with his honorable conduct, that without requiring from him any unbecoming concessions, he continued him a Privy Councillor, appointed him Master of the Rolls,[1] conferred upon him great ecclesiastical preferment crowned with the Bishopric of Ely,—and, by his last will, made him one of his executors. Some of the biographers of Morton state, that he was likewise Lord Chancellor to Edward IV., but this is a mistake. In the year 1473, during the illness of Lord Chancellor Stillington, he for a short time was intrusted with the custody of the Great Seal, and no doubt did the duties of the office, but he then only acted as deputy to the Chancellor.

Being executor of Edward IV., and enjoying the entire confidence of the Queen, he had a sort of guardianship of the royal children, and Richard thought it would be a great point gained to corrupt him as he had corrupted Buckingham and others; but Morton rejected all his overtures with scorn and indignation, and thereby incurred the special hatred of the usurper.

On the very day when Rivers, Gray, and Vaughan, the Queen's relations, were executed by the orders of Richard at Pomfret, there was acted in the Tower of London the scene which is so admirably and truly described by our immortal dramatist. Morton, along with Hastings and the other councillors, took his place at the council-table, according to the summons sent to them,—when Richard, who was capable of committing the most bloody and treacherous murders with the utmost coolness and indifference, appearing among them in an easy and jovial humor, entered into familiar conversation with them before proceeding to business, and complimenting the Bishop on the good and early strawberries which he

[1] 1473.

raised in his garden at Holborn, he begged the favor of having a dish of them.[1] A messenger was immediately despatched for the fruit, but before he returned, Hastings was beheaded, and Morton was a close prisoner in the Tower.

The University of Oxford petitioned King Richard for Morton's liberation, saying, "the bowels of our mother the University, like Rachel weeping for her children, are moved with pity over the lamentable distress of this her dearest son. For if a pious affection be praiseworthy, even in an enemy, much more is it in our University, professing the study of all virtues. Upon the re-admittance of so great a prelate into your favor, who is there that will not extol your divine clemency? Thus gloried the Romans to have it marshalled among their praises that *submissive wights they spared, but crusht the proud.*"[2]

Richard would have cared little for these remonstrances; but lest the confinement of a popular prelate in the Tower might stir up a mutiny among the Londoners, he was given in ward to the Duke of Buckingham, and was shut up by him in the castle of Brecknock.[3] From this prison, however, he escaped, and after lying disguised for some time in the Isle of Ely, he contrived to pass beyond sea, and joined the Earl of Richmond. He was attainted by Richard's parliament which met soon after. He assisted in planning Richmond's invasion, and is said first to have suggested and pressed upon him the plan of putting an end to the civil wars by marrying Elizabeth, the daughter of Edward IV., who had become the heiress of the House of York.

He did not accompany Richmond's expedition, not

---

[1] "*Glo.* My Lord of Ely, when I was last in Holborn
I saw good strawberries in your garden there,—
I do beseech you, send for some of them.
"*Ely.* Marry, and will, my Lord, with all my heart.
* * * * * *
Where is my Lord Protector? I have sent
For these strawberries.
"*Hast.* His Grace looks cheerfully and smooth this morning:
There's some conceit or other likes him well
When he doth bid good-morrow with such spirit."
King Richard III. act iii. sc. 4.

[2] Ath. Ox. i. 640. "Parcere subjectis et debellare superbos."

[3] In Sir Thomas More's Life of Richard III. there is a very long and rather amusing, but evidently a fictitious dialogue, between Morton and the Duke of Buckingham, upon the character and conduct of the usurper.

being of the class of fighting bishops, now nearly extinct, but remained in the Netherlands to watch the event. Immediately after the battle of Bosworth, Henry recalled him,—on the death of Cardinal Bourchier, raised him to the see of Canterbury,—procured a Cardinal's hat for him from Pope Alexander VI.,—and now made him Lord Chancellor.

He continued in this office, and in the unabated favor and confidence of his royal master, down to the time of his death, a period of thirteen years; during which he greatly contributed to the steadiness of the government, and the growing prosperity of the country. Although he appeared merely to execute the measures of the King, he was in reality the chief author of the system for controlling the power of the great feudal barons, and he may be considered the model, as he was the precursor, of Cardinal Richlieu, who in a later age accomplished the same object still more effectually in France.

The first parliament at which he presided was that which met on the 3rd of November, 1488. Lord Bacon, in his "History of Henry VII.," gives a very long account of the speech delivered by the Lord Chancellor on this occasion. The custom of taking a text from the Holy Scriptures was dropped by him, and he rather conformed to the modern fashion of a King's speech, though with more of detail and of reasoning than would now be considered discreet on such an occasion. He thus begins :—

"My Lords and Masters, the King's Grace, our Sovereign Lord, hath commanded me to declare unto you the causes that have moved him at this time to summon this his parliament, which I shall do in few words, craving pardon of his Grace, and of you all, if I perform it not as I would. His Grace doth first of all let you know that he retaineth in thankful memory the love and loyalty shown to him by you at your last meeting in establishment of his royalty: freeing and discharging of his partakers and confiscation of his traitors and rebels ; more than which could not come from subjects to their Sovereign in one action. This he taketh so well at your hands, as he hath made it a resolution to himself to communicate with so loving and well approved subjects in all affairs that are of public nature at home or abroad. Two, therefore, are the causes of your present assembling ; the one a foreign business, the other matter of government at home. The French King (as no doubt you have heard) maketh at this present hot war upon the Duke of Brittaine."

He then enters at great length into the disputes between these two Princes, and the manner in which England was affected by them; whereupon the King prayed their advice, whether he should enter into an auxillary and defensive war for the Brittons against France, pretty clearly intimating an opinion, that this would be the expedient course, but stating that in all this business, the King remitted himself to to their grave and mature advice, whereupon he proposed to rely. He next comes to the government at home, and states, that no King ever had greater cause for the two contrary passions of joy and sorrow than his Grace,—joy in respect of the rare and visible favors of Almighty God in girding the imperial sword by his side,—sorrow for that it hath not pleased God to suffer him to sheathe it as he greatly desired, otherwise than for the administration of justice, but that he hath been forced to draw it so oft to cut off traitors and disloyal subjects. He then enters into topics of political economy, strongly inculcating the doctrine of *protection*, and above all exhorting parliament to take order that the country might not be impoverished by the exportation of money for foreign manufactures. He concludes by urging liberal supplies—

"The rather for that you know the King is a good husband, and but a steward in effect for the public, and that what comes from you is but as moisture drawn from the earth, which gathers into a cloud and falls back upon the earth again." [1]

On the recommendation of the Chancellor, several important statutes were passed for suppressing riots, and for the orderly government of the kingdom. Lord Bacon and Lord Coke particularly celebrate that contrived to extend the jurisdiction of the Star Chamber, which they call "a Court of Criminal Equity, and which, not being governed by any certain rules, they consider superior to any other Court to be found in this or any other nation. It was certainly found a very useful instrument of arbitrary government during the whole continuance of the Tudor dynasty; but its authority being still stretched in

[1] 1 Parl. Hist. 451.

opposition to a growing love of freedom, it mainly led to the unpopularity of the Stuarts and their expulsion from the throne.[1]

Another law of Morton's, of an extraordinary nature, respecting real property, was well adapted to the then existing state of affairs; but we must wonder that it should have been allowed to continue in force down to our times. From the attainders, forfeitures, and acts of violence which had prevailed during the wars of the Roses, property had changed hands so frequently that the title to it had become very uncertain, if it were to be traced backwards according to the common rules of conveyance and pedigree. A power was now given to a person in possession as owner of the fee to go through certain ceremonies in the Court of Common Pleas, and in five years after the time when these were concluded, his title was good against all the world.[2] Morton introduced several acts showing a great jealousy of foreigners, and particularly one, "for avoiding all Scottishmen out of England."

But the most important piece of legislation with which he was connected, was the famous statute protecting from the pains of treason all who act under a *de facto* King. On proofs which even stagger inquirers in our times, a belief had become very prevalent among the people, that the Duke of York, younger son of Edward IV., still survived, and the apprehension that, if he were restored, those who fought for the present King, whose title was so defective, might be tried for treason, or be attainted by act of parliament, deterred many from joining the royal standard. To meet this difficulty the Chancellor, in the parliament which assembled in October, 1497, introduced and passed an act,[3] that no person that did assist, in arms or otherwise, the King for the time being, should afterwards be impeached therefor, or attainted either by

---

[1] 3 Hen. 7, c. 1. I wish that there had been preserved to us the debates on the abolition of the Star Chamber. I make no doubt that its advocates ascribed to it all the prosperity and greatness of the country, and prophesied from its abolition the speedy and permanent prevalence of fraud, anarchy, and bloodshed in England.

[2] 4 Hen. 7, c. 24. This was repealed by an act which I had the honor to introduce, establishing twenty years as the uniform period of limitation, which before had in some cases been five years, and in others might extend to five hundred.   [3] 11 Hen. 7, c. 1.

the course of the law or by parliament ; but if any such attainder did happen to be made, it should be void and of none effect." "The spirit of this law," says Lord Bacon. "was wonderfully pious and noble; being like, in matter of war, unto the spirit of David in matter of plague, who said. *If I have sinned, strike me ; but what have these sheep done ?* Neither wanted this law parts of prudent and deep foresight, for it did the better take away occasion for the people to busy themselves to pry into the King's title ; for that howsoever it fell, their safety was already provided for." Had there been a counter-revolution, the law would probably have been very little regarded, and future parliaments would not have been bound by it. It has never been pleaded in a court of justice, unless by the regicides on the restoration of Charles II., who in vain contended that they came within the equity of it, having acted in obedience to an ordinance of the existing supreme power of the state. However, it still remains on the Statute-book, and we shall undoubtedly be entitled to the benefit of it if the Duke of Modena, the lineal heir of the monarchy, should be restored, notwithstanding our zealous defense of the throne of Queen Victoria.[1]

There are no other parliamentary proceedings of any interest connected with this Chancellor. His great effort was to extract subsidies from the Commons, and when he could not do this in a sufficient degree to satisfy the avarice of his royal master, who was now bent upon accumulating treasure as if it had been the chief end of government, he resorted to the most culpable expedients for levying money upon the subject. Notwithstanding the law of Richard III. so recently passed, forbidding, in the most express and emphatic language, any taxation without authority of parliament, and more particularly the tax called "a Benevolence,"—on pretense of a French war, he issued a commission for levying a "Benevolence" on the people according to their pecuniary ability ;—and that none might escape, he ingeniously instructed the commissioners to employ a dilemma in which every one might be comprehended: "If the persons applied to for the benevolence live frugally, tell them that their parsimony must necessarily have enriched them ; if their

[1] Hall Const. Hist. i. 12.

method of living be hospitable, tell them they must necessarily be opulent on account of their great expenditure." This device was by some called "Chancellor Morton's fork," and by others his "crutch."

Notwithstanding some discontents, there was perfect internal tranquillity during the administration of Morton, with the exception of the rebellion caused by the imposture of Lambert Simnel, which was wisely terminated by making the pretended Plantagenet a scullion in the King's kitchen.

In 1494, Morton's dignities were further increased by his being elected Chancellor of the University of Oxford.

But he became much broken by age and infirmities, and after a lingering illness he died on the 13th of September, 1500, leaving behind him, notwithstanding some arbitrary acts of government, which should be judged of by the standard of his own age, a high character for probity as well as talents. His munificence was great, and he was personally untainted by the vice of avarice which disgraced the Sovereign. Not only did he liberally expend money in raising early strawberries in Holborn, but the great cut or drain from Peterborough to Wisbech, now known as Morton's Leame, was made entirely at his expense while he was Bishop of Ely.[1] His literary attainments reflect still greater splendor upon him, and he is to be considered the author of the first classical prose composition in our language, if the supposition be well founded that the English Life of Richard III., usually attributed to Sir Thomas More, was written by his predecessor Chancellor Morton.

More had, when a youth, been brought up in his family as a page, and his Introduction to the Utopia has left us a very interesting, though rather flattering, character of his patron. "I was then much obliged to that reverend prelate, John Morton, Archbishop of Canterbury, Cardinal and Chancellor of England, a man who was no less venerable for his wisdom and virtue than for the high reputation he bore. He was of a middle stature, in advanced years, but not broken by age: his aspect begot reverence rather than fear. He sometimes took pleasure

[1] He likewise founded four scholarships in St. John's Hospital, which are now enjoyed by St. John's College, Cambridge.

to try the mental qualities of those who came as suitors to him on business, by speaking briskly though decorously to them, and thereby discovered their spirit and self-command; and he was much delighted with a display of energy, so that it did not grow up to impudence, as bearing a great resemblance to his own temperament, and best fitting men for affairs. He spoke both gracefully and mightily; he was eminently skilled in the law; he had a comprehensive understanding, and a very retentive memory; and the excellent talents with which nature had furnished him were improved by study and discipline. The King depended much on his counsels, and the government seemed to be chiefly supported by him; for from his youth he had been constantly practiced in affairs, and having passed through many changes of fortune, he had, at a heavy cost, acquired a great stock of wisdom, which, when so purchased, is found most serviceable." [1]

The day after the death of Cardinal Morton, the King sent messengers with a warrant to Knoll in Kent, where he expired, to bring the Great Seal to him at Woodstock.[2] His Majesty received it from them there on the 19th of September, and kept it in his own custody till the 13th of October following—much puzzled as to how he should dispose of it. He wished to pay the compliment to the Church of having an ecclesiastic for Chancellor, and there was no one at that time in whom he could place entire confidence as he had done in Morton, the companion of all his fortunes. He at last fixed upon HENRY DEANE, Bishop of Salisbury, as a safe if not very able man, and to him he delivered the Great Seal, but with the title of Keeper only.[3]

I do not find any trace of Deane's origin, or any account of him till he was at New College, Oxford. Here he was a diligent student, and before he left the University he took the degree of S. T. D.

In 1493 he was made Prior of Llanthony Abbey, in Monmouthshire; but he resided very little there, liking better to push his fortune at the court of Henry VII. He

---

[1] Utop. lib. i.
[2] The Seal is stated to have been found "apud Knoll, infra Hospicium dci nuper Cardinalis, in quadam alta camera ibidem vocat. *Le Rake chamber*, in quadam bega de albo :orio inclusum."—Rot. Cl. 16 Hen. 7.
[3] Rot. Cl. 16 Hen. 7.

continued to make himself useful to Cardinal Morton, by whose interest, in September, 1495, he was made Lord Chancellor of Ireland. I have not been able to find how his appointment was received in that country, or how he conducted himself there; but, more lucky than some of his successors, he held the office for two years, and only resigned it for a piece of preferment which brought him back to this island,—the Bishopric of Bangor. From that see he was translated, in 1500, to Salisbury. The experience he had as Chancellor in Ireland, was supposed to be the reason for his new elevation.

He continued to hold the Great Seal of England as Keeper during two years, decently discharging the duties of his office, but not rising in favor with the King, nor gaining much reputation with the public.

During this time no parliament sat. Instead of the good old custom of the Plantagenets to call these assemblies yearly, or oftener " if need were," the rule now laid down was to avoid them, unless for the purpose of obtaining money. The King was at first occupied with his inglorious French war, which, although he did once carry an army across the sea, he used as an instrument of extorting a pecuniary supply from the King of France, who was willing to buy him off on any terms, to be at liberty to prosecute his expedition into Italy, and claim the crown of Naples.

The Lord Keeper assisted in negotiating the treaty with Scotland, by which, after near two centuries of war, a perpetual peace was concluded between the two kingdoms, one of the articles being the marriage of Margaret, Henry's eldest daughter, with James, the Scottish King, which in another age brought about the union of the whole island under the House of Stuart.

But the court was soon thrown into mourning by the untimely death of Prince Arthur, a few months after the celebration of his marriage with Catherine of Aragon.

Before the question arose respecting Prince Henry's marriage with his brother's widow, Deane was removed from his office of Lord Keeper, and he escaped the responsibility of that inauspicious measure. In January, 1502, he was advanced to the archiepiscopal see of Canterbury, and feeling himself oppressed by his new duties, and his health declining, he resigned the Great Seal on the 27th of July following.[1] He died at Lambeth on the 15th of February, 1503, having displayed a mediocrity of talent and of character, neither to be greatly extolled not condemned.

The King seems again to have been at a loss to dispose of the Great Seal, as it was allowed to remain near a month in the keeping of Sir William Barons, the Master of the Rolls, who was a mere official drudge, and was restricted in the use of it to the sealing of writs, and the despatch of routine business.

At last, on the 11th of August, it was given to WILLIAM WARHAM, the Bishop of London,[2] well known in English history,—who retained it during the rest of this reign and the early years of the next,—till, his influence being undermined by the arts of a greater intriguer, it was clutched from him by the hand of Wolsey.

CHAPTER XXVI.

LIFE OF ARCHBISHOP WARHAM, LORD CHANCELLOR OF ENGLAND.

WILLIAM WARHAM was born at Okely, in Hampshire, of a small gentleman's family in that county. He studied at Winchester School, and afterwards at New College, Oxford, of which he was chosen fellow in 1475. Having greatly distinguished himself in the study of the civil and canon law, he took the degree of LL.D., and practiced as an advocate in the Court of Arches in Doctors' Commons. Following in the footsteps of Morton, he attacted the notice and gained the patronage of this prelate, who recommended him for employment to Henry VII. He was accordingly sent on a very delicate mission to the court of Burgundy, to remonstrate against the countenance there given to Perkin Warbeck, the pretended Duke of York, younger son of Edward IV. The Duchess of Burgundy, sister of Edward IV., had a deep dislike to Henry as a Lancastrian, and having

[1] Rot. Cl. 17 Hen. 7, n. 47.
[2] This ceremony took place at Fulham, under a warrant from the King, then at Langley, in the forest of Wychewoode.—Rot. Cl. 17 Hen. 7.

formerly patronized Lambert Simnel, now professed to receive Perkin as her nephew, and "the White Rose of England."

Hollinshead gives us an account of a speech supposed to have been delivered by the ambassador on his arrival at Bruges, in the presence of the Duchess as well as of the Duke; but from its very uncourtly terms, it must surely be the invention of the chronicler. "William Warram made to them an eloquent oration, and in the later end somewhat inveighed against the Ladie Margaret, not sparing to declare how she now, in her later age had brought foorth (within the space of a few yeares together) two detestable monsters, that is to saie, Lambert and this same Perkin Warbecke; and being conceived of these two great babes, was not delivered of them in 8 or 9 moneths, as nature requireth, but in 180 months, for both these, at the best, were fiftene yeeres of age yer she would be brought in bed of them, and shew them openlie; and when they were newlie crept out of hir wombe, they were no infants, but lustie yoonglings and of age sufficient to bid battel to kings. These tawnts angred the Ladie Margaret to the hart."[1]

Warham could not succeed in having Perkin delivered up or dismissed, but gained highly useful information respecting the Pretender's history and designs; and gave the King such satisfaction, that on his return he was made Master of the Rolls and Bishop of London. He continued at the Rolls nine years, during which time he had a seat at the council-board, and he was looked forward to by many as the successor of Morton in managing the civil affairs of the kingdom.

When he received the Great Seal he held it at first with the title only of Lord Keeper; and it was not till two years afterwards, when being translated to Canterbury, that he was invested with the full dignity of Lord Chancellor. His installation now took place with extraordinary pomp, the Duke of Buckingham, the first peer of the realm, acting as steward of his household.

Notwithstanding all the cares of the primacy, he applied very diligently to the discharge of his judicial duties. His experience as an advocate must now have been of essential advantage to him; and, besides being assisted

[1] Hollinsh. iii. 506.

by the Masters in Chancery, he prudently continued the practice of calling in the assistance of the common-law judges in all difficult cases. Thus without the appointment of any Vice-Chancellor or deputy, he contrived to keep down arrears of causes in his Court, and to give general satisfaction.

As a statesman he gained great credit by protesting against the proposed marriage between Prince Henry and the Princess Dowager of Wales, pointing out the objections to the legality of such a union, and the serious difficulties in which it might afterwards involve the affairs of the nation; but his advice was neglected on account of the cupidity of Henry, who was not only unwilling to refund that half of the lady's large dowry, which he had received, but was impatient to have the remaining half of it in his coffers.

Lord Chancellor Warham was not connected with any parliamentary proceedings of much importance during this reign. Henry, calling parliaments very rarely, when they did meet, had introduced the custom of opening the session with a speech of his own, instead of trusting to his Chancellor, and there was nothing like free discussion in either House while he was upon the throne.

With the assistance of Warham, and other such dexterous men whom Henry had selected for his tools, he contrived, in the latter part of his reign, to render himself nearly absolute. Thus, in his last parliament, the Commons being desired by the Chancellor to chose a Speaker, they found themselves under the necessity, on his recommendation, of electing Dudley, the Attorney General, who was then universally execrated, and who was afterwards hanged, to the great joy of the nation. The Chancellor confirmed the election with much commendation of the new Speaker.

Perkin Warbeck being taken, and the Earl of Warwick, the last male of the Plantagenet line, being murdered under the forms of law, there was a gloomy tranquillity at the conclusion of this reign, Henry leaving nothing to the Chancellor, or any of his Council, but the discharge of the routine duties of their office.

After the death of the Queen, the Court was a little amused by negotiations for a second marriage; but, on the 22nd of April, 1509, the selfish tyrant was carried off by a sudden fit of illness, in the fifty-second year of his age, and the twenty-fourth of his reign; and his courtiers and subjects did not affect to disguise their satisfaction at the event.

Although no transfer of the Great Seal immediately followed the demise of the Crown, we must here pause to take a short retrospect of jurisprudence during this reign. Although it be looked upon as an era in our annals, and the commencement of modern history, it was not marked by any important legislative acts, or by any change in the constitution of our tribunals, beyond the remodelling of the Star Chamber.[1]

Henry's common-law Judges were men of ability; but they rendered themselves most odious by their rigorous enforcement of obsolete laws, for the purpose of swelling the revenue.

The Chancellors exercised, without disturbance, the equity jurisdiction which had been so much attacked in preceding reigns; but we cannot much admire their reasoning in deciding the cases which came before them.

A judgment of Lord Chancellor Morton's may be given as a specimen. Two persons being appointed executors, one of them released a debt due to the testator without the assent of his companion, who filed a bill in Chancery, suggesting, that on this account the will could not be performed, and praying relief against the other executor and the debtor, to whom the release was granted. Objection was made that there was no ground for interference, as one executor, by the common law, may release a debt. *Archbishop Morton, Lord Chancellor.*—" It is against reason that one executor should have all the goods, and give a release by himself. I know very well that every law should be consistent with the law of God; and that law forbids that an executor should indulge any disposition he may have to waste the goods of the testator; and if he does, and does not make amends, if he is able, he shall be damned in hell."[2]

Equity decisions at this time depended upon each Chancellor's peculiar notions of the law of God, and the manner in which Heaven would visit the defendant for the acts complained of in the Bill; and though a rule is sometimes laid down as to where "a subpœna will lie," that is to say,

[1] 2 Hen. 7, c. 1.   [2] Y. B. 4 Hen. 7, 4, b.

where there might be relief in Chancery, it was not till long after that authorities were cited by Chancellors, or that there was any steady reference by them to "the doctrine of the Court."

In this reign no attention was paid to the improvement of the laws or the administration of justice, except with a view to extorting money from the subject and amassing treasure in the Exchequer, and the Chancellors were much employed in assisting inferior agents to enforce dormant claims of the Crown against the owners of estates, and in compelling corporations to accept new charters for the sake of fees.

A brighter prospect was now supposed to open on the nation. Instead of a monarch jealous, severe, and avaricious, who receded from virtue as he advanced in years, a young prince of eighteen had succeeded to the throne, who, even in the eyes of men of sense, gave promising hopes of his future conduct, and was possessed of qualifications in a high degree to dazzle and captivate the multitude. He nominally took upon himself the goverment without Protector or Regent, but Warham the Chancellor was supreme till superseded by the superior ascendency of Wolsey.

There is no memorandum of the delivery of the Great Seal by Henry VIII. to Warham, but there can be no doubt that he continued Chancellor from his appointment in the preceding reign until his resignation in the year 1515. He is said to have been now placed at the head of the Council, as the least unpopular of the ministers of the King, by the advice of Margaret Countess of Richmond, who still survived, and being much celebrated for prudence and virtue, had great influence over her royal grandson.

The Chancellor, in his capacity of Archbishop of Canterbury, placed the crown on Henry's head, and there being then no Prince of the blood, was the first subject in rank at the ceremony, uniting in himself the highest ecclesiastical and civil offices in the realm.

A great question immediately arose which divided the Council; and the Chancellor, adhering to his original opinion, stood alone against all the other members: this was the completion of the King's marriage with Catherine of Aragon, the widow of his brother, Prince Arthur. The virtues of the Princess and the advantages of the match were universally admitted; but Warham, as a churchman, still doubted its validity, and as a statesman, foresaw the momentous consequences of its being afterwards questioned, and therefore he now strongly remonstrated against it, though, if it should be broken off, a large dowry was to be returned, and the King of Spain, from being a firm and valuable ally, might be converted into a formidable and bitter enemy. Had the Chancellor's opinion prevailed, England might have remained a Roman Catholic country. But the Countess of Richmond took part with the majority;—Henry, not much inclined to this arrangement of convenience, thought he was bound to fulfill the promise given in his father's lifetime, —and the marriage took place which produced our boasted Reformation.

Things went on very smoothly with the Chancellor for some years. Not much to his credit, he concurred in the punishment of Empson and Dudley, whose obnoxious proceedings he had countenanced in the former reign, and for which indeed he was himself responsible, as being at the head of the administration of justice; but he did not choose to oppose the strong cry for their execution, and he saw them suffer for actual offenses to which he was privy, on a pretended charge of treason of which he must have known they were innocent.

Parliament assembling on the first of January, 1510, and the King being on the throne, the Chancellor by his command opened the session according to ancient fashion with a speech from the text,—"Deum timete, Regem honorificate."[1] After various commentaries upon fear and honor, he said it behoved Kings to govern wisely, and he explained the duties of the different officers trusted with the affairs of the public. The judges rightly and duly adminstering justice, he said, were the eyes of the commonwealth; the learned expositors of the law he styled the tongues of it. Others were the messengers of the government, as the sheriffs and magistrates of cities and counties; the former of which who did not execute their offices rightly he compared to Noah's raven. Others were the pillars of the government, as juries of twelve men are. "Lastly," says the reporter, "*cum magno audientium plausu*, he went upon the state of the whole king-

[1] 1 Parl. Hist. 575.

dom, and urged that it was the real interest of each separate body, spiritual, temporal, and commonalty, to unite in supporting the Crown; that justice, which is the queen of virtues may be auspicious in the nation; that both bishop and peer may join in reforming the errors of past times; in utterly abolishing all iniquitous laws; in moderating the rough and severe ones; in enacting good and useful statutes, and when made to see that they should be faithfully, honestly and inviolably observed;—which if this parliament will perform, then he affirmed there was no one could doubt but that God should be feared, the King honored, and for the future the Commonwealth served with good councillors every way useful to the King and kingdom.[1]

The great applause of the audience arose from the belief that the Chancellor, in his conclusion, alluded to the harsh laws and the harsh admininistration of them which had characterized the late reign. In a few days he carried through the House of Lords, the act for the attainder of Empson and Dudley, and it passed *nemine contradicente*.

Lord Chancellor Warham again opened the parliament which met on the 4th of February, 1512, with a speech in the King's presence from this text,—"Justitia et pax osculatæ sunt," in which, rather whimsically for an Archbishop, he explained how war was to be carried on successfully: "He added further what was absolutely necessary in those that took the field and hoped for victory, first, that they should walk in the ways of the Lord, and in him alone place their dependence;—that every man should keep the post he was ordered to,—and that each individual should be content with pay and should avoid plunder." On a subsequent day the Lord Chancellor went down to the Commons and made them another speech explaining the treacherous proceedings of the King of France, and pressing for a supply.[2]

The last parliament in which Warham presided, was that which met on the 5th of February, 1514, when he took for his text,—"Nunc Reges intelligite, erudimini qui judicatis terram." Having dwelt at great length on the duties of a King, "he added what qualities belonged also to good councillors, viz. that they should give such counsel as was heavenly, holy, honorable to the King and

[1] 1 Parl. Hist. 476. [2] Ibid. 479.

useful to the Commonwealth; that they should be speakers of truth and not flatterers; firm and not wavering, and neither covetous nor ambitious."¹

A Speaker being chosen and approved,—a few days afterwards the Lord Chancellor, attended by the Archbishop of York, the Bishops of Winchester and Durham, the Earl of Surrey, Lord Treasurer, with other Peers, went down to the House of Commons, and made another speech to induce them to grant a liberal supply. These visits appear to have been well taken by the Commons, instead of being treated as a breach of privilege, and they rescue the memory of Wolsey from the imputation of having done a violent and unprecedented act when, being Chancellor, he paid a visit to the Commons and remonstrated with them on their tardiness in voting money for the King's use,—which has been considered by some almost as great an outrage as that committed by Charles, when he burst into the House to arrest the five members in their places. On the present occasion Lord Chancellor Warham, to take advantage of national antipathy, and to stimulate the liberality of the Commons, told them " that the Scotch had lately at several times done great injuries to the King's subjects, both by land and sea, and were daily meditating more; by which attempts His Majesty, being sufficiently provoked, had determined to declare war against them." Therefore he exhorted the Commons "diligently to consider these things, and the King's necessary expenses in the defense of the kingdom."²

Soon after, he had a matter of great delicacy to decide in the Lords. Thomas Earl of Surrey, the eldest son of the Duke of Norfolk, being called to the Upper House in his father's lifetime, claimed there the precedence over all Earls, to which he was entitled out of parliament, a claim which was most resolutely resisted. Garter King at Arms and the other heralds were called in; but they declared that, " though well skilled in the genealogy of Peers,—as concerning superiority of seats in parliament they could not determine." Whereupon, the question was referred to the Lord Chancellor, who, after time taken to consider and negotiate between the parties, declared and decreed, " that the Earl of Surrey, with much humility and discretion, had agreed to content himself with his place in

¹ 1 Parl. Hist. 478. ² Ibid. 481.

parliament according to his creation, and not dignity; provided always, that his place of honor and dignity out of parliament should be reserved to him, and that, if hereafter any ancient records should be found in the Tower of London, or elsewhere, proving the said pre-eminent place in parliament to belong to the said Earl, then the said seat should be restored unto him, notwithstanding this present decree against him."[1] We need not wonder that great interest was taken in the controversy, and that no small discretion was required to bring it to a peaceable termination, when we remember that the claimant was warmly supported by his father, who was lately returned from Flodden Field, where, by his superior generalship, the King of Scotland and all the prime nobility of that kingdom had bit the dust, and the Scottish nation had sustained the most fatal defeat recorded in their annals.

This was the last memorable act of Warham, as Chancellor. He had for some time been carrying on an unequal contest which he could support no longer. Wolsey had completely established himself in the favor of the King, was already prime minister with unlimited power, and, having obtained a cardinal's hat, with the appointment of legate *à latere* from the Pope, even in ecclesiastical matters affected supremacy. Nothing in England was wanting to his ambition, except the possession of the Great Seal. Warham had conducted himself so unexceptionably, that there was great difficulty in forcibly depriving him of it, and Wolsey's policy therefore was by a series of affronts and disgusts to induce him to resign it. When they were together in public, he assumed greater state and splendor; he irregularly paraded the cross of York, in the province of Canterbury; he interfered with the patronage and the jurisdiction of the Great Seal; and he caused the retainers and officers of the Chancellor to be insulted.

Warham, conscious that it would be vain to appeal to the King, who was weary of his services, on the 22nd of December, 1515, resigned the Great Seal into his Majesty's hands, and the same day it was bestowed on the haughty Cardinal, who now possessed greater power than has ever belonged to any subject in England.

Warham left behind him in Westminster Hall a high

[1] 1 Parl. Hist. 482.

reputation for strictly watching over the administration of justice. It was said of him that "in his own Court no Chancellor ever discovered greater impartiality or deeper penetration of judgment, and that none of his predecessors who were ecclesiastics had equalled him in a knowledge of law and equity."[1]

He now wholly retired from politics, employing himself in the duties of his diocese and in literary pursuits, which he soon found more agreeable than judicial drudgery, or the anxieties of office. He not only resumed with ardor the studies in which he had once gained distinction, and which he had long been obliged to suspend, but he became famous as a patron of learning and the learned. So much was he now respected and admired, that he excited the envy of Wolsey, who, though himself in the possession of supreme power, still tried to vex and to humble him by extended usurpation on his metropolitan jurisdiction and increased insolence when they necessarily met. Wolsey, with legatine authority, acted as if he had actually worn the triple crown, and as if the Pope were vested with absolute authority to dispose of all ecclesiastical preferment in England, and to tyrannize both over the clergy and the laity. Warham, meek as he was, found himself bound to make complaint to the King, and to inform him of the discontents of the people. Henry displayed a gracious manner, professed his ignorance of the whole matter, and said, "The master of the house often knows least what is passing in it. But do you, father, go to Wolsey, and tell him if anything be amiss that he amend it." The royal command was obeyed, and an admonition so administered (as might have been expected), only served to augment Wolsey's enmity to Warham.

For years the Ex-Chancellor was obliged quietly to submit to the ill-usage he experienced; but at last, as the consequences of a measure which he himself had strenuously opposed, he had the satisfaction of seeing his rival disgraced and ruined. The controversy arose respecting the validity of the King's marrige with Catherine of Aragon. Along with all the English prelates, except Fisher, Bishop of Rochester, Warham concurred in the opinion that the Pope's license to permit a man to marry his brother's

[1] Stowe, 504.

widow was *ultra vires*, and that, the marriage being uncanonical, Henry was entitled to a divorce.

When Wolsey's duplicity and finesse at last terminated in his own downfall, it is said that the office of Chancellor was again offered to Warham; but that he declined it on account of his age and infirmities.[1] I doubt this offer; for Henry had now testified an inclination to break with Rome, and Warham openly declaring himself a champion of the papal see, had latterly shown himself adverse to the divorce, unless with the full consent of his Holiness.

He continued to live at a distance from the Court, and to associate with those who were for supporting the papal supremacy. Shortly before his death he even weakly countenanced the imposture or delusion of the Holy Maid of Kent. The vicar of the parish where she lived went to Warham, and having given him an account of Elizabeth's pretended revelations, wrought so far on the aged and superstitious Prelate, as to receive orders from him to watch her in her trances, and carefully to note down all her future sayings. The regard paid her by a person of such high rank, who was supposed to be very discerning from having so long held the office of Lord Chancellor, rendered her more than ever an object of attention, and persuaded the multitude that her ravings were the inspirations of Heaven,—till the fraud was exposed in the Star Chamber, and she and her chief associates were hanged at Tyburn. No attempt was made to include Warham in the prosecution.

In 1532, he died at St. Stephen's, near Canterbury; and according to her own desire, without funeral pomp was buried in a small chapel which he had erected in the cathedral for his tomb.

When on his death-bed, he asked his steward what money he had in the world, and was answered, "Thirty pounds:" he exclaimed, "Satis viatici in cœlum." His effects were found hardly sufficient to pay his debts and the small expense of his funeral.

His great glory was his connection with ERASMUS. He had early formed a friendship with this distinguished scholar—had constantly corresponded with him—had induced him to visit England—had given him church preferment here,—and had made him munificent presents.

[1] Erasmus, Ep. 1151.

Erasmus showed his gratitude by dedicating to his patron his Edition of the works of St. Jerom, in terms the most flattering; and by celebrating his praises in letters addressed to literati on the Continent of Europe. I offer the translation of one of these written shortly after the Archbishop's death, as the best account of his character and his manners:—

"I have the most tender recollection of a man worthy to be held in perpetual honor, William Warham, Archbishop of Canterbury, and Primate of all England. He was a theologian in reality as well as by title, and profoundly versed both in the civil and canon law. He early gained reputation by his skillful conduct of foreign embassies intrusted to him; and, on account of his consummate prudence, he was much beloved and esteemed by King Henry VII. Thus he rose to be Archbishop of Canterbury, the highest ecclesiastical dignity in the island. Bearing this burden, itself very weighty, one heavier still was imposed upon him. He was forced to accept the office of Chancellor, which among the English is attended with regal splendor and power. As often as he goes into public, a crown and sceptre are carried before him.[1] He is the eye, the mouth-piece, and the right hand of the Sovereign; and the supreme judge of the whole British empire. For many years, Warham executed the duties of this office so admirably, that you would have supposed he was born with a genius for it, and that he devoted to it the whole of his time and thoughts. But all the while he was so constantly watchful and attentive with respect to religion, and all that concerned his ecclesiastical functions, that you would have supposed he had no secular cares. He found leisure for the strict performance of his private devotions—to celebrate mass almost daily—to hear prayers read several times a day—to decide causes in his Court —to receive foreign ministers—to attend cabinets—to adjust all disputes which arose in the church—to give dinners to his friends, whom he often entertained in parties of two hundred—and, along with all this, for reading all the interesting publications which appeared. He proved himself sufficient for such multiplicity of avocations, by wasting no portion of his time on his spirits in field sports,

---

[1] I presume the purse and the mace. Erasmus may have seen Wolsey with his crosses, pillars, and poll-axes.

or in gaming, or in idle conversation, or in the pleasures of the table, or in any profligate pursuit. His only relaxation was pleasant reading, or discoursing with a man of learning. Although he had bishops, dukes, and earls at his table, his dinners never lasted above an hour. He appeared in splendid robes becoming his station; but his tastes were exceedingly simple. He rarely suffered wine to touch his lips; and when he was turned of seventy, his usual beverage was small beer, which he drank very sparingly. But while he himself abstained from almost everything at table, yet so cheerful was his countenance, and so festive his talk, that he enlivened and charmed all who were present. He was the same agreeable and rational companion at all hours. He made it a rule to abstain entirely from supper; yet if his friends (of whom I had the happiness to be one) were assembled at that meal, he would sit down along with them and promote their conviviality, but would hardly touch any food himself. The hour generally devoted to supper he was accustomed to fill up with prayers or reading, or with telling witty stories, of which he had great store, or freely exchanging jests with his friends, — but ever without ill-nature or any breach of decorum. He shunned indecency and slander as one would a serpent. So this illustrious man made the day, the shortness of which many allege as a pretext for their idleness, long enough for all the various public and private duties he had to perform."[1]

Warham was much flattered by the compliments which in his lifetime he knew that Erasmus had paid him, and thus expresses his acknowledgments :—

"Since through you I am to enjoy lasting fame, a boon denied to many great kings and commanders who have utterly vanished from the memory of mankind, unless that their names may be found in some dry catalogue,—I know not what in this mortal life I can offer you in return for the immortality you have conferred. I am overwhelmed when I think of the flattering mention you have made of me in conversation, in letters, and in the works you have given to the world. You would set me down for

---

[1] Erasmus likewise delivers an elaborate panegyric on Warham in his Commentary on 1 Thess. ii. 7, and several of his other letters, but without descending to such interesting particulars of his private life as are here disclosed.

the most ungrateful of men if I did not show a deep sense of your kindness, however unworthy I may be of the praises you have showed upon me."[1]

Although Warham does not occupy the great space in the eye of posterity which he had fondly anticipated, he must be regarded with respect as a man who had passed through the highest offices with general applause,—and who, if he did not by any extraordinary talents influence the events of his age and improve the institutions of his country, could not be accused of any public delinquency, or (the prosecution of Empson and Dudley excepted) of ever having treated any individual with injustice.

CHAPTER XXVII.

LIFE OF CARDINAL WOLSEY FROM HIS BIRTH TILL HIS APPOINTMENT AS LORD CHANCELLOR.

WE now come to the life of the man who enjoyed more power than any of his predecessors or successors who have held the office of Chancellor in England.

THOMAS WOLSEY, destined to be Archbishop of York, Legate à latere, Lord Chancellor, and for many years master of the King and kingdom, was born at Ipswich, in Suffolk, in the year 1471, and though "fashioned to much honor," was "from an humble stock," being the son of a butcher in that town.[2]

---

[1] "Quum non illaudati nominis æternitatem per te sim consecutus, qua multi præclari reges et imperatores carent, et a memoria hominum penitus exciderunt, nisi quod tantum vix nominum eorum catalogus, et id jejune quidem fiat, non video quod satis sit in hac mortali vita quod pro immortalitate reddam. Cogito enim quanta mihi tribueris ubique, vel præsens per colloquia, vel absens per literas, aut communiter per volumina: quæ quidem sunt majora, quam sustinere valeam. Judicabis ergo Cantuariensem ingratissimum nisi tui sit habiturus rationem constantissimam, licet meritis inæqualem et inferiorem."—A.D. 1516.

[2] Some of his admirers have, without reason, questioned the particular vocation of his father; for that he was the son of a low tradesman in a country town is admitted. It cannot detract from his merit that his father was a butcher, and the fact stands on strong evidence. In his own lifetime he was called "the butcher's dog;" and Shakspeare, who must have conversed with

From his cradle he is said to have given signs of those lively parts which led to his buoyant career, but we possess no particulars of his early domestic life to throw light on the formation of his character; and, till he was sent to the University, nothing has reached us respecting his studies, except a statement that the indications of genius he displayed induced some of his townsmen to assist his father in maintaining him at Oxford. He was entered of Magdalen College when still of tender years, and he made such proficiency that, when only fifteen, he took his Bachelor's degree with great distinction, gaining the honorable soubriquet of "the boy Bachelor." In the very zenith of his fortune he used to boast with laudable

persons who well recollected the Cardinal, puts these words in the mouth of Buckingham:—

> "This butcher's cur is venom-mouth'd, and I
> Have not the power to muzzle him."

His origin from the "boucher's stall" is distinctly averred in the contemporary satire of "Mayster Skelton, poete laureate:"—

> "He regardeth Lordes
> No more than pot shordes,
> He ruleth al at will
> Without reason or skyll,
> Howbeit they be prymordyall:
> Of his wretched originall,
> And his base progeny,
> And his gresy genealogy,
> He came out of the sanke roiall
> *That was cast out of a boucher's stall.*"

Luther, in his Colloquies, calls him "a butcher's son." Polydore Virgil speaks of his father as "a butcher;" and Fuller, in his Church History, observes that "to humble the Cardinal's pride, some person or other had set up in a window belonging to his college, at Oxford, a painted mastiff dog gnawing the spade bone of a shoulder of mutton, to remind him of his extraction." Godwyn says, "Patre lanio pauperculo prognatus est." If his father had been of any other trade, the fact might have been easily established; but Cavendish, his gentleman usher and biographer, who must have heard the assertion hundreds of times, is contented with saying that "he was an honest poor man's son," and the only supposed contradiction is the father's will, showing that he had houses and property to dispose of, which he might as well have acquired by slaughtering cattle, as by any other occupation.—The will shows him to have been a very pious Christian. After leaving his soul to "Almighty God, our Lady Sent Mary, and to all the company of Hevyn," he says, "itm, I wyll that if Thomas my son be a prest witn a yer next after my decesse, yan I wylle that he syng for me and my frends be the space of a yer, and he for to haue for his salary x marc." The will bears date September, 1486, and was proved in the month of October following. The testator signs himself Robert *Wuley*, and by this name the son was known, till he changed it *euphoniæ causâ*.

vanity of this appellation, as the best proof of his early devotion to literature.

At an early age he was elected a fellow of Magdalen, and there being a school connected with the college, according to the usage then prevailing, he was appointed head master. He dedicated himself with much diligence and success to the duties of this humble office. While so occupied, he formed an acquaintance with Sir T. More, then an undergraduate, and with Erasmus, who had taken up his residence at Oxford.

The probability at this time was, that he would spend the rest of his days in the University, and that his ambition (which could not have aspired higher) might be crowned with the headship of his college. But it so happened that he had for pupils three sons of the Marquess of Dorset, and during a Christmas vacation he accompanied them to the country seat of their father. Wolsey was now in his twenty-ninth year, of great acquirements, both solid and ornamental,—remarkably handsome in his person, insinuating in his manners, and amusing in his conversation. The Marquess was so much struck with him, that he at once proferred him his friendship, and as a token of his regard presented him to the rectory of Lymington, in Somersetshire, which then happened to fall vacant.[1] Wolsey accordingly took orders, and was instituted parson of this parish on the 10th of October, 1500. He immediately renounced his school and other college appointments,—the more readily on account of a charge brought against him, that he had misapplied the college funds. While bursar he had erected the tower of Magdalen College chapel, known by the name of "Wolsey's Tower," still admired for the chaste simplicity and elegance of its architecture, and he was accused of having clandestinely diverted a portion of the revenue, over which his office of bursar gave him control, to the expense of this edifice,—a heinous offense in the eyes of the fellows, while lamenting their diminished dividend. He certainly seems to have been betrayed into considerable irregularity in this affair from his passion for building, which

[1] It has been denied that there is any place of this name in Somersetshire, and the locality has been changed in a very arbitrary manner to Hampshire; but I have ascertained that there is a very small parish called Lymington, near Ilchester, in Somersetshire,—with the *stocks* still standing near the church.

adhered to him through life; but there is no reason to suspect that he derived any pecuniary advantage from it.

Suddenly emerging from the cloisters of Magdalen, in which he had been hitherto immured,—when he took possession of his living, he seems for a time to have indulged in levities not becoming his sacred calling. By his dissolute manners, or perhaps by his superior popularity, he incurred the displeasure of Sir Amyas Paulet, a neighboring justice of the peace, who lay by for an opportunity to show his resentment. This was soon afforded him. Wolsey being of "a free and sociable temper," went with some of his neighbors to a fair in an adjoining town, where they all got very drunk, and created a riot. Sir Amyas, who was present, selected " his Reverence " as the most guilty, and convicting him " *on the view*," ordered him to be set in the stocks, and actually saw the sentence carried into immediate execution. " Who," says Cavendish, in relating this adventure, " would have thought then that ever he should have attained to be Chancellor of England ! These be wonderful works of God and fortune."[1]

Wolsey afterwards had his revenge of Sir Amyas. " For when the schoolmaster mounted the dignity to be Chancellor of England, he was not oblivious of the old displeasure ministered unto him by Master Pawlet, but sent for him, and after many sharp and heinous words, enjoined him to attend upon the Council until he were by them dismissed, and not to depart without license upon an urgent pain and forfeiture."[2] According to this writer,—for having so affronted the country parson, " Sir Amyas was in reality detained a prisoner in his lodging, in the Gate House of the Middle Temple, next to Fleet Street, for the space of five or six years, although he attempted to appease the Chancellor's displeasure by re-edifying the house, and garnishing the outside thereof sumptuously with hats and arms, badges and cognizances of the Cardinal, with other devices in glorious sort." This anecdote, which rests on undoubted testimony, is not very honorable to Wolsey, who, even if he had been wrongfully put in the stocks, ought not, when Chancellor, to have perverted the law to revenge the wrongs of the country parson. The discipline he then underwent seems

[1] Cavendish, 69.   [2] Ibid. 68.

to have had a salutary effect upon him; for although he did not by any means reform so far as to become faultless in his manners, we do not find him afterwards guilty of any public breach of decorum.

This mischance happened when Wolsey had been about two years resident at Lymington, and he soon after left the country,—as some assert from the scandal it had caused,—but I believe from the necessity he felt of finding a new patron, the Marquess of Dorset, to whom he looked for promotion, having suddenly died. We may suppose that, conscious of his powers, he was glad to leave this rural retreat where they could so little be appreciated. Storer, who published his biographical poem of Wolsey in 1599, describes his feelings on this occasion with some felicity:—

> " This silver tongue methought was never made
>   With rhetoric's skill to teach each common swain;
> These deep conceits were never taught to wade
>   In shallow brooks; nor this aspiring vein
>   Fit to converse among the shepherd train.
> " Just cause I saw my titles to advance,
>   Virtue my gentry, priesthood my descent,
> Saints my allies, the cross my cognizance,
>   Angels the guard that watch'd about my tent,
>   Wisdom that usher'd me where'er I went."

He was soon received as chaplain in the family of Deane, Archbishop of Canterbury,—a proof that his fame had not sustained any permanent blemish, and he was gaining the goodwill of those around him when he was again thrown upon the world by the death of the primate.

However, he was almost immediately after engaged as domestic chaplain by Sir John Nanfant, "a very grave and ancient knight," a special favorite of Henry VII. Sir John held the important office of Treasurer of Calais, and Wolsey now behaved himself so discreetly, that he obtained the special favor of his new master, and all the charge of the office was committed to him. He resided for a considerable time at Calais, and must have materially improved his knowledge of mankind by the variety of company with whom he here mixed. But he panted still for a larger sphere of action, and, through the interest of his employer he was at last gratified with the appointment of chaplain to the King, and he was transferred to the Court. " He cast anchor in the port of promotion,' says his biographer, or rather, he "got his foot in the stirrup resolved to outstrip every competitor in the race."

He had now occasion to be in the presence of the King daily celebrating mass before him in his private closet, and he afterwards gave attendance upon the courtiers who he thought bore most rule in the Council and were highest in favor. These were Fox, Bishop of Winchester, Secretary and Lord Privy Seal, and Sir Thomas Lovel, Master of the King's wards and Constable of the Tower. They soon perceived his merit, and were disposed to avail themselves of his services. He is said now to have displayed that "natural dignity of manner or aspect which no art can imitate, and which no rule or method of practice will ever be able to form."[1] He was eminently favored by nature in dignity of person, and winning expression of countenance. According to Cavendish, he was celebrated for "a special gift of natural eloquence, with a filed tongue to pronounce the same, so that he was able to persuade and allure all men to his purpose;" or, in the words of Shakespeare, he was "exceedingly wise, fair spoken, and persuading." He had, besides, a quick and correct perception of character, and of the secret springs of action, and a singular power of shaping his conduct and conversation according to circumstances. The consequence was, that, placed among men of education and refinement, he seemed to exercise an extraordinary influence over them, amounting almost to fascination,—and this influence was not the less powerful and enduring, that before superiors it was unostentatious, and seemed to follow where it led the way. Fitting himself to the humors of all, we need not doubt that, with the cold-blooded, calculating, avaricious founder of the Tudor dynasty, he tried to make himself remarkable for the laborious assiduity, regularity, steadiness, and thriftiness of his habits.

However he did not contrive to make any progress in the personal intimacy of Henry, till he was recommended to him by Fox and Lovel to conduct a delicate negotiation, in which the King took a very lively interest, and which he was desirous to see brought to a speedy conclusion.

[1] Fiddes' Life of Wolsey, p. 11.

Henry was a widower, with one surviving son and two daughters, and being only fifty years of age, he wished to enter into another matrimonial alliance, in the hope of strengthening the succession in his dynasty;—regardless of the question as to the right to the throne, which, if his son by Elizabeth, the daughter of Edward IV., should die without issue, might arise between a son by a second marriage, and his eldest daughter of the first marriage, who would have been "the white Rose of England." The object of his suit was Margaret, Duchess dowager of Savoy, only daughter of the Emperor Maximilian. They having been sounded, were not unfavorable to the alliance, and it was necessary to employ a person of great address to adjust with the Emperor in person some delicate matters connected with the marriage. Wolsey being pointed out by Fox and Lovel, the King, who as yet had scarcely ever personally conversed with him, "and being a Prince of excellent judgment, commanded them to bring his chaplain whom they so much commended before his Grace's presence. At whose repair thither, to prove the wit of his chaplain, the King fell in communication with him, in matters of weight and gravity, and perceiving his art to be very fine, thought him sufficient to be put in trust with this embassy."[1]

While the preparations were going forward, "he had a due occasion to repair from time to time to the King's presence, who perceived him more and more to be a very wise man and of good intendment."[2]

Wolsey, having at last got his dispatches from the wary monarch, performed the journey with a celerity which even astonishes us, accustomed to steam packets and railways, and which in that slow-travelling age must have appeared almost as marvelous as the boasted exploit of Puck.[3] The Court was then at Richmond, and there taking leave of the King after dinner he arrived in London on a Sunday afternoon about four o'clock. The Gravesend barge was ready to sail with a prosperous tide and wind, and by her he arrived at Gravesend in little more than three hours. There he tarried only till post-horses were provided, and traveling all night he came to Dover next morning, just

---

[1] Cavendish, 10. [2] Ibid. 12.
[3] "I'll put a girdle round about the earth
In forty minutes."—*Shaksp.*

as the passage boat for Calais was about to sail. He stepped on board, and in less than three hours he landed at Calais. Here he immediately got post-horses, and galloping off he arrived that night at Bruges, where the Imperial Court lay. Maximilian, "whose affection for Henry VII. was such that he rejoiced when he had occasion to show him pleasure," received the ambassador forthwith, and the next day he was despatched with all the King's requests fully accomplished. He was conducted back to Calais with such a number of horsemen as the Emperor had appointed, and arrived at that city at daybreak, as the gates were opened. The passage boat for England was about to sail, and before ten o'clock on Wednesday forenoon he was at Dover. He had ordered post-horses to be in readiness for him, and that night he reached Richmond. He now took some repose, but rising early next morning he knelt before the King going from his bed-chamber to his closet to hear mass. The King saw him with some surprise and displeasure, and *checked* him for not having set out on his journey. "Sir," quoth he, "if it may stand with your Highness's pleasure, I have already been with the Emperor, and despatched your affairs, I trust, to your Grace's contention." Thereupon he delivered to the King the Emperor's letters. The King demanded of him whether he encountered not his pursuivant whom he had sent after him yesterday, supposing him to be scarcely out of London, with letters concerning an important matter neglected in his commission and instructions which he courted much to be sped. "Yes, forsooth, Sire," quoth he, "I encountered him yesterday by the way, and having no information by your Grace's letters of your pleasure therein, had notwithstanding been so bold upon mine own discretion (perceiving that matter to be very necessary) to despatch the same. And for as much as I exceeded your Grace's commission I most humbly require your gracious remission and pardon." The King rejoicing, replied,—"We do not only pardon you thereof, but also give you our princely thanks, both for the proceeding therein, and also for your good and speedy exploit,"—commanding him for that time to take his rest, and to repair again to him after dinner, for the farther relation to his embassy. At the appointed time he reported his embassy to the King and Council with such a graceful deportment, and so eloquent language, that he received the utmost applause,—all declaring him to be a person of so great capacity and diligence that he deserved to be farther employed.[1]

The deanery of Lincoln, reckoned one of the most valuable preferments in the church, was immediately bestowed upon him; he was marked as a rising favorite—and, had the King's life been prolonged, there can be no doubt that, accommodating himself to his inclinations, Wolsey would have been promoted under him to the highest offices both civil and ecclesiastical.

But Henry, meditating his second marriage, was attacked by a disease which carried him to the tomb, and Wolsey had to concert fresh plans for his own advancement under a new monarch, only eighteen years of age, gay and folicsome, fond of amusement and averse to business, though not unitiated in the learning of the schools. The royal chaplain, while resident at Court, must have seen the Prince from time to time, but hitherto had made no acquaintance with him,—cautious in showing any accordance with the tastes of the son, lest he should give umbrage to the father.

It luckily happened that the young Marquess of Dorset had been a very intimate friend of Prince Henry, and by his former pupil he was introduced to the new King. This introduction is usually attributed to Bishop Fox, who, jealous of his rival, the Earl of Surrey, the late King's High Treasurer, is supposed to have intended Wolsey as an instrument to keep up the interest of his own party at Court; but in reality all the old ministers had penetrated the Dean of Lincoln's character, and become jealous of his influence.

Wolsey at once conformed to the tastes of the youthful Sovereign, and won his heart. He jested, he rallied, he sang, he danced, he caroused with the King and his gay

[1] Cavendish declares that he had all these circumstances, as above related, from Wolsey's own mouth, after his fall.—Life, p, 78. Storer's metrical Life of Wolsey has the following stanza on this expedition:—
"The Argonautic vessel never past
 With swifter course along the Colchian main,
 Than my small bark with small and speedy blast
 Conveyed me forth and reconvey'd again;
 Thrice had Arcturus driven his rolless wain,
 And Heaven's bright lamp the day had thrice reviv'd,
 From first departure till I last arriv'd.

comp᾽, 1ions, and in a very short time, by his extraordinary address, he not only supplanted Surrey in the royal favor, but also Fox his patron. He was sworn a Privy Councilor, and appointed King's almoner, an office which kept him in constant attendance on the person of the Monarch in his hours of relaxation, and thereby enabled him to acquire over the mind of Henry an ascendency which was imputed to the practice of the magical art. It is said, however, that although Wolsey, for the purposes of ambition, countenanced irregularities at Court unsuitable to the presence of a priest, he was careful, when any proper opportunity offered, to give good advice to the King, as well in respect to his personal as his political conduct, and highly tending on both accounts to his advantage and improvement. He would instil into his mind a lesson on the art of government over a game at primero, and after a roistering party with him at night, he would hold with him in the morning a disputation on a question out of Thomas Aquinas.

As yet without any higher appointment about the Court than that of Almoner, he soon made himself Prime Minister, and exercised supreme power in the state. "The King was young and lusty, disposed to all mirth and pleasure, and to follow his desire and appetite, nothing minding to travail in the busy affairs of the realm; the which the Almoner perceiving very well, took upon him therefore to disburden the King of so weighty a charge and troublesome business, putting the King in comfort that he shall not need to spare any time of his pleasure for any business that necessarily happens in the Council as long as he being there, and, having the King's authority and commandment, doubted not to see all things sufficiently furnished and perfected, wherewith the King was wonderfully pleased. And whereas the other ancient councillors would, according to the office of good councillors, persuade the King to have some time and intercourse into the Council, there to hear what was done in weighty matters, the which pleased the King nothing at all, for he loved nothing worse than to be constrained to do any thing contrary to his royal will and pleasure, and that knew the Almoner very well, having a secret intelligence of the King's natural inclination, and so fast as the other councillors advised the King to leave his pleasures and to attend to the affairs of the realm, so busily did the Almoner persuade him to the contrary, which delighted him much, and caused him to have the greater affection and love for the Almoner."[1]

Wolsey pushed his advantages; and not contented with secret influence, was determined to chase from office those to whom the public had looked with respect as the ministers of the Crown, and openly to engross all power in his own person. He observed to the King, that while he intrusted his affairs to his father's councillors, he had the advantage of employing men of wisdom and experience, but men who owed not their promotion to his own personal favor, and who scarcely thought themselves accountable to him for the exercise of their authority;—that by the factions, and cabals, and jealousies which prevailed among them, they more obstructed the advancement of his affairs than they promoted it, by the knowledge which age and practice had conferred upon them;—that while he thought proper to pass his time in those pleasures to which his age and royal fortune invited him, and in those studies which would in time enable him to sway the sceptre with absolute authority, his best system of government would be, to intrust his authority into the hands of some *one person* who was the creature of his will, and who could entertain no view but that of promoting his service;—and that if the minister had also the same relish for pleasure with himself, and the same taste for literature, he could more easily, at intervals, account to him for his own conduct, and introduce his master gradually into the knowledge of public business, and thus, without tedious restraint or application, initiate him in the science of government.'

Henry said, he highly approved of this plan of administration, and that he knew no one so capable of executing it as the person who proposed it. The two rival ministers of Henry VII., the Duke of Norfolk and Bishop Fox,—who had been continued in office by the advice of Margaret, Countess of Richmond, the young King's Grandmother,—were now treated with neglect and disrespect, and retired from Court. "Thus," says Cavendish, "the Almoner ruled all them that before ruled him; such things did his policy and wit bring to pass. Who was now in

[1] Cavendish, 82.   [1] Lord Herbert, Pol. Virg.

high favor but Master Almoner? Who had all the suit but Master Almoner? And who ruled all under the King but Master Almoner? Thus he proceeded still in favor. At last, in came presents, gifts, and rewards so plentifully, that he lacked nothing that might either please his fantasy or enrich his coffers."

The first earnest of Henry's bounty to his favorite was the grant, on the attainder of Epsom, of a magnificent mansion, with gardens, in Fleet Street which had belonged to that minister. He was soon after made Canon of Windsor, Registrar and Chancellor of the Order of the Garter, and Reporter of the proceedings in the Star Chamber, and various rectories, prebends, and deaneries were conferred upon him,—having obtained an unlimited dispensation from the Pope to hold pluralities in the church. On the resignation of the Duke of Norfolk, in 1512, he was made Lord Treasurer,—and, with the exception of Warham, the Lord Chancellor, who still carried on an unequal struggle against his ascendency, all who filled the offices of state were his creatures and dependents.

The Life of Wolsey henceforth becomes the History of England and of the European states; but I propose to confine myself to those events and circumstances which may be considered to belong to his personal narrative.[1]

In the year 1513, Henry going to war with France, Wolsey was specially appointed by him to direct the supplies and provisions for the use of the army,—or "Commissary General,"—a situation which gave him an opportunity of amassing great wealth, and which, though seemingly inconsistent with his clerical functions, he justified himself for accepting, on the ground that the Pope

[1] "The variety and splendor of the lives of such men render it often difficult to distinguish the portion of time which ought to be admitted into history, from that which should be reserved for biography. Generally speaking, these two parts are so distinct and unlike, that they cannot be confounded without much injury to both; either when the biographer hides the portrait of the individual by a crowded and confined picture of events, or when the historian allows unconnected narratives of the lives of men to break into the thread of history. Perhaps nothing more can be universally laid down than that the biographer never ought to introduce public events except as far as they are absolutely necessary to the illustration of character, and that the historian should rarely digress into biographical particulars, except as far as they contribute to the clearness of his narrative of political occurrences."—Sir James Mackintosh.

approved of the expedition against Louis XII., then at enmity with the See of Rome.

He accompanied the King to the Continent, witnessed the battle of "the Spurs," and assisted at the siege of Tournay. When the city surrendered, it was found that the Bishop had lately died, and that a new Bishop had been elected by the chapter, but had not yet been installed. Henry claimed by right of conquest the disposal of the office, appointed Wolsey to it, and put him in immediate possession of the temporalities.

This step was directly at variance with the canons of the church, and at another time would have been resented by the supreme Pontiff as a sacrilegious usurpation. Wolsey became Bishop *de facto*, but his title to the see was afterwards questioned, and was made the subject of long and intricate negotiations.

On his return to England he was legitimately placed in the episcopal order, by being elected and consecrated Bishop of Lincoln. He is reproached for having been guilty of great rapacity in seizing the goods which had belonged to his predecessor, Bishop Smith; and his gentleman usher is obliged to admit that he had frequently seen with shame some of the stolen furniture of the late Bishop in the house of his master.[1]

A few months after, Bambridge, Archbishop of York, dying, Wolsey was elevated to this archiepiscopal see. He was farther allowed to unite with York—first the see of Durham, and next that of Winchester. He farmed besides, on very advantageous terms, the Bishoprics of Bath, Worcester, and Hereford, filled by foreigners who gladly compounded for the indulgence of residing abroad by yielding up to him a large share of their English incomes. The rich Abbey of St. Alban's, and many other church preferments, he held *in commendam*.

There was only one individual in the kingdom on whom he now looked with envy, Warham, who, as Archbishop of Canterbury and Lord Chancellor, had precedence of him both ecclesiastically and civilly; but though he could not aim at the primacy during the life of his rival, he resolved that he himself should be the first subject under the King in rank as well as in power.

Pope Julius II., styled the "Incendiary of Christen-

[1] Cavendish, 88.

dom," being dead, he was succeeded by the celebrated Leo X., who closely resembled Wolsey in the love of pleasure and love of literature, and was desirous of cultivating the friendship of England against the ambition of France. One of his first acts was to confer a Cardinal's hat on the favorite of Henry, with a Bull creating him Legate *à latere* over the whole kingdom of England, and enabling him to call convocations, and to exercise supreme ecclesiastical authority. The Pope's messenger, conveying the emblems of spiritual precedence and authority, was met on Blackheath by "a great assembly of prelates, and lusty gallant gentlemen, and from them conducted through London with great triumph." The new Cardinal and Legate was confirmed in his dignity in Westminster Abbey by a numerous band of Bishops and Abbots, in rich mitres, copes, and other ornaments, "which," says Cavendish, "was done in so solemn a wise as I have not seen the like, unless it had been at the coronation of a mighty prince or king."[1]

He was now armed with effectual means of annoying and mortifying Warham. As Cardinal he took place of him,[2] and as Legate he was entitled to interfere with his jurisdiction within the province of Canterbury. "Wherefore remembering as well the taunts and checks before sustained by Canterbury which he intended to redress, and having respect to the advancement of worldly honor, he found the means with the King that he was made Chancellor, and Canterbury thereof dismissed."[3]

The transfer of the Great Seal, as we have seen in the life of Lord Chancellor Warham, took place on the 22nd of December, 1515.[4] The affair was conducted with

[1] Cavendish, 91.
[2] This point was settled by the Pope in the case of Cardinal Kempe, Archbishop of York, and authors are mistaken who represent the precedence now assumed by Wolsey as an usurpation dictated by his arrogance.
[3] Cavendish, 93.
[4] The reader may be amused with a translation of the Latin entry in the Close Roll upon the occasion. "Be it remembered that on Sunday, the 22nd of December, in the seventh year of the reign of Henry VIII., about the hour of one in the afternoon, in a certain high and small room in the King's palace at Westminster, near the Parliament Chamber, the Most Reverend Father in Christ, William Archbishop of Canterbury, then Chancellor of England, the King's Great Seal in the custody of the said Chancellor then being inclosed in a certain bag of white leather, and five times sealed with the signet of the said Archbishop, into the hands of our said lord the King surrendered

exterior decency, as if there had been a voluntary resignation on the one side and a reluctant acceptance on the other.

A contemporary letter of Sir Thomas More might lead to the belief that Warham was really eager to retire, and Wolsey afraid of farther promotion. Writing to Ammonius, he says, "The Archbishop of Canterbury hath at length resigned the office of Chancellor, *which burden as you know he had strenuously endeavored to lay down for some years;* and the long-wished-for retreat being now obtained, he enjoys a most pleasant recess in his studies, with the agreeable reflection of having acquitted himself honorably in that high station. The Cardinal of York, *by the King's orders,* succeeds him." Ammonius, writing to Erasmus, says, in the same strain, "Your Archbishop, with the King's good leave, has laid down his post, which that of York, after much importunity, has accepted of, and behaves most beautifully." Nay, Warham himself, in a letter to the same correspondent, says, he desired to give up this magistracy "*quem Eboracensis Episcopus impendio rogatus suscepit.*"

But the testimony of Cavendish, and the internal evidence on the other side, greatly preponderate. Warham, although like other Chancellors resolved to cling to office as long as possible, may from time to time have ex-

and delivered up in the presence of the Most Reverend Father in Christ, Thomas by Divine compassion * Cardinal Priest of the Holy Roman Church, by the title 'Sancti Ariaci in Termis,' Archbishop of York, Primate of England, and Legate of the Apostolic See, of Charles Duke of Suffolk, and of William Throgmorton, prothonotary of the Chancery of our Lord the King. And our said Lord the King, the said seal in the said bag so inclosed, so surrendered and delivered up by the said Archbishop, then and there caused to be opened and taken out, and being opened and taken out, saw and examined the same. And our said Lord the King then immediately, in the presence of those before mentioned, caused the said seal to be again inclosed in the said bag, and the said seal inclosed in the said bag, sealed with the signet of the said most reverend Cardinal, delivered to the said most reverend Cardinal, to be by him kept and used by the said most reverend Cardinal, whom he then and there constituted his Chancellor, with all diets, fees, profits, rewards, robes, commodities, and advantages to the office of Chancellor of England of old due, belonging or appertaining, and the said most reverend Cardinal the said seal, in the presence of the persons before mentioned, then and there received from the aforesaid most invincible King."—Rot. Cl. 7 Hen. 8, m. 1. On the 24th of December following there is an entry on the Close Roll of the new Chancellor being sworn in by the King at his palace at Eltham. The tenor of the oath is set out in English.

* Miseracione divinâ.

pressed a wish to be rid of it, and when the crisis actually came, the parties themselves and their friends deemed it best to avoid, as much as possible, the appearance of compulsion on the retiring Chancellor, or of any intriguing by his successor; but there can be no doubt that Wolsey, from the time of his obtaining the rank of Cardinal with the legatine authority, had taken every opportunity to insult Warham, with a view of driving him from Court, and that the Great Seal had long been an object of ambition to him, on account of the profit and power it would bring him,—and perhaps likewise from the opportunity it would afford him to add to his reputation for learning, ability, and eloquence.

The parade which he immediately made of the trappings of the office of Chancellor, and the manner in which he devoted himself to the discharge of its duties, showed that he had clutched it as eagerly, and that he enjoyed it as intensely, as any preferment ever bestowed upon him.[1]

CHAPTER XXVIII.

LIFE OF CARDINAL WOLSEY FROM HIS APPOINTMENT AS LORD CHANCELLOR TILL HIS FALL.

WOLSEY was now in the zenith of his greatness. At this period the Crown was absolute in England, and he alone wielded all its power. He was in consequence courted with the obsequiousness of Francis I. and Charles V., the rival monarchs, who were contending for superiority on the continent of Europe, and who felt that the result of the struggle depended to a considerable degree on his friendship. They not only flattered him by letters and embassies, but settled large pensions upon him, which there was no law or etiquette then prevailing to prevent him from accepting. The Doge of Venice, likewise, sent him a large pecuniary gratification, with letters containing the most fulsome adulation.[2] "In

---
[1] Cavendish, 93.
[2] As a specimen: "Incredibilis vestræ reverendissimæ Dominationis virtus et sapientia." Again, using the third person: "Ut nihil tam arduum difficileque foret (si modo id honestum esset et conducibile) quod non ipsa sua

all things the Chancellor was honored like the King's person, and sat always at his right hand. In all places where the King's arms were put up, the Chancellor's appeared alongside of them, so that in every honor the Sovereign and his minister were equal."[1] The money coined with the Cardinal's hat upon it was current without objection, though made the ground of one of the charges against him on his fall. The University of Oxford is supposed to have exceeded all the rest of the nation in servility towards him, and to have almost committed treason, by styling him in their addresses, "Your Majesty:"[2] but this appellation had not then been exclusively appropriated to kings, and it had been applied by the same University to Lord Chancellor Warham.[3]

Perhaps the strongest proof of his ascendency is to be found in the private confidential letters written to him by the King's sisters. Margaret, Queen of Scotland, by the battle of Flodden left a widow, with an infant son, and every way destitute, thus concludes a letter asking his interference in her favor, "for next to the King's Grace, my next trust is in you, and you may do me most good of any." Mary, Queen of Louis XII., thus addresses him: "for the payne ye take remembring to write to me soo often I thanke you for it w^h al my hert." She wrote him another letter pressing him to use his influence with the King to permit Lady Guilford to live with her in France as one of her ladies of honor. On the death of her husband, she communicates the intelligence to Wolsey, saying, "My Lord, my trust is in you for to remember me to the King my brother, for now I have none other to put my trust in but the Kyng my brother, *and you*. And so I pray you, my Lord, to show hys Grace, saying, that the Kyng, my housebande, ys departed to God, of whos sole God pardon. And wher as you avyse me that I should make no promas, my Lord, I trust the Kyng my brother *and you* wole not reckon in me soche chyldhode." In spite of the pledge here given against

bonitate ultro vellet; sapientissime ac providentissime disponeret; auctoritate quam meritissime in regno isto supremum tenet, optime possit conficere."
[1] Bellay, the French ambassador, an eye-witness.
[2] "Consultissima tua Majestas: reverendissima Majestas; inaudita Majestatis tuæ benignitas; vestra illa sublimis et longè reverendissima Majestas."
[3] "Et diu felicissime vivat *tua Majestas*."—Fiddes, 178.

her well-known inclination for her lover, Sir Charles Brandon, afterwards Duke of Suffolk, she married him in a few weeks; but as he was a person exciting no political jealousy, Wolsey pardoned them, and they were kindly received in England.

The homage universally paid to the Chancellor had such an effect upon him, that he gradually in his own letters assumed an equality with the King, which was afterwards made a subject of his impeachment.[1]

The fame of his influence was so great that he had many solicitations from other countries for his patronage. Thus, the Earl of Argyle wrote him a very humble letter, asking his interest with the Pope, that Donald Campbell, the Earl's brother, might be appointed Abbot of Cowper: "I beseich ye to forther ye promotionne of my saed brother in the best manner as your Grace thinks expedient; and my lord gief there be any service or labore that I canne do your Gracie in this realme, truly thar shalbe nane in it yat sall accompleis ye same w^t bettir hart nor mynd nor I sall."[2] This Donald Campbell was appointed Abbott of Cowper accordingly, although before entering into religion he had been married, and had children who survived him.

Wolsey's manner of living now eclipsed the splendor of the King's court. His household consisted of eight hundred persons, comprehending one Earl (the Earl of Derby), nine barons, and many knights and squires of great figure and worship. He had a high-chamberlain, a vice-chamberlain, a treasurer, a controller, and other officers corresponding to those of royalty, bearing white staves. He had in his hall-kitchen two master cooks, with many assistants and in his private kitchen a master cook, who went daily in damask, satin, or velvet with a chain of gold about his neck. We should never finish if we were to enumerate all the yeoman, grooms, pages, and purveyors that he he had in his larder, scalding-house, scul-

---

[1] Thus, in his correspondence with Pace, the secretary, and others, he says, "His Highness *and I* give you hearty thanks." "Neither the King's Highness *nor I* will advise them." "Much it is to the King's *and my comfort.*" "The King's Highness *and I* abide daily knowledge." "Arrived here the Archbishop of Capua, whom the King's Highness *and I* like." "The King's Highness *and I* be always of the same mind that the Emperor is." "The King's Highness *and I* gave my own lodgings to him."—MS. Letters in British Museum. [2] MSS. Cott. Lib.

lery, buttery, pantry, ewery, cellar, chaundery, wafery, wardrobe, laundry, bake-house, wood-yard, garner, garden, stable, and almoserie, with the yeoman of his barge, yeoman of his chariot, his master of the horse, saddler, farrier, and muleteer. "Also he had two secretaries, and two clerks of his signet, *and four councillors learned in the laws of the realm.*"[1] Now that he was Chancellor, he was constantly attended by all the officers of the Court, and by four footmen appareled in rich ermine coats,—and whensoever he took any journey, by a herald at arms, a sergeant at arms, a physician, an apothecary, four minstrels, a keeper of his tents and an armorer. Three great tables were daily laid in his hall for this numerous retinue. Many of the nobility placed their children in his family, and for the purpose of winning his favor, allowed them to act as his servants, although they had a separate table, called "the mess of lords," and had numerous menials to attend them.

"When it pleased the King's Majesty, for his recreation, to repair unto the Cardinal's house, such pleasures were then devised for the King's comfort and consolation as might be invented or by man's wit imagined. The banquets were set forth with masks and mummeries in so gorgeous a sort and costly manner, that it was a heaven to behold. There wanted no dames or damsels meet or apt to dance with the maskers, or to garnish the place for the time with other goodly disports. There was there all kinds of music and harmony set forth, with excellent voices, both of men and children."[2]

[1] Cavendish, 97.
[2] Cavendish, who goes on to give an account of the King's coming with maskers like shepherds, from which Shakspeare hath taken the 4th scene of the 1st act of Henry VIII. In one particular the dramatist differs from the biographer. (The twelve maskers, habited like shepherds, being ushered in as foreigners who could not speak English,)

"*Wolsey.* Pray tell them thus much from me:
There should be one amongst them, by his person,
More worthy this place than myself, to whom
If I but knew him, with my love and duty
I would surrender it.

"*Chamberlain.* Such a one they all confess
There is indeed, which they would have your Grace
Find out, and he will take it.

"*Wolsey.* Let me see then; here I'll make
My royal choice,

"*King Henry (unmasking).* You have found him, Cardinal."

But Cavendish relates, "My Lord Chancellor said to my Lord Cardinal,

We have likewise very picturesque descriptions of his march to the Court at Greenwich on Sundays,—riding through Thames Street on his mule, with his crosses, his pillars, his hat, and the Great Seal, till he came to Billingsgate, where he took his barge,—and of the gorgeous celebration of mass in his chapel, where he was attended by Bishops and Abbots. Such was his haughtiness, that he made Dukes and Earls to serve him with wine, and to hold the bason and lavatories.

But for our purpose, the most interesting pageant he exhibited was his procession from York House to the Court of Chancery in Westminster Hall, which is minutely described to us by an eye-witness. Having arisen by day-break, and heard mass, he returned to his private chamber; and his public rooms being now filled with noblemen and gentlemen attending his levee,—

" He issued out unto them appareled all in red, in the habit of a cardinal, which was either of fine scarlet, or else of crimson satin, taffety damask, or caffa, the best that he could get for money; and upon his head a round pillion, with a noble of black velvet set to the same in the inner side; he also had a tippet of fine sables about his neck; holding in his hand a very fine orange, whereof the meat or substance within was taken out, and filled up again with the part of a sponge, wherein was vinegar and other confections against the pestilent airs, the which he most commonly smelt unto passing among the press, or else when he was pestered with many suitors. There was also borne before him—first the Great Seal of England, and then his Cardinal's hat, by a nobleman or some worthy gentleman, right solemnly, bare-headed. And as soon as he was entered into his chamber of presence, where there

'Sir, they confess that among them there is such a noble personage, whom if your Grace can appoint him from the others, he is contended to disclose himself and to accept your place most worthily.' With that the Cardinal, taking a good advisement among them, at the last quoth he, ' Me seemeth the gentleman with the black beard should be even he.' And with that he arose out of his chair and offered the same to the gentleman in the black beard, with his cap in his hand. This turned out to be Sir Edward Neville, a comely knight of a goodly personage, that much resembled the King's person in that mask. The King, perceiving the Cardinal so deceived in his estimation and choice, could not forbear laughing, but plucked down his visor, and Master Neville's also, and dashed out with such a pleasant countenance and cheer, that all noble estates there assembled, seeing the King to be there amongst them, rejoiced very much."—Cavendish, 112.

was attending his coming to wait upon him to Westminster Hall, as well noblemen and other worthy gentlemen as noblemen and gentlemen of his own family; thus passing forth with two great crosses of silver borne before him; with also two great pillars of silver, and his pursuivant at arms, with a great mace of silver gilt. Then his gentleman ushers' cried, and said 'On, my Lords and Masters, on before; make way for my Lord's Grace.' Thus passed he down from his chamber to the Hall; and when he came to the Hall door, there was attendant for his mule, trapped altogether in crimson velvet and gilt stirrups. When he was mounted, with his cross-bearers and pillar-bearers, also upon great horses trapped with fine scarlet, then marched he forward, with his train and furniture in manner as I have declared, having about him four footmen with gilt poll-axes in their hands; and thus he went until he came to Westminster Hall door. And there alighted, and went after this manner up through the Hall into the Chancery; howbeit, he would most commonly stay awhile at a bar made for him a little beneath the Chancery on the right hand, and there commune some time with the Judges, and some time with other persons. And that done he would repair into the Chancery, sitting there till eleven of the clock, hearing suitors, and determining of divers matters. And from thence he would divers times go into the Star Chamber, as occasion did serve; where he spared neither high nor low, but judged every one according to their merits and deserts."

His crosses, pillars, and poll-axes are likewise celebrated by Cavendish in the metrical autobiography, which he imputes to Wolsey:—

> " My crossis twayne of silver long and greate
> That dayly before me were carried hyghe,
> Upon great horses openly in the streett,
> And massie pillars gloryouse to the eye,
> With poll-axes gylt that no man durst come nyghe
> My presence, I was so princely to behold
> Ryding on my mule trapped with silver and golde." [2]

This pagentry, although regarded with great reverence by dependent courtiers, called forth many gibes from the vulgar; and it was a common saying, that "the two

[1] Cavendish being one of them.
[2] We have likewise a metrical description of the Cardinal's equipage from Willam Roy, styled by Bale " vir ætatis suæ non ineruditus," in a satire

crosses showed that the Cardinal had twice as many sins to repent of as any other prelate." The pulpit likewise occasionally resounded with invectives against him. Doctor Barnes, afterwards burnt for heresy, having showed his independent spirit by inveighing against the pomp and luxury of the Cardinal, was summoned before him, and received this admonition: "What, Master Doctor! had you not a sufficient scope in the Scriptures to teach the people but yon; but that my golden shoes, my poll-axes, my pillars, my golden cushions, and my crosses did so far offend you, that you must make us *ridiculum caput* amongst the people? We were jollily that day laughed to scorn. Verily, it was a sermon more fitter to be preached on a stage than in a pulpit." Barnes answered, published about 1530, in the form of a dialogue between two priests' servants, with the motto

"Rede me and be nott wrothe,
For I saye no thynge but trothe."

"*Wat*. Doth he use then on mules to ryde?
"*Jeff*. Yes; and that with so shamfull pryde
That to tell it is not possible,
More like a God celestiall
Than any creature mortall
With worldly pomp incredible.

"Before hym rideth two prestes stronge,
And they beare two crosses right longe,
Gapynge in every man's face:
After theym folowe two laymen secular
And each of theym holdyng a pillar
In their hondes, steade of a mace.

"Then followeth my Lord on his mule
Trapped with gold under her cule
In every poynt most curiously;
On eache syde a pollaxe is borne
Which in none wother use are worne
Pretendynge some hid mystery.

"Then hath he servauntes fyve or six score,
Some behynd and some before,
A marvelous great company:
Of which are lords and gentlemen,
With many gromes and yemen,
And also knaves amonge.

' Thus dayly he proceedeth forthe,
And men must take it at worthe
Whether he do right or wronge.
A great carle he is, and a fatt,
Wearynge on his hed a red hatt
Procured with angel's subsidy."

Supp. to Harl. Misc. 1812

that he had spoken nothing but the truth out of the Scriptures, according to his conscience, and was for that time discharged. With the exception of his prosecution of Buckingham, Wolsey showed no inclination to blood or cruelty.

We must now consider him in the capacity of a Judge.

Unfortunately none of his decisions have come down to us; but it seems to be generally allowed that his elevation to the judgment-seat, by proving the extent of his capacity, seemed to exalt his personal character;—that no Chancellor ever discovered greater impartiality;—that he showed much discrimination and shrewdness in discussing the principles of law and equity,—and that a strict administration of justice took place during his enjoyment of this high office.[1]

We are rather at a loss to imagine how, with all his tact, he was able to get through the business without committing serious errors, and exposing himself to ridicule from his ignorance of legal distinctions. The fashion of a Chancellor having a Keeper of the Seal, or Vice-Chancellor, to act for him had passed away—and Wolsey, although he had probably paid some attention to the civil and canon law while a resident at Oxford, had never, like Morton and many other ecclesiastical Chancellors, practiced in the Arches, or been a clerk or master in Chancery, or assisted a prior Chancellor. The coming event of his Chancellorship had long cast its shadow before, and he probably had, by a course of study, in some degree prepared himself for his office; and he no doubt had the address to avail himself of the assistance of the four lawyers who formed part of his establishment, as well as of the clerks and other officers of the court. "In examining cases," says Fiddes, "which came before the Cardinal as Chancellor, he would take associates with him learned in the laws, and ask their opinions; but in such matters as came before him, and were not very intricate, but might be determined in a rational way of arguing from the com-

---

[1] He is extravagantly praised by Sir Thomas More, writing to Erasmus. "Ita se gerit ut spem quoque omnium, quanquam pro reliquis ejus virtutibus maximam, longe tamen exsuperet; et, quod est difficillimum, post optimum prædecessorem valde probatur et placeat." And Ammonius, writing of the office of Chancellor, coming to Wolsey, says, "Quem Magistratum Eboracensis pulcherime gerit."

mon principles of equity, he would often give sentence according to the light of his own understanding."

However he may have managed it, such reputation did he gain as a judge, that some have ascribed to him the establishment of the equitable jurisdiction of the Court of Chancery; and, from the confidence reposed in him, the number of bills and petitions increased so much that he was obliged to refer some of them to the Master of the Rolls, and to have a commission of common-law Judges to assist him.

Bishop Godwyn, who is severe on many parts of Wolsey's conduct, gives him unqualified praise for improvements he introduced in the administration of justice, and the purity he displayed as a Judge.[1]

Wolsey presided as Chancellor in a session of parliament in the end of 1516; but no account is preserved of any of its proceedings in which he was concerned, except of a very anomalous one,—a bill for a subsidy brought into the House of Lords, and being passed there, ordered to be carried to the Commons by the Lord Chancellor. He, no doubt, appeared in the Lower House with his crosses, his pillars, and his poll-axes, and delivered an eloquent discourse on the duty of supplying the wants of the King. But the bill is supposed to have been thrown out by the Commons; and this may be the reason why no other parliament was called for seven years, and that very arbitrary methods of raising money were resorted to.

In 1518 Wolsey received an addition to his legatine jurisdiction, which gave him the plenary power of the Pope in England, and which he grievously abused by setting up a new Court for the proof of wills, and for the trial of all spiritual offenses in the province of Canterbury, and by presenting to all ecclesiastical benefices which became vacant,—in derogation of the rights of chapters and patrons. When Archbishop Warham wrote him a respectful letter on the subject, signed "your loving brother," Wolsey complained of his presumption, in thus

---

[1] "Multa ordinavit in rebus civilibus popularibus grata, ac nobis in hunc usque diem usurpata. Quibus virum se ostendit sapientissimum necnon Reipublicæ amantem. Certe qui illis temporibus vixerunt asserere non dubitarunt, cum hoc regno nunquam felicius actum, quam cum florente Wolseo, cujus consiliis pacem opulentam et securam qua fruebatur, *et iustitiam equo Jure* civibus omnibus administratam, tribuebatur."—God Ann. 14.

challenging an equality with the Lord Cardinal Legate This distinction he valued more than the Great Seal itself, as we may judge from his observation to Cavendish on his fall: "My authority and dignity legatine is gone, wherein consisted all my honor." Warham was himself unmoved by the insolence of his rival, and having remonstrated in vain, only observed, "Know ye not that this man is drunk with too much prosperity?" But the Judge of his Legatine Court, whom, for a private purpose, he had appointed with a knowledge that he had been guilty of perjury,—having been convicted of some gross malversation, the King himself expressed such displeasure to the Cardinal as made him ever after more cautious in exerting his authority.

These follies would have left no lasting stain on the memory of Wolsey, but he was now instrumental in the violent death of a rival through the forms of law. The Duke of Buckingham, representing the ancient family of Stafford, and hereditary High Constable of England, stood the first in rank and consequence among the nobility. He viewed with envy and jealously the elevation of the butcher's son, who was at no pains to gain his good will, and on several occasions they had passed affronts on each other. Buckingham's character was marked by levity and indiscretion, as well as by ambition and arrogance. Being descended through a female from the Duke of Gloucester, youngest son of Edward III., he pretended that he had a right to the Crown if the King should die without issue,— passing over the claims of the King's sisters, the dowagers of Scotland and France, and their descendants.

Wolsey worked upon Henry's hatred of all collaterally connected with the blood royal, which he showed during the whole course of his reign, and caused Buckingham to be arrested and brought to trial for high treason. The evidence against him consisted almost entirely of idle and vaunting language held with servants who, if they spoke true, betrayed his confidence,—and of certain soothsayers, who had foretold that he should be King. The apologists of Wolsey have insisted that the sentence against Buckingham was just, because it was unanimously pronounced by a Court consisting of a Duke, a Marquess, seven Earls, and twelve Barons,—forgetting that in that age, and for long after, no one charged by the Crown for high treason was ever acquitted, and that trial before a jury, and still more before the Lord High Steward and a selection of Peers, was an empty form. Buckingham, who was a great object of affection with the vulgar, was considered a victim to the resentment of the Cardinal. After the Duke of Norfolk, with hypocritical tears, had condemned him to suffer the death of a traitor, he was ordered to be carried by water from Westminster Hall to the Tower; but owing to the state of the tide at London Bridge, he was landed at the Temple Stairs and conducted through the city. On this occasion, as well as at his execution, the curses were loud and deep upon the "venom-mouthed cur" who was alleged to be the cause of his death.

But in those days slight account was made of the heads of men,[1] and legal murders were so usual that they were not long remembered against those who perpetrated them. The Cardinal's power was rather augmented by thus intimidating the great families from whom so much disquietude had formerly been experienced, and his popularity soon revived.

The excitement of a new object of ambition extinguished any feelings of remorse which might have disturbed his own bosom. He now aimed at the triple crown. The Emperor Charles V., when visiting England, suggested to him his fitness to be the successor of St. Peter, and promised him his interest on a vacancy,—with the less scruple as Leo X., the reigning Pope, was in the flower of his age.

Francis I. tried to do away the effects of this intrigue by contriving the famous interview with Henry in "the field of the cloth of gold,"

> "When those suns of glory, those two lights of men,
> Met in the vale of Andres."

But Wolsey was invited to visit Charles at Bruges, and

[1] I may mention, as an instance of the levity with which cutting off heads was talked of,—the manner in which Henry raised the supplies when there was some reluctance to grant them. He sent for Mr. Montague, an opposition leader in the Commons, and said to him, "Ho, man! will they not suffer my bill to pass?" and laying his hand on the head of Montague, who was then on his knees before him, "Get my bill passed by to-morrow, or else to-morrow this head of yours shall be off." This bill was passed, or some trumped-up charge of treason might have cost him his life, **and made a nine-days' wonder.**

went thither in the character of ambassador from England Cavendish is eloquent in describing the splendor of his train and the sumptuousness of his reception :—

"His gentlemen being in number very many, clothed in heavy coats of crimson velvet of the most purest color that might be invented, with chains of gold about their necks, and all his yeomen and other mean officers were in coats of fine scarlet guarded with black velvet a hand broad. Also the emperor's officers every night went through the town from house to house, where as any Englishman lay or resorted, and there served their liveries for all night, which was done after this manner :—first, the Emperor's officers brought into the house a cast of fine manchet bread ; two great silver pots with wine and a pound of fine sugar ; white lights and yellow ; a bowl or goblet of silver, to drink in, and every night a stafftorch. Thus the Emperor entertained the Cardinal and all his train for the time of his embassy there ; and, that done, he returned home again to England with great triumph."

Charles on this occasion again encouraged Wolsey to aspire to the tiara, and the sincerity of his promise of support was soon unexpectedly put to the test by the sudden demise of his Holiness. Wolsey was immediately in the field with high hopes of success, as the Imperial party was decidedly the strongest in the conclave. Charles wrote a friendly letter to Wolsey, inclosing the copy of one he had written to his ambassador at Rome, enjoining him to urge the Cardinals to elect Wolsey to the papal chair. There were twenty votes for Wolsey, and twenty-six would have been sufficient to carry the election in his favor; but there can be no doubt that he was trifled with, and, to save appearances, the Conclave having sat an unusual length of time, the Emperor's own tutor was raised to the Popedom, under the title of Adrian VI.

Charles, dreading the loss of the English alliance from Wolsey's disappointment, immediately afterward made him another visit in this country, augmented his pension, and renewed the promise of aiding his pretensions on the next vacancy, an event which, from Adrian's age and infirmities, could not be far distant. Wolsey suppressed his resentment, adhered to the Imperial party, and devoted himself to measures for strengthening his interest with the College of Cardinals at Rome.

Adrian died in about a year and a half after his elevation. Wolsey again entered the lists with his characteristic zeal. Henry, at his request, wrote in the most urgent terms to the Emperor, reminding him of his repeated promises, and calling upon him now to fulfill them, as he valued his friendship;—and the English ambassadors and agents at Rome were instructed to spare among the members of the Conclave neither bribes nor promises.[1] But Wolsey was again deceived, and Cardinal Giulio de Medici, with the concurrence of the Imperial party, was elected Pope under the title of Clement VII.

Wolsey secretly resolved to be revenged of the perfidy of Charles by for ever forsaking his alliance; but, meanwhile, he concealed his disgust; and, after congratulating the new Pope on his promotion, applied for a continuation of the legatine powers which the last two Popes had conferred upon him. Clement, knowing the importance of gaining his friendship, granted him the commission for life; and Wolsey was thus reinvested with the whole Papal authority in England.

He now showed in a striking manner that devoted love of learning and ardor for good education which distinguished him through life, and by which his memory has been redeemed from the failings and vices he exhibited. Though ashamed of his low origin if girded by the ancient nobility,—he looked back with satisfaction on that part of his career when he was master of Magdalen school at Oxford, and tutor to the sons of the Marquess of Dorset; and he was at all times willing to render available

---

[1] Wolsey's letter on this occasion to Lord Bath, ambassador at Rome, very undisguisedly exhorts him to exert himself to the utmost amongst the Cardinals, "not sparing any reasonable offers, which is a thing that amongst so many needy persons is more regarded than per-case the qualities of the person; ye be wise, and ye wot what I mean. The King thinketh that all the Imperials shall clearly be with you, if faith be in the Emperor. The young men, which for the most part being needy, will give good ears to fair offers, which shall be undoubtedly performed. The King willeth you neither to spare his authority or his good money or substance."—Fidd. Col. 87. The letter is still preserved in which Wolsey informes the King of his disappointment, which he ascribes entirely to *intimidation*. After stating the threats of violence held out to the Cardinals, he says, " Albeit they were in manner principally bent upon me, yet for eschewing the said danger and murmur, by inspiration of the Holy Goste, without farther difficulty, the xixth day of the last month, in the morning, elected and choose Cardinal de Medicis, who immediately was published Pope, and hath taken the name of Clement VII."—Fidd. Col. 82.

the experience he then acquired. He superintended, with assiduous care, the training of the Earl of Richmond, his godson (natural son of the King); and in his own handwriting drew up, with the utmost minuteness, a plan for the household and for the tuition of the boy when entering his sixth year.

The domestic education of the Princess Mary was likewise under the care of the Prime Minister; and in the height of his power and ambition, after deciding a great cause in Chancery, or dictating a treaty which was to change the face of affairs in Europe, he stooped to detei mine whether or not the Princess should have "spice plates and a ship of silver for the almes dish;" and whether "a trumpet and rebeks were a fitting toye for her pastime hours at the solempne fest of Christmas." He framed the regulations of St. Paul's School, founded by Dean Collet; and he caused a new Latin Grammar to be composed, to which he himself wrote an introduction. He revised and remodelled the statutes of his own and several other colleges at Oxford; and he likewise introduced very salutary reforms at Cambridge, under a power conferred upon him by the senate of that University. Having suppressed a number of smaller monasteries, instead of appropriating their revenues to himself, or bestowing them on some rapacious courtier, he employed them in endowing splendid establishments, which he hoped would spread the blessings of knowledge, with his own fame, through distant generations.

> ———" Ever witness for him
> Those twins of learning that he rais'd in you,
> Ipswich and Oxford, one of which fell with him,
> The other——————— so famous,
> So excellent in art, and still so rising,
> That Christendom shall ever speak his virtue."

After an interval of seven years a parliament was called, as the irregular modes of filling the Exchequer, which had been resorted to, had proved ineffectual. On the first day of the session, on the King's right side, at his feet, sat the Cardinal of York; and at the rail behind stood Tunstal, Bishop of London, who made an eloquent oration to the parliament on the office of a King. Wolsey, it seems, had thought it more for his dignity to depute the task of delivering the speech to another; but he took the lead in all the subsequent proceedings.[1]

At the same time he called a convocation of the clergy, at which, by virtue of his legatine power, he presided, and from which he readily obtained the required grant of one half their revenues spiritual, to be paid in five years.

The Commons, however, were by no means so complaisant. From them was demanded a subsidy of £800,000, which they declared to be more than the whole current coin of the realm.

Now we have the first instance of a complaint of the publication of debates in parliament. This, I presume, was merely by verbal narration; but certain smart sayings of the opponents of the grant, and certain gibes leveled at the Chancellor, had been generally circulated; and reaching his ears, had given him high displeasure. He made formal complaint to the Lords; and insisted that for any member to repeat out of the House what had passed in the House, was a breach of privilege and a misdemeanor—"whereas, at this parliament, nothing was so soon done, or spoken therein, but that it was immediately blown abroad in every alehouse." Not contented with this, he resolved to pay a visit of remonstrance to the Commons,—and in such style that they should be completely overawed by the splendor of his appearance. He calculated, likewise, on the complaisance of the Speaker, whom he had been instrumental in placing in the chair; but the Speaker was Sir Thomas More, the most courageous as well as the mildest man then in England.

As the Chancellor was approaching the house with his immense retinue, a debate arose " whether it was better with a few of his Lords (as the most opinion of the House was), or with his whole train, royally to receive him?" " 'Masters,' quoth Sir Thomas More, 'forasmuch as my Lord Cardinal lately, ye wot well, laid to our charge the lightness of our tongues for things uttered out of this House, it shall not in my mind be amiss to receive him with all his pomp, with his maces his pillars, his crosses, his poll-axes, his hat, and Great Seal too, to the intent that if he find the like fault with us hereafter, we may be the bolder from ourselves to lay the blame on those whom

[1] 1 Parl. Hist. 484.

his Grace bringeth here with him. Whereunto the House wholly agreeing, he received accordingly. When after he had by a solemn oration, by many reasons, proved how necessary it was the demand then moved to be granted, and farther showed that less would not serve to maintain the Prince's purpose; he seeing the company sitting still silent, and thereunto nothing answering, and, contrary to his expectation, showing in themselves towards his request no towardness of inclination, said to them,— 'Masters, you have many wise and learned men amongst you, and sith I am from the King's own person sent hitherto unto you, to the preservation of yourselves and of all the realm, I think it meet you give me some reasonable answer.' Whereat every man holding his peace, he then began to speak to one Master Marney, afterwards Lord Marney. 'How say you, quothe he, 'Master Marney?' who making him no answer neither, he severally asked the question of divers others, accounted the wisest of the company, to whom, when none of them all would give so much as one word, being agreed before, as custom was, to give answer by their Speaker;—'Masters,' quoth the Cardinal, 'unless it be the manner of your House, as or likelihood it is, by the mouth of your Speaker, whom you have chosen for trusty and wise (as indeed he is), in such cases to utter your minds, here is without doubt, a marvelously obstinate silence;' and thereupon he required answer of Mr. Speaker, who first reverently, on his knees, excusing the silence of the House, abashed at the presence of so noble a personage, able to amaze the wisest and best learned in a realm, and then by many probable arguments proving that for them to make answer was neither expedient nor agreeable with the ancient liberty of the House; in conclusion for himself, showed, that though they had all with their voices trusted him, yet except every one of them could put into his own head their several wits, he alone in so weighty a matter was unmeet to make his Grace answer. Whereupon the Cardinal, displeased with Sir Thomas More, that had not in this parliament in all things satisfied his desire, suddenly arose and departed."[1]

The conduct of More on this occasion is supposed to have set the example followed by Lenthall on the visit

[1] 1 Parl. Hist. 487.

by Charles I. to arrest the five members, and to have established the rule, that the House can only communicate with others by the mouth of the Speaker, who can only speak and act by order of the House.

On the Cardinal's departure a debate arose, which was adjourned, and lasted fifteen or sixteen days. The result was, that a subsidy was voted of half the amount required, to be paid by installments. Wolsey and the King were so angry, that, contrary to usage, they compelled the people to pay up the whole subsidy at once; and resolving henceforth to rule entirely by prerogative, no other parliament was called for seven years. When the session was closed, Wolsey, in his gallery at York Place, said to More, " I wish to God you had been at Rome, Mr. More, when I made you Speaker." "Your Grace not offended, so would I too, my Lord," replied Sir Thomas, " for then should I have seen the place I long have desired to visit."

After the lapse of two years, Wolsey made a deliberate attempt to levy a general tax of a sixth part of every man's substance without the authority of parliament. This demand he announced in person to the Mayor and chief citizens of London. They attempted to remonstrate, but were warned to beware, " lest it might fortune to cost some their heads." The rich and poor agreed in cursing the Cardinal as the subverter of their laws and liberties; and said, " if men shall give their goods by a commission, then it would be worse than the taxes of France, and England would be bond, and not free." Happily the commissioners met with forcible resistance in several counties; and such a menacing spirit was generally displayed, that the proud spirit of Wolsey quailed under it, and he was obliged not only to pardon all concerned in these tumults, but, on some frivolous pretext, to recede altogether from the illegal exaction. This was a great crisis in our constitution; for if Wolsey could have procured the submission of the nation to the yoke he attempted to impose, there would have been an end of parliaments for all ordinary purposes, although, like the States-General of France, they might still have been convoked to ratify certain acts of state originating with the executive government. But the courage and love of freedom natural to the

English Commons, speaking in the hoarse voice of tumult, and resorting to the last right of *insurrection*, preserved us in so great a peril.[1]

Various attempts were made to open the eyes of the King to the misconduct of the minister,—and even the stage was resorted to for this purpose. There being a grand entertainment given to the King and his Court by the Society of Gray's Inn, Sergeant Roo, a great lawyer of that time, more eager to show his wit than to be made a Judge, composed for the occasion a masque, which, notwithstanding his asseverations to the contrary, must have been intended as a satire on the Lord Chancellor. Of this Hollinshead, who affects to believe that it was not " miching mallecho," and that it did not " mean mischief," gives the following account:—

"The effect of the play was, that 'Lord Gouvernance' was ruled by 'Dissipation' and 'Negligence,' by whose misgouvernance and evill order 'Lady Public Weale' was put from 'Gouvernance.' Which caused ' Rumor Populi,' ' Inward Grudge,' and ' Disdaine of Wanton Sovereigntie,' to rise with great multitude, to expell 'Negligence' & ' Dissipation,' and to restore ' Publike Welth' again to hir estate,—which was so doone. This plaie was so set foorth with rich and costlie apparell, with strange devises of maskes and morishes, that it was higlie praised of all men, saving of the Cardinall, which imagined that the plaie had been devised of him, and in great furie sent for the said Maister Roo, and took from him his coife and sent him to the Fleet; and after he sent for the yooung gentlemen that plaied in the plaie, and them highly rebuked and threatened, and sent one of them, called Thomas Maile of Kent, to the Fleet, but by means of friends Maister Roo and he were delivered at last. This plaie sore displeased the Cardinall, and yet it was never meant to him. But what will you have of a guilty conscience but to suspect all things to be said of him (as if all the worlde knew his wickedness) according to the old verse,

"'Conscius ipse sibi de se putat omnia dici?'"[2]

Wolsey, now hated by all ranks, began to lose favor even with the King, and tottered to his fall. But before we come to the cause which immediately led to that

---

[1] Hall. Const. Hist. 29.   [2] Hollinsh. iii. 714.

catastrophe, we must accompany him in the last scene of his greatness—negotiating a treaty of alliance with France. The Emperor having defeated his rival Francis at Pavia, and after the sack of Rome having made the Pope his prisoner, had become master of all Italy, and aimed at universal dominion. What weighed still more in English councils than a regard to the balance of power, was the consideration that with his consent there was no chance of Wolsey being raised to the Popedom. For these reasons it was resolved that England should put herself at the head of a league to check the ambition of Charles, and Wolsey was sent on a grand embassy to Paris, accompanied by many Bishops, Lords, and Knights, for the purpose of establishing it. Cavendish was in his suite, and has left us a very amusing account of his adventures:

"Then marched he forward out of his own house at Westminster, passing through all London over London Bridge, having before him of gentlemen a great number, three in rank, in black velvet livery coats, and the most part of them with great chains of gold about their necks. And all his yeomen, with noblemen's and gentlemen's servants following him in French tawny livery coats; having embroidered upon the backs and breasts of the said coats the letters T. C. under the Cardinal's hat. His sumpter mules, which were twenty in number and more, with his carts and other carriages of his train, were passed on before, conducted and guarded with a great number of bows and spears. He rode like a Cardinal, very sumptuously, on a mule trapped with crimson velvet upon velvet, and his stirrups of copper and gilt, and his spare mule following him with like apparel. And before him he had his two great crosses of silver, two great pillars of silver, the Great Seal of England, his Cardinal's hat, and a gentleman that carried his valaunce, which was made altogether of fine scarlet cloth embroidered over and over with cloth of gold very richly, having in it a cloak of fine scarlet."[1]

He by no means traveled so rapidly now as on his mission from Henry VII. to Maximilian. He passed the first night at a gentleman's house near Dartford, the second in the Bishop's palace at Rochester, the third in

[1] Cavendish, 150

the abbey at Feversham, and the fourth in the priory at Canterbury. Here he stopped some days, during which there was a grand jubilee—with a fair in honor of St. Thomas. A solemn office was celebrated in the cathedral for the deliverance of the Pope from captivity, during which it is said that Wolsey, conscious of the instability of his own grandeur, and anticipating his fall, wept tenderly.

Hence Cavendish was sent forward with letters to Calais, and after two days the Cardinal arrived in the haven, "where he was received in procession by all the most worshipfullest persons of the town in most solemn wise. And in the Lantern Gate was set for him a form with carpets and cushions, where he kneeled and made his prayers before his entry any further in the town; and there he was censed with two great censers of silver, and sprinkled with holy water."[1] After an account of his receiving the Captain of Boulogne, with a number of gallant Frenchmen who dined with him, we have a long speech, which he addressed to the noblemen and gentlemen of his train, instructing them respecting the royal honors to be paid to himself, and how they were to conduct themselves to the French whom they were to visit." "For my part I must, by virtue of my commission of Lieutenantship, assume and take upon me in all honors and degrees, to have all such service and reverence as to His Highness's presence is meet and due, and nothing thereof to be neglected or omitted by me that to his royal estate is appurtenant. Now as to this point of the Frenchmen's nature ye shall understand that their disposition is such, that they will be at their first meeting as familiar with you as they had been acquainted with you long before, and commence with you in the French tongue as though you understood every word they spoke; therefore, in like manner, be ye as familiar with them again as they be with you. If they speak to you in the French tongue, speak to them in the English tongue; for if you understand not them, they shall no more understand you." Then, addressing a Welshman, "Rice," quoth he, "speak thine Welsh to him, and I am well assured that thy Welsh shall be more diffuse to him than his French shall be to theee." He concludes with good advice to them all, to practice

[1] Cavendish, 152.

gentleness and humanity for the honor of their prince and country.¹

He left the Great Seal at Calais with Dr. Taylor, the Master of the Rolls, until his return, as he could not regularly take it beyond the dominions of England, although he thought himself at liberty to use it in this place. We have a very curious description of his departure from Calais with a train above three quarters of a mile long, and of his march to Boulogne, Montreuil, and Abbeville, where there were divers pageants for joy of his coming, and he was hailed as "Le Cardinal Pacifique." In his journey he released prisoners, distributed his blessing, and proclaimed indulgences. The French Court came to Amiens to receive him. "In came Madame Regent, the King's mother, riding in a very rich chariot; and in the same with her was her daughter, the Queen of Navarre, furnished with a hundred ladies and gentlewomen, or more, following, riding upon white palfreys, over and besides divers other ladies and gentlewomen, that rode, some in rich chariots, and some in horse litters. Then follows the King, with his Bourgonyan guard, his French guard, and 'the third guard, *pour le corps*, which was of tall Scots, much more comelier persons than all the rest.'"² Wolsey required that Francis should meet him as a sovereign, on equal terms; and, both alighting at the same time, embraced in the midway, between their respective retinues. Francis having placed Wolsey on his right, each English gentleman was marshalled with a Frenchman of equal rank, and the procession extending nearly two miles in length, proceeded to Amiens. After a few days' stay there, the conference was removed to Compiegne.³

---

¹ Cavendish, 155.   ² Ibid. 163.
³ Cavendish describes very minutely the banquets, balls, masses, and boar hunts which took place; but he is most amusing in relating his own visit to the *Chastel de Crequi*, where the Countess received him most gently, having a train of twelve gentlewomen. "And when she with her train came out, she said to me, '*Forasmuch*,' quoth she, "*as ye be an Englishman, whose custom is in your country to kiss all ladies and gentlewomen without offense, and although it be not so here in this realm, yet will I be so bold to kiss you, and so shall all my maidens.*' By means whereof I kissed my lady and all her women." Erasmus celebrates the same custom as then prevalent in England. "Est præterea mos nunquam satis laudatus, sive quo venias omnium osculis exciperis; sive discedas aliquo osculis dimitteris; redis? redduntur suavia venitur ad te? propinantur suavia: disceditur abs te? dividuntur basia

Much artifice and chicanery were displayed by the French negotiators, although they were exceedingly desirous to conciliate England. Wolsey became indignant; and one evening, when Francis himself was present, he lost all patience; and, starting from his seat, said to his brother Chancellor of France, " Sir, it becomes you not to trifle with the friendship between our Sovereigns; and if your master follows your practices, he shall not fail shortly to feel what it is to war against England." Upon that he left the room; and was only at the earnest entreaty of the Queen-mother that he renewed the discussion. By this bold conduct the object of his mission was soon satisfactorily accomplished, and he returned to England.

The French alliance not being much relished,—on the first day of next term he called an assembly in the Star Chamber of noblemen, judges, and justices of the peace of every shire, and there made them a long oration; "declaring to them the cause of his embassy to France, and assuring them that he had concluded such an amity and friendship, as never had been heard of in our time before. All which things shall be perfected at the coming of the great embassy out of France. This peace thus concluded, there shall be such an amity between gentlemen of each realm, and intercourse of merchants, with merchandise, that it shall seem to all men the territories to be but one monarchy. Gentlemen may travel from one country to another for their recreation and pastime; and merchants being arrived in each country, shall be assured to travel about their affairs in peace and tranquillity, so that this realm shall joy and prosper for ever."

The expected embassy sent to ratify the treaty according to the prevailing forms of diplomacy at length arrived, " in number above four score persons, of the most noblest and worthiest gentlemen in all the Court of France, who were right honorably received from place to place after their arrival, and so conveyed through London into the Bishop's palace in Paul's Churchyard, where they were lodged."[1] The Lord Mayor and City of London supplied them with "wine, sugar, wax, capons, wild fowl, beefs, muttons, and other necessaries in great abundance." They were royally entertained by the King at Greenwich,

occurritur alicubi? basiatur affatim: denique quocunque te moveas, suavi orumplena sunt omnia."—*Erasmi Epist.* p. 315. ed. 1642.   [1] Cavendish, 190.

where they invested him with the insignia of the Order of St. Michael; and he declared Francis a Knight of the Order of the Garter. A solemn mass was sung at St. Paul's where my Lord Cardinal associated with twenty-four mitres of Bishops and Abbots, attending upon him by virtue of his legatine authority; "and the Grand Master of France, the chief Ambassador, kneeled by the King's Majesty, between whom my Lord divided the sacrament, as a firm oath and assurance of this perpetual peace." The mass being finished, the Cardinal read the treaty openly, both in French and English, before the King and the assembly, both French and English. The King then subscribed it with his own hand, and the Grand Master for the French King. Last of all, it was sealed with seals of fine gold, and interchanged. The King and the ambassadors rode home with Wolsey to his house at Westminster, and dined with him.

But to give them a just notion of the magnificence of England, it was arranged that, before their departure, he should make them a supper at Hampton Court. Two hundred and eighty beds, with furniture of the costliest silks and velvets, with as many ewers and basons of silver, were prepared for the guests. The halls were illuminated with innumerable sconces and branches of plate. The most celebrated cooks belonging to the King and the nobility, joined with the Cardinal's in preparing the entertainment. Supper was announced by the sound of trumpets, and served with triumphal music. But the master was not yet come. He had been detained in the Court of Chancery hearing a long cause, and concluded that he should best exalt his country in the eyes of foreigners, by showing them that the due administration of justice was with him the highest consideration.

The dessert, consisting of a representation of St. Paul's Cathedral, in confectionery, with castles and tournaments, and other emblems of ecclesiastical pomp and pageants of chivalry, was on the tables, when he suddenly entered, "booted and spurred." Having cordially and gracefully welcomed the guests, he called for a golden bowel, filled with hypocras: the French ambassadors were, at the same time, served with another, and they reciprocally drank to the health of their respective Sovereigns. He then retired to dress; and returning speedily to the company, exerted those convivial talents which had first contributed to his attainment of this excessive grandeur. " Then went cups merrily about, that many of the Frenchmen were fain to be led to their beds. They were all delighted with their reception, and doubted which most to admire,—the mansion, the feast, or the master."[1]

Next morning, after mass and an early dinner, they departed to hunt at Windsor; and, it being in the midst of the term, Wolsey returned to Westminster.

" Thus passed the Cardinal his life and time, from day to day, and year to year, in such great wealth, joy, and triumph and glory." " But," adds the gentleman usher, " Fortune, of whose favor no man is longer assured than she is disposed, began to wax somewhat wroth with his prosperous state, and thought she would devise a mean to abate his high port; wherefore, she procured Venus, the insatiate goddess, to be her instrument, and to work her purpose, she brought the King in love with a gentlewoman, who, after perceiving his good will towards her, and how diligent he was to please her, and to grant all her requests, wrought the Cardinal much displeasure."[2]

> —— " When love could teach a monarch to be wise,
> And Gospel-light first dawn'd from Boleyn's eyes."

Henry's passion for Anne Boleyn certainly produced the fall of Wolsey. But there is a general mistake as to the part which he took in this affair, it being supposed by many that he disapproved of the King's divorce from Catherine; that he intrigued for the purpose of delaying and preventing it; that he opposed, to the last, the elevation of Anne Boleyn to the throne, because she was favorable to the Reformation; and that he fell a sacrifice to his love for the ancient Church. In truth it will be found that he favored the divorce; that he promoted it as far as the forms would permit which he was bound to observe; that though for a time, from motives merely political and personal, he opposed the King's union with Anne, he would at last have willingly consented to it; and that he fell because, from circumstances over which he had no control, he was unable to gratify the inclination of his master.

Before Wolsey's departure on his embassy to France,

---
[1] Cavendish, 198.   [2] Ibid. 118.

the King had imparted to him the scruples which he professed to entertain respecting the validity of his marriage with Catherine—scruples which had been greatly quickened by the progress of her maid of honor in his affections. Wolsey was previously acquainted with the King's new passion, and, at his request, had judicially dissolved the pre-contract between Anne and Lord Percy; but he had then no notion of her becoming Queen, and expected that she would only add to the list of his mistresses, in which the name of her sister Mary is said to have stood. To strengthen the French alliance, on which the Cardinal was bent, he intended that Renée, sister of Louis XII., should be the Queen; and a divorce being proposed by Henry, he immediately offered his aid, and promised complete success to the project from his influence at Rome.

On Wolsey's return from the embassy, "the cunning chastity" of Anne Boleyn having made her resist the royal solicitations in the hope of reaching a throne, Henry told him he did not want a French princess, for that Anne Boleyn should be his wife as soon as the papal dispensation could be obtained. The Cardinal threw himself upon his knees before the King, and used every argument to dissuade him from a step which he represented as calculated to cover him with disgrace. But religion did not enter into the consideration, for although Anne had been represented as a convert to the new faith, she was no more a Lutheran than Henry himself, who, to the last, adhered to all the doctrines of the Church of Rome, with the exception of making himself Pope in England, and who continued to burn and·behead his subjects for doubting the dogma of transubstantiation.

Henry being inexorable, Wolsey became a convert to the measure which he could not avert, and labored, by his subsequent services, to atone for the crime of having dared to dispute the pleasure of his Sovereign. The particulars of the conference being disclosed to the young lady and her family, they became implacable enemies of Wolsey; and, although they dissembled their resentment, and at times treated him with apparent courtesy, they always suspected that he was plotting against them, and they secretly vowed his destruction. In truth, however, there is the best reason to believe, that from this time he did all in his power that the divorce might be obtained, and the wished-for union completed.

All opinions agreed that, as Henry's marriage with his brother's widow had been celebrated under a dispensation from Pope Julius II., it could not be set aside without the sanction of the papal see. Clement VII. had been liberated from captivity by Henry's good offices, and was disposed to oblige him as far as he prudently could from a remaining dread of the Emperor; but Charles strenuously supported the cause of Catherine his aunt, and his Holiness, to use his own language, was " between the hammer and the forge." Wolsey wrote a long letter to him, vindicating the character of Anne Boleyn, and asserting that the suit of Henry proceeded from sincere and conscientious scruples.

Clement so far complied with Wolsey's application as to grant to Henry a conditional license to marry again, nicely adapted to the case of Anne Boleyn,[1] upon the dissolution of his first marriage; and to examine the validity of that marriage, he granted a joint commission to Wolsey and Cardinal Campeggio, an Italian ecclesiastic, who was supposed to be gained over by being appointed Bishop of Salisbury, but who remained an instrument of chicanery under the control of his Holiness.

Although the commission was granted in the month of April, 1528, Campeggio did not reach London till the month of October following. In the mean time there had been great alarm in England from the sweating sickness. Anne Boleyn was sent from Court, and had a smart attack of it; the King, abandoning for the time his "secret matter," joined the Queen in her devotional exercises, confessing himself every day, and receiving the communion every Sunday and festival. During the time of the pestilence he sent regulations to Wolsey for his diet, insisted on receiving daily an account of his health, and invited him to lodge in a house at a short distance, so that if either fell ill they might hear from each other in the

[1] "—— etiamsi talis sit quæ prius cum alio contraxerit, dummodo illud carnali copula non fuerit consummatum ; etiamsi illa tibi alias secundo aut remotiore consanguinitatis aut *primo affinitatis gradu* etiam ex quocunque licito seu *illicito* coitu proveniente invicem conjuncta sit, dummodo relicta fratris tui non fuerit." The dispensation referred to Ann's precontract with Lord Percy, and to Henry's liaison with Mary Boleyn, and in fact assumed the power denied to Julius II.

space of an hour, and might have the benefit of the same medical attendance. The Cardinal, beginning to "order himself anent God," made his will,—sent it to Henry,—and assured him, "as truly as if he were speaking his last words, that never for favor, mede, gyfte, or promysse, had he done or consented to any thing that might in the least poynte redownde to the King's dishonour or disprouffit."

But the sickness passed away; Anne Boleyn returned to Court more beautiful and enticing than ever, and Campeggio's proceedings appeared so dilatory that Wolsey was suspected to be in league with him to defeat the King's wishes, and he daily declined in the royal favor.[1]

Notwithstanding all the efforts of Wolsey, who now saw that despatch was essential for his own safety, months were consumed in preliminary forms after Campeggio's arrival in England.

In the beginning of the following year, when Wolsey had been in daily danger of disgrace, he was very near reaching the grand object of his ambition, the triple crown. Clement VII. had a dangerous fit of illness, and for some time his recovery was despaired of. Historians are agreed that if he had actually died at this juncture, Wolsey, in all probability, would have been his successor. Charles had made himself odious to the great majority of the college of Cardinals by his imprisonment of the Pope; the sack of Rome, and the licentious conduct of the Imperial troops in Italy, had rendered his cause generally unpopular; his arms had recently sustained some disasters; and the Kings of France and England, who had stood by the supreme Pontiff in all his misfortunes, were in general favor. Both these sovereigns, to serve their

[1] It is curious that, even down to this time, Anne's letters to the Cardinal are full of kindness and gratitude. "All the days of my life I am most bound of all creatures, next to the King's Grace, to love and serve your Grace, of the which I beseech you never to doubt that ever I shall vary from this thought as long as any breath is in my body. And as for the coming of the legate, I desire that much, and, if it be God's pleasure, I pray him to send this matter shortly to a good end, and then I trust, my Lord, to recompense part of your great pains. I assure you that, after this matter is brought to pass, you shall find me, as I am bound in the mean time, to owe you my service; and then look what thing in the world I can imagine to do you pleasure in, you shall find me the gladdest woman in the world to do it, and next unto the King's Grace, of one thing I make you full promise to be assured to have it, and that is my hearty love, unfeignedly, during my life."—1 Burnet, 55. Fiddes, 204, 205. There can be no doubt that her uncle, the Duke of Norfolk, with her knowledge, was then meditating Wolsey's overthrow.

own ends, now exerted all their influence to secure the election of Wolsey in case of a vacancy, and they calculated on success.

This event would have had a most powerful influence on the fate of the Western Church, and might have entirely changed the history of our country. Wolsey, a much abler and more enlightened man than Clement, would probably have stopped the Reformation, or given it a new direction; and he certainly would have kept England true to the Papal see by granting Henry his divorce, and conferring new honors upon him as Defender of the Faith. But Clement arose, as it were by miracle, from the grave, Wolsey was disgraced, and England became Protestant.[1]

It was not till the month of May, 1529, that the Legates opened their court in the hall of the Blackfriars' Convent in London, where the parliament in those days usually assembled. The King sat at the upper end in a chair of state, on an elevated platform. The Queen was seated at some distance a little lower. Wolsey and Campeggio were placed in front of the King, three steps beneath him, the one on his right, the other on his left; and at the same table sat the Archbishop of Canterbury and all the Bishops. At the bar appeared as counsel for the King, Dr. Sampson, afterwards Bishop of Chichester, and Dr. Bell, afterwards Bishop of Worcester; — for the Queen, Dr. Fisher, Bishop of Rochester, who was afterwards beheaded on Tower Hill, and Dr. Standish, a grey

---

[1] Wolsey received the first news of Clement's illness by a letter from Peter Vannes, his watchful and zealous agent at Rome. "Dum de Pontificis valetudine beno speraremus, ecce ex secretissimo certissimoque loco nobis nunciature illius morbum ita ingravescere ad delirium usque et vomitum, ut desperenda sit illius salus. Scripsimus ad comitem S'ti. Pauli ut apud C'tianissimum efficiat, quod Gallici Cardinales quam primum ad confinia advolent, ut creationi novi Pontificis, quam vereor plus nimio mature instare, queant interesse, nam nisi factionis nostræ creetur Pontifex, actæ sunt Gallorum actiones."—Fidd. Coll. 211. Wolsey thereupon instantly wrote a despatch to Gardyner, the King's minister at Rome, in which, after showing that he himself is the fittest person to be Pope for the good of Christendom, "absit verbum jactantiæ," he implores him to exert his utmost efforts, "ut ista res ad effectum perduci possit, nullis parcendo sumptibus, pollicitationibus sive laboribus, ita ut horum videris ingenia et affectiones sive ad privata sive ad publica ita accommodes actiones tuas. Non deest tibi et collegis tuis amplissima potestas, nullis terminis aut conditionibus limitata sive restricta, et quicquid feceris scito omnia *apud hunc regem et me* esse grata et rata." This was written with his own hand. "Tuæ salutis et amplitudinis cupidissimus T. Car'lis Ebor propria manu."—Fidd. Coll. 211.

friar, Bishop of St. Asaph,—all very distinguished civilians and canonists.

The Court being constituted, and the Pope's commission read, the apparitor, by Wolsey's order, called the parties. To the summons, "King Henry of England, come into Court," the King answered, "Here, my Lords." The Queen protested against the competency of her judges, as holding benefices in the realm of the gift of her adversary, but they overruled her plea. She then knelt before the King, made a pathetic appeal to him for justice, and withdrew. She was pronounced contumacious, and the suit proceeded;—but very slowly, Wolsey urging despatch, and Campeggio resorting to every artifice for delay.

Henry's impatience and suspicions increasing, he one day at the rising of the Court ordered the Cardinal to attend him at the palace of Bridewell adjoining, and there showered on the head of the devoted minister the most vehement abuse for his supposed misconduct in not bringing the proceedings to a speedy close. The Bishop of Carlisle, who entered the Chancellor's barge with him at Blackfriars to escort him to York Place, seeing him, contrary to custom, silent and moody, observed, "it was a very hot day." "Yes," replied Wolsey, "and if you had been as much chafed as I have been within this hour, you would indeed say it was very hot." On his arrival at home he was so much exhausted and heart-broken, that he went "incontinent to his naked bed;" but he was soon compelled, by a royal message brought by Anne Boleyn's father, to return to Bridewell, and to try to induce the Queen voluntarily to retire into a convent. The interview which then took place between them shows strikingly the spirit as well as the dignity of Catherine. He wished to confer with her in private. "My Lord," quoth she, "if you have anything to say, speak it openly before all these folks." He then began to speak to her in Latin. "Nay, good my Lord," quoth she, "although I understand Latin, speak to me in English, I beseech you." She listened to him, but rejected his proposal; and he had the additional mortification this unlucky day to relate to the King the hopelessness of any voluntary separation from Catherine, who ever pleaded her love for her daughter Mary the heir presumptive to the Crown.

At last the proofs in the suit were completed, and at a meeting of the Court held on the 23rd of July, the King attending in a neighboring room, from which he could see and hear the proceedings, his counsel in lofty terms required that sentence should be pronounced. But Campeggio replied that judgment must be deferred till the whole of the proceedings had been laid before the sovereign Pontiff; that he attended there to do justice, and that no consideration should divert him from his duty. Thereupon the Duke of Suffolk, coming from the King and by his commandment, in a loud and angry tone, spoke these words: " It was never merry in England whilst we had Cardinals among us." Although Wolsey privately regretted the delay, his spirit would not brook this insult to his order. Rising with apparent coolness, he said, " Sir, of all men living, you have the least reason to dispraise Cardinals; for if I a poor Cardinal had not been, you would not at this present have had a head upon your shoulders wherewith to make such a brag in disrepute of us who have meant you no harm, and have given you no cause of offense."[1]

The King now made a progress in the midland counties with Anne, who was using all her arts, under the guidance of her uncle, her father, and other courtiers, to bring about Wolsey's disgrace. There was such apprehension of his influence over the King if they should meet, and the policy adopted was to keep them apart as much as possible.

The Court was fixed for some weeks at Grafton in Northamptonshire. Wolsey stationed himself at the Moore, a county house a few miles distant; but he was never invited to Court. On matters of state his opinion was seldom asked, and then only by a special messenger. His ruin was seen to be at hand; wagers were laid that the King would never again speak to him, and his opponents openly threatened "to humble the pride of all churchmen, and to ease them of that load of wealth which incumbered the successors of the apostles."[2]

[1] I presume he referred to the Duke's marriage with the King's sister, which, without the Cardinal's good offices might have been suddenly dissolved by the decapitation of the bridegroom.

[2] "La fantaisie de ces seigneurs est que, luy mort ou ruiné, ils deferrent incontinent icy l'estat de l'église et prendront tous leur biens. Ils le crient en

Wolsey rested his hopes on the result of a personal interview with the King, and, after many disappointments, he at last obtained permission to accompany Campeggio, when that prelate was to take leave on setting off for Rome. The Italian was received by the officers of the Court with the attention due to his rank; the falling minister found, to his extreme mortification, that though an apartment had been ordered by his companion, none was provided for himself. He was, in some degree, relieved from his embarassment by the delicate attention of Sir Henry Norris, a young knight (afterwards executed as one of the lovers of Anne Boleyn), who begged him to accept of his chamber,—affecting to ascribe the premeditated affront put upon Wolsey to the limited arrangement of the King's present residence. The Chancellor was, however, admitted into the presence hall, and the sun of his fortune cast a parting ray upon him before it set forever.

"Having knelt before the King standing under the cloth of state, then he took my Lord up by both arms and caused him to stand up, and with as an amiable a cheer as ever he did called him aside, and led him by the hand to a great window, where he talked with him and caused him to be covered. Then to behold the countenances of those who had made their wagers to the contrary it would have made you smile; and thus were they all deceived." After some conversation, the King said to him, "My Lord, go to your dinner, and all my Lords here will keep you company."[1]

"The King dined that same day with Mrs. Anne Boleyn in her chamber, who kept there an estate more like a Queen than a simple maid." The alarmed courtiers now strove through her to break off all further intercourse between Henry and their victim. Prompted by them she said during dinner:—"Is it not a marvelous thing to consider what debt and danger the Cardinal hath brought

pleine table."—*Letter of M. de Bellay, Bishop of Bayonne.* Singer's edition of Cavendish, vol. ii. 275.

[1] Cavendish, who was an eye-witness of this scene, adds, that in a long and earnest communication between them, he heard the King say, "How can that be? Is not this your own hand?" but that Wolsey satisfied the King. This is probably the foundation for the second scene of the third act of Shakspeare's Henry VIII., turning upon a paper disclosing secrets, which the Cardinal is supposed by mistake to have sent to the King.

you in with all your subjects?" " How so, sweetheart?" quoth the King. She mentioned the illegal taxation, which the King attempted to justify. " Nay, Sir," quoth she, " besides all that, what things hath he wrought in this realm to your great slander and dishonor? There is never a nobleman within this realm that if he had done but half as much but he were well worthy to lose his head." " Why I then perceive," quoth the King, " ye are not the Cardinal's friend." " Forsooth, Sir," then quoth she, " I have no cause, nor any other that loveth your Grace, no more hath your Grace if ye consider well his doings."[1] He had received the promise of another audience next day, but the same night a solemn engagement was extorted from the King by Anne, that he never again would admit the Cardinal into his presence.[2]

Wolsey had a lodging provided for him that night by his own servants at Euston. When he returned in the morning he found that the King had rode out with the Lady Anne to hunt in Hartwell Park, where she had made provision for the King's dinner, lest he should return before the Cardinal was gone. They never met more.

When the Chancellor found that he was finally cast off by his master, who was now under the entire management of other favorites, and that he must soon bid adieu to all his greatness,—for a time he lost all fortitude,—"he wept like a woman and wailed like a child." On his return to London, however, his spirits rallied, and he resolved with decency to meet the impending blow.

On the first day of Michaelmas Term, which then began in the middle of October, he headed the usual grand procession to Westminster Hall, riding on his mule,—attended by his crosses, his pillars, and his poll-axes, and an immense retinue to defend the Great Seal and the Cardinal's hat. It was remarked that in the procession, and while sitting in the Court of Chancery, his manner was dignified and collected, although he, and all who beheld him, knew that he had touched the highest point of all his greatness, and from the full meridian of his glory he

[1] Cavendish relates this curious dialogue from the report made to him at the time by those who waited on the King at dinner.
[2] This fact is not mentioned by Cavendish, but is proved by a letter from the French ambassador, who was then at Grafton. " Mademoiselle de Boulen a faict promettre a son amy q'il ne l'escoutera jamais parler."—*Letters of Bishop of Bayonne*, 375.

hastened to his setting. This was his last appearance in public as Chancellor.

That same evening he received a private intimation that the King had openly announced his immediate disgrace. The next day he remained at home, hourly expecting the messenger of fate, but it passed on without any occurrence to terminate his suspense. The following day, however, came the Dukes of Norfolk and Suffolk from the King, "declaring to him how the King's pleasure was that he should surrender and deliver up the Great Seal into their hands." He demanded of them "what commission they had to give him any such commandment?" They answered "they were the King's commissioners in that behalf, having orders by his mouth so to do." He denied that this was sufficient without further manifestations of the King's pleasure, and high words passed between them.

The Dukes were obliged to take their departure without accomplishing their object. Bnt the next morning they brought from Windsor letters from the King, under the Privy Seal, demanding the surrender of the Great Seal; whereupon, expressing great reverence for the King's authority so exercised, he delivered it up to them inclosed in a box, of which he gave them the key. They at the same time signified to him his Majesty's pleasure that he should surrender up York Place and all his possessions, and retire to his country-house at Esher.

CHAPTER XXIX.

LIFE OF CARDINAL WOLSEY FROM HIS FALL TILL HIS DEATH.

THE utter destruction of Wolsey had been determined upon immediately after his departure from Grafton; and some days before the Great Seal was taken from him, Hales, the Attorney-General, had filed an information against him, charging him with having, as legate, transgressed the act of Richard II., commonly called "the statute of præmunire," in receiving

[1] Cavendish, 247.

bulls from Rome, and acting upon them, without the King's consent, whereby he was out of the King's protection, his lands and goods were forfeited, and he might be imprisoned at the King's pleasure. Nothing could be more iniquitous than this proceeding, for Henry himself had joined in soliciting the legatine grant to him, and rejoiced in the greatness which the exercise of it conferred upon him. But Wolsey knew the stern and irritable temper of his prosecutor. To have maintained his innocence would have excluded all hope of forgiveness; and there was, moreover, "a night crow," to use his own expression, "which possessed the royal ear, and misrepresented the most harmless of his actions." He therefore pleaded guilty to the information, and threw himself upon the royal clemency. He caused inventories to be made of his plate, furniture, and valuables, showing the immense riches which he had accumulated. These he formally made over to the King, with York Place,—which thenceforth, under the name of Whitehall, became the chief town residence of the Kings of England, and so continued till it was burnt down in the reign of William and Mary. Some time before he had voluntarily made a gift of Hampton Court to the King, in the vain hope of recovering his favor.

When he entered his barge to proceed to Esher, he found the river Thames covered with above a thousand boats, full of men and women of the city of London, who expected to witness the spectacle of his being carried to the tower, and there landing at the Traitor's Gate. It is confessed that he was now greatly hated by people of all degrees, and that there was a general disappointment when the head of his barge was turned towards Lambeth, and when he was seen rowed up the river to Putney.

Here he landed and mounted his mule,—when a horseman was seen descending the hill, who turned out to be Sir Harry Norris, with a message to him from the King, "willing him in any wise to be of good cheer, for he was as much in his Highness's favor as ever he had been, and so should continue to be." And, in token of the King's kindness, he delivered him a ring of gold with a rich stone, being the privy token between the King and him when any important secret communication took place between them. Wolsey was so transported with joy at this gleam of returning good fortune, that he instantly dismounted, knelt in the mud, and returned thanks to God his Maker and to the King his sovereign Lord and Master, who had sent him such comfort. He added, "Gentle Norris, if I were lord of a realm, the one half thereof were an insufficient recompense for your pains and good comfortable news. But good, good Master Norris, consider with me that I have nothing left me but my clothes on my back. Therefore I desire you to take this small reward at my hands." He then gave him a gold chain, with a cross of gold enclosing a piece of the vertable wood of the true cross, which he continually wore around his neck, next his skin.

When Norris was gone a little way he called him back, saying, "I am sorry that I have no condign token to send to the King; but if you would present the King with this poor fool, I trust his Highness would accept him well; for surely, for a nobleman's pleasure, he is worth a thousand pounds." This fool, whose name was "*Patch*," was so much attached to his master, that it required six tall yeomen to force him to accompany Norris to Windsor, although he knew that he was to be transferred from disgrace and want to royalty and splendor. It is a pleasure to be told that the King received him most gladly.[1]

Wolsey, on his arrival at Esher, found the house without beds, sheets, tablecloths, cups, or dishes,—which he was obliged to borrow in the neighborhood; but he remained, with a numerous train of attendants, till the commencement of the following year.

A letter from Erasmus, written at this time to a correspondent on the Continent, though chargeable with some inaccuracies, gives a lively representation of the fallen favorite. "The Cardinal of York has incurred the royal displeasure to such a degree, that, stript of all his dignities, and all his wealth, he is confined, not literally in a prison, but in one of his country houses, attended, or rather guarded, by about thirty servants. Innumerable charges are brought forward against him, so that it is thought he can hardly escape capital punishment. Behold the sport of fortune. From being a schoolmaster,

---

[1] A fool was so necessary to the establishment of a Lord Chancellor, that we shall find one in the household of Sir Thomas More. It is very doubtful when Chancellors ceased to have about them any such character.

he is made ruler of a kingdom; for he, in truth, reigned more than the King himself: feared by all, loved by few —I might say, by no human being."[1]

The King continued, from time to time, to send him consoling messages and tokens of affection, though generally by stealth, and during the night; but[2] at the ur-

[1] "Cardinalis Eboracensis sic offendit animum regium, ut spoliatus bonis et omni dignitate, teneatur, non in carcere, sed in quodam ipsius prædio; adhibitis triginta duntaxat seu famulis seu custodibus. Proferuntur in illum querelæ innumeræ, ut vix existiment effugere posse capitis supplicium. Hic est fortunæ ludus; ex ludi magistro subvectus est ad regnum; nam plane regnabat verius quam ipse rex, metuabatur ab omnibus, amabatur a paucis, ne dicam a nemine."—Ep. 1151. Erasmus thought himself ill-used by Wolsey, who, in return for a flattering dedication of the Paraphrase on the Epistles of St. Peter, and in performance of magnificent promises, had only given him a prebend at Tournay, which produced nothing. On another occasion the disappointed wit writes, "Cardinalis perbenigne pollicetur; verum hæc ætas non moratur lentas spes."—Ep. 352.

[2] Cavendish gives a curious account of one of these nocturnal missions, Sir John Russell, the chief founder of an illustrious house, being the messenger. He was sent off from the Court at Greenwich after dark, with orders to be back before day. It was a dreadful rainy and tempestuous night, and the Cardinal and his household were all in bed before he arrived at Esher. After loud knocking at the gate he was admitted, and saying he had come from the King, was conducted to the bedchamber of the Cardinal, who had risen and put on his night gown. "When Master Russell was come into his presence, he most humbly reverenced him upon his knee, and delivering him a great ring of gold with a *turkis* for a token, said, ' Sir, the King commendeth him unto you, and willeth you to be of good cheer; who loveth you as well as ever he did, and is not a little disquieted for your troubles, whose mind is full of your remembrance, insomuch as his Grace, before he sat to supper, called me unto him and commanded me to take this journey secretly to visit you, to your comfort the best of my power. And sir, if it please your Grace, I have had this night the sorest journey for so little a way that ever I had to remembrance." A great fire was lighted and refreshments prepared, but Master Russell, after being some time in secret communication with my Lord, took leave, saying that, ' *God willing, he would be at the Court at Greenwich again before day, for he would not for anything it were known his being with my Lord that night.*' "

Wolsey soon after received a visit from his capital enemy, the Duke of Norfolk, which illustrates strikingly the manners of the times. All his yeomen were drawn up in the hall, and he and his gentlemen went to the gates and there received my Lord of Norfolk bare-headed. "They embraced each other, and the Duke complimented the Cardinal's attendants on their fidelity to him in his misfortunes. The Cardinal praised the magnanimity of his guest, who he said properly had the lion for his cognizance.

" Parcere prostratis scit nobilis ira Leonis.
Tu quoque fac simile, quisquis regnabis in orbem.

"Water being brought into the dining-chamber for them to wash before dinner, the Cardinal asked the Duke to wash with him, but the Duke said, ' it became him not to presume to wash with him any more now than it did before in his glory.' ' Yes, forsooth,' quoth my Lord Cardinal, ' for my augent request of his enemies, who were under a perpetual apprehension that he might be again taken into favor, and avenge themself upon them, permission was given to institute a proceeding against him in the Star Chamber,—and this being attended with some difficulty,—to prosecute him by parliamentary impeachment, or by a bill of pains and penalties.

Parliament, after a long interval, met in November in this year; and a Committee of the Lords, over which More, the new Chancellor, presided, prepared " articles of impeachment," as they were called, against Wolsey. These were forty-four in number, and were generally of a frivolous description. His illegal commissions to raise taxes without the authority of parliament, and his other unconstitutional acts, were entirely passed over; and he was charged with naming himself with the King, saying, " the King and I;" and, in Latin, " Ego et Rex meus;"[1] —with receiving, first, all letters from the King's ministers abroad—requiring to be the first visited by foreign ministers—and desiring that all applications should be made through him;—practices hardly to be avoided, unless the King were his own minister and his own secretary. Then he is accused of illegally exercising the legatine authority; and of interfering, in an arbitrary manner, with the administration of justice, and drawing into Chancery questions properly cognizable in the courts of common

thority and dignity legatine is gone, wherein consisted all my high honor.' ' A straw,' quoth my Lord of Norfolk, ' for your legacy. I never esteemed your honor the more or higher for that. But I regarded your honor for that you were Archbishop of York and a Cardinal, whose estate of honor surmounteth any Duke now being within this realm; and so will I honor you and bear you reverence accordingly. Therefore I beseech you content yourself, for I will not presume to wash with you, and therefore I pray you hold me excused.' So they washed separately." Another dispute arose as to whether the Duke should sit inside or outside the table at dinner. " The Cardinal wished him to sit inside, but he refused the same with much humbleness. There was then set another chair for my Lord of Norfolk, over against my Lord Cardinal, on the outside of the table, the which was by my Lord of Norfolk based something beneath my Lord Cardinal." Stowe shows us what store was set upon the nasty compliment of washing together, in his account of a banquet during the visit of Charles V. to Henry VIII. " The Emperor, the King, and the Queen did wash together, the Duke of Buckingham giving the water, the Duke of Suffolk holding the towel. Next them did wash the Lord Cardinall, the Queen of Fraunce, and the Queen of Arragon." On this occasion the Cardinal sat on the Emperor's right hand, between the Queen of England and the Queen of Arragon.—*Stowe's Annals.*

[1] A mode of expression justified by the Latim idiom.

law. One of the gravest charges is, that he whispered in the King's ear when he knew that he labored under a particular distemper, then supposed to be communicated by the breath.[1] Lord Herbert goes so far as to affirm, that no man ever fell from so high a station who had so few real crimes objected to him; and we are mortified by finding that the articles were subscribed by the virtuous Sir Thomas More, as Chancellor, and presented by him to the King.[2]

Without any proof, they were unanimously agreed to by the House of Lords, where the Ex-Chancellor was particularly odious on account of his haughty bearing to the ancient nobility, and even to his brother prelates; but when they came down to the House of Commons, they were rejected on a speech made by Thomas Cromwell, formerly a servant of the Cardinal, who defended his unfortunate patron with such spirit, generosity, and courage, as acquired him great reputation, and mainly contributed to his own subsequent extraordinary rise. The King still having returning fits of kindness for his old favorite, royal influence was supposed to have contributed to this result of the parliamentary proceeding against Wolsey; and the French ambassador, unable to foresee what might be the final issue of the struggle, advised his Court to render to the fallen minister such good offices as, without giving cause of offense to the existing administration, might be gratefully remembered by Wolsey, if he should finally triumph over his enemies.

At home, however, he was neglected and slighted, even by those whom his bounty had raised.[3] He was unable

---

[1] Shakspeare dwells upon several other articles equally treasonable.

> —— "that, without the knowledge
> Either of King or Council, when you went
> Ambassador to the Emperor, you made bold
> To carry into Flanders the Great Seal.—
> That, out of mere ambition, you have caus'd
> Your holy hat to be stamp'd on the King's coin.
> Then, that you have sent innumerable substance,
> To furnish Rome, and to prepare the ways
> You have for dignities, to the mere undoing
> Of all the kingdom."
>
> *Hen. VIII.* act iii. scene 2.

[2] 1 Parl. Hist. 492.

[3] Storer, in his metrical history of Wolsey, in describing his feelings at this time, uses one of the most pathetic and original images in poetry, which would have been worthy of Shakspeare:

to pay or to support his dependents who still adhered to him, and he begged them to provide themselves a new master till fortune should prove more auspicious. Tears were copiously shed on both sides, and most of those he addressed refused to leave "so kind a master" in his adversity.[1] A subscription among the chaplains and others of most substance, whom he had promoted, provided a fund from which the most urgent necessities of the establishment were supplied.

These mortifications preyed so much upon his mind that, about Christmas, he fell ill and was supposed to be dying. Henry exclaimed, "God forbid that he should die!—I would not lose him for twenty thousand pounds;"[1] —sent his own physicians to attend him;—conveyed to him assurances of unabated attachment, and even insisted on Anne Boleyn presenting to him a tablet of gold for a token of reconciliation.

Through the management of Cromwell a settlement of his affairs was made with the King, whereby he received a general pardon on making over all his revenues of every description, except those of the Archbishopric of York, and 1,000 marks a year from the Bishopric of Winchester, which he was to be allowed to retain for his sustentation.[2]

> "I am the tomb where that affection lies
> That was the closet where it living kept;
> Yet wise men say affection never dies.
> No, but it turns; and when it long hath slept,
> *Looks heavy like the eye that long hath wept.*"

[1] Cavendish's picture of this scene is very touching. "Afterwards my Lord commanded me to call all his gentlemen and yeomen up into the great chamber, commanding all the gentlemen to stand on the right hand, and the yeomen on the left; at last my Lord came out in his rochet upon a violet gown, like a bishop, who went with his chaplains to the upper end of the chamber, where was a great window. Beholding his goodly number of servants, he could not speak to them until the tears ran down his cheeks, which being perceived by his servants, caused fountains of tears to rush out of their sorrowful eyes, in such sort as would make any heart to relent."—Cavendish, 265.

[2] A difficulty arose respecting the title to York House, which the King had taken possession of, and which belonged to the archiepiscopal see from the gift of a former Archbishop, who had been Lord Chancellor. To sanction this palpable spoliation,—by the discreditable advice of the Judges and the new Chancellor, the form was gone through of a fictitious recovery in the Court of Common Pleas, and Wolsey was required to execute a recognizance that the right was in the King. Judge Shelley was sent to Esher to obtain this from him, but found him very reluctant—on the ground that the property was not his, and that he was robbing his successors of it. At last he said, "Master Shelley, ye shall report to the King's Highness that I am his obedient subject and faithful chaplain and bondsman, whose royal command-

As a further mark of kindness, the King permitted him, for a change of air and better accommodation, to remove from Esher to Richmond, where his health greatly improved, and he again began to gather some society round him.

His enemies, more alarmed than ever by his vicinity to the Court at Windsor, prevailed on Henry to issue a peremptory order that he should thenceforth reside within his archiepiscopal see, and he was supplied with a sum of money to bear the charges of his journey to York.

It is amusing to observe that this journey, which may now be performed in three hours, was then considered as formidable as if it had been to a distant foreign land. Some of Wolsey's servants, though much attached to him, "of their own mind desired him of his favor to tarry still here in the south, being very loath to abandon their native country, their parents, wives and children." [1]

Wolsey, notwithstanding his reduced fortune, had still a train of 160 persons, and twelve carts to carry his baggage. He made short stages, sleeping at different religious houses, where he was hospitably entertained. On Maundy Thursday, being at the abbey of Peterborough, he washed, wiped, and kissed the feet of fifty-nine beggars, on whom he bestowed liberal alms. Having paid a visit to Sir William Fitzwilliam, a wealthy knight of that country, he spent the summer and autumn at Southwell, Scroby, and Cawood Castle, near York,—acquiring immense popularity by his condescension, his kindness, his hospitality, and his piety. "He set an example to all church dignitaries, a right good example how they might win men's hearts." On Sundays and holidays he rode to some country church, celebrated mass himself, ordered one of his chaplains to preach to the people, and distributed alms to the poor. He spent much of his time in adjusting differences in families and between neighbors. His table, plentifully but not extravagantly supplied, was

---

ment and request I will in no wise disobey, but most gladly fulfill and accomplish his princely will and pleasure in all things, and in especial in this matter, inasmuch as ye, the fathers of the laws, say that I may lawfully do it. Therefore I charge your conscience, and discharge mine. Howbeit, I pray you show his Majesty from me that I most humbly desire his Highness to call to his most gracious remembrance that there is both heaven and hell."— We may well believe that Master Shelley did not venture to sound this salutary warning in the royal ear. [1] Cavendish, 307.

open to all the gentry of the country, and he gave employment to hundreds of workmen in repairing the houses and churches belonging to his see.[1]

Wolsey had appointed his installation as Archbishop to take place in York Minster on the 7th of November, and preparations were made to perform the ceremony with great pomp and magnificence. Presents of game and other provisions poured in from all quarters for the entertainment he was that day to give, and on the morrow he had agreed to dine with the Lord Mayor of York, when the greatest efforts were to be made to do him honor. But before the time arrived he was a prisoner on a charge of high treason, and he had sustained a mental shock which soon brought him to his grave.

Henry, who had recommended to the nothern nobility to be courteous to Wolsey, was not a little startled when he heard of the following which the Cardinal now had, independently of the royal favor. The courtiers were still more astounded, and the "night crow," as he styled Anne Boleyn, uttered notes of fear. The divorce suit was still dragging on, and there seemed no chance of bringing it to a favorable conclusion without a rupture with the Court of Rome, which Wolsey might very seriously have impeded.

On Friday, the 4th of November, about noon, when the Cardinal was sitting at dinner in his hall with his officers, suddenly entered the Earl of Northumberland, who had been his page, and whom he had divorced from Anne Boleyn. Wolsey apologized to him that dinner was nearly over, and seeing him attended by the old servants of the family, said: "Ah, my Lord, I perceive well that ye have observed my old precepts and instructions which I gave you when you were abiding with me in your youth,—to cherish your father's old servants, whereof I see here present with you a great number. They will live and die with you, and be true and faithful servants to you, and glad to see you prosper in honor, the which I beseech God to send you with long life." The Cardinal then conducted the Earl to a chamber, where, no one else being present but Cavendish himself, who kept the door as gentleman-usher, "the Earl, trembling, said with a very faint soft voice unto my Lord (laying his hand upon his arm),—

[1] Cavendish, 328.

My Lord, I arrest you of high treason." He refused to submit without seeing the warrant, which was refused; but he surrendered to Walshe, a privy councillor, who, he admitted, had authority to arrest him by virtue of his office.

When he had a moment's time to recover from the stupor caused by this blow, he wept bitterly,—more for the sake of others than himself. He particularly lamented the fate of Cavendish, about to be thrown destitute on the wide world, "who," quoth he, "hath abandoned his country, his wife and children, his house and family, his rest and quietness, only to serve me." At the next meal he summoned firmness to appear in the hall; "but there was not a dry eye among all the gentlemen sitting at table with him."

The particular charge to be brought against Wolsey has never been ascertained; the general opinion is, that Henry had been induced to believe that he was carrying on some clandestine correspondence of a suspicious nature with the Court of France, and that Augustine, a Venetian in his service, had given some false information against him.[1]

The next day after his arrest, he was committed to the special custody of five of his domestics, and sent off under the escort of the Earl of Northumberland's train towards London. But the population of the adjoining country, hearing of his misfortune, met him by thousands as he journeyed on, calling out with a loud voice, "God save your Grace, God save your Grace! The foul evil take all them that have thus taken you from us! We pray God that a very vengeance may light upon them."

His keepers afterwards obliged him to travel in the night time to escape public notice. He expressed deep regret for the loss of a sealed parcel he had left behind him at Cawood. This being sent for was found to contain hair shirts, one of which he now always wore next his skin.

The first night he was lodged in the abbey at Pontefract. In journeying thither he felt great apprehension lest his destination should be Pontefract Castle, where so many had suffered violently; and he said, "Shall I go to the Castle, and die like a beast?" On the Thursday he

[1] A few days before, the silver cross of York standing in the hall, was upset by the velvet robe of the Venetian, which at the moment Wolsey said was *malum omen*.

reached Sheffield Park, where he was eighteen days very kindly entertained by the Earl of Shrewsbury till orders should be received from the Court for his ulterior destination.

At the end of this time arrived Sir William Kingston, Keeper of the Tower, with a guard of twenty-four beefeaters, to conduct him to London. When the name of this officer was mentioned to him,—"*Master Kingston!*" quoth he,—"rehearsing his name once or twice; and with that clapped his hand on his thigh, and gave a great sigh." He no doubt then recollected the prophecy by some fortunetellers, respecting which Cavendish is silent, but which is mentioned by Fuller and other writers, *that he should have his end near Kingston.* This had induced him always to make a wide circuit to avoid Kingston-on-Thames when he approached that town, and the emotion he now displayed is accounted for by his anticipation that he was about to finish his career on Tower Hill, in the custody of Kingston, " too late perceiving himself deceived by the father of lies."[1]

For some days he was afflicted with a dysentery; but as soon as he was able to travel he set forward for London, although so much reduced in strength, that he could hardly support himself on his mule. When his servants saw him in such a lamentable plight, they expressed their pity for him with weeping eyes; but he took them by the hand as he rode, and kindly conversed with them. In the evening of the third day, after dark, he arrived with difficulty at the Abbey of Leicester. The Abbot and Monks met him at the gates with many torches. As he entered he said, " Father Abbot, I am come to lay my weary bones among you."

He was immediately carried to his chamber, and put into a bed, from which he never rose. This was on Saturday night, and on Monday he foretold to his servants, that by *eight of the clock next morning* they should lose their master, as the time drew near that he must depart out of this world."

Next morning, about seven, when he had confessed to a priest, Kingston asked him how he did. " Sir," quoth he, " I tarry but the will and pleasure of God, to render my simple soul into his divine hands. If I had served God

[1] Fuller's Church History, book v.

as diligently as I have done the King, he would not have given me over in my gray hairs. Howbeit, this is the just reward that I must receive for my worldly diligence and pains that I have had to do him service; only to satisfy his main pleasure, not regarding my godly duty. Wherefore, I pray you, with all my heart, to have me most kindly commended unto his royal majesty; beseeching him, in my behalf, to call to his most gracious remembrance all matters proceeding between him and me, from the beginning of the world unto this day, and the progress of the same, and most and chiefly in the weighty matter yet depending:[1] then shall his conscience declare, whether I have offended him or no. He is a sure prince of a royal courage, and hath a princely heart: and rather than he will either miss, or want any part of his will or appetite, he will put the loss of one half of his realm in danger. For, I assure you, I have often kneeled before him in his Privy Chamber, on my knees, the space of an hour or two, to persuade him from his will and appetite; but I could never bring to pass to dissuade him therefrom. Therefore, Master Kingston, if it chance hereafter you to be one of his Privy Counsel, as for your wisdom and other qualities ye are meet to be, I warn you to be well advised and assured what matter ye put in his head, for ye shall never put it out again." After a strong admonition to suppress the Lutheran heresy, he thus concluded: "Master Kingston, farewell, I can no more, but wish all things to have good success. My time draweth on fast. I may not tarry with you. And forget not, I pray you, what I have said and charged you withal; for, when I am dead, ye shall, peradventure, remember my words much better."

He was then annealed by the Father Abbot; and, as the great Abbey Clock struck *eight*, he expired—" KINGSTON" standing by his bedside.

His body was immediately laid in a coffin, dressed in his pontificals, with mitre, crosses, ring, and pall; and, lying there all day open and barefaced, was viewed by the Mayor of Leicester and the surrounding gentry, that there might be no suspicion as to the manner of his death. It was then carried into the Lady Chapel, and watched, with many torches all night;—whilst the monks sung dirges and other devout orisons At six in the morning mass

[1] The divorce. [2] Cavendish, 392.

was celebrated for his soul; and as they committed the body of the proud Cardinal to its last abode, the words were chanted, "Earth to earth, ashes to ashes, dust to dust!" No stone was erected to his memory; and the spot of his interment is unknown.

" Here is the end and fall of pride and arrogancy."[1]

I shall not attempt to draw any general character of this eminent man. His good and bad qualities may best be understood from the details of his actions, and are immortalized by the dialogue between Queen Catherine and Griffith, her secretary, which is familiar to every reader.[2]

But the nature of this work requires that I should more deliberately consider him as a Judge; for, although he held the Great Seal uninterruptedly for a period of fourteen years, and greatly extended its jurisdiction, and permanently influenced our juridical institutions, not only historians, but his own biographers, in describing the politician and the churchman, almost forget that he ever was Lord Chancellor.

From his conference with Justice Shelley respecting York Place, we know exactly his notions of the powers and duties of the Chancellor as an Equity Judge. When pressed by the legal opinion upon the question, he took the distinction between law and conscience, and said, "It is proper to have a respect to conscience before the rigor of the common law, for *laus est facere quod decet non quod licet*. The King ought of his royal dignity and prerogative to mitigate the rigor of the law where conscience has the most force; therefore, in his royal place of equal justice he hath constituted a Chancellor, an officer to execute justice with clemency, where conscience is opposed to the rigor of the law. And therefore the Court of Chancery hath been heretofore commonly called the Court of Conscience, because it hath jurisdiction to command the high ministers of the Common Law to spare execution and judgment, where conscience hath most effect."[3] With such notions he must have been considerably more arbitrary than a Turkish Kadi who considers himself bound by a text of the Koran in point, and we are not to be surprised when we are told that he chose to exercise his

---

[1] Cavendish, p. 394.   [2] Hen. VIII. act iv. sc. 2.   [3] Cavendish, p 283.

equitable authority over every thing which could be a matter of judicial inquiry.

In consequence, bills and petitions multiplied to an unprecedented degree, and notwithstanding his despatch there was a great arrear of business. To this grievance he applied a very vigorous remedy, without any application to parliament to appoint Vice-Chancellors;—for of his own authority he at once established four new Courts of Equity by commission in the King's name. One of these was held at Whitehall before his own deputy; another before the King's almoner, Dr. Stoherby, afterwards Bishop of London; a third at the Treasury Chamber before certain members of the Council; and a fourth at the Rolls, before Cuthbert Tunstall, Master of the Rolls, who, in consequence of this appointment, used to hear causes there in the afternoon.[1] The Master of the Rolls has continued ever since to sit separately for hearing causes in Chancery. The other three Courts fell with their founder.

Wolsey himself used still to attend pretty regularly in the Court of Chancery during term, and he maintained his equitable jurisdiction with a very high hand, deciding without the assistance of common law judges, and with very little regard to the maxims of the common law.

If he was sneered at for his ignorance of the doctrines and practice of the Court, he had his revenge by openly complaining that the lawyers who practiced before him were grossly ignorant of the civil law and the principles of general jurisprudence; and he has been described as often interrupting their pleadings, and bitterly animadverting on their narrow notions and limited arguments. To remedy an evil which troubled the stream of justice at the fountain-head, he, with his usual magnificence of conception, projected an institution to be founded in London, for the systematic study of all branches of the law. He even furnished an architectural model for the building, which was considered a master-piece, and remained long after his death as a curiosity in the palace at Green-

[1] In Reeves's History of the Law it is said that this is the first instance of the Master of the Rolls ever hearing causes by himself, he having been before only the principal of the council of Masters assigned for the Chancellor's assistance; but there have lately been found in the Tower of London, bills addressed to the Master of the Rolls as early as the reign of Edward IV.—See ; Reeves, 369.

wich. Such an institution is still a desideratum in England; for, with splendid exceptions, it must be admitted that English barristers, though very clever practitioners, are not such able jurists as are to be found in other countries where law is systematically studied as a science.

On Wolsey's fall his administration of justice was strictly overhauled; but no complaint was made against him of bribery or corruption, and the charges were merely that he had examined many matters in Chancery after judgment given at common law;—that he had unduly granted injunctions;—and that when his injunctions were disregarded by the Judges, he had sent for those venerable magistrates and sharply reprimanded them for their obstinacy. He is celebrated for vigor with which he repressed perjury and chicanery in his Court, and he certainly enjoyed the reputation of having conducted himself as Chancellor with fidelity and ability,—although it was not till a later age that the foundation was laid of that well-defined system of equity now established, which is so well adapted to all the wants of a wealthy and refined society, and, leaving little discretion to the Judge, disposes satisfactorily of all the varying cases within the wide scope of its jurisdiction.

I am afraid I cannot properly conclude this sketch of the Life of Wolsey without mentioning that " of his own body he was ill, and gave the clergy ill example." He had a natural son, named Winter, who was promoted to be Dean of Wells, and for whom he procured a grant of " arms " from the Heralds' College. The 38th article of his impeachment shows that he had for his mistress a lady of the name of Lark, by whom he had two other children: there were various amours in which he was suspected of having indulged,—and his health had suffered from his dissolute life. But we must not suppose that the scandal arising from such irregularities was such as would be occasioned by them at the present day. A very different standard of morality then prevailed: churchmen debarred from marriage, were often licensed to keep concubines, and as the Popes themselves were in this respect by no means infallible, the frailties of a Cardinal were not considered any insuperable bar either to secular or spiritual preferment.[1]

---

[1] Many gibes, however, seem to have been current against the licentious

In judging him we must remember his deep contrition for his backslidings; and the memorable lesson which he taught with his dying breath, that, to ensure true comfort and happiness, a man must addict himself to the service of God, instead of being misled by the lures of pleasure and ambition.

The subsequent part of Henry's reign is the best panegyric on Wolsey; for, during twenty years, he had kept free from the stain of blood or violence the Sovereign, who now, following the natural bent of his character, cut off the heads of his wives and his most virtuous ministers, and proved himself the most arbitrary tyrant that ever disgraced the throne of England.[1]

conduct of the Cardinal, as we may judge from Lord Surrey's speech to him:—

"I'll startle you
Worse than the sacring bell, when the brown wench
Lay kissing in your arms, Lord Cardinal."

Skelton likewise was probably only embodying in rhyme the common talk of the town when he wrote,—

"The goods that he thus gaddered
Wretchedly he hath scattered,—
To make windows, walles, and dores,
And to maintain bauds and whores."

[1] See Fiddes's Life of Wolsey, folio, 1724. Gall's Life of Wolsey, 4to. 1812.

www.ingramcontent.com/pod-product-compliance
Lightning Source LLC
Chambersburg PA
CBHW032028150426
43194CB00006B/187